T0388903

NARRATIVES ON TRANSLATION ACROSS EURASIA AND AFRICA

CONTACT AND TRANSMISSION

INTERCULTURAL ENCOUNTERS FROM LATE ANTIQUITY TO THE EARLY MODERN PERIOD

VOLUME 3

Narratives on Translation across Eurasia and Africa

From Babylonia to Colonial India

Edited by

SONJA BRENTJES

in cooperation with

JENS HØYRUP *and* BRUCE O'BRIEN

BREPOLS

British Library Cataloguing in Publication Data
A catalogue record for this book is available from the British Library.

ISBN: 978-2-503-59489-7
e-ISBN: 978-2-503-59490-3
ISSN: 2736-6952
e-ISSN: 2736-6960
DOI 10.1484/M.CAT-EB.5.123706

Printed in the EU on acid-free paper.

D/2022/0095/12

Table of Contents

List of Illustrations

Acknowledgements

Narratives on Translation emerged from a project (FFI2012-38606) that questioned major historiographical approaches to translating scientific, medical, philosophical, alchemical, and related texts between the eighth and the thirteenth centuries in various Islamicate and Christian societies around the Mediterranean and in Abbasid Baghdad. The problems that we struggled with are presented in the introduction. Here, we wish to express our gratitude to the institutions and colleagues who supported our research and our debates financially, intellectually, and materially.

During the course of the project, the idea was born to trace, question, and re-contextualize narratives on translation across a major part of the Old World before and beyond the centuries and cultures dealt with in our original research project. In the workshop held at the Autonomous University of Barcelona, we decided to combine our expertise with that of many other colleagues and produce a book on the various manners in which translating was narrated in Eurasia both by actors in the past and by academic historians in the twentieth and twenty-first centuries. We also wished to open this part of history of science, medicine and philosophy to recent theoretical debates about translating to see whether and if so how such a cross-disciplinary dialogue might help understanding cross-cultural exchanges and transformations of knowledge.

The way from the idea of exploring issues of historiography and history with respect to translation in Eurasia from the second millennium BCE to the nineteenth century CE to the final production of this book was long. It took us six years from the decision to create the book until the presentation of the finished manuscript to our publisher Brepols and the colleagues who conceived the series CAT (Contact and Transmission. Intercultural Encounters from Late Antiquity to the Early Modern period). We thank in particular Görge Hasselhoff, who agreed to present and recommend our work to his colleagues on the editorial board of CAT and all the members of CAT's board, who agreed to our temporal and geographical extension of their focus. We also thank Guy Carney from Brepols, who helped us through the many formal challenges of producing a collection of papers that cover an unusual number of languages, themes, periods, and spaces.

For their financial and material support of the research project and its substantive conceptual and temporal extension in the form of our book we are very pleased to thank the Ministry of Economy and Competitiveness, Spain; the Department of Philosophy, Logic and Philosophy of Science, University of Sevilla; ICREA, Autonomous University of Barcelona; the Max Planck Institute for the History of Science (MPIWG), Berlin, and the

Alexander Humboldt Foundation, Bonn (Annelies Maier Prize, Maribel Fierro, CSIC, Madrid).

Four workshops (2012–2016) and one conference (2015) were organized by José Luis Mancha (Seville), Maribel Fierro (Madrid), Alexander Fidora (Barcelona), Jürgen Renn (Berlin), Dagmar Schäfer (Berlin), and Sonja Brentjes (Berlin) in Madrid, Seville, Berlin, and Barcelona. We thank all of them for their intellectual support and their active involvement in the organization of these scholarly encounters.

The four workshops discussed

1. Stories of Medieval and Early Modern Exchanges of Knowledge: Narrators and Interlocutors, Objects and Practices, Values and Beliefs (Meeting 1); CSIC, Madrid, 25 September 2013;
2. Stories of Medieval and Early Modern Exchanges of Knowledge: Narrators and Interlocutors, Objects and Practices, Values and Beliefs (Meeting 2); Department of Philosophy, Logic and Philosophy of Science, University of Sevilla, 26 November 2013;
3. Participant and Observer Narratives about Medieval Cross-Cultural Knowledge Transfer: Missing, Single or Multiple Translations, 21–22 November 2014, MPIWG, Department I, Berlin;
4. Discussion of the Book Plan about Narratives on Translation, 8–9 September 2016, Autonomous University of Barcelona.

The conference 'Narratives on Translations' took place at the MPIWG, Department I, Berlin, 17–20 November 2015 with a preceding public lecture 'Narratives, Translations and a Global History of Science' by Dagmar Schäfer, MPIWG, Department III on 16 November 2015.

We also give thanks to Dagmar Schäfer and Michael Friedrich (CMCS, University Hamburg) for expanding our possibilities for cooperation to colleagues working on translation in East Asian cultures.

Scholarly meetings, the writing of papers, and book production are not accomplished by scholars alone. Hence, we thank all the members of the publication groups of Departments I and III at the MPIWG for their valuable help in copy-editing and formatting our texts as well as the administrative and the student support staff of both departments, who helped organize our workshops and conference in all practical respects.

Sonja Brentjes, Jens Høyrup, and Bruce O'Brien

SONJA BRENTJES
IN COOPERATION WITH
JENS HØYRUP AND BRUCE O'BRIEN

Poetry is more philosophical and more elevated than history, since poetry relates more of the universal, while history relates particulars.

Aristotle, *Poetics*, 1451^b5–7, ed. and trans. by Stephen Halliwell

The question may actually be raised whether the working-out of general views can at all be reconciled with that accuracy of research that alone can give it certainty and specificity. Historical research is indeed by its very nature directed toward particulars. But it will be granted me that it fails its aim if it gets stuck in these.

Leopold von Ranke, *Zwölf Bücher preußischer Geschichte*, p. xi (trans. by Høyrup)

Introduction

History of science as well as of belief systems, when not confining themselves to the strictly patriotic, will by necessity have to confront the ways one region interacts with others, often involving translation. When presented as a history of translation, the past *could* (perhaps) be described in the form of a catalogue, listing which translations from a specific place and period and between specific languages are known to have existed. If the current historian is not satisfied with mere catalogue-making in the style of much

Sonja Brentjes is a historian of science in Islamicate societies and Christian Europe; she is an affiliated scholar at the Max Planck Institute for the History of Science, Berlin. Her research includes the history of the mathematical sciences, mapmaking, institutions, cross-cultural exchange of knowledge, and the involvement of the arts in the sciences. Among her recent publications are S. Brentjes and A. Fidora, *Premodern Translation: Comparative Approaches to Cross-Cultural Transformations* (Brepols, 2021) and *Teaching and Learning the Sciences in Islamicate Societies, 800–1700* (Brepols, 2018).

Jens Høyrup (jensh@ruc.dk) is a professor emeritus, Section for Philosophy and Science Studies, Roskilde University. His main research areas are the history of Mesopotamian and European medieval mathematics and premodern practitioners' mathematics.

Bruce O'Brien is professor at the University of Mary Washington, Fredericksburg, Virginia. He received his PhD in history from Yale University (1990). His research focuses on the history of England from the tenth to the twelfth centuries, in particular on legal history, history of translation, and multilingualism. On these themes, he published *God's Peace and King's Peace: The Laws of Edward the Confessor* (University of Pennsylvania Press, 1999) and *Reversing Babel: Translation among the English during an Age of Conquests, c. 850 to c. 1200* (Rowman & Littlefield, 2011). Since 2007, he has chaired as academic lead the international project of reediting and translating online all English legal texts before the Magna Carta (1215).

Narratives on Translation across Eurasia and Africa: From Babylonia to Colonial India, ed. by Sonja Brentjes in cooperation with Jens Høyrup and Bruce O'Brien, CAT 3, pp. 11–23 (Turnhout: Brepols, 2022) BREPOLS PUBLISHERS 10.1484/M.CAT-EB.5.127931

early modern philology, and thus with writing 'history' in Aristotle's sense, history of science as of belief systems will need to go with a general view which, when formulated, becomes a 'narrative'. To trace such 'narratives' as constructed in the distant as well as in the more recent past and to question through them our own historiographical practices are the two main purposes of this collection of invited papers. In order to achieve a better understanding of our current strengths and weaknesses when telling histories of premodern sciences through histories of translations, two historians of non-Western sciences, Jens Høyrup and Sonja Brentjes, joined forces with a historian of translation in medieval England, Bruce O'Brien. Together we designed the book's profile, invited the contributors, edited the papers, and worked on this introduction.

This cross-disciplinary collaboration is the first of our answers — both in a historiographical and in a pragmatic sense — to the questions we wish to raise in this volume and the problems that we see in how translations and their histories are treated by historians of premodern sciences. All three of us believe that histories of translations should not be told as a sub-category of histories of premodern sciences but as histories of cultural practices cutting synchronically and diachronically through the entire fabric of the investigated societies. We propose to disentangle histories of translations from specialized intellectual fields such as science, religion, law, or literature — to name just a few of such domains in which translations occurred in past societies and are treated today in isolation from each other by historians of respective specializations. If we wish to improve our chances for understanding the complexities involved in any kind of translation activity and all the more so when wishing to study them as sociocultural processes, it is necessary to investigate translating as synchronic practices across all fields of a society where they occurred and all languages, communities, and actors that were involved. Treating histories of translations as subcategories of other histories has led to separations of historical practices according to modern expectations and goals which in the past either did not exist at all or at least not in the kind of boxes that our academic desires and qualifications invented. Breaking with such artificial divisions is our second effort to gain new insights. That is why we invited specialists for cultures that used several languages in their scientific, legal, literary, religious, or political activities but were never praised for their translating activities. This goal also motivated us to go far beyond the usual cultural, temporal, and disciplinary boundaries that so far characterize discussions of translations in the premodern sciences. Investing serious attention to contextual features of translating whether done by an individual or a group should by now be a quite ordinary, standard element of any study of intellectual history. However, this is either rarely done in depth or still all too often fully neglected. In this book, our approach to the all too often vexing quest for data about motivations for and conditions of translating in specific circumstances is two-pronged. In the first part, we asked our authors to reflect on the histories of the approaches to translating in their specific fields of competence in order to learn what shaped our questions, theoretical and practical tools, arguments, and willingness to accept certain kinds of evidence but not others. The second part explores how translators and authors from long-ago centuries presented their motivations and circumstances.

Translation Narratives

No man is an island, according to John Donne. Even less is any culture.

One may discuss to what extent the hypostasized notion of cultures as well-defined entities corresponds to what we encounter in the real world. That problem we shall not attack directly here. Instead, we shall concentrate on one of the ways in which cultures learn from and about each other — the process broadly known as 'translation'. We hope that this indirect way will also teach us about the general question, what a culture *is*.

Even when pursuing this indirect way, we are not going to look at translation in general but — as just stated — through a mirror: reports, beliefs, statements, claims *about* translations — made either by the translators themselves or others from their times and environments, or by modern historians. This is what we call *translation narratives*. Confronting such narratives with what we suppose to know from other sources and from diverging analyses will, for its part, teach us about aspects of translation 'in itself'.

In recent historiography (which we call 'observer narratives'), processes where suddenly a larger number of translations into a target language were made than we know about in the preceding period are regularly referred to as 'translation movements' — in particular if religious or scientific (including medical, astrological, and magical) texts were translated. At first the concept was used for the translations into Arabic made between the late eighth and the early eleventh century CE and then for the translations into Latin made from the twelfth century onward; in recent years the term has also been applied in other cases and has become — such is our impression — a marker of cultural excellence.

Obviously, such processes have had different characteristics — in some cases, for instance, translations were made exclusively or predominantly from a single source language; other cases involved several source languages. But the features on which modern historians concentrate, and the descriptions they offer, are no less different — so different indeed that the phrase 'translation movement' can be seen to be not an analytical tool but, precisely, *a phrase* simply describing that suddenly more translations were made in the environment in question than usually. Each historian may intend something more precise, but such usage is not intersubjective.

As an offer for improving the intersubjectivity of our usage of terms and stories, we sketch a framework with which we can reflect on current or less current observer narratives.

Firstly, can we meaningfully model the sociocultural processes around an accumulation of translations in a given epoch and context in terms of 'translation movements' and if so, what should this concept mean to us? This question includes several sub-questions, for instance:

1.1. Since originally one spoke of only two 'translation movements', when was this concept introduced, by whom and with which (if any) interpretive goals?

1.2. Why was the concept traditionally not applied to other cultural processes in which translating played an important role, whether in Europe, Asia, Africa, or the Americas?

1.3. What were the qualitative and quantitative properties that called for the application of the concept to the events that took place in Abbasid Baghdad between the second half of the eighth and the first half of the eleventh centuries, and in different regions and cities of the Iberian Peninsula, southern France, Sicily, southern Italy, and Byzantium in the twelfth and thirteenth centuries?

1.4. How can we be certain that all translation efforts in a given period and space belong to one and the same cultural process and not to different coterminous processes?

1.5. Given the existence of different kinds of translation — authored translations, anonymous translations, multiple translations, invented translations, plagiarized translations, etc. — and thus different kinds of actors with different kinds of professional, social, cultural, and ethnic identities: what are our criteria to decide that they all contributed to one and the same cultural process which we rightfully may baptize a 'movement'?

1.6. Why do we less often or never call other accumulated translations a 'movement', even those which took place within a single cultural sphere? Examples are translations into Armenian, Coptic, New Persian, Hebrew, Ottoman Turkish, Byzantine Greek, Tangut, Mongol, or Japanese.

A second main question concerns issues of choice. Why do we single out certain kinds of actors, subject matters, languages, periods, cultures, and regions when designating 'translating' as an important cultural process worthy of our sustained attention? Here too, several sub-questions can be easily formulated:

2.1. Why do we privilege in the case of the Abbasid 'movement' Christians as translators and Muslims as patrons, while ignoring mostly Zoroastrians, Jews, and other groups also involved in such activities?

2.2. In contrast, why do we focus with regard to medieval translations into Latin on the Catholic actors and downgrade often the Mozarab and Jewish participants?

2.3. Why do we not include in the concept of the 'translation movement' translations into the vernaculars?

2.4. Why do we insist on telling different narratives about scientific, medical, and philosophical translations in comparison to translations of religious, literary, historical, legal, economic, and other texts?

A third type of question applies to issues of context. Which kinds of context do we privilege in different academic fields and different time periods?

Here, we have no sub-questions to offer, but comments. When two of our editorial trio entered the field of history of science in Islamicate societies or Latin Europe in the 1970s, very few contexts were considered relevant for analysing any given translation in particular or the entire phenomenon of translating scientific, medical, and philosophical texts in general. Those that were considered relevant in the Abbasid case were religious debates between Muslims and Christians, practical needs like healing or prognostication, and courtly patronage. Nonetheless, there is — to the best of our knowledge — no study by a historian of science in Islamicate societies of the first and the third type of context for the second half of the eighth century available until now that goes beyond declarations of belief. The analysis of religious polemics is undertaken primarily by colleagues in Religious Studies who, on their side, do not really pursue links to the translation of scientific, medical, or philosophical texts at or around the Abbasid court. Courtly patronage in the eighth century is difficult to assess due to a lack of sources and a lack of training among historians of science, medicine, and philosophy in Islamicate societies with regard to sophisticated qualitative research methods. As a result, central beliefs about 'courtly patronage' as a sociocultural context are not built on sufficient direct evidence nor on reliable methodological investigations of indirect evidence. Let us present one example.

Many historians, art historians, economic historians, and a few historians of philosophy in Islamicate societies are convinced that the Abbasid dynasty consciously built its legitimacy, politics, economy, and culture on Sasanian models. The arguments for this belief include: the circular structure of the new capital Baghdad; the use of imagery and material from Ktesiphon, the last Sasanian capital; the employment of Iranian secretarial families and astrologers recently converted to Islam or still adhering to the Zoroastrian faith; the rise of astrology as a court office and policy; the reported translation of Middle Persian historical, political, and astrological texts; stories by tenth-century historical writers about the Sasanian character of Abbasid institutions; the alleged existence of a Sasanian narrative of translation. Since we are not historians of architecture or art, we ignore the first two points and focus on the issues of astrology and storytelling. It is certainly true that Iranian secretarial families and astrologers who had recently converted to Islam or continued to adhere to their paternal faith worked for the Abbasid dynasty. Examples are Ibn al-Muqaffaʿ, his father, and his son; the Nawbakht and the Ibn Sahl families; the Bānu Munajjim and the Bānu Mūsā; and the famous

Barmakids. It is equally reasonable to assume that Middle Persian astrological texts were translated into Arabic and that the Sasanian usage of astrology as a historical narrative, unknown in Mesopotamian, Hellenistic, Roman, or Indian astrology — as far as we know — was quickly applied by Iranian astrologers to Muḥammad's birth and prophecy. But does this evidence suffice to speak of an emulation of Sasanian precedents by Abbasid caliphs; and if so, what would be the political, cultural, and religious meaning of such an emulation within Abbasid politics and for the acquisition of different kinds of foreign knowledge through translating?

One of the difficulties when facing such issues is that the Umayyad dynasty, preceding the Abbasids, had already hired Iranian secretaries and administrators, among them the father of Ibn al-Muqaffaʿ and Ibn al-Muqaffaʿ himself as well as Khālid b. Barmak. Would that mean that already the Umayyads followed Sasanian precedents and the Abbasids merely continued Umayyad custom? What should we then think of the absence of any major translation activity under the Umayyad dynasty? Are we just too blind to see it or is the claimed link between material and social continuity in the Near East too weak for explaining the translation activities that took place under the Abbasids? And where had the astrologers acquired their knowledge and skills who cast the horoscope for Baghdad in 762? We know that Nawbakht came from Ahwaz in Khuzistan and the Iranian Jew Māshāʾallāh from Basra. Does this mean that in the regions of southern Iraq (or at least within its Jewish segment) and western Iran astrology was sufficiently established for those men to learn their professions and textual traditions? And how did a Sasanian courtly science survive a century without a court to sustain it? Had astrology migrated into some other sociocultural context after the fall of the Sasanian dynasty? In a discussion about these and other questions concerning the survival and translation of Sasanian knowledge and institutions until the early ninth century, Götz König proposed the Zoroastrian clergy as this protective umbrella (which would be a parallel to the conservation of Babylonian scholarly scribal culture within the temples of Babylon and Warka (Uruk) after the collapse of the Assyrian and Neobabylonian political structures). König's reflections on the traces of natural philosophy in Zoroastrian literature of that period, presented within this volume, complicate the situation and challenge our traditional understanding. Māshāʾallāh moreover lived in an Umayyad garrison city, i.e. in a military settlement founded by Arab troops in the period of expansion and conquest. It had now become the seat of the Umayyad governor and intense political intrigues. It also was one of the two earliest cities of Muslim intellectual activity in the domain of grammar. Where could an Iranian Jew have learned and practised astrology in such a cultural context? We simply do not know, because to the best of our knowledge nobody has yet explored this issue. But the Iranian astrologers were not the only people who participated in casting the horoscope for Baghdad. Although the stories told about this event are contradictory and incomplete, at least one Arab had sufficient skills to be seen by later transmitters of the stories as a legitimate practitioner of the art and a member of the group of experts — Ibrāhīm al-Fazarī. According to David Pingree, al-Fazarī is believed to have come from an Arab family which settled in Kufa, the other early centre of Arabic grammatical studies and, like Basra, a military settlement of Muslim troops. Why an allegedly old Arab family agreed to let their son learn an art practised by Iranian Zoroastrians and Jews and with whom then Ibrāhīm might have studied the methods, theories, and instruments is another problem that we have apparently no information about. But according to the sparse documentation of his life and scholarly achievements in medieval sources, he was the first Muslim to write about and construct astronomical instruments. Thus, he was an important actor in what became labelled the 'translation movement'. Exploring the Kufan context in the eighth century is thus as important a task as exploring the contexts of Basra and Ahvaz if we wish to better understand these cultural changes and transformations. Turning to colleagues who study the emergence of Arabic grammatical studies is one of the possible points of entry into such an inquiry. We might discover some nuggets of information that could reshape our views about the impact that Sasanian memories, Zoroastrian and Jewish practices, and Arab social organization in southern Iraq and western Iran under the late Umayyads may have exercised on the emergence of astrology as an accepted courtly practice under the early Abbasids. Such potential new bits of knowledge may help us to better understand the growing interest in foreign knowledge. But what is already clear today is what Dimitri Gutas has argued, although in too general terms, namely that the Sasanian connection — whether invented as a narrative or upheld as continued knowledge — was of a decisive importance for the phenomenon of translating scientific texts into Arabic as narrated by some of its participants and later, in particular Buyid, writers of histories about Abbasid times.

Which Narratives Do We Tell?

In a previous paper, Brentjes, Fidora, and Tischler offered critical comments on the main observer narratives on Latin translations of Greek and Arabic scientific, medical, philosophical, and occult texts before 1400. They described the dominating observer narrative constructed and maintained during the twentieth century as 'teleological, linear, mono-cultural, and static'.[1] In their view, the key components of this long-term successful observer narrative are the concept of a twelfth-century renaissance, the recovery of Ancient Greek philosophy, medicine, and science, and a purposeful intellectual movement that stood at the beginning of the renewed rise of rational knowledge in Europe

1 Brentjes, Fidora, and Tischler, 'Towards a New Approach', pp. 9, 11–13.

and continued in an uninterrupted manner up to our own times with their sciences, philosophies, and technologies.[2]

This observer narrative resulted from and encouraged practices of exclusion and isolation. The post-Second World War form of the narrative defined the translations of scientific, medical, and philosophical texts of the twelfth and thirteenth centuries as a translation movement silently assuming that every participant in these activities had the same goals and ambitions. Earlier translations were explicitly excluded from the narrative. Translations after the thirteenth century were not merely ignored. It was believed that there were none or at least none of relevance to the history of science, medicine, and philosophy. Translations into vernaculars remained somehow in limbo, being mentioned but not seen as truly belonging to the great story of recovery and the new beginning. Translations into Hebrew were recognized in observer narratives, when the source language was Arabic.[3] Translations from Latin into Hebrew or from Hebrew into Latin were rarely included in such narratives, despite the material already provided by Steinschneider in the late nineteenth century and despite the fact that the Hebrew translations of Latin texts emerged in the twelfth century.[4] In some specialized works they are described as rare or even less relevant until the early twenty-first century.[5] Participating translators received similarly asymmetric treatments, in particular, when they cooperated across linguistic and religious boundaries.[6]

The sciences also suffered under this observer narrative. Modern views of what was scientific were imposed on the intellectual trends of those much earlier periods. As a result, not only famous texts on astrology, magic, alchemy, and other so-called occult disciplines for which no translators were and are known, but also those translated by well-known translators, received only limited attention. Their central meaning for the so-called translation

---

2 Brentjes, Fidora, and Tischler, 'Towards a New Approach', p. 11.

3 Langermann, 'Science in the Jewish Communities', pp. 172, 175, 177, 179–80.

4 Langermann, 'Science in the Jewish Communities', pp. 172, 181–82; Steinschneider, *Die hebräischen Übersetzungen des Mittelalters*. For more recent works on Hebrew translations of Latin works, see for instance, Ferre, 'Traducciones'; Ferre, 'Hebrew Translations'; Hasselhoff, *Dicit Rabbi Moyses*. For a list of Hebrew translations of Latin works see Zonta, 'Medieval Hebrew Translations', pp. 20, 22–24, 27–29, 31–32, 36–37, 39–41, 44–56, 58–72.

5 See, despite his other important new evaluations and perspectives, both in his own papers and those of other contributors to his edited volume, Freudenthal, 'Arabic and Latin Cultures as Resources for the Hebrew Translation Movement', pp. 74–105; Langermann, 'Science in the Jewish Communities', p. 172.

6 D'Alverny, 'Translations and Translators'; D'Alverny, 'Les traductions à deux interprètes'; Burnett, *Arabic into Latin in the Middle Ages*; Langermann, 'Science in the Jewish Communities', p. 172; Hasse, 'The Social Conditions', p. 72. Recent changes in attention and interpretation are signaled, for instance, in works by Zonta, 'The Jewish Mediation', p. 102; Zonta, 'Medieval Hebrew Translations', pp. 17–18.

movement took a long time before finally being fully recognized in the last third of the twentieth century.[7]

Translations in other areas such as law, trade, diplomacy, history, geography, or war were not considered necessary for understanding the societal activities and desires that enabled translation to occur as a cultural phenomenon. Asymmetries between the geographies of translation in medieval Europe were a further problem that characterizes the observer narrative on translations in the sciences, medicine, and philosophy dominating in the twentieth century. The separation of research on Muslim-ruled societies in al-Andalus, Sicily, southern Italy, or eastern Europe and Oriental Christian societies in Byzantium, the Balkans, Bulgaria, or the Rus from research on Occidental Christian societies and hence the separate investigation of translations even of medical, philosophical, occult, or scientific texts is a well-known outcome not merely of the observer narrative on Latin translations of Arabic and Greek texts but of the grand narrative that shaped the historical profession institutionally and mentally over the last two centuries, if not longer.

During the last two to three decades, this Eurocentric, Occidental Christianity observer narrative which priviledged science, medicine, and philosophy has begun to crumble. Numerous new research efforts have demonstrated its flaws and weaknesses both on the historiographical level and on the levels of historical detail. Therefore, we regret it all the more that all our efforts were unsuccessful to motivate a colleague to write a new analysis of these changes in perspective and methodology with regard to medieval and early modern translations in Europe.

Encouraged by the historian in our editorial team, we offered the invited colleagues to reflect about their experience with applying theoretical tools in the study of translations in their fields of expertise. We are grateful to Benjamin Wright who responded enthusiastically to this invitation. Four other contributors to the first part accepted another focus of our invitation and reflect on how interpretations of translations of scientific, medical, philosophical, occult, or religious texts into Syriac, Arabic, or Tangut and their contexts evolved over the last century or slightly more (Martelli, Shefer-Mossensohn, Hjälm, Galambos). Crisostomo argues for a daily practice of translating in the surviving cuneiform tablets from one Babylonian scribal family. König challenges parts of Gutas' thesis of a Sasanian narrative and culture of translating by pointing to the Abbasid context of some of the philosophical terms and ideas in famous Middle Persian works compiled during the ninth century that previously were taken as evidence for such an antecedent. Fierro, finally, addresses both a specific narrative of translating in Umayyad al-Andalus and the absence of translation from Andalusian knowledge cultures.

7 Lemay, *Abu Maʿshar*; Lemay, 'The True Place of Astrology'; Brentjes, 'Reflexionen'; Burnett, 'Astrology, Astronomy and Magic'.

While discussions of translations focused traditionally on the analysis of translated texts and their translators' techniques, in recent years, introductions to Latin translations of scientific, medical, philosophical, or occult texts have attracted more systematic analytic attention. Extracts from forty such reports from the ninth to the fourteenth century were recently published together with other texts and are thus now more easily accessible.[8] We call such stories 'participant narratives'. The narrational thread that Martínez Gázquez derived from those reports is one of poverty of knowledge, eagerness to learn, admiration for knowledge expressed in Greek and Arabic, and of the translators seeing themselves at the threshold of a new era that their labour would usher in.[9] It is clear that he identifies here exclusively a narrative constructed by Christians mostly foreign to the worlds of the Iberian Peninsula (and, by extension, Byzantium). The threads constructed by Jewish and Mozarab translators and authors also found in some of the introductions cannot be summarized in such a manner. When found in Latin translations, they rather highlight their pride in their knowledge, their willingness to share it, and their conviction that such knowledge in new garb would be more than useful to the new lords of the land. Narrational points shared among translators of different faith and language concern self-representation and criticism at rivals. The introduction of Stephen of Antioch's translation of ʿAlī b. al-ʿAbbās al-Majūsī's *al-Kitāb al-malikī* (*The Royal Book*) makes this clear for a Christian translator from Italy with regard to a Christian translator from North Africa.[10] The extracts published by Martínez Gázquez reveal several other strands of narration that deserve attention and challenge a too credulous reading of the traditionally emphasized ones listed above.

A comparison between all those strands present in prologues, as well as comments, descriptions, and other textual components of translations from Arabic into Latin with narratives offered in true or pretended translations in other linguistic and thus cultural contexts is our main proposal in this book for approaching issues of context. We are aware, of course, that several other options also exist as richly documented in Bruce O'Brien's book *Reversing Babel*. This book encouraged us to look beyond translations of scientific, medical, philosophical, and occult texts to simultaneous translations in other fields of knowledge and larger cultural practices. Instead of describing the movement of source texts through successive translations done from antiquity to the Middle Ages, O'Brien directs attention to the linguistic ideas and translation practices current when any individual translation was done. He charts these ideas and practices as comprehensively as possible, noting all languages used and all translations (in all genres) done at the time. This

8 Martínez Gázquez, *The Attitude*.

9 Martínez Gázquez, *The Attitude*, pp. 11–12; see also his evaluation of such narrational threads in Martínez Gázques, 'Auctor et auctoritas', pp. 697–704.

10 Martínez Gázquez, *The Attitude*, pp. 25–26.

broader context for translation as the basis for analysis offers an alternative to a traditional approach which would follow a text as it passed from one language through a series of other languages over as long a period as 1500 years. In O'Brien's view, each individual translation done over this long span of time is best understood in the context of the full range of translation ideas and practices current at that time of the translation's creation. The starting point is where languages come into contact. We need to keep in mind that places where language contact occurred were real, three-dimensional meetings between people who used different languages and were engaged in everything from haggling in the market over the price of silk, hearing testimony in a court, journeying on pilgrimage to the other side of the Mediterranean, as well as reading an Arabic text of a treatise by Aristotle. All of these contact situations occurred in a world governed by natural geographies — not only the linkages created by the sea road that joined England to Byzantium and the Islamic states, but also the divisions between highland and lowland, the barriers and bonds made by rivers and roads, and the rise of multicultural urban centres. This cacophonous portrait of the ideas and practices in evidence in a culture at a given moment is not just the noise from which one rescues a key translation, but is the very fabric of sound in the ears and minds of the translators, and should, therefore, be the foundation of any paradigm that hopes to explain translation.

O'Brien's study emboldened us to include in this book studies of participant narratives in poetry (Wilden), texts on erotica (Gurevich), conversion and pseudepigraphy (Fiori), alchemical fiction (Braun), law and religious controversy (Fidora), Kabbala (Dal Bo), freemasonry and diplomacy (Soto), or trade (Clemens). These ventures into territories unexplored by historians of science and largely unknown to historians of Latin Christianity are accompanied by new stories about participant narratives or fragments thereof in medical (Carpentieri, Finotto) and mathematical works (Raina).

Bibliography

d'Alverny, Marie-Thérèse, 'Translations and Translators', in *Renaissance and Renewal in the Twelfth Century*, ed. by Robert Louis Benson and Giles Constable (Cambridge, MA: Harvard University Press, 1982), pp. 421–62; [there are several reprints of the entire volume]; [repr. *La transmission*, no II and Addenda et corrigenda, 1]

——, 'Les traductions à deux interprètes, d'arabe en langue vernaculaire et de langue vernaculaire en latin', in *Traduction et traducteurs au moyen âge*, Actes du Colloque international du CNRS organisé à Paris, Institut de recherche et d'histoire des textes, les 26–28 mai 1986, ed. by Geneviève Contamine (Paris: Éditions du CNRS, 1989), pp. 193–206 [repr. *La transmission*, no III]

——, *La transmission des textes philosophiques et scientifiques au moyen âge*, ed. by Charles Burnett, Collected Studies Series, 463 (Aldershot: Variorum, 1994)

Brentjes, Sonja, 'Reflexionen zur Bedeutung der im 12. Jahrhundert angefertigten lateinischen Übersetzungen wissenschaftlicher Texte für die europäische Wissenschaftsgeschichte', in *Europa. Die Gegenwärtigkeit der antiken Überlieferung*, ed. by Justus Cobet, Carl Friedrich Gethmann, and Dieter Lau, Essener Beiträge zur Kulturgeschichte, 2 (Aachen: Shaker, 2000), pp. 269–305

Brentjes, Sonja, Alexander Fidora, and Matthias Tischler, 'Towards a New Approach to Medieval Cross-Cultural Exchanges', *Journal of Transcultural Medieval Studies*, 1.1 (2014), 9–50

Burnett, Charles, 'Astrology, Astronomy and Magic as the Motivation for the Scientific Renaissance of the Twelfth Century', in *The Imaginal Cosmos: Astrology, Divination and the Sacred*, ed. by Angela Voss and Jean Hinson Lall; Introduction by Geoffrey Cornelius (Canterbury: The University of Kent, 2007), pp. 55–61

——, *Arabic into Latin in the Middle Ages: The Translators and their Intellectual and Social Context*, Collected Studies Series, 939 (Farnham: Ashgate Variorum, 2009)

Ferre, Lola, 'Traducciones al hebreo de obras médicas en los s. XIII y XIV', *Miscelánea de estudios árabes y hebraicos*, 33.2 (1985–86), 61–74

——, 'Hebrew Translations from Medical Treatises of Montpellier', *Korot*, 13 (1998–89), 21–36

Freudenthal, Gad, 'Arabic and Latin Cultures as Resources for the Hebrew Translation Movement: Comparative Considerations, Both Quantitative and Qualitative', in *Science in Medieval Jewish Cultures*, ed. by Gad Freudenthal (Cambridge: Cambridge University Press, 2011), pp. 74–105

Hasse, Dag Nikolaus, 'The Social Conditions of the Arabic-(Hebrew-)Latin Translation Movements in Medieval Spain and in the Renaissance', in *Wissen über Grenzen. Arabisches Wissen und lateinisches Mittelalter*, ed. by Andreas Speer and Lydia Wegner (Berlin: de Gruyter, 2006), pp. 68–86

Hasselhoff, Görge, *Dicit Rabbi Moyses: Studien zum Bild von Moses Maimonides im lateinischen Westen vom 13. bis 15. Jahrhundert* (Würzburg: Königshausen und Neumann, 2004) [enlarged edn 2006]

Langermann, Y. Tzvi, 'Science in the Jewish Communities', in *The Cambridge History of Science, Vol. 2: Medieval Science*, ed. by David C. Lindberg and Michael H. Shank (Cambridge: Cambridge University Press, 2013), pp. 1688–89

Lemay, Richard [Joseph], *Abu Ma'shar and Latin Aristotelianism in the 12th century. The recovery of Aristotle's Natural Philosophy through Arabic astrology*, Publications of the Faculty of Arts and Sciences. Oriental Series, 38 (Beirut: American University of Beirut, 1962)

——, 'The True Place of Astrology in Medieval Science and Philosophy: Towards a Definition', in *Astrology, Science and Society: Historical Essays*, ed. by Patrick Curry (Woodbridge: Boydell, 1987), pp. 57–73

Martínez Gázquez, José, 'Auctor et auctoritas en las traducciones del griego y el árabe al latín', in *Auctor et auctoritas in latini medii aevi litteris. Author and Authorship in Medieval Latin Literature, Proceedings of the VIth Congress of the International Medieval Latin Committee (Benevento-Naples, November 913, 2010)*, ed. by Edoardo D'Angelo and Jan Ziolkowski (Florence: Sismel, Editioni del Galluzzo, 2014), pp. 691–708

——, *The Attitude of the Medieval Latin Translators Towards the Arabic Sciences*, Micrologus Library (Florence: Sismel, Eidzioni Galluzzo, 2016)

O'Brien, Bruce, *Reversing Babel: Translation Among the English During an Age of Conquests, c. 800 to c. 1200* (Newark: University of Delaware Press, 2011)

Steinschneider, Moritz, *Die hebräischen Übersetzungen des Mittelalters und die Juden als Dolmetscher. Ein Beitrag zur Literaturgeschichte des Mittelalters, meist nach handschriftlichen Quellen* (Berlin: Kommissionsverlag des Bibliographischen Bureaus, 1893) [there are several reprints]

Zonta, Mauro, 'The Jewish Mediation in the Transmission of Arabic-Islamic Science and Philosophy to the Latin Middle Ages: Historical Overview and Perspectives of Research', in *Wissen über Grenzen. Arabisches Wissen und lateinisches Mittelalter*, ed. by Andreas Speer and Lydia Wegner (Berlin: de Gruyter, 2006), pp. 89–105

——, 'Medieval Hebrew Translations of Philosophical and Scientific Texts: A Chronological Table', in *Science in Medieval Jewish Culture*, ed. by Gad Freudenthal (Cambridge: Cambridge University Press, 2011), pp. 17–73

Part 1

Observer Narratives

C. JAY CRISOSTOMO

Scholarly Translation in the Ancient Middle East

Ancient and Modern Perspectives

Translation was an important aspect of the cuneiform cultures of the ancient Middle East. The people who invented and subsequently adapted the cuneiform writing system existed in a multilingual culture and the documents they wrote often reflected such to varied extent. Cuneiform scribes composed and translated narratives, lists, prayers, royal propaganda, and many other genres primarily in scholarly, non-vernacular languages. Often lacking in our modern appreciation of these translations, however, is the recognition that, like modern translators, ancient translators adopted multiple roles and thereby utilized varied modes of translation. In other words, their cultures of translation reflected different ways of knowing and thus variegated outcomes. Considering these modes of translation and accepting how and why cuneiform translators translated historically and situationally invites us to reconsider what counts as *translation*.

In what follows, I look carefully at one of these modes — *scholarly translation*. I demonstrate that scholarly translations, particularly those in word lists, were not intended to convey semantic meaning about one word or phrase in another language — a mode of translation I call here *communicative translation* — but were instead part of a larger project of knowledge production, an integral dynamic of scholarly ingenuity and cuneiform writing cultures in general. In the word lists which formed the backbone of cuneiform scholarly production for nearly 3000 years, scholarly translation could result in equivalencies such as Sumerian 'sun' is Akkadian 'donkey', Sumerian 'to know' is Akkadian 'silver', and Sumerian 'ten' is Akkadian 'hand'. Moreover, the scholars who produced these scholarly translations were — in practice, but not in theory — apathetic about language boundaries. Through their

C. Jay Crisostomo (PhD, University of California, Berkeley) (cjcrisos@umich.edu) is Associate Professor of Assyriology at the University of Michigan. His research focuses on language use and the intellectual history of cuneiform cultures of the ancient Middle East. His first book, *Translation as Scholarship* (De Gruyter, 2019), examined the role of interlingual analogical reasoning in scribal education in the early second millennium BCE. He is currently writing a book on the social uses of Sumerian over its 3000-year history.

Narratives on Translation across Eurasia and Africa: From Babylonia to Colonial India, ed. by Sonja Brentjes in cooperation with Jens Høyrup and Bruce O'Brien, CAT 3, pp. 27–44 (Turnhout: Brepols, 2022) BREPOLS PUBLISHERS 10.1484/M.CAT-EB.5.127932

activities and products, they demonstrated that the cuneiform writing system rather than the semantics, grammars, or contents of individual languages was their primary objective of knowledge. This view contrasts with previous work in Assyriology.

Throughout its relatively brief history, Assyriology — the study of cuneiform languages and cultures — has until recently assumed, like most predominantly Western presumptions about translation, that translation in cuneiform was principally *communicative* in nature and, as such, largely unremarkable. That is, translation was viewed as simply transferring meaning from one language to another. Any variation in translation practice has generally been regarded as atypical or language play. Certainly, communicative translation was an important facet of multilingual literature, but this was not the only mode of translation that cuneiform translators utilized. This brief discussion accords with recent calls in translation studies to broaden definitions of translation and text types traditionally associated with translation.[1]

In the introduction to her overview of translation in the twenty-first century, Susan Bassnett remarks on the difference between what she calls the layman's view of translation and the reality. The former, she writes, assumes translation 'involves a simple process of linguistic transfer, whereby whatever is written in one language [...] can be transferred unproblematically into another language', a viewpoint which minimalizes the role of the translator. Bassnett contrasts this simplistic notion with a reality in which translators are required to engage in a complex navigation of languages, constituting a form of rewriting. Ultimately, Bassnett — continuing the call of numerous others working on translation — emphasizes the translator and the importance of understanding the translator's role, purpose, and creativity in translation.[2] Yet, like most considerations of translation, Bassnett's historical overview begins with Cicero and, moreover, retains a view of translation that is largely literary and communicative in character. Long before Cicero, translation in all its complexity is first recorded in the ancient Middle East.

In this paper, after a brief introduction to the cuneiform writing system and its potential, I introduce the writing cultures of the ancient Middle East, the social worlds in which translation took place, and the modes of translation scribes and scholars utilized. I then discuss ancient metalinguistic conceptualizations of translation and language ideology. I next consider the work of a particular Babylonian scholar, Nabû-kuṣuršu (*c.* 450 BCE) of the city of Borsippa, his work on translation, and conclude with the implications of his work and the culture of scholarly translation for modern conceptions of ancient languages and translation.

---

1 Tymoczko, 'Reconceptualizing Translation Theory', pp. 13–32.

2 Bassnett, *Translation*, p. 2.

Cuneiform Writing

In its initial form, the cuneiform writing system that developed in what is now the Middle East was primarily iconic in nature. By the time the writing system was conventionalized into the familiar wedge-shaped signs with which the general public is familiar, each sign — now more indexical or even symbolic — had acquired multiple phonetic values and potential meanings. A given sign could be used syllabically or logographically, representing either part of a word or morpheme or a whole word on its own. For example, the sign KA (𒅗), originally shaped as a head with markings to indicate the region of the mouth, could represent the Sumerian words kag 'mouth' as well as a series of Sumerian words related to the mouth and things emanating from the mouth including gu$_3$ 'voice', inim 'word', kir$_3$ 'nose', zu$_2$ 'tooth' or dug$_4$ 'to say' in addition to the syllabic equivalents or approximants for each of these words such as /ka/ or /qa/.[3] By virtue of the rebus principle, the sign could also be used to represent words that sounded similar to words the sign already represented such as kiri$_4$ 'hyena' which sounded like kir$_3$ 'nose'. When the writing system was adapted to languages other than Sumerian, particularly Akkadian (see below), signs further acquired the phonetic values of a Sumerian word's Akkadian counterparts. So, KA could represent the Akkadian words *pû* 'mouth', *rigmu* 'voice', *amātu* 'word', *appu* 'nose', *šinnu* 'tooth', and various verbs for 'to say' such as *epēšu* or *qabû*. In addition, depending on local conventions, KA could potentially represent syllabic apocopations or approximants of some of these words such as /pu/ as well as conjugated variations of this word such as /pi/. Although at first encounter, such a writing system may seem overwhelming, cumbersome, and ambiguous, much of the theoretical potential outlined here was limited by local writing conventions. It is worth noting that the *potential* exists and was accordingly exploited by scholars in esoteric ways and occasionally for scholarly translation. Whereas communicative translation regularly relied upon typical writing conventions, scholarly translation capitalized upon the potential inherent in the writing system and embedded within the languages which used it.

Writing Cultures

Cuneiform writing was invented in southern Mesopotamia in the latter half of the fourth millennium. Initially developed for bureaucratic purposes, this iteration of the writing system was largely a semiotic system which could theoretically represent any language.[4] By the middle of the third millennium

3 The subscripted numbers are modern scholarly conventions intended to indicate which sign is written with the given value — i.e., the sign ka$_2$ is differentiated from the sign ka$_3$. The numbers are not pronounced.

4 Most likely this writing represented Sumerian; nevertheless, some doubt remains and the

BCE, cuneiform was undoubtedly used to represent Sumerian and some Semitic languages. At this same time, uses for writing expanded from a bureaucratic context. Genres such as incantations, royal propaganda, property transfers, and narratives were recorded through the medium of cuneiform writing. Multilingualism is evident even in the earliest documents written in Semitic.[5] Translation, however, particularly in the form of bilingual texts, is not known until around 2400 BCE at the city of Ebla (Tell Mardikh, Syria), such as that preserved in a literary composition — a hymn to the sun god — written in Sumerian from the southern Mesopotamian city of Abū Ṣalābīḫ and in a Semitic language from Ebla.[6] Soon afterwards, when Sargon of Agade created a large polity in southern Mesopotamia, he instituted a new scribal culture, placing Akkadian, a Semitic language, at the centre of his bureaucracy. Akkadian and Sumerian then co-existed as written cuneiform languages for the next two thousand years.

Sometime in the late third millennium, Sumerian was restricted to a literary, ritual, and documentary language, no longer vernacular. This resulted in a rise of a different scribal culture, which focused on Sumerian as a learned language, acquired through copying texts, memorization and, ostensibly, recitation. During this period, referred to in modern scholarship as the Old Babylonian period (the first half of the second millennium BCE), translation became a fundamental aspect of scribal culture, part of the expectation for scribes mastering the cuneiform writing system and the languages which utilized it. Because the scribes were all native speakers of a language other than Sumerian, translation must have been a requisite aspect of their education despite the relative paucity of bilingual texts (i.e., objects with multiple languages explicitly translated). But more importantly, the ability to translate demonstrated that a scribe-in-training could actively engage in scholarship, manipulating the language and writing to effectively create new and innovative translations that had little to do with learning to read and write literary Sumerian. In this way scholarly translation became an important aspect of cuneiform scribal culture and would remain so until the end of the written tradition.

The latter half of the second millennium BCE saw cuneiform scribal culture flourish throughout the ancient Middle East. Cuneiform tablets have been discovered in Egypt, Turkey, Israel/Palestine, Lebanon, Syria, Iran, Bahrain, and of course Iraq. The writing system was the medium for the main diplomatic language of the period, Akkadian, and used for correspondence throughout the eastern Mediterranean and Middle East, from Cyprus to Egypt, from Western Anatolia to Iran. In each location there is evidence of

---

ambiguity reflects the lack of necessary linguistic affiliation (see further Englund, 'Texts from the Late Uruk Period', pp. 56–81 and Rubio, 'On the Linguistic Landscape').

5 Gelb, Steinkeller, and Whiting, *Earliest Land Tenure Systems*, pp. 11–14.

6 See Lambert, 'The Language of ARET V 6 and 7', pp. 41–62 and Civil and Rubio, 'An Ebla Incantation against Insomnia and the Semiticization of Sumerian', pp. 263–66.

some degree of training in this particular scribal culture. With the spread of the writing system came further innovations in multilingualism, including the adaptation of existing cuneiform compositions to other languages and cultures as well as the creation and innovation of new works and experiments in multiple writing systems and languages. As a result, translation continued to play an important role, not just for communication but also for ongoing exploration of the potential and limits of cuneiform writing. The adaptation of cuneiform to Indo-European Hittite and other languages of Anatolia as well as the creation of a cuneiform abjad at Ugarit (Syria) resulted in extensive experimentation with local languages both separate from and alongside the traditional cuneiform languages and scripts.

During the first millennium, as Assyrian and Babylonian states spread throughout the ancient Middle East, cuneiform scribal cultures continued to flourish. Yet Akkadian — following the example of Sumerian 1000 years earlier — faded from vernacular use.[7] Nevertheless, both Akkadian and Sumerian retained their status as the primary languages of scholarship written on clay tablets.[8] Scholars worked to both preserve and expand ancient traditions as well as innovate and reproduce cuneiform knowledge, with translation playing perhaps even a greater role in the process than ever before. Translation at this time — especially scholarly translation — often focused less on necessarily replicating Sumerian in Akkadian (or other languages) and more on grounding knowledge of the cuneiform writing system in the guise of its traditional languages.

In cuneiform scribal cultures, translation manifested in multiple forms within these varied political and social environments. Scholarly translation existed alongside other modes of translation, especially literary (communicative) translation. In cuneiform scholarly culture, literary translation often invoked transformation. Here, I use transformation to capture the sense in which we typically think of translation, but also other modes that extended a discourse beyond its original capacity and social world. Indeed, the innovation of multilingual texts at Ebla mentioned above apparently arose from a desire to transfer some aspects of southern Mesopotamian writing culture to northern cultures and the local Eblaite culture. Among the tablets discovered in Ebla are bilingual word lists that replicate those found in southern Mesopotamia during the period with 'translations' into the local dialect as well as aforementioned local 'translations' of literary texts that were written in Sumerian in the south as early as the third millennium.[9]

---

7 On the languages of the later first millennium and the replacement of Akkadian in cuneiform cultures, especially by Aramaic languages, see Beaulieu, 'Official and Vernacular Languages', and Hackl, 'Zur Sprachsituation in Babylonien'.

8 Other scholarly languages may have been preserved on more permeable media such as parchment, papyri, wax writing boards, or wood.

9 On these lists, see especially Veldhuis, *History of the Cuneiform Lexical Tradition*, pp. 129–39.

Similar instances of transformative translations from the second millennium include the well-known re-imaginations of the stories of the goddess Inana's (Ištar) descent to the Netherworld, the legends of the demi-god-king Gilgamesh, and the hero who built a life-preserving boat and gained eternal life (the 'Flood Story'). These literary narratives were written in Sumerian and were substantially revised and redacted in Akkadian iterations.[10] These edited and translated compositions may be considered original works in themselves and not merely translations or simulacra, but nevertheless speak to the role of translation in bridging linguistic varieties. Presumably these transformations served to preserve these well-known stories for perceived literary revolutions, allowing for direct transmission over time. But in the particular examples of the Inana/Ištar stories and Gilgamesh stories, Sumerian and Akkadian versions existed simultaneously, sometimes even in the same social environment, such as a scribal school.[11]

In the first millennium, Sumerian-Akkadian translators utilized translation as transformation to foster a different kind of cultural transfer despite the restricted use of both languages. Select classic works composed in these languages continued to be copied and transmitted, including works from the whole range of literary genres such as narratives, proverbs, incantations, prayers and hymns to gods, and so-called laments. New translations in these genres, such as the story of the god Ninurta's heroic exploits (often called 'Lugal-e') could be utilized in innovative ways for political or literary purposes.[12] But beyond mere cultural conservation, new compositions could be created in either or even both languages, featuring translations from one to the other language. Among these are compositions which draw on ancient compositions, such as narratives praising the goddess Ištar or the scribal school (see below).[13]

In contrast to literary, communicative translation, scholarly translation focused primarily on innovation and knowledge production. In this way,

---

10 There is some discussion about whether the two traditions were rather co-existing and independent or whether the Akkadian versions were dependent upon the Sumerian. Regardless, the existence of two linguistic traditions of the same narrative indicates that translation and transformation played a part at some point in the transmission and textual production of these narratives. On the development of the Gilgamesh stories, see especially Tigay, *The Evolution of the Gilgamesh Epic*, pp. 241–50 and George, *The Babylonian Gilgamesh Epic*, pp. 17–22.

11 At least one fragment of the story of Gilgamesh's journey to the Cedar Forest in Akkadian seems to have been found in the same context as similar stories written in Sumerian that served as part of the curriculum of Sumerian schools. One Akkadian version of the 'Flood Story' was copied by a scribe who also produced several important Sumerian literary stories, again suggesting the two linguistic literary traditions belonged, at least in part, to the same scribal culture (Koppen, 'The Scribe of the Flood Story', and Löhnert, 'Ipiq-Aja und die Klage über Ur').

12 See Seminara, *La Versione Accadica del LUGAL-E*, pp. 519–48, and Seminara, 'The Babylonian Science of the Translation'.

13 On the Ištar composition, see Veldhuis, 'Translation in the Elevation of Ištar'.

scholars utilized translation as a critical social commodity within their community. Through scholarly translation, scholars could demonstrate their competency, creativity, and indeed mastery of their craft, namely the cuneiform writing system. During the early second millennium, the innovative mode of scholarly translation was systematically habitualized as part of scribal training in the practice of analogical hermeneutics. Scholars could create interlingual correspondences based on analogical criteria without necessary recourse to a notion of (near) semantic equivalence. Such correspondents could be based instead on phonological resemblance, graphic similarity, or semantic proximity even antinomy as well as any combinations of these analogues. Word lists produced in scribal schools included occasional interlingual glossing which illustrate the varieties of bases for correspondents.[14]

For example, the word list 'Izi' from the early second millennium BCE offers the following Akkadian glosses for various Sumerian words written with the sign UD (𒌓).

219.	*ūmum* ud	'day' = 'day'
220.	*ṣētum* ud	'light' = 'light'
221.	*šamaš* utu	'sun' = 'sun'
222.	*imērum* utu	'donkey' = 'sun'
223.	*ummidum* ud	'abcess' = ?

(Crisostomo, *Translation as Scholarship*, pp. 253–54; Old Babylonian Nippur Izi I: 219–23)

These five entries illustrate differing modes of translation. The first three present simple semantic correspondences. The fifth provides an Akkadian gloss *ummidum*, but this meaning for Sumerian ud is unknown elsewhere. The fourth entry, however, offers a clear example of translation based on multiple analogies. In this case, utu 'sun' is a close phonological approximant to udu 'sheep' which is typically translated by Akkadian *immerum*, which itself is nearly homophonous to *imērum* 'donkey'. Thus, via an A (utu) ≈ B (udu) = C (*immerum*) ≈ D (*imērum*) sequence of analogical reasoning (A = D), 'sun' is translated 'donkey'. Such analogically based translations are not rare; more than 30 per cent of tokens of Akkadian glosses in this particular word list offer similar examples and similar and even greater ratios exist for other advanced word lists from this period and later.

Word lists were not the only genre in which this mode of translation was realized. Not only could literary translations utilize the correspondents

14 These word lists, particularly during this period of cuneiform history, were not fundamentally about literacy acquisition (see briefly Veldhuis, 'Ancient Mesopotamia', pp. 26–27) and the very rare explorations into bilingualism are similarly not tools for translation, but expressions of aptitude in the writing system and participation in the social field of scholarship (see Crisostomo, *Translation as Scholarship*, pp. 179–84).

provided by word lists to craft 'pseudo-translations', but whole compositions could be generated by the same scholarly methods used to produce the word lists. In this way, scholars demonstrated their mastery of the cuneiform script and ability to manipulate the languages which used the writing system, even to the point of complete fabrication. The composition 'Scholars of Uruk' exhibits how scribes could create meaningless Sumerian translations. In other words, the Sumerian lines are crafted to look like Sumerian but are incomprehensible standing on their own. They are thus semantically null.

e-zu e-zu e-zu e-zu ĝa$_2$-am$_3$ na-ĝa$_2$-ah me-en
ina ēhiz talmadu ahmuṭku kīma ana yâšim nûhum atta
i$_3$-la$_2$ i$_3$-la$_2$ i$_3$-la$_2$ i$_3$-la$_2$ za-am$_3$ pe-el he$_2$-me-en
aṭṭul uṣappî uššir āmurma ana kâšim pehûm anāku
e-gi$_4$ e-gi$_4$ e-gi$_4$ e-gi$_4$ ĝa$_2$-am$_3$ na-ĝa$_2$-ah me-en
tur šini mitlik āpul kīma ana yâšim nûhum atta
i$_3$-ĝen(DU) i$_3$-ĝen(DU) i$_3$-gub(DU) i$_3$-DU za-am$_3$ pe-el he$_2$-me-en
allik erde ina ša ašṭuruma naṭû ana kâšim pehûm anāku

((Even) in the knowledge you have learned, I was faster than you; compared to me, you are a brute
I observed, I scrutinized, I checked, I read; Am I a blockhead to you?
Respond! Reconsider! Advise! Answer! Compared to me, you are a brute
I went, I advanced. In whatever I wrote, it was fitting.
Am I a blockhead to you?)

(George, *The Babylonian Gilgamesh Epic*, pp. 84–85, (text) 14. 17–20)

Here, the Sumerian lines all begin with repeated sequences of Sumerian homonymic words and signs, each translated by a different Akkadian word. The Sumerian is largely senseless without the guide of the Akkadian translation. Nevertheless, as Andrew George has demonstrated, each translation can be decoded if considered through multiple steps of analogical reasoning such as abbreviation or homophony.[15] The point in producing such apparent gibberish was not, therefore, about conveying meaning from one language to another or representing a source text in a new context. The act of translation was not conceptualized as an exercise in communicative translation but as a creative practice, knowledge production of linguistic and scribal nous.

Innovative, scholarly translation became a standard method of translation until the end of cuneiform culture and was the basis for an extensive exegetical programme.[16] This mode of translation, so pervasive in the extant texts — scholarly, literary, and religious alike — offers an alternative perspective on the use of translation, one that seems somewhat outside the established

15 George, *Babylonian Literary Texts*, pp. 95–96.

16 See especially Frahm, *Babylonian and Assyrian Text Commentaries*, pp. 12–19, 59–85 and Gabbay, *The Exegetical Terminology*, pp. 13–35, 264–65.

norms and expectations of translation typically associated with literary and translation studies in the European and North American tradition. In short, translation in the world of the ancient Middle East could be whatever the translators needed it to be. And these translators founded all modes of translation as part of typical cuneiform writing cultures.

Given that translation was a fundamental aspect of written cultures of the cuneiform world, it might be somewhat surprising that there is little metalinguistic reflection on translation. Most discourse on translation from cuneiform scribal cultures emerges from one of two scholarly worlds — the scribal schools of the early second millennium or the scholarly circles of the first millennium. The former included several statements made in collections of short sayings and compositions satirizing life as a scribal student (known as Eduba texts by modern scholars); discourse from the latter recreates the dialogic drama of the Eduba texts in newly invented compositions.

> eme-ĝir$_{15}$ a-na i$_3$-zu niĝ$_2$ dul-bi ur$_5$-ra bur-ra [i-zu-u]
>   *ina šumerî mala tāhuzu kātim[tašu kīam še…]*
> inim bal inim šar$_2$-šar$_2$ an-ta uri^{ki}-ra ki-ta eme-
> [ĝir$_{15}$-ra an-ta eme-ĝir$_{15}$-ra ki-ta eme-ur$_x$-ra i-zu-u]
>   INIM BAL *šutābulu eliš akkadâ [šapliš šumerû šapliš] akkadâ eliš šumērû [idê]*
> ki-bi ĝar-ra niĝ$_2$ gilim-gilim-bi zu$_2$-keš$_2$-ta […] eme-ur^{ki}-ra si-
> [sa$_2$-e-de$_3$ nu-ĝar-ra i-zu-u]
>   *[pūh]ti egirti kaṣir[ti šumerû … šulūšā] ša akkadû ana šutē[šuru la naṭû tīdê]*
>
> (What have you learned about Sumerian?
> Do you know how to unravel its secrets?
> [Do you know how] to translate and interpret Akkadian above to Sumerian below and Sumerian above to Akkadian below?
> [Do you know] the substitutions, the complementary correspondents, and compounds(?), Sumerian with [two or] three meanings each that are not suitable for translating into Akkadian?)
>
> (Sjöberg, 'Der Examenstext A', pp. 140–42;
> Exam at the Scribal School, 13–15)[17]

This composition intentionally draws attention to the varieties of both Sumerian and Akkadian that true scholars should be able to write and recite; the difficult terminology employed in the text underscores that those who could read and copy this composition had truly mastered the ancient tradition of the scribal arts. Here, we are given a sense about how scholars viewed their responsibilities with regard to translation. At least in their explicit ideology, scholars were expected to know the ins and outs of Sumerian-Akkadian translation and how to manipulate these two languages in juxtaposition.

---

17 On these lines with respect to translation, see recently George, *Babylonian Literary Texts*, pp. 106–07.

These ideals perpetuate the discourse of romanticized scholarly achievement from one thousand years prior as recorded in the texts from the scribal schools, such as these sentiments from collections of sayings copied by student scribes.

> A scribe who does not know Sumerian — how will he produce a translation?
> A scribe incapable of grasping meaning — how will he produce a translation?
>
> (Alster, *Proverbs of Ancient Sumer*, 2.49, 56)

Taken at face value, these texts describe the task of translation in much the same terms we might expect from typical narratives of translation from Cicero to modern textbooks. They attest an idealized view of Sumerian and the process of communicative translation. In practice, however, scholarly translation was a normative scholarly practice that prevailed especially in the most foundational of cuneiform scholarly texts, the word lists which, moreover, inform practices of translation in all cuneiform textual genres.[18] Cuneiform translators understood the interlingual space not in terms of reinforcing language boundaries or for communicative translation but as opportunities for scholarly exploration.

From the Notebooks of a Babylonian Scholar

In order to evaluate scholarly translation in practice, we can look at the work of particular scholars. Nabû-kuṣuršu, son of Bel-eriba of the Huṣabu family, was a scholar in the city of Borsippa sometime in the fifth century BCE during the reign of Artaxerxes, king of Persia.[19] He was a particularly productive scholar, with more than thirty tablets attributed to him deposited as votive offerings to the scribal god Nabû in his Ezida temple.

Nabû-kuṣuršu's family was one of the few prominent priestly families to survive the Persian king Xerxes' reprisals against uprisings in 484 BCE.[20] At that time, the economic and religious foundations of Babylonia were uprooted and many important families were replaced with those who demonstrated fealty to the Persian crown. As a result, scholarship in Borsippa experienced similar trauma.[21] Nabû-kuṣuršu was among a handful of individuals who transmitted scholarly knowledge after the so-called end of archives.

18 See, for example, Veldhuis, 'Translation in the Elevation of Ištar', pp. 185–98 on how the scholarly and esoteric translations in word lists negotiate literary value in a hymn to the goddess Ištar.

19 It is not clear which of the four Artaxerxes is referenced in the dated tablets, but Artaxerxes I is most likely.

20 Waerzeggers, 'The Babylonian Revolts', p. 162; Waerzeggers, *The Ezida Temple of Borsippa*, p. 169.

21 Robson, 'The Socio-Economics of Cuneiform Scholarship', pp. 460–63; Robson, *Ancient Knowledge Networks*, pp. 221–35.

Most prominent among his works is a set of tablets belonging to the sign list series 'Aa = *nâqu*', an expansion of another sign list known as 'Ea = *nâqu*'. Both lists offer various readings of cuneiform signs and their translations in Akkadian, but the list 'Aa = *nâqu*' pushes these translational possibilities to esoteric extremes, illustrating the potential of scholarly translation. Whereas 'Ea = *nâqu*' is complete in eight chapters, 'Aa = *nâqu*' expands on that material in forty-two chapters. The following illustrates the difference between the two series as well as the utilization of scholarly translation in innovative ways.[22]

•	u_2	〈	*ubān*	'finger'
•	u_2	〈	*ešeret*	'ten'

(*Materials for the Sumerian Lexicon XIV*, ed. by Civil, 'Ea = *nâqu*' 2: 146–47)

• u_2	〈	*ešeret*	'ten'
	ubānu	'finger'	
	Anum	'the god Anu'	
	Antum	'the goddess Antum'	
	Enlil	'the god Enlil'	
	Sîn	'the god Sîn'	
	Šamaš	'the god Šamaš'	
	Adad	'the god Adad'	
	Ištar	'the goddess Ištar'	
	Ištar kakkabi	'the goddess Ištar of the stars'	
	kiššātum	'totality; world'	
	uznu	'ear; wisdom'	
	hasīsu	'wisdom'	
	šīlum	'depression, hole'	
	īlum	'god'	
	šarrum	'king'	
	bēlum	'lord'	
	bēltum	'lady'	
	banû	'beautiful, well-formed; created'	
	šaqû	'cup-bearer; steward'	
	manû	'to count'	
	biblu	'marriage gift'	

22 The columns here represent the layout of the entries on the tablet: entry marker — pronunciation gloss — cuneiform sign — Akkadian gloss; omitted is the column with the ancient name of the cuneiform sign.

qīštum	‘gift’
GIRtum	‘?’
Ibrātum	‘outdoor shrine, cultic niche’
sulû	‘street’
sūtum	‘*sūtu* capacity (*c.* 10 litres)’
qātum	‘hand’
qūlum	‘silence’
qaqqarum	‘ground, earth’
ṣîrum	‘exalted’
qabrum	‘grave’
bītum	‘house’
āli	‘city’
ša gigurû	‘the U sign’
tēltum	‘the syllabic value /u/’

(*Materials for the Sumerian Lexicon XIV*, ed. by Civil, ‘Aa = *nâqu*’ 12: 1–36)

The entries deal with the cuneiform sign U ‹ when read /u/. In ‘Ea = *nâqu*’, the sign with this reading is treated in two entries, with the Akkadian correspondences *ubān* ‘finger’ and *ešeret* ‘ten’. Already, scholarly translation creates the translation; in no context would U mean ‘finger’; instead, the translation *ubānu* ‘finger’ is based on the meaning indicated by *ešeret* ‘ten’ and, of course, related to the number of fingers a person has. By contrast, ‘Aa = *nâqu*’ treats the same data, U read /u/, in thirty-six entries. According to ‘Aa = *nâqu*’, U means *manû* ‘to count’ and *qātum* ‘hand’, both extensions presumably based on the created correspondence U = *ubānu* ‘finger’. ‘Aa = *nâqu*’ also gives the opaque correspondence U = *bītum* ‘house’.[23] Furthermore, in ‘Aa = *nâqu*’, U means *īlum* ‘god’ as well as several particular deities. This equation is constructed on the basis that elsewhere in this list, the sign U can be read /umun/, a (Emesal) dialect variant for normative Sumerian en (often translated by Akkadian *bēlu* ‘lord’). And *bēlu* ‘lord’ may be conceptually connected to *īlum* ‘god’. Thus, ‘Aa = *nâqu*’ uses one semantic extension from umun = *bēlu* ‘lord’ to *īlum* ‘god’ to subsequently generate further analogous translations of particular gods and goddesses. However, when the U sign is used to mean *lord*, it would not have been read as u in Sumerian but as umun. Thus, ‘Aa = *nâqu*’ is not concerned with proper pronunciations of Sumerian; instead, it features any potential readings for a given cuneiform sign and any Akkadian translations related to the *sign*, not a Sumerian word. In one sense, then, the pronunciations given in ‘Aa = *nâqu*’ are artificially Sumerian, proxies for the

23 Potentially, this correspondence may be based on a loose vocalic analogy of /u/ and /e/, since Sumerian e_2 is typically translated by Akkadian *bītum* ‘house’.

sign itself. This conception thereby underscores the inherent interlingual potential of cuneiform, particularly in this later period. The series 'Aa = *nâqu*' deals extensively, even speculatively, with all possible readings and meanings for any given sign. It is the epitome of scholarly translation at work.

Modern Translation Assumptions

The scholar Nabû-kuṣuršu is responsible for most of our present knowledge of the important sign list series 'Aa = *nâqu*'. Of the seventy-three extant exemplars of the series from the first millennium, Nabû-kuṣuršu is almost certainly responsible for thirteen, about eighteen per cent, and potentially another five for a total of nearly twenty-five per cent. For good or ill, the series 'Aa = *nâqu*' has been an important reference in modern lexicography, often containing sole attestations of particular words. Thus, a single individual — Nabû-kuṣuršu — controls nearly a quarter of our knowledge of 'Aa = *nâqu*' and therefore exhibits a great influence on modern scholarship.

Moreover, if, as I have shown, the sign list series 'Aa = *nâqu*' features scholarly translation rather than communicative translation, then the assumption that the series can offer lexicographic insight into ancient languages is invalid or at least tenuous, with lasting ramifications for our interpretations of compositions and the creation of our dictionaries. Here then is the requisite warning about the necessity of critically considering the nature and purpose of our sources and appreciating the social and literary forms employed by ancient scholars and scribes.

To cite a concrete example, in his commentary on the Sumerian literary composition 'Enki and Ninmah' line I 28, W. G. Lambert gives the translation 'After Enki had in wisdom reflected upon his own blood and body', based on his supposition that the meaning of the verb (that he reads) ù-mu-e-ni-ri-ge is found in 'Aa = *nâqu*' where ri = *hasāsu* 'to be mindful (of something); to plan'.[24] Lambert, however, has misunderstood the basis of the ancient scholars' (not, in this case, Nabû-kuṣuršu's) consideration of the writing system. Sumerian ri does not mean Akkadian *hasāsu*. Rather, the translation is based on one of two analogies: either a simple qualified or abbreviated analogy where ri (read deg) is part of an idiomatic verbal compound ĝeštug — deg 'to gather wisdom; to plan' which may be translated *hasāsu*.[25] The scholar who wrote this entry in 'Aa = *nâqu*' has introduced a qualified correspondence, but the modern scholar has taken the ancient's work at face value and thereby misunderstood the nature of scholarly translation.

---

24 Lambert, *Babylonian Creation Myths*, pp. 336–37, 504. The verb here should probably be read ù-mu-e-ni-de$_5$-ge with the more concrete meaning of 'gathered up his own blood and body', ultimately with the same outcome in general meaning (see Ceccarelli, *Enki und Ninmah*, p. 103 no. 494).

25 See Ceccarelli, *Enki und Ninmah*, pp. 156–58.

Similarly, our modern assumptions about the purposes of translation lead to a failure to understand and thereby appreciate the work of ancient scholars. So to once again use an illustration from Lambert who is discussing various translations and readings of the sign TIR (𒌁), typically *qištu* 'forest' but in lists such as 'Aa = *nâqu*' given meanings *šubtu* 'residence', *ašābu* 'to sit', and *mūšabu* 'seat': 'it may be suspected that the post-Old Babylonian lists *ignorantly failed* to gloss the sign [TIR] with tu for the meanings such as "sit"'.[26] Because of his own ideas of what should be included, Lambert regards the lack of a particular sign reading an ignorant failing. Rather, the ancient scholars' conceptualization of how to interpret the cuneiform writing system and how that knowledge is presented in sign lists does not necessitate the type of information that Lambert seeks. Lambert, however, is not alone in his assumptions.

Comparable notions appear in standard dictionary entries, particularly for lemmas which are only known from the cuneiform lexical tradition. For example, the most recent volume of the *Chicago Assyrian Dictionary* U-W (2010), the standard dictionary for Akkadian, assigns the lemma *uttūtu* the meaning 'fright, terror'. The meaning is given on the basis of the Sumerian correspondent ul_4 'to hurry (toward)' and its semantic extension 'to harass' and thus potentially 'to frighten'[27] as well as preceding entries in the list 'Aa = *nâqu*' (40: 257–59) with the Akkadian correspondents *pirittu* 'fear' and *hattu* 'panic, fear'. On these bases, the assumption that *uttūtu* should then fall into the same semantic category is not unreasonable. However, as we have already seen, the notion that 'Aa = *nâqu*' reflects communicative translations either in its Sumerian and Akkadian correspondents or even in surrounding entries is unsustainable.

Similarly, the *Electronic Sumerian Pennsylvania Dictionary* suggests for Sumerian sa the meaning 'jewellery' on the basis of the Akkadian correspondent *šukuttum* given in some lexical lists; the Akkadian translation, however, reflects an abbreviation of Sumerian gil-sa. So Sumerian sa does not, by itself, mean 'jewellery'. These examples illustrate simple ways that modern scholarly expectations lead to uncritical acceptance of translations and misleading entries in dictionaries. Because scholarly translation was an important aspect of cuneiform translation, modern lexicographers must account for the ways that the writers of cuneiform texts practised translation.

Scholarly Translation and the History of Translation

What then do the cultures of cuneiform scholarly translation suggest for translation studies and for the history of linguistic knowledge? It is strikingly clear that for Assyrian and Babylonian scholars, translation was not merely a

26 Lambert, *Babylonian Creation Myths*, p. 502, emphasis mine.

27 See Sjöberg, 'Nungal in the Ekur', p. 44 and Civil 'On Mesopotamian Jails', p. 74.

literary activity, but also *science* inasmuch as all forms of knowledge creation in cuneiform cultures were *science*. That is, translation participated in the same systems of knowledge production that we recognize in other forms of cuneiform scholarship such as divination, mathematics, medicine, commentary, grammar, and astronomy. By focusing exclusively on communicative translation or by assigning what I have discussed here as scholarly translation to the realms of mere scribal play, modern scholarship has ignored the inventiveness and craft required for ancient practices of translation. The practice of scholarly translation was not isolated to occasional outlandish correspondences in word lists or whimsical equations in otherwise standard literary translations but was rather a fundamental part of ancient cuneiform writing culture.

Modern introductions to translation theory and the history of translation and, indeed, the field of Assyriology itself have failed to understand and thus incorporate the varied modes of translation that cuneiform translator-scribes employed. By ignoring translation in the ancient Middle East and the ways that ancient translators acted through their translations, modern scholarship has cultivated a generally simplistic view that elevates communicative translation as normative and standard throughout the history of translation. Communicative translation existed alongside multiple modes of translation, including scholarly translation. Our concept of translation has historically been restricted, constructed based on our expectations and assumptions about translation rather than how translators actually translated. The ways of knowing on display in 'Aa = *nâqu*' and the purposes of scholarly translation exhibited within particular cuneiform cultures force us to both recognize where our notions of translation differ from the ancient cuneiform scholars' as well as to adjust our expectations for our own scholarship and pragmatic needs. Our etic perspectives and definitions of translation should be reevaluated in light of practices of translation in historical contexts. In so doing, we revivify the spirit of cuneiform translator–scholars and invite their translations, their scholarship, into the broader discourses of the history of knowledge production and translation studies.

Bibliography

Primary Sources

Alster, Bendt, *Proverbs of Ancient Sumer: The World's Earliest Proverb Collections*, 2 vols (Bethesda: CDL Press, 1997)

Ceccarelli, Manuel, *Enki und Ninmaḫ: Eine mythische Erzählung in sumerischer Sprache*, Orientalische Religionen in der Antike, 16 (Tübingen: Mohr Siebeck, 2016)

Civil, Miguel, and Gonzalo Rubio, 'An Ebla Incantation against Insomnia and the Semiticization of Sumerian: Notes on ARET 5 8b and 9', *Orientalia*, 68 (1999), 254–66

Gelb, Ignace J., Piotr Steinkeller, and Robert M. Whiting, Jr., *Earliest Land Tenure Systems in the Near East: Ancient Kudurrus*, 2 vols, Oriental Institute Publications, 104 (Chicago: The Oriental Institute of the University of Chicago, 1991)

George, Andrew, *The Babylonian Gilgamesh Epic: Introduction, Critical Edition and Cuneiform Texts*, 2 vols (Oxford: Oxford University Press, 2003)

——, *Babylonian Literary Texts in the Schøyen Collection*, Cornell University Studies in Assyriology and Sumerology [CUSAS], 10 (Bethesda: CDL Press, 2009)

Materials for the Sumerian Lexicon, XIV. *Ea A = nâqu, Aa A = nâqu, with their Forerunners and Related Texts*, ed. by Miguel Civil, with the collaboration of Margaret W. Green, and Wilfred G. Lambert (Rome: Pontificium Institutum Biblicum, 1979)

Sjöberg, Åke W., 'Der Examenstext A', *Zeitschrift für Assyriologie*, 64 (1974), 137–76

Secondary Studies

Bassnett, Susan, *Translation* (New York: Routledge, 2014)

Beaulieu, Paul-Alain, 'Official and Vernacular Languages: The Shifting Sands of Imperial and Cultural Identities in First-millennium B.C. Mesopotamia', in *Margins of Writing, Origins of Cultures*, ed. by Seth L. Sanders, Oriental Institute Seminars, 2 (Chicago: The Oriental Institute of the University of Chicago, 2006), pp. 191–219

Civil, Miguel, 'On Mesopotamian Jails and Their Lady Warden', in *The Tablet and the Scroll: Near Eastern Studies in Honor of William W. Hallo*, ed. by Mark E. Cohen, Daniel C. Snell, and David B. Weisberg (Bethesda: CDL Press, 1993), pp. 72–78

Crisostomo, C. Jay, *Translation as Scholarship: Language, Writing, and Bilingual Education in Ancient Babylonia*, Studies in Ancient Near Eastern Records, 22 (Berlin: de Gruyter, 2019)

Englund, Robert K., 'Texts from the Late Uruk Period' in *Mesopotamien: Späturuk-Zeit und Frühdynastische Zeit*, ed. by Josef Bauer, Robert K. Englund, and Manfred Krebernik, Orbis Biblicus et Orientalis, 160/1 (Freiburg: Universitätsverlag, 1998), pp. 15–233

Frahm, Eckart, *Babylonian and Assyrian Text Commentaries: Origins of Interpretation*, Guides to the Mesopotamian Textual Record, 5 (Münster: Ugarit-Verlag, 2011)

Gabbay, Uri, *The Exegetical Terminology of Akkadian Commentaries*, Culture and History of the Ancient Near East, 82 (Leiden: Brill, 2016)

Hackl, Johannes, 'Zur Sprachsituation im Babylonien des ersten Jahrtausends v. Chr. Ein Beitrag zur Sprachgeschichte des jüngeren Akkadischen', in *Mehrsprachigkeit: Vom Alten Orient bis zum Esperanto*, ed. by Sebastian Fink, Martin Lang, and Manfred Schretter, dubsar, 2 (Münster: Zaphon, 2018), pp. 209–38

Koppen, Frans van, 'The Scribe of the Flood Story and His Circle', in *The Oxford Handbook of Cuneiform Culture*, ed. by Karen Radner and Eleanor Robson (Oxford: Oxford University Press, 2011), pp. 140–66

Lambert, W. G., 'The Language of ARET V 6 and 7', in *Literature and Literary Language at Ebla*, ed. by Pelio Fronzaroli, Quaderni di Semitica, 18 (Florence: Dipartimento di linguistica Università di Firenze, 1999), pp. 41–62

——, *Babylonian Creation Myths*, Mesopotamian Civilizations, 16 (Winona Lake: Eisenbrauns, 2013)

Löhnert, Anne, 'Ipiq-Aja und die Klage über Ur', *Journal of Cuneiform Studies*, 63 (2011), 65–72

Robson, Eleanor, 'The Socio-Economics of Cuneiform Scholarship after the "End of Archives": Views from Borsippa and Uruk', in *At the Dawn of History: Ancient Near Eastern Studies in Honour of J. N. Postgate*, ed. by Yağmur Heffron, Adam Stone, and Martin Worthington (Winona Lake: Eisenbrauns, 2017), pp. 459–74

——, *Ancient Knowledge Networks: A Social Geography of Cuneiform Scholarship in First-Millennium Assyrian and Babylonia* (London: UCL Press, 2019)

Rubio, Gonzalo, 'On the Linguistic Landscape of Early Mesopotamia', in *Ethnicity in Ancient Mesopotamia: Papers Read at the 48th Rencontre Assyriologique Internationale Leiden, 1–4 July 2002*, ed. by W. H. van Soldt, PIHANS, 102 (Leiden: Nederlands Instituut voor het Nabije Oosten, 2005), pp. 316–32

Seminara, Stefano, *La Versione Accadica del LUGAL-E: La tecnica babilonese della traduzione dal sumerico e le sur regole*, Materiali per il Vocabolario Sumerico, 8 (Rome: Università degli studi de Roma 'La Sapienza', 2001)

——, 'The Babylonian Science of the Translation and the Ideological Adjustment of the Sumerian Text to the "Target Culture"', in *Ideologies as Intercultural Phenomena: Proceedings of the Third Annual Symposium of the Assyrian and Babylonian Intellectual Heritage Project held in Chicago, USA, October 27–31, 2000*, ed. by A. Panaino and G. Pettinato, Melammu Symposia, 3 (Milan: Università di Bologna & Islao, 2002), pp. 245–55

Sjöberg, Åke W., 'Nungal in the Ekur', *Archiv für Orientforschung*, 24 (1973), 19–46

Tigay, Jeffrey, *The Evolution of the Gilgamesh Epic* (Philadelphia: The University of Pennsylvania Press, 1982)

Tymoczko, Maria, 'Reconceptualizing Translation Theory: Integrating Non-Western Thought about Translation', in *Translating Others*, ed. by Theo Hermans (London: Routledge, 2006), pp. 13–32

Veldhuis, Niek, *History of the Cuneiform Lexical Tradition*, Guides to the Mesopotamian Textual Record, 6 (Münster: Ugarit-Verlag, 2014)
——, 'Translation in the Elevation of Ištar', in *The Scaffolding of Our Thoughts: Essays on Assyriology and the History of Science in Honor of Francesca Rochberg*, ed. by C. Jay Crisostomo, Eduardo A. Escobar, Terri Tanaka, and Niek Veldhuis, Ancient Magic and Divination, 13 (Leiden: Brill, 2018), pp. 183–206
——, 'Ancient Mesopotamia', in *The Cambridge World History of Lexicography*, ed. by John Considine (Cambridge: Cambridge University, 2019), pp. 11–35
Waerzeggers, Caroline, 'The Babylonian Revolts Against Xerxes and the "End of Archives"', *Archiv für Orientforschung*, 50 (2003–2004), 150–73
——, *The Ezida Temple of Borsippa: Priesthood, Cult, Archives*, Achaemenid History, 15 (Leiden: Nederlands Instituut voor het Nabije Oosten, 2010)

BENJAMIN G. WRIGHT III

Interdisciplinary Interactions

Septuagint Studies, Classics, and Translation Studies

Over the last number of years interdisciplinarity has become the buzzword of secondary education in the United States, although that term gets applied to many different configurations of activity.[1] The drive for interdisciplinary work likely has been nowhere more prevalent than in the humanities, where for a long time, humanities disciplines were just as embedded in their academic silos as any other in the university. One area ripe for interdisciplinary work is the study of translation, especially in the ancient world, a primary interest of mine. Questions concerning the nature and function of ancient translation, who was doing it, where, and why still remain largely open, even if some scholars have thought about aspects of that problem. Three modern fields of study have an interest in these questions, although for different reasons — Septuagint Studies, in which I work, Classics, and Translation Studies. Unfortunately, until now scholars in these fields have worked in relative isolation from one another, although those sands are beginning to shift in positive directions. The extent to which scholars in these three fields can translate their methods and results to each other successfully in order to collaborate in their research, however, will determine how we answer the questions I posed above as well as ones as yet unanticipated.

In a volume focused on narratives of translation, I begin with a personal translation narrative that highlights, at least in Septuagint Studies, the shifts that have begun to take place. When I began my graduate work in the Department of Religious Studies at the University of Pennsylvania in the late 1970s, something of my future scholarly direction was determined by a research project on the corpus of translations made from Hebrew to Greek, usually called the Septuagint or the translation of the Seventy (LXX/OG), directed

1 My thanks to Sonja Brentjes for her valuable feedback and to Irene Peirano for her advice on the section on Classics.

Benjamin G. Wright III (bgw1@lehigh.edu) is University Distinguished Professor in the Department of Religion Studies at Lehigh University in Bethlehem, Pennsylvania. His primary areas of research are the Septuagint and Ancient Translation, Second Temple Jewish Wisdom Literature, and the Dead Sea Scrolls.

Narratives on Translation across Eurasia and Africa: From Babylonia to Colonial India, ed. by Sonja Brentjes in cooperation with Jens Høyrup and Bruce O'Brien, CAT 3, pp. 45–66 (Turnhout: Brepols, 2022) BREPOLS PUBLISHERS 10.1484/M.CAT-EB.5.127933

by Robert Kraft at the University of Pennsylvania and Emanuel Tov of the Hebrew University of Jerusalem.[2] The idea was to create a searchable, electronic database of the Hebrew text of the Bible together with its Greek translations. For my PhD dissertation, I studied aspects of the translation technique of the Greek translator of the *Wisdom* of Ben Sira, since this translator had written a prologue in which he reflected on the problems of translating from Hebrew to Greek, something rare in an ancient translation.[3] The methodological basis for my work came exclusively from scholars who worked in Septuagint Studies. The year after I completed my PhD, as I was looking for a permanent academic position, I attended Professor Kraft's graduate seminar, whose theme was issues related to ancient translation. Only then did I discover that scholars in Classics had been interested in translation for quite a while, since Roman philhellenism necessitated rendering works from Greek into Latin, and some Roman writers, most notably Cicero and Horace, had discussed translation. As I began to read even more broadly, I wandered into the field of Translation Studies, which in the scholarship that I first read dealt primarily with theories of modern translating and secondarily with the history of its development. Those histories almost exclusively were indebted to Classics and classical writers, which created a mostly Western-oriented theory.[4] So, for example, all of these histories cited and discussed the remarks on translation made by Cicero, Horace, and later Jerome, but I discovered that none even recognized the prologue to the Greek of Ben Sira, even though (a) the translator wrote about the process of translating and (b) it was older than Cicero, Horace, or Jerome.[5] I was surprised that with so much work being done on translation in these three fields that scholars in each seemed so unaware of work being done in the others. An opportunity arose for me at a conference in 2001 to try my hand at pulling together some insights from Septuagint Studies, Classics, and Translation Studies. Using Louis Kelly's idea of personal and positional

---

2 The abbreviation LXX refers technically to the translations of the Pentateuch and OG refers to the translations of the other books. See Wright, 'The Septuagint and its Modern Translators', pp. 104–05. For the Penn/HU project, see Tov, *A Computerized Data Base.*

3 See Wright, *No Small Difference.* The book of Ben Sira is in the so-called Apocrypha or Deuterocanonical texts of the Bible. It is canonical for Roman Catholics and the Orthodox traditions, but not for Protestants. It was composed in Hebrew in the early part of the second century BCE and was translated into Greek sometime in the latter part of the second century BCE by a translator who claims to be the author's grandson.

4 For a discussion of Eurocentrism in Translation Studies, see Dooslaer, 'Eurocentrism'. There were, however, scholars in Biblical Studies who were interested in thinking about translation for the purposes of rendering the Bible into modern languages, see especially, the work of Eugene Nida and the Nida Institute (http://www.nidainstitute.org/).

5 So, for example, Susan Bassnett (Bassnett, *Translation Studies*) cites George Steiner, who sees the history of translation theory beginning with Cicero, and Eric Jacobsen, who claims that the Romans invented translation. Venuti, *Translation Studies Reader,* which is organized chronologically, begins with Jerome, skipping not only Ben Sira but Cicero as well, although he mentions 'frequently cited theorists' beginning with Cicero (p. 4). See below.

structures of authority, I argued that the particular authority stance that Cicero, the translator of Ben Sira, and the translators of the Septuagint took toward their source texts conditioned the interactions among translation, their relationship to their source texts, and their audiences.[6]

Septuagint Studies

At about this time, I began work as the co-editor of *A New English Translation of the Septuagint* (NETS) with Albert Pietersma of the University of Toronto, a project to translate into English the LXX/OG corpus (and some compositional works) for the first time since the translation of Sir Lancelot Charles Lee Brenton in 1844.[7] One of our first problems was how to approach translating a translation, a very different task from translating an original Greek composition.[8] Questions like how important a role should the Hebrew source text play or how should one do lexicography on a translated corpus loomed large. Already in 1998, Pietersma had given the basic outlines of what would be called the 'interlinear model' on which NETS would be based.[9] In 2000, Pietersma gave his fullest articulation of the interlinear model in his paper 'A New Paradigm for Addressing Old Questions'.[10] There he developed a model or paradigm, that is, a theory of translation, for the relationship between the Hebrew and Greek that governed the work in NETS, and in support of the necessity of such a theory he cited translation theorists Gideon Toury and Itamar Even-Zohar.[11] Significantly, in this article Pietersma made a first foray into the target/product-oriented theory of descriptive translation studies — later to become the theoretical frame for NETS — in which

6 The conference was 'From Hellenistic Judaism to Christian Hellenism: An International Colloquium', which was held at the Institute for Advanced Studies, Jerusalem, Israel. See Wright, 'Access to the Source', employing Kelly, *The True Interpreter*. The term 'text' can have a variety of referents. For Septuagint Studies, particularly, but also for Classics in most cases, the translations that I am treating in this article were made from works that had achieved and been transmitted in written form, whether they had or were attributed to a specific author or not. In this article, the term 'text' refers to a written instantiation of an ancient work. Of course, translation also took place on the oral level, and we hear about ancient 'translators' who apparently did not know how to write. For some examples, see Wright, 'The Jewish Scriptures in Greek' and the literature cited there.

7 For a brief discussion of Brenton and his predecessor in translating the LXX/OG, Charles Thompson, see Pietersma and Wright, 'To the Reader of NETS', p. xiii.

8 See the comments in Pietersma and Wright, 'To the Reader of NETS', pp. xvi–xviii.

9 Published as Pietersma, 'A New English Translation of the Septuagint'.

10 Published as Pietersma, 'A New Paradigm for Addressing Old Questions'.

11 Toury's work ultimately played the most important role in NETS. He argued that translations were facts of their target cultures and the intended position/function of that translation determined the product or the textual-linguistic makeup of the translation, which in turn governed the process or strategies that translators use to achieve that textual-linguistic makeup. See Toury, 'A Handful of Methodological Issues in DTS', pp. 11–14 and below.

one significant component was the claim that interference from the source text, both positive and negative, plays a critical role in the realization of the target text. In 2001, Cameron Boyd-Taylor employed Toury's target-oriented approach in order to question the methodological feasibility of producing a lexicon of the Septuagint, a subject of discussion since the earliest days of the International Organization for Septuagint and Cognate Studies, the major scholarly organization in Septuagint Studies.[12] By that time, Pietersma's interlinear paradigm and Toury's theoretical views in *Descriptive Translation Studies – and beyond* (DTS) had significantly shaped the work of NETS.[13]

Several factors suggested that Toury's views should apply to NETS and to Septuagint Studies more comprehensively. Most importantly, Toury's product-oriented approach — the (prospective) systemic position and function of a translation determines its appropriate surface realization (= textual linguistic makeup), which governs the strategies that the translator employs in order to derive the target text from its original — undergirded Pietersma's (and hence NETS's) fundamental distinction between the point of a translation's *production* and its subsequent history of *reception*, that is, between what the translator(s) did when a translation was made and how later readers received/read that translation.[14] Pietersma argued that contrary to most previous thinking, the translations of the LXX/OG were not intended to function at their point of production independently of the source text(s) — that is, in their systemic position and function, they were not supposed to *replace* the Hebrew source text but rather to provide a gateway to the source text, which remained the point of authoritative focus — even though they later functioned that way in their reception. Thus, the Septuagint translations had a two-dimensional orientation that needed to be taken into account when translating them into a modern language: horizontally in the way that the Greek text was constructed via its own grammar, lexical elements, and syntax, and vertically since 'the parent text forms the *de facto* context for units of meaning'.[15] Thus, translators were to work within the Greek linguistic system but with the Hebrew text in view, since often the Hebrew helped to explain best specific elements of the translation. DTS also helped to account for a distinctive feature of LXX/OG translations, the coexistence, often side by side, of unidiomatic Greek, which can sometimes be unintelligible from the perspective of a native Greek reader, and perfectly intelligible, idiomatic Greek.[16]

---

12 Boyd-Taylor, 'The Evidentiary Value of Septuagintal Usage'.

13 Toury, *Descriptive Translation Studies*. See the papers by Albert Pietersma, Cameron Boyd-Taylor, and me given at a conference in 2002 at Bangor Theological seminary and published in Kraus and Wooden, *Septuagint Research*. For reflections on NETS after its publication, see the papers from a 2008 conference held at Trinity Western University published in Hiebert, *'Translation is Required'*.

14 See the chart in Toury, *Descriptive Translation Studies*, p. 13.

15 Pietersma, 'A New Paradigm for Addressing Old Questions', pp. 351–52.

16 See the comments in Pietersma, 'Exegesis in the Septuagint', pp. 37–39.

A target-oriented approach also had important implications for lexicography, as Boyd-Taylor had shown already, offering a basis from which to critique the frequent practice of ascribing, on the basis of their equivalence in the LXX/OG but without sufficient methodological warrant, Hebrew meanings to Greek words, a practice prevalent in the major classical Greek lexica, such as Liddell, Scott, Jones. So, Pietersma's initial articulation of the interlinear paradigm found solid theoretical grounding on Toury's conceptual base.[17]

By the mid-2000s, scholars in Septuagint Studies had begun to engage Translation Studies in a more comprehensive way, and the fruits of their labours were beginning to appear.[18] In the years preceding the appearance of NETS in 2007, the project's use of the interlinear paradigm and DTS spawned publications from a growing number of its translators illustrating the utility of this theoretical foundation. Yet, Pietersma had argued that the interlinear paradigm offered a model of the LXX/OG for Septuagint Studies generally and not only for the NETS project, and the debate over the merits of this paradigm became one of the foci of Septuagint Studies in these years.[19] The most extensive articulation of how the paradigm and its theoretical underpinnings applied to Septuagint Studies came from Boyd-Taylor in his 2005 University of Toronto dissertation 'Reading Between the Lines — Towards an Assessment of the Interlinear Paradigm for Septuagint Studies', written under Pietersma's supervision, in which he gave detailed theoretical and methodological argumentation for the interlinear paradigm as firmly grounded in DTS.[20]

At the same time as Boyd-Taylor was writing in Toronto, Theo A. W. van der Louw was doing his PhD at Leiden University with supervisors from both Septuagint Studies and Translation Studies, and as such he was the first person working in Septuagint Studies of whom I am aware that had specific training in Translation Studies. His dissertation, 'Transformations in the Septuagint', had the primary goal of bringing Septuagint Studies and Translation Studies together, as the subtitle, 'Towards an Interaction of Septuagint Studies and

---

17 The interlinear paradigm also forms the basis for the Society of Biblical Literature Commentary on the Septuagint Series, which will publish textual commentaries on LXX/OG books based of the NETS translations.

18 Within the world of Bible translation, Eugene Nida and the Nida Institute had been thinking about translation since the 1960s. See Nida, *Towards a Science of Translating*. Nida makes a distinction between formal and dynamic equivalence in translation that has become axiomatic in discussions of translating the Bible into modern languages. NETS, however, did not conceive of itself as a Bible translation. On Nida and Translation Studies, see the discussions in Bassnett, *Translation Studies*, pp. 39–41 and Munday, *Introducing Translation Studies*, pp. 38–44.

19 NETS was not without its critics, of course. For an overview of some criticisms and a response, see Pietersma, 'Beyond Literalism', pp. 3–21. For different approaches to the Septuagint and translating it into a modern language, see Harl, Dorival, and Munnich, *La Bible Grecque des Septante*; Dogniez and Harl, ed., *La Bible des Septante*; Kraus and Karrer, *Septuaginta*; and Fernández Marcos and Spottorno, ed., *La Biblia griega*.

20 Published as Boyd-Taylor, *Reading Between the Lines*. See van der Louw, 'Review'.

Translation Studies', explicitly indicates.[21] Van der Louw pointed to several earlier publications from Jan de Waard that in his view had not received extensive scholarly notice as well as to Boyd-Taylor's and my more recent studies and to a 2004 panel on Septuagint Studies and DTS that included Gideon Toury's participation.[22] He sums up the situation in the early 2000s well, however, when he writes,

> Translation Studies is a relatively recent discipline that consists of a variety of approaches for the study of translation. The Septuagint *is* a translation. It is, in fact, the most important translation of the pre-Christian era and intensively researched. But Septuagint Studies and Translation Studies lead separate lives. Although one of the first major translations, the Septuagint has been neglected by Translation Studies, and, although a translation, it has barely been studied with the help of methods from Translation Studies.[23]

In his Chapter 2, 'Translating and Translations in Antiquity', van der Louw discusses together the Septuagint and classical sources, and thus, his dissertation engages at least briefly in concert Septuagint Studies, Classics, and Translation Studies. In response to van der Louw's dissertation, Raija Sollamo, one of the doyens of the study of translation technique in the Septuagint, investigated the relationship between translation universals and translation technique in the Septuagint. She concluded that several features that van der Louw had identified — 'interference, explicitation, untypical lexical patterning, and under-representing of target language specific items' — find strong support in translation technical studies and that interference was a universal '*par excellence*' in the LXX/OG. Although she did not specifically interact with the work of NETS, she did engage Toury's work in DTS, and her emphasis on the importance of interference in the LXX/OG coincides with the approach of NETS on that issue.[24]

Since the first decade or so of the interaction of these two disciplines, a steady stream of research in Septuagint Studies has engaged or at least invoked Translation Studies. Boyd-Taylor and van der Louw continue to be important participants in the conversation, and the discussion has broadened within the field, both with respect to wider scholarly participation and the ways that Translation Studies insights have been employed. Several PhD dissertations have interacted with different approaches from Translation Studies in order

21 See van der Louw, *Transformations in the Septuagint*, also in a more preliminary way, van der Louw, 'Approaches in Translation Studies'.

22 See Pietersma, 'LXX and DTS'; Toury, 'A Handful of Methodological Issues in DTS'; Boyd-Taylor, 'Toward the Analysis of Translational Norms'; Wright, 'The *Letter of Aristeas* and the Reception History'; Fraade 'Locating Targum'.

23 van der Louw, *Transformations in the Septuagint*, p. 1.

24 See Sollamo, 'Translation Technique and Translation Studies', p. 351 for her conclusions. For an early example of discussions of interference in the NETS project, see Pietersma, 'A New Paradigm for Addressing Old Questions'.

to illuminate the LXX/OG translations, notably those of Dries De Crom on Song of Songs, of Randall Gauthier on Psalms 38 and 146, of John Screnock on Exodus 1–14, and of Marieke Dhont on Old Greek Job.[25]

Boyd-Taylor has pointed out that scholars in the field have started to shift their attention from an earlier focus on source-oriented questions, such as textual criticism of the Hebrew text, to target-oriented concerns (thus the turn towards Translation Studies), which has resulted in two concurrent trends. First, scholars have begun to study in more detail the Greek of the translations, and Septuagint scholars such as James Aitken at the University of Cambridge, who have training in Classics, have brought that expertise to the Greek text, focusing on elements such as rhetoric or vocabulary.[26] Second, more attention also has been paid to translation narratives, both ancient and modern. The *Letter of Aristeas*, which was written in the latter part of the second century BCE and which transmits the earliest legend of the translation of the Pentateuch, has experienced something of a renaissance. For centuries, scholars mined it for historical clues to the origins of the LXX, but recently scholars have looked to the narrative for how it constructs the *idea* of the translation and how that construction functions discursively in the Alexandrian Jewish community of the late second century BCE.[27]

With respect to the consideration of translation narratives, Naomi Seidman's *Faithful Renderings: Jewish-Christian Difference and the Politics of Translation* stands out for her engagement with multiple fields of study and theoretical perspectives.[28] While the Septuagint forms only one component of her study, which ranges from antiquity to contemporary translations of Yiddish into English, Seidman employs Translation Studies, Feminist Theory, and Postcolonial Theory in order 'to read the recurring controversies of translation discourse — the question of translatability, the choice of word-for-word versus sense-for-sense translation, or of "fidelity" versus "treason", or of the "invisibility" of the translator — as religious and political rather than "purely" linguistic questions'.[29] Thus, Seidman takes a decidedly different tack on the Septuagint (and Jewish translation more generally), but one that remains grounded in current trends in Translation Studies along with other areas of critical theory. In this conjunction of theoretical perspectives, at least as far as the Septuagint is concerned, Seidman's study is unique.[30]

---

25 De Crom's dissertation, 'The LXX Text of Canticles: A Descriptive Study in Hebrew-Greek Translation', remained unpublished until 2019. Gauthier, Screnock, and Dhont have published their dissertations; see Gauthier, *Psalm 38 and 145*; Screnock, *Traductor Scriptor*; and Dhont, *Style and Context of Old Greek Job*.

26 See, for example, Aitken, 'The Language of the Septuagint'.

27 For an overview of the issues, see Wright, 'The *Letter of Aristeas* and the Question of Septuagint Origins Redux' and Wright, *The Letter of Aristeas: 'Aristeas to Philocrates'*.

28 Seidman, *Faithful Renderings*. See also Boyd-Taylor, 'Review'.

29 Seidman, *Faithful Renderings*, pp. 30–31.

30 Tessa Rajak appeals to post-colonial theories to account for the LXX, although not within a Translation Studies framework. See Rajak, *Translation & Survival*.

Although as a rule Septuagintalists across the board have not embraced Translation Studies to the extent that the debates of the first decade of the twenty-first century might have led us to expect, increasingly those who work in Septuagint Studies are looking to Translation Studies to help them understand this corpus of Hebrew to Greek translations, using ever more diverse methodological approaches. To this point, Septuagintalists have engaged Classics primarily with a view to Greek education in the Hellenistic and Roman periods in order to understand better the possible backgrounds of the LXX/OG translators, but they have not as yet incorporated to a great extent the work of scholars in Classics who have employed Translation Studies. Thus, this leg of the methodological triangle remains largely unlinked.[31]

Classics

Translation, both ancient and modern, has been at the heart of Classics almost since its beginning. Indeed, many classicists trace the beginnings of Latin literature to Livius Andronicus's translation of Homer's *Odyssey*. As Glenn Most writes, 'The first line of Greek literature is the opening of Homer's *Iliad*; the first line of Latin literature is the opening of Livius Andronicus' translation of Homer's *Odyssey*'.[32] We can distinguish, then, two separate interests in Classics: (1) a focus on the *history* of translation, especially within Latin literature and (2) a concern with the translation of classical texts into modern languages. In recent years, Classicists have begun to employ insights from Translation Studies as a means to think about both of these foci. Since translations are ubiquitous in Latin literature, the main object of their analysis understandably has been Latin. Greeks, for their part, although they owed much to non-Greeks in philosophy and science, were more interested in the content of that knowledge rather than the genres and texts that transmitted them. As a result, translation of written texts played a much smaller role in Greek literature than it did in Latin literature, and so it does in Translation Studies.[33]

An interest in bringing Translation Studies to bear on the history of translation can be found in studies such as Astrid Seele's on Latin translation in which she examines Latin literature through the lens of Translation Studies. She argues that in their earliest forms ancient ideas about translation differed fundamentally from modern conceptions, but as Latin literature developed, especially with Cicero, conceptions of translation come closer to modern ones, even though in classical and post-classical translations, translators exercised

---

31 Van der Louw is the one scholar who has incorporated into his work that of scholars in Classics who are using Translation Studies in their work. See, for example, the bibliography to van der Louw, *Transformations in the Septuagint*.

32 Most, 'Violets in Crucibles', p. 388.

33 For more detail on this point, see Most, 'Violets in Crucibles'.

a certain freedom 'to which modern translators are no longer entitled'.[34] She emphasizes the ideal for Latin translators of *aemulatio*, competing with the Greek original in order to surpass it, and thus, Latin translations, because their readers likely knew and could read the source language, often served as metatexts to the Greek originals.

More extensive engagement with Translation Studies, involving both foci mentioned above, becomes more prevalent in the same period that Septuagint Studies was beginning its investment in that field. Several articles in the 2008 collection *Translation and the Classic* illustrate this trend.[35] Richard Armstrong, for instance, brings together both the history of Latin translation and its modern translators. He examines the translation of Homer into Latin and the developing epic genre in Latin, employing Even-Zohar's polysystem theory, in order to show how 'our "classic" translations of Homer in English hang very much on the Latin tradition in a manner that is thoroughly interwoven with its techniques and concerns [...]'.[36] In the same volume, both Deborah Roberts and Edith Hall treat aspects of the modern reception of the classics through translation. Roberts reflects on modern translations of the vocabulary of sex, elimination, and the body parts associated with them. She maps the translation of these terms onto changing justifications about 'defending', 'protecting', and 'preserving' the classics together with their readers, society more generally, and social attitudes about what constitutes obscenity.[37] Hall assesses the early history of modern translations of Greek and Latin texts that made them available to a reading audience wider than just elites (usually men of a certain social and educational background) who could read the original languages. She notes that these translations have had a similar impact on European culture as translations of the Bible, even though 'the history of the translation of the Greek and Latin classics into English enjoys no equivalent of the veritable industry attaching to the activities of John Wyclif and William Tyndale'.[38] In arguing for the value and worth of such translations, she observes that these texts 'have historically been accessed far more of the time in the languages spoken by their post-Renaissance consumers than in the languages spoken in the Greco-Roman Mediterranean two thousand years ago'.[39]

More recent interaction of scholars in Classics with Translation Studies has occurred in conjunction with the incorporation of a wider range of theoretical perspectives, particularly a focus on the discursive practices of these ancient texts, and a more self-conscious and explicit interdisciplinary thrust. The volume *Tradition, Translation, Trauma: The Classic and the Modern*,

34 Seele, *Römische Übersetzer*. See especially her conclusions on pp. 102–08.

35 Lianeri and Zajko ed., *Translation and the Classic*.

36 Armstrong, 'Classical Translations of the Classics'.

37 Roberts, 'Translation and the "Surreptitious Classic"'.

38 Hall, 'Navigating the Realms of Gold', p. 320, where she also refers to Bruce's *The English Bible*.

39 Hall, 'Navigating the Realms of Gold', p. 334. Most recently, see also the 'Translator's Note' in Emily Wilson's translation of the Odyssey (Wilson trans., *The Odyssey*).

for instance, contains a prologue by Susan Bassnett, one of the early theorists in Translation Studies, and the volume's introduction invokes her challenges and the way that the contributors have tried to respond to them. As Jan Parker writes there:

> [I]t is time to release 'translation' from its disciplinary home into an interdisciplinary questioning: of how a text affects over time and space. For the metaphorical power of translation embraces travel between cultures and between times; embraces personal experience and active transformation of self by a text.[40]

While the volume is eclectic in its topics and methodologies, the translation and reception of the Classics forms a consistent theme in essays such as Pat Easterling's 'Sophoclean Journeys', Matthew Fox's 'Cicero: Gentleman and Orator: Metaphors in Eighteenth Century Reception', Jane Montgomery Griffiths's 'The Abject Eidos: Trauma and the Body in Sophocles' *Electra*', and Parker's 'What's Hecuba to him [...] that he should weep for her?'.

Although classicists have begun increasingly to employ the methods and theoretical insights of Translation Studies, they typically have taken little notice of work in Septuagint Studies. Sometimes one finds an article or two in a footnote (often published in journals that classicists read), but as a rule, Septuagint scholarship on translation seems relatively unknown. One study, however, emerges from among those in Classics that engage Translation Studies, Maurizio Bettini's *Vertere: Un'antropologia della traduzione nella cultura antica*. One of the concerns that sets Bettini's study apart is his chapter 'Alla ricerca della traduzione perfetta' in which he treats the LXX/OG, noting that 'a God who speaks in writing represents a great cultural shift'.[41] Although he does not treat the translations in the Septuagint *per se*, that is, their translation techniques or linguistic characters, he does examine the major translation narratives *about* the Septuagint in the *Letter of Aristeas*, Philo, Irenaeus, Ps.-Justin, Epiphanius, Augustine, and Jerome. Bettini, more than any other scholar in Classics that I have read, understands ancient translation to include literary translations from across the ancient world. His book, then, is the fullest interdisciplinary study that I have encountered that takes account of all three academic fields.[42]

---

40 See Bassnett's 'Prologue' and Parker's comments in Parker and Matthews, *Tradition, Translation, Trauma*, pp. 1–9 and 11–25. The quote comes from Parker, p. 17.

41 Bettini, *Vertere*, p. 191; 'Un Dio che parla per iscritto costituisce una grande mutazione culturale'.

42 The book, unlike most that deal with ancient translation, also treats aspects of translation in Egypt, albeit mostly through the testimony of Herodotus and via the terms *hermeneus* in Greek and *interpres* in Latin.

Translation Studies

In the Preface to the fourth edition of her seminal survey, *Translation Studies*, Susan Bassnett writes,

> When this book first appeared in 1980, there seemed to be little interest in the study of translation. Indeed, the notion of an independent field, some would say discipline in its own right, focusing on the theory and practice of translation would have been viewed with astonishment in the academic world. Translator programmes, mostly outside the English-speaking world, provided professional courses for business and industry, but translation was not a mainstream university subject and when it was taught, appeared only as an adjunct to foreign language learning. Today that world has changed.[43]

As the foundation for theory and practice, Translation Studies constructed a skeletal history of translation theory that built on Cicero's and Horace's distinction between word-for-word and sense-for-sense translation, Quintilian's advocating of translation as a stylistic exercise, and Jerome's comments about the use of word-for-word translation for Scripture. Indeed, as early as 1958, Eric Jacobsen declared that 'translation is primarily an invention of the Romans', which Bassnett seems to accept, calling the claim 'a *bit* [italics mine] of critical hyperbole'.[44] This fundamental connection between Latin translation and the history of translation theory as Translation Studies has (re)constructed it remains the regnant paradigm for tracing this history, and it established the framework for early theoretical discussions of translations as either free or literal, two poles of approach derived from the ancient sources of which modern conceptions of translation such as 'formal' or 'dynamic' seem to be variations. So, for example, Jeremy Munday, in his influential *Introducing Translation Studies*, begins with the distinction in Latin writers between sense-for-sense and word-for-word, although he notes that these same distinctions also were made by translators in China and in the Arabic World. Nonetheless, Cicero's comments serve as the launching pad for the discussion.[45] He then moves to concepts of equivalence and the labels of formal and dynamic.

While the connection between Translation Studies and Classics, at least as far as the history of translation theory is concerned, can be traced to some of the early scholarship in the budding field of Translation Studies, van der Louw notes that, as a rule, general surveys of Translation Studies do not take

---

43 Bassnett, *Translation Studies*, p. 1.

44 Jacobsen, *Translation*, p. 43; Bassnett, *Translation Studies*, p. 53.

45 Munday, *Introducing Translation Studies*, pp. 19–23. See also Bassnett, *Translation Studies*, p. 54. Rener, *Interpretatio* traces a theory of language to the Greeks and Romans, beginning explicitly in his title from Cicero.

full enough account of more extensive scholarship on the history and practice of translation in antiquity, much of which originates within Classics.[46] Even so, the attachment within Translation Studies to the origins of translation and translation theory as beginning within Latin literature becomes clear in the *absence* of any mention of the prologue to Ben Sira or the Septuagint in almost any general work within Translation Studies, which in my view constitutes a critical lacuna. Van der Louw gives a couple of examples within Translation Studies that refer to the Septuagint, but they are the exceptions that prove the rule.[47]

Furthermore, almost all discussions of translations of the Bible in Translation Studies begin with Jerome and not with the LXX/OG. Both Bassnett and Munday start with Jerome and move forward from him, often skipping centuries from the Latin church father to much later translators.[48] Lawrence Venuti's *Translation Studies Reader* opens with Jerome's 'Letter to Pammachius' in which he claims that only in the case of Scripture should word-for-word translation be used, because 'the very order of the words is a mystery'. Otherwise, Jerome translates in a sense-for-sense mode, even quoting Cicero and Horace on the matter of translation approach. The second reading in that volume comes from Nicolas Perrot d'Ablancourt in the seventeenth century, a full thirteen centuries later.

In the face of the equivalence models of translation long held in Western translation theory that originate in the Latin language with Cicero, Horace, and Jerome, Venuti has offered a different model, what he calls the 'hermeneutical model', using Jerome's letter as a starting point and a foil.[49] In Venuti's view, Jerome exemplifies this equivalence approach, which he calls the 'instrumental model' that assumes that some 'invariant' — whether in a sense-for-sense mode or a word-for-word mode — can be transferred from the source text to the target text. Thus, approaches to translation that rely on conceptions such as free or literal or dynamic and formal assume that there is some equivalence between a source text and its translation in the target language, some 'thing', what Venuti calls an invariant, that can be evaluated and understood to be equivalent between the two texts. In Venuti's view, however, translation is a hermeneutical project in which no invariant exists to transfer between source and target. This understanding of translation is founded on a materialist theory of language in which language is mediated by linguistic

46 van der Louw, *Transformations in the Septuagint*, p. 26. In footnotes 3 and 4 on this page van der Louw gives a fuller list of bibliographical references that includes Rener, *Interpretatio*; Ballard, *De Ciceron à Benjamin*; van den Broeck, *Over de grenzen van het vertaalbare*; Seele, *Römische Übersetzer*; and Albrecht, *Literarische Übersetzung*.

47 van der Louw, *Transformations in the Septuagint*, pp. 11–12.

48 Munday skips from Jerome to Luther; Bassnett moves from Jerome to Wyclif. Rener has no entry for Bible translation in his index, although he does discuss Jerome's comments on translation at various points.

49 Venuti, 'Genealogies of Translation Theory'. Still, however, Jerome serves as the starting point.

and cultural determinants. A translation does not transfer anything from the source because there is nothing to transfer; rather, translation inscribes in the target language one possible interpretation among many of the source text through the translator's application of formal and thematic 'interpretants', of which there are two kinds, formal and thematic, that mediate between the two languages.[50]

Venuti argues that Jerome took this model from classical authors, especially Cicero, through his classical education. To the extent that Jerome's views derive from Cicero, Horace, and the Roman tradition of translation, then, Western translation theory, grounded in an instrumental model of translation and flawed as it is according to Venuti, derives from Rome. So, even though Venuti challenges the regnant paradigm of translation within Translation Studies, he reinforces the conclusion that the field remains indebted to that Roman tradition via Classics, both for its history and for concepts that continue to play a central role in theoretical thinking about translation.

Prospects

As I have sketched it out here, then, since the mid- to late 1990s, Septuagint Studies has increasingly looked beyond its disciplinary boundaries, primarily toward Translation Studies but also somewhat in the direction of Classics, for methods and approaches that help scholars understand this monumental project of translation. This shift was at least partially triggered by the initiation in this period of several major projects to translate the LXX/OG into modern languages, which made thinking about how to translate a translation a priority: NETS (English), Bible d'Alexandrie (French), Septuaginta Deutsch (German), and La Biblia griega — Septuaginta (Spanish).[51] This flurry of translation activity resulted in more theoretical thinking about the LXX/OG in new and innovative ways, primarily because these projects by virtue of their objectives were target-oriented.

Translation Studies and Classics traditionally have had a much closer relationship, although Translation Studies mostly draws on Classics, albeit selectively, for its history of translation. Scholars in Classics, like those in

50 Formal interpretants encompass ideas such as semantic correspondence or style and syntax related to particular genres or discourses. Thematic interpretants are codes that involve 'specific values, beliefs, and representations; a discourse in the sense of a relatively coherent body of concepts problems, and arguments; or a particular interpretation of the source text that has been articulated independently in a commentary' (Venuti, 'Genealogies of Translation Theory', p. 23). In Venuti's view, analysis of the translator's use of formal and thematic interpretants demystifies the process of translation. For more detail, see Venuti, 'Genealogies of Translation Theory', pp. 21–44. On these models applied to the book of Ben Sira, see Wright, 'Translation, Reception, and the Historiography of Early Judaism'.

51 See Dogniez and Harl ed., *La Bible des Septante*; Kraus and Karrer, *Septuaginta*; Fernández Marcos and Spottorno ed, *La Biblia griega*.

Septuagint Studies, have more and more looked to methodological insights from Translation Studies for their work. Classics and Translation Studies, for their part, have taken almost no notice of the Septuagint and ancient testimony about it. Several reasons might be suggested for this neglect: (1) Septuagint Studies requires a specialized knowledge, particularly of ancient Hebrew along with Greek, which many (most?) researchers in Classics and Translation Studies might not have; (2) the scholarly literature in Septuagint Studies usually appears in venues that Classics and Translation Studies scholars typically do not read; (3) the traditional home of Septuagint Studies in Biblical Studies and/or Theology determined many of its methods, which were source oriented toward textual criticism of the Hebrew Bible and theology; (4) the confessional interests of many within Biblical Studies could have been viewed with some suspicion, although that has certainly changed with the advent of Religious Studies as an academic field; and (5) the Septuagint translators remain anonymous figures, and, outside of the prologue to Ben Sira, they did not make statements about their approaches to translation, even though we see a variety of modes of translation in the texts themselves.[52]

In order to point to the importance of the LXX/OG for Translation Studies and Classics, I want to look briefly at two texts that predate the Roman writers, that give us an indication of how some ancient Jews thought of translation, and that ought to have broader recognition outside of Septuagint Studies, particularly with respect to the history of translation and its development in Western thought.

(1) The most direct reflection on translating comes from the prologue to Ben Sira, written by the translator who claims to be a descendant/grandson of the author. It consists of three sentences in good *koine* Greek, the second of which reads:

> You are invited, therefore, to a reading with goodwill and attention, and to exercise forbearance in cases where we may be thought to be insipid with regard to some expressions that have been the object of great care in rendering; for what was originally expressed in Hebrew does not have the same force when it is in fact rendered in another language. And not only in this case, but also in the case of the Law itself and the Prophets and the rest of the books the difference is not small when these are expressed in their own language.[53]

Here the translator recognizes the difference between Hebrew and Greek with which he has to wrestle. Not only that, he points to 'the Law itself, the Prophets, and the rest of the books' that exhibit these same differences, which are 'not small'. This passage has been the subject of much debate in Septuagint Studies, particularly over the meaning of the verb 'to have the same force',

52 See van der Louw, *Transformations in the Septuagint*, p. 12.

53 Wright, 'Sirach', p. 719; Ziegler, *Septuaginta*; NETS.

but the point at hand is that this passage reveals a translator who reflects on translation, and unlike Cicero — whose translations of Demosthenes and Aeschines have not survived or perhaps never got made — we can then look at how he translates to see to what degree the concern expressed in the prologue has a practical effect in his translation.[54] We can see the most obvious effect in the quality of the Greek in the prologue compared with that of the translation. Whereas the translator's prologue is written in good koine Greek, the Greek of the translation does not rise to the syntactic and stylistic level of the prologue, often being unidiomatic, representing in Greek features of the Hebrew source text, and sometimes not even making much sense. Of course, we see the same kind of translation in the 'the Law itself, the Prophets, and the rest of the books', and the translator of Ben Sira seems to have accepted that translation in what could be called an isomorphic process of translation was the 'right' way to do it.[55] Although he does not rely on these earlier translations in most cases for his lexical choices, he does seem to have taken them as models for how translation ought to be done.[56]

(2) The *Letter of Aristeas*, a second century BCE Jewish text, offers the oldest version of the legend of the translation of the Pentateuch from Hebrew to Greek. Although much of the work concerns the translation, little is said about translating *per se*. The author uses the vocabulary of translating and transcribing in ambiguous ways throughout the text. In § 121, however, we are told,

> Thus, Eleazar selected excellent men who excelled in education, inasmuch as indeed they were the product of parents of high distinction. These had not only acquired skill in the literature of the Judeans, but also not incidentally they had given heed to preparation in Greek literature.[57]

In this short sentence, we see the author's ideal of the translator and his conception of the translation of the Pentateuch. His translators had education in *literature*, both Judean and Greek. Due to this preparation, they were eminently capable of taking the laws of the Jews and rendering them into a form that comported with the standards of Greek literature, and at the same time the piety of these men, mentioned on numerous occasions, confirmed that the

54 On this debate, see Wright, 'Translation Greek in Sirach', and Aitken, 'The Literary Attainment', pp. 101–08.

55 Isomorphism refers to the practice of translating each word, morpheme, or phrase in the Hebrew essentially in sequence with little regard for the overall discursive structure of the source text. In the LXX/OG corpus, this practice results in Greek that can be sensible, if not necessarily literary, but also in Greek that can range from awkward to opaque. On isomorphism in the LXX/OG, see Boyd-Taylor, 'A Place in the Sun', and Boyd-Taylor, *Reading Between the Lines*.

56 See Wright, *No Small Difference*; Wright, 'Access to the Source'; and Wright, 'Translation Greek in Sirach'.

57 Wright, *The Letter of Aristeas: 'Aristeas to Philocrates'*, p. 236.

Greek translation would contain all that was necessary to fulfil the law for Greek-speaking Jews.[58] This claim furthers a larger argument made in *Aristeas* that the LXX was every bit scripture for those Judeans living in Hellenistic Alexandria while at the same time it could claim *bona fides* as a work of Greek literature worthy of the Alexandrian Library, which in the narrative provided the motivation for the translation in the first place (§§ 9–11).[59]

Conclusion

By way of conclusion, we have seen that the intersections among Septuagint Studies, Classics, and Translation Studies have been somewhat uneven and halting. Yet, as I see it, with important questions remaining about ancient translation as an activity and about the varied social and cultural sites of translation in antiquity, collaboration among these three fields is more of a desideratum in the current interdisciplinary environment in the academy. Certainly, translation activity was more pervasive in antiquity than our textbooks generally recognize, whether we encounter it in ancient comments about translations and translators, such as Herodotus makes, or in multi-language papyri, or in word lists, or via the back-and-forth cultural traffic that we know happened in the ancient Mediterranean. Translation in antiquity took place in varied contexts, not all of which were literary or even written. In these contexts, we know little about the everyday speech of ancient peoples and how speech habits and practices might affect the process of translation in written contexts. At least in Egypt, where numerous papyri document people's daily lives, we get a glimpse of daily speech or at least of the ordinary *koine* Greek of the period and the extent to which that Greek is reflected in the Septuagint.[60] Likewise, as ancient texts continue to be translated into modern languages for new audiences, new questions will arise about how best to do that work. For both of these enterprises, interdisciplinary cooperation in these disciplines will enable us to learn more about the ancient world and to bring the texts into new and different contexts than any single discipline could.

What, then, are the prospects of Septuagint Studies (and more generally the study of ancient religious texts), Classics, and Translation Studies coming more closely into conversation? While I think that the process is underway, three avenues appear fruitful. First, as scholars in Septuagint Studies and Classics continue to incorporate Translation Studies into their work, scholars in Translation Studies will have to take notice, whether for

---

58 See Wright, *The Letter of Aristeas: 'Aristeas to Philocrates'*.

59 Of course, the Greek of the Septuagint does not achieve the literary levels claimed in *Aristeas*. Its author is constructing an argument for the importance of the translations for Jews as a foundational text comparable to those of the Greeks and for their status as compared to authoritative texts written in Greek.

60 See, for example, Aitken, 'The Language of the Septuagint'.

constructing a more complete history of translation or for thinking about how this work has an impact of theoretical perspectives within Translation Studies. Second, interdisciplinary conferences and working seminars that include scholars from these three disciplines will enhance the possibilities for interdisciplinary conversation. Third, scholars in these three fields ought to think about publishing in venues outside of their own disciplines that would be more accessible to scholars in the other two. Up until now, some projects within Classics have interacted with Translation Studies theorists, such as the volumes that I highlighted above edited by Lianeri and Zajko, in which the lead article is by Lawrence Venuti, and by Parker and Matthews, which has a prologue by Bassnett that sets the stage for the volume's essays. In Septuagint Studies, the 2004 panel at the international meeting of the IOSCS entitled 'LXX and Descriptive Translation Studies — Making the Connection' included the translation theorist Gideon Toury. These enterprises, however, only link two of the three legs of the triangle. They are a beginning, but the next steps remain to be taken.

More broadly, such interdisciplinary collaboration has potential benefits for thinking about translation in other ancient corpora, such as scientific, philosophical, medical, or occult texts. One paradigmatic example comes to mind. The *Potter's Oracle*, an Egyptian text of nationalist propaganda likely dating from the middle to the end of the second century BCE, survives in five fragmentary Greek papyri from the second to third centuries CE. Uncertainty surrounds its original language of composition. The text itself hints that it was translated from Egyptian into Greek: 'The Potter's Defense made t[o] Amenophis the king, translated as b[es]t as possible. Concerning the things that wil[l hap]pen in Egypt' (P_2 54–57).[61] Was the text indeed translated? When might it have been translated? Does the Greek text bear the marks of translation? If the text was originally written in Greek, can that date be determined? Stefan Beyerle has remarked, 'What would be helpful for further clarification is the identification of clear Egyptian phrases and Egyptian grammatical phenomena in the Greek edition of the oracle'.[62] I would argue that the question of whether this is a translation or a pseudotranslation requires not only an understanding of Demotic (the likely original language of the text if it was a translation) but also theoretical awareness of the use of pseudotranslations and why a text might claim to be translated when it was not.[63] In order to understand the Greek text in its own context would require knowledge of papyrology, *koine* Greek, and its developments, and Hellenistic and Roman period history. I am certain that this example could

61 Cited in Beyerle, 'Authority and Propaganda', p. 176, from Alan Kerkeslager's translation.

62 Beyerle, 'Authority and Propaganda', p. 176.

63 On including pseudotranslations under the umbrella of Translation Studies, see Toury, *Descriptive Translation Studies*, pp. 40–52.

be multiplied with ease.[64] The dilemma of the language and interpretation of the *Potter's Oracle*, then, exemplifies the way that interdisciplinary work across multiple scholarly disciplines, and particularly with Translation Studies, can hold out the potential to help scholars investigate ancient translations and pseudotranslation beyond the corpora of texts studied in Septuagint Studies and Classics.

---

64 The case of the so-called *Corpus Hermeticum* also comes to mind, since it as well purports to be a translation from Egyptian into Greek.

Bibliography

Primary Sources

Wilson, Emily, trans., *The Odyssey. Homer* (New York: W. W. Norton & Company, 2018)

Wright, Benjamin G., *The Letter of Aristeas: 'Aristeas to Philocrates' or 'On the Translation of the Law of the Jews'*, Commentaries on Early Jewish Literature (Berlin: de Gruyter, 2015)

Secondary Studies

Aitken, James K., 'The Literary Attainment of the Translator of Greek Sirach', in *The Texts and Versions of the Book of Ben Sira: Transmission and Interpretation*, ed. by Jan Joosten and Jean-Sébastien Rey, JSJSup, 150 (Leiden: Brill, 2011), pp. 95–126

——, 'The Language of the Septuagint and Jewish Greek Identity', in *The Jewish-Greek Tradition in Antiquity and the Byzantine Empire*, ed. by James K. Aitken and James Carleton Paget (Cambridge: Cambridge University Press, 2014), pp. 120–34

Albrecht, J., *Literarische Übersetzung. Geschichte, Theorie, kulturelle Wirkung* (Darmstadt: Wissenschaftliche Buchgesellschaft, 1998)

Armstrong, Richard H., 'Classical Translations of the Classics: The Dynamics of Literary Tradition in Retranslating Epic Poetry', in *Translation and the Classic: Identity as Change in the History of Culture*, ed. by Alexandra Lianeri and Vanda Zajko (Oxford: Oxford University Press, 2008), pp. 169–202

Ballard, M., *De Ciceron à Benjamin. Traducteuers, traductions, reflexions* (Lille: Presses Universitaires de Lille, 1992)

Bassnett, Susan, *Translation Studies*, 4th edn (London: Routledge, 2014)

Bettini, Maurizio, *Vertere: Un'antropologia della traduzione nella cultura antica*, Piccolo Biblioteca Einaudi, Nuova serie, 573 (Torino: Giulio Einaudi, 2012)

Beyerle, Stefan, 'Authority and Propaganda – The Case of the *Potter's Oracle*', in *Sibyls, Scriptures, and Scrolls: John Collins at Seventy*, vol. 1, ed. by Joel Baden, Hindy Najman, and Eibert Tigchelaar, JSJSup, 175/1 (Leiden: Brill, 2017), pp. 167–84

Boyd-Taylor, Cameron. 'A Place in the Sun: The Interpretative Significance of LXX-Psalm 18:5c', *BIOSCS*, 31 (1998), 71–105

——, 'The Evidentiary Value of Septuagintal Usage for Greek Lexicography: Alice's Reply to Humpty Dumpty', *BIOSCS*, 34 (2001), 47–80

——, 'Toward the Analysis of Translational Norms: A Sighting Shot', *BIOSCS*, 38 (2006), 27–46

——, review of Naomi Seidman, *Faithful Renderings: Jewish-Christian Difference and the Politics of Translation*, Review of Biblical Literature (2008) <http://rblnewsletter.blogspot.com/2008/05/> [accessed 17 November 2019]

——, *Reading Between the Lines: The Interlinear Paradigm for Septuagint Studies*, BTS, 8 (Leuven: Peeters, 2011)

Broeck, R. van den, *Over de grenzen van het vertaalbare. Een historische verkenning in het gebied van de vertaaltheorie*, Nieuwe Cahiers voor Vertaalwetenschap, 1 (Antwerp: Fantom, 1992)

Bruce, Frederick Fyvie, *The English Bible: A History of Translation* (London: Lutterworth, 1961)

Crom, Dries de, 'The LXX Text of Canticles: A Descriptive Study in Hebrew-Greek Translation' (doctoral thesis, KU Leuven, 2009). Published (Göttingen: Vandenhoek & Ruprecht, 2019)

Dhont, Marieke, *Style and Context of Old Greek Job*, JSJSup, 183 (Leiden: Brill, 2018)

Dogniez, Cécile, and Marguerite Harl, ed., *La Bible des Septante. Le Pentateuque d'Alexandrie. Texte grec et traduction* (Paris: Les Éditions du CERF, 2001)

Dooslaer, Luc van. 'Eurocentrism', in *Handbook of Translation Studies: Volume 3*, ed. by Yves Gambier and Luc van Doorslaer (Amsterdam: John Benjamins Library, 2012), pp. 47–51

Fernández Marcos, Natalio, and Maria Victoria Spottorno, ed., *La Biblia griega. Septuaginta. I. Pentateuco*, Biblioteca de Estudios Bíblicos, 125 (Salamanca: Edíciones Segueme, 2008)

Fraade, Steven D., 'Locating Targum in the Textual Polysystem of Rabbinic Pedagogy', *BIOSCS*, 38 (2006), 69–91

Gauthier, Randall X., *Psalm 38 and 145 of the Old Greek Version*, VTSup, 166 (Leiden: Brill, 2014)

Hall, Edith, 'Navigating the Realms of Gold: Translation as Access Route to the Classics', in *Translation and the Classic: Identity as Change in the History of Culture*, ed. by Alexandra Lianeri and Vanda Zajko (Oxford: Oxford University Press, 2008), pp. 315–40

Harl, Marguerite, Gilles Dorival, and Olivier Munnich, *La Bible Grecque des Septante: Du Judaïsme Hellenistique au Christianisme Ancien*, Initiations au Christianisme Ancien (Paris: Les Éditions du Cerf, 1988)

Hiebert, Robert J. V., ed., *'Translation is Required': The Septuagint in Retrospect and Prospect*, SCS, 56 (Atlanta: Society of Biblical Literature, 2010)

Jacobsen, Eric, *Translation: A Traditional Craft* (Copenhagen: Nordisk Forlag, 1958)

Kelly, Louis, *The True Interpreter* (New York: St Martin's, 1979)

Kraus, Wolfgang, and Martin Karrer, *Septuaginta Deutsch. Das griechische Alte Testament in deutscher Übersetzung* (Stuttgart: Deutsche Bibelgesellschaft, 2009)

Kraus, Wolfgang, and R. Glenn Wooden, ed., *Septuagint Research: Issues and Challenges in the Study of the Greek Jewish Scriptures*, SCS, 53 (Atlanta: Society of Biblical Literature, 2006)

Lianeri, Alexandra, and Vanda Zajko, ed., *Translation and the Classic: Identity as Change in the History of Culture* (Oxford: Oxford University Press, 2008)

Louw, Theo van der, 'Approaches in Translation Studies and their Use for the Study of the Septuagint', in *XII Congress of the International Organization for Septuagint and Cognate Studies. Leiden 2004*, ed. by Melvin K. H. Peters, SCS, 54 (Atlanta: Society of Biblical Literature, 2006), pp. 17–28

——, *Transformations in the Septuagint: Towards an Interaction of Septuagint Studies and Translation Studies*, CBET, 47 (Leuven: Peeters, 2007)

——, review of Cameron Boyd-Taylor, *Reading Between the Lines: The Interlinear Paradigm for Septuagint Studies*, JSCS, 44 (2011), pp. 145–50

Most, Glenn W., 'Violets in Crucibles: Translating, Traducing, Transmuting', *Transactions of the American Philological Association (1974–)*, 133 (2003), 381–90

Munday, Jeremy, *Introducing Translation Studies: Theories and Applications*, 2nd edn (London: Routledge, 2008)

Nida, Eugene A., *Towards a Science of Translating: With Special Reference to Principles and Procedures Involved in Bible Translating* (Leiden: Brill, 1964)

Parker, Jan, and Timothy Matthews, *Tradition, Translation, Trauma: The Classic and the Modern* (Oxford: Oxford University Press, 2011)

Pietersma, Albert, 'A New English Translation of the Septuagint', in *X Congress of the International Organization for Septuagint and Cognate Studies, Oslo 1998*, ed. by Bernard A. Taylor, SCS, 51 (Atlanta: Society of Biblical Literature, 2001), pp. 217–28

——, 'A New Paradigm for Addressing Old Questions: The Relevance of the Interlinear Paradigm for the Study of the Septuagint', in *Bible and Computer: The Stellenbosch AIBI-6 Conference. Proceedings of the Association Internationale Bible et Informatique 'From Alpha to Byte'. University of Stellenbosch 17–21 July, 2000*, ed. by Johann Cook (Leiden: Brill, 2002), pp. 337–64

——, 'Exegesis in the Septuagint: Possibilities and Limits (The Psalter as a Case in Point)', in *Septuagint Research: Issues and Challenges in the Study of the Greek Jewish Scriptures*, ed. by Wolfgang Kraus and R. Glenn Wooden, SCS, 53 (Atlanta: Society of Biblical Literature, 2006), pp. 33–45

——, 'LXX and DTS: A New Archimedean Point for Septuagint Studies?' *BIOSCS*, 38 (2006), 1–11

——, 'Beyond Literalism: Interlinearity Revisited', in *'Translation is Required': The Septuagint in Retrospect and Prospect*, ed. by Robert J. V. Hiebert, SCS, 56 (Atlanta: Society of Biblical Literature, 2010), pp. 3–21

Pietersma, Albert, and Benjamin G. Wright, 'To the Reader of NETS', in *A New English Translation of the Septuagint and the Other Greek Translations Traditionally Included under that Title*, ed. by Albert Pietersma and Benjamin G. Wright (New York: Oxford University Press, 2007), pp. iii–xx

Rajak, Tessa, *Translation & Survival: The Greek Bible of the Ancient Jewish Diaspora* (Oxford: Oxford University Press, 2009)

Rener, Frederick M., *Interpretatio: Language and Translation from Cicero to Tyler*, Approaches to Translation Studies, 8 (Amsterdam: Rodopi, 1989)

Roberts, Deborah H., 'Translation and the "Surreptitious Classic": Obscenity and Translation', in *Translation and the Classic: Identity as Change in the History of Culture*, ed. by Alexandra Lianeri and Vanda Zajko (Oxford: Oxford University Press, 2008), pp. 278–311

Screnock, John, *Traductor Scriptor: The Old Greek Translation of Exodus 1–14 as Scribal Activity*, VTSup, 174 (Leiden: Brill, 2017)

Seele, Astrid, *Römische Übersetzer, Nöte, Freiheiten, Absichten* (Darmstadt: Wissenschaftliche Buchgesellschaft, 1995)

Seidman, Naomi, *Faithful Renderings: Jewish-Christian Difference and the Politics of Translation*, Afterlives of the Bible (Chicago: University of Chicago Press, 2006)

Sollamo, Raija, 'Translation Technique and Translation Studies: The Problem of Translation Universals', in *XIII Congress of the International Organization for Septuagint and Cognate Studies. Ljubljana, 2007*, ed. by Melvin K. H. Peters, SCS, 55 (Atlanta: Society of Biblical Literature, 2008), pp. 339–51

Toury, Gideon, *Descriptive Translation Studies – and Beyond*, Benjamins Translation Library, 4 (Amsterdam: John Benjamins Library, 1995)

——, 'A Handful of Methodological Issues in DTS: Are They Applicable to the Study of the Septuagint as an Assumed Translation?', *BIOSCS*, 38 (2006), 13–25

Tov, Emanuel, *A Computerized Data Base for Septuagint Studies: The Parallel Aligned Text of the Greek and Hebrew Bible*, CATSS, 2, JNSL, Sup 1 (Stellenbosch: Journal of Northwest Semitic Languages, 1986)

Venuti, Lawrence, 'Genealogies of Translation Theory: Jerome', *Boundary 2*, 37.3 (2010), 5–28

——, ed., *The Translation Studies Reader*, 3rd edn (London: Routledge, 2012)

Wright, Benjamin G., *No Small Difference: Sirach's Relationship to its Hebrew Parent Text*, SCS, 26 (Atlanta: Scholars Press, 1989)

——, 'The Jewish Scriptures in Greek: The Septuagint in the Context of Ancient Translation Activity', in *Biblical Translation in Context*, ed. by Frederick W. Knobloch, Studies and Texts in Jewish History and Culture, 10 (Bethesda: University of Maryland Press, 2002), pp. 3–18

——, 'Access to the Source: Cicero, Ben Sira, the Septuagint and their Audiences', *JSJ*, 39 (2003), 1–27

——, 'The *Letter of Aristeas* and the Reception History of the Septuagint', *BIOSCS*, 38 (2006), 1–11

——, 'Sirach', in *A New English Translation of the Septuagint and the Other Greek Translations Traditionally Included under that Title*, ed. by Albert Pietersma and Benjamin G. Wright (New York: Oxford University Press, 2007), pp. 715–62

——, 'The Septuagint and its Modern Translators', in *Die Septuaginta–Texte, Kontexte, Lebenswelten: Internationale Fachtagung veranstaltet von Septuaginta Deutsch (LXX.D), Wuppertal 20.-23. Juli 2006*, ed. by Wolfgang Kraus and Martin Karrer, WUNT, 219 (Tübingen: Mohr Siebeck, 2008), pp. 103–14

——, 'The *Letter of Aristeas* and the Question of Septuagint Origins Redux'. *Journal of Ancient Judaism*, 2 (2011), 304–26

——, 'Translation Greek in Sirach in Light of the Grandson's Prologue', in *The Texts and Versions of the Book of Ben Sira: Transmission and Interpretation*, ed. by Jan Joosten and Jean-Sébastien Rey, JSJSup, 150 (Leiden: Brill, 2011), pp. 75–94

——, 'Translation, Reception, and the Historiography of Early Judaism', in *'When the Morning Stars Sang': Essays in Honor of Choon Leong Seow on the Occasion of his Sixty-Fifth Birthday*, ed. by Christine Roy Yoder and Scott C. Jones, BZAW, 500 (Berlin: de Gruyter, forthcoming)

Ziegler, Joseph, *Septuaginta: Vetus Testamentum Graecum Auctorite Academiae Scientiarum Gottingensis editum XII/2 Sapientia Iesu Filii Sirach*, 2nd edn (Göttingen: Vandenhoeck & Ruprecht, 1980)

MATTEO MARTELLI

A Plurality of Voices

Fragmented Narratives on Syriac Translations

Introduction

Many texts pertaining to diverse domains of ancient science and philosophy — from medicine to logic, from alchemy to astronomy/astrology — were translated into Syriac between the sixth and the thirteenth century.[1] Within this wide chronological framework, works originally produced in distinct cultural *milieux* and written in various languages (Greek, Middle Persian, Arabic)[2] were read, translated, and commented on by members of Christian communities who used Syriac as a spoken and/or liturgical language and were settled across different countries and empires: a vast geographical area that stretches from Turkey to south-western China and includes modern Syria, Iraq, Iran as well as a number of cities along the Silk Road.

Such a long and articulated history of translations and cultural exchanges, which were often promoted by key figures operating in highly multilingual settings, has not yet been fully told and systematically described in a monographic study. Scholars have certainly highlighted the contributions made by different actors of this complex process in various areas, but the overall picture is still fragmented, as I shall examine in the following pages.

1 For lists of translated works (especially from Greek), see Brock, 'The Syriac Commentary Tradition', pp. 11–15 (Aristotelian works); Fiori, 'Translations from Greek into Syriac'; Takahashi, 'Between Greek and Syriac', pp. 32–35; McCollum, 'Greek Literature in the Christian East', pp. 37–46.

2 If we broaden our scope to religious and hagiographical texts, Syriac writings can derive from Armenian or Coptic sources as well: for Armenian, see van Esbroek, 'Le résumé syriaque de l'Agathange'; for Coptic, see Toda, 'Syriac Translation in Egypt'; Nau, 'Une version syriaque inédite de la Vie de Schenoudi', pp. 362–63.

Matteo Martelli (matteo.martelli@unibo.it) has a PhD in Greek Philology from the University of Bologna (2007) and in History of Science from the University of Pisa (2012). Currently professor in History of Science at the University of Bologna, he has edited and translated the Greek and Syriac sections of Pseudo-Democritus' alchemical books *The Four Books of Pseudo-Democritus* (Maney, 2014). In L. Lehmhaus and M. Martelli, eds, *Collecting Recipes: Byzantine and Jewish Pharmacology in Dialogue* (De Gruyter, 2017), he explored various aspects of Byzantine and Syriac medicine.

Narratives on Translation across Eurasia and Africa: From Babylonia to Colonial India, ed. by Sonja Brentjes in cooperation with Jens Høyrup and Bruce O'Brien, CAT 3, pp. 67–82 (Turnhout: Brepols, 2022) BREPOLS PUBLISHERS 10.1484/M.CAT-EB.5.127934

Indeed, secondary literature devoted to this topic is vast and its complexity is also due to the key role played by translations in the development of Syriac literature. As Adam McCollum has recently observed,

> Syriac literature, by far the richest of Aramaic dialects in terms of surviving texts, is almost impossible to conceive apart from the presence of translated Greek literature, whether we mean straightforward translations or Hellenistically influenced commentaries, treatises, etc.[3]

In this paper, I will first survey some features of modern scholarship on Syriac translations by emphasizing common tendencies, more recent trends, and *desiderata* in the field; in the second part, closer attention will be devoted to two specific issues, namely the main types of periodization that have been so far proposed by scholars as well as the much-debated question of the role played by Syriac in the origins and development of the Abbasid translation movement.

The State of the Art: A Complex Picture

Already at the turn of the nineteenth century, in their first efforts to give a structured picture of the main phases of Syriac literature, eminent Syriacists did make scanty references to Syriac translations of philosophical and scientific works. These mentions, however, are scattered throughout the pages of introductory studies on Syriac literature and *belles-lettres*, which are organized according to different criteria. William Wright, for instance, followed a chronological order, and briefly introduced Syriac translations of Greek treatises (or Syriac commentaries on these works) in the sections devoted to specific figures. It is possible to artificially extract the following list of translators of Greek treatises (or commentators on these texts) from the continuous narrative of Wright's *Syriac Literature*:[4]

1. Probus (fifth century in Wright's opinion), who would have translated Aristotle's *De Interpretatione* (and perhaps other parts of the *Organon*);[5]
2. Sergius of Rēšʿaynā (d. 536), who translated pseudo-Dionisius's writings, Aristotelian works, and a selection of Galen's medical treatises;

3 McCollum, 'Greek Literature in the Christian East', p. 16.

4 The book is not easy to navigate, since the final index only includes references to a few translations.

5 More recent studies on this figure have cast serious doubt on the traditional fifth-century dating (Probus was rather active in the sixth century) and better defined his works: he wrote commentaries on Porphyry's *Isagoge* as well as Aristotle's *De Intepretatione* and *Prior Analytics* (first part), two books that he probably also translated; see Brock, 'The Commentator Probus'; Hugonnard-Roche, 'Le commentaire syriaque de Probus sur l'Isagoge de Prophyre'.

3. Paul the Persian (sixth century), who composed a treatise on Aristotelian logic;[6]
4. Severus Sēbōḵt (d. 667), active in the monastery of Qennešre, who wrote treatises and commentaries on Aristotelian logic;
5. Jacob of Edessa, prolific author, pupil of Severus Sēbōḵt; Wright only mentions the *Encheiridion* among his philosophical writings;[7]
7. Athanasius of Balad (d. 686/687), who, according to Wright's opinion, translated Porphyry's *Isagoge* and edited, at the same time, an earlier version of the same work;[8]
8. George, bishop of the Arabs (d. 724), who is credited with translations of *De Interpretatione, Prior Analytics* and *Categories*;
9. Ḥenanīšū I (d. 699/700), who wrote a commentary on *Prior Analytics*;
10. Moše bar Kēphā (d. 903), who wrote a commentary on Aristotelian dialectic;[9]
11. Ḥunayn ibn Isḥāq (d. 873), whose contribution as translator of medical works is briefly sketched by Wright;
12. Denḥā (ninth century), who wrote commentaries on Aristotle's *Organon*;[10]
13. David bar Paulos (early thirteenth century in Wright's opinion), who enumerated Aristotle's *Categories*;[11]
14. the polymath Bar Hebraeus (d. 1286);
15. along these figures, Wright briefly mentions anonymous translations, such as the Syriac versions of the *Physiologus*, Pseudo-Callisthenes' *Life of Alexander*, and Aesop's *Fables*.[12]

Such a dry list of names and treatises is instrumental in giving us a sense of the kind of information that was collected by exploring unpublished

---

6 Namely, a short commentary on Aristotle's *De Interpretatione*; see Hugonnard-Roche, 'Sur la lecture tardo-antique du *Peri Hermeneias*', pp. 47–67; Teixidor, *Aristote en Syriaque*, pp. 79–121.

7 Furlani, 'L'*Encheiridion* di Giacomo di Edessa'. Wright does not mention Jacob's translation of Aristotle's *Categories*, which was partially edited by Salomon Schüler in 1897; see now Georr, *Les Catégories d'Aristote*, pp. 253–316.

8 Scholars today agree that Athanasius wrote an introduction to Aristotelian logic (edited by Furlani, 'Contributi alla storia della filosofia greca in Oriente') and revised an earlier translation of the *Isagoge* (see Freimann, *Die Isagoge des Porphyrius*).

9 A brief fragment on *Categories* is extant in MS Med. Pal. Or. 200, fol. 179[r]; see King, *The Earliest Syriac Translation*, p. 19.

10 On this figure and his *oeuvre*, see Kessel, 'Neoplatonic Treatment', pp. 140–45.

11 David actually dates to the eighth–ninth century; see King, *The Earliest Syriac Translation*, p. 19.

12 Wright, *A Short History*, pp. 132–33 (*Physiologus*), pp. 139–40 (*Life of Alexander*), p. 242 (Aesop).

manuscripts and medieval accounts provided by encyclopaedic writers, from Bar Hebraeus to ʿAbdīšōʿ bar Brīḵā (d. 1318). The data obviously reflect the state of the art of the period, and they have been reorganized, expanded, and rectified in more recent publications.[13] Already in the first half of the twentieth century, Anton Baumstark substantially enriched our knowledge of the works of Syriac translators in his monumental and still valuable work on Syriac literature (*Geschichte der syrischen Literatur*). He adopted a chronological order and recognized two main historical periods: before and after Islam. He organized the authors accordingly, by dividing them on the basis of the churches they belonged to. In addition to the above-mentioned figures, who mainly translated (and commented on) philosophical and medical texts, Baumstark took into account anonymous Syriac translations pertaining to fields that had been dismissed in previous scholarship, such as agriculture (the so-called Syriac *Geoponica*), alchemy, and astrology (the anonymous Syriac translation of Ptolemy's *Tetrabiblos*, that he tentatively ascribed to Severus Sēbōḵt).[14] A similar attention to a broader spectrum of disciplines and sciences is also recognizable in Rubens Duval's overview of Syriac literature (*La littérature syriaque*), especially in two sections respectively devoted to philosophy and sciences.[15] The section on sciences includes chapters dealing with medicine, natural philosophy, astronomy (along with cosmography and geography), chemistry (*lege* alchemy) and mathematics, where translations are also considered.

The overwhelming mass of data that has been accumulated by these scholars is difficult to handle, and it was never reduced to a 'holistic' narrative on the origins and developments of Syriac translations. A certain need for systematization, shared by both Eastern and Western scholars, is certainly observable in other (often more recent) studies, some of which took the form of catalogues. In his *The Scattered Pearls*, whose second edition was published in 1956, the Patriarch of Antioch Ignatius Aphram I Barṣoum tried to give a complete list of Syriac translators, even though he mainly focused on translators of religious texts.[16] Among Western scholars, Sebastian Brock more recently published an invaluable repertory of all the Syriac translations and commentaries on the *Organon* which are known to us; Grigory Kessel

---

13 In the previous notes, I briefly referred to up-to-date literature on some of the mentioned figures.

14 Baumstark, *Geschichte der syrischen Literatur*, pp. 171–73 (*Geoponica* and alchemical literature, both described in a section devoted to 'profane Übersetzungsliteratur'), p. 247 (Ptolemy's *Tetrabiblos*; see also Nau, 'La cosmographie au VIIe siècle', pp. 228–29 ; Dimitrov, 'Fort. Recte').

15 Duval, *La littérature syriaque*, pp. 235–84.

16 Here, I refer to Moosa's English translation of *Kitāb al-Lu'lu' al-manṯūr fī tārīḫ al-ʿulūm wa-l-ādāb al-suryāniyya* (الؤلؤ المنثور في تاريخ العلوم والآداب السريانية); see Barṣoum, *The Scattered Pearls*, pp. 196–97. Syriac translations of Greek philosophical and scientific texts are mentioned in the sections devoted to philosophy, medicine, and natural sciences (pp. 179–95).

provided a full list of the extant Syriac translations of Galen's treatises.[17] More specific lists also appear in studies devoted to particular works, such as in Daniel King's recent edition of the earliest (anonymous) translation of the *Categories*: indeed, the book mentions all the known Syriac translations of the *Categories* as well as the Syriac scholars who wrote 'treatises and commentaries in some way connected to it [i.e. the *Categories*]'.[18] A broader approach is recognizable in Hidemi Takahashi's studies, which give a valuable summary of all the extant Syriac translations of non-religious texts.[19]

Despite these efforts to systematize a critical mass of facts and figures, the scholarly community did not devote the same attention to each phase and actor of this long and complex historical process. Recent scholarship is certainly marked by a growing interest in Syriac secular literature, and a plurality of studies have started to focus on single figures, thus enlarging our knowledge of their translations. A progressive specialization led scholars to narrow the scope of their inquiries to more discrete subjects, focusing on single sciences or specific areas of philosophy;[20] Aristotelian logic and medicine especially have been the subject of new and deeper examinations, being often investigated from a variety of points of view. In these fields, fresh textual investigations currently respond to the urgent need of making unedited and poorly known primary sources available.[21] In fact, general statements and long-lasting assumptions on Syriac translations are sometimes based on second-hand information or, in the worst cases, on cultural bias, which can be dismantled only through a more rigorous study of the primary sources. Two case-studies can help to make this new trend clear. Siam Bhayro has recently shown how a common criticism against Sergius of Rēšʿaynā's translations of medical texts — often judged too mechanical and unintelligible in places — has never been substantiated by a direct examination of his extant translations of Galen's writings, which remain largely unedited.[22] A new analysis of the sources led scholars to dismiss the long held argument for a fifth-century origin of Aristotelian studies among Syrians: Sergius of Rēšʿaynā was rather the 'founder' of Syriac Aristotelianism. Moreover, scholars now tend to downplay the role attributed to Christian controversies as the original motivation for the study of Aristotelian logic

17 Brock, 'The Syriac Commentary Tradition', pp. 3–7; Kessel, 'Inventory of Galen's Extant Works in Syriac'.

18 King, *The Earliest Syriac Translation*, pp. 19–23.

19 See, e.g., Takahashi, 'Between Greek and Arabic', pp. 33–35. See also Takahashi 'Syriac as the Intermediary', pp. 66–74; Troupeau, 'Le role des syriaques dans la transmission', pp. 2–3.

20 For an up-to-date description of the state of the art in the study of different sciences (mathematics, geography, astronomy, alchemy, agriculture, medicine, botany, pharmacology), see Villey ed., *Les sciences en syriaque*.

21 For an up-to-date discussion of the state of the art in modern studies on Syriac philosophy and medicine, see respectively: King, 'Continuities and Discontinuities'; Kessel, 'Syriac Medicine'.

22 Bhayro, 'Galen in Syriac', pp. 133–43.

among Syrians: in compliance with the Alexandrian tradition, Sergius used the *Organon* as a tool to study philosophy.[23]

Cultural bias or a simple lack of interest may also explain why other important and rich branches of knowledge have often been disregarded. Astrology and alchemy, for instance, remain largely underestimated and understudied, if we exclude a few pioneering efforts to explore the main Syriac sources pertaining to these disciplines. The chronology of these sources, as well as their possible dependence on (perhaps lost) earlier texts in different languages, still remain hypothetical.

In other cases, the lack of primary sources impairs a full understanding of relevant segments of this history. For instance, it is currently very difficult to assess the real circulation of Middle Persian works within Syriac-speaking intellectual circles or communities. Modern narratives usually refer to Paul the Persian, who operated at the court of Chosroes II (531–578): his short treatise on Aristotle's *De Interpretatione*, in fact, was originally composed in Persian, but it is only preserved in a Syriac translation attributed to Severus Sēbōḵt.[24] Nevertheless, this important evidence is somehow isolated. If scholars agree that Syro-Persian bilingualism was widespread among Christians living under Sasanian rule,[25] the impact of this phenomenon on Syriac sciences and philosophy is difficult to measure properly. Modern scholars have often emphasized the bilingualism of the physicians in Gondēšāpūr (Khūzistān); however, the importance (and even the existence) of a school of medicine there has been often questioned,[26] and the penetration of Persian elements into Syriac medicine remains only a possibility. Two Persian pharmacological fragments written in Syriac script certainly survive from the Turfan collection.[27] Nevertheless, these scattered (although precious) pieces of information come from 'remote' areas, which have begun being included in general studies on Syriac translations only recently.[28] So far, close attention has been directed mainly to the Greek influences on the development of a philosophic and scientific discourse among Syriac-speaking intellectuals, physicians, and men of letters. We cannot exclude the possibility that ancient scholars working in specific geographical and cultural contexts could also accommodate the legacies of other learned traditions as well. For instance,

---

23 See, in particular, King, *The Earliest Syriac Translation*, pp. 3–8; McCollum, 'Greek Literature in the Christian East', p. 20.

24 On this work by Paul, see above, n. 6. On the possible use of Persian in other works by Paul, see Hugonnard-Roche, *La logique d'Aristote*, pp. 234–35.

25 See, e.g., Ciancaglini, *Iranian Loanwords*, pp. 14–20 with references to other religious and literary texts in Syriac (e.g. the Syriac version of the *Kalīla wa-Dimna*) presumably translated from Persian. A Middle Persian model has been recently postulated for a Syriac alchemical treatise attributed to the Graeco-Egyptian alchemist Pebichius (second century CE): see van Bladel, *The Arabic Hermes*, pp. 56–57.

26 See, for instance, Pormann and Savage-Smith, *Medieval Islamic Medicine*, pp. 19–20.

27 Sims-William, 'Early New Persian in Syriac Script', pp. 361–73.

28 Takahashi, 'Syriac as a Vehicle', pp. 41–44.

Siam Bhayro has recently pointed to possible traces of Mesopotamian science that might be detectable in Syriac astronomy,[29] an important observation that seems to be substantiated by a well-known passage from a letter attributed to Severus Sēbōḵt:

> Concerning the fact that some of the Greeks who are with you, as you wrote, say that the Syrians can know nothing at all of such things (I mean, the computation of the stars and the eclipse of the sun and the moon), believing that all knowledge belongs to the Greeks alone because they speak Greek, they ought to know, since there are the wise Babylonians, that the Babylonians were the first inventors of knowledge, and not the Greeks, as all the writings of the Greeks themselves testify; and after the Babylonians came the Egyptians, and then the Greeks — I do not think anyone will dispute that the Babylonians were Syrians.[30]

Periodization and the Abbasid Translation Movement

The expression 'translation movement' is nowadays commonly used by scholars to refer to a key moment in the early history of the Abbasid caliphate in Bagdad, namely the two and a half centuries that produced Arabic translations of a great amount of Greek (and, to a lesser extent, Indian and Persian) writings on a variety of sciences and all branches of philosophy: logic, metaphysics, ethics, physics, zoology, botany, meteorology, along with astronomy and astrology, theory of music, mathematics and geometry, medicine, alchemy, and military science. As stressed by Dimitri Gutas, 'from the middle of the eighth century to the end of the tenth, almost all non-literary and non-historical secular Greek books that were available throughout the Eastern Byzantine Empire and the Near East were translated into Arabic'.[31] The growing interest on this historical and cultural phenomenon left its mark on studies devoted to Syriac science and philosophy. On the one hand, many scholars addressed the question of the possible relationships between the Abbasid translation movement and the earlier or contemporary translations into Syriac. On the other, in contrast to the discrete (both in time and in space) extent of the Abbasid translation movement, it has been stressed how Syriac translations appear to be scattered within a much wider chronological and geographical framework. For instance, Muriel Debié recently spoke of various Syriac translation movements: indeed, a variety of cultural, political, and economic forces fostered the production of Syriac translations, and these motivations

---

29 Bhayro, 'On the Problem of Syriac Influence', pp. 212–17.

30 Syriac text edited by Reich, 'Ein Brief des Severus Sēbōḵt', pp. 479–80; translation (slightly modified) by Takahashi, 'Syriac as a Vehicle', p. 34.

31 Gutas, *Greek Thought, Arabic Culture*, p. 1.

could have varied according to the different historical phases or geographical areas under consideration.[32]

The simple opposition between a period before versus a period after the Arabs[33] has been further complicated in more recent scholarship. Slightly different periodizations have been proposed, in some cases according to criteria that show a certain degree of variation. Some scholars recognized two main phases connected by a transition period (eighth to tenth centuries), in which the above-mentioned Abbasid translation movement must be located. The first phase stretched for over four hundred years, from the second/third century to the seventh century, and it featured a deep influence of Greek culture on Syriac authors and translators. This was the foundational moment for Syriac science and philosophy, much influenced by the late antique Alexandrian tradition. A second phase, often referred to as 'the Syriac Renaissance' (from tenth to thirteenth centuries), saw a strong influence of Arabic writings over Syriac authors.[34] This phase seems to be dominated by the work of the Syrian Orthodox polymath Gregory Bar Hebraeus: indeed, most recent studies devoted to the Syriac Renaissance focused on this figure, active in the thirteenth century.

If such a periodization is marked by a broader emphasis on the development of Syriac science and philosophy, slightly different chronologies were proposed with a stronger focus on translations of Greek works into Syriac — basically, on the first phase of the division sketched above. In this regard, scholars have devoted closer attention to variations and trends in the translation technique: while the first translations from Greek were free and reader-oriented (fourth/fifth century), a progressively stronger tendency towards literal or text-oriented translations is observable in the sixth/seventh century. This tendency — that produced Syriac texts imitating the Greek syntax and including many Greek loanwords — mirrored the great esteem that Greek language had among Syriac scholars, also under the first Umayyad caliphs, who — it is worth mentioning — kept Greek as the main language of the administration.[35] On the contrary, as Sebastian Brock observes, when Arabic replaced Greek in the civil service, especially under the Abbasid caliphs, 'these new circumstances demanded a move away from text-oriented translations to reader-oriented ones: the original language no longer enjoyed the importance and prestige that it formerly had'.[36] With some degree of approximation, these observations might lead to a distribution of Syriac translations of Greek treatises into the following four periods:[37]

---

32 Debié, 'Sciences et savants syriaques', p. 13.

33 See above, p. 70; see also Troupeau, 'Le role des syriaques dans la transmission', p. 2.

34 See, for instance, Debié, 'Sciences et savants syriaques', pp. 12–13.

35 Brock, 'Towards a History'; for a critical discussion of this scheme, see McCollum, 'Greek Literature in the Christian East', pp. 29–31.

36 Brock, 'Changing Fashions in Syriac Translation Technique', pp. 6–7.

37 See, for instance, Takahashi, 'Between Greek and Arabic', who, however, further divides the

(1) An early stage (third to fifth centuries), when translators paid particular attention to works of popular philosophy and moral sayings attributed to ancient sages, such as Menander, Socrates, or Plato. Recent investigations of the manuscript tradition of this material have emphasized its close intertwining with the fourth- and fifth-century Christian educational system as well as its reception in later Syriac religious literature.[38]

(2) A second period (sixth century), in which Aristotelian works (primarily on logic), Porphyry's *Isagoge*, and medical texts (especially by Galen) were translated into Syriac. One of the key figures of this phase is Sergius of Rēšʿaynā, whose work — both as translator and as author of original treatises — received particular attention in recent studies on Syriac science and philosophy. As recently summarized by Grigory Kessel,

> The origins of Syriac medicine must be traced in the context of the medical tradition as practised and studied in late ancient Alexandria. It is now widely accepted that Sergius of Rēšʿaynā's contribution to the field of philosophy cannot be detached from the commentary tradition of the Neoplatonic school of Alexandria. The same pattern can be safely applied to his contribution to medicine. Moreover, Sergius himself exemplifies the Alexandrian type of scholar who combines Aristotelian philosophy and Galenic medicine. Both in his selection of texts to be translated and their interpretation he is heavily dependent on Alexandrian models.[39]

On the other hand, the absence of any Platonic text among Sergius's translations is certainly remarkable: after all, the Alexandrian tradition used Aristotle's texts instrumentally as an introduction to (Neo)platonic 'theology'. This absence has been often explained by assuming the use of Ps.-Dionysius's corpus as a substitute of Plato in the philosophical curriculum set by Sergius of Rēšʿaynā.[40]

(3) A third period, between the seventh and the eighth centuries, in which Sergius's legacy seems to have been inherited and expanded by his 'successors' belonging to the Western Syrian Church, especially by those scholars whose activities centred around the monastery of Qennešre, on the bank of Euphrates. Sergius's translation of Ps.-Dionysius was probably known in the monastery, where it was studied and revised by Athanasius of Balad (as we read in the introduction of the new translation by Phokas of Edessa). We might therefore wonder whether the scholars working in Qennešre

---

third period into two segments: (A) Seventh–Early Eight Century and (B) Eight Century; Fiori, 'Translations from Greek into Syriac', pp. 1333–34 (with further bibliography), who joins the third and the fourth periods together.

38 See Arzhanov, 'Menander in Syriac' (with reference to earlier literature on this topic).

39 Kessel, 'Syriac Medicine', p. 441 (with further bibliography).

40 For a summary of this thesis, discussed by many scholars such as Sebastian Brock, Emiliano Fiori, Henri Hugonnard-Roche, or John Watt, see King, 'Continuities and Discontinuities', pp. 236–37.

followed Sergius's pattern in combining Aristotle with Ps-Dionysius's corpus.[41] Along with Athanasius, figures such as Severus Sēbōḵt, Jacob of Edessa, and George of the Arabs were certainly driven by strong interests for astronomy and Aristotelian logic. Some doubts, however, remain as to the circulation of Sergius's translations of secular works in Western Syriac cultural centres as well as in the East. This holds particularly true for medicine. For instance, we have no information about medical books read or copied in Qennešre. If Sergius translated about thirty works by Galen according to Ḥunayn ibn Isḥāq, none of these translations can be located in the library of the monastery, even though one must bear in mind that most manuscripts of Sergius's translations are actually of Syrian Orthodox provenance.[42] As for the East, scholars have sometimes suggested that Sergius's choice of Galen's medical treatises to be translated into Syriac set the agenda for the study of medicine in the schools of Nisibis or Gondēšāpūr;[43] however, more recent investigations are much more cautious about this point.[44] The earliest sources providing solid evidence for an Eastern circulation of Sergius's medical works date to the ninth century. On the other hand, already at the end of the eighth century, the letters of the Eastern patriarch Timothy I (727–823) include references to his search for earlier philosophical texts (in particular, translations of Aristotle's *Posterior Analytics* and *Topics*, as well as of a Neo-Platonic treatise *On Principles and Matter.*) in the libraries of Orthodox monasteries, such as Mār Mattai, near Mossul.[45]

(4) A fourth period (ninth to tenth centuries) featuring the activities of many Christian scholars who translated Greek scientific and philosophical texts into Syriac and Arabic. Needless to say, the most famous figure is Ḥunayn ibn Isḥāq (d. 873): in the 'letter' (*risāla*) on his own translations of Galen's medical works, he drew up a list of the many Syriac and Arabic translations that were produced or, in the case of earlier Syriac translations, revised in his school.[46] Moreover, to this period — often to Ḥunayn himself — scholars often ascribe Syriac translations of Greek mathematical writings as well as of treatises on natural philosophy — such as Theophrastus's *Meteorology* or Nicolaus of Damascus's *Compendium of Aristotle's Philosophy* — which expand the focus on logical treatises that marked out the work of earlier Syriac scholars and translators.[47] On the contrary, the chronology of other anonymous translations, such as texts on alchemy or agriculture, still remains

41 See, for instance, Watt, 'The Syriac Aristotle', pp. 37–38.

42 Kessel, 'Inventory of Galen's Extant Works in Syriac', p. 171.

43 See, for instance, Le Coz, *Les médecins nestoriens*, pp. 17–66.

44 Becker, *Fear of God*, pp. 94–95. See also Kessel, 'Syriac Medicine', p. 441.

45 Berti, 'Libri e biblioteche cristiane' (with further bibliography) and Arzhanov, *Porphyry on Principles and Matter*, p. 4. See also Takahashi, 'Syriac as the Intermediary', pp. 82–83; Watt, 'The Syriac Aristotle'', p. 42.

46 See Lamoreaux, *Ḥunain ibn Isḥāq*, pp. 2–131 (edition and English translation of Ḥunayn's *risāla*).

47 See, for instance, Takahashi, 'Between Greek and Syriac', pp. 34–35; King, 'Continuities and Discontinuities', p. 240.

tentative; the dating of these texts to this period certainly requires further investigation.[48]

These hesitations aside, the fact remains that we are here at the core of the Abbasid translation movement, whose relationship with Syriac translations has been recently summarized by Hidemi Takahashi as follows:

> When those groups of people using Syriac as their principal literary medium started translating Greek scientific works into their language, they did not do so with the aim of becoming 'intermediaries' and passing them on to the Arabs, but by an accident of history the Syriacs and the Syriac language came to play an indispensable role in the transmission of scientific knowledge from the Greek-speaking to the Arabic-speaking world.[…] It is true that the Syriac reception of Greek philosophy and other sciences facilitated, and in many ways determined the course of, the reception of the same sciences in Arabic. The exact manner in which the Syriac-language material functioned as intermediaries in this process, however, is less well known, mainly because of the loss of a large proportion of the relevant literature in Syriac, especially the Syriac translations made in the 'Abbāsid period that served as the immediate *Vorlage* of the Arabic translations.[49]

This passage touches upon the main problems that scholars must currently face in evaluating the role played by Syriac in the rise and development of the Abbasid translation movement. Syriac is often presented as the key intermediary between Greek and Arabic and almost any account on Graeco-Arabic translations includes a section devoted to the contribution given by Syriac scholars. This contribution is, however, differently assessed. General studies on the Abbasid translation movement tend to downplay the role played by Syriac translations when considered in a broader cultural perspective. Even though single Eastern Christian physicians and translators were certainly important actors in the process, the economic and historical reasons that made the Abbasid translation movement possible are to be found in other elements linked to the Abbasid politics. After all, as Peter Pormann and Emilie Savage-Smith pointed out for medicine, the vast majority of Graeco-Syriac translation activity took place under the aegis of the Abbasids and depended on 'the historical and intellectual forces at work in ninth-century Bagdad, where the ruling elite and their entourage set not only the political, but also the cultural and scientific agenda'.[50] Dimitri Gutas drew attention to the state

48 For instance, Takahashi tends to attribute these translations to an earlier phase (fifth century); see 'Between Greek and Syriac', p. 32, and 'Syriac as the Intermediary', p. 68. On alchemy and agriculture, see the contributions of Matteo Martelli and Christophe Guignard in Villey, ed., *Les sciences en syriaque*, Martelli, 'L'alchimie syriaque et l'oeuvre de Zosime', pp. 191–214 and Guignard, 'L'agriculture en syriaque l'*Anatolius Syriacus*', pp. 215–51 respectively.

49 Takahashi, 'Syriac as the Intermediary', pp. 66–67.

50 Pormann and Savage-Smith, *Medieval Islamic Medicine*, p. 28.

ideology of the Abbasid rulers, 'followers' of the Persians, who considered all Greek science and philosophy as ultimately depending on Iranian wisdom, which had been stolen by Alexander the Great. By supporting and promoting the translations of Greek texts, the Abbasids wanted to regain access to a knowledge that originally began in Persia.[51] On the other hand, George Saliba emphasized the role of bureaucrats: the Graeco-Arabic translation movement would have taken root in the Umayyad period, in particular under the caliph ʿAbd al-Malik (685–705 CE), who promoted the switch from Greek to Arabic as the language of administrative offices (see also above).[52] More recently, Saliba expanded his thesis, by stressing how this process would have first excluded Syriac-speaking people from any occupation in the civil service. However, since the bureaucrat (or a member of the *dīwān*) was expected to have basic knowledge of Greek science, Syriacs were somewhere forced to 'learn the most sophisticated Greek sciences' in order to become more competitive. This led to the formation of highly specialized figures, who could serve the first Abbasid caliphs and orient the Arabic translation movement towards a strong focus on Greek science and philosophy.[53]

Be that as it may, critical ninth- or tenth-century sources, such as Ḥunayn's personal account on his own Galenic translations or al-Nadīm's *Book of Catalogue*, point to a plurality of Syriac translations produced during the Abbasid translation movement. The same Greek treatises were often translated both into Syriac and into Arabic — either by two different translators or by the same author, in some cases with the version in one language (more often in Syriac) being the basis for the translation into the other. By relying on al-Nadīm's *Book of Catalogue* and Ibn Abī Uṣaybiʿa's *Lives of Physicians*, Gérard Troupeau counted all the names of translators operating between the end of the eighth and the end of the tenth centuries: according to his calculation, 78 per cent might have been Syriac.[54] Both for philosophical and medical texts, the choice of the target language was likely to depend on the will, creed, and language of the client.[55] If the traditional narrative on Syriac translations emphasized their use as intermediary texts to be translated into Arabic, some scholars are currently more prudent about the actual scale of this phenomenon. Ninth-century Syriac translations had their own market and circulation, regardless of their use as textual basis for further translations into Arabic.[56]

A worrying fact, however, remains unchanged: most ninth-century Syriac translations have not come down to us. This textual loss is usually explained by

---

51 Gutas, *Greek Thought, Arabic Culture*.

52 Saliba, *Islamic Science*, pp. 26–72.

53 Saliba, 'Revisiting the Syriac Role'.

54 Troupeau, 'Le role des syriaques dans la transmission', pp. 4–5.

55 See, for instance, Watt, 'Why did Ḥunayn, the Master Translator into Arabic, Make Translations into Syriac?', pp. 363–77 and 382–83.

56 See, for instance, Bhayro, 'Galen in Syriac', pp. 145–52.

pointing to a lack of interest in early Syriac translations of Greek philosophical or medical texts by copyists working after the thirteenth century.[57] In front of this shortage of primary sources, from the late 1980s academic research was reoriented towards fresh investigations of the available manuscripts — a promising field that led to new discoveries. This invaluable work paved the way for further textually-based research on Syriac philosophy and its impact on the development of Arabic *falsafa*.[58] As far as medicine is concerned, a wealth of new textual discoveries has been promoted by important European projects, which are currently exploring key-texts that still remain unedited: for instance, Ḥunayn's *Book on the Medicinal Properties of Foodstuffs* (extant both in Syriac and in Arabic) or the rich Syriac-Arabic tradition of Galen's pharmacology.[59]

Most scholars agree that only a constant effort leading to new editions, translations, and commentaries of previously neglected texts can provide the necessary basis to look for 'signs of continuities and discontinuities' between the Greek and the Syriac traditions as well as between the Syriac and the Arabic world, as recently pointed out by Daniel King.[60] Such textual work cannot miss the opportunity to study each Syriac text and translation in its context: the cultural, political, and historical *milieux* that produced our primary sources must be investigated along with their reception and reuse. By mapping the available manuscripts, editing the texts that they preserve, and integrating this information with other indirect pieces of evidence, it will hopefully be possible to combine our fragmented data into a more articulated picture, in which the contributions of Syriac scholars may also vary according to the sciences and disciplines under consideration. In fact, as recently suggested, the Syriac tradition could not be equally important in the transmission of all Greek sciences to the Arabs: if it seems central for philosophy, it might be less strong for astronomy, or not exclusive for medicine, in which other traditions — such as the indigenous Mesopotamian tradition — could have played a relevant role as well.[61]

---

57 See Kessel, 'Inventory of Galen's Extant Works in Syriac', pp. 170–71; Watt, 'The Syriac Aristotle', p. 30.

58 Especially for philosophy, see the works of scholars such as Yury Arzhanov, Sebastian Brock, Emiliano Fiori, Henri Hugonnard-Roche, Hidemi Takahashi, John Watt, or Daniel King (to name but a few).

59 See, in particular, the ERC projects 'From Babylon to Baghdad: Toward a History of the Herbal in the Near East' (led by Robert Hawley), and 'Transmission of Classical Scientific and Philosophical Literature from Greek into Syriac and Arabic' (led by Grigory Kessel); the AHRC funded project 'The Syriac Galen Palimpsest: Galen's *On Simple Drugs* and the Recovery of Lost Texts through Sophisticated Imaging Techniques' (led by Peter Pormann and Siam Bhayro). Within the framework of the ERC project 'Alchemy in the Making: From Ancient Babylonia via Graeco-Roman Egypt towards the Byzantine, Syriac and Arabic Traditions', I am currently working on an edition and translation of the Syriac alchemical treatises ascribed to the Graeco-Egyptian author Zosimus of Panopolis (third/fourth century).

60 King, 'Continuities and Discontinuities', p. 243.

61 See Bhayro, 'On the Problem of Syriac "Influence"'.

Bibliography

Primary Sources

Arzhanov, Yury N., *Porphyry, on Principles and Matter* (Berlin: De Gruyter, 2021)

Freimann, Aron, *Die Isagoge des Porphyrius in den syrischen Übersetzungen* (Berlin: H. Itzkowski, 1897)

Georr, Kamil, *Les Catégories d'Aristote dans leurs versions syro-arabes* (Beirut: Institut français de Damas, 1948)

King, Daniel, *The Earliest Syriac Translation of Aristotle's 'Categories'* (Leiden: Brill, 2010)

Secondary Sources

Arzhanov, Yury N., 'Menander in Syriac: From Euthalian Apparatus to Scholia on Gregory of Nazianzus', *Studia Graeco-Arabica*, 7 (2017), 57–74

Barṣoum, Ignatius Aphram I, *The Scattered Pearls: A History of Syriac Literature and Sciences*, trans. by Matti Moosa (Piscataway: Gorgias Press, 2003)

Baumstark, Anton, *Geschichte der syrischen Literatur* (Bonn: A. Marcus and E. Webers Verlag, 1922)

Becker, Adam H. *Fear of God and the Beginnings of Wisdom: The School and Christian Scholastic Culture in Late Antique Mesopotamia* (Philadelphia: University of Pennsylvania Press, 2006)

Berti, Vittorio, 'Libri e biblioteche cristiane nell'Iraq dell'VIII secolo: una testimonianza dell'epistolario del patriarcasiro-orientaleTimoteo I (727–823)', in *The Libraries of the Neoplatonists*, ed. by Cristina D'Ancona (Leiden: Brill, 2007), pp. 307–17

Bhayro, Siam, 'On the Problem of Syriac "Influence" in the Transmission of Greek Science to the Arabs: The Cases of Astronomy, Philosophy, and Medicine', *Intellectual History of the Islamicate Word*, 5 (2017), 211–27

——, 'Galen in Syriac: Rethinking Old Assumptions', *Aramaic Studies*, 15 (2017), 132–54

Brock, Sebastian, 'Towards a History of Syriac Translation Technique', in *III Symposium Syriacum 1980*, ed. by Réné Lavenant, Orientalia Christiana Analecta, 221 (Rome: Pontificium Institutum Studiorum Orientalium, 1983), pp. 1–14

——, 'The Syriac Commentary Tradition', in *Glosses and Commentaries on Aristotelian Logical Texts*, ed. by Charles Burnett (London: Warburg Institute Surveys and Texts, 1993), pp. 3–18

——, 'Changing Fashions in Syriac Translation Technique: The Background to Syriac Translations under the Abbasids', *Journal of the Canadian Society for Syriac Studies*, 4 (2004), 3–11

——, 'The Commentator Probus: Problems of Date and Identity', in *Interpreting the Bible and Aristotle in Late Antiquity*, ed. by Josef Lössl and John W. Watt (Farnham: Ashgate, 2011), pp. 195–206

Ciancaglini, Claudia A., *Iranian Loanwords in Syriac* (Wiesbaden: Ludwig Reichert Verlag, 2008)

Debié, Muriel, 'Sciences et savants syriaques: une histoire multiculturelle', in *Les sciences en Syriaque*, ed. by Émilie Villey (Paris: Geuthner, 2014), pp. 9–66

Dimitrov, Bojidar, 'Fort. Recte: Witness to the Text of Ptolemy's Tetrabiblos in its Near Eastern Transmission', in *Ptolemy's Science of the Stars in the Middle*

Ages, ed. by David Juste, Benno van Dalen, Dag Nikolaus Hasse, and Charles Burnett (Turnhout: Brepols, 2020), pp. 97–113

Duval, Rubens, *La littérature syriaque* (Paris: V. Lecoffre, 1907)

Esbroeck, Michel van, 'Le résumé syriaque de l'Agathange', *Analecta Bollandiana*, 95 (1977), 291–358

Fiori, Emiliano, 'Translations from Greek into Syriac', in *Encyclopedia of Medieval Philosophy*, ed. by Henrik Lagerlund and Cristina d'Ancona (Heidelberg: Springer, 2011), pp. 1333–35

Fiori, Emiliano, and Henri Hugonnard-Roche, ed., *La philosophie en syriaque* (Paris: Geuthner, 2019)

Furlani, Giuseppe, 'Contributi alla storia della filosofia greca in Oriente, Testisiriaci VI. Una introduzione alla logica aristotelica di Atanasio di Balad', *Rendiconti della Reale academia dei Lincei. Classe di scienze morali, storiche e filologiche*, serie quinta, 25 (1916), 717–78

——, 'L'*Encheiridion* di Giacomo di Edessa nel testo siriaco', *Rendiconti della Reale Accademia Nazionale dei Lincei. Classe di Scienze morali, storiche e filologiche*, 6.4 (1928), 222–49

Guignard, Christophe, 'L'agriculture en syriaque: l'*Anatolius Syriacus* ("Géoponiques syriaques")', in *Les sciences en Syriaque*, ed. by Émilie Villey (Paris: Geuthner, 2014), pp. 215–51

Gutas, Dimitri, *Greek Thought, Arabic Culture: The Graeco-Arabic Translation Movement in Baghdad and Early 'Abbāsid Society (2nd–4th / 8th–10th Centuries)* (New York: Routledge, 1998)

Hugonnard-Roche, Henri, *La logique d'Aristote du grec au syriaque* (Paris: Vrin, 2004)

——, 'Le commentaire syriaque de Probus sur l'Isagoge de Prophyre. Une étude préliminaire', *Studia Graeco-Arabica*, 2 (2012), 227–43

——, 'Sur la lecture tardo-antique du *Peri Hermeneias* d'Aristote: Paul le Perse et la tradition d'Ammonius. Édition du texte syriaque, traduction française et commentaire de l'élucidation du *Peri Hermeneias* de Paul le Perse', *Studia Graeco-Arabica*, 3 (2013), 37–104

Kessel, Grigory, 'Neoplatonic Treatment of Clytemnestra's Infidelity: An East Syriac Philosopher Denḥā on the Power of Music', in *De l'Antiquité tardive au Moyen Âge. Études de logique aristotélicienne et de philosophie grecque, syriaque, arabe et latine offertes à Henri Hugonnard-Roche*, ed. by Elisa Coda and Cecilia Martini Bonadeo (Paris: Vrin, 2014), pp. 123–48

——, 'Inventory of Galen's Extant Works in Syriac', in *Ḥunain ibn Iṣḥāq on His Galen Translations*, ed. by John C. Lamoreaux (Provo: Brigham Young University Press, 2015), pp. 168–92

——, 'Syriac Medicine', in *The Syriac World*, ed. by Daniel King (Oxford: Oxford University Press, 2018), pp. 438–59

King, Daniel, 'Continuities and Discontinuities in the History of Syriac Philosophy', in *De l'antiquité tardive au Moyen Âge: études de logique aristotélicienne et de philosophie grecque, syriaque, arabe et latine offertes à Henri Hugonnard-Roche*, ed. by Elisa Coda and Cecilia Martini Bonadeo (Paris: Vrin, 2014), pp. 225–43

Lamoreaux, John C., *Ḥunain ibn Iṣḥāq on His Galen Translations* (Provo: Brigham Young University Press, 2015)

Le Coz, Raymond, *Les médecins nestoriens au Moyen Âge. Les maîtres des Arabes* (Paris: L'Harmattan, 2004)

Martelli, Matteo, 'L'alchimie en syriaque et l'oeuvre de Zosime', in *Les sciences en Syriaque*, ed. by Émilie Villey (Paris: Geuthner, 2014), pp. 191–214

McCollum, Adam Carter, 'Greek Literature in the Christian East: Translations into Syriac, Georgian and Armenian', *Intellectual History of the Islamicate World*, 3 (2015), 15–65

Nau, François, 'Une version syriaque inédite de la Vie de Schenoudi', *Revue sémitique d'épigraphie et d'histoire ancienne*, 7 (1899), 356–63

——, 'La cosmographie au VIIe siècle chez les Syriens', *Revue de l'orient chrétien*, 15 (1910), 225–54

——, 'L'Araméen chrétien (Syriaque). Les traductions faites du grec en syriaque au VIIe siècle', *Revue de l'histoire des religions*, 99 (1929), pp. 232–87

Pormann, Peter E., and Emilie Savage-Smith, *Medieval Islamic Medicine* (Washington, DC: Georgetown University Press, 2007)

Reich, Edgar, 'Ein Brief des Severus Sēbōḵt', in *Sic Itur ad Astra. Studien zur Geschichte der Mathematik und Naturwissenschaften. Festschrift für den Arabisten Paul Kunitzsch zum 70. Geburtstag*, ed. by Menso Folkerts and Richard Lorch (Wiesbaden: Harrassowitz, 2000), pp. 478–89

Saliba, George, 'Revisiting the Syriac Role in the Transmission of Greek Sciences into Arabic', *Journal of the Canadian Society for Syriac Studies*, 4 (2004), 27–32

——, *Islamic Science and the Making of the European Renaissance* (Cambridge, MA: MIT Press, 2007)

Sims-William, Nicholas, 'Early New Persian in Syriac Script: Two Texts from Turfan', *Bulletin of the School of Oriental and African Studies*, 74 (2011), 361–73

Takahashi, Hidemi, 'Between Greek and Arabic: The Sciences in Syriac from Severus Sebokht to Barhebraeus', in *Transmission of Sciences: Greek, Syriac, Arabic and Latin*, ed. by Haruo Kobayashi and Mizue Kato (Tokyo: Waseda University Press, 2010), pp. 16–44

——, 'Syriac as a Vehicle for Transmission of Knowledge across Borders of Empires', *Horizons*, 5 (2014), 29–52

——, 'Syriac as the Intermediary in Scientific Graeco-Arabica: Some Historical and Philological Observations', *Intellectual History of the Islamicate World*, 3 (2015), 66–97

Teixidor, Javier, *Aristote en syriaque. Paul le Perse, logicien du VIIe siècle* (Paris: CNRS Éditions, 2003)

Toda, Satoshi, 'Syriac Translation in Egypt: The Case of the Life of Saint Macarius the Egyptian', *Orientalia*, 75 (2006), 96–106

Troupeau, Gérard, 'Le rôle des syriaques dans la transmission et l'exploitation du patrimoine philosophique et scientifique grec', *Arabica*, 38 (1991), 1–10

Van Bladel, Kevin, *The Arabic Hermes: From Pagan Sage to Prophet of Science* (Oxford: Oxford University Press, 2009)

Villey, Émilie, ed., *Les sciences en syriaque* (Paris: Geuthner, 2014)

Watt, John W., 'The Syriac Aristotle between Alexandria and Baghdad', *Journal for Late Antique Religion and Culture*, 7 (2013), 26–50

——, 'Why did Ḥunayn, the Master Translator into Arabic, Make Translations into Syriac? On the Purpose of Syriac Translations of Ḥunayn and his Circle', in *The Place to Go: Contexts of Learning in Baghdād, 750–1000 C.E.*, ed. by Jens J. Scheiner and Damien Janos (Princeton: Darwin Press, 2014), pp. 363–88

Wright, William, *A Short History of Syriac Literature* (London: Adam and Charles Black, 1894)

MIRI SHEFER-MOSSENSOHN

Revisiting the Translation Narratives

The Multiple Contexts of the Arabic Translation Projects

One of the most significant cultural phenomena in the Arab Islamicate Middle East of the ninth and tenth centuries was the massive volume of translation into Arabic from different Middle Eastern and Asian languages, like Greek, Syriac, Persian, and Sanskrit, of a vast number of works on a variety of subjects. It was a profound cultural, social, technological, and scientific force in the Islamicate world.

This translation process is also one of the most studied topics of the medieval Middle East and of the history of translation and knowledge circulation. Many a scholar has studied the subject, including key figures in the field, dealing with linguistic aspects, the scientific contents, and more. This is also one of the best-known 'facts' about the Arab Islamicate Middle East outside the circle of scholars. In the popular discourse among Muslims and non-Muslims alike, the so-called 'Age of Translation' attracts great attention as an important element in the perception of the 'Golden Age of Islam'.

Nevertheless, despite the certainty that the translated materials played a major role in the evolution of Arabo-Islamic civilization, some of the key elements in the process are less than clear: what did translation mean to the people engaged in the process? How did they articulate it to themselves and others? What were the practices for transforming texts into Arabic? What were the goals? Who resisted the translation activities and why?[1]

* The first version was presented at the 14th Biennial Conference of Asian Studies in Israel in the panel 'Eurasian Transmissions of Knowledge', organized by Ronit Yoeli-Tlalim (May 2018, Jerusalem).

1 Paraphrasing Ricci, *Islam Translated*, p. 31.

Miri Shefer-Mossensohn is the head of the Zvi Yavetz School of Historical Studies and associate professor in the Department of Middle Eastern & African History at Tel Aviv University. She is a social historian of medicine, health, and wellbeing in the early modern Ottoman world in its Arabic- and Turkish-speaking regions. Her publications include *Ottoman Medicine: Healing and Medical Institutions 1500–1700* (SUNY Press, 2009) and *Science among the Ottomans: The Cultural Creation and Exchange of Knowledge* (University of Texas Press, 2015).

Narratives on Translation across Eurasia and Africa: From Babylonia to Colonial India, ed. by Sonja Brentjes in cooperation with Jens Høyrup and Bruce O'Brien, CAT 3, pp. 83–98 (Turnhout: Brepols, 2022) BREPOLS PUBLISHERS 10.1484/M.CAT-EB.5.127935

These and other vital questions are still open, as these translated texts do not elaborate on the translation process. They may also include formulae rather than historical information. The void between translators and the translated texts is being filled by scholars who retrospectively try to reconstruct the narratives of these translations. Such narratives try to explain how and why knowledge that was produced by 'the other', which was foreign and maybe strange, was translated to become familiar, domesticated, and part of 'us'. This is translatability — a set of features, both universal and particular, embedded in the text, the people involved in its translation, and the cultural atmosphere of the period, that determine the possibility (or lack thereof) of 'converting' stories and ideas to a new language and culture. The narratives of translation scholars suggest are also the product of their own understanding of the process of 'translation', of their own specific cultural circumstances.

This article is devoted to scrutinizing the different approaches in the modern scholarship on the translation projects to Arabic of the eighth, ninth, and tenth centuries. The historiographical change that has been taking place in recent years on this very topic is a good opportunity to reflect on the scholarly narratives. The premise is that each approach is based on distinct images of the flow of knowledge into and within the Islamicate world. Each narrative thus offers not only an explanation of the historical process of translations of a large corpus of scientific texts into Arabic, but also reframes the Islamicate world in different civilizational contexts. Most of the evidence is drawn from medicine, on which my own research focuses. The aim is to discuss the overall process of translation and how it was understood by modern scholars instead of demonstrating how it materialized in each and every body of knowledge.

The Original Narrative: 'The Translation Movement'

One of the best-known narratives regarding the Arab Islamicate Middle East is that of a dramatic cultural-intellectual project of mass translations of texts from languages for a new audience, namely Arab Muslims. The gist of the narrative is that from about 750 to about 900, there was a very elaborate and intentional effort to transmit the whole legacy of Greek science to the Islamic world. Non-Greek materials were translated as well, but they were an addendum, and not the central intellectual attention.

One of the key figures in this narrative is Franz Rosenthal (1914–2003). His works on the translation projects are still a point of reference, more than forty years later. In his canonical *The Classical Heritage of Islam*, published originally in 1975, Rosenthal says: 'Here seems to have been a direct line to the Muslim world for the transmission of Greek philosophy that originated in Alexandria'.[2] The context is Rosenthal's discussion of the

2 Rosenthal, *The Classical Heritage of Islam*, p. 6.

historical and ideological motivations for the translations and the men capable of concerting it.

Rosenthal has become the anchor for the Greek-to-Arabic translation narrative. However, he was far from being the first. As Dimitri Gutas discussed in his survey of Graeco-Arabic Studies, the historical and philological analysis of the translations has started some 200 years ago with the French scholar Amable Jourdain (1788–1818) who studied translations of Aristotle into Arabic and Latin.[3] The phrase 'Greek into Arabic', which was adopted as a title to the whole scholarly translation narrative, was coined by Richard Walzer (1900–1975), a Classicist and philologist.[4]

Another central term, 'the translation movement', predates Rosenthal as well; in fact, it predates his major works on the subject by almost half a century. The term 'movement' appears frequently in the 1931 *The Legacy of Islam*, a joint publication by the two eminent British Orientalists, Thomas Walker Arnold (1864–1930) and Alfred Guillaume (1888–1965). 'Movement' occurs quite frequently in the book to denote changes, trends, and developments in the religious, cultural, and social realms throughout Islamicate history.

Among other things, Arnold and Guillaume use the term to describe the translation projects in the Abbasid period. The following citation is a typical text in the book: 'At the end of the period of translation, the physicians and scientists of the Islamic world stood on a firm foundation of Greek science, increased by a large share of Persian and Indian thought and experience'.[5] This and many other passages share the same tone since the purpose of the monograph, as explained in the preface, was to seek 'to give an account of those elements in the culture of Europe which are derived from the Islamic world'.[6] Further down the reader is told that one

> will learn from this book that there is little that is *peculiarly* Islamic in the contributions which Occidental and Oriental Muslims have made to European culture [...] It was under the protection and patronage of the Islamic Empire that the arts and sciences which this book describes flourished [...] Arabic is the Greek of the Semitic world, and it was a fortunate thing for Islam that its message was delivered at a time when Arabic was potentially at its zenith. Aramaic was a poverty-stricken tongue compared with Arabic, and not even classical Hebrew at its best could rival Arabic in its astonishing elasticity.[7]

---

3 Gutas, *Greek Thought, Arabic Culture*, pp. 1–2.

4 See the obituaries: Zimmermann, 'Richard Walzer (1900–1975)', pp. 1–4; Wehrli, 'Richard Walzer', pp. 221–22. Also Gutas, *Greek Thought, Arabic Culture*, p. 2.

5 Arnold and Guillaume, *The Legacy of Islam*, p. 322.

6 Arnold and Guillaume, *The Legacy of Islam*, p. v.

7 Arnold and Guillaume, *The Legacy of Islam*, pp. v–vi.

Rosenthal may have not conceived the fundamental terms of the scholarly discourse, but he became the well-known and articulate voice of that discourse. Furthermore, by his time, the terms that were utilized to explain various cultural and religious shifts in the early Islamicate world were appropriated as a specific paradigm in history of science.

This narrative that focuses on the transfer of Greek science and philosophy to the Arabic-speaking Middle East has been exhaustively studied. The main stages can be summarized as follows.[8] There were three main stages of contact. The first encounter occurred during the seventh century, when the Umayyads founded their caliphate in Damascus. This encounter blossomed during the early Abbasid era, which is the second stage. Since the late eighth century, and with more force during the ninth and tenth centuries, there was a wave of translations from Greek to Arabic, which kept Greek tradition alive. Centuries later, this tradition was transmitted back to Europe, via Latin and vernaculars, thereby transferring Greek science from the eastern Mediterranean to the western parts of Europe. This phase in the translation process was one of the important factors driving universal science in general in Europe and toward the Renaissance in particular.[9] The third stage, in Buyid Baghdad, continued the interest in Greek philosophy and science but with other characteristics. First, the main activity focused not on producing new translations but rather adaptations, commentaries, summaries, and encyclopedias based on existing works of translation. Second, Greek science was appropriated (to use A. I. Sabra's term)[10] by Islamic culture to the point that it was disassociated from its original Hellenic context. Third, by this period, the scholarly community developed into sometimes competing professional groups. Fourth and last, the rise of the *madrasa* institution in the eleventh century oriented Islamic learning toward law and the religion and the spotlight was diverted from independently studying and teaching the sciences. This narrative presented a clear process of progress which explains why it gained popularity despite the problems with such a linear view.

The Greek-to-Arabic narrative depicts an interfaith arena of cultural and scientific activity. This activity was carried out by circles of learned scholars made up of Muslims and Christians (mainly) of various denominations, with some Sabians. Yet this narrative also assigns a crucial role to Middle Eastern Christians, especially Nestorian Christians. They are depicted as translators to Arabic, usually from intermediate versions in Syriac, as procurers of manuscripts, and as scholars of the original and translated works.[11]

---

8 Following D'Ancona, 'Greek into Arabic'.

9 For instance, Saliba, *Islamic Science and the Making of the European Renaissance*, especially pp. 193–232.

10 Sabra, 'The Appropriation and Subsequent Naturalization of Greek Science in Medieval Islam'.

11 Rosenthal, *The Classical Heritage of Islam*, pp. 5–9.

This narrative also accentuates the sponsorship of the Abbasid upper echelon. It highlights early sources, like Ibn al-Nadīm's tenth-century *Kitāb al-Fihrist*, which portrayed the Abbasid caliphs themselves as initiators and directors of the translation movement.[12] It follows, then, that the narrative identifies a centre of activity and situates it in Baghdad, the newly founded Abbasid capital. Within Baghdad, one particular institution — *Bayt al-Ḥikma* — was depicted as the central organization for this large-scale movement.[13] Overall, we are presented with a top-down, elite-sponsored, and institutionalized intellectual-cultural project.

The Greek-to-Arabic narrative gained such an authority that it is known simply in catch-phrases like 'the translation movement', 'the age of translation', and similar phrases. There is no need any more to elaborate or cite sources and evidence. Dimitri Gutas, a key figure in this discourse since his doctorate in Yale in 1974, incorporated the term into the title of his 1998 monograph: *Greek Thought, Arabic Culture: The Graeco-Arabic Translation Movement in Baghdad and Early ʿAbbāsid Society (2nd–4th / 8th–10th Centuries)*.[14]

The 'translation movement' became a commonplace that has been appropriated by scholars outside the specializations of the transition from Late Antiquity to Islam and early Abbasid times. One such example is the introduction to a double issue of *Science in Context* in 2001. The guest editors, historians of premodern science in general rather than Islamicate science, titled their introductory essay 'Transmission as Transformation: The Translation Movements in the Medieval East and West in a Comparative Perspective'.[15]

This narrative has been adapted and updated over the years. One particular point that has received significant attention and amendment is the subject of the supposed passivity of Arab and Muslim agency. According to Arnold and Guillaume, Arabic was a vehicle of transmission. Future generations of scholars have shown the degree of dynamism, innovation, contribution, and change. Whatever the translated Arab Islamicate science was when it was transferred into Europe, it was not simply Greek science in Arabic. Rather, it was a new creation. However, the spatial context remained the same: the discussion was quite limited to Baghdad.

The 'translation movement' narrative endured several decades, probably for several intertwined reasons. The paradigm of the 'translation movement' seems to offer a convincing and comprehensive explanation. Some of the top names in the field contributed to its status. They were charismatic scholars and teachers, who had much sway over their numerous students, many of whom became influential scholars in their own right. Perhaps the paradigm

12 D'Ancona, 'Greek into Arabic'.

13 van Koningsveld, 'Greek Manuscripts in the Early Abbasid Empire', pp. 345–71; Gutas and van Bladel, 'Bayt al-Ḥikma'.

14 Gutas, *Greek Thought, Arabic Culture*.

15 Abattouy, Renn, and Weinig, 'Transmission as Transformation'.

survived also because it conforms to the ideological stance of the scholars themselves regarding the place of Christians and Christianity in Arab culture, past and present.

New Narratives

In the opening decades of the twenty-first century, new scholarship has raised several important questions about various aspects of the 'translation movement' narrative. New questions are being asked regarding finance, translation, patronage, motivation, logistics, and more. Although a new paradigm is yet to be fully formulated, it is already clear that it is far from being a narrative of a neat and linear transmission of high-end, well-articulated, theoretical Greek science, from the Hellenized eastern Mediterranean, to medieval Europe via the Muslim Middle East. In fact, these new studies promote parallel narratives which complement rather than replace each other. The discursive map is further complicated by the fact that there are not necessarily clear breaks of 'before' and 'after'. Some scholars present a different or a more nuanced position than their pre-2000 studies suggest, and others may now contribute to several narratives at the same time.

Multiple Centres of Translations, Multiple Phenomena of Translation

One trajectory of rethinking touches upon the spatial dimensions of the translation activities. New studies put in the limelight the translation activity beyond the Baghdad-centred narrative sketched before. The broadening of the prism is at once geographical and social.

A large part of the translations in Baghdad were made possible by the cultural activities that took place elsewhere in Syria at large and outside the Muslim elite, which was still a small minority. Furthermore, this literary activity was going on not in cities, where it had traditionally taken place, but rather in monasteries in rural areas.

Moreover, while the Christians who were involved in producing these texts were an intellectual elite in their own communities, they belonged to churches which were seen as heretical in late antique Byzantium; they offered an alternative cultural blooming.[16] Likewise, translations were a significant culturally activity in the monasteries of Palestine and Antioch from the eighth to the tenth century and beyond. This translation phenomenon was distinct from the Baghdadi one. The translation activity in the Levant focused on religious Christian materials for the benefit of the Christian communities of the Middle East rather than for the benefit of the Muslim community, as in Baghdad. Yet the two activities were connected in various ways: they were

16 Tannous, *The Making of the Medieval Middle East*, p. 217.

the fruits of the same social and cultural context, and apparently shared at least some patrons and translators.[17]

Continuation of Late Antique Modes of Intellectual Production

Some new studies understand the various translation activities as mediums that were at once a vehicle of change in the Middle East from one civilization (Byzantine) to another (Arab Islam) and a mode of preserving some enduring intellectual characteristics of Late Antiquity.

Connecting the translations into Arabic made in the Abbasid period to translation activities from Greek, undertaken as part of the cultural enterprise of Christian communities in the Byzantine Levant, was quite commonplace among scholars. The previous view envisioned clear historical stages that laid the ground for the next stages. According to this approach, the activity carried out in the Byzantine period paved the way to the more mature and sophisticated Abbasid translation activity. During the Byzantine period, important scientific texts were transmitted from Greek to Syriac, which later enabled translators, who had already acquired expertise by the Muslim period, to render the texts into Arabic. This approach depicts the later Islamic translation phase as replacing the earlier (and inferior) Byzantine one.[18]

The current position, however, draws attention to the endurance of the intellectual and cultural patterns from Late Antiquity that passed into the Islamic period rather than claiming them as new Abbasid enterprises. Scholars had discussed already the continued respect for Greek learning, even during the 'dark' medieval period,[19] but now this claim stands centre stage. According to this line of thought, the shared linguistic identity of the translators of Abbasid Baghdad as Syriac-speaking was not perceived to be coincidental.

Scholars of Byzantine Studies or Late Antique Christianity suggest an overarching continuation of the Graeco-Arabic Byzantine project even if for modern scholars it was later overshadowed by the Abbasid project. They perceive Late Antiquity as a period that did not end with the arrival of the Islamicate world, although there were changes. In the words of Jack Tannous: 'In the movement from the world of Justinian to that of Hārūn al-Rashīd — the streams and rivers of antique learned culture flowed unbroken'.[20] These scholars emphasize that this period was culturally independent and creatively flourished in its own right, much more than an inferior fossilized version of an earlier period would have,[21] and a conduit to what came after. Some scholars, such as Maria Mavroudi, even propose that in certain bodies of knowledge, the translators into Arabic were not interested in what was ancient knowledge

17 Treiger, 'Christian Graeco-Prolegomena'.
18 Bhayro and Brock, 'Three Syriac Galen Palimpsests', pp. 41–42.
19 Wasserstein, 'Greek Science in Islam'.
20 Tannous, *The Making of the Medieval Middle East*, p. 215.
21 Mavroudi, 'Translations from Greek into Latin and Arabic during the Middle Ages', p. 30.

as such, but in the version that had remained current and relevant practice in their contemporary world where they encountered it via the Byzantine and the Syriac communities.[22]

The Circulation of Knowledge from Asia

Another trajectory of rethinking the Greek-to-Arabic narrative is the greater weight scholars have recently attached to the scientific traditions that entered Arabic and Islamic civilizations from sources other than the Greek world. This is part of a growing scholarly interest in the interchange between various Asian intellectual and scientific traditions, including Islamicate traditions. Admittedly, part of this new scholarship deals with later Islamic periods than those discussed here.[23] However, all these new studies attest to the current reflections on the framing of knowledge by Asian and Eurasian cultures and their relations with the Islamicate world. For instance, one study looks at the interaction between Indian and Muslim medicine and physicians during the eighth and ninth centuries; it proposes that while the contact did not yield significant long-term fruits, it was not an atypical phenomenon at the time. Furthermore, while the contact may have been rather brief, it did have a long-lasting impact with the presence of Indian physicians in Baghdad in and around the Abbasid court, and the emergence of early Muslim hospitals.[24]

Within the context of scientific exchanges between Islamicate science and sources other than the Greek world, two aspects regarding the translations of texts into Arabic in the Abbasid period are considered. One aspect is the integration of pre-Islamic non-Greek Middle Eastern scientific literature in Arabic. Even if the direct contact of Arab Muslims was with Greek- and Syriac-written texts and Syriac-speaking scholars, materials on astronomy, astrology, and mathematics, for instance, were in fact indebted to earlier compilations from Mesopotamia.[25] The state of the art is such that traces of Babylonian components in later Middle Eastern written texts are well attested. However, through the process of transmission and adaptation to make it more relevant to new historical contexts, these materials have changed; they are not 'truly' Babylonian or Akkadian, although they originated in those texts, but something else for which we have no name yet.

A second aspect of knowledge exchange in an Asian context now considered with more attention is the complexities of the east, that is knowledge derived from Iran, Transoxiana, central Asia, India, and China. In medicine, mathematics, astronomy, and other bodies of science, scholars are finding social links and

---

22 Mavroudi, 'Translations from Greek into Latin and Arabic during the Middle Ages', pp. 45–46.

23 Some examples are: Langermann, 'The Chapter on *Rasāyana*'; Weil, 'The Fourteenth-Century Transformation'.

24 Shefer-Mossensohn and Abbou Hershkovits, 'Early Muslim Medicine and the Indian Context'.

25 Bohak and Geller, 'Babylonian Astrology in the Cairo Genizah'; Langermann, 'Babylonian and Indian Wisdoms'.

intellectual similarities between Sasanian-Zoroastrian, eastern Iranian and Buddhist materials and Arabo-Islamic works. The connections were the products of contact between Abbasid, and Buddhist and Iranian-Bactrian scholars: physicians, alchemists, and more. They also point to references in the sources to debates in the Abbasid court regarding these materials.[26] Currently some of the findings are viewed in part as somewhat speculative, especially the portions that refer to frontier contacts with Chinese envoys. Yet, such polemics in the Islamicate cultural centres indicate that contemporaries noticed the transmission of eastern materials into the Islamicate world, even if we ought to take the exact cultural-ethnic identification of the sources and their couriers with a pinch of salt.

The earlier scholarship, which subscribed to the original narrative, did not neglect non-Greek wisdom. Gutas himself devoted his *Greek Thought, Arabic Culture* to demonstrate a revival of Sasanian and Zoroastrian ideology in the Abbasid court. But Gutas and others emphasized the Greek basis to Sasanian materials and discussed the translations of Greek texts to Middle Persian. The new narrative, however, reviews Persian and Indian learning on their own merit and emphasizes much more than before the high degree of connectivity of goods and ideas in and around the Asian Islamicate world. Similarly, and as with the current position on the function of Mesopotamian materials in the Islamicate world, the present idea is that certain parts of the pre-Islamic Iranian materials were revised via Arabic and that these revisions were impacted by the cultural and intellectual concerns of the Abbasid court.

Languages

The reconstruction of the complexities of knowledge exchange crisscrossing premodern Asia puts the practice of translation at the forefront of scholarly attention, which also underscores the roles of languages in both connecting and separating. Indeed, the transfer of knowledge is often seen as essentially linguistic.[27] As Rosenthal wrote, 'Every term translated is a term distorted'.[28] But while the linguistic change to Arabic was dramatic, complex, and non-uniform, such changes enriched the target language and opened new possibilities for knowledge production.[29]

26 Kevin van Bladel's work is especially noteworthy regarding the Iranian world and east: van Bladel, 'The Arabic History of Science of Abū Sahl ibn Nawbkht (fl. ca. 770–809)'; van Bladel, 'Graeco-Arabic Studies in Classical Near Eastern Studies'; van Bladel, 'Eighth-Century Indian Astronomy in the Two Cities of Peace'. With regard to India, see Wujastyk, 'From Balkh to Baghdad'.

27 For instance, Rashed, 'Problems of the Transmission of Greek Scientific Thought into Arabic', pp. 199–200.

28 Rosenthal, *Knowledge Triumphant*, p. 3.

29 Wasserstein, 'Why Did Arabic Succeed Where Greek Failed?'.

Much research has been done in the past regarding the linguistic aspects of the translations in the Abbasid period. This line of enquiry was in accord with the traditional emphasis given to philology and lexicography within the discipline in previous decades. The new scholarship looks at languages in a different way. In addition to rigorous linguistic analysis of translations and their correspondences with source texts, as in the past, the new wave rethinks the civilizational context of languages.

The original wave in the scholarship would have emphasized the role of either Greek *or* Syriac,[30] but now attention is focused on the cultural reality of bi- and even multi-lingualism. Scholars reconstruct parallel translation projects from and to several languages. They also challenge the label 'Greek to Arabic' and suggest in its stead 'Greek to Arabic/Syriac'. Different areas of knowledge were translated from different languages depending on the history of that specific science. For instance, the role of Syriac in transmitting Greek science into Arabic was not important in astronomy but was significant in philosophy and medicine. Decisions regarding the target language also rested with the confessional identity of the client for whom translations were made.[31] Scholars also point out that the function of a *lingua franca* was not exclusive and stable: multiple languages simultaneously acted as a mode of contact, exchange, and mediation.[32] In other words, the current position is one that considers inclusive modes of transmission via multiple languages.

The Translators and their Translations

Another lead for research is not about languages per se but rather focuses on the process of translation and the people who carried it out, namely the translators. These too are not new research agendas, but they are given greater emphasis now due to the historiographical context of the Social Turn and Translation Studies.

As mentioned above, the profile of the translators has been broadened. It now includes figures who are not only outside the patronage of the tight Muslim elite circles, but also connected with the smaller (marginal?) groups within Orthodox Christianity. Questions are now asked regarding their motivation and remuneration.[33]

The enquiry into the translators' self-perception is both social and professional. Translation Studies remind us to consider the theory and practice of translation as a medium of cultural communication, adaptation/localization, and transformation at the centre of attention. Hence this line of

30 Bhayro and Brock, 'Three Syriac Galen Palimpsests', pp. 41–42.

31 Bhayro, 'On the Problem of Syriac "Influence" in the Transmission of Greek Science to the Arabs'; Bhayro, 'Galen in Syriac'.

32 Yoeli-Tlalim, 'The Silk-Roads as a Model for Exploring Eurasian Transmissions of Medical Knowledge'

33 Bhayro, 'Galen in Syriac', pp. 148–52.

enquiry brings to the fore questions regarding the methods and self-image of translators, as individuals and as professional networks and circles.[34] The linguistic issues are emblematic of the wide-ranging cultural and scientific changes. Scholars remind us that the concept and profession of translation is historically embedded and we should explain how it was understood and practised by the medieval translators themselves.[35]

Hybridity

Scientific texts in Islamicate societies written in Arabic are thought of as a fairly thoroughly hybridized body of knowledge. Answering questions of 'sources', 'origins', and 'originality' is currently less often the goal of an investigation. The choice to use terms like 'hybrid', 'hybridization', and 'hybridity' reframes what has already been accepted, namely that all science, indeed all cultures, are the product of engagement with others. This is a shift from the previous position that used the terms 'transmission', 'transformation', and 'appropriation' as analytical tools. These studies looked at the trajectories of theories, facts, methodologies, and attitudes from one culture to another. They identified different types of transmission (transference of entire traditions or of selected parts) and the mechanisms of naturalization of this new information or resistance to it.[36]

By concentrating on hybridity, that is the blending of themes, attitudes, practices, knowledge from two or more sources, the emphasis is not on the knowledge and how it is transferred and accommodated in the receiving culture. Instead, the focus is the culture that absorbs new ideas and the implications to it. The outcome of such acts of translation is that the traces of one culture exist in other cultures. Cultures are deeply entwined and interdependent. The growing scholarship attests to this phenomenon in the Mediterranean basin, the Near East, and across Asia.[37]

One possible cause of this new direction is the multiplicity and diversity of knowledge sources. As mentioned above, the proponents of the Greek-to-Arabic narrative place particular importance on the Hellenic link, including in cases where the body of knowledge in question derived from non-Hellenistic origins.

---

34 For example, Overwien, 'The Art of the Translator'.

35 Vagelpohl, 'The Abbasid Translation Movement in Context'; Vagelpohl, 'Cultural Accommodation and the Idea of Translation'; Vagelpohl, 'In the Translator's Workshop'.

36 For instance, Ragep and Ragep, with Livesey ed., *Tradition, Transmission, Transformation*; Gutas, *Greek Thought, Arabic Culture*, pp. 91–101.

37 See the programmatic agenda in Wisnovsky, Wallis, Fumo, and Fraenkel, 'Introduction'.

Why Now?

The sum total of these new narratives is a picture of multiple, complex, and competitive translation projects in the first Islamic centuries. Historiographical changes are routine and normal. Already in the late 1990s, some scholars pointed out the need to distinguish fiction and fact in the commonplace narrative of the translations under the Abbasid patronage. They looked into the profile of the people who carried out the translation enterprise and enquired about the agenda that brought them to describe it in the way they did.[38] However, what encouraged scholars in the last decade to question explanations accepted since the mid-twentieth century? And why did the change take the characteristics outlined above? Two possible interconnected causes are intellectual and social: the stimulation from the discourse about the history of knowledge, and a change in the profile of a new generation of scholars.

In the twenty-first century there is a growing cohort of scholars with the language skills to situate Islam in various Eurasian contexts, namely Mediterranean, Near Eastern, Persian, central Asian, eastern Iranian, Turkic, Indic, and Chinese. They are able to execute research projects that look at the circulation of texts and knowledge between the Islamicate world, central Asia, and eastern Asia. The linguistic skills scholars have (or lack) dictate the accessibility (and lack thereof) of sources and delineates the contours of the discussion. A new generation of scholars, whose linguistic skills are more comprehensive and inclusive than earlier generations, is better equipped to notice cultural encounters less observed before, and consider hybridized and non-compartmental shifts and transitions of knowledge. Such a change in the profile of the scholars is at once random and deliberate due to life experience, personal interests, and conscious professionalism. They may be few and scattered, but their work accumulates and has already had an impact on the field.[39]

The emergence of the history of knowledge as a scholarly approach in its own right in the twenty-first century is another possible factor in the historiographical shift. During the 2000s, the subject of the history of knowledge has become more popular and institutionalized, mainly in the German-speaking world but not limited to it. Collectively, this body of scholarship puts knowledge — rather than science, ideas, etc. — at the centre of historical analysis and asks about the concepts of knowledge, the monopolies of knowledge, the processes of producing, analysing, disseminating, and implementing knowledge. Under this umbrella, the discussion includes the circulation of knowledge between people, groups, and institutions; the organization

38 For instance, Rashed, 'Problems of the Transmission of Greek Scientific Thought into Arabic'; van Koningsveld, 'Greek Manuscripts in the Early Abbasid Empire'.

39 Yoeli-Tlalim, 'The Silk-Roads as a Model for Exploring Eurasian Transmissions of Medical Knowledge', pp. 49–50, 61.

of knowledge including cataloguing and classification; its appearance and disappearance; how knowledge transcends space and time; and more.[40] All these issues are highly relevant to the phenomena of the translation projects in the Abbasid period.

This recent energized research conducted by more linguistically prepared researchers seems to bring us closer to a very new understanding of the significant phenomenon of massive translations of pre-Islamic materials in the Middle East. These translations took place exactly at the time when Islamicate civilization took its shape and contours. Hence the possible gains from the new historical understanding are a better understanding of the Islamicate enterprise as a whole.

40 Burke, *What is the History of Knowledge?*; Östling, Sandmo, Heidenblad, Hammar, and Nordberg ed., *Circulation of Knowledge: Explorations in the History of Knowledge.*

Bibliography

Abattouy, Mohammed, Jürgen Renn, and Paul Weinig, 'Transmission as Transformation: The Translation Movements in the Medieval East and West in a Comparative Perspective', *Science in Context*, 14.1–2 (2001), 1–12

Arnold, Thomas Walker, and Alfred Guillaume, *The Legacy of Islam* (Oxford: Oxford University Press, 1931)

Bhayro, Siam, 'On the Problem of Syriac "Influence" in the Transmission of Greek Science to the Arabs: The Cases of Astronomy, Philosophy, and Medicine', *Intellectual History of the Islamicate World*, 5 (2017), 211–27

——, 'Galen in Syriac: Rethinking Old Assumptions', *Aramaic Studies*, 15.2 (2017), 132–54

Bhayro, Siam, and Sebastian Brock, 'Three Syriac Galen Palimpsest and the Role of Syriac in the Transmission of Greek Medicine in the Orient', *Bulletin of the John Rylands Library*, 89 suppl. 1 (2013), 25–43

Bohak, Gideon, and Mark Geller, 'Babylonian Astrology in the Cairo Genizah', in *Envisioning Judaism: Studies in Honor of Peter Schäfer on the Occasion of His Seventieth Birthday*, vol. 1, ed. by Raʿanan S. Boustan, Klaus Herrmann, Reimund Leicht, Annette Y. Reed, and Giuseppe Veltri, with the collaboration of Alex Ramos (Tübingen: Mohr Siebeck, 2013), pp. 607–22

Burke, Peter, *What is the History of Knowledge?* (Cambridge: Polity, 2016)

D'Ancona, Cristina, 'Greek into Arabic', *Encyclopaedia of Islam Three*, vol. 2016–1, 116–34

Gutas, Dimitri, *Greek Thought, Arabic Culture: The Graeco-Arabic Translation Movement in Baghdad and Early 'Abbāsid Society (2nd–4th / 8th–10th Centuries)* (London: Routledge, 1998)

——, 'The Greek and Persian Background of Early Arabic Encyclopedism', in *Organizing Knowledge: Encyclopaedic Activities in the Pre-Eighteenth Century Islamic world*, ed. by Gerhard Endress (Leiden: Brill, 2006), pp. 91–101

——, 'Introduction: Graeco-Arabic Studies from Amable Jourdain through Franz Rosenthal to the Future', *Intellectual History of the Islamicate World*, 3.1–2 (2015), 1–14

Gutas, Dimitri, and Kevin van Bladel, 'Bayt al-Ḥikma', *Encyclopaedia of Islam Three*, vol. 2009–2, 133–37

Koningsveld, P. S. van, 'Greek Manuscripts in the Early Abbasid Empire: Fiction and Facts about their Origin, Translation and Destruction', *Bibliotheca Orientalis*, 55.3–4 (1998), 345–71

Langermann, Y. Tzvi, 'The Chapter on *Rasāyana* (Medications for Rejuvenation) in *Miʿrāj al-duʿāʾ*, a Shiʿite Text from the 12th/18th Century', *Intellectual History of the Islamicate World*, 6 (2018), 14–83

——, 'Babylonian and Indian Wisdoms in Islamicate Culture', *Oriens*, 46.3–4 (2018), 435–75

Mavroudi, Maria, 'Translations from Greek into Latin and Arabic during the Middle Ages: Searching for the Classical Tradition', *Speculum*, 90.1 (2015), 28–59

Overwien, Oliver, 'The Art of the Translator, or: How Did Ḥunayn ibn ʾIsḥāq and His School Translate?', in *Epidemics in Context: Greek Commentaries on Hippocrates in the Arabic Tradition*, ed. by Peter E. Pormann (Berlin: de Gruyter, 2012), pp. 151–69

Östling, Johan, Erling Sandmo, David Larsson Heidenblad, Anna Nilsson Hammar, and Kari Hernæs Nordberg, ed., *Circulation of Knowledge: Explorations in the History of Knowledge* (Lund: Nordic Academic Press, 2018)

Ragep, F. Jamil, and Sally P. Ragep, with Steven Livesey, ed., *Tradition, Transmission, Transformation* (New York: Brill, 1996)

Rashed, Roshdi, 'Problems of the Transmission of Greek Scientific Thought into Arabic: Examples from Mathematics and Optics', *History of Science*, 27 (1989), 199–209

Ricci, Ronit, *Islam Translated: Literature, Conversion, and the Arabic Cosmopolis of South and Southeast Asia* (Chicago: Chicago University Press, 2011)

Rosenthal, Franz, *The Classical Heritage of Islam* (London: Routledge, 1992)

——, *Knowledge Triumphant: The Concept of Knowledge in Medieval Islam* (Leiden: Brill, 2007)

Sabra, Abdelhamid I., 'The Appropriation and Subsequent Naturalization of Greek Science in Medieval Islam: A Preliminary Statement', *History of Science*, 25 (1987), 223–43

Saliba, George, *Islamic Science and the Making of the European Renaissance* (Cambridge, MA: MIT Press, 2007)

Shefer-Mossensohn, Miri, and Keren Abbou Hershkovits, 'Early Muslim Medicine and the Indian Context', *Medieval Encounters*, 19 (2013), 274–99

Tannous, Jack, *The Making of the Medieval Middle East: Religion, Society, and Simple Believers* (Princeton: Princeton University Press, 2018)

Treiger, Alexander, 'Christian Graeco-Prolegomena to a History of the Arabic Translations of the Greek Church Fathers', *Intellectual History of the Islamicate World*, 3 (2015), 188–227

Vagelpohl, Uwe, 'The Abbasid Translation Movement in Context. Contemporary Voices on Translation', in *Abbasid Studies II. Occasional Papers of the School of Abbasid Studies. Leuven, 28 June – 1 July, 2004*, ed. by John Nawas (Leuven: Peeters, 2010), pp. 245–67

——, *'Cultural Accommodation and the Idea of Translation'*, *Oriens*, 38.1–2 (2010), 165–84

——, 'In the Translator's Workshop', *Arabic Sciences and Philosophy*, 21 (2011), 249–88

Van Bladel, Kevin, 'The Arabic History of Science of Abū Sahl ibn Nawbakht (fl. ca. 770–809) and its Middle Persian Sources', in *Islamic Philosophy, Science, Culture, and Religion*, ed. by Felicitas Opwis and David Reisman (Leiden: Brill, 2012), pp. 41–62

——, 'Graeco-Arabic Studies in Classical Near Eastern Studies: An Emerging Field of Training in Its Broader Institutional Context', *Intellectual History of the Islamicate World*, 3.1–2 (2015), 316–25

——, 'Eighth-Century Indian Astronomy in the Two Cities of Peace', in *Islamic Cultures, Islamic Contexts: Essays in Honor of Professor Patricia Crone*, ed. by

Behnam Sadeghi Asad, Q. Ahmed, Adam Silverstein, and Robert Hoyland (Leiden: Brill, 2015), 257–94

Wasserstein, David J., 'Greek Science in Islam: Islamic Scholars as Successors to the Greeks', *Hermathena*, 147 (1989), 57–72

——, 'Why Did Arabic Succeed Where Greek Failed? Language Change in the Near East after Muhammad', *Scripta Classica Israelica*, 22 (2003), 257–72

Wehrli, Fritz, 'Richard Walzer', *Gnomon*, 48.2 (1976), 221–22

Weil, Dror, 'The Fourteenth-Century Transformation in China's Reception of Arabo-Persianate Astronomy', in *Knowledge in Translation: Global Patterns of Scientific Exchange, 1000–1800*, ed. by Patrick Manning and Abigail Owen (Pittsburgh: Pittsburgh University Press, 2018), pp. 262–74

Wisnovsky, Robert, Faith Wallis, Jamie C. Fumo, and Carlos Fraenkel, 'Introduction', in *Vehicles of Transmission, Translation, and Transformation in Medieval Textual Culture*, ed. by Robert Wisnovsky, Faith Wallis, Jamie C. Fumo, and Carlos Fraenkel (Turnhout: Brepols, 2011), pp. 1–22

Wujastyk, Dominik, 'From Balkh to Baghdad: Indian Science and the Birth of the Islamic Golden Age in the Eighth Century', *Indian Journal for History of Science*, 51 (2016), 679–90

Yoeli-Tlalim, Ronit, 'The Silk-Roads as a Model for Exploring Eurasian Transmissions of Medical Knowledge: Views from the Tibetan Medical Manuscripts of Dunhuang', in *Entangled Itineraries: Materials, Practices, and Knowledge across Eurasia*, ed. by Pamela H. Smith (Pittsburgh: University of Pittsburgh Press, 2019), pp. 47–62

Zimmermann, Friedrich W., 'Richard Walzer (1900–1975)', *Der Islam*, 53.1 (1976), 1–4

GÖTZ KÖNIG

Philosophical Pahlavi Literature of the Ninth Century

In this paper I approach the difficult and contentious problem of possible translations of Greek or Syriac philosophical texts into Middle Persian from the perspective of the ninth century, when we first have reliable documentation of philosophical activities among Zoroastrian clerics. I start with a survey of the problem and focus then on possible alternative interpretations.

Greek Philosophy and Pahlavi Literature

As a consequence of Bailey's famous study on *Zoroastrian Problems* (pub. 1943) and of de Menasce's edition of the Middle Persian treatise *Škand Gumānīg Wizār* (pub. 1945), it is a common assumption in Iranian Studies that the literature in Pahlavi, i.e., the Middle Persian literature of the Zoroastrians in the ninth/tenth century, is to a certain extent an heir of Greek philosophy, especially of the philosophy of Aristotle. The basis for such a heritage were probably translations from the Greek — or from an intermediary language (Syriac) — into an Iranian, most likely into a West Middle Iranian language. It is indeed obvious that some Pahlavi works remain incomprehensible if we do not read a good number of Middle Persian words — Greek loanwords are missing — as *calques* from the Greek, as philosophical terms. However, it is unclear when such translations have been made, and it is much disputed in Oriental Studies whether such a Greek-Iranian knowledge transfer belongs to the fundaments of the Abbasid translation movement. Because of the scarcity of significant historical sources and because of the absence of texts that are to be identified as translation texts, the scholars had to work in a

Götz König (goetz.koenig@fu-berlin.de) is a German Iranist whose work focuses on Old and Middle Iranian texts related to Zoroastrianism. Currently he is preparing a new edition of the texts belonging to the *Xorde Avesta* within the project *Corpus Avesticum Berolinense* at the Freie Universität Berlin. He has published books and articles on the intellectual and religious history of ancient and late antique Iran, including *Studien zur Rationalitätsgeschichte im Älteren Iran. Ein Beitrag zur Achsenzeitproblematik* [*Studies on the history of rationality in Ancient Iran: A contribution to the theory of Axial Age*] (Harrassowitz, 2018), and on Zoroastrian texts belonging to the Avesta, the translation of the Avesta, and the Pahlavi literature of the ninth/tenth century.

Narratives on Translation across Eurasia and Africa: From Babylonia to Colonial India, ed. by Sonja Brentjes in cooperation with Jens Høyrup and Bruce O'Brien, CAT 3, pp. 99–117 (Turnhout: Brepols, 2022) BREPOLS PUBLISHERS 10.1484/M.CAT-EB.5.127936

circular process. The Pahlavi texts themselves — the assumed late output of a Greek-Iranian knowledge transfer — had to be taken as a proof for the existence of such a transfer. In the following I shall revise the established historical model of the Greek-Iranian knowledge transfer; and I shall put forward the hypothesis that (at least) parts of the Pahlavi literature belong to what I call the 'Philosophical Zoroastrian School' of the ninth century (a school that reformulates the Zoroastrian teachings by means of philosophical terms of Greek origin).

The Age and Type of a Philosophical Tradition in the Pahlavi Literature

The approach of Bailey and de Menasce was further developed by Shaki since 1970[1] on the basis of the third book of the *Dēnkard* (Dk) which became better known through its translation in de Menasce.[2] While Bailey had made *ad hoc* re-translations of Middle Persian words into Greek (Aristotelian) philosophical terms, Shaki tried to explore the philosophical contexts in the Pahlavi texts, to compare them with Aristotelian and Platonic theories and concepts, and to make these comparisons plausible by a reconstruction of a historical scenario of the philosophical and scientific knowledge transfer. As those Arabo-Graecists who stress the importance of pre-Islamic Iran for the medieval reception of Greek philosophy in the Abbasid empire, Shaki's historical reconstruction is led by two assumptions: a) Greek philosophy and science has had a reception in Iran since the Hellenic period and especially in the Sasanian times, i.e., the times that were shaped by Zoroastrianism; b) although the main part of the Pahlavi literature was produced late, in the ninth century, this literature is nevertheless a true heir of this antique/late antique reception of philosophy.

Historical Continuity?

This historical reconstruction is certainly not wrong in general. A small number of Pahlavi accounts[3] on the transmission of the Avesta indeed show that Zoroastrianism adapted Greek philosophy during the third century. These accounts report that Šābuhr I 'collated' (*abāz handāz-*) Greek 'books' with the Avesta. Among these books were writings, for instance, on *bawišn ud wināhišn ud *jadag-wihīrīh*[4] 'on becoming and decaying and transformation'.[5] As already

1 Shaki 1970, 1973, 1975, 1981, 1998, 1999, 2003.

2 Menasce, trans., *Le troisième livre du Dēnkart.*

3 See König, 'A Re-thinking of Mansour Shaki's Contributions', with literature.

4 Bombay, Mulla Firuz, MS 55 (= B) ytkʿ ʾylyh/*jadag-ērīh*. For *jadag-wihīrīh* see *Dēnkard* 3.369 (B 271.5–272.2; Bailey, *Zoroastrian Problems in the Ninth-Century Books*, pp. 204–05; Zaehner, *Zurvan*, p. 33 with references to *Physics* 1.7 (190b5); *De Caelo* 270a27; *De Gen. et Corr.* 319b10; *Metaph.* 1022b15.

5 It follows: *ud gowāgīh* 'and logic'. Bailey reads *gavākīh* 'growth' (root *gu-*) and brings

Bailey had recognized, the term *bawišn ud wināhišn* refers to Aristotle's περὶ γενέσεως καὶ φθορᾶς, better known as *de generatione et corruptione*, and one may suggest, that the (difficult) term *jadag-wihīrīh* 'transformation' points to the second part of this text, a *locus classicus* of Aristotle's theory of elements.[6] According to the information on the Avesta of Šābuhr I, we have to expect that Aristotle's theory of the elements was transported by means of the Pahlavi translation of the Avesta, the *Zand*, and was then part of the cosmological scientific tools of the Zoroastrian priests. At least in some Pahlavi books from the ninth century this expectation is fulfilled.

Besides the traces of Aristotelianism, Shaki was able to detect some elements of Neoplatonic philosophy in (more or less) the same Pahlavi books (*Dēnkard* 3, *Greater Bundahišn*),[7] especially the concept of hypostasis/ emanation, a concept that — I dare to say — allowed to bridge the sharp border of the Zoroastrian ontological dualism of spiritual and material (*mēnōg / gētīg*), and to re-formulate a cosmological concept based on correspondence and analogy as a concept based on continuity and transition. I believe that further analysis could show that some key-terms of *Dēnkard* 3 (being; the Good; soul [of the world]) cannot be understood without their Platonic-Neoplatonic background. The detection of Neoplatonic elements in some Pahlavi books leads to two conclusions: first, it shows that the Zoroastrian writings were influenced by Greek philosophy more than once; second, the merger of Aristotelian and Neoplatonic elements evokes the design of the Neoplatonism of many post-Plotinian philosophers. Such philosophers are well known in the early late Sasanian period. The report of Agathias[8] on the exiled philosophers from Athens testifies to the presence of Neoplatonic commentators of Aristotle at the court of the young Xosrō I (*c.* 530). Priscianus, one of seven philosophers, wrote a treatise for his host Xosrō I, the *Solutiones*,[9] which is, besides the Aristotelian logic of Paulus

---

this in conjunction with the following term ('change and growth'), see also Zaehner, *Zurvan*, p. 55. Bailey points to *Yašt* 13.142 *ərədat̰.fəδrī-* → *Dēnkard Madan* 674.16 gwb'k AB' (according to West, *Pahlavi Texts* v, p. 115, the words should be read as *gōwāk pit* 'having a testifying father', a Pahlavi translation that is 'sehr zweifelhaft' according to AiW 350). Bailey thinks that in *Dēnkard Madan* 230.8–9 the word *gayōmart* is explained as *zīndagīh gawāgīh ī mīrāg* 'mortal life and growth' (cf. *Dādestān ī dēnīg* 63 *zīwandag ī mīr<ā>g*), not accepted by de Menasce (*Le troisième livre du Dēnkart*, p. 220, 'vivant, raisonnable, mortel'). A reading *gōwāgīh* (understood as 'logic') seems much more acceptable. The Pahlavi term *star-gōwišnīh* 'astrology' which is used in the report on Šābuhr's I Avesta in *Dēnkard* 4 shows clearly that *gōwišnīh* is a loan translation of -λογία. The logic of the Indians (*tark* < Skr. *tarka-*) is mentioned in *Dēnkard* 4.99 (see Shaki, 'The Dēnkard Account', p. 116 no. 8).

6 This theory is the scientific reflection of the philosophical term 'becoming and decaying' that is discussed in book I of *De Generatione et Corruptione*.

7 Shaki, 'Some Basic Tenets of the Eclectic Metaphysics of the Dēnkart'.

8 *Histories* 2.28–32.

9 See Quicherat, 'Solution des problèmes par Chosroës'; Bywater, *Supplementum Aristotelicum*,

Persa, the most important evidence for the presence of Neoplatonism/Aristotelianism in Iran.[10] I assume that with the new redaction of the Avesta under Xosrō I Neoplatonic thoughts found their way into the authoritative Zoroastrian writings.

A Historical Counter Model

Although we have left behind a historical model according to which the Pahlavi literature is *only* a late reflection of an early Sasanian Aristotelianism by emphasizing that Zoroastrianism was affected by Greek philosophy (better: by Greek philosophies) more than once, we stick with the former model still in one point. We continue to regard the literature of the ninth/tenth century as an heir of earlier periods.

However, two observations that I was able to make concerning the Pahlavi literature induce me to modify this model. My starting point for the short sketch below is the following assumption. If Greek terms and theories were borrowed by the Iranians/Zoroastrians in antiquity/Late Antiquity and implemented in the authoritative writings (the *Zand*), one should see a more or less even distribution of these terms and theories among Pahlavi texts of the same genre. However, this is not the case.

Distribution of the Aristotelian Theory of Elements

Let us consider first the case of the Aristotelian theory of elements. The theory of Aristotle is in competition with an old Zoroastrian doctrine of six elements or six plus one element. This Zoroastrian doctrine could not be abandoned by Zoroastrians because of its close ties to the design of the highest pantheon.[11] For this reason, the Pahlavi literature has both theories side by side, and sometimes we see even attempts to merge both theories. But it is remarkable that the *loci* of the Greek/Aristotelian theory are restricted

---

I, 2; Erhart, 'Priscianus of Lydia at the Sasanian Court'; Huby and others, trans., Priscian, *Answers to King Khosroes of Persia*.

10 *Treatise on the Logic of Aristotle the Philosopher addressed to King Khhuosrowousrowau* (in Syriac; London, British Museum, MS 988 [Add. 144660], fols 55^{v}–67^{v}, translated into Latin by Land, *Anecdota Syriaca*; Wright, *Catalogue of Syriac Manuscripts*, III, p. 1161 [see also p. xxv]). See further Christensen, *L'Iran sous les Sassanides*, pp. 427–28; Gutas, 'Paul the Persian on the Classification of the Parts of Aristotle's Philosophy', especially pp. 250–54 on the Arabic translation, attributing it to Abū Bishr Matta. On the Aristotelian corpus in MP, see Panaino, 'Aristotelian Corpus'.

11 It seems that the construction of the Aməṣ̌a Spəṇta pantheon is based on the theory of the six elements or six plus one element. However, the sequence of the elements is modified according to the sequence of the Aməṣ̌a Spəṇta pantheon; see Kellens, 'Sur l'Origine des Aməṣ̌as Spəṇtas'. The connection of the elements and the deities is, as far as I see, the oldest formulation of a thinking in correspondences which is then, especially in Late Antiquity, of fundamental importance in Iran.

to very few scriptures. It is a constitutive element in *Dēnkard* 3 and *Škand Gumānīg Wizār* (ŠGW). The leading topic of both books is the apologia/defence of the teaching of the *dō bun*, the fundamental dualism of Good and Evil. This teaching was reformulated by means of the theory of elements: the world is based on two distinct substances, the hot-moist, and the cold-dry. Besides *Dēnkard* 3 and *Škand Gumānīg Wizār*, the Aristotelian theory is prominent in the so-called *Bundahišn*, the Zoroastrian world history 'from the first creation to the resurrection'. Luckily, this work is transmitted in two recensions of different length (the so-called *Iranian/Greater* and the *Indian Bundahišn*). When comparing both recensions, we recognize that the theory of elements can be found only in those parts of the *Bundahišn* that belong to the longer version exclusively (made around 900 CE), while the elements are absent in the shorter version (that cannot be dated).

On the Age of the Aristotelian Theory of Elements in Iran

According to Aristoxenos, the pupil of Aristotle, the doctrine of the four elements is not of Greek, but of Iranian origin. He gives the following account on Pythagoras who came to the Chaldean Zaratas (= Zaraϑuštra). This Zaratas instructed him as follows: 'that from the beginning on there are two principles of the existing things, "father" and "mother": "father" is the light, "mother" the darkness; parts of the light are the warm, dry, light, swift, parts of the darkness are the cold, wet, heavy, slow. The whole world is made from these <principles>, from the female and the male'.[12] Be that as it may be,[13] the statement of Aristoxenos proves that the teaching of the (four) elements or the teaching of the qualities of elements (on which the teaching of mixture and transformation is based) has a very long tradition in Iran.[14] A clear reflection of Aristotle's theory can already be found in Manichaean teachings. The Greek theory is modified and enlarged according to the Manichaean dualism and the Manichaean abhorrence of the solid material as shown in the table on the following page.

12 Hippol. ref. I 2,12 = Aristoxenos fg. 13 (ed. by Wehrli); quoted after Burkert, *Die Griechen und der Orient*, p. 124.

13 Compare, for instance, the qualities of the male and female semen (*garm* and *husk*; *sard* and *xwēd*) according to *Greater Bundahišn* (GrBd) 15.5–6, cf. also the long discussion of the qualities of light and heavy in Aristotle's *De Caelo*.

14 For a comprehensive discussion of the topic, see König, *Studien zur Rationalitätsgeschichte im Älteren Iran*, II.

	father of greatness	mother of life	
the Good (not material)	light[16] (light-air, light-earth[17])	?	air (= light-air [ethe
the Evil (material)	darkness (+ hyle[21])	?	smoke[22]
	(zoomorphic[24]) prince of darkness[25]	Āz[26]	

15 Compare in the *Gyān wifrās* (GW) the sequence of the 'five gods' (pnj bg'n), the 'children of the god Ohrmazd' (' (hrm)yzd (bg) [z'dg'n]) (GW § 21). These five gods, the Righteous Frawardīn (≈ air) and the *yazds* of wind, light, water and fire, were interestingly — in a 'nsk/nsg' with the name 'the Living Nask' ((n)s(g) jyw'ng) — identified with the five Avestan *Gāϑās* (see GW § 32, 46, 65).

16 The ontological position of the light is not totally clear. It is, of course, strictly separated from matter, see Severus of Antioch, *Hom.* 123, ed. by Brière and Graffin (Syriac version), PO XXIX, fasc. 1, pp. 164.10–167. 15 (Böhlig, *Die Gnosis*, pp. 135–37, 136): 'Denn in jener Welt des Lichtes gibt es kein brennendes Feuer, um gegen das Böse eingesetzt zu werden, noch Eisen, das schneidet, noch Wasser, das ertränkt, oder irgend etwas anderes Böses, das ihm gleicht. Alles nämlich ist Licht und freier Raum' (translation Böhlig, *Die Gnosis*, p. 136); for the concept of 'freier Raum' = 'world of light' see König, *Yašt* 3, pp. 263–75. But its relation to the good elements seems to be ambiguous, as it is the relation to god. In an-Nadīm, *Kitâb al-Fihrist*, ed. by Flügel, 329.1–331.2 (see Böhlig, *Die Gnosis* pp. 144–49, 144) the light is identified with god who is 'außerhalb des Zahlenbegriffs', i.e., he is beyond diversity.

17 According to an-Nadīm, *Fihrist*, ed. Flügel, *Kitâb al-Fihrist*, pp. 329.1–331.2 (Böhlig, *Die Gnosis*, pp. 144–49, 144–45), air and earth are together with the light/god. The light-air has the five parts *nous*, thinking, insight, secret, and consideration. The light-earth compasses the five elements. It is remarkable that in Zoroastrianism not air and earth, but fire and water are seen as first elements.

18 See Böhlig, *Die Gnosis*, p. 310 no. 110. Aš-Šahrastānī's text on the Manichaeans (Cureton, ed., *Book of Religious and Philosophical Sects*, 1, 188.11–192.18; Haarbrücker, *Abu-'l-Fath' Muhammad asch-Schahrastanis Religionspartheien und Philosophenschulen*, 1, pp. 285–91; Böhlig, *Die Gnosis*, pp. 149–56, 151) says that the both series of elements are made of one spiritual and four physical elements. The spiritual elements are the fresh air / the smoke.

19 See Augustinus, *de haeresibus*, text according to its translation in Böhlig, *Die Gnosis*, pp. 138–40.

20 See Augustinus, *de haeresibus*, text according to its translation in Böhlig, *Die Gnosis*, pp. 138–40.

21 For the identification of darkness and hyle cf. the Manichaean selections in Severus of Antioch, *Hom.* 123, ed. by Brière and Graffin (Syriac version), PO XXIX, fasc. 1, pp. 148.23–25; 150.8–10 (Böhlig, *Die Gnosis*, p. 133).

22 On the mixture of smoke and fire in the Zoroastrian theory, see *Greater Bundahišn* 4.27.

23 On the dark fire, see Brinkmann ed., *Alexandri Lycopolitani contra Manichaei opiniones disputatio*, pp. 4.23–8.4 (Böhlig, *Die Gnosis*, pp. 130–33, 130).

24 See an-Nadīm, *Fihrist*, ed. by Flügel, pp. 329.1–331.2 (Böhlig, *Die Gnosis*, pp. 144–49, 145).

25 According to aš-Šahrastānī's texts on the Manichaeans (Cureton, ed., *Book of Religious and Philosophical Sects*, 1, 188.11–192.,18; Haarbrücker, *Abu-'l-Fath' Muhammad asch-Schahrastani's Religionspartheien und Philosophenschulen*, I, pp. 285–91; Böhlig, *Die Gnosis*, pp. 149–56, 153) the Evil emerged from darkness (i.e., both are not identical).

26 On the Āz as the 'evil mother of all demons', see the hymn from S 9 (in Middle Persian) (Salemann, 'Manichaica III', pp. 9–13; Henning, 'Ein manichäischer kosmogonischer Hymnus', pp. 214–18; Boyce, *A Reader in Manichaean Middle Persian and Parthian*, pp. 100–01; Asmussen, *Manichaean Literature*, pp. 133–34; Böhlig, *Die Gnosis*, pp. 121–23, 121).

27 On the opposition of god and *hyle*, see Brinkmann ed., *Alexandri Lycopolitani contra*

	first man		
the five parts of his living soul[15]:			
wind	light (= light-earth)	water (> moon[19])	fire (> sun[20])
wind	darkness	water	fire[23]
	hyle[27]		

Distribution of Neoplatonic Concepts

Even more surprising is the examination of the distribution of Neoplatonic concepts in the Pahlavi literature. The famous first cosmogonic chapter of the *Bundahišn* is contained in both above-mentioned recensions of the text, but the shorter version brings only 50 per cent of the text. The other 50 per cent of Chapter 1 are not transmitted in the *Indian Bundahišn*. As it is proved by internal references in the longer version of the text, the editor of the *Iranian/Greater Bundahišn* made textual additions. He distinguished his text from the material that goes back to a *Vorlage*:

***Greater Bundahišn* 1.33** (beginning of the first intersection)	
dām dahišnīh mēnōgīhā ***gōwom*** *ud pas gētīgīhā*	and **I shall speak** about the spiritual (see *Greater Bundahišn* 1.34–53) and then the material creation (see *Greater Bundahišn* 1.57–1A24)'

These textual additions (and only these additions) contain a theory according to which the entities of the world are connected with each other in a model of 'creative emanation' (C is made by a creator from B is made by a creator from A):

Greater Bundahišn 1.1–32	≈ *Indian Bundahišn*	
Greater Bundahišn 1.33–53	Ø *Indian Bundahišn*	created emanations (spiritual world)
Greater Bundahišn 1.53a–55	≈ *Indian Bundahišn* (shortened)	
Greater Bundahišn 1.55–59	Ø *Indian Bundahišn*	created emanations (material world)
Greater Bundahišn 1A	Ø *Indian Bundahišn*	

Manichaei opiniones disputatio, pp. 4.23–8.4 (Böhlig, *Die Gnosis*, pp. 130–33, 130–31); Hegemonius, *Acta Archelai*, chapters VII–XIII, ed. by Beeson, ch. XI (Böhlig, *Die Gnosis*, pp. 123–30, 128); Theodoret of Kyrrhos, *Haereticarum fabularum compendium*, text according to its translation in Böhlig, *Die Gnosis*, p. 137. According to *Acta Archelai*, ch. VIII, the *hyle* is in opposition to the Living Spirit.

Conclusions from the Above-mentioned Observations

It appears that those parts of the *Greater Bundahišn* that are without a parallel in the *Indian Bundahišn* are rooted in an intellectual milieu that was familiar with Aristotle and Neoplatonism. Nevertheless, both versions of the *Bundahišn* refer to themselves as *Zand-āgāhīh*, 'Knowledge from the *Zand*'. From these observations, two (slightly different) historical conclusions can be drawn:

1. The Pahlavi literature is divided into two parts that are related to the *Zand* in different ways. Only one part accepted those *Zand* texts that contained Greek theoretical/philosophical concepts. For this scenario to be plausible we would have to reconstruct the ninth century as a struggle between two hermeneutic schools of the *Zand*.
2. In the early times of the Abbasids, when the Mu ʿtazilite doctrines were formulated, there was a new study of Greek philosophy among (at least some) Zoroastrian priests.[28] This philosophical interest lasted during the whole ninth century. Other priests did not participate in this new scholarship, or they refused some of the new scientific/philosophical elements.

Both conclusions would point to a participation of some Zoroastrian priests in the new intellectual activities of early Muslim theological factions. Conclusion 1 describes such a participation in a weak manner (emphasis on Greek concepts that were already part of the *Zand*). Conclusion 2 describes such a participation in a strong manner (acceptance of Greek concepts that were/are not part of the *Zand*). Both conclusions can be supported by further arguments. The strong conclusion can point to the fact that the Zoroastrian key figure in the early ninth century, the leading high-priest Ādurfarrbay ī Farroxzādān, the author of *Dēnkard* 3 and other works, took part in the inter-denominational discussion-rounds at the Abbasid court in Baghdad, at which Mu ʿtazilite scholars were highly influential. Especially *Dēnkard* 3 and *Škand Gumānīg Wizār*, a book produced in the school of Ādurfarrbay ī Farroxzādān, show the rise of the new style of thinking. The 420 chapters of *Dēnkard* 3 have one overarching theme, the defence of the postulate of the two fundamental principles (substances). About sixty chapters of *Dēnkard* 3 have polemic *addenda* against the so-called *kēšdārān* — most often Muslim theologians. The structure of these (shorter or longer) essays is a transformation of the old Indo-Iranian *frašna* structure (question — authoritative answer) into a discussion-structure. *Škand Gumānīg Wizār* develops this new structure systematically.

28 The earliest materials are collected in van Ess, *Theologie und Gesellschaft*.

The Pahlavi Translation of the Avesta and Greek Philosophy

Conclusion 1 is based on the conjecture of a 'philosophical *Zand*'. Since the 1980s a new interest in the Pahlavi translation of the Avesta arose.[29] It culminated in 2004 in Cantera's work.[30] The focus lay on the comparison of the Avestan and the Pahlavi translation text. Unfortunately, a comparison of the vocabulary/terminology of the Pahlavi translation with the vocabulary/terminology of the Pahlavi books of the ninth century was not part of those studies. However, it seems that the traces of Greek philosophy that can be found in Ādurfarrbay's *Dēnkard* are missing in *all* Pahlavi translations, i.e., in the translations of the Sasanian period *and* of the post-Sasanian period. It is unclear how we should interpret this fact. The assumption that the lack of philosophical terminology is simply the consequence of the age of the canonical Pahlavi translation has difficulties to explain why also the (probably late) Pahlavi translation of the *Yasna* and the *Xorde Avesta* has not adopted this new terminology. For this reason, it seems more plausible to assume that the whole *Zand* literature is based on a fixed and stable vocabulary/terminology. However, an analysis of passages in *Dēnkard* 8, the reports of the Avesta/*Zand*, shows that at least these reports participated to a certain extent in the new terminology.

The Emergence of a Philosophical Zoroastrian School

Within the Pahlavi literature of the ninth and tenth centuries, two authors and their work have an exceptional position. One is (the already mentioned) Ādurfarrbay ī Farroxzādān, the first editor of the post-Sasanian *Dēnkard*.[31] The other is Mardānfarrox, the son of Ohrmazddād, author of the *Škand Gumānīg Wizār*. Ādurfarrbay was the first *hudēnān pēšōbāy*[32] 'the leader of those of the Good Religion' of the (Iranian) Zoroastrian community, whose term in office overlaps with the caliphate of al-Maʾmūn (caliph 813–33).[33] The time of Mardānfarrox is to establish only *post* (and probably also *ante*) *quem*.

29 See especially: Taraf, *Der Awesta-Text Niyāyiš*; Deghan, *Der Awesta-Text Srōš Yašt t.*

30 Cantera, *Studien zur Pahlavi-Übersetzung des Avesta*.

31 *Dēnkard* 3.420; see also *Dēnkard* 3.299, 3.142.

32 See Anklesaria, *The Pahlavi Rivāyat*, II, p. 5; cf. Kreyenbroek, 'The Zoroastrian Priesthood', p. 160 (*hudēnān pēšōbāy* 'leader of the orthodox people' ≈ designation of the caliph as *ʿamīr ul-muʾmanīn*; Asha, 'The traditional history of the Zoroastrian Scriptures', n. 30, mentions aram. *rēš gālūṯā* 'exilarch'). The *pēšōbāy* was also the *pārs āsrōnān pēšag framādār* and the *mōbedān-iz ī pārs sālār* (*Dādestān ī dēnīg* 44.5; see Kreyenbroek, 'The Dādestān ī dēnīg on priests', pp. 201–02; on the titles, see also Macuch, *Rechtskasuistik und Gerichtspraxis*, pp. 58–59).

33 See the text *Gizistag Abāliš*.

In contrast to most of the other authors of Pahlavi books,[34] Mardānfarrox refers several times to the *Dēnkard*, especially to passages that originated in the work of Ādurfarrbay and of Ādar-Pādiiāβaṇdą. (Ādurbād ī *Jāwandān/°dād)[35] who was probably the teacher (? *bun-spās*[36]) of Ādurfarrbay[37] and maybe the author of *Dēnkard* *1,*2,[38] and to the work of Ādurfarrbay's son Rōšn.[39] Because Ādurfarrbay's son Rōšn is already called *hūfarβard* 'blessed' in *Škand Gumānīg Wizār*, Mardānfarrox was probably not in personal contact with Ādurfarrbay anymore who has the epithet *ašō* 'blessed' in *Škand Gumānīg Wizār*.[40] In contrast to the network of the other Pahlavi books, there are no hints to family ties between Ādurfarrbay and Mardānfarrox. It seems that Mardānfarrox's discipleship was the discipleship of an intellectual that did not belong to the very dense circle of Persian high priests. The passages *Škand Gumānīg Wizār* 10. 50–58 and 9. 1–3 allow to reconstruct Mardānfarrox's 'intellectual homeland', as well as an important string in the Zoroastrian *Geistesgeschichte* of the ninth century. Especially *Škand Gumānīg Wizār* 10. 50–58 gives us insight in the genetic and intellectual relations of the school of Ādurfarrbay:

---

34 For references on the *Dēnkard* see also *Dādestān ī dēnīg* 88(87).8; *Nāmagīhā Manuščihr* 1.3.9; in the New Persian *Rewāyats*, see MU I pp. 103.2 ff., 118.11–13 (Dhabhar, *The Persian Rivayats*, pp. 104–05, 123).

35 *Škand Gumānīg Wizār* 4.106–07, 9.1–3, 10.50–58, 1.38.

36 West, *Pahlavi Texts* III, p. 162 '*from* the original thanksgiving (spâs)'; de Menasce, *Une apologétique mazdéenne du IXe siècle*, p. 109 'par son fidèle disciple'.

37 *Škand Gumānīg Wizār* 9.1–3.

38 West, *Pahlavi Texts* III, pp. 138–39 no. 9, says in the context of *Škand Gumānīg Wizār* 4.10–07 on that (otherwise unknown) Ādurbād ī Jāvandān (West: Âtûr-pâdîyâvand): 'This writer is also mentioned in Chaps I,38, IX,2 X,52, but his name has not yet been found elsewhere. As he does not appear to be mentioned in that portion of the Dînkard known to be extant, his writings were probably embodied in the first two books of that work, which have not yet been discovered'.

39 *Škand Gumānīg Wizār* 10.50–58. His quite unusual name ('light') may express a penchant of some Zoroastrians for a metaphysics of light (cf. *Dēnkard* 3.420). West, *Pahlavi Texts* III, p. 169 no. 4, identifies him with the commentator Rōšn who is mentioned for example in *Šāyest-nē-Šāyest* and *Pahlavi-Vīdēvdād* (10x in *Pahlavi-Vīdēvdād*, see Cantera, *Studien zur Pahlavi-Übersetzung des Avesta*, pp. 208–10) where he is one time in a dispute with Abarag, the last commentator from the school of Ādurfarrbay-Narsē (Ādurfarrbay-Narsē > Sōšans > Abarag).

40 *Škand Gumānīg Wizār* 4.107 says, Ādurfarrbay 'was' the Zoroastrian leader (*Ādur Farrbay ī Farroxzādan ī hudēnān pēšōbāy būd*; cf. *Dēnkard* 3.420 [B 317.5–21; K43 II 2^{v15}–3^{r12}]; *Dēnkard* 3.142 [B 110.15–18]; *Dēnkard* 5.1.2–3 [B 494.1–5]).

Škand Gumānīg Wizār 10. 50–58	
əž. ham. zōr. i. dīn. dānāī. u. nißə̇. <*i.*> *x^{v}aškār. i. dānāgą. u. *awē.*[41] *aṇgōšīdaa.*[42] *nißəgą. i. faržąnaa. ādar.pādiiāßaṇdą. u. əž. ą. nißə̇. yaš. kard. hūfarßard. rōšan. adar-farōbagą. yaš. rōšan. nißə̇. nąm. nahāṯ. ąca. i. ōi. ayrə̇. faržąnaa. ašō. ādar. farōbag. i. frōxzādą. i. hūdīną. pə̇šaßāē. əž. dīn. vazārd(an). dīn.kard. nißə̇. nąm. nahāt. buxt. hom. əž. vas. gumąnī. u. ə̇raṇg. u. frəß. u. dōšī. i. kə̇šą.*	By the *syn(en)ergeia*[43] of the (book?) *dīn. dānāī.* ('philosophy of religion') and of the book '*x^{v}aškār.* of the philosophers' (**xwēškār*<*īh*>*/*ōšyār*<*īh*> *ī dānāgān?*) and of the incomparable books[44] of the wise Ādarpād, son of Jāßaṇd and of that book which was composed by the blessed *Rōšan*, son of *Adar-Farōbag*, under the title *Rōšan Niwē* ('Book of Rōšan/Light') and of the (book) that was compiled (? *vazārd*)[45] by the highest intellectual, the blessed *Ādar-Farōbag*, son *Frōxzād*, the leader of the Mazdayasnians, from the *Dīn* (= *Zand*?) that is called the book *Dīn-Kard*,[46] I am saved from many doubts and errors and deceptions and follies.[47]

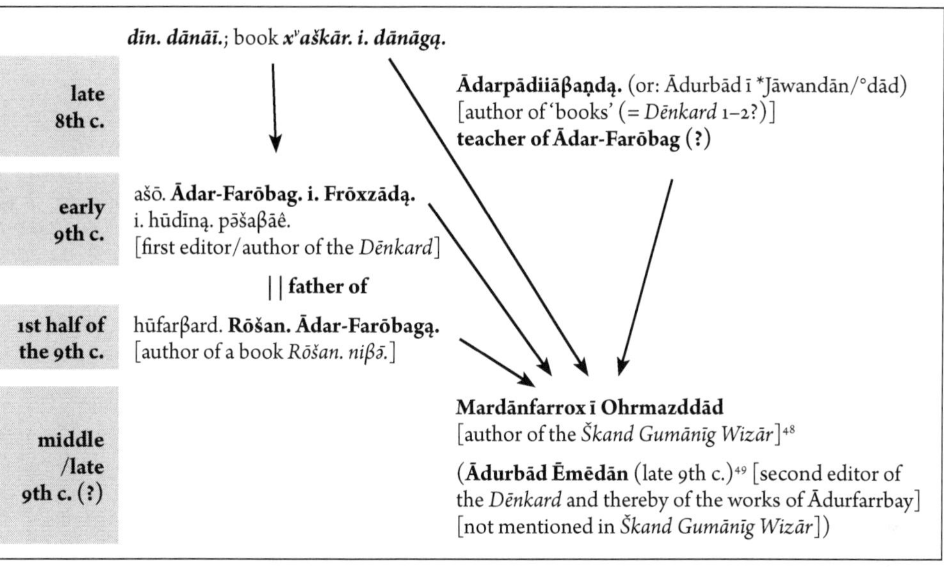

41 *aßaṯ.*; correction de Menasce.

42 Cf. Col. 1 of Bombay, Mulla Firuz, MS 55 (= B) (*im an-hangōšīdag ud anarz ud ahamtāg Dēnkard nibēg*); the word *hangōšīdag* is used several times in *Dēnkard* 3.420 but in the sense of a conjunction ('like').

43 On *hamzōr*, *hamzōrīh*, *hamzōrān*, with the prepositions *az* or *pad*, see *Greater Bundahišn* 2.3, 11.7; *Dēnkard* 3.0; *Šāyast-nē-šayast* 10.10; *Dādestān ī dēnīg* 36.55, 36.62, 36.91, and *Wizīdagīhā ī Zādspram* 1.31, 4.1, 8.6, 30.26, 30.43, 34.38.

44 West, *Pahlavi Texts* III, p. 170 'the marvellous allegorical writings'.

45 de Menasce, *Une apologétique mazdéenne du IXe siècle*, p. 117 'parce qu'il explique la Dēn'; see also West, *Pahlavi Texts* III, p. 170.

46 West, *Pahlavi Texts* III, p. 170 'appointed the name of the Dînkar*d* manuscript — owing to its explaining the religion'; de Menasce, *Une apologétique mazdéenne du IXe siècle*, p. 117 'qui, parce qu'il explique la Dēn, est intitulé: le livre du *Dēnkart*'.

47 See West, *Pahlavi Texts* III, p. 170; Nyberg, *A Manual of Pahlavi*, p. 65; de Menasce 'l'attrait'.

48 Thrope, 'Contradictions and Vile Utterances', prefers the tenth century as the date of the *Škand Gumānīg Wizār*.

49 As a contemporary mentioned by Farrbay in *Greater Bundahišn* 35a8. For Arabic and New Persian sources on Ādurbād and Ēmēd ī Ašawahištān see de Menasce, *Une Encyclopédie mazdéenne, le Dēnkart*, pp. 10–11, with literature. For suggestions on the genealogy see Tavadia, *Šāyast-nē-šayast*, p. 5; Tavadia, 'Zum iranischen Feuertempel', col. 61; Anklesaria, *Rivâyat-î Hêmît-î Asavahištân*, p. 3; Anklesaria, *The Pahlavi Rivāyat*, II, pp. 5 and 21 ('Âṭar-frenabag's sixth descendant'); Boyce, 'Middle Persian Literature', p. 46 (Ēmēd ī Ašawahištān is perhaps the grandson of Ādurbād ī Ēmēdān).

Surprisingly, in his autobiographical sketches Mardānfarrox never describes himself as a priest.[50] Little is known about his biography. Early wanderings[51] led him, as he says, *ō-iz was kišwār ud zrēh wimand* (to the borders of many countries and seas).[52] Perhaps being of Manichaean origin,[53] at some time, he found his 'salvation',[54] especially in the scriptures of the mentioned Ādurbād ī *Jāwandān and Ādurfarrbay ī Farroxzādān. Hence, it is not surprising that his work shows some anomalies. It is 'not made and arranged for the wise and experienced men, but for pupils and novices'.[55] It is, as he says, transmitted in India in a considerable number of manuscripts. A good number of them were as it seems produced in Pāzand (Middle Persian in Avestan characters),[56] maybe to make the text known also among the Indian community. In 1925, Schaeder commented on the *Škand Gumānīg Wizār* that it replaced the assertorical style of the older Persian writings by an effort to rationally justify the doctrines.[57] Mardānfarrox completes what has had its beginnings in Ādurfarrbay's work. *Dēnkard* 3 and *Škand Gumānīg Wizār* are connected in two important points: a) the development of polemical/demarcating thoughts, i.e., thoughts that are the results of a reflection and discussion of non-Zoroastrian positions; b) the development of a philosophical terminology and system.

Intellectual Landscape

In Chapter 35a of the *Greater Bundahišn* called *dūdag ī mōbedān* 'family of the Mōbeds' the editor Farrbay presented his own genealogy. His family included many high priests (*hudēnān pēšōbāy*)/authors of the ninth century.

50 *Škand Gumānīg Wizār* 1.35–57; 10.43–63.

51 *Škand Gumānīg Wizār* 1.36–37, 10.43–49.

52 *Škand Gumānīg Wizār* 1.37; cf. 10.47.

53 See his sharp polemic against Mani ['Mānāe'] in *Škand Gumānīg Wizār* 1.59–60.

54 *Škand Gumānīg Wizār* 1.54, 10.58.

55 *Škand Gumānīg Wizār* 1.40 *u-m nē dānāgān ud abzārōmandān bē frahangiyān <ud> nōg-abzārān rāy kard ud ārāst*).

56 *Škand Gumānīg Wizār* is transmitted only in parts in Pahlavi, but completely in Pāzand. However, some mistakes in the Pāzand and Sanskrit text point to the higher age of the Pahlavi text (see West, *Pahlavi Texts* III, p. xxviii; de Menasce, *Une apologétique mazdéenne du IXe siècle*, p. 159). *Škand Gumānīg Wizār* belongs to the very few Pahlavi works that were translated into Sanskrit. The MS from the former private library of Dastur Hoshangji, AK2, written 1569 by the famous scribe Āsadīn Kākā, proves a higher age of the Bombay MS AK which was Āsadīn's Vorlage (see Jâmâsp-Âsânâ and West, *Shikand-Gûmânîk Vijâr*, pp. xxvii, xxxvii–xxxviii; Cereti, 'Škand Gumānīg Wizār').

57 Schaeder 'Die islamische Lehre', pp. 200–201, no. 3: 'An die Stelle der rein assertorischen Darstellung der älteren persischen Lehrschriften, deren letzter Rekurs das "Es steht geschrieben" ist, ist hier der Versuch einer rationalen Begründung des Dogmas … getreten …'. According to Sundermann, 'Das Manichäerkapitel des Škand Gumānīg Wizār', p. 325, the *Škand Gumānīg Wizār* is a 'Schlüsseltext(es) der nahöstlichen Religionsgeschichte'.

***Greater Bundahišn* 35a7**	
*ud man Farrbay [ī xwānēnd Dādagīh] ī Ašwahišt ī Gušnjam ī Wahrām-šād ī Zarduxšt ī (Zarduxšt) Ādurbād Māraspandān Zādsparām ī *Juwānjam Ādurbād *Ēmēdān ud Ašawahišt ī Frāy-srōš ud abārīg mōbedān az hamdūdag būd hēnd*	And I, **Farrbay** [who is called Dādagīh[58]], <son> of **Ašawahišt**, <son> of ***Juwānjam**, <son> of **Wahrām-šād**, <son> of **Zardušt**, <descendant> of Ādurbād Māraspandān; **Zādsparām**, <son> of **Juwānjam**; **Ādurbād *Ēmēdān** and **Ašawahišt**, <son> of Frāy-Srōš, and other Mōbeds were <all> of the same family.

Farrbay's information is remarkable for two reasons:

1. Farrbay mentions his uncles Zādsparam and Ašawahišt, but he remains silent about his uncle Manuščihr, the famous and mighty high-priest of Pārs. This Manuščihr did not only write a treatise in the old dogmatic *frašna*-style, but he also wrote three letters. These letters were his reaction on a change in the ritual that was decreed by his brother Zādsparam. Probably because of his scientific and medical interests, Zādsparam had tried to shorten the very lengthy purification ritual. While *Nāmagīhā Manuščihr* 2. 1. 8 sketches a great assembly of priests,[59] *Nāmagīhā Manuščihr* 2. 1. 10–12 points to two assemblies of priests, one that seems to have taken place in *Šīrāz (?),[60] and one assembly of the Tuγazguz.[61] The passage *Nāmagīhā Manuščihr* 2. 1. 8–12 is difficult to understand, but we dare to assume that the topics of these councils were not only discussions of Zādsparam's heteropraxis, but also of the scientific and philosophical concepts and interests that had provoked Zādsparam's decision.

2. Farrbay's genealogic list neither mentions the name of Mardānfarrox. Should we assume that Mardānfarrox lived after Farrbay? For two reasons, I think we should not: a) Mardānfarrox mentions the *Dēnkard* several times but never its last editor Ādurbād Ēmēdān; b) the chapter *Škand Gumānīg Wizār* 9. 1–4 shows that Mardānfarrox still knew and used a sequence of the chapters of *Dēnkard* 3 that is not the same as the sequence of the chapters after the edition by Ādurbād Ēmēdān. When Farrbay does not mention Mardānfarrox in his genealogy then simply because Mardānfarrox did not belong to his own family (and maybe not to the high clergy at all).

From these two points, we can derive the following characteristics of the Zoroastrian *Geistesgeschichte* in the ninth century:

58 An alternative reading of the name is Jādagī, see Cereti, *La letteratura Pahlavi.*

59 *ka-iz pad šādurwān ī mowān hanjaman ī Pārs dar ud abārīg was ham-rasišnīh uskārdan ud 1000 hu-dēn mow padiš* [...] (Also, when within the compass (*pad šādurwān*) of the considering of the assembly of the *mobeds* of the temple (*dar*) of Pārs and of many other conventions and of 1000 *mobeds* of good religion [...]).

60 *Nāmagīhā Manuščihr* 2.1.11. The manuscripts give slʾp/cʿ and sylʾp/cʿ.

61 *Nāmagīhā Manuščihr* 2.1.12.

1. In the late ninth century, a philosophical Zoroastrian theology that was dominating in the family of Ādurfarrbay (i.e., in the family of the highest priests in Iran) was probably not appreciated by the mighty Manuščihr, a conservative high-priest from the same family.[62] In contrast to the books of Farrbay and Zādsparam, Manuščihr's treatise *Dādestān ī dēnīg* 'Religious decision' did not participate in the 'new theology' of the school of Ādurfarrbay.

2. In the succession of Ādurfarrbay's philosophical theology a student body emerged. These educated people — Mardānfarrox is their known representative — did not belong to the highest clergy. It seems that their aim was to spread the new ideas and the new style of thinking among the Zoroastrians.

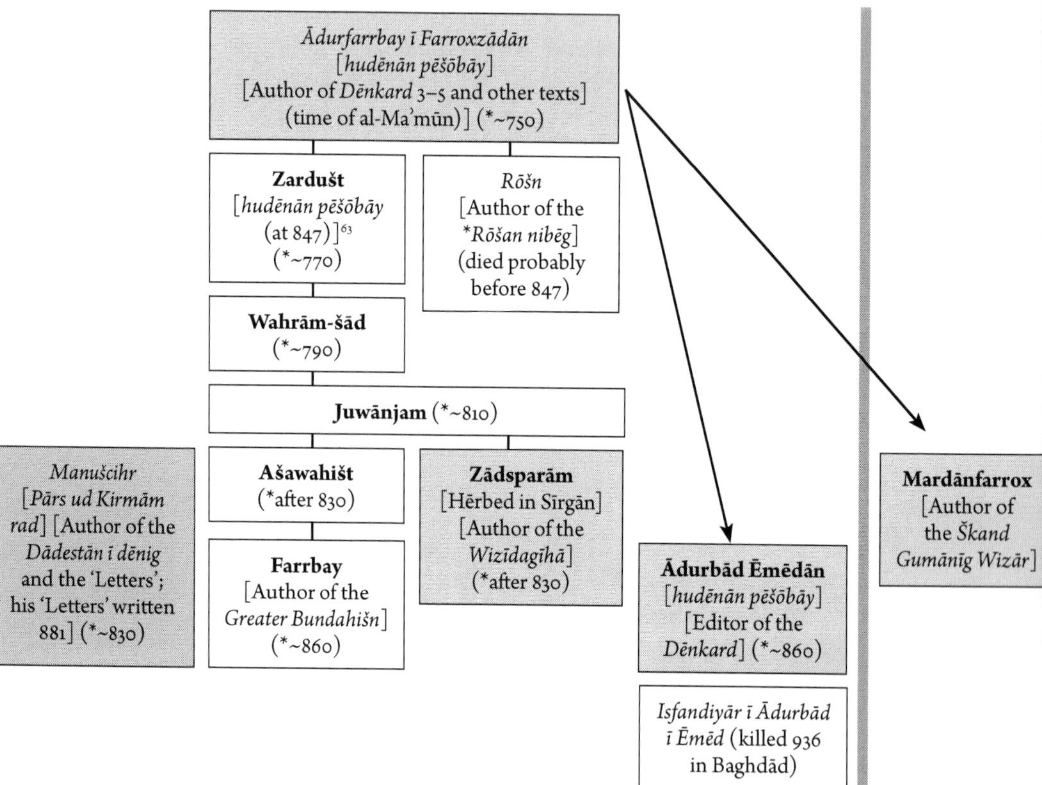

62 A closer examination of the vocabulary/terminology of Manuščihr is still missing.

63 On Zardušt see West, *Pahlavi Texts* IV, p. xxxii (*Dēnkard* 3.420); Browne, *The Literary History of Persia*, pp. 323–36 (participation in the process against Afšīn); Anklesaria, *Vichitakiha-i Zatsparam*, pp. vii, xxi; Anklesaria, *The Pahlavi Rivāyat*, II, p. 13. According to Asha, Zartošt was not an apostate, but a martyr. Asha's interpretation of *Dēnkard* 3.420 is based on the words pṯ' škpt' 'lm W wznd y 'L zltwhšt, words that show that something happened to Zardušt (*ī ō Zardušt*).

Summary

1. It is likely that translations of Greek philosophical texts were adopted by the authoritative Zoroastrian tradition in the early (Šābuhr I) and late Sasanian (Xosrō I) period, i.e., they were adopted more than once.
2. However, it seems that the canonical Pahlavi translation of the Avesta was not affected by an Aristotelian or Neoplatonic terminology. In the Pahlavi literature of the ninth century, only a few books adopted the (translated) Greek philosophical terminology and a 'Greek style of philosophical thinking'.
3. Especially the school of Ādurfarrbay participated in the philosophical interests of the Muʿtazilite court of Baghdad. Ādurfarrbay's school was successful during the whole ninth century. However, at the end of the century a conservative fraction came to power (Manušcihr).
4. The translation and adaptation of Greek philosophy (especially of Aristotle and Neoplatonism) is probably the most important tool in the late antique/medieval process of a transformation of Zoroastrian theology.

Bibliography

Manuscripts

Bombay, Mulla Firuz Library (today Cama Oriental Institute), MS 55 (= B)
Copenhagen, Det Kongelige Bibliotek, MS K43
Navsari, Meherji Rana Library, MS T12 (= AK)
Poona, Private Library Hoshangji Jamaspji, MS AK2 (manuscript probably lost)
For manuscript MU see Unvala, *Dârâb Hormazyâr's Rivâyat.*

Primary Sources

Anklesaria, Behramgore T., *Rivâyat-î Hêmît-î Asavahištân*, I: *Pahlavi Text* (Bombay: Parsi Punchayet Funds and Properties, 1962)

——, *Vichitakiha-i Zatsparam, with Text and Introduction*, I (Bombay: Parsi Punchayet Funds and Properties, 1964)

——, *The Pahlavi Rivāyat of Āturfarnbag and Farnbag-Srōš*, 2 vols (Bombay: Parsi Punchayet Funds and Properties, 1969)

Brinkmann, August, ed., *Alexandri Lycopolitani contra Manichaei opiniones disputatio*, Bibliotheca scriptorum Graecorum et Romanorum Teubneriana (Leipzig: Teubner, 1895 [Stuttgart: Teubner, 1989])

Bywater, Ingram, *Supplementum Aristotelicum*, I, 2: *Prisciani Lydi. Quae Extant Metaphrasis in Theophrastum et Solutionum ad Chosroem Liber* (Berlin: G. Reimer, 1886)

Cureton, William, ed., *Book of Religious and Philosophical Sects, by Muhammad al-Sharastāni* (London: Society for the Publication of Oriental Texts, 1842–1846 [reprint: Leipzig 1923])

Dhabhar, Ervad Bamanji N., *The Persian Rivayats of Hormazyar Framarz and Others: Their Version with Introduction and Notes* (Bombay: The K. R. Cama Oriental Institute 1932)

Deghan, Keyvan, *Der Awesta-Text Srōš Yašt (Yasna 57)* (München: R. Kitzinger, 1982)

Erhart, Victoria, 'Priscianus of Lydia at the Sasanian Court: Solutionum ad Chosroem', *Falsafeh*, 37 (2009), 21–31

Haarbrücker, Theodor, *Abu-'l-Fath' Muhammad asch-Schahrastani's Religionspartheien und Philosophenschulen. Zum ersten Male vollständig aus dem Arabischen übersetzt und mit erklärenden Anmerkungen versehen* (Halle: C. A. Schwetschke und Sohn, 1850–1851)

Hegemonius, *Acta Archelai*, ed. by Charles H. Beeson, Die griechischen christlichen Schriftsteller der ersten Jahrhunderte, 16 (Leipzig: J. C. Hinrichs'sche Buchhandlung, 1906)

Henning, Walter B., 'Ein manichäischer kosmogonischer Hymnus', *NGWG*, 1932, 214–28 (= *Selected Papers* I, pp. 49–64)

Huby, Pamela, Sten Ebbesen, David Langslow, Donald Russell, Carlos Steel, and Malcolm Wilson, trans., *Priscian, Answers to King Khosroes of Persia* (London: Bloomsbury, 2016)

Jâmâsp-Âsânâ, Hoshangji J., and Edward W. West, *Shikand-Gûmânîk Vijâr: The Pazand-Sanskrit Text Together with a Fragment of the Pahlavi* (Bombay: Government Central Book Depot 1887)

König, Götz, *Yašt 3. Der avestische Text und seine mittel- und neupersischen Übersetzungen. Einleitung, Text, Kommentar* (Girona: Estudios Iranios y Turanios, 2016)

Land, Jan P. N., *Anecdota Syriaca*, vol. 4 (Leiden: Brill, 1875)

Macuch, M., *Rechtskasuistik und Gerichtspraxis zu Beginn des siebenten Jahrhunderts in Iran. Die Rechtssammlung des Farroḫmard i Wahrāmān* (Wiesbaden: Harrassowitz, 1993)

Menasce, Jean de, *Une apologétique mazdéenne du IXe siècle. Škand-Gumānīk vičār. La solution décisive des doutes. Texte pazend-pehlevi transcrit, traduit et commenté* (Fribourg: Librairie de l'Université, 1945)

Menasce, Jean de, trans. *Le troisième livre du Dēnkart. Traduit du pehlevi* (Paris: Klincksieck, 1973)

al-Nadīm, Muḥammad ibn Isḥāq Ibn, *Kitâb al-Fihrist*, ed. by Gustav Flügel, 2 vols (Leipzig: F. C. W. Vogel, 1871–1872)

Piras, Andrea, trans. *Hādōxt Nask 2. Il raccontro zoroastriano della sorte dell'anima. Edizione critica del testo avestico e pahlavi, traduzione e commento*, SOR, 88 (Rome: Istituto italiano per l'Africa e l'Oriente, 2000)

Quicherat, Jules, 'Solution des problèmes par Chosroës: traité inédit de Priscien le philosophe', *Bibliothèque de l'École des Chartes*, 14 (1853), 248–63

Salemann, Carl, 'Manichaica III', *Bulletin de l'Acad. Imp. des Sciences de St Pétersbourg* (1912), 1–32

Severus of Antioch, *Hom. XXIX*, ed. by Maurice Brière and François Graffin, Patrologia Orientalis 36, Nr. 170 (Turnhout: Brepols, 1974)

Taraf, Zahra, *Der Awesta-Text Niyāyiš mit Pahlavi- und Sanskritübersetzung* (München: R. Kitzinger, 1981)

Tavadia, Jehangir C., *Šāyast-nē-šayast: A Pahlavi Text on Religious Customs Edited, Transliterated and Translated with Introduction and Notes*, Alt- und Neu-Indische Schriften, 3 (Hamburg: Friederichsen, 1930)

Unvala, Manockji R., *Dârâb Hormazyâr's Rivâyat, with an Introduction by J. J. Modi. 2 vols* (Bombay, British India Press) (= MU)

West, Eduard W., *Pahlavi Texts*, III: *Dīnā-ī Maīnōg-ī Khirad, Sikand-Gümānīk Vigār, Sad Dar,* Sacred Books of the East, 24 (Oxford: Oxford University Press, 1885)

——, *Pahlavi Texts*, IV: *Contents of the Nasks*, Sacred Books of the East, 37 (Oxford: Oxford University Press, 1892)

——, *Pahlavi Texts*, V: *Marvels of Zoroastrianism*, Sacred Books of the East, 47 (Oxford: Oxford University Press, 1897)

Secondary Studies

Asha, Rahim: 'The Traditional History of the Zoroastrian Scriptures', http://www.rahamasha.net/uploads/2/3/2/8/2328777/dk_iii__420.pdf (accessed 11 November 2019)

Asmussen, Jes P., *Manichaean Literature: Representative Texts Chiefly from Middle Persian and Parthian Writings* (New York: Scholar's Facs., 1975)

Bailey, Harold W., *Zoroastrian Problems in the Ninth-Century Books* (Oxford: Clarendon Press, 1943 [1971])

Böhlig, Alexander, ed., *Die Gnosis. Der Manichäismus* (Düsseldorf and Zürich: Artemis, 1997)

Boyce, Mary, 'Middle Persian Literature', in *Handbuch der Orientalistik* 1.4.2.1 (Leiden: Brill, 1968), pp. 32–66

Boyce, Mary, *A Reader in Manichaean Middle Persian and Parthian*, Acta Iranica, 9 (Leiden: Brill, 1975)

Browne, Edward G., *The Literary History of Persia, Vol. 1: From the Earliest Times until Firdawsi* (London: Curzon, 1902)

Burkert, Walter, *Die Griechen und der Orient* (München: Beck, 2003)

Cantera, Alberto, *Studien zur Pahlavi-Übersetzung des Avesta* (Wiesbaden: Harrassowitz, 2004)

Cereti, Carlo G., *La letteratura Pahlavi. Introduzione ai testi con riferimenti alla storia degli studi e alla tradizione manoscritta* (Milano: Mimesis, 2001)

——, 'Škand Gumānīg Wizār', in *Encyclopædia Iranica* (Mazda Publishers) (digital electronic version)

Christensen, Arthur, *L'Iran sous les Sassanides. Deuxième édition revue et augmentée* (København: Ejnar Munksgaard, 1944 [Osnabrück: Zeller, 1971])

Ess, Josef van, *Theologie und Gesellschaft im 2. und 3. Jahrhundert der Hidschra. Eine Geschichte des religiösen Denkens im frühen Islam* (Berlin: de Gruyter, 1993–1995)

Gutas, Dimitri, 'Paul the Persian on the Classification of the Parts of Aristotle's Philosophy: A Milestone Between Alexandria and Baghdad', *Der Islam* 60 (1983), 231–67

Josephson, Judith, *The Pahlavi Translation Techniques as Illustrated by Hōm Yašt* (Uppsala: Uppsala University Library, 1997)

Kellens, Jean, 'Sur L'Origine des Aməṣ̌as Spəṇtas', *Studia Iranica*, 433 (2014), 163–75

König, Götz, 'A Re-thinking of Mansour Shaki's Contributions to the Philosophical Writings in Pahlavi', *Quarterly Journal of Language and Inscription: Dedicated to Professor Mansour Shaki*, 1.1 (2016), 4–26

——, *Studien zur Rationalitätsgeschichte im Älteren Iran*, II (Wiesbaden: Harrassowitz, forthcoming)

Kreyenbroek, Philip G., 'The Dādestān ī dēnīg on priests', *Indo Iranian Journal*, 30 (1987), 185–208

——, 'The Zoroastrian Priesthood after the Fall of the Sasanian Empire', *Studia Iranica (Transition Periods in Iranian History)*, 5(1987), 151–66

Menasce, Jean de, *Une Encyclopédie mazdéenne, le Dēnkart* (Paris: Presses Univiversitaires de France, 1958)

Nyberg, Henrik S., *A Manual of Pahlavi*, Part II: *Ideograms, Glossary, Abbreviations, Index, Grammatical Survey, Corrigenda to Part I* (Wiesbaden: Harrassowitz, 1974)

Panaino, Antonio, 'Aristotelian Corpus: Translations into Pahlavi (200–900 CE)', in *Encyclopedia of Ancient Natural Scientists: The Greek Tradition and its Many Heirs*, ed. by Paul T. Keyser and Georgia L. Irby-Massie (London: Routledge, 2012)

Schaeder, Hans H., 'Die islamische Lehre vom Vollkommenen Menschen, ihre Herkunft und ihre dichterische Gestaltung', *ZDMG*, 79 (1925), 192–268

Shaki, Mansur, 'Some Basic Tenets of the Eclectic Metaphysics of the Dēnkart', *Archiv Orientálni*, 38 (1970), 277–312

——, 'A Few Philosophical and Cosmological Chapters of the Denkart', *Archiv Orientálni*, 41 (1973), 133–64

——, 'Two Middle Persian Philosophical Terms LYSTK' and M'TK'', in *Iran ancien: Actes du XXIXe Congrès international* (Paris: L'Asiatique, 1975), 52–57

——, 'The Dēnkard Account of the History of the Zoroastrian Scriptures', *Archiv Orientálni*, 49 (1981), 114–25

——, 'Elements', in *Encyclopædia Iranica*, 8, ed. by Eshan Yarshater (London: Mazda Publishers, 1998), 357–60

——, 'Falsafa I. Pre-Islamic Philosophy', in *Encyclopædia Iranica*, 9, ed. by Eshan Yarshater (London: Mazda Publishers, 1999), 176–82

——, 'Greek Influence on Persian Thought', in *Encyclopædia Iranica*, 11, ed. by Eshan Yarshater (London: Mazda Publishers, 2003), 321–26

Sundermann, Werner, 'Soziale Typenbegriffe altgriechischen Ursprungs in der altiranischen Überlieferung', in *Soziale Typenbegriffe im alten Griechenland VII*, ed. by E. Ch. Welskopf (Berlin: Akademieverlag, 1982), 14–38

——, 'Das Manichäerkapitel des Škand Gumānīg Wizār in der Darstellung und Deutung Jean de Menasces', in *Augustine and Manichaeism in the Latin West: Proceedings of the Fribourg-Utrecht Symposium of the International Symposium Association of Manichaean Studies (IAMS)* ed. by Johannes van Oort, Otto Wermelinger, and Gregor Wurst (Leiden: Brill, 2001), 325–37

Tavadia, Jehangir C., 'Zum iranischen Feuertempel', *Orientalische Literaturzeitung*, 46 (1943), 57–66

Thrope, Samuel F., 'Contradictions and Vile Utterances; The Zoroastrian Critique of Judaism in the *Škand Gumānīg Wizār*' (unpublished doctoral dissertation, University of California, Berkeley, 2012), https://escholarship.org/uc/item/14b43599#page-14 (accessed 19 November 2019)

Wright, William, *Catalogue of Syriac Manuscripts in The British Museum acquired since the year 1838*, 3 vols (London: British Museum, 1870–1872)

Zaehner, Robert C., *Zurvan: A Zoroastrian Dilemma* (Oxford: Clarendon Press, 1955 [reprint: New York: Biblo and Tannen, 1972])

IMRE GALAMBOS

Changing Perceptions of Tangut Translations of Chinese Texts in Modern Scholarship

The Tangut state in present-day north-west China was in existence from the first half of the eleventh century until the Mongol conquest in 1227. Originally a vassal of the Song Empire, the Tangut ruler Li Yuanhao 李元昊 (r. 1032–1048) formally declared independence from the Song court in 1038 and assumed the title of emperor. As part of his nation-building projects, he introduced a native script, which was then used to record Tangut translations of a larger body of Buddhist texts and an array of works from the Chinese literary tradition. By the second half of the sixteenth century, the language and the script fell into oblivion and were deciphered only in the early twentieth century. Even though the majority of the surviving material consists of Buddhist writings, including scriptures, commentaries, and liturgical texts, the smaller portion of Tangut translations of Confucian classics and Chinese literary works held a particular fascination for modern scholars. Some of the Tangut texts did not correspond to known Chinese works, and these were considered either to have been translated from now lost originals, or written and compiled by the Tanguts. As scholarship advances, our understanding of the relationship of Tangut texts with the Chinese written tradition also evolves; for some texts we are able to identify their Chinese originals, while for others we may be able to verify their status as native compositions.

This brief paper proposes to look at how our perception changes as our knowledge of Tangut texts, and their potential links with Chinese ones, improves. Each new discovery slightly shapes our image of how Tangut translations were produced, yet this is a gradual process that is not always apparent when working on individual texts. Nevertheless, it is useful to take a step back and observe not only the Tangut books and manuscripts but also ourselves as we are studying this material. This, in turn, may help us develop

* I am grateful to Gábor Kósa and Sonja Brentjes for their valuable comments and suggestions.

Imre Galambos (iig21@cam.ac.uk) is a specialist of Chinese manuscript culture and palaeography. He completed his PhD at the University of California, Berkeley in 2002 with a dissertation on the orthography of the early Chinese script. After graduating, he worked for ten years at the British Library for the International Dunhuang Project, after which, in 2012, he moved to Cambridge to pursue a career in teaching. Now Professor of Chinese Studies at the University of Cambridge, his research interests include Chinese and Tangut manuscripts, codicology, as well as East-West contacts.

Narratives on Translation across Eurasia and Africa: From Babylonia to Colonial India, ed. by Sonja Brentjes in cooperation with Jens Høyrup and Bruce O'Brien, CAT 3, pp. 119–134 (Turnhout: Brepols, 2022) BREPOLS PUBLISHERS 10.1484/M.CAT-EB.5.127937

new methodologies and lead to a more nuanced view of the translation techniques employed in the Tangut state. My focus here is primarily on non-Buddhist texts as these were the ones most commonly cited as having undergone various degrees of adaptation, which may very well be due to the fact that, at least in the early stages of Tangut studies, they had been studied more closely. An analysis of Buddhist translations, including the differences between various types and genres of texts, would no doubt be an equally interesting endeavour, resulting in new insights into the process of translation and acculturation. Nonetheless, because of my own lack of expertise in this area, I choose to leave the assessment of Buddhist texts, as well as the equally interesting topic of translations from Tibetan, to those more qualified to do this.

In 1908–1909 the team of the Russian explorer Pjotr K. Kozlov (1863–1935) conducted excavations at the ruins of Khara-khoto in Inner Mongolia and discovered a large body of printed and handwritten texts, the majority of which was in Tangut and Chinese. Although Kozlov took credit for the discovery of the site, the ruins had in fact been found a year earlier by Tsokto Badmazhapov (1879–1937), a young Buryat officer who not only knew Kozlov personally but had accompanied him on an earlier expedition. Badmazhapov sent a report and some photographs to Kozlov and the Imperial Russian Geographical Society. Fearing that Russian interests would be compromised by a premature publication of such a report, especially since at that very moment the Hungarian-born British archaeologist M. Aurel Stein (1862–1943) was exploring the neighbouring Gansu province, the Society decided to suppress Badmazhapov's notice and instead sent Kozlov with an expedition directly to Khara-khoto to 'discover' it in a manner that was better suited for Russian colonial and scientific interests.[1] Even though Kozlov was not the first person to locate the site of the city, he certainly deserves credit for excavating thousands of books and documents at the ruins. The spoils of the expedition were shipped to St Petersburg where Russian scholars studied the texts, gradually leading to the development of a new field of research called Tangut studies.

In terms of its content, the overall majority of the Tangut material is of Buddhist orientation. At least in part this may be the consequence of most of the finds having been excavated from inside a stupa, which also contained a skeleton of a woman and had thus probably been a burial site. Still, within the rich body of Buddhist literature, there were also, on a much more modest scale, translations of Chinese texts, including Confucian classics, military treatises, didactic primers, compendia on statecraft, legal texts, popular encyclopaedias, and historiographic works. Due to the predominantly sinological approach of contemporary scholarship, the texts that could be directly linked with the Chinese tradition generated a disproportional amount

1 For Badmazhapov's role in the discovery of Khara-khoto and his subsequent sidelining, see Galambos, *Translating Chinese Tradition*, pp. 29–37.

of interest until relatively recently.[2] Aleksej I. Ivanov (1878–1937), the first scholar to work on the Tangut material after their arrival in St Petersburg, did a preliminary categorization of the collection and picked out the 'secular' texts, and this smaller selection was the part that subsequently received the most attention.[3] The binary distinction between religious and 'secular' texts played an important role in how scholars in the following decades perceived and studied the Kozlov collection.

Cataloguing Tangut Texts

Without doubt, the most important contribution during the early history of Tangut studies was that of Nikolaj A. Nevskij (1892–1937), a brilliant linguist and a former student of Ivanov. From the late 1920s, he devoted much of his time to working on the collection and deciphering the language. His groundbreaking research was brought to a halt by Stalin's Great Purge of 1937–1938, to which he also fell victim.[4] The ensuing World War II further delayed research,[5] which only began to revive in the late 1950s, mainly in Russia and Japan. In China, the Cultural Revolution (1966–1976) created another decade-long disruption and it was only from the late 1970s that Chinese scholars were able to join their Soviet and Japanese colleagues in directing scholarly attention to Tangut texts. The renewed interest in the Tangut material kept in St Petersburg (then called Leningrad) drew attention to Nevskij's unpublished research, which was published posthumously in two big volumes.[6] His series of articles and, most importantly, a large dictionary of the Tangut language provided much-needed tools for a new generation of researchers.[7]

---

2 This is not to say, of course, that there was no research on the Tangut translations of Buddhist texts. In fact, the first steps in trying to decipher the language were done on Buddhist texts, such as the Juyongguan inscriptions 居庸關 (Bushell, 'The Tangut script in the Nank'ou Pass') and a Tangut copy of the *Lotus sutra* found in Beijing in the aftermath of the Boxer Rebellion (Morisse, *Contribution preliminaire*). Yet considering that most of the discovered texts were Buddhist in nature, the non-Buddhist material received an unwarranted amount of attention.

3 Kychanov, *Katalog tangutskikh buddijskikh pamjatnikov*, p. 2.

4 Nevskij was arrested and executed in 1937 on charges of espionage, which must have been due to the fact that he had lived in Japan between 1915 and 1929, and had also married a Japanese national. Stalin's repressions were catastrophic for the field of Asian studies, as most scholars had international connections and had at one point or another lived abroad. Because of this, hundreds of them were charged with espionage or conspiracy against the Soviet state. The online bibliographical dictionary of Orientalists repressed during the Soviet regime lists 750 people; http://memory.pvost.org. For a paper version of the dictionary, see Vasil'kov and Sorokina, *Ljudi i sud'by*.

5 The Siege of Leningrad between 1941 and 1944 likewise had a devastating impact on the Institute of Oriental Studies, where Asian manuscripts were kept and studied. Aside from human casualties, the bombing and shelling of the city inflicted serious damages to the building of the Institute, including the manuscript rooms; see Marakhonova, 'Institut vostokovedenija AN SSSR v Leningrade', pp. 25–26.

6 Nevskij, *Tangutskaja filologija*, vols 1–2.

7 Parallel with Nevsky's research, the British linguist Gerard Clauson (1891–1974) was also

Among the first tasks in this new wave of scholarship was the compilation of the catalogue of identifiable Tangut texts in the Kozlov collection, the contents of which had been largely invisible to the outside world since their discovery.[8] This was accomplished by Zoja I. Gorbacheva and Evgenij I. Kychanov, who based their catalogue on Nevskij's inventory from the 1930s, which in turn had been heavily influenced by Ivanov's original division of the collection. The organization of texts in the catalogue was of significance because, on the one hand, it exemplified the current understanding of the nature of the Tangut corpus and, on the other hand, determined how researchers in the years to come would approach the material. Undeniably, the catalogue was extremely useful at the time of its publication and had a strong impact on the development of the field. In fact, it is still among the first tools one consults when examining or describing a Tangut text.

The catalogue divided the 405 identified texts in the Kozlov collection into secular and Buddhist texts. Of these, the secular category was further split into six subcategories, whereas Buddhist texts merely appeared as a long list. Thus, the overall structure of the catalogue, including the total number of titles in each category, was as follows:

(i) Secular texts	
1. Translations from Chinese (nos 1–12)	12
2. Dictionaries and phonetic tables (nos 13–24)	12
3. Original Tangut texts (nos 25–39)	15
4. Calendars, tables, diagrams (nos 40–46)	7
5. Spells and medical texts (nos 47–54)	8
6. Tangut legal texts (nos 55–60)	6
(ii) Buddhist texts (nos 61–405)	345

Merely considering the number of items in each category, we can illustrate the composition of the collection (as presented in the catalogue) using a pie chart (Fig. 1A), in which the largest slice represents the Buddhist texts, with each of the smaller ones taking up about 15 per cent of the total number. If we zoom in on this 15 per cent with non-Buddhist texts (Fig. 1B), we can see the relative size of the six subcategories (in clockwise order, starting from 12:00 at the top).

We should keep in mind, however, that the catalogue uses texts (i.e. titles) as the basic units, rather than physical copies (i.e. manuscripts, printed books,

---

compiling a Tangut dictionary which he eventually left unfinished when publications of Tangut texts from the Kozlov collection ceased in the late 1930s. He deposited a manuscript copy of the dictionary along with his research notes in the Library of the School of Oriental and African Studies, thereby making it available for others to consult. A facsimile edition of the dictionary was published only recently (Clauson, *Gerard Clauson's Skeleton Tangut*).

8 Gorbacheva and Kychanov, *Tangutskie rukopisi i ksilografy*. Among the early introductions to the contents of the collection available in western languages was a brief paper by Paul Pelliot (Pelliot, 'Les documents chinois trouvés par la mission Kozlov').

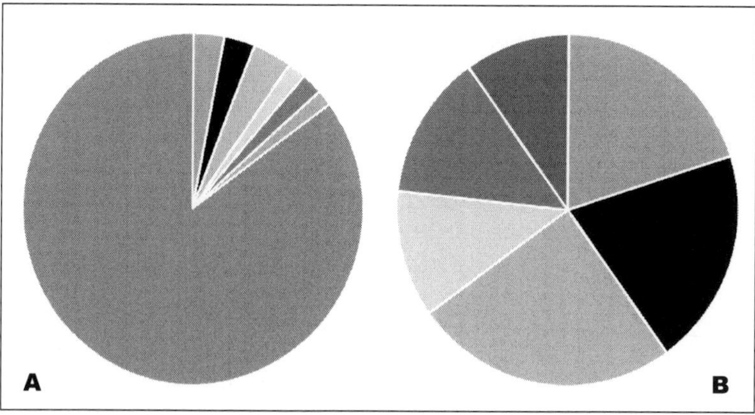

Figure 1. (A): A quantitative display of the types of texts in the Kozlov collection, as recorded in the 1963 catalogue. (B): A division of the six non-Buddhist categories.

or fragments). Consequently, even though the *Mahāprajñāpāramitā sūtra* survives in nearly three hundred copies and fragments, it counts only as one title (no. 334) in the list. While this was by far the most popular sutra, several others, such as the *Vajracchedikā prajñāpāramitā sūtra* or the *Mahāratnakūṭa sūtra*, also survive in thirty-some copies. In contrast with this, the number of physical copies of any particular secular texts does not seem to go beyond ten items per title and is in most cases well below that. Consequently, if we look at the collection from the point of view of the number of books or manuscripts originally in existence, even if we take into account that some of the fragments may have once belonged to the same physical book, we end up with an even higher ratio of Buddhist material in the collection. It is hard not to see that the numbers have major implications for assessing the nature of the entire collection.

It is all the more surprising then that the catalogue, in sharp contrast with the contents of the collection itself, primarily focused on the secular material. Buddhist texts, despite their exceedingly high ratio in the collection, only featured as a simple list in the last category of the catalogue (nos 61–405). In contrast, the much fewer non-Buddhist titles (nos 1–60) were treated in considerably more detail, including bibliographical and codicological observations. To make up for the imbalance, twenty-seven years later Kychanov published a catalogue of Buddhist texts, which he claimed to be a continuation of the 1963 catalogue, and in this he provided a more substantial description of Buddhist texts in the collection.[9] The Buddhist catalogue identifies, whenever possible, the

9 This catalogue greatly benefitted from the inventory of Buddhist texts in Tangut compiled over two decades earlier by Nishida Tatsuo (Nishida, *Seikabun Kegonkyō*, III, 13–59). This is especially true for indicating the language of the source text for the Tangut translations.

source of Tangut texts, which is invariably Chinese or Tibetan. In comparison, none of the secular texts in the 1963 catalogue was identified as coming from a Tibetan source: all texts were considered translations from Chinese or not translations. The difference between the two catalogues demonstrates the significant shift in scholarly attitudes between the early 1960s and the late 1990s. During these three decades, excellent catalogues of Dunhuang manuscripts have been published and these provided a much-needed model for the compilation of catalogues of medieval manuscripts from Central and East Asia.[10] Among the main innovations were an increased attention to the materiality of manuscripts and an interest in Buddhist literature.

* * *

To trace the evolution of modern scholarly views concerning Tangut texts, let us examine the group of non-Buddhist texts in the 1963 catalogue. This part of the catalogue has a total of sixty texts in six categories (see above). Of these, only two categories are defined in terms of their origin (no. 1. 'Translations from Chinese' and no. 3. 'Original Tangut texts'), whereas the other four bear descriptive titles. There is clearly a degree of arbitrariness to this division because dictionaries (no. 2) or medical texts (no. 5) can just as easily be classified into translations or indigenous compositions. Leaving the issue of inconsistency aside, the division of the dictionary and the categorization of texts are symptomatic of how scholars perceived Tangut texts at the time.

The very first category in the section was 'Translations from Chinese', demonstrating the overall concern of contemporary scholarship with identifying translations of known Chinese texts. In a sense, it is entirely reasonable to approach a new body of texts in a difficult language from the point of view of its connections with a familiar culture. Yet at the same time, the sequential order of categories reflected a predisposition to assess Tangut written culture in light of the Chinese tradition. As part of this trend, the first wave of scholarly translations of Tangut texts from the Kozlov collection focused precisely on these translations, resulting in monographs on the Chinese Classics, on the *Sunzi bingfa* 孫子兵法 (Art of War of Master Sun), and a lost Chinese encyclopaedia called *Leilin* 類林 (Forest of Categories).[11]

---

10 The catalogue of the Russian collection of Dunhuang manuscripts was compiled under the leadership of Lev N. Men'shikov (Men'shikov, Vorob'eva-Desjatovskaja, Gurevich, Spirin, and Shkoljar, *Opisanie kitajskikh rukopisej Dun'khuanskogo fonda, 1*; Men'shikov, Vorob'eva-Desjatovskaja, Zograf, Martynov, and Smirnov, *Opisanie kitajskikh rukopisej Dun'khuanskogo fonda, 2*); the four volumes of the catalogue of the French collection were published between 1970 and 1995 (Gernet and Wu, *Catalogue des manuscrits chinois de Touen-houang*; Soymié, Drège, Dzo Ching-chuan, Eliasberg, Hou, Magnin, Monnier, Quiquemelle, Schneider, Trombert, and Wu, *Catalogue des manuscrits chinois de Touen-houang, III*; Soymié, Drège, Eliasberg, Magnin, Mollier, Schneider, and Trombert, *Catalogue des manuscrits chinois de Touen-houang, IV*; Soymié, Drège, Eliasberg, Magnin, Mollier, Schneider, Trombert, Wang-Toutain, Zhang, and Thote, *Catalogue des manuscrits chinois de Touen-houang, V*).

11 Kolokolov and Kychanov, *Kitajskaja klassika v tangutskom perevode*; Kepping, *Sun'dzy v*

The category 'Original Tangut texts' was only no. 3 in the list but the fifteen items grouped here were also interesting because they had the potential to offer insights into the relatively obscure world of 'native' Tangut culture. Although some items were damaged or fragmentary and thus did not have any titles to guide modern researchers, many of them preserved the original titles:[12]

1. Untitled; collection of Tangut poetry, dated 1185–1186.[13]
2. Untitled; fragment of court odes.
3. *Collection of Bright Sayings from Three Generations*; collection of Tangut literary compositions in prose and verse.
4. *Ode on Praising Forbearance*; religious ode, dated 1195.
5. Untitled; an ode.
6. *Newly Collected Grains of Gold in the Palm*; a primer.
7. *Newly Collected Notes on Paternal Love and Filial Piety*; collection of exemplary biographies chosen from Chinese dynastic histories.
8. *Sea of Meanings Established by the Sages*; a Chinese-type encyclopedia.
9. *Collection of Inspired Wisdom*; collection of teachings in prose and verse.
10. Untitled.
11. *Newly Collected Precious Dual Maxims*; collection of Tangut proverbs.
12. *Compendium on Virtuous Conduct*; collection of translations from Chinese Confucian sources.
13. Untitled.
14. *Reaching Wisdom*; collection of Buddhist compositions on morality.
15. *Seating of Subordinates(?)*; possibly a composition related to official subordination.

Naturally, this was merely a preliminary list of native compositions and there are texts in the other categories that could have just as easily been placed here. Even so, this is not a long list and it stands in stark contrast with the immense

---

tangutskom perevode; Kepping, *Les Kategorij*.

12 The translations and descriptions here are based on the ones provided in the catalogue, even if newer scholarship has since then improved our reading of the text or its title.

13 The dates obviously refer to the time when the physical copy of the text was produced, rather than to that of the composition of the text itself.

volume of manuscripts and printed books discovered at Khara-khoto. It is all the more remarkable then that, as scholarship progressed, one or two texts were shown to have been translations of Chinese works, further reducing the number of items in this category. One of these was the text called *Compendium on Virtuous Conduct* (no. 12). This, in fact, turned out to be two separate texts which had the same title but were different in content. Originally, Nevskij noted that this was a Tangut work compiled by culling material from Chinese texts, which is probably why it was placed into the 'Original Tangut texts' category in the 1963 catalogue.[14]

New Interpretations and Perspectives

Almost forty years after the publication of the catalogue, in a monograph devoted to one of the two texts with this title, Nie Hongyin for the first time proposed that it was a work translated from a Chinese original, even though at the time he was unable to locate the source text. In addition, he drew attention to the fact that the text was not, as claimed earlier, purely Confucian in content but also contained elements that could be associated with Huayan and Chan Buddhist teachings.[15] Finally in 2011, Sun Bojun successfully identified the source text as the *Zhengxing ji* 正行集 (A Compendium on Proper Conduct) compiled by Qingjue 清覺 (1043–1121), founder of the popular Buddhist sect White Cloud School 白雲宗. She further advocated the view that the translation most likely postdated the fall of the Tangut Empire (1227) and came from the Yuan period (1271–1368), an observation that is significant for our understanding of the general time frame of the textual material found at the ruins of Khara-khoto.[16] In retrospect, it is apparent that the main reason why the text was considered a native Tangut compilation in the first place was because the Chinese source text was still unidentified.

Another example is a Tangut manuscript entitled *Newly Collected Records of Parental Love and Filial Piety*, of which only the last volume survives.[17] According to a note at the beginning of the volume, the text had been 'translated and reassembled' by a Chinese person whose name could be reconstructed as Cao Dao'an 曹道安 or Cao Daole 曹道樂. The note, however, did not resolve the question of the degree of this person's involvement in the construction of the text, and whether he was the author or translator. The Russian scholar Ksenia B. Kepping published a monograph with a study and a translation, and in this she reiterated Nevskij's opinion that the text was compiled from Chinese sources by a Tangut translator.[18] Several years later,

14 Nevskij, *Tangutskaja filologija*, 1, pp. 86–87.

15 Nie, *Xixiawen* Dexingji *yanjiu*, pp. 5–10.

16 Sun, 'Xixiawen *Zhengxingji* kaoshi', pp. 87–94.

17 Gorbacheva, and Kychanov, *Tangutskie rukopisi i ksilografy*, p. 56.

18 Nevskij, *Tangutskaja filologija*, 1, p. 86; Kepping, *Vnov' sobrannye zapiski*, p. 9.

however, Chinese scholars suggested that the entire work a translation from a Chinese original.[19] Efforts to locate the source text led to matching individual passages with — sometimes much earlier — precedents in Chinese historical and literary works, without being able to identify the direct source of the entire compilation.[20] It was only in 2009 that Nie Hongyin demonstrated a close connection of the Tangut text to Sima Guang's 司馬光 (1001–1086) *Jiafan* 家範 (Family Models), a work from the Song period, relatively close in time to the Tangut version.[21] Even though the *Jiafan* is not identical with the Tangut version, there are numerous parallels between the two both in overall composition and on the level of individual stories, and the similarities seem to corroborate the theory that the Tangut text could not have been entirely composed by a translator-cum-editor, at least not without relying on an existing Chinese model. Our inability to locate a Chinese text that is closer to the Tangut text than Sima Guang's *Jiafan*, understandably brings the issue of adaptation into the foreground.

These two examples show how in the course of the past two decades one of the original fifteen items in the 'Original Tangut texts' category turned out to be a direct translation from Chinese, and another one a compilation that was either translated from or closely modelled after an existing Chinese text. Although this is merely two texts out of fifteen, it demonstrates how our understanding of the relationship between Tangut and Chinese texts may change as we discover more and more connections between texts in these two languages. Without suggesting that any more of the remaining titles will turn out to be straightforward translations, it is clear that our perception of the nature of surviving Tangut texts continues to evolve.

The change in perception is not limited to the 'Original Tangut texts' category of the catalogue. Some of the texts in other categories or those not listed in the catalogue have also been reinterpreted and their relationship with potential source texts has been clarified. A case in point is item no. 5 in the category 'Translations from Chinese', listed there as 'Untitled'. Even without a title it was clear that this was a collection of quotes from Chinese sources, which is why it was considered a translation of a lost Chinese work. Based on its content, Chinese scholars tentatively titled it **Jingshi zachao* 經史雜抄 (*Excerpts from the Classics and Histories) and with time it became apparent that it was closely related to the *Xinji wenci jiujing chao* 新集文詞九經鈔 (Newly Collected Words and Phrases from the Nine Classics), a collection of loose quotes from Confucian works specifically targeting beginners.[22] The Chinese text had been lost sometime before the modern era but copies of it were discovered among the Dunhuang manuscripts. Although it was clear

19 Shi and Nie, 'Ecang Xixiawen shisu wenxian mulu', pp. 87–95.

20 Kepping, *Vnov' Sobrannye zapiski*; and Jacques, *Textes tangoutes*.

21 Nie, *Xixiawen* Xinji cixiao zhuan *yanjiu*.

22 Nie, 'Xixiaben *Jingshi zachao* chutan'; and Huang, 'Xixiawen *Jingshi zachao* kaoyuan'.

that the Tangut text was not a translation of the Chinese, there were many common points, including specific mistakes in the quotes, the presence of which attested to a direct connection between the two texts.

Yet another text that illustrates a shift in our understanding is a manuscript, the title of which was translated into Russian as *Record at the Altar about Confucius's Conciliation* and subsequently into Chinese as *Kongzi hetan ji* 孔子和壇記.[23] The text retells the story of Confucius meeting an old sage and learning from him a type of wisdom that transcends what he himself had been propagating. Noticing the similarity of the plot with the 'Old Fisherman' chapter of the *Zhuangzi* 莊子 from over a millennium earlier, Kychanov suggested that this may have been a lost version of a story describing the meeting of Confucius and the Daoist sage Laozi 老子. Nie Hongyin, however, correctly noted that this must have been a translation of a text that was relatively close to the time of the Tangut translator, and drew attention to the difficulties in interpreting the word *he* 和 ('peace, conciliation') in the title.[24] In a recent study, tracing the story in the Chinese tradition, I have shown that the original title must have been *Fuzi xingtan ji* 夫子杏壇記 (Record of the Master at the Apricot Platform).[25] I was also able to locate a related Chinese version of the story in a sixteenth-century edition of a popular religious work, providing tangible evidence of the existence of a literary tradition involving this story, even if it was not a word-for-word match to the Tangut manuscript.[26]

This brings us to the issue of adaptation. Assumptions about the translator's intervention have been commonly voiced for texts with matching Chinese counterparts. In a number of instances, discrepancies between translation and source text were clearly the result of intentional adaptation on the part of the translator, who may have introduced details in order to make the translation more suitable for a Tangut audience. In her study of the Tangut translation of the famous military treatise *Sunzi*, Kepping addressed the issue of adaptation in some detail.[27] She observed that translations of the Confucian Classics have been completed with great accuracy, whereas the translator of the *Sunzi* allowed himself much more flexibility and introduced a range of changes in order to make the text more accessible for his readers. Thus, the translator used everyday terms in place of abstract ones; omitted metaphors and allegories or translated them in a descriptive manner; had a preference for being descriptive when rendering military terms; added contextual details for names by specifying where a person was from or whether a toponym referred to a city, a state, or a region. Kepping was undoubtedly correct in her analysis and the translator must have implemented many smaller adjustments, since

23 Kychanov, *Zapis' u altarja o primirenii Konfutsija*.

24 Nie, '*Kongzi hetan ji* de Xixia yiben'.

25 The Apricot Platform was the place where, according to the Confucian tradition, Confucius taught his disciples.

26 Galambos, 'Confucius and Laozi at the Altar'.

27 Kepping, *Sun'dzy v tangutskom perevode*, pp. 19–24.

his readers lacked much of the historical and cultural background that would have been obvious for Chinese readers. Turning to larger divergences between the Chinese original and the translation, such as the occasional addition or omission of commentary entries, Kepping came to the conclusion that these must have been the result of the translator using a source text that differed from the editions that have come down to us.[28] Considering the thorough standardization of military works during the Song dynasty, and the scarcity of surviving textual witnesses from the preceding centuries, this conjecture is not only reasonable but also very likely.

Yet in other cases Kepping continued to emphasize the role of translator in reshaping the source text. One such example is her discussion of another military work called *Jiangyuan* 將苑 (The General's Garden), the Chinese version of which has the sentence 'when folly overcomes wisdom, this is going against the current' 以愚克智逆也. The Tangut translation of the text in place of the expression 'going against the current' uses the word *ljo* ('good luck, fortune'). Trying to resolve the seeming contradiction why folly overcoming wisdom would be considered good luck, Kepping suggested that the Tangut word should be understood in this place as 'supernatural' and that the general point of the statement was that the victory of folly over wisdom was a phenomenon that went against the normal course of nature.[29] She considered this case an example of the type of adaptations Tangut translators introduced into the text. However, some of the sixteenth- and seventeenth-century editions of the Chinese text have the word *ming* 命 ('fate, fortune') in place of *ni* 逆 ('to go against the current'), which is a reasonable match for the Tangut translation and eliminates the need to explain the translation as an adaptation. Thus, the Tangut text simply says — matching some of the early editions — that 'when folly overcomes wisdom, this is a matter of fate'. In other words, the Tangut translator relied on a version with the word *ming* in it, which matches the earliest surviving Chinese editions but not the edition in common circulation today.[30]

Conclusions

The above examples attempt to shed light on how our perception of Tangut translations changed in the past decades. Taking the 1963 catalogue as our departure point, we have seen the initial emphasis on non-Buddhist texts, despite the fact that the vast majority of surviving Tangut material is Buddhist in content. Although there has always been some interest in Buddhist texts,[31]

28 Kepping, *Sun'dzy v tangutskom perevode*, p. 18.

29 Kep[p]ing and Gong 'Zhuge Liang's "The General's Garden"', pp. 18–19.

30 Galambos, *Translating Chinese Tradition*, pp. 236–37.

31 See, for example, Nishida Tatsuo's monumental study of the *Avataṃsaka sūtra* (Nishida, *Seikabun Kegonkyō*).

until the late 1980s Russian and Chinese scholars primarily focused their attention on the non-Buddhist part of the collection. Naturally, this was a much wider scholarly trend (primarily in China), not limited to Tangut studies. Since then, the study of Tangut Buddhism has been on the rise and is today one of the main directions of research throughout the world.[32] In addition, the Buddhist material is also regularly used in other fields, such as linguistics and art history.[33]

With regards to the relationship of Tangut texts to their potential Chinese sources, we have seen that the 1963 catalogue made a division between translations, which were invariably from Chinese, and texts perceived as original Tangut compositions. The division was relatively arbitrary but it provided a basic breakdown of the material that at the time was still largely unpublished. Later scholarship, however, improved our understanding of particular texts and one of those listed as a native text turned out to be a translation. Another text was shown to be closely related to a known Song-dynasty text and was likely also a translation. Few as they are, these examples demonstrate how limited our knowledge of contemporary Chinese literature still is. If anything, the Tangut manuscripts and printed books discovered at Khara-khoto serve to remind us to be careful to consider the possibility that when we cannot match a Tangut text to a Chinese one, this may be because the Chinese text was lost before the modern period.

As to texts listed in the catalogue under the 'Translations from Chinese' category, in some cases subsequent research has been able to clarify their relationship with the Chinese source text. Whenever we can locate the Chinese version of the text, we typically gain a much better understanding of the context and function of the translation, which are often extremely difficult to reconstruct from fragments that survive in Tangut only. In addition, access to the Chinese version greatly benefits our ability to decipher the text accurately and provides an opportunity to study the process and techniques of translation.

Even texts confidently identified as translations of known Chinese works, when differing from the received versions of the source text, are in some cases considered to reflect a creative intervention on the part of the translators. This may very well be the case but there are also examples when textual scholarship is able to locate variant editions or manuscripts that are closer to the Tangut version. In many cases the assumption that a particular discrepancy is the result of intentional adaptation will remain a hypothesis that can never be positively proved, only disproved.

---

32 Just to cite a few representative works, see Shi, *Xixia fojiao shilue*; Matsuzawa, 'Seika bunken shūi *Ga zō Karahoto*'; Matsuzawa, 'Sutain shōrai Karahoto chutsudo Seika bunken ni tsuite'; Solonin, 'Hongzhou Buddhism in Xixia'; Solonin, 'Sinitic Buddhism in the Tangut state', 157–83; and Arakawa, *Seikabun Kongōkyō no kenkyū*.

33 For example, Sun, 'A Textual Research on the Tangut Version of "Bazhong cuzhongfanduo"'; Linrothe, 'Xia Renzong and the Patronage of Tangut Buddhist Art'.

Considering the various scenarios outlined above, it is striking that in some of the cases it is difficult to decide whether a particular Tangut text should be considered a translation, an adaptation, or a native compilation. These examples show that not all texts can be grouped under these binary divisions but there are quite a number of intermediate possibilities between faithful translation to native composition. If a text consists of content culled from Chinese histories that was brought together and arranged into its final form by a Tangut individual, should we regard this as a native Tangut text? What if this individual was a Chinese person living in the Tangut state? It is entirely possible that such a collection would have been first compiled in Chinese, even if for the sake of having it immediately translated into Tangut. It is also possible that the Chinese prototype was then also circulated. Such cases blur the borderline between native texts and translations and it is not hard to see that some of the titles listed in the 1963 catalogue are precisely of this kind. The Tangut state was a multilingual and multicultural empire where Tangut and Chinese were both in use. The types of texts that survive attest to this complex situation.

On a final note, we should remember that Buddhist texts in Tangut comprise a much larger pool of material, and include both native compositions and translations from Chinese and Tibetan. Therefore, this material has an even greater potential for the study of translations to and from Tangut, involving several other languages.

Bibliography

Arakawa Shintarō 荒川慎太郎, *Seikabun Kongōkyō no kenkyū* 西夏文金剛経の研究 (Kyoto: Shōkadō, 2014)

Bushell, Stephen W., 'The Tangut Script in the Nank'ou Pass', *The China Review*, 24.2 (1899), 5–68

Clauson, Gerard, *Gerard Clauson's Skeleton Tangut (Hsi Hsia) Dictionary: A Facsimile Edition* (Portlaoise: Evertype, 2016)

Galambos, Imre, 'The Northern Neighbors of the Tangut', *Cahiers de Linguistique – Asie Orientale*, 40 (2011), 69–104

——, *Translating Chinese Tradition and Teaching Tangut Culture* (Berlin: de Gruyter, 2015)

——, 'Confucius and Laozi at the Altar: Reconsidering a Tangut Manuscript', *Studies in Chinese Religions*, 2.3 (2016), 237–64

Gernet, Jacques, and Wu Chi-Yu, *Catalogue des manuscrits chinois de Touen-houang (Fonds Pelliot chinois), Volume I, N°s 2001–2500* (Paris: Bibliothèque nationale, 1970)

Gorbacheva, Zoja I., and Evgenij I. Kychanov, *Tangutskie rukopisi i ksilografy* (Moscow: Nauka, 1963)

Huang Yanjun 黃延軍, 'Xixiawen Jingshi zachao kaoyuan' 西夏文《經史雜抄》考源. *Minzu yanjiu* 民族研究, 2 (2009), 97–103

Jacques, Guillaume, *Textes tangoutes I: Le nouveau recueil sur l'amour parental et la piété filiale* (München: Lincom Europa, 2007)

Kepping, Ksenija B., *Sun'dzy v tangutskom perevode* (Moscow: Nauka, 1979)

——, *Les Kategorij: utrachennaja kitajskaja lejshu v tangutskom perevode* (Moscow: Nauka, 1983)

——, *Vnov' sobrannye zapiski o ljubvi k mladshim i pochtenii k starshim* (Moscow: Nauka, 1990)

Kep[p]ing, Ksenia, and Gong Hwang-cherng, 'Zhuge Liang's "The General's Garden" in the Mi-nia Translation', in Ksenia Kep[p]ing, *Last Works and Documents* (St Petersburg: Omega,2003), pp. 13–23

Kolokolov, Vsevolod S. and Evgenij I. Kychanov, *Kitajskaja klassika v tangutskom perevode (Lun' juj, Men dzy, Sjao tzyn)* (Moscow: Nauka, 1966)

Kychanov, Evgenij I., *Katalog tangutskikh buddijskikh pamjatnikov Instituta vostokovedenija Rossijskoj Akademii Nauk* (Kyoto: Kyoto University, 1999)

——, *Zapis' u altarja o primirenii Konfutsija* (Moscow: Vostochnaja Literatura, 2000)

Linrothe, Rob, 'Xia Renzong and the Patronage of Tangut Buddhist Art: The Stūpa and Ushnīshavijayā Cult', *Journal of Song-Yuan Studies*, 28 (1998), 91–121

Marakhonova, S. I., 'Institut vostokovedenija AN SSSR v Leningrade v gody vojny I blokady', *Pis'mennye pamjatniki vostoka*, 1.8 (2008), 21–36

Matsuzawa Hiroshi 松澤博, 'Seika bunken shūi *Ga zō Karahoto bunken* shoshū dampen shiryō wo chūshin to shite' 西夏文獻拾遺『俄藏黒水城文献』所収斷片資料を中心として, *Ryūkoku shidan* 龍谷史壇, 116 (2001), 1–93

——, 'Sutain shōrai Karahoto chutsudo Seika bunken ni tsuite' スタイン將來黒水城出土西夏文獻について, *Tōyō shien* 東洋史苑, 77 (2011), 1–126

Men'shikov, Lev N., M. I. Vorob'eva-Desjatovskaja, I. S. Gurevich, V. S. Spirin, and S. A. Shkoljar, *Opisanie kitajskikh rukopisej Dun'khuanskogo fonda Instituta narodov Azii, Vypusk 1* (Moscow: Izdatel'stvo vostochnoj literatury, 1963)

Men'shikov, Lev N., M. I. Vorob'eva-Desjatovskaja, I. T. Zograf, A. S. Martynov, and B. L. Smirnov, *Opisanie kitajskikh rukopisej Dun'khuanskogo fonda Instituta narodov Azii, Vypusk 2* (Moscow: Izdatel'stvo Nauka, 1967)

Morisse, M. G., *Contribution preliminaire à l'étude de l'écriture et de la langue Si-hia* (Paris: Imprimerie nationale, 1904)

Nevskij, Nikolaj A., *Tangutskaja filologija: issledovanija i slovar'*, 2 vols (Moscow: Nauka, 1960)

Nie Hongyin 聶鴻音, *Xixiawen* Dexingji *yanjiu* 西夏文《德行集》研究 (Lanzhou: Gansu wenhua chubanshe, 2002)

——, 'Xixiaben *Jingshi zachao* chutan' 西夏本《經史雜抄》初探 *Ningxia shehui kexue* 寧夏社會科學, 5 (2002), 84–86

——, '*Kongzi hetan ji* de Xixia yiben' 《孔子和壇記》的西夏本譯, *Minzu yanjiu* 民族研究, 3 (2008), 89–95

——, *Xixiawen* Xinji cixiao zhuan *yanjiu* 西夏文《新集慈孝傳》研究 (Yinchuan: Ningxia renmin chubanshe, 2009)

Nishida Tatsuo 西田龍雄, *Seikabun Kegonkyō* 西夏文華嚴經, 3 vols (Kyoto: Kyōto daigaku Bungakubu, 1975–1977)

——, *Seikabun Kegonkyō III* 西夏文華厳経 III (*The Hsi-Hsia Avataṃsaka Sūtra, Volume III*) (Kyoto: Faculty of Letters, Kyoto University, 1977)

Pelliot, Paul, 'Les documents chinois trouvés par la mission Kozlov à Khara-Khoto', *Journal Asiatique*, 11e série 3 (1914), 503–18

Shi Jinbo 史金波, *Xixia fojiao shilüe* 西夏佛教史略 (Yinchuan: Ningxia renmin chubanshe, 1988)

Shi Jinbo 史金波 and Nie Hongyin, 'Ecang Xixiawen shisu wenxian mulu' 俄藏西夏文世俗文獻目錄, *Chuantong wenhua yu xiandaihua* 傳統文化與現代化, 2 (1998), 87–95

Solonin, Kirill Ju., 'Hongzhou Buddhism in Xixia and the Heritage of Zongmi (780–841): A Tangut Source', *Asia Major*, 16.2 (2003), 57–103

——, 'Sinitic Buddhism in the Tangut State', *Central Asiatic Journal*, 57 (2014), 157–83

Soymié, Michel, Jean-Pierre Drège, Dzo Ching-chuan, Danielle Eliasberg, Hou Ching-lang, Paul Magnin, Marie-Pascale Monnier, Marie-Claire Quiquemelle, Richard Schneider, Eric Trombert, and Wu Chi-yu, *Catalogue des manuscrits chinois de Touen-houang, Fonds Pelliot chinois de la Bibliothèque nationale, Volume III, N*os *3001–3500* (Paris: Éditions de la Fondation Singer-Polignac, 1983)

Soymié, Michel, Jean-Pierre Drège, Danielle Eliasberg, Paul Magnin, Christine Mollier, Richard Schneider, and Eric Trombert, *Catalogue des manuscrits chinois de Touen-houang, Fonds Pelliot chinois de la Bibliothèque nationale, Volume IV, N*os *3501–4000* (Paris: École française d'Extrême-Orient, 1991)

Soymié, Michel, Jean-Pierre Drège, Danielle Eliasberg, Paul Magnin, Christine Mollier, Richard Schneider, Eric Trombert, Françoise Wang-Toutain, Zhang

Guangda, and Alain Thote, *Catalogue des manuscrits chinois de Touen-houang, Fonds Pelliot chinois de la Bibliothèque nationale, Volume V, N*[os] *4001–6040* (Paris: Éditions de la Fondation Singer-Polignac, 1995)

Sun Bojun 孫伯君, 'Xixiawen *Zhengxingji* kaoshi' 西夏文《正行集》考釋, *Ningxia shehui kexue*, 1.164 (2011), 87–94

Sun, Bojun, 'A Textual Research on the Tangut Version of "Bazhong cuzhongfanduo" Excavated from Khara-Khoto', in *Tanguty v Tsentral'noj Azii: Sbornik Statej v Chest' 80-letija Prof. E. I. Kychanova*, ed. by Irina Popova (Moscow: Oriental Literature, 2012), pp. 437–42

Vasil'kov, Jaroslav V. and Marina Ju. Sorokina, *Ljudi i sud'by: Bibliograficheskij slovar' vostokovedov – zhertv politicheskogo terrora v sovetskij period (1917–1991)* (St Petersburg: Peterburgskoe vostokovedenie, 2003)

MIRIAM L. HJÄLM

Biblical Theology, Scholarly Approaches, and the Bible in Arabic

A century or two after the Muslim conquests in the seventh century, a substantial number of Near Eastern Christians increasingly adopted Arabic as a trade language, a cultural-intellectual *lingua franca*, and, at least partly, as a vernacular and a liturgical language. Arabic was already spoken by Arab Christian tribes in the area yet during the early Abbasid period, Christians of diverse provenance were increasingly Arabized and commenced an extensive translation process wherein a large portion of their religious heritage, including biblical books, was translated mainly from Greek and Syriac. Over the centuries, a great number of Arabic Bible renditions — and revisions of these — appeared, which reflect various *Vorlagen*, translation techniques, functions, and communal interests.

The study of the Bible in its Arabic garb is still struggling to uncover and describe basic features of this corpus. Only sparse information has come down to us from which we may try to reconstruct the purpose, use, and perception of these translations. In the first part of this chapter, observations from the production and character of Arabic Bible translations are offered and searched for clues to their contextual settings. The second part focuses on the purposes that motivated modern scholars to approach the corpus of Christian Arabic translations and tries to catch shifts in focus that caused research to choose new routes. In the third part, trends in contemporary scholarship relating to the field are discussed. Throughout the survey, we will keep an eye to how

* This paper was written with the support of the Swedish Research Council (2017–01630). I sincerely wish to thank Sonja Brentjes, Jens Høyrup, and Bruce O'Brien for their valuable comments and improvements on the draft version.

Miriam Lindgren Hjälm (miriam.hjalm@sanktignatios.org) is senior lecturer in Eastern Christian Studies at Stockholm School of Theology, Sankt Ignatios College. Before that, she was a member of *the Biblia Arabica* project at Ludwig-Maximilians-Universität Munich (2015–2017). Her research focuses on premodern Bible translations composed by Christian Arabic speakers and on use and perception of the Bible among these communities. In addition, she is interested in the Jewish-Christian interactions that took place in the East in medieval times. Her publications include *Christian Arabic Versions of Daniel* (Brill, 2016), and *Senses of Scriptures, Treasures of Tradition* (ed., Brill, 2017).

Narratives on Translation across Eurasia and Africa: From Babylonia to Colonial India, ed. by Sonja Brentjes in cooperation with Jens Høyrup and Bruce O'Brien, CAT 3, pp. 135–156 (Turnhout: Brepols, 2022) BREPOLS PUBLISHERS 10.1484/M.CAT-EB.5.127938

'the Bible in Arabic' reflects notions of Scripture prevalent in the society in which these compositions were made or studied.

It is impossible to wholly cover the rich and multifaceted sources in the current study. Thus, the results herein are preliminary, yet to the best of my knowledge representative.[1]

Arabic Bible Translations in the Near East

An overview of extant Arabic material indicates that certain biblical books were frequently reproduced and thus responded to a communal interest, whereas others did not, or only marginally so. The uneven use and the hierarchical status of biblical books are more discernable before the technical advancements in the modern era made it possible to reproduce the voluminous content of the Bible in identical copies. For instance, in the early Islamic era (eighth–tenth centuries), the Book of Daniel and the Book of Job are overrepresented. The choice to translate the apocalypses in Daniel describing various empires that will rise and fall, as well as the sufferings of the righteous Job, suggest that these topics were important for Christians, likely as a means of tackling the new societal stresses brought by Islam.

Whereas some biblical books were produced in a high number, others were seemingly not translated until the sixteenth century when complete versions of the Bible were produced in connection to Western missionary activities, a topic to which we will return below. In addition, lists of canonical Bible books composed in Near Eastern communities exhibit notable variation and obscurities. Thus, the discussions on the biblical canon, which became so important in modern times, apparently did not play a significant and practical role in these communities in late antique and medieval times. There is a substantial overrepresentation of Gospels, Epistles, and Psalms; i.e. books that were frequently used during liturgy in their entirety.[2] We may conclude, then, that a primary reason to translate biblical books was to supply Christians with a liturgy in a language ordinary people understood after the Arabization of Christians in the Near East had occurred, at least in certain areas.[3]

Yet, far from all manuscripts containing Arabic Bible translations include liturgical marks and divisions. Some translations are characterized by non-literal translation techniques such as explicative additions, short commentaries, or

---

1 I am trained in Semitic languages and philology and currently hold a position in Eastern Christian Studies where I focus on historical aspects, translation, and use of the Bible. These perspectives will dominate the scope of the current chapter. To my knowledge, Arabic Bible translations are rarely discussed in translational studies. On the use of Arabic Bibles in literary studies, see n. 42 below.

2 In contrast, Esther and some deuterocanonical books are not found in the early corpus. On the production of Arabic Bible translations, see Hjälm, 'The Arabic Canon'; Hjälm, 'Hazy Edges', pp. 569–87.

3 Cf. Griffith, 'When Did the Bible Become an Arabic Scripture?', pp. 20–21.

expansions, apparently a result of literary concerns, which seemingly made them unfit for liturgical use. Instead, they appear to have served exegetical and literary purposes. Many non-literal renditions of this kind are based on the standard Syriac Bible version, the Peshitta, and are frequently attested especially in Arabic Old Testament translations produced up to the printing era.

We seldom find the type of 'mirror-translations' associated with the Jewish Karaites as a means of instructing students in biblical Hebrew. In early Islamic times, the Karaites used the advantage of the similarities in structure and vocabulary offered by the two Semitic languages, Hebrew and Arabic, to create 'see-through' texts.[4] With some exceptions, it appears that Christian Arabic speakers, regardless of Church affiliation,[5] focused on the reader-audience, yet these renditions are not necessarily self-contained in the sense that they were made to replace their source texts. It has been argued that some Christians wished to contest the Muslim notion of *iʿjāz* (the inimitability of the Qurʾān) by rendering the Christian Scripture into Arabic translations that reflected the elevated biblical language as they understood it.[6] It has also been suggested in connection to early translators that some dressed their Holy Writ in a typically 'Islamic vocabulary' (cf. below) either as a missionary strategy, or because Christians shared a theological language with Muslims.[7]

Thus, judged by their translational character, Arabic translations must have served a range of different purposes, depending on audience, time, and geographical location.[8] Arabic renditions were often revised or, at least up to around the thirteenth century, replaced by new translations, which indicates that they functioned in parallel to biblical texts written in Syriac, Greek, Coptic, and Latin. Furthermore, a substantial number of manuscripts are bilingual or contain up to five different languages, arranged in parallel columns, which enables a close study of the same biblical passage in various versions. In the thirteenth and fourteenth centuries in particular, certain renditions began to be standardized although new translations and revisions still appeared. Before we move into the modern era, it is worthwhile to have a deeper look into some extra-textual material in an attempt to trace some further aspects of the notion of Scripture in these communities.

---

4 For instance, Judaeo-Arabic translators could coin artificial Arabic words so that the translation would become as transparent as possible vis-à-vis the Hebrew source text, see Polliack, *The Karaite Tradition*, pp. 173–74.

5 Arabic-speaking Christians were mainly divided into Byzantine/*Rūm* Orthodox (Melkite), East Syriac (Nestorian), West Syriac (Jacobite), and Coptic communities (later also Maronite).

6 Sadan, 'In the Eyes of the Christian Writer al-Ḥārit', pp. 1–26.

7 Hjälm, 'Scriptures beyond Words' pp. 49–69; Leemhuis, Klijn, and Van Gelder, *The Arabic Text of the Apocalypse of Baruch*, p. 5; Drint, 'Some Notes', pp. 171–72.

8 For comparative summaries of translation techniques in early Arabic renditions, see Hjälm, *Christian Arabic Versions*, esp. pp. 377–98; Hjälm, 'Scriptures beyond Words', pp. 53–65.

We know from scribal notes that copies were requested from monks at different monasteries, or from other learned men, and that they were bought and sold before a large number of translations finally ended up at the library of Saint Catherine's Monastery in Sinai. Many premodern manuscripts are annotated with marginal notes. Such comments may include longer interpretations or short references connecting biblical and historical events. Most often, these notes are made up of single glosses with reference to a biblical *Vorlage* or to renderings in a different Arabic translation, as well as various kinds of extra-textual markers such as alternative chapter divisions, typically noted when a translation was borrowed from a Christian denomination with a different biblical tradition. Thus, there is an unmistaken interest in the multitude of biblical *Vorlagen*, including the Hebrew text, in several copies, especially Coptic and Andalusi ones.[9] Yet, such notes should not necessarily always be regarded as showing an interest in the original version of the Bible but also a care to reflect 'Tradition' as it has come down to the community. This is exceptionally clear in the Coptic case where 'maximalist' biblical versions were created in which non-protocanonical material was sometimes incorporated where it seemed to fit in historically and literarily.[10]

A number of premodern Arabic introductions to biblical books have survived. These prologues normally focus on the content and theological meaning of the biblical books to which they are attached rather than informing us why they were made or how they were used. We do know that some translations supplied with commentaries were composed by highly educated men, such as Abū al-Faraj ibn al-Ṭayyib (d. 1043) and the contemporary scholar ʿAbdallāh ibn al-Faḍl al-Anṭākī, both known for their theological and philosophical works.[11] Thus, the activity of copying was seemingly part of the intellectual and pietistic life of monasteries and commenting and writing introductions in particular were tasks connected to intellectual activity on the highest communal level, where exegetical works were integrated with philosophical principles and theories of knowledge.

Of particular interest for the perception of the Bible in the early era of the Arabic Bible production is al-Ḥārith b. Sinān b. Sunbāṭ's introduction to the Pentateuch. Seemingly, al-Ḥārith was active in the tenth century in Ḥarrān, in modern Turkey. In his introduction, we learn that his client, who requested the Arabic translation of the Septuagint, is unsettled with the Arabic translations from the Syriac Peshitta (*al-tafsīr al-baṣīṭ*) he has read, since these are 'full of shortcomings'. Al-Ḥārith then relates the transmission

9 Cf. Vollandt, 'The Conundrum', pp. 66–76.

10 Both deuterocanonical biblical books and what are today labelled Apocrypha were incorporated in Arabic translations of Daniel, Jeremiah and probably other books. Cf. Sucio, 'Jeremiah's Prophecy to Pesher', forthcoming; Hjälm, 'The Christian Arabic Book of Daniel', pp. 115–78.

11 Faultless, 'Ibn al-Ṭayyib', pp. 667–97; Treiger, 'Abdallāh ibn al-Faḍl al-Antākī', pp. 89–113.

history of the Septuagint and we are told that there are six Greek renditions: that by the seventy-two (i.e. the Septuagint); those by Aquila, Symmachus, and Theodotion; and two anonymous ones. He then states that the Church Father Origen (d. *c.* 253) compared various Greek versions with the Hebrew text (cf. the Hexapla) and, according to our scribe, arranged these texts in eight columns. Al-Hārith must have had at least partial access to such a work, since he provides examples of these renditions in Arabic letters.[12]

The 'struggle over Scripture' that took place between Jews, Christians, and Muslims in this environment seemingly impelled Christians to create and reinforce narratives on the reception of Scripture to mark their ownership over this contested heritage. Al-Ḥārith did not mince his words when accusing the Jews of being unable to understand the Scriptures they had transmitted. Yet, tacitly he had to acknowledge the role of the Jews in conveying and translating the Scriptures, whose reliable Greek transmission he is then vouching for. A more outright criticism of the Jews was voiced by the tenth-century writer and historian Agapius of Manbij (in modern Syria). Agapius rebukes his peers for using the Syriac version of the Bible, the Peshitta, because it is based on the 'distorted' Hebrew text where Messianic information was deliberately hidden by Jewish leaders.[13] Already in early Patristic times, some Christians accused Jews of having tampered with Scripture in order to hide passages proving that Jesus was the Messiah. Such passages include entire biblical books (deuterocanonical books such as Wisdom and Baruch), or only certain key words and phrases. However important this narrative was for the Christian appropriation of the Hebrew Scriptures in its Greek dress in Patristic times, the significance of the correct version of the Bible must have been no less important under Islam, at least in certain contexts, where not only specific renderings but the entire reception of God's words were put into question by the existence of the Qur'ān: God's words sent down to Muḥammad. Muslims too soon noted that the Hebrew version and the Greek Septuagint differed in many details.[14]

* * *

Up to the sixteenth century, the history of the Bible in Arabic developed rather independently from the West and, as we will soon see, the treatment of it in the West was for a long time largely detached from its Near Eastern context. However, there were times in history when East and West met and

---

12 For relevant manuscripts, see Vollandt, *Arabic Versions*, pp. 60–62. I have prepared a study on al-Ḥārith and the sources discussed above, which will be forthcoming by the title 'Texts Attributed to al-Ḥāriṯ b. Sinān b. Sinbāṭ al-Ḥarrānī: Notes on Prologues, Translation Techniques and New Manuscripts'.

13 Cf. Treiger, 'From Theodore Abū Qurra', pp. 11–57; Lamoreaux, 'Agapius of Manbij', pp. 136–59.

14 On so-called *taḥrīf*, i.e. distortion of the meaning or form of the original version of the Bible, see among others, Accad, 'Muḥammad's Advent', pp. 218–19; Adang, *Muslim Writers*, pp. 223–24; Keating, 'Revisiting the Charge of Taḥrīf', pp. 211–16. On Christian *kalām*, see for instance Thomas, 'The Bible and the *Kalām*', pp. 175–91.

interacted intensively, in particular in the early missionary era, right before the dawn of biblical criticism.

The invention of the printing press and the rifts within the Roman Catholic Church in the sixteenth century came to shape the modern history of Eastern Christianity in general and that of the Bible in Arabic in particular to a remarkable degree. Motivated by the opportunity to enlarge their ecclesiastical jurisdictions, Roman Catholics readily utilized printed Arabic Bible translations for missionary purposes and successfully attracted converts from Orthodox and Oriental churches (rather than from among Muslims), so that fractions from them, the so-called 'Uniate churches' or 'Eastern Catholic churches', entered into communion with Rome.[15] To various extents, native speakers from these communities were involved in producing complete Arabic translations of the Bible sponsored by Catholic institutions (cf. the *Sacra Congregatio de Propaganda Fide*). At the first stage, extant Arabic manuscripts were adopted and to various degrees brought in line with the Latin Vulgate and its canon before they were sent back to Near Eastern Christians under Catholic jurisdiction (cf. the *Biblia Sacra Arabica:* 1671–1673).[16] In due time, Presbyterians, Anglicans, and other Protestant Christians followed suit on route to harvesting souls in the area. As a consequence, and often under the auspices of Bible societies, several Protestant Bibles appeared, including the popular Smith-Bustānī-van Dyke Bible (1865), sponsored by the American Bible Society.[17] So great was the influence and accessibility of these Bibles that Christians who remained in communion with the Eastern Orthodox and the Oriental churches to various degrees began to use these translations as well.[18]

As in any modern language, the work of producing translations suitable for various creeds, audiences, and purposes never ceases and new translations or revisions of popular Arabic Bibles constantly appear.

Studies of Arabic Bible Translations in the West

The subversion of the Catholic Church as the guarantor of the correct transmission and interpretation of Scripture, in parallel to an unquenchable

15 On this process, see for instance Haddad, 'On the Melkite Passage to the Unia', pp. 67–90; Walbiner, 'Melkite (Greek Orthodox) Approaches', pp. 53–61; and Kilpatrick, 'Meletius', pp. 63–73.

16 On the *Biblia Sacra Arabica*, see for instance Vollandt, 'Che portono', pp. 401–18 and Féghali 'The Holy Books', pp. 37–51.

17 On the so-called van Dyke Bible, see Issa, 'Biblical Reflections', pp. 58–67; Grafton, *The Contested Origins*, pp. 1–41; Binay, 'Revision', pp. 75–84. Protestant missionaries were in general more committed to texts in the original languages, than to the rich tradition of Arabic Bible translations. The Anglican missionary and translator Henry Martyn (d. 1812), for instance, argues that previous translations are unimportant. Many thanks to Rana Issa for discussing the topic with me.

18 Hjälm, 'Arabic Texts', pp. 483–95 and further references there.

thirst for the original biblical version, resulted in notable scholarly interest in ancient Bible versions in the sixteenth and seventeenth centuries. As Alastair Hamilton has shown, reformists such as William Bedwell (d. 1632) saw in Christian Arabic sources potential allies, i.e. a simple form of Christianity freed from 'papism' and other disliked Catholic practices.[19] Ronny Vollandt has recently demonstrated the extent to which scholars took pains in finding and studying Arabic renditions of the Bible and how they were included in printed editions destined for a European market, sporadically accompanied by grammars and lexicons.[20]

The focus on philology and the perception of the Bible that motivated these impressive compositions becomes especially evident in the production of Polyglots by both Roman Catholics and Reformists. These Polyglots, wherein ancient versions of the Bible were printed side by side, were produced right before 'the collapse of *historia sacra*' and the rise of biblical criticism that ultimately relegated ancient texts to editorial notes.[21] Of great interest in this regard are the thoughts of the Anglican archbishop Brian Walton (d. 1661), the compiler of the famous London Polyglot (1653–1657). Walton defended the existence of the original text, the inspired word of God, but acknowledged that since it was entrusted into faulty human hands, every now and then the sacred text had been corrupted. In his eyes, the truth is found somewhere between ancient versions since they reflect a less corrupted time closer to the original composition and could therefore be used to solve ambiguities and evident mistakes in the transmitted biblical text. As such, Walton's perspective, quite common in his days, is reminiscent of Origen's, the forefather of biblical polyglots (cf. the Hexapla), mentioned above. It is no surprise then that Walton held Origen in high esteem.[22]

Another assumption that prompted early scholars to include Arabic was that since they were written in a Semitic language, Arabic renditions might throw light on the original Hebrew text. Thus, in Robert Wakefield's work entitled *On the Three Languages* (1524), the author's reverence for the biblical languages (Hebrew and Aramaic), led him to value also their sister language, Arabic.[23]

Walton's monumental work was the last of its kind. The seventeenth century yielded a range of scholarly developments that eventually caused systematic theology — that related to the Bible as a whole — and biblical criticism to part ways.[24] Biblical criticism increasingly ousted other conceptions of the Bible (typically those not concretely measurable) and scholarly enthusiasm for Arabic traditions somewhat faltered. Since these translations are normally

19 Hamilton, *William Bedwell*, p. 79.
20 Vollandt, *Arabic Versions*, esp. pp. 12–14; 109–28.
21 Miller, 'Antiquarianization', p. 472.
22 Miller, 'Antiquarianization', pp. 467–78.
23 Cf. Vollandt, 'Che portono', pp. 401–02.
24 Nellen and Steenbakkers, 'Biblical Philology', pp. 16; 28–36.

tertiary renditions based on Greek, Syriac, or Latin *Vorlagen*, they have little to offer in the search for the Hebrew *Urtext*, its univocal (literal) meaning, and the biblical context. In particular, many of the Syriac-based Arabic translations clearly had a different aim than establishing a literal version of God's written word. The premise that the best text equals the most original (Hebrew) rendering and that this is the truest version of God's words, thus made Arabic Bible translations uninteresting by default and caused most scholars to treat the rich Arabic heritage as marginal notes, at the best.

Although editors normally reached the conclusion that they had little to contribute, Arabic versions, those in the Polyglots in particular, were still consulted in many text-critical works.[25] The increasing attention paid to textual criticism of the Septuagint even made the Arabic tradition moderately interesting. Already in 1784, the German biblical scholar and text-critic Samuel G. Wald approached the Polyglot versions of Daniel, primarily to establish whether or not the Hebrew text was its primary source. By doing so, he noted that it contained the so-called *Greek Additions*, that it was based on Theodotion's Greek rendition, and more explicitly, the Alexandrian recension thereof.[26] The Semitist and exegete Wilhelm Gesenius included the Arabic Polyglot translation in his *Philologisch-kritischen und historischen Commentar über den Jesaia* (1821), and noted that it too represented the Alexandrian recension and contained a special set of divisions, perhaps of a liturgical character.[27] This kind of short, basic description of Arabic Bible translations included in text-critical works or Bible encyclopedias continued to appear during the nineteenth and early twentieth centuries in particular. In general, scholars used translations in the printed missionary works or Polyglots of the early modern era.[28] In Rudolf Kittel's edition of *Biblia Hebraica* (1st edn 1906), for instance, the siglum appertaining to *versio Arabica* refers to the translations of various origins that were incorporated into the Paris Polyglot,[29] without providing the reader with an explanation as to why these Arabic versions were more important for textual criticism than other Arabic renditions. Clearly, this was the Arabic text accessible to scholars at the time and therefore treated as *the* Arabic Bible, as if it was the only, or the official rendition in that language. The extensive Arabic legacy tucked away in monastery libraries in the Middle East was largely unknown to them.[30]

---

25 Cf. Margoliouth, *An Essay on the Place of Ecclesiasticus*, p. 5; cf. Vollandt, *Arabic Versions*, pp. 18–19.

26 Wald, 'Über die Arabische Übersetzung', 204–11.

27 Gesenius, *Der Prophet Jesaia*, esp. pp. 97–106. For further references, see Hjälm, 'Latter Prophets', pp. 723–30.

28 Vollandt, 'Historiographical Remarks', pp. 31–33.

29 Vollandt, *Arabic Versions*, pp. 18–19. Several New Testament editions such as Holmes (1822), Von Tischendorf (1849), and Alford (1859–1871) referred to Arabic manuscripts, yet the latter removed them in later editions, see Vollandt, *Arabic Versions*, pp. 18–19.

30 A large portion of these translations are today available online, for instance through The

Subsequent to the works of the philologist Karl Lachmann (d. 1851), known for his rapture with *textus receptus* and associated with the introduction of a new methodology that aimed at reconstructing the archetypes of texts based on the genealogical relationships of manuscripts, scholars, beginning with Ignazio Guidi (1888), increasingly began to discover and take interest in the variety of Arabic recensions.[31] Around the same time, biblical scholars such as Constantin von Tischendorf (d. 1874) and later the Semitic scholars Agnes Smith Lewis (d. 1926) and her sister Margaret Dunlop Gibson (d. 1920), travelled to the Middle East in search for documents. Thus, the last century has offered a range of works concentrating on finding and describing several translations of the same biblical book. Most notably, the German Orientalist Georg Graf categorized every Arabic translation accessible to him in European and Egyptian libraries and in library catalogues in his *Geschichte der christlichen arabischen Literatur*, vol. 1 (1944). This work is still the most impressive and important contribution to the study of Arabic Bible translations and constitutes a game changer in the Western approach to this rich heritage.

In the decades following World War II, the field saw but sporadic studies of the Arabic Bible but, with regard to this corpus, also an increasing disentanglement of Oriental Studies from Biblical Studies. Furthermore, although Near Eastern Christians had long been consulted about the production of missionary Bibles, scholars from the Middle East now begun to participate in the field in greater numbers and for a variety of reasons. These developments led to a greater focus on the material as witnesses to the Near Eastern context and eventually also to a growing interest in the translations in their own right. Thus, whereas the first shift in focus occurred when biblical criticism began to be separated from (systematic) theology in the seventeenth century, a second major shift is traceable to the past century where scholars were no longer necessarily trained in both Oriental philology and biblical criticism. In the same time, Biblical Studies increasingly developed new approaches, including reception history (see below).

An example that marks this gradual shift in focus is the use of Arabic Bible translations for discussions on the emergence of Islam. Already in 1931, the Orientalist and liturgist Anton Baumstark claimed to find evidence for pre-Islamic Bible translations in some extant manuscripts, such as liturgical marks inserted to indicate when certain biblical passages were read in service that coincided with a more ancient use.[32] The excitement (and provocation) with this theory was that, should it be true, the Christian Bible — and not the Qurʾān — represents the first literary work of significant length composed

Library of Congress: https://www.loc.gov/manuscripts/?q=Sinai. Accessed 3 October 2018.

31 Vollandt, *Arabic Versions*, pp. 16–17.

32 See, for instance, Baumstark, 'Die sonntägliche Evangelienlesung', pp. 350–59. For an overview of the debate, see Kashouh, *The Arabic Versions of the Gospels*, pp. 17–21; 34–35; and Griffith, *The Bible in Arabic*, pp. 46–53.

in Arabic. Other scholars at that time, including Graf and the theologian and Orientalist Arthur Vööbus (1954), questioned these claims and argued that such evidence could be explained elsewise.[33] In the 1980s, the Orientalist Irfan Shahīd gathered an impressive amount of documentation of pre-Islamic Christian material and argued for the *rationale* behind a pre-Islamic use of the Bible in Arabic. He drew attention to the fact that traces of such use should be searched for in liturgy (not the other way around), perhaps already in the fourth century, yet his findings were still based on assumptions, which the author admitted.[34] For instance, the fact that a pagan liturgy had developed in Arabic at the time made it fit to function as a liturgical language, but this does not prove that Christians used it as such, since liturgies in Syriac and Greek could still have fulfilled basic communal needs.[35] Sidney Griffith has lately argued that Christians used oral translations of the Bible in pre-Islamic times. In his opinion, this idea harmonizes well with what we know about the oral culture on the Peninsula as well as contributing to the question of how Muḥammad and his contemporaries came to be familiar with the biblical narratives.[36] Indeed, the Qurʾān is replete with references to these narratives, which gives witness to the wide dispersion of them in the area, albeit often in alternative forms.[37]

As noted above, the language employed in Arabic Bible translations was attended to by Western scholars early on, initially to study Arabic, a cognate language of Hebrew, and such compositions were thus incorporated into chrestomathies and grammars.[38] It was soon noted, however, that the rules of Classical Arabic were not necessarily followed in Christian manuscripts and these divergences were simply labelled bad Arabic.[39] Especially thanks to the efforts of Joshua Blau from the 1960s onwards, interest in these 'mistakes' grew and trends were established in various corpuses and sorted into categories.[40] These features are often termed 'Middle Arabic', and are in fact not restricted

33 Graf, *Geschichte*, I, pp. 142–46; Vööbus, *Early Versions of the New Testament*, pp. 271–97. Here it is argued that old liturgical marks in Arabic Bible manuscripts could simply be translated from an old Greek manuscript. In addition, liturgical change was likely slow and heterogeneously implemented.

34 Shahīd, *Byzantium and the Arabs in the Fourth Century*, pp. 435–43; Shahīd, *Byzantium and the Arabs in the Fifth Century*, pp. 196–99.

35 Shahīd, *Byzantium and the Arabs in the Fourth Century*, pp. 288–93. In like manner, Shahīd suggests that Jerome's recording of the liturgical use of the Syriac word *barekh* 'bless' could very well have been mixed up with the Arabic *bārik* with the same meaning, idem. More recently, Kashouh has argued for the plausibility of a pre-Islamic date of some early translations, Kashouh, *Arabic Versions of the Gospels*, pp. 142–71. However, it is difficult to move beyond speculation here since there is no unequivocal documentation of such use.

36 Griffith, *The Bible in Arabic*, pp. 1–96.

37 For more on the Bible in the Qurʾān, see for instance Reynolds, *The Qurʾān and the Bible*.

38 Vollandt, *Arabic Versions*, pp. 13–14.

39 See for instance, Gibson, *An Arabic version of the Acts of the Apostles*, p. vii.

40 A sum of these trends is found in Blau, *A Handbook of Early Middle Arabic*, pp. 14–56; 68–96.

to Christian texts but found in Muslim texts as well, especially in Arabic documents.[41] Blau's findings are thus an example of how the field of Arabic Bible translations was opened up to linguistic studies outside of the realm of Biblical Studies.[42]

Most of the surveys on the Arabic Bible composed during the last century are, or contain, necessary updates on Graf's findings, i.e. they include an inventory of manuscripts together with basic descriptions of various versions of a specific biblical book. During the last decades, the scholarly production has intensified with scholars such as Juan Pedro Monferrer-Sala and Hikmat Kashouh.[43] A number of recent studies include descriptions of translation techniques in one or several versions of a biblical book. The most prominent work in this area is Polliack's *The Karaite Tradition* (1997), wherein translation techniques in Judaeo-Arabic renditions were systematized. Most subsequent works on translation techniques in Arabic Bible translations, including Christian Arabic ones, relate to Polliack's work.[44] Common translation techniques have already been discussed in the first part of this paper. A related feature frequently attended to by contemporary scholars is the use of 'Islamic' vocabulary vs. 'imitation' vs. 'neutral' Arabic. In essence, the possibility to dress the Christian and Jewish Bibles in Islamic vocabulary has been utilized by translators and missionaries in all times either to demonstrate their ability to master literary Arabic, or as a means of attracting Muslims who presumably would become favourably inclined towards Christianity if only its message was dressed up in a familiar terminology. For scholars, the borders between 'Islamic' vocabulary, 'imitation', and 'neutral' Arabic are nevertheless often blurred. The Qurʾān and other Islamic compositions naturally contain cognates of Syriac and loanwords; if there existed oral pre-Islamic translations in Arabic from Syriac *Vorlagen*, we cannot know with certainty whether extant copies reflect a vocabulary that was adopted to sound Islamic or that preceded what we

41 Christian Arabic texts are mainly written according to common rules of Classical Arabic, but more or less sporadically deviate from them through replacing them with 'Middle Arabic' forms, depending on various factors such as period, region, genre, and personal preferences or education.

42 Although beyond the competence of the present author, it should be mentioned in this connection, that recent studies have yielded important findings with regard to the literary influence of the Arabic missionary Bibles and related works. See the works in notes 15–17 above as well as Saliba, 'The Bible in Arabic', pp. 254–63; Somekh, 'Biblical Echoes', pp. 186–200; Issa, 'Al-Shidyāq-Lee Version', pp. 305–23; and further references there. My gratitude to Rana Issa for providing me with these works.

43 Monferrer-Sala has published a substantial number of articles on Arabic Bible translations, as well as several editions. See for instance Monferrer-Sala, 'Between Hellenism and Arabicization', pp. 445–71. Kashouh's dissertation on Arabic Gospel translations has also received a great deal of attention. See for instance his categorization of various gospel versions in *Arabic Versions of the Gospels*, pp. 46–77. In addition, see the many recent works referred to in this article.

44 See for instance Hjälm, *Christian Arabic Versions*, pp. 118–19; 124–376; Vollandt, *Arabic Versions*, pp. 159–216; Zaki, 'Textual History', pp. 392–424.

understand to be Islamic. Whereas we have statements regarding deliberate translational choices in printed books of modern times and from the Bible societies, we know less about the incentives governing ancient and medieval translations, as mentioned above.[45]

The discussion of Islamic vocabulary is an expression of the increasing attention contemporary scholarship pays to interreligious encounters. Another example of this tendency is the Israeli-German project *Biblia Arabica: The Bible in Arabic among Jews, Christians and Muslims*, initiated by Camilla Adang, Meira Polliack, and Sabine Schmidtke (and later, Ronny Vollandt).[46] In this project, experts in Judaeo-Arabic literature and in the more understudied field of Christian Arabic, as well as specialists in the reception of the Bible in Muslim works, joined forces and, together with a substantial number of doctoral and post-doctoral students, they got the opportunity to focus on this material in a concentrated manner for several years (2013–2018).[47] In connection with this project, several studies that deepen our knowledge of how translations moved between Jews and Christians appeared as well as how Muslims utilized biblical material for their own purposes.[48] It should be noted that not only did Christians sometimes adopt Judaeo-Arabic translations, the most famous example being the adaptation of Saadia Gaon's translation of the Pentateuch by the Copts,[49] but also that Karaite translations may have been influenced by Christians in terms of techniques.[50] Most evidently, the use of alternate renderings, where one unit in the source text is reflected by two or more in the target text, which became associated with Karaites in the tenth century, are found in Christian translations from the same period or earlier, as well as in philosophical and scientific renditions.[51]

---

45 There are a number of studies discussing the use of Islamic-sounding language among Jews and Christians. For early Christian Arabic translations, see Frank, 'The Jeremias of Pethion', pp. 136–70; Martin, 'An Anonymous Mozarab', pp. 125–52; Hjälm, 'Scriptures beyond Words', pp. 49–69 and further references there; for Judaeo-Arabic, see for instance Freidenreich, 'The Use of Islamic Sources', pp. 353–95; Polliack, *The Karaite Tradition*, p. 174. For examinations of *Vorlage* dependence and the use of Syriac-Arabic cognates, see for instance Monferrer-Sala, 'Pauline Epistle to Philemon', pp. 341–71; Hjälm, *Christian Arabic Versions*, 238–74; 377–98; Bassal, 'Syriac-Aramaic', pp. 17–36.

46 Sponsored by the DFG-DIP: http://biblia-arabica.com (accessed 26 November 2019).

47 As for Christian works, Vevian Zaki is preparing an inventory of Pauline Epistles in Arabic.

48 Some recent contributions on the Muslim reception of the Bible include Adang, 'Guided to Islam by the Torah', pp. 57–71; Schmidtke and Adang, 'Muʿtazilī discussions', pp. 701–42; Schmidtke, 'Notes on an Arabic Translation', pp. 72–129; Halft, 'Ismāʿīl Qazvīnī', pp. 280–304; Halft, 'Towards a New Perception of Islam', pp. 225–39; McCoy III, 'What Hath Rome to do with Seville?', pp. 240–52. On conceptual developments in Judaeo-Arabic texts, see Polliack, 'Inversion', pp. 243–302; Polliack, 'Deconstructing the Dual Torah', pp. 113–30.

49 Graf, *Geschichte*, I, pp. 101–02 and further references there; Vollandt, 'An Unknown Medieval Coptic Hebraism?', pp. 183–99; Vollandt, 'Coptic Hebraists', pp. 71–86.

50 Polliack, *The Karaite Tradition*, pp. 7–9.

51 Cf. Polliack, *The Karaite Tradition*, pp. 181–99. For a summary of early Christian translations with a large number of alternate renderings, see Hjälm, *Christian Arabic Versions*, 377–98.

Besides the focus on interreligious encounters in this project, considerable attention has been paid to recent trends within manuscript studies.[52] The latter is also connected to several new digitization projects that have made the accessibility of manuscripts possible. Other works focused on gender and literary studies and other recent research trajectories within Biblical Studies.[53] In addition, manuscript inventories on specific biblical books continued to appear and several overviews of the manuscript production have been prepared.[54]

In order to facilitate future research and also to create an interest in the topic, the *Biblia Arabica* project has aspired to make the field accessible to a broader readership through conferences and publications. Besides providing entries on most biblical books in Arabic, and thus updating Graf's monumental work,[55] an online bibliography on Christian Arabic Bible material is currently being prepared by Vollandt and others.[56] The book series *Biblia Arabica: Texts and Studies* was initiated with Brill in connection with the commencement of the project and several edited volumes have seen the light or are currently being prepared for publication, as are a handful of editions.[57]

Notes on Future Avenues

Despite the many valuable studies that the last decades have yielded, much work remains, both on a descriptive, philological level, including making sources available, and on an analytical level. It is therefore often pointed out that the field of Christian Arabic Bible translations is still in its infancy. This is certainly true. Yet, the reason it is at this stage is not only connected to the lack of basic studies but also to a lack of thorough integration of the various genres in the Christian Arabic corpus, such as Bible translations, liturgy,

---

Scholars have sometimes connected this feature with the East Syriac community, see for instance, Vollandt, *Arabic Versions*, p. 135. For the use of synonymous renderings in philosophical and scientific translations, see 'hendiadyoīn' in Arabic translations of Aristotle, in Edzard and Köhnken, 'A New Look', pp. 222–64.

52 More encompassing studies on paleography are underway by members in the project.

53 Sasson, '"The Matter Applies Not Only to Man"', pp. 71–96; Sasson, 'Gender Equality', pp. 51–74; Zawanowska, 'Was Moses the *mudawwin* of the Torah?', pp. 7–35; Sasson, 'The Mudawwin Revisited', pp. 327–39; Nadler-Akirav, 'The Literary-Historical Approach of Yefet', pp. 171–200.

54 Vollandt, *Arabic Versions*, pp. 40–138; Hjälm, 'Arabic Texts', pp. 483–95; Hjälm, 'Arabic Canon', pp. 280–98. A number of studies focused on translation techniques, see Zawanowska, 'In the Border-Land of Literalism', pp. 179–202; Zawanowska, 'Reading Divine Attributes', pp. 153–81; Polliack, 'On the "Literal Sense"', pp. 390–415; Hjälm, 'Changing Face of the Arabic Bible', pp. 832–48.

55 Several members of the project are contributing such entries to the multi-volume encyclopedia *The Textual History of the Bible*, ed. by Lange and others, forthcoming in several volumes.

56 https://biblia-arabica.com/bibl/index.html (accessed 26 November 2019).

57 https://biblia-arabica.com/book-series/ (accessed 26 November 2019.

historiography, and theology.[58] In addition, the Arabic material should be more systematically compared with sources written in other Eastern Christian languages, which were used by the very same communities that produced the Arabic corpus (especially Syriac, Coptic, Latin, and Greek), as these communities were bilingual, if not trilingual.

It is sometimes stated that 'the field' of Christian Arabic is not — and should not be — a separate field but instead be defined as a corpus of texts which can be approached from a multitude of scholarly disciplines. A main purpose of this corpus is to provide insights for adjacent fields and in return, methods and theories are borrowed from these fields. This has been a strength in terms of advancing the field and making it relevant and known. Yet the question is whether the time has come for a development of Christian Arabic Studies into a discipline proper, perhaps within the broader discipline of Eastern Christian Studies, whose various parts suffer from the same dilemma (cf. Syriac Studies, etc.). Eastern Christian sources are sometimes inevitably approached by axioms, theories (perspectives) and methods, which are developed to answer questions in other disciplines. The clearest example is textual criticism, which for so long used Arabic translations to answer questions within that discourse. Whereas some axioms, theories, and methods, for sure, transcend disciplinary borders, others do not and need to be established from within in order to catch the particularities of a specific tradition. Such a development may eventually help to transform Christian Arabic Studies from a corpus to a discipline so that its various parts develop and throw light on one another in the best possible ways (e.g. the more integrated field of Jewish Studies, or Late Antiquity that was transformed from a time period to a discipline famous for its methodology). A progressive development into a more integrated field, which takes pains in developing and adapting appropriate methodologies, would, in my opinion, mark a third, necessary, shift in focus; one which, among other things, would unravel how these translations functioned in their own context.

To be sure, interdisciplinary studies will still contribute to our understanding of Eastern Christian sources. As we have seen, the theology of Scripture that biblical criticism rests upon (the interest in the *Urtext* and its context) made Arabic Bible translations rather superfluous for modern scholars. However, since the accessibility of the text and its context in a strict sense has been problematized by late modernity and postmodern philosophy and literature studies in particular, the venue for the history of translation and interpretation has opened up considerably. Perhaps more than ever, scholars and Church leaders cross confessional lines in trying to cope with the challenge of making Scripture relevant in post-secular societies.[59] Furthermore, the

---

58 For valuable studies on the use of the Bible in theological texts in Arabic, see Treiger, 'From Theodore Abū Qurra', pp. 11–57; Tarras, 'Spirit before Letter', pp. 79–103; and Martin 'An Anonymous Mozarab', pp. 125–52.

59 Already in the seventeenth century, the dilemma of keeping the biblical text sacred for the

growing interest in Bible reception often makes the borders between various traditions less demarcated. Translations are highly interesting as theological and hermeneutical texts and precisely here, the Arabic traditions can come to their own: as documents archiving the reception of the Bible in the Islamic world. This draws the attention away from the original composition, to the extent that this existed, to the interpretative community in which a translation was made. Thus, the adoption of modern literary theory by biblical scholars as well as more multifaceted debates on theologies of Scriptures pave the way for a greater scholarly interest in the Bible in its Arabic garb. In this light, Arabic Bible translations cannot be discarded as less relevant than other traditions.[60]

Concluding Remarks

The gap between the world of the source material and research relating to this material is still far from bridged, yet the process has come a long way. As an example, the tenth-century al-Ḥārith's introduction to the Pentateuch, discussed in the first part of this paper, was briefly attended to by scholars from the seventeenth to the nineteenth centuries to trace the Hexapla, (via the Syrohexapla) in search of the original version of Scripture.[61] In the nineteenth and twentieth centuries, scholars became increasingly more interested in the author himself, his confessional belonging, the date of his lifetime, etc. There are still important aspects of this introduction (and similar texts)

---

community while at the same time emending it according to text-critical principles was resolved by Roman Catholics who contrasted *sola scriptura* with tradition, an ongoing process in which the Holy Spirit was still active. Some Protestants had already endorsed similar positions in the seventeenth century, or tried to solve the dilemma by carefully distinguishing between textual-historical and theological aspects of the Bible (the latter took recourse to the Bible as a whole), Nellen and Steenbakkers, 'Biblical Philology', pp. 28–36. The notion of *sola scriptura* is to various extents defended, not least to question the interpreting authority of the Pontifical Biblical Commission in the Catholic Church, cf. Ebeling, *The Word of God and Tradition*, p. 136. An outspoken critic to this approach, the theologian and philosopher Hauerwas, argues that biblical criticism, just like literal fundamentalism, rests on the assumption that the Bible can and should be understood objectively. Hauerwas, who is known for his call to remove the Bible from the hands of ordinary Christians since they do not know how to read it, instead places the authority with the Church, the assembly of rightful Christians, 'the community of interpreters', to decide how the Bible should be interpreted. Hauerwas, *Unleashing the Scripture*, pp. 7–44. This is not the place to discuss the theology of Scripture, yet it should be noted that this kind of reasoning is essential in creating a greater interest in the Bible from various aspects, including the relation between standardization of translations and power structures, systematic theology as reflected in renditions, etc.

60 On 'misreadings' as historical documents in their own right, see McKenzie, *Bibliography and the Sociology of Texts*, p. 22.

61 See for instance, Nestle, 'Jacob von Edessa', pp. 465–508; Tregelles, 'Arabic Versions', p. 1615; Assemani, *Bibliothecae Mediceae Laurentianae*, p. 61. For more on this translation, see Vollandt, *Arabic Versions*, esp. pp. 60–62..

to unravel, which would enhance our understanding of exegetical trends, perception of Scripture, interreligious encounters, and these communities' struggles to form and preserve their identity in an increasingly Islamic society. Other observations, such as the relative disinterest in a biblical canon in the premodern stages of Arabic Bible translations as well as its place in the large, understudied corpus of liturgical texts, may enrich our understanding of how the Bible was perceived and functioned in practice.

As systematic theology was severed from biblical criticism (including philology and Orientalist studies) in the Christian West, the Bible in Arabic was largely transferred to the realm of the latter. By the turn of the past century, Oriental Studies, including philology, rapidly developed independently of Biblical Studies and the Bible in Arabic submerged into several disciplines. In contemporary research, the study of Christian Arabic Bible translations in the West is connected as often with Semitic and Arabic/Islamic departments as with biblical departments and often disconnected from systematic theology. Recent developments have improved our knowledge of the field considerably, especially thanks to the adoption and development of new philological methods and online research tools.[62] We also find an unmistakable interest in the interface between religious communities and the subsequent exchange of knowledge, which easily crossed communal borders. Here, it is the movement itself that attracts scholarly attention, but also the incentives and structures governing not only polemic and apologetic works in which such knowledge was often transmitted, but also Bible translations. Yet as Bible translations essentially are theological tracts and made to serve a religious function, one can only hope that a new generation of theologians who attend to the contextual settings of the sources will resume interest in these translations in a larger number. In addition, and with continued focus on interreligious studies, philology, and biblical exegesis, these sources should in my opinion be studied closely in connection to other Eastern Christian material and with the propositions underpinning Eastern theology.

Scholarship is always driven by a certain perspective, which ultimately makes the sources relevant for a community of scholars and their context. Yet, awareness of our own outlook might help decreasing the gap between the source objects and the scholarly subject that might arise as a result. Although the current paper has not been able to compare the narratives of the translators (that still largely needs to be uncovered) with those of recent scholarship as closely as one might wish, it is my hope that it has contributed a little to our understanding of the development of the study of Christian Arabic Bible translations, in light of general trends in Western scholarship.

---

62 For instance, textual criticism has advanced remarkably on internet-based sites with various search functions as have technical advancements used to decipher readings in old manuscripts, especially palimpsests: see http://www.sinaipalimpsests.org/technologies. See also Schulthess, 'The Role of the Internet in New Testament Textual Criticism', pp. 71–82, and other works by her and several other contemporary scholars.

Bibliography

Primary Sources

Assemani, Stefano E., *Bibliothecae Mediceae Laurentianae et Palatinae codicum mms. [sic] orientalium catalogus* (Florence: Ex Typographio Albiziniano, 1742)

Gesenius, Wilhelm, *Der Prophet Jesaia: uebersetzt und mit einem vollständigen philologisch-kritischen und historischen Commentar begleitet* (Leipzig: Friedr. Christ. Wilh. Vogel, 1820–1821)

Gibson, Margaret Dunlop, *An Arabic version of the Acts of the Apostles and the seven Catholic Epistles from an eighth or ninth Century MS. in the Convent of St Catherine on Mount Sinai; with a Treatise on the triune nature of God, with translation, from the same Codex* (London: Clay, 1899)

Secondary Studies

Accad, Martin, 'Muḥammad's Advent as the Final Criterion for the Authenticity of the Judeo-Christian Tradition: Ibn Qayyim al-Jawziyya's Hidāyat al-ḥayārā fī ajwibat al-yahūd wa-l-naṣārā', in *The Three Rings: Textual Studies in the Historical Trialogue of Judaism, Christianity and Islam*, ed. by Barbara Roggema, Marcel Poorthuis, and Pim Valkenberg (Leuven: Peeters, 2005), pp. 217–36

Adang, Camilla, *Muslim Writers on Judaism and the Hebrew Bible: From Ibn Rabban to Ibn Hazm* (New York: Brill, 1996)

——, 'Guided to Islam by the Torah: The Risāla al-Hādiya by ʿAbd al-Salām al-Muhtadī al-Muḥammadī', in *Contacts and Controversies between Muslims, Jews and Christians in the Ottoman Empire and Pre-Modern Iran*, ed. by Camilla Adang and Sabine Schmidtke (Würzburg: Ergon Verlag, 2010), pp. 57–71

Bassal, Ibrahim, 'Syriac-Aramaic Words in an Early Christian Arabic Copy of the Pentateuch (Ms. Sin. Ar. 2)', *Collectanea Christiana Orientalia*, 10 (2013), 17–36

Baumstark, Anton, 'Die sonntägliche Evangelienlesung im vorbyzantinischen Jerusalem', *Byzantinische Zeitschrift*, 30.1 (1930), 350–59

Binay, Sara, 'Revision of the Manuscripts of the So-called "Smith-van Dyke Bible": Some Remarks on the Making of this Bible Translation', in *Translating the Bible into Arabic: Historical, Text Critical, and Literary Aspects*, ed. by Sara Binay and Stefan Leder (Beirut: Orient-Institut Beirut, 2012), pp. 75–84

Blau, Joshua, *A Handbook of Early Middle Arabic* (Jerusalem: Max Schloessinger Memorial Foundation and the Hebrew University of Jerusalem, 2002)

Drint, Adriana, 'Some Notes on the Arabic versions of IV Ezra and the Apocalypse of Baruch in ms. Mount Sinai Arabic 589', in *Actes du 5e Congrès international d'études arabes chrétiennes (Lund, août 1996)*, ed. by Samir Khalil Samir (Kaslik: Université Saint-Esprit, 1999–2000), pp. 165–77

Ebeling, Gerhard, *The Word of God and Tradition: Historical Studies Interpreting the Divisions of Christianity*, translated by S. H. Hooke (Collins, Fortress Press, 1968); from *Wort Gottes und Tradition: Studien zu einer Hermeneutik der Konfessionen* (Göttingen: Vandenhoeck & Ruprecht, 1964)

Edzard, Lutz, and Adolf Köhnken, 'A New Look at the Greek, Syriac, and Arabic Versions of Aristotle's Poetics', in *Grammar as a Window onto Arabic Humanism: A Collection of Articles in Honour of Michael G. Carter*, ed. by Lutz Edzard and Janet C. E. Watson (Wiesbaden: Harrassowitz, 2006), pp. 222–64

Faultless, Julian, 'Ibn al-Ṭayyib' in *Christian-Muslim Relations: A Bibliographical History: Volume 2 (900–1050)*, ed. by David Thomas and Alexander Mallett (Leiden, Brill, 2010), pp. 667–97

Féghali, Paul, 'The Holy Books in Arabic: The Example of the *Propaganda Fide* Edition', in *Translating the Bible into Arabic: Historical, Text Critical, and Literary Aspects*, ed. by Sara Binay and Stefan Leder (Beirut, Orient-Institut Beirut, 2012), pp. 37–51

Frank, Richard M., 'The Jeremias of Pethion ibn Ayyūb al-Sahhār', *The Catholic Biblical Quarterly*, 21.2 (1959), 136–70

Freidenreich, David M., 'The Use of Islamic Sources', *The Jewish Quarterly Review*, 93.3–4 (2003), 353–95

Graf, Georg, *Geschichte der christlichen arabischen Literatur*, vols 1–2 (Vatican: Biblioteca Apostolica Vaticana, 1944; 1947)

Grafton, David D., *The Contested Origins of the 1865 Arabic Bible: Contributions to the Nineteenth Century Nahḍa* (Leiden: Brill, 2015)

Griffith, Sidney H., *The Bible in Arabic: The Scripture of the 'People of the Book' in the Language of Islam* (Princeton: Princeton University Press, 2013)

——, 'When Did the Bible Become an Arabic Scripture?', *Intellectual History of the Islamicate World*, 1 (2013), 7–23

Haddad, Robert M., 'On the Melkite Passage to the Unia: The Case of Patriarch Cyril al-Zaʿīm (1672–1720)', in *Christians and Jews in the Ottoman Empire: The Functioning of a Plural Society*, vol. 2, ed. by Benjamin Braude, and Bernard Lewis (New York: Holmes & Meier Publishers, 1982), pp. 67–90

Halft, Dennis, 'Ismāʿīl Qazvīnī: A Twelfth/Eighteenth-Century Jewish Convert to Imāmī Šīʿism and his Critique of Ibn Ezra's Commentary on the Four Kingdoms (Daniel 2:31–45)', in *Senses of Scripture, Treasures of Tradition: The Bible in Arabic among Jews, Christians and Muslims*, ed. by Miriam L. Hjälm (Leiden: Brill, 2017), pp. 280–304

——, 'Towards a New Perception of Islam: The Influence of Marie-Dominique Chenu's Theology of Incarnation on Christian-Muslim Relations', in *The Promise of Renewal: Dominicans and Vatican II*, ed. by Michael Attridge and others (Adelaide: ATF Theology, 2017), pp. 225–39

Hamilton, Alastair, *William Bedwell: The Arabist 1563–1632* (Leiden: Brill, 1985)

Hauerwas, Stanley, *Unleashing the Scripture: Freeing the Bible from Captivity to America* (Nashville: Abingdon Press, 1993)

Hjälm, Miriam L., 'The Christian Arabic Book of Daniel: Extant Versions, Canonical Constellations, and Relation to the Liturgical Practice, with an Appendix of "The Song of the Three Young Men"', *Collectanea Christiana Orientalia*, 12 (2015), 115–78

——, '6–9.2.8 Latter Prophets: Arabic Translations', in *Textual History of the Bible*, vol. 1: *The Hebrew Bible*, part 1b: *Pentateuch, Former and Latter Prophets*, ed. by Armin Lange and Emanuel Tov (Leiden: Brill, 2016), pp. 723–30

——, 'The Changing Face of the Arabic Bible: Translation Techniques in Early Renditions of Ezekiel', *Open Theology*, 2, issue 1 (2016), 832–48

——, *Christian Arabic Versions of Daniel: A Comparative Study of Early MSS and Translation Techniques in MSS Sinai Ar. 1 and 2* (Leiden: Brill, 2016)

——, 'The Hazy Edges of the Biblical Canon: A Case Study of the Wisdom of Solomon in Arabic', in *The Embroidered Bible: Studies in Biblical Apocrypha and Pseudepigrapha in Honour of Michael E. Stone*, ed. by Lorenzo DiTommaso, Matthias Henze, and William Adler (Leiden: Brill, 2017), pp. 569–87

——, 'Scriptures beyond Words: "Islamic" Vocabulary in Early Christian Arabic Bible Translations', *Collectanea Christiana Orientalia*, 15 (2018), 49–69

——, '1.2.12 Arabic Texts', in *The Textual History of the Bible*, vol. 2A, ed. by Matthias Henze, and Frank Feder (Leiden: Brill, 2020), pp. 483–95

——, '1.1.10 The Arabic Canon', in *The Textual History of the Bible*, vol. 2A, ed. by Matthias Henze, and Frank Feder (Leiden: Brill, 2020), pp. 280–98

Issa, Rana, 'Biblical Reflections in the Arabic Lexicon: A Very Modern Translation Phenomenon', *Babylon: nordisk Tidsskrift for Midtöstenstudier*, 2 (2012), 58–67

——, 'Al-Shidyāq-Lee Version (1857): An Example of a Non-Synchronous Nineteenth-Century Arabic Bible', in *Senses of Scripture, Treasures of Tradition: The Bible in Arabic among Jews, Christians and Muslims*, ed. by Miriam L. Hjälm (Leiden: Brill, 2017), pp. 305–23

Kashouh, Hikmat, *The Arabic Versions of the Gospels: The Manuscripts and their Families* (Berlin: de Gruyter, 2012)

Keating, Sandra Toenies, 'Revisiting the Charge of Taḥrīf: The Question of Supersessionism in Early Islam and the Qurʾān', in *Nicholas of Cusa and Islam: Polemic and Dialogue in the Late Middle Ages*, ed. by Ian Christopher and others (Leiden: Brill, 2014), pp. 202–17

Kilpatrick, Hilary, 'Meletius Karmah's Specimen Translation of Genesis 1–5', in *Translating the Bible into Arabic: Historical, Text Critical, and Literary Aspects*, ed. by Sara Binay and Stefan Leder (Beirut: Orient-Institut Beirut, 2012), pp. 63–73

Lamoreaux, John C., 'Agapius of Manbij', in *The Orthodox Church in the Arab World (700–1700): An Anthology of Sources*, ed. by Samuel Noble and Alexander Treiger (DeKalb: Northern Illinois University Press, 2014), 136–59

Lange, Armin, and others, *The Textual History of the Bible*, vols 1 and 2 (Leiden: Brill, 2016–)

Leemhuis, Frederik, Albertus F. J. Klijn, and Gert J. Van Gelder, *The Arabic Text of the Apocalypse of Baruch: Edited and Translated with a Parallel Translation of the Syriac Text* (Leiden: Brill, 1986)

Margoliouth, David S., *An Essay on the Place of Ecclesiasticus in Semitic Literature* (Oxford: Clarendon, 1890)

Martin, Geoffrey K., 'An Anonymous Mozarab Translator at Work', in *Senses of Scripture, Treasures of Tradition: The Bible in Arabic among Jews, Christians and Muslims*, ed. by Miriam L. Hjälm (Leiden: Brill, 2017), pp. 125–52

McCoy III, Roy Michael, 'What Hath Rome to do with Seville? Exploring the Latin-to-Arabic Translation of the Gospel of Matthew in Ibn Barrajān's (d. 536/1141) Qurʾān Commentary', in *Senses of Scripture, Treasures of Tradition:*

The Bible in Arabic among Jews, Christians and Muslims, ed. by Miriam L. Hjälm (Leiden: Brill, 2017), pp. 240–52

McKenzie, Donald F., *Bibliography and the Sociology of Texts* (Cambridge: Cambridge University Press, 1999)

Miller, Peter N., 'The "Antiquarianization" of Biblical Scholarship and the London Polyglot Bible', *Journal of the History of Ideas*, 62 (2001), 463–82

Monferrer-Sala, Juan Pedro, 'Between Hellenism and Arabicization. On the Formation of the Melkite Community in the Heart of Muslim Rule', *Al-Qanṭara*, 32.2 (2012), 445–71

——, 'The Pauline Epistle to Philemon from Codex Vatican Arabic 13 (Ninth Century CE). Transcription and Study', *Journal of Semitic Studies*, 60.2 (2015), 341–71

Nadler-Akirav, Meirav, 'The Literary-Historical Approach of Yefet Ben 'Eli in his Commentary of the Book of Amos', in *European Journal of Jewish Studies*, 10.2 (2016), 171–200

Nellen, Henk J. M., and Piet Steenbakkers, 'Biblical Philology in the Long Seventeenth Century: New Orientations', in *Scriptural Authority and Biblical Criticism in the Dutch Golden Age: God's Word Questioned*, ed. by Dirk van Miert, Henk Nellen, Piet Steenbakkers, and Jetze Touber (Oxford: Oxford University Press, 2017), pp. 16–58

Nestle, Eberhard, 'Jacob von Edessa über den Schem hammephorasch und andere Gottesnamen. Ein Beitrag zur Geschichte des Tetragrammaton'. *Zeitschrift der Deutschen Morgenländischen Gesellschaft*, 32 (1878), 465–508

Polliack, Meira, *The Karaite Tradition of Arabic Bible Translation: A Linguistic and Exegetical Study of Karaite Translations of the Pentateuch from the Tenth and Eleventh Centuries C.E.* (Leiden: Brill, 1997)

——, 'On the "Literal Sense" in Medieval Jewish Exegesis and Daniel Al-Qumisi's Contribution to the Semanitc Study of the Hebrew Bible', in *Zer Rimonim: Studies in Biblical Literature and Jewish Exegesis Presented to Professor Rmon Kasher*, ed. by Michael Avioz, Elie Assis, and Yael Shemesh (Atlanta: Society of Biblical Literature, 2013), pp. 390–415

——, 'Inversion of "Written" and "Oral" Torah in Relation to the Islamic Arch-Models of Qur'an and Hadith', *Jewish Studies Quarterly*, 22.3 (2015), 243–302(60)

——, 'Deconstructing the Dual Torah: A Jewish Response to the Muslim Model of Scripture', in *Interpreting Scriptures in Judaism, Christianity and Islam: Overlapping Inquiries*, ed. by Mordechai Z. Cohen and Adele Berlin (Cambridge: Cambridge University Press, 2016), pp. 113–30

Reynolds, Gabriel Said, *The Qur'ān and the Bible. Text and Commentary* (New Haven: Yale University Press, 2018)

Sadan, Joseph, 'In the Eyes of the Christian Writer al-Ḥāriṯ ibn Sinān Poetics and Eloquence as a Platform of Inter-Cultural Contacts and Contrasts', *Arabica*, 56 (2009), 1–26

Saliba, Issa A., 'The Bible in Arabic: The 19th Century Protestant Translation', *The Muslim World*, 65 (1975), 254–63

Sasson, Ilana, 'Gender Equality in Yefet ben Eli's Commentary and Karaite Halakhah', *AJS Review*, 37.1 (2013), 51–74

——, '"The Matter Applies Not Only to Man": Gender Equality in Yefet ben Eli's Biblical Commentary and in the Karaite Legal System', *Ben Ever La-Arav*, 6 (2014), 71–96 [in Hebrew]

——, 'The Mudawwin Revisited: Yefet ben Eli on the Composition of the Book of Proverbs', *Journal of Jewish Studies*, 67.2 (2016), 327–39

Schmidtke, Sabine, 'Notes on an Arabic Translation of the Pentateuch in the Library of the Twelver Shīʿī Scholar Raḍī al-Dīn ʿAlī b. Mūsā Ibn Ṭāwūs (d. 664/1266)', *Shii Studies Review*, 1 (2017), 72–129

Schmidtke, Sabine, and Camilla Adang, 'Muʿtazilī Discussions of the Abrogation of the Torah: Ibn Ḫallād (4th/10th Century) and his Commentators', *Arabica*, 60 (2013), 701–42

Schulthess, Sara, 'The Role of the Internet in New Testament Textual Criticism: The Example of the Arabic Manuscripts of the New Testament', in *Digital Humanities in Biblical, Early Jewish and Early Christian Studies*, ed. by C. Clivaz, A. Gregory, D. Hamidović, with the collaboration of S. Schulthess (Leiden: Brill, 2013), pp. 71–82

Shahīd, Irfan, *Byzantium and the Arabs in the Fourth Century* (Washington, DC: Dumbarton Oaks, 1984)

——, *Byzantium and the Arabs in the Fifth Century* (Washington, DC: Dumbarton Oaks, 1989)

Somekh, Sasson, 'Biblical Echoes in Modern Arabic Literature', *Journal of Arabic Literature*, 26 (1995), 186–200

Sucio, Alin, 'Jeremiah's Prophecy to Pesher', in *The Textual History of the Bible*, vol. 2, ed. by Armin Lange and others (forthcoming)

Tarras, Peter, 'The Spirit Before the Letter: Theodore Abū Qurra's Use of Biblical Quotations in the Context of Early Christian Arabic Apologetics', in *Senses of Scripture, Treasures of Tradition: The Bible in Arabic among Jews, Christians and Muslims*, ed. by Miriam L. Hjälm (Leiden: Brill, 2017), pp. 79–103

Thomas, David, 'The Bible and the *Kalām*', in *The Bible in Arab Christianity*, ed. by David Thomas (Leiden: Brill, 2007), pp. 175–91

Tregelles, Samuel P., 'Arabic Versions', in *A Dictionary of the Bible Comprising its Antiquities, Biography, Geography, and Natural History*, ed. by William Smith and others (London: John Murray, 1896), 3.1614–16

Treiger, Alexander, "Abdallāh ibn al-Faḍl al-Anṭākī', in *Christian-Muslim Relations: A Bibliographical History: Volume 3 (1050–1200)*, ed. by David Thomas and Alexander Mallett (Leiden: Brill, 2011), pp. 89–113

——, 'From Theodore Abū Qurra to Abed Azrié: The Arabic Bible in Context', in *Senses of Scripture, Treasures of Tradition: The Bible in Arabic among Jews, Christians and Muslims*, ed. by Miriam L. Hjälm (Leiden: Brill, 2017), pp. 11–57

Vollandt, Ronny, 'Che portono al ritorno quì una Bibbia Arabica integra: A History of the Biblia Sacra Arabica (1671–73)', in *Græco-latina et orientalia. Studia in honorem Angeli Urbani heptagenarii*, ed. by Juan-Pedro Monferrer-Sala and Samir Khalil Samir (Beirut: CEDRAC, 2013), pp. 401–18

——, 'Some Historiographical Remarks on Medieval and Early-Modern Scholarship of Biblical Versions in Arabic: A Status Quo', *Intellectual History of the Islamicate World*, 1 (2013), 25–42

——, *Arabic Versions of the Pentateuch: A Comparative Study of Jewish, Christian, and Muslim Sources* (Leiden: Brill, 2015)

——, 'Coptic Hebraists in The Middle Ages? On the Transmission of Rav Saʿadiah Gaon's Tafsīr'. *Tarbiz*, 83.1–2 (2015), 71–86 [in Hebrew]

——, 'An Unknown Medieval Coptic Hebraism? On a Momentous Junction of Jewish and Coptic Biblical Studies', in *Canonical Texts and Scholarly Practices: A Global Comparative Approach*, ed. by Anthony Grafton and Glenn Most (Cambridge: Cambridge University Press, 2016), pp. 183–99

——, 'The Conundrum of Scriptural Plurality: The Arabic Bible, Polyglots, and Medieval Predecessors of Biblical Criticism', in *The Text of the Hebrew Bible and its Editions; Studies in Celebration of the Fifth Centennial of the Complutensian Polyglot*, ed. by Andrés Piquer Otero and Pablo Torijano Morales (Leiden: Brill, 2017), pp. 56–85

——, Nathan Gibson, and others, *Bibliography of the Arabic Bible*, online [forthcoming]

Vööbus, Arthur, *Early Versions of the New Testament* (Stockholm: Estonian Theological Society in Exile: Papers 6, 1954)

Wakefield, Robert, *On the Three Languages [1524]*, ed. and trans. by G. Lloyd Jones (Binghamton: Medieval and Renaissance Texts and Studies, 1989)

Walbiner, Carsten, 'Melkite (Greek Orthodox) Approaches to the Bible at the Time of the Community's Cultural Reawakening in the Early Modern Period (17th–early 18th Centuries)', in *Translating the Bible into Arabic: Historical, Text Critical, and Literary Aspects*, ed. by Sara Binay and Stefan Leder (Beirut: Orient-Institut Beirut, 2012), pp. 53–61

Wald, Samuel Gottlieb, 'Über die arabische Übersetzung des Daniel in den Polyglotten', *Repertorium für Biblische und Morgenländische Litteratur*, 14 (1784), 204–11

Zaki, Vevian, 'The Textual History of the Arabic Pauline Epistles: One Version, Three Recensions, Six Manuscripts', in *Senses of Scripture, Treasures of Tradition: The Bible in Arabic among Jews, Christians and Muslims*, ed. by Miriam L. Hjälm (Leiden, Brill, 2017), pp. 392–424

Zawanowska, Marzena, 'In the Border-Land of Literalism: Interpretative Alterations of Scripture in Medieval Karaite Translations of the Bible into Arabic', *Intellectual History of the Islamicate World*, 1 (2013), 179–202

——, '"Was Moses the *mudawwin* of the Torah?" The Question of Authorship of the Pentateuch According to Yefet ben 'Eli', in *Studies in Judaeo-Arabic Culture: Proceedings of the Fourteenth Conference of the Society for Judaeo-Arabic Studies*, ed. by Haggai Ben-Shammai, and others (Tel Aviv: Tel Aviv University, 2014), pp. 7–35

——, 'Reading Divine Attributes into the Scriptural Text in Medieval Karaite Bible Translations', in *Senses of Scripture, Treasures of Tradition: The Bible in Arabic among Jews, Christians and Muslims*, ed. by Miriam L. Hjälm (Leiden: Brill, 2017), pp. 153–81

MARIBEL FIERRO

Translating Inside al-Andalus

From Ibn Rushd to Ibn Juljul

Most of Aristotle's works were not translated into Latin during the time of the Roman Empire. Around 1260, the first Latin translation of Aristotle's *Politics* was carried out by the Dominican William of Moerbeke (d. *c.* 1286) — perhaps at the suggestion of Thomas of Aquinas (d. 1274) — using a copy of the Greek text from Byzantium as no Arabic translation existed.[1] In fact, the *Politics* was one of the few works by Aristotle that were not translated into Arabic.[2] Thus, much to his disappointment, in al-Andalus (i.e. Muslim Spain and Portugal) Ibn Rushd al-Ḥafīd (1126–1198), our Averroes[3] and the great commentator of Aristotle, could not access the text in spite of his longing for it. Did he ever consider the possibility of searching for the Greek original and having it translated?[4] Could he also have considered the possibility of learning

* This paper was carried out within the project *Practicing knowledge in Islamic societies and their neighbours*, Anneliese Maier Award 2014. Alexander von Humboldt Foundation. Previous versions of this paper were presented at the Conference *Narratives on Translations*, organized by S. Brentjes and J. L. Mancha, 16–20 November 2015, Max Planck Institute for the History of Science, and at the Advanced School in the Humanities, *Judaism, Christianity, and Islam: Religious Communities and Communities of Knowledge*, organized by G. Stroumsa and S. Schmidtke, 12–14 June 2017, Institute of Advanced Study, Princeton. I wish to thank Luis Molina and Mayte Penelas for their help.

1 Schütrumpf, *The Earliest Translations of Aristotle's Politics.*

2 Brague, 'Note sur la traduction arabe de la Politique d'Aristote', pp. 423–33; Syros, 'A Note on the Transmission of Aristotle's Political Ideas', pp. 303–09.

3 From now onwards this will be the name employed to refer to this figure.

4 Contacts between the Islamic world and the Byzantine Empire continue to be attested at the time: El Cheikh, 'Byzantium through the Islamic Prism', pp. 53–69, and thus — at least

Maribel Fierro is research professor at the Institute of Languages and Cultures of the Mediterranean at the High Council for Scientific Research (CSIC-Spain). She has worked and published on the political, religious, and intellectual history of al-Andalus and the Islamic West, on Islamic law, on the construction of orthodoxy and on violence and its representation in medieval Arabic sources. Among her publications: *Abd al-Rahman III: The First Cordoban Caliph* (2005) and *The Almohad Revolution: Politics and Religion in the Islamic West during the Twelfth–Thirteenth Centuries* (2012). She is the editor of *Orthodoxy and heresy in Islam: Critical Concepts in Religious Studies* (2013) and the *Routledge Handbook on Muslim Iberia* (2020).

Narratives on Translation across Eurasia and Africa: From Babylonia to Colonial India, ed. by Sonja Brentjes in cooperation with Jens Høyrup and Bruce O'Brien, CAT 3, pp. 157–173 (Turnhout: Brepols, 2022) BREPOLS PUBLISHERS 10.1484/M.CAT-EB.5.127939

Greek as William of Moerbeke did in order to read Aristotle's works in the language in which they were written? Was there any Andalusi local tradition of translation and of learning languages other than Arabic that would have facilitated direct access to the legacy of antiquity?

In the eleventh century, the Toledan Ṣāʿid (d. 1070), the famous author of the *Ṭabaqāt al-umam* (Categories of Nations) which dealt with the history of the sciences of the ancients, documented how for him and like-minded scholars the sciences were universal, Aristotle was a crucial intellectual figure for mankind, and the Greek philosophical and scientific tradition was maintained in al-Andalus. According to Ṣāʿid, Andalusi Muslims and Jews were now in charge of what before had been centred in Baghdad after the Abbasids had fallen under the influence of both women and Turks, thus abandoning the pursuit of philosophy since the caliphate of al-Rāḍī (r. 934–940) with only a few Muslims and non-Muslims left to cultivate sciences such as astronomy, geometry, and medicine under the protection of some rulers.[5] With their increased self-esteem, by the sixth/twelfth century — especially after the Almohad revolution which famously proclaimed that knowledge now resided in the Maghrib — Andalusis seem to have been less and less interested in the scientific and philosophical works authored in the Eastern regions of the Islamic world.[6] If the scientific and philosophical legacy of antiquity was kept alive in al-Andalus and if the East had lost its centrality, why would Andalusis not look for the original texts of that legacy and have them translated as had happened under the early Abbasids?

For all the expenses that this may have occasioned, Averroes counted on the support of the Almohad caliphs whom he served as judge, physician, and also as philosopher. Averroes' commitment to commenting on Aristotle was initially supported by the second Almohad caliph Abū Yaʿqūb Yūsuf (r. 1163–1184) when he was still a prince, thus in an initiative that originated in the caliphal court.[7] By then, the Almohad caliphs needed to establish their legitimacy in new ways after the charismatic phase that had brought the dynastic founder ʿAbd al-Muʾmin to power and to empire-building by means of a Messianic figure, the Mahdī Ibn Tumart (d. 1130). Abū Yaʿqūb Yūsuf's interest in philosophy and encyclopaedism was a way to redirect Mahdism after the initial phase of conquest and revolutionary violence, in a process that bears similarities with developments that took place among the Ismailis during the early Fatimid

---

in theory — the Muslims could have tried to obtain a copy of the Greek text of Aristotle's *Politics* as Moerbeke did.

5 Balty-Guesdon, 'Al-Andalus et l'héritage grec', pp. 231–342.

6 Richter-Bernburg has shown how in the fields of medicine and astronomy, Ṣāʿid's information on the Mashriq rapidly decreased from the end of the tenth century: Richter-Bernburg, 'Ṣāʿid, the *Toledan Tables* and Andalusī Science', pp. 373–401. See also Samsó, *On Both Sides of the Strait of Gibraltar.*

7 Morata, 'La presentación de Averroes en la corte almohade', pp. 101–22.

caliphate.[8] The Almohad caliphs Abū Yaʿqūb Yūsuf and Abū Yūsuf Yaʿqūb (r. 1184–1198) gave support to the study and teaching of the sciences of the ancients among their learned elites — support that had also previously existed on a minor scale in Umayyad caliphal Cordoba and in the Taifa kingdoms of Toledo and Saragosse. The Almohad programme of intellectual renovation directed to philosophically orient Revelation faced, however, opposition in different sectors, not only among the traditional Maliki scholars but also among the Almohad elites, specifically among those who saw in such an orientation the danger of having the figure of Ibn Tūmart diminished, which would in turn affect their own legitimacy and authority. In 1197, Averroes' persecution and that of those who occupied themselves with the rational sciences took place, to be followed shortly after by the death of the philosopher. Philosophy lost then the prominent place it had gained during Averroes' life.[9] Had the context in which Averroes operated lasted and especially had the numbers of those involved in the study of philosophy increased and given a stable place among the *ṭalaba* (the Almohad learned elites), things may have evolved different as William Montgomery Watt explained in a thought-provoking article in which he analysed the intellectual and related social developments that had taken place under the Almohads.[10] With continuing caliphal support, a stable place among the Almohad elites given to the practitioners of the ancient sciences, and an educational programme adapted to different types of audience, the conditions may have been created for initiating the search of Greek originals in order to translate or retranslate Aristotle's works — an endeavour that counted on the prestigious model offered by the Abbasid caliphate.[11] Eastern Arabic sources both Christian and Muslim mention that the Byzantine emperors had sent books to the Abbasid caliphs, especially during the second iconoclast period (815–843) that coincided with the reign of al-Maʾmūn (r. 813–833). No sending of books from Byzantium to Bagdad is mentioned from the middle of the third/ninth century. This may have been caused by internal developments in Byzantium, some scholars have argued, specifically the classical renaissance that started with the Macedonian dynasty in 867 — and perhaps even with the last iconoclast emperor, Teophilus (829–842) — as the Byzantines would not have been willing any longer to part with books they now valued.[12] In any case, apart from the Abbasid model, the Almohads also counted on the precedent of the Cordoban Umayyad caliphate during which two books (Dioscorides' *Materia Medica* and Orosius' *History*) were

8 Fierro, 'Ibn Ṭufayl's *Ḥayy b. Yaqẓān*'.

9 Fierro, 'Averroes' "Disgrace" and his Relations with the Almohads', pp. 73–118.

10 Watt, 'Philosophy and Theology under the Almohads', pp. 101–07.

11 Gutas, *Greek Thought, Arabic Culture*; Yücesoy, 'Translation as Self-Consciousness', p. 552, quoting the Maghribi al-Ḥimyarī for the Abbasid caliph al-Maʾmūn's (r. 198/813–218/833) search of ancient manuscripts: al-Ḥimyarī, *Rawḍ al-miʿṭār*, p. 16.

12 Signes Codoñer, 'La diplomacia del libro en Bizancio', pp. 153–87; Sypianski, 'Arabo-Byzantine Relations', pp. 465–78.

said to have been sent by the Byzantine emperor to be translated into Arabic. This was a relevant precedent given that in their search for legitimacy, the Almohads insisted on connecting themselves with the Cordoban Umayyads.

However, the place of translation in Andalusi culture and society was in fact rather limited as we shall see. This may come as a surprise, as translating activities are prominently associated with medieval Iberia, but they refer to the process of translating Arabic books on sciences and philosophy into Latin and Hebrew on the part of Christians and Jews who lived outside al-Andalus. Compared to the large amount of research carried out on the translations from Arabic into other languages that took place outside the territory under Muslim rule,[13] there is little regarding translating activities made by Muslims and dhimmis (Christian and Jews) inside al-Andalus.[14] There are reasons for this. Balty-Guesdon has shown how for Ṣāʿid al-Ṭulayṭulī pre-Islamic Iberia had no scientific legacy to offer. Even if other sources record some scientific activities on the part of the Christians living in al-Andalus that drew on pre-Islamic intellectual traditions,[15] by the fourth/tenth century for both Andalusi Muslims and non-Muslims access to philosophy and the sciences of the ancients meant Arabization. The scientific legacy of Antiquity — together with the contributions made within the Islamicate world — arrived in the Iberian Peninsula in Arabic, and thus it was as Arabic sciences that Andalusi Muslims, Jews, and Christians became familiar with them.[16] For Isabel Toral, the fact that the range of languages spoken in al-Andalus did not include either Greek or Syriac — only Latin — meant that in Cordoba there was no material basis for a translation movement similar to that in Baghdad.[17] In the field of the sciences of the ancients — together with some translations from Latin and some updating of Dioscorides' *Materia Medica* as we shall see — Andalusi activity concentrated on the reception of texts already translated in the East.

Christians translated some of their religious works from Latin into Arabic: Ḥafṣ b. Albar al-Qūṭī's translation of the *Psalms* is usually dated to the second half of the third/ninth century and in the first half of the fifth/eleventh century the Canons of the Visigothic Church were translated.[18] Evidence regarding

13 Two examples: Gutas, 'What was there in Arabic for the Latins to Receive?' pp. 3–21, and in the same volume Hasse, 'The Social Conditions of the Arabic-(Hebrew-)Latin Translation Movements', pp. 68–86.

14 An overview in Vernet, *Lo que Europa debe al Islam de España*. Gilbert's study *Reading Cultures* is unpublished. For a more general perspective see Santoyo, *La traducción medieval en la Península Ibérica (siglos III–XV)*.

15 A recent overview in Aillet, *Mozarabes*.

16 Balty-Guesdon, 'Al-Andalus et l'héritage grec', pp. 231–342.

17 Toral, 'Translations as Part of Power Semiotics' http://hdl.handle.net/10261/13949 (accessed 19 June 2017). Cf. van Koningsveld, 'Greek Manuscripts in the Early Abbasid Empire', pp. 345–72.

18 See footnote 15. The Arabic translation of the Canons is now being studied in the Gerda Henkel Foundation research project *Christian Society under Muslim Rule: Canon Collections from Muslim Spain* directed by A. Echevarría and Matthias Maser https://lisa.

other translating activities — apart from the case of Orosius' *History* to be discussed below — is not as clear as these two. The Christians of al-Andalus seem to have known some or parts of the translations of the Bible into Arabic made outside al-Andalus, and perhaps they also carried out their own.[19] In the field of science, there is some scanty evidence about translations of medical and astrological Latin knowledge that was of interest to the Muslims.[20] In the field of history such interest is more apparent. The *Chronica Pseudo-Isidoriana* was initially the translation of a Latin source into Arabic,[21] and at least some parts of Isidore of Seville's *Etymologies* were also available in Arabic,[22] while there has been much discussion about other possible Latin sources in Andalusi Arabic historiographical and geographical writings, with Orosius' *History* occupying a prominent position.[23]

As for the Andalusi Jews, translations of their religious literature into Arabic carried out in the East such as those by Saadia Gaon (892–942) circulated among them, but there were no translations made in al-Andalus.[24] The Jews' deep Arabization allowed them to read Arabic books on grammar, belles lettres, poetry, science, philosophy, and mysticism without any need to translate them into Hebrew. They also wrote in Arabic in those fields and this eventually led to the need to translate some of their Arabic production into Hebrew, but this took place outside al-Andalus to cater for the needs of those co-religionists who knew no Arabic.[25]

In terms of the Muslims, translations made in the East circulated in al-Andalus although no general overview tracing when, how, and why they were introduced exists, except for certain disciplines such as astrology and medicine.[26] By the fifth/eleventh century, the reception of the works of the

---

gerda-henkel-stiftung.de/christian_society_under_muslim_rule_canon_collections_from_muslim_spain?nav_id=8609&focus_comments=1.

19 A useful overview referring to the research carried out on this topic by scholars such a P. Sj. van Koningsveld, M.-Th. Urvoy and J. P. Monferrer among others in López Guix, 'Las primeras traducciones bíblicas', http://www.raco.cat/index.php/1611/article/viewFile/275764/363728. Among more recent studies, Monferrer, '"You brood of vipers!"', pp. 187–21. The materials found in Ibn Barrajān's (d. 1141) works are now to be added: Casewit, 'A Muslim Scholar of the Bible', pp. 1–48.

20 Samsó, *Las ciencias de los antiguos en al-Andalus.*

21 *La Chronica Gothorum Pseudo-Isidoriana (ms. Paris BN 6113).*

22 Ducène, 'Al-Bakrī et les *Étymologies* d'Isidore de Séville', pp. 379–97.

23 Sánchez-Albornoz, *Fuentes latinas de la historia romana de Rasis,* and Vallvé, 'Fuentes latinas de los geógrafos árabes', pp. 241–60. Both scholars tend to stress such a use, while Molina, 'Orosio y los geógrafos hispano-musulmanes', pp. 63–92, Penelas in a number of studies (such as 'Contribución al estudio de la difusión de la Cosmografía de Julio Honorio', pp. 1–18) and Christys, *Christians in al-Andalus. 711–1000*, are more cautious with the extant evidence.

24 Judah ha-Levi translated some Hebrew verses into Arabic: Tobi, 'Yehudah Ha-Levi's Translations of Arabic Poems', pp. 369–86. I owe this information to Jonathan Decter.

25 See, for example, Freudenthal, 'Arabic into Hebrew', pp. 125–43.

26 For the sciences of the ancients, see above notes 11 and 17, as well as Samsó, 'Al-Andalus, a Bridge between Arabic and European Science', pp. 101–25. For philosophy, see Plessner,

Arab *falāsifa* and of the 'Arabic' Aristotle is well attested, while the circulation of Hermetic and alchemical literature translated into Arabic is attested already in the tenth century.[27] Together with the circulation of medical works such as those by Galen, this tenth-century interest in Greek learning can be connected with the establishment of the Cordoban Umayyad caliphate and with the need to compete in the intellectual arena with both the Abbasids and the Fatimids, a process in which the figure of the 'wise' al-Ḥakam II, before and during his reign (r. 961–976), was crucial as also was the exchange of embassies with Byzantium.[28] It is in the context of such an embassy that translations being undertaken in al-Andalus with the involvement of Muslims are mentioned.

As noted above, the translations involved Dioscorides' *Materia Medica* and Orosius' *History*, the books that were sent by the Byzantine emperor to the Cordoban Umayyad caliph. The Cordoban scholar and doctor Ibn Juljul (943–994) is the main source on this episode in a narrative that must have been included in the lost prologue to his work *Tafsīr asmāʾ al-adwiya al-mufrada min Kitāb Diyusqūrīdus* (Commentary on the Names of the Simple Remedies of the Book of Dioscurides),[29] and that has been preserved by Ibn Abī Uṣaybiʿa (d. 1270).[30] There are other related texts,[31] but here we shall concentrate on Ibn Juljul's narrative. Ibn Abī Uṣaybiʿa may have recorded it faithfully, although there is no way to ascertain if he introduced any changes in it.

Ibn Juljul was five years old when the Byzantine embassy arrived in Cordoba in 948.

قال ابن جلجل وورد هذا الكتاب إلى الأندلس وهو على ترجمة إصطفن منه ما عرف له أسماء بالعربية ومنه ما لم يعرف له أسماء فانتفع الناس بالمعروف منه بالمشرق وبالأندلس إلى أيام الناصر عبد الرحمن بن محمد وهو يومئذ صاحب الأندلس فكاتبه أرمانيوس الملك ملك

'Hispano-Arabic vs. Eastern Tradition of Aristotle's and al-Fārābī's writings', pp. 109–14; Ramón Guerrero, 'Para la historia de al-Andalus: Primera presencia de al-Fārābī', pp. 1191–208; Cruz Hernández, 'La recepción de los *falāsifa* orientales en al-Andalus: problemas críticos', pp. 37–51.

27 See *Historia de los Autores y Transmisores Andalusíes (HATA)*, sections XII and XV at http://kohepocu.cchs.csic.es/.

28 al-Ḥajjī, 'Al-ʿAlāqāt al-diblūmasiyya bayna al-Andalus wa-l-Bizanta', pp. 53–91; Wasserstein, 'Byzantium and al-Andalus', pp. 76–101.

29 On Ibn Juljul and his works, see Garijo Galán, 'Ibn Ŷulŷul, Sulaymān', pp. 163–66, nº 1396. See also Cabo-González, 'Action et interaction entre les peuples de la Méditerranée'.

30 Ibn Abī Uṣaybiʿa, *ʿUyūn al-anbāʾ fī ṭabaqāt al-aṭibbāʾ*, pp. 37–41 (Arabic)/36–40 (translation); a version in al-ʿUmarī (d. 1349), *Masālik al-abṣār*, IX, pp. 311–12. Rosenthal translated it into English in *The Classical Heritage in Islam*, pp. 194–96. A new translation has been carried out by E. Savage-Smith, S. Swain and G. J. van Gelder: Ibn Abī Uṣaybiʿa, *A Literary History of Medicine*, ed. and trans. by Savage-Smith, Swain, and van Gelder [https://brill.com/view/db/lhom].

31 For example, Ibn Khaldūn (d. 1406) refers to this event in his *Kitāb al-ʿibar* (Būlāq edn: II, pp. 88, 197; Beirut edn: II, pp. 169, 401–02). The problematic character of these passages has been discussed by Penelas in her study accompanying her edition of Orosius' history (see below note 37).

قسطنطينية أحسب في سنة سبع وثلاثين وثلاثمائة وهاداه بهدايا لها قدر عظيم فكان في جملة هديته كتاب ديسقوريدس مصور الحشائش بالتصوير الرومي العجيب وكان الكتاب مكتوباً بالإغريقي الذي هو اليوناني وبعث معه كتاب هروسيس صاحب القصص وهو تأريخ للروم عجيب فيه أخبار الدهور وقصص الملوك الأول وفوائد عظيمة.

وكتب أرمانيوس في كتابه إلى الناصر أن كتاب ديسقوريدس لا تجتنى فائدته إلا برجل يحسن العبارة باللسان اليوناني ويعرف أشخاص تلك الأدوية فإن كان في بلدك من يحسن ذلك فزت أيها الملك بفائدة الكتاب وأما كتاب هروسيس فعندك في بلدك من اللطينيين من يقرأه باللسان اللطيني وإن كشفتهم عنه نقلوه لك من اللطيني إلى اللسان العربي.

قال ابن جلجل ولم يكن يومئذ بقرطبة من نصارى الأندلس من يقرأ اللسان الإغريقي الذي هو اليوناني القديم فبقي كتاب ديسقوريدس في خزانة عبد الرحمن الناصر باللسان الإغريقي ولم يترجم إلى اللسان العربي وبقي الكتاب بالأندلس والذي بين أيدي الناس بترجمة إسطفن الواردة من مدينة السلام بغداد.

فلما جاوب الناصر أرمانيوس الملك سأله أن يبعث إليه برجل يتكلم بالإغريقي واللطيني ليعلم له عبيداً يكونون مترجمين فبعث أرمانيوس الملك للناصر براهب كان يسمى نقولا فوصل إلى قرطبة سنة أربعين وثلاثمائة وكان يومئذ بقرطبة من الأطباء قوم لهم بحث وتفتيش وحرص على استخراج ما جهل من أسماء عقاقير كتاب ديسقوريدس إلى العربية وكان أبحثهم وأحرصهم على ذلك من جهة التقرب إلى الملك عبد الرحمن الناصر حسداي بن شبروط الإسرائيلي وكان نقولا الراهب عنده أحظى الناس وأخصهم به.

> (Ibn Juljul said: 'This book [Dioscorides on simples] reached al-Andalus in the translation of Iṣṭifan,[32] a book in parts of which the translator either did not know the name [of the simple] in Arabic or did not know the original name. People profited from what was clear in it in both the Mashriq and al-Andalus until the days of ʿAbd al-Raḥmān b. Muḥammad [i.e. ʿAbd al-Raḥmān III al-Nāṣir] who was at the time the ruler of al-Andalus. Armāniyūs,[33] the emperor (*mālik*) who reigned in Constantinople, wrote to ʿAbd al-Raḥmān in the year 337/948 sending him presents of great value and among those presents there was the *Book* of Dioscorides with illustrations of the herbs according to the admirable Byzantine/Christian (*rūmī*) way of illuminating. The book was written in Greek that is Ionian (*al-yunānī*). The emperor also sent the *Book* by Orosius, the historian (*ṣāḥib al-qiṣaṣ*) which is an admirable

32 Iṣṭifan b. Basīl, as previously explained by Ibn Juljul, had translated the *Materia medica* during the reign of al-Mutawakkil, and Ḥunayn b. Isḥāq had added glosses to it. But a number of simples had been left un-translated. For an overview on the complex history of the Arabic Dioscorides, see Gutas' review of Ullmann's seminal work (*Untersuchungen zur arabischen Überlieferung*), 'The Arabic Transmission of Dioskurides', pp. 457–62.

33 This name has been understood as referring to Romanus I (r. 920–944), but it may refer also to Constantine VII (r. 944–959), whose reign corresponds to the dates given in the text, as the Byzantine emperors from 867 to 1065 belonged to the Macedonian dynasty also called Armenian. I owe this point to S. Brentjes.

history of the Christians (*al-rūm*) which contains stories of the past, narratives on the kings of earlier times, and important useful lessons.

Armāniyūs wrote in his letter to al-Nāṣir: 'The utility of the *Book* of Dioscorides could not be harvested by you except with a man who mastered its expression in the Greek language and knew the plants of those simples. Is there in your land such a person who masters the language so that you — oh, King! — could profit from the utility of the book? As regards the *Book* of Orosius, you have in your land among the people who speak Latin someone who could read it in the Latin language so that if you make them study it they will translate it (*naqalūhu*) for you from Latin to the Arabic language'.

Ibn Juljul said: 'There was at that time among the Christians of al-Andalus none who could read the Greek language that is called ancient Greek (*al-yunānī al-qadīm*).[34] The *Book* of Dioscorides remained in the library of ʿAbd al-Raḥmān al-Nāṣir in the Greek language without being translated (*lam yutarjam*) into the Arabic language. The *Book* remained in al-Andalus while what circulated among the people was the translation by Iṣṭifan that had arrived from *Madīnat al-salām*, i.e. Baghdad'.

When al-Nāṣir answered the emperor Armāniyūs, he asked him to send him a man who spoke Greek and Latin to teach, thanks to him, slaves (*ʿabīd*) who would then become translators. The emperor Armāniyūs then sent to al-Nāṣir a monk called Nicholas. He arrived in Cordoba in the year 340/951. There were at that time in Cordoba among the doctors a group who were involved in investigation and scrutiny (*qawm lahum baḥth wa-taftīsh*) and who desired to figure out in Arabic what was ignored of the names of the medicaments mentioned in the *Book* of Dioscorides. The most inquisitive and willing (*wa-kāna abḥathahum wa-aḥraṣahum*) in this thanks to his proximity (*taqarrub*) to the king ʿAbd al-Raḥmān al-Nāṣir was Ḥasdāy b. Shaprūṭ al-Isrāʾīlī and the monk Nicholas became most esteemed by him and most intimate with him'.)[35]

Scholars who have dealt with this text have paid attention to the chronological problems related to the emperor mentioned in the text,[36] and to the identification of the translators of Orosius' *History* from Latin into Arabic,[37] but among other relevant issues largely left untouched is why a Byzantine

34 When I presented this paper at the Advanced School in the Humanities (see note *), some of the attendants expressed their surprise at the terminology used in this text to refer to the Greek language.

35 The reference to Ibn Abī Uṣaybiʿa's work in note 30 above.

36 This refers to those who understood the text as mentioning the emperor Romanus I (r. 920–44), but cf. what is said in note 33.

37 Levi Della Vida, 'La traduzione araba della storie di Orosio', pp. 257–93; Christys, *Christians*

emperor would have decided to include books among the presents sent to a Muslim ruler and why specifically those two.

Regarding the first issue and as already noted, books had been sent from Byzantium to the Abbasids,[38] and receiving the same type of gift in al-Andalus made the Cordoban Umayyads equal to their Abbasid rivals, in the same way that having mosaics sent from Byzantium to Cordoba made them equal to their Umayyad ancestors in Damascus.[39] Taking this into account, contrary to what the narrative implies, the Umayyad court may have suggested that books were appropriate gifts to be sent as part of the exchange of embassies. We should note that contemporary Byzantine embassies to the other Umayyad caliphal rival, the Fatimid imam-caliph, did not include books or at least they are not mentioned in the reports at our disposal.[40] The fact that relics were included among the presents in this case can be connected with Fatimid interests.[41] It is also noteworthy that a letter sent by the Byzantine emperor to al-Ḥakam II (r. 961–976) when he was still a prince reveals the eagerness with which the Cordoban Umayyads were demanding books by the philosophers and men of science (*al-ḥukamāʾ*) from Byzantium.[42] In that letter, the emperor states: 'As regards your request that I should present him with (such) books ….'[43] As part of the Umayyad construction of the Cordoban caliphate, the initiative must have originated in Cordoba, but Ibn Juljul later obscured the demand that put the Cordoban caliph in a position of inferiority vis-a-vis the emperor so that in his narrative the emperor sends the books on his own initiative.

Regarding the second issue, for some modern scholars the mention of Orosius' *History* among the presents sent by the emperor is puzzling for a number of reasons.[44] Not least because many copies of this Latin text circulated in the

---

in al-Andalus (711–1000), pp. 140–45; Penelas, 'A Possible Author of the Arabic Translation of Orosius' *Historiae*', pp. 113–35.

38 See above note 22.

39 Fierro, 'En torno a la decoración con mosaicos de las mezquitas omeyas', pp. 131–44.

40 A Byzantine embassy to the Fatimids in North Africa took place in 957–958: Stern, 'An Embassy of the Byzantine Emperor', pp. 239–58 (Halm, *The Empire of the Mahdi*, p. 331, mentions a previous embassy dated in 946). Among the presents sent by the Emperor Nikephoros Phokas to al-Muʿizz (r. 953–975) there was the sword of Muḥammad that had been captured in Palestine: Cutler, 'Significant Gifts', pp. 90 and 92; later the saddles of Alexander the Great were sent by Michael IV Stratiotikos to the mother of the Fatimid caliph al-Mustanṣir: Mango, 'Hierarchies of Rank and Materials', p. 369, quoting Hamidullah, 'Nouveaux documents', pp. 286–88.

41 Walker, 'Purloined Symbols of the Past', pp. 364–87.

42 Stern, 'A Letter of the Byzantine Emperor', pp. 37–42 and Krönung, 'Ein Schreiben des Konstantinos VII. Porphyrogennetos', pp. 93–99. The letter has been preserved with a copy (now lost) of the Arabic translation of Apollonius of Tyana's *Kitāb al-ʿilal*, a magical text.

43 The request is done not by the Umayyad himself but by one of his courtiers, most probably Ḥasdāy b. Shaprūṭ, of whom a fragment of a letter that he sent to the Byzantine emperor has been preserved: Ashtor, *The Jews of Moslem Spain*, pp. 188–91; Mann, *Texts and Studies in Jewish History and Literature*, pp. 10–12. I owe these references to Jonathan Decter.

44 While al-Ḥakam's request was for philosophical and scientific books, the embassy

Iberian Peninsula and a translation seems to have been undertaken before the embassy given that materials taken from Orosius were quoted by Aḥmad al-Rāzī (d. 955). Thus, the translation would have taken place within the Christian community in Cordoba with the aim of providing that community — by then largely Arabized — with a universal history written from a Christian point of view (roughly at the same time, Orosius' *History* was being translated into Old English to cater for the needs of another Christian community). This context would explain why the Arabic translation at our disposal incorporated a summary of Visigothic history: it is implausible that a copy brought from Byzantium would have contained such details.[45] But such a summary could have been added during the process of translation, as caliphal needs cannot be completely ruled out: the Umayyad caliphal political and religious project involved the desire to integrate the history of the communities who had lived in the Iberian Peninsula prior to the arrival of the Arabs.[46] The project was of course larger; it involved the creation of a distinctive Andalusi culture — no longer dependent on Iraq — in which Muslims, Christians, and Jews would equally participate with Umayyad intellectual patronage embracing them all. Regarding the Jews, as D. Wasserstein notes, Ḥasdāy is portrayed in Ibn Juljul's text as acting in concert with his employer, the caliph of Cordoba:

> Ḥasdāy's work, in separating the Jews of al-Andalus from those of Iraq, and in offering the patronage and creating the conditions in which a distinctive Jewish cultural identity came into being in the Iberian Peninsula, parallels that of his own patron, al-Ḥakam II al-Mustanṣir, in which exactly the same happened, at exactly the same time, for the Muslims of al-Andalus.[47]

Doubts can thus be reasonably expressed about the inclusion of a copy of the Latin Orosius among the books sent by the Emperor to the Cordoban caliph. What about the case of Dioscorides's *Materia Medica*? As noted, the book had been translated incompletely into Arabic for the Abbasids in Baghdad towards the middle of the third/ninth century: in the translation made from a Greek original by Iṣṭifan b. Basīl — with glosses by Ḥunayn b. Isḥāq — no Arabic equivalents had been found for a number of technical terms.[48] According to Ibn Juljul's narrative, the Byzantine emperor warned the caliph that someone

---

mentioned by Ibn Juljul included a historical text. We do not know if it had been requested (see the discussion below) or if was included on the Byzantine emperor's initiative.

45 Penelas, introduction to *Kitāb Hurūšiyūš*, pp. 27–30. See also Penelas, '¿Hubo dos traducciones árabes independientes?', pp. 223–52 (the answer is negative), and 'Fuentes no identificadas y contenidos no conservados del Libro 7 del Orosio árabe', forthcoming (available at https://digital.csic.es/handle/10261/159608). See also Matesanz Gascón, 'Desde Bizancio hasta Córdoba', proposing that Apianus' historical writings may have been those sent by the Byzantine emperor.

46 Sahner, 'From Augustine to Islam', pp. 1–27.

47 Wasserstein, 'The Muslims and the Golden Age of the Jews in al-Andalus', p. 194.

48 See note 31. Which simples were those is not known.

familiar with 'old Greek' would be needed, as if assuming that persons (such as slaves and merchants) who could speak what can be termed 'colloquial Greek' were available in al-Andalus but they would be unable to access the original medical text.[49] The monk Nicholas was thus sent to Cordoba after 'Abd al-Raḥmān requested someone capable of speaking Greek (*ighrīqī*) as no one with such expertise had been found in al-Andalus. The caliph intended to have this person teach slaves who would eventually act as translators,[50] but if that was the case the slaves are not mentioned again. Among the group of doctors who were mentioned by Ibn Juljul as having been involved in the investigation and scrutiny (*qawm lahum baḥth wa-taftīsh*)[51] and who desired to work out what would be the Arabic names for the remedies in Dioscorides' book, some are specifically named: Muḥammad al-Shajjār, al-Basbasī, Abū ʿUthmān al-Jazzār al-Yābisa, Muḥammad b. Saʿīd al-Ṭabīb, ʿAbd al-Raḥmān b. Isḥāq b. Haytham, and one Abū ʿAbd Allāh al-Ṣiqillī.[52] These names suggest neither slaves nor Christians, except perhaps in the case of the Sicilian (Abū ʿAbd Allāh al-Ṣiqillī) of whom it is said that he spoke Greek[53] and knew the remedies. A Sicilian connection appears in another report having to do with Muslims trying to understand the text of Dioscorides. The Sevillan poet and litterateur Abū l-Ḥasan ʿAlī b. ʿAbd Allāh, known as Ghulām al-Ḥurra, travelled to the East, made the pilgrimage to Mecca and visited many regions of the Maghrib looking for plants. He was interested in medicine and had knowledge of plants, writing a *Sharḥ fī Kitāb Diyāsqūrīdūs* from which people derived many benefits as he was able to point to the specific plants behind the terms mentioned by Dioscorides. He did so by using the knowledge of a slave woman he owned called Ana the Greek and of whom he had taken possession from among the captives taken in Syracuse (Sicily). This slave-girl's mother had been a midwife expert in plants and simples.[54] Direct and

---

49 This point was made by Vernet, 'Los médicos andaluces', pp. 445–62. The use of the expression '*al-yunānī al-qadīm*' deserves to be studied in itself. A tenth-century copy of the Greek Dioscorides is preserved in New York, Pierpont Morgan Library, MS 652: http://ica.themorgan.org/manuscript/page/3/143825.

50 On the prominent role played by slaves in translating activities, see P. S. van Koningsveld, 'Muslim Slaves and Captives in Western Europe during the Late Middle Ages', pp. 5–23. For the view that most Muslims regarded the study of non-Islamic languages as demeaning, see Lewis, *The Muslim Discovery of Europe*, pp. 71–88.

51 Insistence on the importance of investigation, research, and reasoning is paramount in Ibn Juljul's *Ṭabaqāt al-aṭibbāʾ wa-l-ḥukamāʾ*.

52 Ibn Abī Uṣaybiʿa, *ʿUyūn al-anbāʾ fī ṭabaqāt al-aṭibbāʾ*, p. 39 (Arabic)/38 (translation). Ibn Juljul met them all during the caliphate of al-Ḥakam II.

53 Which means that between 948 (embassy) and/or 951 (arrival of the monk) and the time when Ibn Juljul's team was active someone had been found who spoke Greek.

54 al-Marrākushī (d. 1302), *al-Dhayl wa-l-Takmila li-kitabay al-Mawṣūl wa-l-Ṣila*, vol. 1, p. 239 (483), in Luis de Mármol Carvajal, *Description de l'Afrique*, ed. and trans. by d'Ablancourt. Given the absence of any other chronological data in this scholar's biography, the mention of the conquest of Syracuse has led some scholars to conclude that Ghulām al-Ḥurra lived in the third/ninth century, as when Syracuse was conquered in 264/878, many captives were

practical knowledge of the plants appears to have been more helpful than any 'old Greek' for improving the existing Arabic translation of the *Materia Medica* by making it understandable in the local Andalusi context.[55] Thus, in the case of Dioscorides' book it may have been included among those sent by the Emperor to the Cordoban caliph, most probably also including books on the occult sciences such as Apolonius of Tyana's *Kitāb al-ʿilal*.[56] Writing under al-Manṣūr b. Abī ʿĀmir — responsible for the purge of al-Ḥakam II's library during which the books dealing with the science of the ancients were burned excepting those considered to be acceptable for Muslim needs — Ibn Juljul would have omitted such suspicious books and added Orosius, an historical book that was not problematic.[57]

Returning now to Averroes, if the presents sent by the Byzantine emperor to the Cordoban Umayyads and the Fatimids reflected the interests of both dynasties (books and relics), a further differentiation can be added. The Fatimids as Ismaili imam-caliphs were endowed with supernatural knowledge and had no need of being enlightened by foreign books, thus the Fatimids — who could have had easier access to Greek translators through Sicily — do not appear to have started any translating movement. On their part, the Cordoban Umayyad caliphs were Sunnis and thus for them knowledge was acquired, not given, and the possession and study of books was part of such an acquisition process. The Almohads were influenced by both precedents, but in the case of the Andalusi Averroes he would have been more inclined to stress the Cordoban Umayyad model which could have opened the way for an Almohad project of translating into Arabic the legacy of Classical Antiquity, including Aristotle's *Politics*. Luis de Mármol Carvajal (1524–1600), in his *Description of Africa*, states that the Maghribis use a book on agriculture that was translated from Latin into Arabic in Cordoba during the reign of Yaʿqūb al-Manṣūr, i.e., the third Almohad caliph who ruled from 1184–1198.[58] No evidence exists of such a translation, but the mention is indicative that the Almohad period was remembered as one in which translating activities could have taken place.

---

taken and enslaved: Haremska, 'Gulām al-Ḥurra, Abū l-Ḥasan'. But other episodes may be behind: in the fourth/tenth century, the Byzantines conquered the city and held it for three years; in 1086, the Normans conquered it; later there was a Muslim expedition from Ifriqiya and in 1127 an Almoravid attack. One of these later dates and most especially the twelfth century seems to be the most probable period for Ghulām al-Ḥurra's life which coincides with Ullmann's view: *Untersuchungen zur arabischen Überlieferung*, p. 65.

55 The need to pay attention to practical expertise has been highlighted by Zuccato, 'Arabic Singing Girls, the Pope, and the Astrolabe', pp. 99–120.

56 See above note 42. On the Cordoban Umayyads' interest in such sciences, see Fierro, 'Plants, Mary the Copt, Abraham, Donkeys and Knowledge', pp. 125–44.

57 For Ibn Juljul's relations with al-Manṣūr b. Abī ʿĀmir, see Balty-Guesdon, 'Les *Ṭabaqāt al-aṭibbāʾ wa-l-ḥukamāʾ* d'Ibn Ǧulǧul', pp. 49–59, and cf. Alvarez Millán, 'Medical Anecdotes in Ibn Juljul's Biographical Dictionary', pp. 141–58.

58 Mármol Carvajal, *Description de l'Afrique*, 1, p. 15.

Bibliography

Primary Sources

Al-Ḥimyarī, *Kitāb al-rawḍ al-miʾṭār*, partial edition and translation by E. Lévi-Provençal, La Péninsule Iberique au Moyen Age (Leiden: Brill, 1938)

La Chronica Gothorum Pseudo-Isidoriana (ms. Paris BN 6113), ed. and trans. by Fernando González Muñoz (A Coruña: Toxosoutos, 2000)

Ibn Abī Uṣaybiʿa, *ʿUyūn al-anbāʾ fī ṭabaqāt al-aṭibbāʾ. Médecins de l'Occident musulman*, ed. by H. Jahier and A. Noureddin (Alger: Librairie Ferraris, 1377/1958)

——, *A Literary History of Medicine*, ed. and trans. by E. Savage-Smith, S. Swain, and G. J. van Gelder (Leiden: Brill, 2020), Open Access at: https://brill.com/view/db/lhom

Ibn Khaldūn, *Kitāb al-ʿibar*, 7 vols (Būlāq, 1867 / Beirut: Dār al-Kitāb al-Lubnānī, 1959)

Kitāb Hurūšiyūš, traducción árabe de las 'Historiae adversus paganos' de Orosio, ed. by Mayte Penelas (Madrid: CSIC, 2001)

Luis de Mármol Carvajal, *Description de l'Afrique*, ed. and trans. by Chevalier d'Ablancourt (Paris, 1667), vol. 1 : al-Marrākushī. *al-Dhayl wa-l-Takmila li-kitabay al-Mawṣūl wa-l-Ṣila*; vols IV–V : ed. by Iḥsān ʿAbbās (Beirut: Dār al-thaqāfa, n.d.)

al-ʿUmarī, *Masālik al-abṣār*, facsimile ed. by F. Sezgin and others (Frankfurt am Main: Johann Wolfgang Goethe University, 1988), vol. IX

Secondary Studies

Aillet, Cyrille, *Mozarabes: christianisme, islamisation et arabisation en Péninsule Ibérique (IXᵉ–XIIᵉ siècle)* (Madrid: Casa de Velázquez, 2010)

Alvarez Millán, Cristina, 'Medical anecdotes in Ibn Juljul's Biographical Dictionary', *Suhayl*, 4 (2004), 141–58

Ashtor, Eliyahu, *The Jews of Moslem Spain* (Philadelphia: The Jewish Publication Society of America, 1973–1984), I: pp. 188–91

Balty-Guesdon, Marie-Geneviève, 'Les *Ṭabaqāt al-aṭibbāʾ wa-l-ḥukamāʾ* d'Ibn Ǧulǧul: une condamnation du régime ʿāmiride', *Cahiers d'Onomastique Arabe* (1988–1992), 49–59

——, 'Al-Andalus et l'héritage grec d'après les *Ṭabaqāt al-umam* de Ṣāʿid al-Andalusī', in *Perspectives arabes et médiévales sur la tradition scientifique et philosophique grecque*, ed. by Ahmed Hasnaoui, Abdelali Elamrani-Jamal, and Maroun Aouad (Louvain: Peeters, Institut du monde arabe, 1997), pp. 231–342

Brague, Rémi, 'Note sur la traduction arabe de la Politique d'Aristote, derechef, qu'elle n'existe pas', in P. Aubenque and A. Tordesillas, *Aristote Politique. Études sur la Politique d'Aristote* (Paris: Presses Universitaires de France, 1993), pp. 423–33

Cabo-González, Ana M., 'Action et interaction entre les peuples de la Méditerranée. La traduction en arabe de textes scientifiques grecs dans le califat de Cordoue: la version revisée du *Materia medica* de Dioscorides', in *Re-Defining a Space of Encounter. Islam and Mediterranean: Identity, Alterity and Interactions: Proceedings of the 28th Congress of the Union Européenne des Arabisants et Islamisants, Palermo 2016*, ed. by A. Pellitteri, N. Elsakaan, M. G. Sciortino, and D. Sicari, Orientalia Lovaniensia Analecta (Leuven: Peeters, 2019), pp. 415–25

Casewit, Yousef, 'A Muslim Scholar of the Bible: Prooftexts from Genesis and Matthew in the Qur'an Commentary of Ibn Barrajan of Seville (d. 536/1141)', *Journal of Qur'anic Studies*, 18 (2016), 1–48

El Cheikh, Nadia, 'Byzantium through the Islamic Prism from the Twelfth to the Thirteenth Century', in *The Crusades from the Perspective of Byzantium and the Muslim World*, ed. by Angeliki E. Laiou and Roy Parviz Mottahedeh (Washington, DC: Dumbarton Oaks, 2001), pp. 53–69

Christys, Ann, *Christians in al-Andalus: 711–1000* (Richmond: Curzon, 2002)

Cruz Hernández, Miguel, 'La recepción de los *falāsifa* orientales en al-Andalus: problemas críticos', *Anaquel de Estudios Arabes*, 4 (1993), 37–51

Cutler, Anthony, 'Significant Gifts: Patterns of Exchange in Late Antique, Byzantine, and Early Islamic Diplomacy', *Journal of Medieval and Early Modern Studies*, 38 (2008), 79–101

Ducène, Jean-Charles, 'Al-Bakrī et les *Étymologies* d'Isidore de Séville', *Journal Asiatique*, 297.2 (2009), 379–97

Fierro, Maribel, 'En torno a la decoración con mosaicos de las mezquitas omeyas', *Homenaje al Prof. Jacinto Bosch Vila*, 2 vols (Granada: Editorial Universidad de Granada, 1991), I: pp. 131–44

——, 'Plants, Mary the Copt, Abraham, Donkeys and Knowledge: Again on Batinism during the Umayyad Caliphate in al-Andalus', *Differenz und Dynamik im Islam. Festschrift für Heinz Halm zum 70. Geburtstag*, ed. by Hans-Hinrich Biesterfeldt and Verena Klemm (Würzburg: Ergon Verlag, 2012), pp. 125–44

——, 'Averroes' "Disgrace" and his Relations with the Almohads', in *Islamic Philosophy from the 12th to the 14th Century*, ed. by Abdelkader Al Ghouz (Bonn: V&R, 2018), pp. 73–118

——, 'Ibn Ṭufayl's *Ḥayy b. Yaqẓān*: An Almohad Reading', *Islam and Christian-Muslim Relations*, 34.1 (2020), 385–405

Freudenthal, Gad, 'Arabic into Hebrew: The Emergence of the Translation Movement in Twelfth-Century Provence and Jewish-Christian Polemic', in *Beyond Religious Borders: Interaction and Intellectual Exchange in the Medieval Islamic World*, ed. by David M. Freidenreich and Miriam Goldstein (Philadelphia: University of Pennsylvania Press, 2011), pp. 125–43

Garijo Galán, Ildefonso, 'Ibn Ŷulŷul, Sulaymān', *Biblioteca de al-Andalus*, vol. 6: *De Ibn al-Ŷabbāb a Nubḏat al-ʿaṣr*, ed. by Jorge Lirola Delgado (Almería: Fundación Ibn Tufayl de Estudios Árabes, 2009), pp. 163–66, nº 1396

Gilbert, Claire, *Reading Cultures: The Textual Transmission between Muslim and Christian Communities in al-Andalus* (unpublished Senior Honors Thesis, Department of History, Stanford, May 14, 2004)

Gutas, Dimitri, *Greek Thought, Arabic Culture: The Graeco-Arabic Translation Movement in Baghdad and Early ʿAbbāsid society (2nd–4th/8th–10th centuries)* (London: Routledge, 1998)

——, 'What was there in Arabic for the Latins to Receive? Remarks on the Modalities of the Twelfth-Century Translation Movement in Spain', in *Wissen über Grenzen. Arabisches Wissen und lateinisches Mittelalter*, ed. by Andreas Speer und Lydia Wegener (Berlin: de Gruyter, 2006), pp. 3–21

——, 'The Arabic Transmission of Dioskurides: Philology Triumphant', *Journal of the American Oriental Society*, 132.3 (2012), 457–62

Hamidullah, Muhammad, 'Nouveaux documents sur les rapports de l'Europe avec l'Orient musulman au moyen âge', *Arabica*, 7 (1966), 286–88

Haremska, Julia, 'Gulām al-Ḥurra, Abū l-Ḥasan', in *Biblioteca de al-Andalus*, ed. by Jorge Lirola Delgado (Almería: Fundación Ibn Tufayl de Estudios Árabes, 2012), Apéndice, pp. 48–49, no. 1958

Hasse, Dag Nikolaus, 'The Social Conditions of the Arabic-(Hebrew-)Latin Translation Movements in Medieval Spain and in the Renaissance', in *Wissen über Grenzen. Arabisches Wissen und lateinisches Mittelalter*, ed. by Andreas Speer und Lydia Wegener (Berlin: de Gruyter, 2006), pp. 68–86

al-Ḥajjī, Abderrahman, 'Al-ʿAlāqāt al-diblūmasiyya bayna al-Andalus wa-l-Bizanta ḥattà nihāyat al-qarn al-rābiʿ al-hijrī', *Revista del Instituto Egipcio de Estudios Islámicos*, 22 (1983–1984), 53–91

Halm, Heinz, *The Empire of the Mahdi: The Rise of the Fatimids*, trans. by M. Bonner (Leiden: Brill, 1996)

Historia de los Autores y Transmisores Andalusíes (HATA), dir. Maribel Fierro, available online at http://kohepocu.cchs.csic.es/

Krönung, Bettina, 'Ein Schreiben des Konstantinos VII. Porphyrogennetos an den umayyadischen Prinzen al-Ḥakam in Cordoba', *Byzantinische Zeitschrift*, 105 (2012), 93–99

Levi Della Vida, Giorgio, 'La traduzione araba della storie di Orosio', *Miscellanea G. Galbialti III*, (Milano, 1951), 185–203, reprint in *Al-Andalus*, 109 (1954), 257–93

Lewis, Bernard, *The Muslim Discovery of Europe* (New York: W. W. Norton, 1982)

López Guix, Juan Gabriel, 'Las primeras traducciones bíblicas en la Península Ibérica', *Revista de Historia de la Traducción*, 7 (2013), n. p. http://www.raco.cat/index.php/1611/article/viewFile/275764/363728

Mango, M. Mundell, 'Hierarchies of Rank and Materials: Diplomatic Gifts Sent by Romanus I in 935 and 938', *Deltion tēs Christianikēs Archaiologikēs Hetaireias*, 4th ser., 24 (2003), 365–74

Mann, Jacob, *Texts and Studies in Jewish History and Literature* (Philadelphia: Hebrew Press Jewish Publication Society of America, 1935), I, 10–12

Matesanz Gascón, Roberto, 'Desde Bizancio hasta Córdoba: Orosio, Apiano y la *Crónica del Moro Rasis*', *Edad Media. Revista de Historia* 6 (2003–2004), 209–24

Molina, Luis, 'Orosio y los geógrafos hispano-musulmanes', *Al-Qanṭara*, 5 (1984), 63–92

Monferrer-Sala, Juan Pedro, '"You brood of vipers!" Translations and Revisions in the Andalusi Arabic Version of the Gospels', *Le Muséon*, 131.1–2 (2018), 187–21

Morata, Nemesion, 'La presentación de Averroes en la corte almohade', *La Ciudad de Dios*, 153 (1941), 101–22

Penelas, Mayte, 'Contribución al estudio de la difusión de la Cosmografía de Julio Honorio en la Península Ibérica', *Al-Qanṭara*, 22 (2001), 1–18

——, 'A Possible Author of the Arabic Translation of Orosius' *Historiae*', *Al-Masāq*, 13 (2001), 113–35

——, '¿Hubo dos traducciones árabes independientes de las *Historias contra los paganos* de Orosio?', *Collectanea Christiana Orientalia*, 6 (2009), 223–52

——, 'Fuentes no identificadas y contenidos no conservados del Libro 7 del Orosio árabe. Nuevos datos para su identificación', forthcoming (available at https://digital.csic.es/handle/10261/159608)

Plessner, Martin, 'Hispano-Arabic vs. Eastern Tradition of Aristotle's and al-Fārābī's writings', *Actas del Primer Congreso de Estudios Arabes e Islámicos* (Madrid: Comité permanente del Congreso de Estudios Árabes e Islámicos, 1964), pp. 109–14

Ramón Guerrero, Rafael, 'Para la historia de al-Andalus: Primera presencia de al-Fārābī', in *Homenaje al Prof. Jacinto Bosch Vilá* (Granada: Editorial Universidad de Granada, 1991), II: pp. 1191–208

Richter-Bernburg, Lutz, 'Ṣāʿid, the *Toledan Tables* and Andalusī Science', in *From Deferent to Equant: A Volume of Studies in the History of Science in the Ancient and Medieval Near East in Honor of E. S. Kennedy*, ed. by David A. King and George Saliba (New York: New York Academy of Sciences, 1987), pp. 373–401

Rosenthal, Franz, *The Classical Heritage in Islam*, translated from the German by Emile and Jenny Marmorstein (London: Routledge and Kegan Paul, 1975)

Sahner, Christian, 'From Augustine to Islam: Translation and History in the Arabic Orosius', *Speculum*, 88.3 (2013), 1–27

Samsó, Julio, *Las ciencias de los antiguos en al-Andalus* (2nd edn with *addenda et corrigenda* by J. Samsó and M. Forcada) (Almería: Fundación Ibn Tufayl, 2011)

——, 'Al-Andalus, a Bridge between Arabic and European Science', *Alhadra*, 1 (2015), 101–25

——, *On Both Sides of the Strait of Gibraltar. Studies on the History of Medieval Astronomy in the Iberian Peninsula and the Maghrib* (Leiden: Brill, 2020)

Sánchez-Albornoz, Claudio, *Fuentes latinas de la historia romana de Rasis* (Buenos Aires: Publicaciones del Instituto Cultural Argentino-Hispano-Arabe, 1942)

Santoyo, Julio-César, *La traducción medieval en la Península Ibérica (siglos III–XV)* (León: Universidad de León, 2009)

Schütrumpf, Eckart, *The Earliest Translations of Aristotle's Politics and the Creation of Political Terminology*, Morphomata Lectures Cologne, Herausgegeben von Günter Blamberger und Dietrich Boschung, 8 (Paderborn: Wilhelm Fink, 2014)

Signes Codoñer, Juan, 'La diplomacia del libro en Bizancio. Algunas reflexiones en torno a la posible entrega de libros griegos a los árabes en los siglos VIII-X', *Scrittura e Civiltà*, 20 (1996), 153–87

Stern, Samuel M., 'An Embassy of the Byzantine Emperor to the Fatimid Caliph Al-Muʿizz', *Byzantion*, 20 (1950), 239–58

——, 'A Letter of the Byzantine Emperor to the Court of the Spanish Umayyad Caliph al-Hakam', *Al-Andalus*, 26 (1969), 37–42

Sypianski, Jakub, 'Arabo-Byzantine Relations in the 9th and 10th Centuries as an Area of Cultural Rivalry', in *Proceedings of the International Symposium Byzantium and the Arab World Encounter of Civilizations*, ed. by A. Kralides and A. Gkoutzioukostas (Thessaloniki: Aristotle University of Thessaloniki, 2013), pp. 465–78

Syros, Vasileios, 'A Note on the Transmission of Aristotle's Political Ideas in Medieval Persia and Early-Modern India: Was there any Arabic or Persian Translation of the Politics?', *Bulletin de Philosophie Médiévale*, 50 (2008), 303–09

Tobi, Yosef, 'Yehudah Ha-Levi's Translations of Arabic Poems', in Yosef Tobi, *Between Hebrew and Arabic: Studies in Medieval Spanish Hebrew Poetry* (Leiden: Brill, 2010), pp. 369–86

Toral, Isabel, 'Translations as Part of Power Semiotics: The Case of Caliphal Cordova' <http://hdl.handle.net/10261/13949> [accessed 19 June 2017]

Ullmann, Manfred, *Untersuchungen zur arabischen Überlieferung der Materia medica des Dioskurides* (Wiesbaden: Harrassowitz, 2009)

Vallvé, Joaquín, 'Fuentes latinas de los geógrafos árabes', *Al-Andalus*, 32.2 (1967), 241–60

van Koningsveld, P. S., 'Muslim Slaves and Captives in Western Europe during the Late Middle Ages', in *Islam and Christian-Muslim Relations*, 6.1 (1995), 5–23

——, 'Greek Manuscripts in the Early Abbasid Empire: Fiction and Facts about their Origin, Translation and Destruction', *Bibliotheca Orientalis*, 55 (1998), 345–72

Vernet, Juan, 'Los médicos andaluces en el *Libro de las generaciones de médicos* de Ibn Ŷulŷul', *Anuario de estudios medievales*, 5 (1968), 445–62

——, *Lo que Europa debe al Islam de España* (Barcelona: El Acantilado, 1999)

Walker, Paul, 'Purloined Symbols of the Past: The Theft of Souvenirs and Sacred Relics in the Rivalry between the Abbasids and the Fatimids', in *Culture and Memory in Medieval Islam: Essays in Honour of Wilferd Madelung*, ed. by Farhad Daftary and Josef Meri (London: I. B. Tauris, 2003), pp. 364–87

Wasserstein, David J., 'Byzantium and al-Andalus', *Mediterranean Historical Review*, 1.2 (1987), 76–101

——, 'The Muslims and the Golden Age of the Jews in al-Andalus', *Israel Oriental Studies*, 17 (1997), 179–96

Watt, William Montgomery, 'Philosophy and Theology under the Almohads', *Actas del Primer Congreso de Estudios Arabes e Islámicos (Córdoba, 1962)* (Madrid: Comité Permanente del Congreso de Estudios Arabes e Islámicos, 1964), pp. 101–07; also published in *The Islamic Quarterly*, 8 (1964), 46–51

Yücesoy, Hayrettin, 'Translation as Self-Consciousness: Ancient Sciences, Antediluvian Wisdom and the Abbasid Translation Movement', *Journal of World History*, 20.4 (2009), 523–57

Zuccato, Marco, 'Arabic Singing Girls, the Pope, and the Astrolabe: Arabic Science in Tenth-Century Latin Europe', *Viator*, 45.1 (2014), 99–120

Part 2

Participant Narratives

EMILIANO FIORI

From *Opheleia* to Precision

Dionysius the Areopagite and the Evolution of Syriac Translation Techniques

The pseudo-epigraphic Corpus of Greek writings attributed to Dionysius the Areopagite (an Athenian judge converted by Paul during the latter's visit to Athens, as narrated in *Acts* 17. 34), abruptly appeared in the third decade of the sixth century and immediately enjoyed a wide success among Christian theologians of all confessions. It consists of four treatises (*On the Divine Names, On the Mystical Theology, On the Ecclesiastical Hierarchy,* and *On the Heavenly Hierarchy*) and of ten epistles addressed to known individuals of the apostolic age. The first half of the sixth century was an age of harsh Christological controversies concerning the way the human and divine components united in Christ. Since the first half of the fifth century, such controversies had been a matter of increasing political concern for the rulers of the eastern part of the empire, and by the first decades of the following century they had become a major reason for division among Christians, under both Roman and Sasanian rule. The writings of Pseudo-Dionysius, initially used by one of the Christological parties, the Miaphysites, as a source in their support, soon became a transversally appreciated theological authority. Their apostolic aura (they were allegedly written by a disciple of Saint Paul) also determined their apparent lack of interest in Christological controversy: Dionysius was instead interested in highly philosophical explanations of the divine names, in describing and interpreting the angelic and the Church orders, or in

* I am deeply indebted to Lucas Van Rompay for his valuable suggestions and for his careful revision of my translation of Phokas' preface.

Emiliano Fiori earned his PhD at the University of Bologna and the École pratique des hautes études of Paris in 2010. He is an associate Professor of Early Christian Literature at Ca' Foscari University of Venice. He has written numerous articles on the transfer of theological, philosophical, and scientific knowledge from Greek to Syriac, and has authored a two-volume critical edition and translation of the earliest Syriac version of the Pseudo-Areopagitic corpus (Louvain, 2014). Currently, he is the Principal Investigator of the Venice-based ERC Starting Grant project 'Florilegia Syriaca. The Intercultural Dissemination of Greek Christian Thought in Syriac and Arabic in the First Millennium CE'.

Narratives on Translation across Eurasia and Africa: From Babylonia to Colonial India, ed. by Sonja Brentjes in cooperation with Jens Høyrup and Bruce O'Brien, CAT 3, pp. 177–197 (Turnhout: Brepols, 2022) BREPOLS PUBLISHERS 10.1484/M.CAT-EB.5.127940

justifying and supporting the ineffability of God. These characteristics explain their peaceful and widespread reception; their apostolicity remained almost undisputed until the Italian Renaissance, when the style and content of the Corpus did not thwart the investigations of Lorenzo Valla. It became evident that Dionysius was a Christian disciple, or reader, of the last Neoplatonic philosopher Proclus, whose thought and language are pervasive and accurately reproduced (and, on crucial points, decisively modified to fit the Christian dogma) in the Dionysian oeuvre, especially in the treatise *On the Divine Names*. Dionysius's language was difficult and oracular, bursting with neologisms and with elaborated syntactic castles, but this did not discourage translators from rendering his works into Latin and into many languages of the Christian East throughout the first millennium and beyond. The Syriac translation made by Sergius, the archiater (i.e. physician-in-chief, d. 536) of the North-Mesopotamian city of Rešʿayna (today's devastated town of Raʾs al-ʿAyn in northern Syria), presumably within the last four years of his life, is particularly important, insofar as it is the first translation of the Dionysian Corpus into any other language and as it was made only a few years after the first public appearance of the Corpus, and the only manuscript that preserves it in its entirety is the earliest witness to the text of the Corpus in any language. Because of its great relevance, this version has already enjoyed a partial critical edition and a certain number of studies.[1]

The second Syriac translation of the pseudo-Dionysian writings, on the contrary, has not been the object of a deep-rooted scholarly attention, a fate it shares with the great majority of Syriac patristic translations of the period starting from the second half of the seventh century. Although a few of these translations enjoyed editions in the twentieth century (the seventh-century versions of Gregory Nazianzen's *Orations* being a particularly remarkable case of a Syriac patristic translation in the good hands of a whole editorial team),[2] a more sustained philological engagement with them and a detailed investigation of their translation style is still lacking and represents a desideratum of Syriac studies. It is a commonly accepted truth,[3] and is evident indeed from an even cursory reading of the published texts, that translations made by monks and clerics between the seventh and the ninth centuries, especially by those educated or active in the monastery of Qenneshre, on the eastern bank of the upper course of the Euphrates,[4] were often highly literal. The particular

1 For the edition, see *Dionigi Areopagita*, ed. and trans. by Fiori.

2 *Sancti Gregorii Nazianzeni Opera. Versio Syriaca I*, ed. by Haelewyck; *Sancti Gregorii Nazianzeni Opera. Versio Syriaca II*, ed. by Schmidt; *Sancti Gregorii Nazianzeni Opera. Versio Syriaca III*, ed. by Haelewyck; *Sancti Gregorii Nazianzeni Opera. Versio Syriaca IV*, ed. by Haelewyck; *Sancti Gregorii Nazianzeni Opera. Versio Syriaca V*, ed. by Haelewyck. See also Taylor, 'Les Pères cappadociens', pp. 43–61.

3 Brock, 'Towards a History of Syriac Translation Technique', pp. 1–14; Brock, 'Changing Fashions in Syriac Translation Technique', pp. 3–14.

4 For a first orientation on this monastery, founded around 530 and a most prominent centre

linguistic features of this literalism and the methodological principles inspiring it, however, have hardly ever been investigated in any detail.[5]

The second translation of the Dionysian Corpus dates indeed from this period. It was composed in the last quarter of the seventh century, and, what is more relevant, the second translator prefaced his work with an introduction in which he reflected on his choices, illustrating the methodological reasons that led him to produce a new version of the Dionysian writings. Of this translator we know little more than the name, Phokas bar Sargis of Edessa, the approximate dates (second half of the seventh century), and the fact that he translated Dionysius while being also distracted by 'worldly affairs'.[6] Unlike Sergius's translation, which has come down to us in only one manuscript and in a bunch of anthologized fragments,[7] Phokas's version apparently enjoyed a wider circulation,[8] which may prove that it actually succeeded in replacing the previous one.

This case study intends to be a brief discussion of the translation principles of Phokas's age on the basis of a comparison between the two versions of the Dionysian Corpus. In the following pages I shall take a first step towards the linguistic study of Phokas's Dionysius, by 1) illustrating the conceptual foundations of his method as expounded in the preface, and 2) by comparing two representative samples of his translation with the corresponding passages in Sergius's version.

---

of Greek learning for Western Syrians between the sixth and the ninth centuries, see at least Tannous, 'Qenneshre, Monastery of', Tannous, *The Making of the Medieval Middle East*, pp. 169–76, and Al-Dabte, 'Iktishāf Dayr Qinnisrīn'.

5 With the notable exception of the groundbreaking work of King, *The Syriac Versions of the Writings of Cyril of Alexandria*. Mention must also be made of Lash, 'Techniques of a Translator', pp. 365–83, and of Van Rompay, 'Jacob of Edessa and the Sixth-Century Translator of Severus of Antioch's Cathedral Homilies', pp. 189–204. Both these works highlight the 'passion for accuracy' (so Lash, 'Techniques of a Translator', p. 375) of the seventh-century translator, which reminds one of 'precision' as a methdological principle in Phokas's formulation (see below).

6 BL, MS Add. 12151, fol. 173r.

7 For the manuscript tradition of Sergius's version, see *Dionigi Areopagita*, ed. by Fiori, text volume, pp. xiii–xvii and xxii–xxvii.

8 After the pioneering investigations of the tradition of Phokas's translation by Sherwood, 'Sergius of Reshaina', pp. 174–84 and Hornus, 'Le Corpus dionysien en syriaque', pp. 69–93, Gernot Wiessner offered a much more precise assessment, which still remains the state of the art on the topic (Wiessner, 'Zur Handschriftenüberlieferung der syrischen Fassung des Corpus Dionysiacum', pp. 165–216; Wiessner, 'Beobachtungen', pp. 73–82). The oldest manuscript containing Phokas's version is dated to the year 804 (BL, MS Add. 12151), and it is the witness I will use in the present contribution.

Phokas of Edessa's Methodological Preface

Phokas's preface to his version of the Dionysian corpus is a document of the first rank for the history of Syriac translation techniques, but it has not received much critical attention.[9] Phokas's preface is particularly rich in indications, as it reveals much about the view West Syrians had of both what is required for a good translation from Greek into Syriac and of the historical development of translation techniques. In this respect, this short piece of writing (see the *Appendix* for the integral text) is one of the most important programmatic statements on translation in all of Syriac literature: the three prefaces of the sixth century that have reached us (to Severus's anti-Julianist works by Paul of Callinicum, to Cyril's *Glaphyra* by Moses of Inghilene, and to Gregory of Nyssa's *Commentary on the Song of Songs* by an anonymous translator) actually give no indications of how their authors saw, and whether they were aware of, their historical position within the evolution of translation techniques. This must not surprise us: in the sixth century, many Greek texts were being translated for the very first time, whereas the seventh century saw a large movement of revisions, starting with the Bible (the Harklean and the Syro-Hexaplaric versions) up to philosophical and patristic texts. This means that at the end of the seventh century, after cultivated West Syrians had witnessed, and still were taking part in, a long and productive wave of revisions of earlier translations, they had also reached a theoretical elaboration of this process. The nature itself of a revision process obliges the reviser to interrogate the historical difference that separates his own approach to language from his predecessors'. Phokas sees himself as a reviser, although his work, as we shall shortly see, can be better defined as a new translation. He ascribes the shortcomings in Sergius's translation to what he deems to be the insufficient development of translation techniques in Sergius's times:

> *perhaps*, as I believe — he writes —, [...] not many at that time had yet been amply instructed in this art of translating from Greek. [Things went thus] until [...] time passed by and with its alternations brought other lovers of toil, like the saint | and renowned Athanasius, patriarch of Antioch, and Jacob, bishop of Edessa — they who with their skill paved the way as far as it was possible, in a certain sense married the two languages, and produced profitable fruits from their joining, together with yet other anonymous people who had come before them.[10]

---

9 It was translated into French by Michel van Esbroeck in 1997: van Esbroeck, 'La triple préface syriaque', pp. 167–86. Unfortunately, however, van Esbroeck's translation misunderstands the meaning of the Syriac to such an extent that it is of no use for further research.

10 BL, MS Add. 12151, fols 2^{r-v}.

The seventh-century translator Phokas, then, not only is aware of the progress made by the translation art in the previous 150 years, but he also underpins the expression of his awareness by explicitly mentioning the names of two representative figures of this progress, Athanasius of Balad (d. 687) and Jacob of Edessa (d. 708). In Phokas, however, this historical consciousness is filtered through the rhetoric of reverence, and does not feature as a dismissal of Sergius's achievements as a translator, as is the case of Ḥunayn ibn Isḥāq's commentaries on most of Sergius's Galenic version one and a half century after Phokas.[11] Indeed, after a short introduction on the necessity of giving up the attachment to material things, Phokas sets out to discuss the translation of Dionysius made by the 'pious and skilful Sergius, priest and archiater'. All the Syrians, Phokas goes on to say, read Sergius's version of the Dionysian Corpus, so that they 'highly admired and praised [it] on account of the highness of its thoughts, i.e., of its divinity'.[12] We have also read above how he introduces his statement on the development of translation techniques with a nuancing 'perhaps' (ܟܒܪ). Phokas, however, immediately expounds the main problem with Sergius's Dionysian version, though downplaying it through a declaration of humility:

> [I] also [re-translated] those [words] that I found in the earlier translation of Sergius, which are not translated with *precision* […]. And this [I did] not in order to take pride in things like these, or to blame the erudition of that [earlier translator], far be it; but in order to clearly show that […] by conforming to the Syriac language and taking pains to teach [the reader] by all means the things said [by Dionysius], [Sergius] simplified his wordings in various passages, lest the reader's mind be dulled […] on account of the difficulty and the intricacy of the sentences, and their reading be found useless.[13]

As can be seen, Phokas does not limit himself to the rhetoric of humility here, but he tells us something substantial and points to a historical truth. He admits

11 Of course, Phokas's respect might also be due to the fact that he shared with Sergius the Miaphysite confession, whereas Ḥunayn belonged to the East Syriac Church. In Ḥunayn's case, however, it is difficult to believe that his critical attitude may be attributed to a difference in ecclesiastical denomination. Moreover, Ḥunayn was not always critical toward Sergius: as he declares in the 'auto-bibliographic' letter on his Galenic translations (see *Ḥunain ibn Isḥāq über die syrischen und arabischen Galen-Übersetzungen*, ed. by Bergsträsser, p. 30 text, 24 transl.; see also the most recent English translation in Lamoreaux, *Ḥunayn ibn Isḥāq on his Galen Translations*), he did not re-translate Galen's *On Simple Drugs*, which Sergius had (integrally?) already translated into Syriac, but simply revised it; and indeed, in his own compilation based on Galen's *On the Properties of Foodstuffs* he integrated some passages from Sergius's version of *On Simple Drugs*, often in the form of a simple copy-paste (see Bhayro and Hawley, 'La littérature botanique et pharmaceutique en langue syriaque', p. 301 n. 39).

12 BL, MS Add. 12151, fol. 1^{v}.

13 BL, MS Add. 12151, fol. 2^{r}.

that Sergius's version, in his opinion, lacks *precision* (ܚܬܝܬܘܬܐ), which is thus indicated as a major criterion for assessing a translation, and he explains why: because Sergius intended to adapt Dionysius's difficult Greek to the Syriac language, although without sacrificing the content ('to teach [the reader] by all means the things said [by Dionysius]', ܕܢܣܟܠܘܗܝ، ܐܟܠܡ ܕܡܬܐܡܪ̈ܢ) and thus simplifies the wording (ܠܡܠܠܬܗ). The appropriateness of this analysis can be demonstrated through an accurate investigation of Sergius's translation style: the archiater's translation actually showcases a successful balance of care for the reader and attention to the content.[14] Phokas does not blame Sergius's choice, insofar as he understands that it aimed to the *opheleia*, the profit of the reader, as to its main goal; nevertheless, he now intends to abandon this orientation, and highlights precision as the major goal. Precision is also explicitly stressed as the synthesis of the 'profitable fruits' Jacob of Edessa, Athanasius of Balad, and many others have brought about (see the quotation above): thanks to their efforts 'the art [of translation] is being refined and clarified, and thanks to their diligence [they, *scil.* the translators] are adopting from the precise rendering [ܚܬܝܬܘܬܗ] of the Greek words that are unusual for the Syrians'.[15] If precision was the main goal, we must assume that Phokas's intended audience no longer was a generically broad cultivated clergy but rather a relatively small, highly learned circle of (monastic) scholars, who took the comprehension of the content of the translated texts for granted and concentrated on the correct application of an increasingly formalized set of translation rules.

Sketches for a Comparative Study, or, Did Phokas Follow His Own Principles?

In the following I shall offer a comparative study of Sergius's and Phokas's translations of two selected passages from the *Divine Names* and the *Mystical Theology*, in order to understand 1) to what extent, and on what linguistic and stylistic levels, Phokas applied the criteria he sketched in his preface; 2) to what extent his Dionysian translation can actually be deemed a 'revision' of Sergius's version.[16] Let us delve into the first text, a particularly complicated eschatological passage from the *Divine Names*.

---

14 See Fiori, 'Sergius of Reshaina and Pseudo-Dionysius', and *Dionigi Areopagita*, ed. by Fiori, translation volume, pp. xxxii and more in general pp. xxxi–lxxxv.

15 BL, MS Add. 12151, fol. 2^{v}.

16 The foundations for this comparison were laid by Werner Strothmann in 1977, when he published a parallel edition and translation of Sergius's and Phokas's versions of Dionysius's treatment of the consecration of the *myron* in his *Ecclesiastical Hierarchy* (Strothmann, *Das Sakrament der Myron-Weihe*). The Greek-Syriac index to this edition is an excellent starting point for any further comparative study of the two versions. A further, shorter comparative lexical sounding in Quaschning-Kirsch, 'Die Frage der Benennbarkeit Gottes', pp. 117–26.

Divine Names 1. 4

Greek[17] (Suchla 114. 7–115. 3)	**Sergius**[18] (Fiori 8)	**Phokas** (BL, MS Add. 12151, fols 79r–80v)
Τότε δέ, ὅταν ἄφθαρτοι καὶ ἀθάνατοι γενώμεθα καὶ τῆς χριστοειδοῦς καὶ μακαριωτάτης ἐφικώμεθα λήξεως, 'πάντοτε σὺν κυρίῳ' κατὰ τὸ λόγιον 'ἐσόμεθα' τῆς μὲν ὁρατῆς αὐτοῦ θεοφανείας ἐν πανάγνοις θεωρίαις ἀποπληρούμενοι φανοτάταις μαρμαρυγαῖς ἡμᾶς περιαυγαζούσης ὡς τοὺς μαθητὰς ἐν ἐκείνῃ τῇ θειοτάτῃ μεταμορφώσει, τῆς δὲ νοητῆς αὐτοῦ φωτοδοσίας ἐν ἀπαθεῖ καὶ ἀΰλῳ τῷ νῷ μετέχοντες καὶ τῆς ὑπὲρ νοῦν ἑνώσεως ἐν ταῖς τῶν ὑπερφανῶν ἀκτίνων ἀγνώστοις καὶ μακαρίαις ἐπιβολαῖς.	ܡܐ ܕܢܗܘܐ ܕܝܢ ܠܐ ܡܝܘܬܐ ܘܠܐ ܡܬܚܒܠܢܐ: ܗܘܝܢ ܡܬܥܠܝܢ ܐܦ ܠܘܬ ܗ̇ ܛܟܣܐ ܛܘܒܬܢܝܬܐ ܕܡܬܕܡܝܐ ܒܡܫܝܚܐ. ܟܕ ܗ̇ܘܝܢ ܒܟܠܙܒܢ ܥܡ ܡܪܢ. ܐܝܟ ܕܐܡܪܐ ܒܪܬ ܩܠܐ ܚܝܬܐ. ܘܡܬܡܠܝܢ ܒ̈ܓܠܝܢܐ ܕܕܟܝܢ ܒܟܠ: ܐܦ ܡܢ ܕܢܚܐ ܡܬܚܙܝܢܐ ܕܐܠܗܢ. ܟܕ ܡܙܠܓ ܥܠܝܢ ܒ̈ܙܠܩܐ ܡ̈ܢܗܪܢܐ: ܐܝܟ ܕܥܠ ܬܠܡ̈ܝܕܐ ܒܗ̇ܘ ܫܘܚܠܦܗ ܐܠܗܝܐ ܕܒܛܘܪܐ.܀ ܥܡ ܡܘܗܒܬܐ ܕܝܢ ܡܥܠܝܬܐ ܕܢܘܗܪܗ ܡܬܝܕܥܢܐ ܡܫܬܘܬܦܝܢ: ܒܡܕܥܐ ܪܘܚܢܐ ܘܠܐ ܚܫܘܫܐ. ܘܡܬܚܠܛܝܢ ܠܡ ܚܢܢ ܒܚܕܝܘܬܗ ܪܡܬ ܡܢ ܟܠ ܡܕܥ: ܒܙ̈ܘܥܐ ܛܘܒܬܢܐ ܘܠܐ ܡܬܕܪܟܢܐ: ܕܙܠ̈ܩܐ ܡܢ̈ܗܪܝ ܠܟܠ ܡܢ ܟܠ: ܕܪܘܚܢܘܬܗ ܕܡܕܥܢ: ܗ̇ܘ ܕܡܢ̈ܝ ܨܠܡ ܐܠܗܐܝܬ ܒܕܡܘܬܐ ܐܠܗܐܝܬ: ܕܗ̈ܘܢܐ ܕܠܥܠ ܡܢ ܫܡܝܐ	ܗ̇ܝܕܝܢ ܕܝܢ: ܐܡܬܝ ܕܠܐ ܡܝܘܬܐ ܘܠܐ ܡܬܚܒ̈ܠܢܐ ܢܗܘܐ: ܘܠܘܬ ܫܘܡܠܝܐ ܕܡܕܡܐ ܠܡܫܝܚܐ ܘܛܘܒܬܢܐ ܢܡܛܐ: ܗܘܝܢ ܒܟܠܙܒܢ ܥܡ ܡܪܢ. ܐܝܟ ܟܬܒܐ: ܘܡܬܡܠܝܢ ܡܢ ܡܬܚܙܝܢܘܬܐ ܕܡܬ ܓܠܝܢܘܬܗ ܐܠܗܝܬܐ ܒܝܕ ܬܐܘܪ̈ܝܣ ܕܕܟܝܬ ܒܟܠ: ܟܕ ܡܢ̈ܗܪܢܐ ܠܢ ܙܗܪ̈ܝܐ ܕܝܬܝܪ ܕܢܨܝܚܝܢ: ܐܝܟ ܕܐܦ ܠܬܠܡ̈ܝܕܐ ܒܫܘܚܠܦ ܕܡܘܬܐ ܗ̇ܘ ܐܠܗܝܐ܀ ܥܡ ܡܘܗܒܬ ܢܘܗܪܐ ܕܝܢ ܡܬܝܕܥܢܝܬܐ ܕܝܠܗ: ܘܚܕܝܘܬܗ ܕܠܥܠ ܡܢ ܗܘܢܐ ܡܫܬܘܬܦܝܢ: ܒܗܘܢܐ ܠܐ ܚܫܘܫܐ ܘܠܐ ܗܝܘܠܝܐ: ܒܝܕ ܡܚ̈ܬܢܘܬܐ ܟܣܝ̈ܬܐ ܘܛܘܒܬ̈ܢܝܬܐ ܕܙܠܝ̈ܩܘܗܝ ܝܬܝܪ ܕܢܗܝܪܐ:
But hereafter, when we are incorruptible and immortal and attain the blessed lot of being like unto Christ, then (as the Scripture saith), we shall be for ever with the Lord, fulfilled with His visible Theophany in holy contemplations, which shall shine about us with radiant beams of glory (even as once of old it shone around the Disciples at the Divine Transfiguration); and so shall we, with our mind made passionless and spiritual, participate in a spiritual illumination from Him and in a union transcending our mental faculties, and there, amidst the blinding blissful impulsions of His dazzling rays, we shall, in a more divine manner than at present, be like unto the heavenly Intelligences.[19]	But when we become immortal and incorruptible, then we shall be raised to the blessed order that is assimilated to Christ, being forever with our Lord, as the vivifying Word says; and we shall also be filled, through completely pure revelations, by the visible manifestation of our God, when it shines upon us with dazzling rays, as upon the disciples in that divine metamorphosis of His on the mountain. In the sublime gift of His intelligible light we shall partake with a spiritual and impassible mind, and we shall be mingled in His union, which is higher than any mind, through the blissful and incomprehensible stirrings of the rays — brighter than all — of the spiritual component of our mind, which is divinely shaped to divinely resemble those intellects that [abide] above the heaven.	But then, when we become immortal and incorruptible, and we reach the perfection similar to Christ and blessed, we shall be forever with our Lord, according to the Scripture, and we shall be filled by the appearance of His divine revelation through completely pure contemplations, as the brightest glares will shine upon us, just as on the disciples, too, in that divine metamorphosis. In the gift of His intelligible light and in His union, which is above the intellect, we shall partake with an impassible and immaterial intellect, through the secret and blissful descents of His over-bright rays.

17 *Corpus Dionysiacum I. De divinis nominibus*, ed. by Suchla.

18 See no. 1.

19 *Dionysius the Areopagite on the Divine Names and the Mystical Theology*, trans. by Rolt, p. 58.

The following Greek sentence is a good starting point for the analysis:

> Τότε δέ, ὅταν ἄφθαρτοι καὶ ἀθάνατοι γενώμεθα καὶ τῆς χριστοειδοῦς καὶ μακαριωτάτης ἐφικώμεθα λήξεως, 'πάντοτε σὺν κυρίῳ' κατὰ τὸ λόγιον 'ἐσόμεθα'
>
> (But hereafter, when we are incorruptible and immortal and attain the blessed lot of being like unto Christ, then [as the Scripture saith], we shall be for ever with the Lord.)

Sergius renders it by:

> ܡܐ ܕܗܘܝܢ ܕܝܢ ܠܐ ܡܝܘܬܐ ܘܠܐ ܡܬܚܒܠܢܐ: ܗܝܕܝܢ ܡܬܥܠܝܢ ܐܦ ܠܘܬ ܗ̇ܝ ܛܟܣܐ ܛܘܒܬܢܝܬܐ ܕܡܬܕܡܝܐ ܒܡܫܝܚܐ. ܟܕ ܗ̇ܘܝܢ ܒܟܠܙܒܢ ܥܡ ܡܪܢ. ܐܝܟ ܕܐܡܪܐ ܒܪܬ ܩܠܐ ܚܝܬܐ.
>
> (But when we become immortal and incorruptible, then we shall enter the blessed order that is assimilated to Christ, being forever with our Lord, as the vivifying Word says.)

We can observe that τότε is translated but postponed, giving the Syriac sentence a more natural flow: ܗܝܕܝܢ [...] ܡܐ (when [...] then); in Phokas, on the contrary, the syntactical structure of the Greek is carefully mirrored:

> ܗ̇ܝܕܝܢ ܕܝܢ: ܐܡܬܝ ܕܠܐ ܡܝܘܬܐ ܘܠܐ ܡܬܚܒܠܢܐ ܢܗܘܐ: ܘܠܘܬ ܫܘܡܠܝܐ ܡܕܡܝܐ ܒܡܫܝܚܐ ܘܛܘܒܬܢܝܬܐ ܢܡܛܐ: ܗܘܝܢ ܒܟܠܙܒܢ ܥܡ ܡܪܢ ܐܝܟ ܟܬܒܐ:
>
> (But then, when we become immortal and incorruptible, and we reach the perfection similar to Christ and blessed, we shall be forever with our Lord, according to the Scripture.)

ܗ̇ܝܕܝܢ (then), translating τότε, is put forward as well as τότε is in Greek and, as in Greek, the subordinate clause precedes the main clause that τότε introduces. Thus, it is clear from the outset that for Phokas syntax is the first relevant level on which his literal orientation is applied. Phokas, however, does not push this as far as to radically mirroring the word order: if a structure is not reproducible in Syriac, he avoids it. This is evident from his translation of the phrase τῆς χριστοειδοῦς καὶ μακαριωτάτης ἐφικώμεθα λήξεως (we [...] attain the blessed lot of being like unto Christ), which cannot be mirrored in Syriac without distorting the language. Phokas renders it through the expression ܘܠܘܬ ܫܘܡܠܝܐ ܡܕܡܝܐ ܒܡܫܝܚܐ ܘܛܘܒܬܢܝܬܐ ܢܡܛܐ: (we reach the perfection similar to Christ and blessed), which preserves the order of the adjectives and the position of the verb but does not postpone the translation of λήξεως, which would produce an unnatural effect in Syriac. Although his rendering cannot be defined a mirror translation, Phokas is, however, much stricter than Sergius in following the word order. If we turn to Sergius's rendering (ܡܬܥܠܝܢ ܐܦ ܠܘܬ ܗ̇ܝ ܛܟܣܐ ܛܘܒܬܢܝܬܐ ܕܡܬܕܡܝܐ ܒܡܫܝܚܐ, we shall enter the blessed order that is assimilated to Christ), we see that he has been more flexible in transposing the order: the verb is in the first position and not at the end as in Phokas, who in this regard tries to keep closer to the original, and the order of the adjectives is reversed. Moreover, Sergius adds the adverb ܐܦ, 'also', which does not find any parallel in Greek. On the lexical level, the most macroscopic difference consists in the different rendering of λήξεως, which Sergius apparently interprets as coming from λαγχάνω (ܬܟܣܐ, order/rank) whereas Phokas views it as linked to λήγω (ܫܘܡܠܝܐ, perfection). Besides these different interpretations, other significant shifts must be stressed: the use of the verb ܡܛܐ, 'to come' for ἐφικνέομαι in Phokas, which is semantically closer to the Greek, while Sergius prefers a much freer rendering through the verb ܥܠܐ, 'to raise, elevate', and the participle-adjective ܕܡܝܐ (similar) in Phokas, which mirrors the adjectival component -ειδοῦς more closely than Sergius's typical periphrastic choice, ܕܡܬܕܡܝܐ (that is assimilated). Even more interesting is the difference between Phokas's translation of the recurrent Dionysian expression κατὰ τὸ λόγιον by ܐܝܟ ܟܬܒܐ (according to the Scripture), which mirrors the Greek both semantically and syntactically, and Sergius's preference for a paraphrase: on the one hand, he uses a Semitic idiom (ܒܪܬ ܩܠܐ, word) to render τὸ λόγιον, and on the other hand, he adds an adjective to it, 'vivifying', ܚܝܬܐ, and a verb: 'as the vivifying Word says'[20] (ܐܝܟ ܕܐܡܪܐ ܒܪܬ ܩܠܐ ܚܝܬܐ). On all levels, then, we can observe that Phokas faithfully follows the methodology of 'marrying the two languages', as he brings them as close as possible to one another, whereas Sergius, though not sacrificing the contents of the original, tries to make one of Dionysius's most characteristic phrases readable for an audience that did not know Greek. Both Phokas's analysis of Sergius's technique and his own translation principles, as stated in the preface, are confirmed by this first sample.

This is further confirmed by the evident effort made by Phokas to account for the radical signification of the Greek words. Indeed, he reformulates Sergius's wording wherever the latter, though *lato sensu* correct, is not perfectly focused on the *basic* semantic level of the corresponding Greek word. An appropriate example is the shift observed above from Sergius's ܥܠܐ (raise) to Phokas's ܡܛܐ (arrive) for the verb ἐφικνέομαι. While the choice for ܥܠܐ does not compromise at all the comprehension of the text, yet Phokas is driven towards a more basic verb. An even more significant example of this tendency in Phokas is the very slight change from Sergius's ܡܘܗܒܬܐ (gift) to ܝܗܘܒܘܬܐ (act of giving, gift) to render the component -δοσία in φωτοδοσία. From the noun formed on the *af'el* used by Sergius, Phokas switches to a plainer pattern and reflects -δοσία more immediately (more basically) than ܡܘܗܒܬܐ does. Indeed, the latter implies the idea of 'gift, present', whereas ܝܗܘܒܘܬܐ conveys no more than the simple concept of 'giving' and thereby the basic meaning of -δοσία. Despite all precision of the sixth-century translator, Sergius, allowing for a penetration

20 This expansion of Dionysius's τὸ λόγιον is quite typical in Sergius; that it does not indicate Christ but the Scripture is unambiguous because of the use of ܒܪܬ ܩܠܐ, which, differently from the noun ܡܠܬܐ, does not usually indicate Christ as the Word of God.

of the second semantic level of 'gift', comes closer to the implied meaning of Dionysius's term than Phokas does with his greater accuracy.

Phokas, however, proves flexible in cases of excessive complexity of the Greek syntax. The clause

> τῆς δὲ νοητῆς αὐτοῦ φωτοδοσίας ἐν ἀπαθεῖ καὶ ἀΰλῳ τῷ νῷ μετέχοντες καὶ τῆς ὑπὲρ νοῦν ἑνώσεως ἐν ταῖς τῶν ὑπερφανῶν ἀκτίνων ἀγνώστοις καὶ μακαρίαις ἐπιβολαῖς
>
> > (and so shall we, with our mind made passionless and spiritual, participate in a spiritual illumination from Him and in a union transcending our mental faculties, amidst the blinding blissful impulsions of His dazzling rays.)

cannot be rendered literally in Syriac as far as the word order is concerned. Phokas translates it as:

> ܒܡ ܡܘܗܒܬ ܢܘܗܪܐ ܕܝܢ ܡܬܝܕܥܢܝܬܐ ܕܝܠܗ: ܘܒܚܘܝܕܗ ܕܠܥܠ ܡܢ ܗܘܢܐ ܡܫܬܘܬܦܝܢ: ܒܗܘܢܐ ܠܐ ܚܫܘܫܐ ܘܠܐ ܗܘܠܢܝܐ܂ ܒܝܕ ܡܚܬܢܘ̈ܬܐ ܟܣܝ̈ܬܐ ܘܛܘܒܬܢܝܬܐ ܕܙܠܝ̈ܩܘܗܝ ܝܬܝܪ ܕܢܗܝܪܐ܂
>
> > (In the gift of His intelligible light and in His union, which is above the intellect, we shall partake with an impassible and immaterial intellect, through the secret and blissful descents of His over-bright rays.)

This sentence is particularly interesting insofar as its complexity probably derives from a textual corruption. Indeed, it would seem reasonable here to expect a second verb besides μετέχοντες, as a parallel structure seems to be needed. The whole sentence consists of two syntactically identical members, made up of a genitive (τῆς φωτοδοσίας – τῆς ἑνώσεως) and of a phrase introduced by ἐν (ἐν ἀπαθεῖ καὶ ἀΰλῳ τῷ νῷ – ἐν ταῖς ἀγνώστοις καὶ μακαρίαις ἐπιβολαῖς). The participle μετέχοντες of the first member, however, does not find any parallel in the second one. This may be due to an *apo koinou* structure, both genitives being related to μετέχοντες; alternatively, the second verb may have fallen in the course of the tradition. Sergius either read a different and more complete Greek original or added to it: not only does he have a second verb parallel to μετέχοντες, but as a matter of fact he also expands the whole sentence with contents that for various reasons[21] may well be deemed to be Dionysian. One must also consider that Sergius pays much attention to the rhetorical level of Dionysius's style,[22] making an effort to render it. Be this as it may, Phokas also perceived that something was not in order in this sentence, to the point that he postponed the translation of μετέχοντες, putting it after the renderings of both genitives φωτοδοσίας and ἑνώσεως; as a result, he grouped both the phrases with ἐν at the bottom of the sentence, one after another

---

21 I have illustrated them in Fiori, 'Mélange eschatologique et "condition spirituelle" de l'intellect'.

22 See the analyses in *Dionigi Areopagita*, ed. by Fiori, translation volume, pp. xl–lvii.

ܒܗܘܢܐ ܠܐ ܚܫܘܫܐ ܘܠܐ ܗܘܠܢܝܐ: ܒܝܕ ܡܚܬܘܬ̈ܐ ܟܣܝܬ̈ܐ ܘܛܘܒܬܢܝܬ̈ܐ ܕܙܠܝ̈ܩܘܗܝ(ܝܬܝܪ ܢܗܝܪܐ, with an impassible and immaterial intellect, through the secret and blissful descents of His over-bright rays). Thus, while trying to make sense of the slightly awkward syntax, Phokas's translation of this sentence does not reflect its rhetorical structure and is on the whole less faithful than Sergius's, even if the latter showcases an elaboration that may be the result of an editing process. On the other hand, however, on the lexical level Phokas confirms his drive to precision. For example, he translates the Greek words ἀπαθεῖ καὶ ἀΰλῳ with the perfect Syriac parallels ܠܐ ܚܫܘܫܐ ܘܠܐ ܗܘܠܢܝܐ (with an impassible and immaterial [intellect]), whereas Sergius renders them (with an inversion) as ܪܘܚܢܝܐ ܘܠܐ ܚܫܘܫܐ (spiritual and impassible), where the second adjective is translated according to similarity of meaning (not material = spiritual) and not through a semantically equivalent root. This cannot be considered as an occasional imprecision, as Sergius employs this rendering consistently throughout his translation.[23] The phrase ἐν ταῖς τῶν ὑπερφανῶν ἀκτίνων ἀγνώστοις καὶ μακαρίαις ἐπιβολαῖς demonstrates, however, that Phokas allows for a certain degree of freedom and flexibility, even on the lexical level, on which he generally proves more coherent. His translation ܟܣܝܬ̈ܐ (secret) for ἀγνώστοις is something the reader would rather expect from Sergius, as it bears a similar meaning but is not formed on a semantically equivalent root; Sergius, on the contrary, gets closer (although he does not employ an exactly equivalent root either) to the original with ܠܐ ܡܬܕܪ̈ܟܢܐ (incomprehensible, lit. inaccessible). The latter example also proves that a clear-cut distinction free/literal does not account for all the possible situations with which Dionysius confronts our translators. Yet this is only an exception to the general rule that Phokas evidently imposed on himself. Indeed, whereas the pioneering translator Sergius is clearly at a loss to translate the Greek technical term ἐπιβολή (relatively common in Plotinus and Proclus) and renders it generically as 'stirrings' (ܙܘ̈ܥܐ), Phokas opts once more for a greater semantic precision, using the noun ܡܚܬܘܬ̈ܐ (lit. descents). As we have observed in the case of ܡܘܗܒܬܐ/ܡܘܗܒܘܬܐ (giving/gift) however, Phokas's literalism impoverishes the Dionysian text as it does not display the philosophical connotations of the Greek word and lays it flat on the very basic sense of the root.[24]

Mystical Theology II

The previous example was useful to underline the methodological differences between Sergius and Phokas, as the divergence between their translation choices was quite remarkable. The following example, drawn from the second chapter of the *Mystical Theology*, is perhaps even more significant insofar as

23 See *Dionigi Areopagita*, ed. by Fiori, text volume, p. 138.

24 It must be recalled, however, that the root of ܡܚܬܘܬ̈ܐ is also rich in connotations throughout the history of Syriac literature: see Brock, 'Passover, Annunciation and Epiclesis', pp. 222–33.

the distance between the two translations is minimal. Phokas exhibits here a greater closeness to his predecessor, whose renderings he mostly preserves; but the changes he introduces, precisely because they are fairly slight, are all the more significant to illustrate the methodological difference between the two versions.

Greek[25] (Ritter 145. 2–7)	**Sergius** (Fiori 109–10)	**Phokas** (BL, MS Add. 12151, fol. 153[vab])
Κατὰ τοῦτον ἡμεῖς γενέσθαι τὸν ὑπέρφωτον εὐχόμεθα γνόφον καὶ δι' ἀβλεψίας καὶ ἀγνωσίας ἰδεῖν καὶ γνῶναι τὸν ὑπὲρ θέαν καὶ γνῶσιν αὐτῷ τῷ μὴ ἰδεῖν μηδὲ γνῶναι — τοῦτο γάρ ἐστι τὸ ὄντως ἰδεῖν καὶ γνῶναι — καὶ τὸν ὑπερούσιον ὑπερουσίως ὑμνῆσαι διὰ τῆς πάντων τῶν ὄντων ἀφαιρέσεως, ὥσπερ οἱ αὐτοφυὲς ἄγαλμα ποιοῦντες ἐξαιροῦντες πάντα τὰ ἐπιπροσθοῦντα τῇ καθαρᾷ τοῦ κρυφίου θέᾳ κωλύματα.	ܣܓܝ ܗܟܝܠ܆ ܠܗܕܐ ܥܪܦܠܐ ܕܠܥܠ ܡܢ ܟܠ ܢܗܝܪ̈ܝܢ ܡܨܠܝܢ ܠܡܥܠ. ܘܒܗ̇ ܠܐ ܚܙܬܐ ܘܠܐ ܝܕܥܬܐ܆ ܠܚܙܐ ܘܠܡܕܥ܆ ܠܗ̇ܘ ܡܢ ܕܐܝܬܘܗܝ܆ ܠܥܠ ܡܢ ܚܙܬܐ ܘܝܕܥܬܐ. ܗܢܘ ܕܝܢ ܗ̇ܝ ܗܕܐ܆ ܕܠܐ ܢܚܙܐ ܘܠܐ ܢܕܥ. ܡܛܠ ܕܗܕܐ ܐܝܬܝܗ̇ ܒܫܪܪܐ܆ ܗ̇ܝ ܕܢܚܙܐ ܫܪܝܪܐܝܬ܆ ܘܢܕܥ ܘܢܫܒܚ܆ ܠܗ̇ܘ ܕܐܝܬܘܗܝ ܠܥܠ ܡܢ ܟܠ ܐܝܬܝܐܝܬ܆ ܒܝܕ ܦܘܪܫܢܐ ܕܡܢ ܟܠܗܘܢ ܟܝܢܐ. ܘܢܥܒܕ ܗܕܐ ܗܟܢܐ܆ ܒܕܡܘܬܐ ܕܗ̇ܢܘܢ ܕܓܠܦܝܢ ܠܗ ܨܠܡܐ ܡܕܡ ܒܟܐܦܐ ܐܘ ܒܩܝܣܐ܆ ܕܦܪܫܝܢ ܘܫܩܠܝܢ ܡܢ ܟܠ ܥܒܝܘܬܗ̇ ܟܠܗܘܢ ܥܘܟ̈ܒܐ܆ ܐܝܠܝܢ ܕܐܝܟ ܬܟܣܝܬܐ ܡܟܠܝܢ ܗܘܘ܆ ܠܚܙܬܐ ܕܫܦܝܬܐ ܕܟܣܝܬܐ ܗܘܬ ܠܓܘ	ܒܗܕܐ ܥܪܦܠܐ ܡܥܠܝܬ ܢܘܗܪܐ ܡܨܠܝܢ ܠܡܗܘܐ. ܘܒܗ̇ ܠܐ ܚܙܬܐ ܘܠܐ ܝܕܥܬܐ ܠܚܙܐ ܘܠܡܕܥ ܠܗ̇ܘ ܕܠܥܠ ܡܢ ܚܙܬܐ ܘܝܕܥܬܐ ܒܗ̇ ܒܗ̇ܝ ܕܠܐ ܚܙܐ ܘܠܐ ܝܕܥ. ܗܕܐ ܓܝܪ ܐܝܬܝܗ̇ ܗ̇ܝ ܕܫܪܝܪܐܝܬ ܚܙܐ ܘܝܕܥ. ܘܠܗ̇ܘ ܕܠܥܠ ܡܢ ܐܘܣܝܐ ܠܥܠ ܡܢ ܐܘܣܝܐ ܢܫܒܚܝܘܗܝ ܒܝܕ ܦܘܪܫܢܐ ܕܡܢ ܟܠܗܘܢ ܐܝܠܝܢ ܕܐܝܬܝܗܘܢ ܐܝܟ ܐܝܠܝܢ ܕܗ̇ܢܘܢ ܕܓܠܦܝܢ ܠܗ ܒܟܐ̈ܦܐ܆ ܕܦܪܫܝܢ ܠܟܠܗܘܢ ܥܘܟ̈ܒܐ ܕܡܟܠܝܢ ܠܚܙܬܐ ܕܟܝܬܐ ܕܗ̇ܘ ܡܢ ܕܟܣܝܐ
I pray we could come to this darkness so far above light! If only we lacked sight and knowledge so as to see, so as to know, unseeing and unknowing, that which lies beyond all vision and knowledge. For this would be really to see and to know: to praise the Transcendent One in a transcending way, namely through the denial of all beings. We would be like sculptors who set out to carve a statue. They remove every obstacle to the pure view of the hidden image, and simply by this act of clearing aside they show up the beauty which is hidden.[26]	Thus we pray to enter this mist, which is above all lights and, through non-sight and non-knowledge, to see and know Him who is above sight and knowledge: [by 'non-sight' and 'non-knowledge' I mean] the fact of not seeing and not knowing — for this is actually seeing truly and knowing and celebrating Him who is essentially above all through separations from all natures, and doing this similarly to those who sculpt an image in stone or wood, who set apart and take [from] its whole thickness all the obstacles that, like a covering, obstructed the pure sight that was hidden inside.	In this mist superior to light we pray to be and, through non-sight and non-knowledge, to see and to know Him who is above sight and knowledge. By not seeing and not knowing — for this is truly seeing and knowing — we shall celebrate above ousia Him who is above ousia, through separations from all that is: like those who sculpt an image in stones, who remove all the obstacles obstructing the pure sight of what is hidden.

If we observe the structure and the wording of the third clause, we realize that Sergius and Phokas overlap almost perfectly in every respect: syntax, word order, vocabulary.

25 *Corpus Dionysiacum II*, ed. by Heil and Ritter.

26 Dionysius, *The Mystical Theology*, trans. by Dysinger.

Sg: ܘܒܝܕ ܠܐ ܚܙܬܐ ܘܠܐ ܝܕܥܬܐ܆ ܚܙܐ ܘܝܕܥ܆ ܗܘ ܡܢ ܕܐܝܬܘܗܝ ܠܥܠ ܡܢ ܚܙܬܐ ܘܝܕܥܬܐ (and, through non-sight and non-knowledge, (we pray) to see and know Him who is above sight and knowledge)

Ph: ܘܒܝܕ ܠܐ ܚܙܬܐ ܘܠܐ ܝܕܥܬܐ ܚܙܐ ܘܝܕܥ ܠܗܘ ܕܠܥܠ ܡܢ ܚܙܬܐ ܘܝܕܥܬܐ (through non-sight and non-knowledge, [we pray] to see and to know Him who is above sight and knowledge)

Phokas has clearly imported Sergius's formulation into his version, but the small changes he introduces show the specific character of his methodology. Whereas Sergius expresses the verb 'to be' in ܗܘ ܡܢ ܕܐܝܬܘܗܝ ܠܥܠ ܡܢ ܚܙܬܐ ܘܝܕܥܬܐ (who is above sight and knowledge), Phokas corrects him by implying the verb (ܠܗܘ ܕܠܥܠ ܡܢ ܚܙܬܐ ܘܝܕܥܬܐ, who [is] above sight and knowledge), as he wants to mirror the Greek wording τὸν ὑπὲρ θέαν καὶ γνῶσιν more literally: indeed, the Greek does not include the verb. The same logic drives the correction of Sergius's antecedent of the relative ܗܘ ܡܢ (him) into ܠܗܘ. Both the elimination of ܡܢ and the addition of the preposition ܠ- also obey to a principle of literalism: the first one as it is superfluous in order to render the original, the second one because it marks the direct object more precisely than the simple ܗܘ.

It is noteworthy that both Sergius and Phokas prefer to avoid translating the difficult adjective αὐτοφυές[27] referred to the noun ἄγαλμα. As I have demonstrated elsewhere,[28] the phrase 'of stone and wood' by which Sergius renders it is typically associated with sculpture (of idols) in the Bible[29] and also used by Sergius in a similar philosophical context in his commentary on Aristotle's *Categories*. Phokas omits ܒܩܝܣܐ, 'in wood', yet he maintains 'in stone(s)', which he can only have taken from Sergius.

The rest of Phokas's wording in this sentence is also influenced by Sergius's choices, but Phokas corrects Sergius in the usual way:

Sg: ܒܕܡܘܬܐ ܕܗܢܘܢ ܕܓܠܦܝܢ ܠܨܠܡܐ ܡܕܡ ܒܟܐܦܐ ܐܘ ܒܩܝܣܐ܆ ܕܦܪܫܝܢ ܘܡܦܩܝܢ ܡܢ ܟܠ ܥܒܝܘܬܗ ܟܠܗܘܢ ܟܠܝ̈ܢܐ܆ ܐܝܠܝܢ ܕܐܝܟ ܬܚܦܝܬܐ ܡܟܠܝܢ ܗܘܘ܆ ܠܐܦ ܚܙܬܐ ܕܫܦܝܬܐ ܕܟܣܝܐ ܗܘܬ ܠܓܘ

(similarly to those who sculpt an image in stone or wood, who set apart and take [from] its whole thickness all the obstacles that, like a covering, obstructed the pure sight that was hidden inside.)

Ph: ܐܝܟ ܕܗܢܘܢ ܕܓܠܦܝܢ ܠܨܠܡܐ ܒܟܐ̈ܦܐ܆ ܕܡܪܚܩܝܢ ܠܟܠܗܘܢ ܟܘ̈ܠܝܐ ܕܡܟܠܝܢ ܠܐܦ ܚܙܬܐ ܕܟܣܝܬܐ ܕܗܘ ܡܢ ܕܒܓܘ

27 Around Sergius's times it mostly recurred in the Neoplatonists Proclus and Simplicius.
28 Fiori, 'Sergius of Reshaina and Pseudo-Dionysius', pp. 192–93.
29 See e.g. Deuteronomy 4. 28; 2 Kings 19. 18; Isaiah 37. 19; Ezra 20. 32.

(like those who sculpt an image in stones, who remove all the obstacles obstructing the pure sight of what is hidden.)

In order to reflect the Greek ὥσπερ more faithfully, Phokas substitutes Sergius's adverbial locution ܒܕܡܘܬܐ (similarly to) with ܐܝܟܢܐ (like), which is closer to the original; he eliminates ܡܕܡ (something, 'one' as an indefinite pronoun) as it does not find any proper correspondence in Greek; and where Sergius used one of his typical translation devices, the doublet, to render a composite Greek verb, in this case ἐξαιροῦντες (in his version ܦܪܫܝܢ ܘܢܣܒܝܢ, 'set apart and take', which translate ἐξ- and -αιροῦντες respectively), Phokas employed one single verb, restoring a 1:1 lexical correspondence and a more proper semantic proximity. Once again, he adds the preposition ܠ- to the direct object (ܟܠܗܘܢ ܟܣܘ̈ܝܐ — ܠܟܠܗܘܢ ܟܣܘ̈ܝܐ); he cares for a more precise rendering of τοῦ κρυφίου, which in Sergius became an adjective of θέᾳ whereas Phokas translates it as it is, namely as a substantivized adjective; Sergius's explicative editing, i.e. his additions ܡܢ ܟܠ ܥܘܒܝܗ, (from its whole thickness), ܐܝܟ ܬܟܣܝܬܐ (like a covering), and ܠܓܘ (inside), is abolished. Thus, the typical features of Phokas's version, grammatical and lexical precision, are manifest here, but at the same time they are implanted in the body of Sergius's version, which remains clearly recognizable under Phokas's.

Provisional Conclusions

Much work remains to be done in order to generalize or inversely to limit the purport of the few notes offered above. From the samples I analysed, however, it seems evident that Phokas conceives of 'precision' as of the closest possible mirroring of the original on all levels, from syntax to vocabulary. Such closeness, however, on the one hand does not exclude flexibility and thus does not reach the excess of some extreme cases of mirror translations like those produced by the Armenian Hellenizing translators or,[30] in some cases, in later Syriac versions (e.g. of Gregory Nazianzen's *Carmina*).[31] Phokas's Dionysius can be read without a facing Greek text. On the other hand, I have observed that the constant search for linguistic precision can and does sometime impoverish the rich stratification of Dionysius's style; whereas Sergius's frequent periphrastic and paraphrastic twists, as they reflect the translator's wandering through the labyrinth of the Dionysian discourse, do end up capturing and conveying its deepest implications.

30 For a representative study, see Muradyan, 'The Hellenizing School', pp. 321–48.

31 For a very imperfect edition of the texts, see *Sancti Gregorii Theologi liber Carminum Iambicorum*, ed. by Bollig and Gismondi; see also the observations of Crimi, 'Fra tradizione diretta e tradizione indiretta', pp. 83–93, of Sembiante, 'Appunti sulla tradizione siriaca', and, most recently, Fiori, 'Appendice seconda', especially pp. 223–41.

Appendix: Text and Translation of Phokas's Preface to his Syriac Version of the Dionysian Corpus (from BL, MS Add. 12151, fols 1v–2v)

First, the introduction that was composed by Phokas bar Sargis of Edessa on the translation and illustration of the scholia that he found to the writing of Dionysius, who is among the judges of the Areopagos.

All things material and that are received materially provide those who possess them with little satiety and with a burden of anxieties — whether concerning the material part in us or those things that grow outside, I mean abundance of foods and richness in belongings —, and the more they increase and the love of the one who cares about possessing them clings to them, the more they drag him down, so as to make the mistress in him a handmaiden. But of the things immaterial and that nourish in an intelligible way the intelligible [part in us], satiety can in no case be found, for the more [knowledge] rises and fixes its gaze, is lifted up from contemplation to contemplation, and senses the great beauty of Him who is truly covetable, the more it longs for that which it has not yet comprehended, acquiring, in the contact with this, a life that is higher. Of such an ascent it is made worthy by meditations of the sacred books, not only of each of them, but also of every chapter and verse: a new ray of light comes toward it, if it meditates on it with diligence and love for toil. These things I said briefly when considering this writing that came into my hands of Saint Dionysius the Areopagite, which was translated long time ago from the Greek language into the Syriac tongue by the pious and skilful priest and archiater Sergius, [a writing] that we all, Syrians, who read it highly admired and praised on account of the highness of its thoughts, i.e., of its divinity which is truly worthy of admiration. But as we found in it | hidden thoughts that are higher than most people [can conceive], we passed them over in uncertainty, except maybe for some (of us), who, because of the purity of their mind — while they receive a brighter splendour and investigate more deeply than the others — maybe also penetrate in the knowledge of those thoughts to a greater extent than the others like us. But now, since, as I said, a new light gushes forth every day from the investigation and the meditations of the sacred books for those who muse upon them, this holy book that I mentioned, written in Greek, came into the hands of my smallness from the divine providence and it included scholia, i.e., wondrous explanations of those words whose comprehension was difficult, as we sufficiently said, which were composed by an orthodox man, worthy of good memory, a *scholastikos*[32]

32 A lawyer.

by [his] profession, John by name, from the city of Bishan.[33] I took pains — as an incompetent of course, who nevertheless desires to take part in such a common profit within the limits of his ability — to translate those scholia from the Greek language into Syriac. Together with them, however, [I] also [re-translated] those [words] that I found in the earlier translation of Sergius, which are not translated with precision, having put my trust in God, who says: *the one who seeks finds and the one who asks receives and to the one who knocks, [the door] will be opened* (Matthew 7. 8). And this [I did] not in order to take pride in things like these, or to blame the erudition of that [earlier translator], far be it; but in order to clearly show that either by conforming to the Syriac language and taking pains to teach [the reader] by all means the things said [by Dionysius], [Sergius] simplified his wordings in various passages, lest the reader's mind be dulled right from the beginning of hearing the writing and, so to speak, from the first encounter, on account of the difficulty and the intricacy of the sentences, their reading be found useless; or perhaps, as I believe, also because not many at that time had yet been amply instructed in this art of translating from Greek. [Things went thus] until, as time passed by and with its alternations brought other lovers of toil, like the saint | and renowned Athanasius, patriarch of Antioch, and Jacob, bishop of Edessa — they who with their skill paved the way as far as it was possible, in a certain sense married the two languages, and produced profitable fruits from their joining, together with yet other anonymous people who had come before them — from that time, the art is being refined and clarified, and thanks to their diligence [they] are adopting from the precise rendering of the Greek words that are unusual for the Syrians. But you, too, o reader, lover of profit, come nigh with limpid mind as far as possible and, becoming examiner and corrector, if you are able, and abstaining from injurious blames without discernment, consider that, while we are copying the holy writing in the main body, we range the scholia, i.e., the shorter explanations, in the margin surrounding it, whereas we put the longer ones at the end of the book, marking with a certain sign every interpreted word that is within the [main] body [of the text], and [marking] it again at the head of its scholion, so that, if you want to read each of the scholia, of whatever word which is explained, you will be able to recognize its scholion without effort on the basis of the marking of the sign. But again, I put apart in the margin of the page, in small tables, also those words that I found in the scholia [and] that need to be explained further.

I also put, after this introduction and before the [already] mentioned holy writing, a useful discourse that was composed by the pious John the *scholastikos*, who was mentioned before, who also composed these scholia to the writing; and after it, again [another discourse] by another pious and orthodox man from the same Bishan, George the priest. But read and

33 The old Scythopolis, capital of Palaestina Secunda, and modern-day Beit Shean in northern Israel.

understand, and benefit and give benefit, and the Lord will give you wisdom, while you also pray for me, the sinner, that [His] grace may take pity on me on the day of the just judgement as on the prodigal son (cf. Luke 15. 11–32) and the robber on the right (cf. Luke 23. 40–43).

Text[34] (A = London, British Library, MS Add. 12151; B = London, British Library, MS Add. 12152)

ܡܩܕܡܘܬ ܥܒܘܪ، ܡܡܠܠܐ ܕܟܬܒ݂ ܠܦܘܩܐ ܒܪ ܣܪܓܝܣ ܐܘܪܗܝܐ ܡܛܠ ܦܘܫܩܐ ܘܫܘܪܪܐ
ܕܡܟܬ̈ܒܢܘܬܐ ܕܐܬܥܒܕ ܗܘܐ ܠܡܟܬܒܢܘܬܐ ܕܕܝܘܢܘܣܝܘܣ. ܗܘ ܕܡܢ ܕܘܟܐ ܕܐܪܝܘܣ ܦܓܘܣ.
ܟܠܗܘܢ ܬ̈ܐܘܠܘܓܝܐ ܘܕܗܘܠܝܐܡܘܬ ܡܬܐ̈ܠܝܨܝܢ. ܡܫܡܫܐ ܘܡܠܐܟܐ ܘܡܘܬܪܐ ܕܡܬܝܠܕܘܬܐ ܬ̈ܚܘܝܬܐ
ܠܩ̈ܢܘܡܐ. ܐܝܟ ܠܚܝܘܬܐ ܡܘܠܝܬܐ ܕܐܢ. ܐܘ ܐܝܟ ܠܗܠܝܢ ܕܡܢ ܠܒܪ ܡ̈ܢܝܢ. ܡܬܡܠܠܘܬܐ
ܐܡܪ ܐܢܐ ܕܡܬ̈ܟܠܬܐ ܘܡܬܪܬܐ ܕܩܕܝܫܐ. ܘܡܟܢܐ ܕܬܗܦܟܝܢ ܘܢܦܪܘܢ ܩܕܡܝܢ ܗܘܘܢ
ܕܐܡܢܐ ܕܟܠܝܠ ܠܗ ܟܠ ܡܢܝܢܐ: ܟܠܗ ܗܘܐ ܢܩܦ ܠܗ ܠܠܗܘܬ. ܐܡܟܢܐ ܕܠܡܪܬܐ ܕܒܗ
ܐܠܗܐ ܢܚܒܝܢ. ܕܗܠܝܢ ܕܝܢ ܠܐ ܡ̈ܠܝܠܘܬܐ: ܘܕܡܬܪܒܝܢܘܬ ܡܬܪ̈ܬܝܢ ܠܡܬܪܒܝܢܘܬܐ.
ܗܟܢܐ ܘܠܐ ܚܕ ܐܝܬ ܠܡܥܒܕܗ. ܡܛܠ ܕܗܟܢܐ ܕܠܟܠ ܬܘܪܨ ܬܘܒ ܕ ܚܘܪܗ: ܘܡܢ ܬܐܘܪܝܐ
ܠܘܬ ܬܐܘܪܝܐ ܬܬܬܠܐ: ܘܡܒܝܢܘܬ ܦܐܝܘܬܗ ܕܗܘ ܕܡܫܪܪܐ ܪ ܠܡܠܐܟܐ ܬܪ ܠܐܦ: ܕܐܝܟ
ܡܠܟܐ ܠܗܘ ܡܢ ܕܐܠܐ ܒܥܠ ܐܪܘܓܬ ܡܫܘܚܐ: ܐܝܟ ܗܢ ܕܫܢܝܐ ܕܗܘܐ ܢܚܝܡ: ܦܢܝܐ
ܒܢܦܫܗ ܕܗܢܐ. ܠܡܫܡܫܘܬܐ ܕܝܢ ܕܐܝܟ ܗܕܐ: ܡܢ ܗܪܟܐ ܕܡܟܬ̈ܒܐ ܩܕܝܫܐ ܡܬܝܕܥܢܐ.
ܟܕ ܠܐ ܗܘܐ ܒܟܠܚܕ ܚܕ ܡܢܗܘܢ ܟܠܗܘܢ: ܐܠܐ ܐܦ ܒܟܠ ܦܪܨܘܦܐ ܘܗܘܪ ܠܗܢܐ. ܘܠܗܟܢ
ܡܕܡ ܒܗܬܬܐ ܕܗܘܦܟܐ ܦܬܘܪܐ ܕܟܬ: ܐܘܟܡܐ ܕܡܢ ܣܦܠܝܬܐ ܘܒܗܬܬܐ ܚܓܝܠܐ ܬܬܬܗ ܠܢ.
ܘܗܠܝܢ ܐܬܪܘܬ ܒܦܩܘܬܐ: ܟܕ ܐܬܟܬܒܬ ܒܡܟܬܒܢܘܬܐ ܗܕܐ ܕܡܢ ܐܢܘܢ: ܕܡܫܝܚܐ
ܕܝܘܢܘܣܝܘܣ ܗܘ ܕܡܢ ܐܪܝܘܣ ܦܓܘܣ. ܐܢܫܐ ܕܡܦܫܩܐ ܗܘܬ ܡܢ ܝܘܢܝܐ ܠܣܘܪܝܐ ܡܢ ܠܫܢܐ
ܝܘܢܝܐ ܠܟܪܬ ܦܠܐ ܕܡܫܘܚܐ: ܠܒܣܦܐ ܘܡܗܡܝܢܐ ܗܘ ܠܗܘܢ ܡܫܝܚܐ ܘܐܪܬܝܩܘܣ ܒܗ̇، ܕܟܠ
ܡܫܘܚܐ ܕܦܣܡ ܗܘܘܢ ܒܗ̇: ܠܐ ܡܬܕܪܟܝܢ ܗܘܘ ܘܡܬܠܗܝܢ: ܡܛܠ ܡܬܠܡܝܬܐ ܕܡܫܘܠܡܗ̇.
ܚܘܬ ܘܐܠܗܘܬܗ̇: ܗ̇ܝ ܕܐܝܟ ܕܦܬܪܪܐ ܚܢܦܐ ܠܗܘܪܝܐ. ܟܕ ܕܝܢ ܡܦܪܚܝܢ ܗܘܘ ܒܗ̇
[2r] ܡܫ̈ܘܚܬܐ ܠܒܢܝܐ ܕܐܢܫܐ ܡܢ ܩ̈ܘܦܠܐܬܐ ܒܡܘܪܬܐ ܠܗܠܝܢ ܚܕ̈ܝܢ[35] ܗܘܘ. ܡܛܠ ܡܢ
ܬ̈ܝܒܘܬܐ ܚܕ: ܗ̇ܢܘܢ ܕܡܛܠ ܕܒܝܬܐ ܕܡܘܢܘܢ. ܟܕ ܝ ܡܚܢܐ ܕܡܠܐ ܢܚܘ ܡܦܠܝܢ.
ܘܡܛܠ ܡܢ ܗ̇ܢܘܢ ܕܥܒܕܐ ܡܚܝܢܝܢ. ܚܕ ܐܦ ܡܠܬ ܡܢ ܐܢܫܐ ܕܐܟܘܬ. ܟܕ ܒܚܝܠܗܘܢ
ܕܗܘܐ ܣܡܠܐ ܡܬ ܚܠܡ. ܟܕ ܕܝܢ ܗܟܢܐ ܐܝܟ ܡܢ ܕܐܢܕܪܬ ܕܡܢ ܒܚܠܬܐ[36] ܘܗܘܪ ܠܢ
ܕܡܟܬܒܐ ܩܕܝܫܐ: ܢܘܗܪܐ ܒܗܬܐ ܢܚܬ ܟܠܗܘܢ ܠܡܫܟܚܘܢ ܒܗܘܢ: ܡܢ ܟܠܝܠܘܬܐ
ܐܠܗܝܬܐ: ܐܝܟ ܠܐܢܫܐ ܕܚܝ ܢܗܘܝ: ܗܘ ܗܢܐ ܟܬܒܐ ܩܕܝܫܐ ܕܐܡܪ: ܕܟܬܒ ܡܢ
ܟܬܒܝܬܐ ܢܘܚܬܐ: ܐܝܬ ܒܗ ܕܝܢ ܡܫܠܡܢܐ ܐܘܟܝܬ ܢܘܗܪܐ ܬܫܡܫܬܐ ܕܬܟܠܐ ܗܠܝܢ
ܕܚܒܫ ܡܣܠܡܝܢ ܐܝܟ ܕܐܡܪܝܢ ܠܟܐܡܪ. ܕܚܕ̈ܝܢ[37] ܠܟܠ ܬܘܪܝ ܥܡܟܢܐ. ܚܝܐ ܠܗܘܢܐ
ܦܬܟܐ: ܡܬܠܡܠܡܐ ܡܢ ܟܐܡܪܢܐ: ܡܫܚ ܕܝܢ ܒܥܠܡܐ: ܡܢ ܡܕܡܝܬܐ ܕܝܢ ܟܢܫܝ: ܐܬܦܫܛܬ
ܐܝܟ ܠܐ ܡܫܡܫܐ ܡܢ: ܕܡܬܐܡܪ ܕܝܢ ܕܡܬܬܦ ܐܝܟ ܫܠܡܐ ܟܡܬܪܬܐ ܠܚܝܫܐ ܕܐܝܟ
ܗܢܐ: ܠܡܦܩܡܘܬܗܘܢ ܠܗܘܢ ܠܡܫ̈ܠܡܐ. ܡܢ ܠܒܪܐ ܢܚܝܐ ܠܗܘܪܝܐ. ܟܡܫܡܗܘܢ ܕܝܢ
ܐܦ ܠܗܠܝܢ ܕܐܝܬܘܗܝ ܒܗ ܒܦܘܫܩܐ ܕܡܢ ܗܘܢ: ܠܐ ܗܘܐ ܒܡ ܢܬܬܬܐ

34 The present text is not a critical edition of Phokas' introduction, but only a collation of the text as found in two ancient MSS, BL Add. 12151 of 804 (the oldest one, which serves as the collation basis) and BL Add. 12152 of 837.

35 ܚܕ̈ܝܢ Add. 12151] ܚܕܝ̈ܢ Add. 12152

36 ܒܚܠܬܐ A] ܬ̈ܚܠܬܐ B

37 ܕܚܕ̈ܝܢ A] ܕܚܕܝܢ B

ܡܦܩ̈ܢ. ܒܗ̇ ܦܣܩܬ ܬܬܡܠܠܐ ܕܠܘ: ܠܐܠܗܐ ܕܐܡܪ: ܕܕܒܪܐ ܡܫܡܫ: ܘܕܫܬܐܠ ܢܦܫ: ܘܠܕܢܦܩ ܡܬܦܬܚ ܠܗ. ܘܡܕܪܐ: ܠܐ ܗܘܐ ܐܝܟ ܗ̇ܝ ܕܠܡܬܚܘܝܘ ܒܕܐܝܟ ܗܠܝܢ ܡܢ ܦ ܐܢܐ: ܐܘ ܠܕܘܡܬܗ ܕܗܘ ܠܡܦܩ ܠܗ: ܠܐ ܗܘܝܬܐ. ܐܠܐ ܕܐܣܘܪܐ ܢܡܘܣܐܝܬ: ܕܐܘ ܒܗ ܡܬܢܣܝܢ ܒܢ ܠܢܦܫܐ ܗܘܢܝܐ: ܘܒܚܠܝܒܘܬ ܡܬܢܦܩ ܕܢܦܩܠܘܢܗ̇ ܐܠܝܢ ܕܡܬܐܡܪ̈ܢ: ܥܘܒܕܗ̇ ܒܝܘܡ ܕܝܘܡ ܠܚܠܬܗ: ܕܠܐ ܒܗ ܡܢܗ ܕܥܒܕܐ ܥܒܕܗ̇ ܕܡܬܠܒܘܬܐ ܘܐܝܟ ܕܠܐܡܪ ܡܢ ܦܓܪܐ ܡܕܡܝܐ: ܢܦܩܘܢ ܗܘܐ ܗܘܝܘ ܕܦܘܪܢܐ ܒܥܘܡܩܬܐ ܘܢܦܠܬܐ ܘܡܦܠܘܪ̈ܐ[38] ܕܡܠܐ: ܕܠܐ ܡܬܕܪܐ ܢܬܐܚܕ ܠܗ ܡܢܗܘܢ. ܐܘ ܒܒܪ ܐܝܟ ܕܡܬܡܠܟܐ ܠܝ: ܕܐܦ ܡܠܠ ܕܠܐ ܗܘܐ[39] ܦܬܓܡܐ ܒܚܒܠ. ܐܬܕܪܫܘ ܗܘܘ ܦܠܓ̈ܘܬܐ ܒܐܘܡܢܘܬܐ ܗܕܐ ܕܦܫܛܐ ܕܡܢ ܠܥܠܐ ܢܘܚܐ ܒܗܘ ܕܒܗ. ܒܕܡܐ ܕܒܗ ܡܬܬܦܩ ܗܘܐ ܕܒܗ. ܘܒܡ̈ܠܘܗܝ ܠܐܚܪܢܐ ܕܝܢܐ ܒܒܠܐ ܚܝܠܬܐ ܗܘܐ. ܐܚܪܢܐ ܕܩܕܡܝܐ [2v] ܘܦܠܚܘܬܐ. ܐܬܚܫܒܘ ܦܠܝܓܘܬܐ ܕܐܬܦܢܝܬܐ. ܘܡܦܫܩ ܐܦܣܩܘܦܐ ܕܐܪܥܐ، ܗ̇ܘ ܕܡܫܡܫܬܘܗܝ ܢܦܠܘ ܠܐܪܥܐ ܗܕܐ ܐܝܟ ܕܡܢ ܠܗ. ܘܗܘܘ ܒܗܕܐ ܡܢܗ ܗ̇ܘ ܒܗܝ ܕܬܪܝܢܘܗܝ ܠܓܒܐ. ܘܡܢ ܢܦܩܘܗܝ ܐܘܠܘ ܦܐܪܐ ܘܬܪܝܢܐ. ܡܢ ܐܚܪܢܐ ܗܘܐ ܠܐ ܡܬܦܩܕܐ ܕܡܬܚܫܒܘܢ. ܘܗܘܝܘܢ ܡܬܕܪܫܐ ܘܡܬܢܣܪܐ ܐܘܡܢܘܬܐ. ܘܡܢܝܢ ܒܣܘܦܠܬܗܘܢ ܡܢ ܚܬܝܬܘܬܗ ܕܗܘܝܐ ܦܬܓܡܐ ܠܐ ܬܬܚܫܒ ܠܗܘܢܝܐ. ܐܠܐ ܐܦ ܐܝܬ ܐܘ ܦܘܩܕܐ ܕܝܢ ܘܬܪܝܢܐ: ܒܗܘܝܐ ܥܡܠܐ ܐܝܟ ܕܡܢ ܠܗ ܐܬܟܢܝ. ܘܒܗ[40] ܗ̇ܘܐ ܐܝܬ ܡܒܣܝܢܐ ܘܡܬܪ̈ܝܢ ܐ ܐܢ ܫܡܫ ܐܝܬ: ܘܡܢ ܚܕ̈ܠܝܐ ܡܫܟܚܢܐ ܕܕܠܐ ܦܘܪܫ ܗ̇ܘܝܢ ܡܬܬܣܡ ܐܝܬ: ܐܬܟܡܐ. ܕܒܗ ܠܗ̇ ܠܡܬܟܢܘܬܐ[41] ܡܬܥܝܬܐ ܒܬܟܝܢ ܒܡܫܬܐ. ܠܫܘ̈ܠܝܐ ܐܘܟܝܬ ܠܢܗܘܪܐ ܘܒܗܪ̈ܐ.[42] ܒܐܝܡܪܐ ܕܚܕܪܗ̇ ܡܬܠܒܫܝܢ.[43] ܗ̇ܢܘܢ ܕܝܢ ܪܘܟܐ. ܒܫܘܠܡܗ ܕܟܠܬܐ ܫܦܝܪܝܢ.[44] ܒܗ ܐܦ ܢܒܝܐ ܡܢܗ ܪܥܝܢ ܥܠ ܟܠ ܡܠܬܐ ܕܟܠܗ ܠܡܫܡܥܐ ܗ̇ܝ، ܕܡܬܦܫܩܐ. ܘܠܗ ܬܘܒ ܐܦ ܥܠ ܪܫܐ ܕܡܟܘܠܝܗܘܢ ܕܠܗ. ܐܡܟܢܐ ܕܒܗ ܬܘܢܝ ܒܗ ܠܓܡܪܐ ܠܟܠ ܚܕ ܡܢ ܡܟܘ̈ܠܝܐ ܕܐܢܫܐ ܕܝܗ̇، ܡܠܬܐ ܕܡܬܢܣܪܐ. ܬܬܒܪܝ ܐ ܕܕܠܐ ܒܒܠܐ ܬܕܟܝܗ̇ ܠܡܟܘܠܝܗܘܢ ܕܠܗ̇. ܡܢ ܪܘܫܡܗ ܕܒܕܟܐ.[45] ܬܘܒ ܕܝܢ ܐܦ ܠܟܠܗ ܡܢܗ ܕܐܫܟܚܬ ܐܦ ܒܗܘܢ ܒܡܟ̈ܘܠܝܐ ܕܪܕܦ ܕܬܪܝܢ ܢܬܦܬܚ ܫܡܥܬ ܒܗ ܒܐܝܡܪܐ ܕܫܦܪ ܘܠܦܐ ܠܫܦܝܪ ܒܠܚܘ̈ܝܘܬܐ.[46] ܫܡܥܬ ܕܝܢ ܬܘܒ ܒܬܪ ܥܘܕܪ، ܡܟܠܠܐ ܗܢܐ ܘܡܢܗ ܡܬܟܢܘܬܐ ܡܬܥܝܬܐ ܕܐܝܡܪܐ ܐܦ ܡܟܠܐ ܡܢܗ ܢܦܫܐ. ܕܒܗ ܠܗ ܠܒܢܝܐ ܐܠܗܐ[47] ܢܘܚ ܡܫܠܡܢܘܬܐ ܕܡܢܗ ܐܬܥܒܕܗ: ܗ̇ܘ ܕܐܦ ܡܟ̈ܘܠܝܐ ܗܠܝܢ ܒܒܪ ܕܝܠܗ̇ ܕܡܬܟܢܘܬܐ. ܘܒܬܪܗ[48] ܬܘܒ ܕܐܝܟ ܐܚܪܢܐ ܡܢܗ ܕܒܢܝܢ ܢܦܩܐ ܘܬܪܝܢ ܥܘܡܩܐ ܒܐܘܪ ܠܟ ܡܫܬܐ. ܐܠܐ ܦܢ، ܘܐܫܬܟܠ. ܘܐܬܪ ܘܐܘܬܪ. ܘܡܢܗܐ ܢܚܒܝܢ. ܒܗ ܐܦ ܟܠ ܢܦܠܐ ܡܢ ܠܗ ܐܝܬ: ܕܬܘܒ ܦܩܘܕܬܐ ܒܝܘܡ ܕܒܗ ܕܒܐܢܘܬܐ. ܐܝܟ ܕܠܒܪܐ ܐܘܟܦܐ ܘܦܢܝܐ ܕܡܢ ܡܢܗ.

38 ܘܡܦܠܘܪ̈ܐ A] ܘܡܣܣܦܪܐ B
39 ܕܠܐ ܗܘܐ A] ܕܠܐ B
40 ܘܒܗ A] ܒܗ B
41 ܠܗ̇ ܠܡܬܟܢܘܬܐ A] ܠܟܠܗ̇ ܡܬܟܢܘܬܐ B
42 ܘܒܗܪ̈ܐ A] om B
43 ܡܬܠܒܫܝܢ A] ܡܢ ܟܠ ܟܠܗܘܢ ܡܬܠܒܫܝܢ B
44 ܕܝܢ ܗ̇ܢܘܢ ... ܫܦܝܪܝܢ A] om B
45 ܕܒܕܟܐ A] add alia manus in marg
46 ܒܠܚܘ̈ܝܘܬܐ B] ܒܠܚܘܝܘܬܐ A
47 ܐܠܗܐ A] ܠܐܠܗܐ B
48 ܘܒܬܪܗ A] ܘܒܬܪܗ̇ B

Bibliography

Manuscripts

London, British Library, MS Add. 12151
London, British Library, MS Add. 12152

Primary Sources

Corpus Dionysiacum I. De divinis nominibus, ed. by Beate R. Suchla, Patristische Texte und Studien, 33 (Berlin: de Gruyter, 1990)

Corpus Dionysiacum II, ed. by Günther Heil and Adolf M. Ritter, Patristische Texte und Studien, 36 (Berlin: de Gruyter, 2012)

Dionigi Areopagita. Nomi divini, teologia mistica, epistole: La versione siriaca di Sergio di Rēšʿaynā (VI secolo), ed. and trans. by Emiliano Fiori, Corpus Scriptorum Christianorum Orientalium, 656–57, Scriptores Syri, 252–53 (Louvain: Peeters, 2014)

Dionysius the Areopagite on the Divine Names and the Mystical Theology, trans. by C. E. Rolt (London: Society for Promoting Christian Knowledge; New York: MacMillan, 1920)

Dionysius the (Pseudo-)Areopagite, *The Mystical Theology*, trans. by Luke Dysinger, http://www.ldysinger.com/@texts/0500_dion_aer/03_dion-mys_th.htm [accessed 23 November 2019]

Ḥunain ibn Isḥāq über die syrischen und arabischen Galen-Übersetzungen, ed. by Gotthelf Bergsträsser, Abhandlungen für die Kunde des Morgenlandes, 17.2 (Leipzig: Deutsche morgenländische Gesellschaft, 1925)

Sancti Gregorii Nazianzeni Opera. Versio Syriaca I: Oration XL, ed. by Jean-Claude Haelewyck, Corpus Christianorum Series Graeca, 49, Corpus Nazianzenum, 14 (Louvain: Brepols, 2001)

——, *Versio Syriaca II: Orationes XIII, XLI*, ed. by Andrea Barbara Schmidt, Corpus Christianorum Series Graeca, 47, Corpus Nazianzenum, 15 (Louvain: Brepols, 2002)

——, *Versio Syriaca III: Orationes XXVII, XXXVIII, XXXIX*, ed. by Jean-Claude Haelewyck, Corpus Christianorum Series Graeca, 53, Corpus Nazianzenum, 18 (Louvain: Brepols, 2005)

——, *Versio Syriaca IV: Orationes XXVIII, XXIX, XXX, XXXI*, ed. by Jean-Claude Haelewyck, Corpus Christianorum Series Graeca, 65, Corpus Nazianzenum, 23 (Louvain: Brepols, 2008)

——, *Versio Syriaca V: Orationes I, II, III*, ed. by Jean-Claude Haelewyck, Corpus Christianorum Series Graeca, 77, Corpus Nazianzenum, 25 (Louvain: Brepols, 2011)

Sancti Gregorii Theologi liber Carminum Iambicorum: Versio Syriaca antiquissima e cod. Vat cv. ed. by Johann Bollig (Beirut: Ex typographia catholica, 1895)

Sancti Gregorii Theologi liber Carminum Iambicorum: Versio Syriaca antiquissima e codicibus londinensibus Musaei Britannici, ed. by Henri Gismondi (Beirut: Ex typographia catholica, 1896)

Secondary Studies

Bhayro, Siam, and Robert Hawley, 'La littérature botanique et pharmaceutique en langue syriaque', in *Les sciences en syriaque*, ed. by Émilie Villey, Études syriaques, 11 (Paris: Paul Geuthner, 2014), pp. 285–318

Brock, Sebastian P., 'Passover, Annunciation and Epiclesis: Some Remarks on the Term *Aggen* in the Syriac Versions of Lk. 1:35', *Novum Testamentum*, 24.3 (1982), 222–33

——, 'Towards a History of Syriac Translation Technique', in *III Symposium Syriacum, 1980: Les contacts du monde syriaque avec les autres cultures (Goslar 7–11 Septembre 1980)*, ed. by René Lavenant, Orientalia Christiana Analecta, 221 (Roma: Pontificium Institutum Studiorum Orientalium, 1983), pp. 1–14

——, 'Changing Fashions in Syriac Translation Technique: The Background to Syriac Translations under the Abbasids', *Journal of the Canadian Society for Syriac Studies*, 4 (2004), 3–14

Crimi, Carmelo, 'Fra tradizione diretta e tradizione indiretta: note alla versione siriaca dei "Carmi" di Gregorio Nazianzeno', in *La diffusione dell'eredità classica nell'età tardoantica e medievale: Forme e modi di trasmissione. Atti del Seminario Nazionale (Trieste, 19–20 settembre 1996)*, ed. by Alfredo Valvo, L'eredità classica nel mondo orientale, 1 (Alessandria: Edizioni dell'Orso, 1997), pp. 83–93

Al-Dabte, Youssif, 'Iktishāf Dayr Qinnisrīn (Monastery of Qinnisre)', *Mahd al Ḥaḍarāt* 2 (2007), 83–99

Fiori, Emiliano, 'Mélange eschatologique et "condition spirituelle" de l'intellect dans le Corpus Dionysiacum syriaque: un cas remarquable de divergence entre le corpus dionysien grec et sa traduction par Serge de Reš'aynā', *Parole de l'Orient*, 35 (2010), 261–76

——, 'Sergius of Reshaina and Pseudo-Dionysius: A Dialectical Fidelity', in *Interpreting the Bible and Aristotle in Late Antiquity: The Alexandrian Commentary Tradition between Rome and Baghdad*, ed. by Josef Lössl and John W. Watt (Aldershot: Ashgate, 2011), pp. 179–94

——, 'Appendice seconda', in *Gregorio di Nazianzo. Tra autobiografia e teologia* [*carm.* II,1,68. II,1,30], ed. by Antonella Conte, Poeti Cristiani, 9 (Pisa: ETS, 2019), pp. 223–55

Hornus, Jean-Michel, 'Le Corpus dionysien en syriaque', *Parole de l'Orient*, 1 (1970), 69–93

King, Daniel, *The Syriac Versions of the Writings of Cyril of Alexandria: A Study in Translation Technique*, Corpus Scriptorum Christianorum Orientalium, 626, Subs. 123 (Leuven: Peeters, 2008)

Lamoreaux, John C., *Ḥunayn ibn Isḥāq on his Galen Translations: A Parallel English-Arabic Text*, Eastern Christian Texts (Provo, Utah: Brigham Young University Press, 2016)

Lash, Christopher J.A., 'Techniques of a Translator: Work-Notes on the Methods of Jacob of Edessa in Translating the Homilies of Severus of Antioch', in *Überlieferungsgeschichtliche Untersuchungen*, ed. by Frany Paschke, Texte und Untersuchungen, 125 (Berlin: Akademie-Verlag, 1981), pp. 365–83

Muradyan, Gohar, 'The Hellenizing School', in *Armenian Philology in the Modern Era. From Manuscripts to the Digital Text*, ed. by Valentina Calzolari and Michael E. Stone, Handbook of Oriental Studies, Section 8 Uralic & Central Asian Studies, 23.1 (Leiden: Brill, 2014), pp. 321–48

Quaschning-Kirsch, Matthias, 'Die Frage der Benennbarkeit Gottes in den syrischen Versionen des Corpus Dionysiacum Areopagiticum', in *Symposium Syriacum VII: Uppsala University, Department of Asian and African Languages, 11–14 August 1996*, ed. by René Lavenant, Orientalia Christiana Analecta, 256 (Roma: Pontificio Istituto Orientale, 1998), pp. 117–26

Sembiante, Antonio, 'Appunti sulla tradizione siriaca delle opere di Gregorio Nazianzeno', *Koinonia*, 41 (2018), 607–35

Sherwood, Polycarpe, 'Sergius of Reshaina and the Syriac Versions of the Pseudo-Denis', *Sacris Erudiri*, 4 (1952), 174–84

Strothmann, Werner, *Das Sakrament der Myron-Weihe in der Schrift De ecclesiastica hierarchia des Pseudo-Dionysios Areopagita in syrischen Übersetzungen und Kommentaren*, Göttinger Orientforschungen, I, Syriaca, 15 (Wiesbaden: Otto Harrassowitz, 1977–1978)

Tannous, Jack, 'Qenneshre, Monastery of', in *Gorgias Encyclopedic Dictionary of the Syriac Heritage*, ed. by Sebastian P. Brock, Aaron M. Butts, George A. Kiraz, and Lucas Van Rompay (Piscataway, NJ: Gorgias Press, 2011) pp. 345–46

Tannous, Jack, *The Making of the Medieval Middle East. Religion, Society, and Simple Believers* (Princeton: Princeton University Press, 2018)

Taylor, David G. K., 'Les Pères cappadociens dans la tradition syriaque', in *Les Pères grecs en syriaque*, ed. by Andrea Barbara Schmidt and Dominique Gonnet, Études syriaques, 4 (Paris: Paul Geuthner, 2007), pp. 43–61

Van Esbroeck, Michel, 'La triple préface syriaque de Phocas', in *Denys l'Aréopagite et sa postérité en Orient et en Occident. Actes du Colloque International, Paris, 21–24 septembre 1994*, ed. by Ysabel de Andia, Collection des Études Augustiniennes, Série Antiquité, 151 (Paris: Institut d'Études Augustiniennes, 1997), pp. 167–86

Van Rompay, Lucas, 'Jacob of Edessa and the Sixth-Century Translator of Severus of Antioch's Cathedral Homilies', in *Jacob of Edessa and the Syriac Culture of his Day*, ed. by Bas ter Haar Romeny, Monographs of the Peshitta Institute Leiden, 18 (Leiden: Brill, 2008), pp. 189–204

Wiessner, Gernot, 'Zur Handschriftenüberlieferung der syrischen Fassung des Corpus Dionysiacum', *Nachrichten der Akademie der Wissenschaften in Göttingen, I. Philologisch-historische Klasse*, 3 (Göttingen: Vandenhoeck & Ruprecht, 1972), pp. 165–216

——, 'Beobachtungen an zwei syrischen Handschriften mit Kommentaren zum syrischen Corpus Dionysiacum', in *A Tribute to Arthur Vööbus: Studies in Early Christian Literature and Its Environment, Primarily in the Syrian East*, ed. by Robert H. Fischer (Chicago: The Lutheran School of Theology at Chicago, 1977), pp. 73–82

CHRISTOPHER BRAUN

Wisdom in Disguise

Translation Narratives and Pseudotranslations in Arabic Alchemy

Introduction

The transmission of Graeco-Roman learning into Arabic by way of translation represents a significant moment in the intellectual history of the medieval Middle East and North Africa. From the second/eighth century onward, a substantial number of mostly philosophical and scientific texts such as Aristotle's (d. 322 BCE) *Metaphysics* and Galen's (d. *c.* 216 CE) vast corpus of medical treatises were translated into Arabic, either directly from Greek into Arabic or via Syriac as an intermediate language.[1] Similar translation processes must have introduced Greek alchemical knowledge to Arab and Arabic-speaking scholars and intellectuals.[2] The exact circumstances and protagonists as well as the ways of transmission, appropriation, and assimilation remain still shrouded in darkness. Arabic alchemy's Greek origins, however, betrays already its Arabic denomination, *al-kīmīyāʾ*, a loan word that very likely derives from the Syriac *kīmīyā*, which in its turn goes back to the Greek χυμεία or χημεία, 'the art of casting or alloying metals'.[3] While most of the Arab and Arabic-writing practitioners were aware of alchemy's non-Islamic origins and classified it, like philosophy and medicine, among 'the sciences of the ancients' (*ʿulūm al-awāʾil*), they disagreed about the actual 'inventors'

1 For an overview of this historical phenomenon, see the excellent study by Gutas, *Greek Thought, Arabic Culture*, and the recent encyclopaedic entry by D'Ancona, 'Greek into Arabic'.
2 Schütt, *Auf der Suche nach dem Stein der Weisen*, p. 15; Ullmann, 'al-Kīmiyā'', p. 110b.
3 Ullmann, 'al-Kīmiyā'', p. 110 and Ullmann, *Wörterbuch*, s. v. كيمياء. Gotthard Strohmaier proposes a non-Greek etymology of this noun, see Strohmaier, 'Elixir, Alchemy, and the Metamorphoses of Two Synonyms'.

Christopher Braun (christopher.braun@uzh.ch) studied Arabic, French, and the history of the Middle East in Berlin and Paris. In 2016, he earned a PhD on Arabic 'treasure hunter manuals' at the Warburg Institute in London. He currently holds a postdoc position at the University of Zurich. His research interests include the Arabic occult sciences, the cultural history of medieval Islamicate societies, and Arabic lexicography.

Narratives on Translation across Eurasia and Africa: From Babylonia to Colonial India, ed. by Sonja Brentjes in cooperation with Jens Høyrup and Bruce O'Brien, CAT 3, pp. 199–217 (Turnhout: Brepols, 2022) BREPOLS PUBLISHERS 10.1484/M.CAT-EB.5.127941

or 'initiators' of this occult science.[4] Various theories and legends of its inception emerged. Some argued that alchemical wisdom was first revealed to prophets such as Adam, Moses, or Abraham and provided, thereby, alchemy with a monotheistic pedigree. Others regarded the syncretistic deity Hermes Trismegistus, often equated with the prophet Enoch (or Idrīs in Arabic), or other (pre-Islamic) civilizations as the inventors or initiators of alchemy and other occult sciences.[5]

Reminiscences of the earliest stage of Arabic alchemy, that is to say the acquisition of Greek alchemical knowledge through translation into Arabic, might represent the legends of commissioned translations of Greek alchemical treatises into Arabic (or into Arabic via Syriac). Perhaps influenced by such legendary accounts, some Arab and Arabic-writing alchemists employed the literary strategy of fictitious or pseudotranslations to link their treatises to the very beginnings of this occult science and, as will be proposed below, to alleviate their readers' resistance to some of Arabic alchemy's rather heterodox ideas.

The Umayyad Prince Khālid b. Yazīd as Promotor of Alchemy

One of the most prominent legends about the transmission of Greek alchemical knowledge into Arabic accredits to the Umayyad prince Khālid b. Yazīd (d. in 85/704 or 90/709), an otherwise rather less known historical figure, the first commissioned translations of alchemical treatises into Arabic.[6] Khālid is said to have studied the art of alchemy under a Byzantine monk named Maryānos, or, according to other sources, Stephanos. Furthermore, the Umayyad prince is said to have asked Greek scholars from Egypt to translate Greek and Coptic works on alchemy, medicine, and astronomy into Arabic.[7] The German Arabist and Classicist Manfred Ullmann has shown that this legendary account is ahistorical. He was able to trace back Khālid b. Yazīd's reputation as an alchemist and promoter of this occult science to the misinterpretation of a particular anecdote. The anecdote deals with Khālid's unsuccessful attempt to regain his right of succession to the caliphate. The prince, it says, wasted his time in 'striving for something he cannot attain' (*ṭalab mā lā yuqdaru ʿalayhi*).[8] In later times, this sentence was misinterpreted. While it expressed

4 On the term *ʿulūm al-awāʾil*, see Endreß, 'Die wissenschaftliche Literatur', p. 400.

5 On some of these origin narratives in Arabic alchemy, see Braun, '"Who Began with this Art?"' and below. For Hermes Trismegistus in the Arabic tradition, see the recent study by Van Bladel, *The Arabic Hermes*. On the late antique Hermes, see Fowden, *The Egyptian Hermes*.

6 On his life, see Ullmann, 'Khālid b. Yazīd'.

7 For references in Arabic literature to Khālid b. Yazīd and his interest in sciences and alchemy, see Ullmann, *Natur- und Geheimwissenschaften*, p. 192, no. 1.

8 Manfred Ullmann closely scrutinized the historical sources dealing with Khālid b. Yazīd and his alchemical expertise, see Ullmann, "Ḫālid ibn Yazīd und die Alchemie: Eine Legende'.

Khālid's hopeless attempts to reclaim the caliphate for himself, later authors interpreted the passage as the prince's endeavour to master alchemy and thereby to transmute metals such as lead and iron into silver and gold.[9] Thus, this was the aim 'he could not attain'. Khālid b. Yazīd had suddenly turned from being an unfortunate prince to a disciple and promoter of the art of alchemy. Several Arabic alchemical works were attributed to him thereafter such as *The Book of the Paradise of Wisdom* (*Kitāb Firdaws al-ḥikma*), a collection of alchemical didactic poems.[10] The Umayyad prince even became an authority in alchemical matters in the Latin West, where he was known as Calid filius Jazidi.[11] The legendary account of Khālid b. Yazīd's interest in alchemy and his commissioned translations is not the only myth that linked Arabic alchemy to a former age.

The Byzantine Emperor Heraclius and the Commissioned Translation into Syriac

Another, less well-known legend introduces Heraclius (*Hiraqal* or *Hirqil* in Arabic), the Emperor of the Byzantine (Eastern Roman) Empire who ruled from 610 to 641, as a protagonist in the transmission of Ancient Greek alchemical wisdom into Syriac. This legend is preserved in several extant Arabic manuscripts, some of which are written in Garshūnī or Karshūnī, that is to say in Arabic using the Syriac alphabet.[12] The legend begins with Aristotle, the 'First Teacher' as he was known among Arab philosophers. Aristotle, it is said, wrote a book on alchemy for Alexander the Great (d. 323 BCE). This book survived the vicissitudes of fate and reached, several centuries later, the emperor Heraclius who commissioned a monk named John to translate the work into Syriac. Again several centuries later, the bishop of Nisibis, Eliyā bar Shīnāyā (d. after 1049), examined its content and approved its veracity and the bishop of Sinjār and later of Nisibis, ʿAḇdišōʿ bar Brīḵā (d. 1318), composed a commentary on this book in Syriac of which an Arabic translation is said to be extant.[13] This narrative account advances the idea, like the legend of

9 Ullmann, 'Ḫālid ibn Yazīd und die Alchemie'. Fuat Sezgin argues for the historicity of Khālid's occupation with alchemy, see Sezgin, *Geschichte des arabischen Schrifttums (GAS)*, IV, pp. 120–26.

10 Ullmann, *Natur- und Geheimwissenschaften*, 192–94; Sezgin, *GAS*, IV, pp. 120–26.

11 Ullmann, *Natur- und Geheimwissenschaften*, p. 194.

12 Beirut, Bibliothèque Orientale de l'Université Saint-Joseph, MS 252; Gotha, Forschungsbibliothek, MS 85, 1 and 2 (fols 1–22), Vatican City, Vatican Apostolic Library, MS 926. For a manuscript in Rampur in the Indian state of Uttar Pradesh, see Stapleton, 'Further Notes'. On the extant manuscripts, see Ullmann, *Natur- und Geheimwissenschaften*, p. 157 and Sezgin, *GAS*, IV, p. 102.

13 Manfred Ullmann presents this myth in his survey of Arabic treatises on the natural and occult sciences, see Ullmann, *Natur- und Geheimwissenschaften*, p. 157. There existed indeed an interest in alchemy among those literate in Syriac, as attested by several preserved

Khālid b. Yazīd, that Greek alchemical treatises were translated into Arabic, either directly or via Syriac, and that these translations were commissioned by a powerful ruler. The similarities between these narrative accounts and the already mentioned historical translations of Greek works on philosophy, medicine, and other sciences into Arabic (at times via Syriac), which were also commissioned in most of the cases by influential and affluent patrons, is telling.[14]

In contrast to the legend about the Umayyad prince Khālid b. Yazīd and his alchemical interests, however, the second account serves in the extant manuscripts to disguise a presented thereafter Arabic alchemical text as the translation of a work formerly written down in Ancient Greek.[15] Such false claims are not uncommon in Arabic occult sciences, in general, and in Arabic alchemy in particular. Authors of medieval occult literature occasionally resorted to the literary strategy of disguising their treatise as a translation of an ancient text. The authors claimed that the knowledge they are going to reveal to their readers is neither based on their own thoughts nor inspired by the works of their Arab and Arabic-writing predecessors or contemporaries. Instead, these texts are said to have existed long before and were once written down in an ancient language such as Greek, Syriac, or Coptic.[16] These claims are more often than not spurious. The texts show no signs of being translated and appear to be the authors' genuine compositions. They are, therefore, 'pseudo-' or 'fictitious translations'.

Pseudotranslations in Arabic Occult Literature

The Israeli scholar Gideon Toury defined pseudotranslations or fictitious translations as 'texts which have been presented as translations with no corresponding source texts in other languages ever having existed'.[17] The Turkish scholar Şehnaz Tahir Gürçağlar, in contrast, considers pseudotranslations as 'texts that are regarded as translations in the target culture although they lack a corresponding source text in any foreign culture'.[18] In the case of Arabic alchemy, however, it remains unknown whether the readers of such texts did perceive the author's translation narratives as truthful accounts or if they were aware

---

alchemical works in Syriac. The Italian scholar of alchemy, Matteo Martelli, recently received an ERC Consolidator grant to study this often neglected alchemical tradition (https://www.unibo.it/sitoweb/matteo.martelli/).

14 On the patronage of Greek translations into Arabic, see Gutas, *Greek Thought, Arabic Culture*, pp. 121–50. There existed indeed a Syriac alchemical tradition, see Martelli, 'L'alchimie en syriaque et l'œuvre de Zosime'.

15 See Ullmann, *Natur- und Geheimwissenschaften*, p. 157.

16 Manfred Ullmann refers to such accounts in his survey of Arabic literature on the natural and occult sciences, see Ullmann, *Natur- und Geheimwissenschaften*.

17 Toury, *Descriptive Translation Studies*, p. 42.

18 Gürçağlar, 'Pseudotranslations', p. 516.

or at least suspected their deceptive character. It seems, therefore, adequate to propose, as Toury did, that pseudotranslations are texts which the authors simply disguised as translations and of which no source text ever existed.

Pseudotranslations in Arabic alchemical and occult literature have not attracted much scholarly attention yet. So far, the phenomenon has only been once debated among orientalists. A mysterious author known as Ibn Waḥshiyya (d. 318/930–931?) provided the bone of contention. He claimed in the preface of his *Nabatean Agriculture* (*al-Filāḥa al-nabaṭiyya*), an agronomical treatise interspersed with various magical and astrological passages, to have translated and compiled this work from texts written in 'Old Syriac' (*al-Suryāniyya al-qadīma*), which he later defines as the language of the Nabateans (*lughat al-Nabaṭ*). The term 'Nabatean' in this context designates the (pre-Islamic) rural population of Iraq (*nabaṭ al-ʿIrāq*), not the inhabitants of the Jordanian city of Petra who were known in Arabic as *nabaṭ al-Shām* ('the Nabateans of Greater Syria').[19] Ibn Waḥshiyya asserted, furthermore, that the material he translated had once been a compilation of works written by a group of scholars in ancient Mesopotamia. These works were later collected by the scholar Qūthāmā. The oldest parts of the *Nabatean Agriculture* were written, according to the author, some 20,000 years ago.[20]

Ibn Waḥshiyya's assertion provoked a heated debate among scholars of the Middle East in the second half of the nineteenth century. The Russian orientalist Daniel Chwolson (d. 1911) took Ibn Waḥshiyya's claim for granted and praised the work as a major discovery of old Babylonian lore.[21] He dated the material to the sixteenth century BCE.[22] Shortly after Chwolson's appraisal of the *Nabatean Agriculture* and its enormous potential for the study of the ancient Near East, the German orientalists Alfred von Gutschmid (d. 1887) and Theodor Nöldeke (d. 1930) began to study this text more closely and strongly criticized Chwolson's approach. They pointed out inconsistencies and provided some compelling arguments that Ibn Waḥshiyya's text was not a genuine work of Babylonian literature.[23] Nöldeke passed a final verdict. He argued that any further research into this material would be a waste of time.[24] The considerable progress in the decipherment of the cuneiform script provided the last piece of evidence and it became obvious that Chwolson was mistaken.[25] Ibn Waḥshiyya's *Nabatean Agriculture* turned out to be a pseudotranslation.

---

19 On this distinction, see Fahd, 'Nabaṭ'.

20 The author of the *Nabatean Agriculture* claims such an old age in the introduction to this work, see Ibn Waḥshiyya, *al-Filāḥa al-nabaṭiyya*, pp. 5–10 (Arabic text); pp. 93–99 (English trans.).

21 Chwolsohn, *Über die Überreste*.

22 Chwolsohn, *Überreste*, p. 65.

23 Gutschmid, 'Nabatäische Landwirthschaft'; Nöldeke, 'Noch Einiges'.

24 Nöldeke, 'Noch Einiges', p. 445.

25 On this debate, see Hämeen-Anttilla, *The Last Pagans of Iraq*, pp. 3–9.

The Finnish Arabist Jaakko Hämeen-Anttila published in 2006 the latest study on this text. He argues that the *Nabatean Agriculture* might be partially based on a translated Syriac text.[26] He thus rehabilitated Ibn Waḥshiyya who might have been translating at least parts of the *Nabatean Agriculture* from Syriac into Arabic. Instead of having translated some piece of Babylonian literature, the author resorted to more recent sources which were composed in late antique and Islamic times. Thus, Ibn Waḥshiyya's *Nabatean Agriculture* blurs the borders between pseudo- and actual translations, a phenomenon one encounters as well in medieval Europe. The Italian scholar Andrea Rizzi has shown, by referring to a translation of an early fourteenth-century Latin text into northern Italian vernacular, that Gideon Toury's clear-cut distinction between actual and fictitious or pseudotranslation needs to be reconsidered.[27]

Ibn Waḥshiyya's *Nabatean Agriculture* is the only pseudotranslation in Arabic occult literature that attracted some interest among orientalists. Similar cases in Arabic alchemy have not been studied so far. Historians of science who were the first and for a long time the only scholars who investigated Arabic alchemical texts seldom took an interest in the authors' narrative strategies. The German scholar of Arabic alchemy Julius Ruska (d. 1949) once called these narratives 'literarisches Rankenwerk', implying their insignificance for the study of alchemy.[28] Only recently has the study of Arabic alchemical treatises as literary texts gained new momentum.[29] Given this emerging interest in the aesthetic quality of Arabic alchemical works and the literary strategies of its composers, the phenomenon of pseudotranslations in Arabic alchemy rightly deserves to be looked at more closely. Since the field of Arabic alchemical literature remains to date an insufficiently charted territory, it is impossible to provide any comprehensive overview of pseudotranslational accounts in Arabic alchemy yet. Therefore, I will restrict myself to the presentation of a quite elaborate example of such an account in the alchemical treatise *Kitāb Sidrat al-muntahā* and to explore the reasons that might have pushed the author to devise such a detailed narrative framework to explain the translation.

26 Hämeen-Anttila, *The Last Pagans of Iraq*, p. 33.

27 See Rizzi, 'When a Text is Both a Pseudotranslation and a Translation'.

28 Despite Ruska's rather negative attitude toward such narratives, he was the first who attempted to categorize the very common origin narratives in Arabic alchemy. See Ruska, 'Quelques problèmes de littérature alchimiste'.

29 Regula Forster, for example, offers in her latest study a thorough analysis of the very common dialogue form in Arabic alchemy. See her forthcoming publication on dialogues in medieval Arabic literature.

The Translation of Hermes' Tablet in Pseudo-Ibn Waḥshiyya's Kitāb Sidrat al-muntahā

The alchemical treatise *The Book of the Ziziphus Tree of the Furthest Boundary* (*Kitāb Sidrat al-muntahā*) is spuriously attributed to the aforementioned occultist Ibn Waḥshiyya. Only one textual witness of this alchemical treatise, the composite manuscript (*majmūʿa*) Gotha 1162, survived.[30] The copyist of this manuscript was the Egyptian Copt Yūḥannā b. ʿUbayr Abū l-Faraj al-Manfalūṭī. He finished copying the manuscript on a Thursday, the 15 Rabīʿ al-Ākhir 1000, which corresponds to 1 February 1592.[31] The German orientalist and explorer Ulrich Jasper Seetzen (d. 1811) acquired the manuscript in 1809 in Cairo when he was hunting for manuscripts, various antiquities, Pharaonic relics, 'objets d'arts', and mirabilia in Egypt.[32]

The Book of the Ziziphus Tree of the Furthest Boundary was written in the form of a dialogue between the protagonist, Ibn Waḥshiyya, and an alchemist from the Islamic West, al-Maghribī al-Qamarī. It begins with an introductory dialogue between these two characters. In the course of the discussion between Ibn Waḥshiyya and al-Maghribī al-Qamarī on the origins of alchemy, the latter relates the discovery of an ancient book in Memphis. This book is said to have been written in hieroglyphic script. Hermes Trismegistus was the only one able to decipher it. He translated it into Coptic. One such Coptic version of this text was finally translated into Arabic. The narrative account starts with Ibn Waḥshiyya inquiring about the beginnings of 'the art' (*al-ṣanʿa*), i.e. alchemy.[33]

قلتُ: من الذي ابتدأ بهذه الصنعة ومن أين مخرجها وأيّ أمّة من الأمم استنبطها واستجرّها إن كانت مستخرجة بالعقول والقياس؟ وإن كان في غير ذلك فمن أيّ موضع كان ابتدأ ظهورها وفي أيّ أمّة [٥و] وجيل ظهرت في المبدأ؟

قال المغربيّ: لقد سألتَ عن شيء كبير وسألتَ عن فائدة جليلة. واعلم أنّ ذلك مختلف فيه.

زعم قوم أنّ الله تعالى علّمها آدم عليه السلام حين أخرجه من الجنّة وعلّمه إيّاها وهو في الجنّة يعلّمه بما هو صائر إليه من الخطيّة. فلمّا هبط إلى الأرض وكثر نسله علّمها ابنه شيثًا وعلّمها شيث ابنه وكذلك حتّى ظهرت.

وزعم قوم أنّ الله عزّ وجلّ أوحاها إلى إدريس الذي هو هرمس بلغة اليونانيّين ليستعين بها على دنياه صيانة من الله تعالى له عن المكاسب الدنيسة والمعايش المذلّة للناس. وزعم قوم

30 Pertsch, *Die orientalischen Handschriften*, II, pp. 375–76.

31 For the description of the manuscript, see Pseudo-Ibn Waḥshiyya, *Das Kitāb Sidrat al-muntahā*, p. 53.

32 See his note on MS Gotha 1162, fol. 1r: 'Kahira 1809 No. 1552'. On Seetzen's journey to Egypt, see Wallenstein, '"Ich habe mehr gefunden"', pp. 65–76.

33 Arab and Arabic-writing authors frequently referred to alchemy as *ʿilm al-ṣanʿa* ('the science of the art'), or just simply *al-ṣanʿa* ('the art'), see Ullmann, 'al-Kīmiyāʾ', p. 110; Ullmann, *Wörterbuch*, s. v. كيمياء; Sezgin, *GAS*, IV, p. 4.

إنّما عملت من قبله وأنّه وضع فيها الكتب ورمزها محبّة منه أن تصل بعده إلى الحكماء الألباب الطالبين لها من بعده.

وزعم آخرون أنّ الله تعالى علّمها إبراهيم عليه السلام مبتدئًا له بها ومن قبله ظهرت.

وزعم قوم أنّ السحرة من أهل بابل استنبطوها واستجرّوها. قالوا وإنّما يسمّوا النبط لاستنباطهم العلوم الغامضة. بل قالوا إنّ العلوم كلّها والصنائع النافعة من جهتهم انتشرت وظهرت.

وزعم آخرون أنّ المبتدئين بها العقلاء من الفرس وأنّهم بذلك فخروا على جميع الأمم وقهروا الملوك ودوّخوا البلاد وكانوا أكثر الأمم أموالًا وفضّةً وذهبًا حتّى [٥ظ] أنّ جميع ملوك الأرض كانوا دونهم. ولم تزل تضرب بهم الأمثال بكثرة أموالهم.

وزعم آخرون أنّ المستخرجين لها فلاسفة اليونان الذين استخرجوا بأفكارهم العميقة وعقولهم الجيّدة العلوم الغامضة المستصعبة. واستدلّوا على ذلك بأنّه لا يوجد لأحد من الأمم ما لهم في عمل الطبّ خاصّة. قالوا وهذه الصناعة نوع من الطبّ وأصحاب علم الطبّ هم أصحابها.

وزعم قوم أنّ المنجّمين من الهند استخرجوها بعقولهم الحادّة وذكائهم العظيم وذلك أنّها صناعة تحت علم النجوم وتسمّى أخت النجوم والطبّ وأنّها باستخراج الهند أليق لجودة قرائحهم وحدّة أذهانهم.

وزعم قوم أنّها وُجِدَتْ في هيكل قديم كان برومانس في كتاب بلغة قديمة وأنّ رومانس لمّا نبأ هذه المدينة أودع الكتاب في بيت يكون في هذا الهيكل وأنّ أصلها إنّما أخذ من ذلك الكتاب ثمّ انتشر في أيدي الناس.

وزعم قوم أنّ سحرة اليمن استخرجوها وأنّها لم يزل يظهر باليمن رجل بعد رجل وامرأة بعد امرأة يتكهّنون فيخبرون بالغيوب ويقدّمون في معرفة ما هو كائن ويظهر منهم في ذلك العجائب العجيبة ويخبرون بضمائر القلوب وتخبّأ لهم الخبايا فيخبرون بها. قالوا فهؤلاء تكهّنوا عليها واستخرجوها وعلّموها وعملوها. قالوا من الدليل على صحّة ذلك أنّه ليس يكاد أن يفطن لها إلّا من فيه كهانة وإصابة في الأخبار بما يكون دائمًا لطبيعة فيه تدلّه على ذلك لا على سبيل العلوم الرياضيّة.

> (Ibn Waḥshiyya: 'Who began this art (*al-ṣanʿa*)? From whence did it emerge? Which community (*umma*) invented it and sought to bring it into being (*istajarrahā*), if it was indeed brought forth through the intellect and through the reasoning by analogy (*qiyās*)? And if it was other than that, from which location had it begun to appear and to which community (*umma*) and to which generation did it appear at the beginning?'
>
> Al-Maghribī al-Qamarī: 'You asked after an important aspect and a significant benefit. Hear! Opinions differ as to where it emerged.
>
> One group claimed that God the Sublime taught it (*ʿallamahā*) to Adam, peace be upon him, when He expelled him from Paradise. He taught it to him while he was still in Paradise, teaching him what kind of sin would befall him. When he descended to the earth and

his progeny increased, he taught it to his son Seth, and Seth taught it to his son, until it [i.e. alchemy] appeared.

Another group argued that God, He is mighty and sublime, revealed it (*awḥāhā*) to Idrīs, who is Hermes in the language of the Ancient Greeks. [He revealed it to him] so that he could make use of it for his worldly existence and as a protection granted by God the Sublime to protect him from unclean profits and the commoner's disgraceful ways of living. A group claimed nothing more than having learned it [i.e. alchemy] from him, and that he composed books on it and referred to it in symbolic language out of his desire that — after his own lifetime — it should reach the wise men of great intellect who would be striving for it.

Others said that God the Sublime taught it to Abraham, peace be upon him, making him its first practitioner. From him it arose.

One group believed that the Babylonian sorcerers (*al-saḥara*) invented it and brought it into being. They say that not only are they called Nabataens (*al-nabaṭ*) because of their invention (*istinbāṭ*) of the occult sciences (*al-ʿulūm al-ghāmiḍa*), but that they originated all the sciences and useful arts and disseminated them.

Others, in turn, argue that those who began with it were the Persian wise men (*al-ʿuqalāʾ min al-Furs*). For this reason, they prided themselves above all other communities (*jamīʿ al-umam*), subjugated kings and conquered countries. They were the richest community (*umma*) in silver and gold so that eventually all the kings of the earth were below them. Proverbs on the wealth of their possessions continue to be cited.

Others claim that those who brought it into being were the philosophers of Ancient Greece (*falāsifa al-Yūnān*), who through their profound reasoning and excellent intellectual capacities brought forth those occult sciences that were deemed difficult [to understand]. They come to this conclusion from the fact that no other community (*umma*) has what they have especially not in medical practice. They say: "This art is a kind of medicine and the practitioners of the science of medicine are the practitioners of it [i.e. alchemy]".

One group holds that the Indian astrologers (*munajjimīn min al-Hind*) brought it forth through their sharp intellectual capacities and powerful mental acuteness. This is because it [i.e. alchemy] is an art under the influence of astrology (*ʿilm al-nujūm*), and it is called "Sister of [the Science of] the Stars and Medicine" (*ukht al-nujūm wa-l-ṭibb*). That it should have emerged in India is more appropriate because of the excellence of their talented men and the sharpness of their minds.

> Some practitioners claimed that it [i.e. alchemical knowledge] was discovered in an old temple dedicated to Romanus in a book written in an old language, and that Romanus, after he had informed this city [of this discovery], deposited the book in a chamber in this same temple. [They claim] that its origin was nothing more than what was derived from this book. Thereafter, it circulated among the common people. Finally, some maintained that the sorcerers of Yemen (*saḥara al-Yaman*) brought it forth and that in Yemen man after man and woman after woman continue to appear who can predict the future (*yatakahhanūna*), provide information about invisible things (*fa-yukhbirūna bi-l-ghuyūb*) and offer knowledge of what will be. Wondrous miracles arise from this. They predict with the innermost part of their hearts. The secrets are hidden from them, [but] they predict about them. They say [i.e. the aforementioned group] that they predicted it [i.e. alchemy] and that they brought it forth, taught it and put it into practice. They say that the proof of the truth of this is that one can hardly comprehend it [i.e. alchemy] without [the gift of] soothsaying and the ability of always predicting what will be, as a result of one's natural disposition, not through the method of mathematics'.)[34]

After al-Maghribī al-Qamarī's presented these ten theories on the origins of alchemy, Ibn Waḥshiyya asks him about his opinion and expresses doubts as to whether al-Maghribī is acquainted with this occult science. The latter rebukes Ibn Waḥshiyya's criticism and finally reveals his view on alchemy's origins:

> قال: نعم. إنّ الذي ظنّ أنّها خرجت من مصر وهو ظنّ لا يلوح عليه دليل قويّ لأنّي رأيتُ الكتب القديمة فيها كان مخرجها كلّها من مصر. وما كان في يد غيرهم من الأمم والكتب فيها فإنّما هي منقولة من لغتهم كما يوجد علم الطبّ عند أكثر الأمم [٦ظ] أو كلّهم وإنّما هو منقول من لغة اليونانيّة إلى تلك اللغة. وهاهنا وجه لم أذكره وكان لنا شيخ من أهل الغرب يذكره.
>
> قلتُ: وما هو؟
>
> قال: كان لنا شيخ يزعم أنّه لم يزل على وجه الدهر في القديم كتاب موجود في مدينة منف من أرض مصر مكتوب بلغة من لغات القبط المتروكة. وكان ورق هذا الكتاب أبيض شديد البياض باقٍ على الدهر ما يُدرى مِمَّ هو سطور مكتوبة بخضرة ويعلوها صفرة ما يُدرى ما هي إلّا أنّ من يشاهده كان يزعم أنّه ذهب محلول. وأنّ أهل تلك النواحي كانوا يقصدون الكتاب فينظرون إليه ولا يعلمون ما فيه إلى أن ظهر هرمس. فنظر فيه ففطن له وعلم ما فيه. وزعموا أنّه كان فيه علم الطلسمات مبيّن وعلم الكيمياء مشروح وعلم السحر والنِيرَنْجَات وغير ذلك من العلوم الغامضة السرّيّة. قد كُتِبَتْ بحروف كانوا يظنّوها بلغة حِمْيَر مرّة ومرّة يتوهّمونها بلغة القبط القديمة المتروكة. وأظنّها لم تكن بلغة من اللغات بتّةً. إنّما كانت بحروف تدلّ ذوي الفطن على معانيها لأنّهم زعموا أنّ حروف ذلك الكتاب كلّها كانت معمولة على صُوَر جميع الحيوان من دوابّ البرّ والبحر والطائر. يبتدئ الحرف ثمّ يضيف إيه آخر ثمّ آخر

34 Pseudo-Ibn Waḥshiyya, *Das Kitāb Sidrat al-muntahā*, pp. 65–66 (Arabic text); pp. 102–05 (German trans.).

ويؤلّف بينهما صورة ما. وكانت كتابة ذلك المصحف صُوَرًا كلّها من أوّله إلى آخره. فرزق الله عزّ وجلّ هرمس الفطنة والهداية. فعرف جميع ما فيه وعلمه وعلّمه.

قلتُ للمغربيّ: هل ذكر لكم شيخكم شيئًا مما كان فيه أيّ كانت [٧و] ترجمته؟

قال: نعم. ذكر شيخنا أنّ ترجمته كانت الكتاب الحاوي للحكمة كلّها. وقد كان يذكر من أوّله شيئًا يحفظه. ثمّ أخبرنا بعد مدّة أنّ الكتاب صار إليه ترجمته وتفسيره بلغة القبط وأنّ ذلك أُخِذَ من قبل هرمس وتداوله الناس. قال وهو لوح هرمس الذي كان من زمرّد أخضر مكتوب بالذهب المحلول.

قلتُ للمغربيّ: فهل عندك الكتاب؟

قال: نعم. هو عندي وأنا أعطيك هو ولكن أوصيك ثمّ أوصيك بكتمانه وترك إظهاره.

(Al-Maghribī al-Qamarī: 'Indeed, those are right who suppose that it [i.e. alchemy] emerged in Egypt. No convincing counter-arguments against this assumption exist. I have seen the old books on it and these were all composed in Egypt. The knowledge other people had of it and the books circulating amongst them were translated from the ancient Egyptian language. In this regard, it is no different than the medical science. Its practice amongst most or all civilizations derives simply from translations of Greek works into their respective languages. There is an aspect I have not mentioned yet. I knew a shaykh from the Maghrib who mentioned it [to me]'.

Ibn Waḥshiyya: 'And what is it?'

Al-Maghribī al-Qamarī: 'I knew a shaykh who claimed that a book once existed in the city of Memphis in Egypt. It was written in one of the languages of the Copts which was no longer in use. Its paper was plain white and did not fall into decay. It was not known of what material it consisted. Lines were written in green colour and above them some yellow colour was applied. It was not known of what it [i.e. the yellow colour] consisted, but those who looked at it believed that it was liquid gold.

The local population sought this book out, looked at it and did not comprehend its content until Hermes appeared. He looked at it, comprehended its content, and knew what it contained. They claimed that it illustrated the talismanic art (*ʿilm al-ṭilasmāt*), explained the art of alchemy (*ʿilm al-kīmiyāʾ*) and described black magic (*siḥr*), the production of phylacteries (*nīranjāt*) and other occult sciences (*al-ʿulūm al-ghāmiḍa*) with the help of letters of which they believed that they either belonged to the Himyarite language or to an old language of the Copts no longer in use. I believe, that these letters did not belong to any language. They rather belonged to a script that points the knowledgeable to its meaning, since they claimed that the letters of this book were symbols resembling the complete fauna, those dwelling on earth, those living in the sea and the birds. [...] The whole script of this book consisted of images. God, mighty and majestic is He, granted Hermes intelligence and divine guidance. Therefore, he recognized all it contained, obtained knowledge about it, and taught it'.

Ibn Waḥshiyya: 'Did your shaykh mention some of its content and did he mention its translation?'

Al-Maghribī al-Qamarī: 'Yes, our shaykh told us that its translation would be *The Book That Contains the Complete Wisdom* (*al-Kitāb al-Ḥāwī li–l-ḥikma kullihā*). Indeed, he recited some parts of its beginning which he could remember. He informed us after a while, that he obtained this book in form of a translation and a commentary in the Coptic language. It was written by Hermes and the people disseminated it. He said: "This is Hermes' tablet (*lawḥ Hirmis*) which consists of green emerald written with liquid gold"'.

Ibn Waḥshiyya: 'Do you possess this book?'

Al-Maghribī al-Qamarī: 'Yes! I possess this book and I will bequeath it to you on the condition that it will be kept secret and will not be made public'.)[35]

Thereupon, al-Maghribī confesses that he does not possess the whole book but only a part of it, respectively the part which the shaykh got his hands on. The next day, al-Maghribī al-Qamarī hands over the book to Ibn Waḥshiyya. The latter opens it and discovers that it has already been translated into Arabic. 'A translator (*mutarjim*)', Ibn Waḥshiyya explains, 'translated it from Coptic into Arabic'.[36]

This lengthy account consists of several *topoi* in Arabic alchemical and Hermetic literature, such as the reference to Hermes (Trismegistus) as initiator of alchemy and 'the tablet' as the ultimate source of alchemical wisdom, which is referred to in this treatise as 'Hermes' tablet' (*lawḥ Hirmis*), but it was commonly known as 'the Emerald tablet' (in Arabic *al-lawḥ al-zumurrudī*, in Latin *tabula smaragdina*) in other alchemical treatises.[37] The frame story on the origins of alchemy and the ensuing legend of discovery (Fundlegende) are thus not particularly surprising elements in this alchemical treatise. Such aetiological narratives abound in Arabic alchemical as well as occult treatises.[38]

---

35 Pseudo-Ibn Waḥshiyya, *Das Kitāb Sidrat al-muntahā*, pp. 68–69 (Arabic text); pp. 106–08 (German trans.).

36 Pseudo-Ibn Waḥshiyya, *Das Kitāb Sidrat al-muntahā*, p. 69 (Arabic text); p. 108 (German trans.).

37 On the Emerald Tablet as the alchemists' founding document, see Ruska, *Tabula Smaragdina*.

38 Weisser, 'Hellenistische Offenbarungsmotive', p. 101. Similar aetiological narratives are found

Other 'origin narratives' in the Arabic occult sciences refer, for example, to the prophets Daniel, Enoch (Idrīs in Arabic), or Solomon as originators of various arts. Like in the presented example, these accounts are sometimes accompanied by tales of the discovery of material in graves or caves.[39]

While these accounts would deserve a closer examination in their own right, it is the pretended translation of the tablet written in the hieroglyphic script into Coptic and eventually into Arabic that interests us here. Arab and Arabic-writing authors called the hieroglyphic script 'the temple script' (*al-qalam al-birbawī*), 'the bird script' (*qalam al-ṭayr*), or 'the diviner's, respectively hieratic script' (*al-qalam al-kāhinī*).[40] The knowledge of these signs had long been lost before the Islamic conquest of Egypt just before the middle of the seventh century and medieval Arab and Arabic-writing authors generally agreed that no one knew how to decipher them.[41] Since the exact meaning of the Hieroglyphs remained unknown, they gave rise to ongoing speculations on what knowledge they might contain. It was often assumed that this script dealt with the former knowledge (mostly of an occult nature) of the ancient Egyptians or Hermes Trismegistus. The cosmographer al-Dimashqī (d. 727/1327), for example, informs us that the images (*taṣāwīr*) in the temple of Akhmīm were believed to be signs (*rumūz*) referring to the sciences of the ancient Egyptians, such as talismanic art, medicine, alchemy, and astrology.[42] In one of the works attributed to the occultist al-Būnī (d. 622/1225) it is said that Idrīs (as was said before, this prophet mentioned in the Qurʾān was often equated with Hermes Trismegistus in Arabic occult literature) saved his alchemical knowledge from the Deluge by inscribing it on the ancient temples.[43] In the introduction to al-Qurṭubī's *Ghāyat al-ḥakīm*, a famous

---

in treatises on Arabic medicine, see Brentjes, 'Narratives of Knowledge in Islamic Societies'.

39 Savage-Smith, 'Introduction', p. xxxi. On the authenticating function of such introductions, see Fodor, 'The Origins of the Arabic Legends of the Pyramids'.

40 For *al-qalam al-birbāwī* or *al-aqlām al-birbāwiyya*, see Abū Jaʿfar al-Idrīsī, *Ahrām*, p. 60,9 and p. 61,7. For *qalam al-ṭayr*, see Abū Jaʿfar al-Idrīsī, *Ahrām*, p. 65,14, and Wüstenfeld, 'Die älteste Aegyptische Geschichte', p. 332. Further references provide Haarmann, 'Schatz', p. 369 n. 10. For *al-qalam al-kāhinī*, see Abū Jaʿfar al-Idrīsī, *Ahrām*, 62,11, 63,10 and 95,9.

41 ʿAbd al-Laṭīf al-Baghdādī, for example, states that nobody knew the meaning of the scripts in the temples and that he neither met nor heard of anyone able to decipher them. See al-Baghdādī, *Ifāda*, p. 118 (Arabic facs.); p. 119 (English trans.). The traveller Ibn Baṭṭūṭa also writes that no one understood the 'writings of the ancients', which he saw in the then still standing temples of Akhmīm. See Ibn Baṭṭūṭa, *The Travels*, I, p. 65.

42 Al-Dimashqī, *Nukhbat al-dahr*, p. 44. On the concept of 'deciphering the signs' (*ḥall al-rumūz*) in the Arabic occult sciences, see Heinrichs, 'Ramz'. On an Arabic treatise that claims to provide the exact meaning of several hieroglyphs, see Ibn Waḥshiyya, *Kitāb Shawq al-mustahām fī maʿrifat rumūz al-aqlām*.

43 Ullmann, *Natur- und Geheimwissenschaften*, p. 234. The inscription of occult wisdom to safeguard it from the deluge is an idea that was already expressed in Coptic writings. The Christian monk John Cassian (*c.* 360–435 CE) transmits some ancient Coptic monastic traditions according to which the magical art was taught to Ham, the son of Noah. Since he was aware that he could not bring a book dealing with magic onto the Ark, he inscribed

magical compendium known in the Latin West as *Picatrix*, the author writes that the ancient philosophers inscribed their wisdom in the form of images (*nuqūshāt al-ṣuwar*) on the ancient Egyptian temples and monuments (*barābī*). Furthermore, they preserved their wisdom in books using symbols (*rumūz*) and concealing expressions (*taʿmiyāt*) so that only the philosophers who are like them (*liʾ-lā yafhamahā illā al-ḥakīm mithluhum*) can comprehend them.[44]

The author of the pseudepigraphical treatise *Kitāb Sidrat al-muntahā* thus tries to present its own work as the occult knowledge of a distant, ancient Egyptian past. However, while he might have had the possibility to simply acknowledge his indebtedness to this 'revelation' of alchemical wisdom, he claims that his own genuine work is an Arabic translation of a Coptic version of this hieroglyphic book discovered in Memphis. Although we will never be able to ascertain the reasons that induced him to make such a false claim, one can at least speculate about what might have inspired him to present his work as a pseudotranslation.

The author might have intended to respond to 'the reader's voyeuristic desire to gain access to the inaccessible'.[45] He might have employed this strategy in order to authenticate the presented knowledge and to provide authority to an text otherwise divested of any reliable authoritative means such as the chain of transmitters (*isnad*) in the science of *ḥadīth*, as has already been suggested in regard to such 'origin narratives'.[46] Moreover, the composers of Arabic alchemical treatises might have employed pseudotranslations for another, hitherto ignored reason. It is possible that the author of the presented treatise and other Arab and Arabic-writing alchemists employed this literary strategy of disguising their treatise as pseudotranslations, that is to say the false claim to present their text as an Arabic translation of a text written in an ancient language, to render rather unorthodox and uncommon material more 'palatable' and acceptable to their prospective readers. Research on pseudotranslations in European literature has proposed that this literary strategy was often employed for exactly such a reason. Gideon Toury argued that cultures manifest a certain resistance to cultural changes but, at the same time, are reliant on change and renewal for their survival. For that reason, some novelties are 'introduced under disguise' to alleviate the inherent resistance to such changes.[47] He argues that the authors tried to 'enhance cultural changes by means of fictitious translations'. Thus, in order to introduce change in a given culture, the authors 'put the cultural gate-keepers to sleep by presenting a text as if it were translated, thus lowering the threshold of resistance to the

---

magical recipes on metal blades and hard stones. They withstood the water, so that this 'forbidden wisdom' was preserved. See Viaud, *Magie*, p. 35.

44 Pseudo-al-Majrīṭī, *Ghāyat al-ḥakīm*, p. 2 (Arabic text); p. 2 (German trans.).

45 Rath, 'Pseudotranslation'.

46 Fodor, 'The Origins of the Arabic Legends of the Pyramids'.

47 Toury, 'Enhancing Cultural Changes', p. 3.

novelties it may hold in store and enhancing their acceptability, along with that of the text incorporating them as a whole'.[48]

Arabic alchemical texts offer quite novel and at times 'unorthodox' ideas and the status of this 'science' remained contested. The historian Ibn Khaldūn (d. 808/1406), for example, denounced the alchemists' cryptic utterances and argued that alchemy is a species of magic and therefore prohibited.[49] In order to counteract such resistance towards their genuine compositions and, at the same time, to cater for the ongoing interest in the hidden and occult knowledge of past civilizations among the readers of medieval Islamicate societies, Arab and Arabic-writing alchemists might have chosen to present their own treatises as translations of ancient works.

But could the author of the alchemical work *Kitāb Sidrat al-muntahā* really have chosen this strategy for such a reason? Did he perceive the content of his treatise as a body of knowledge alien, extrinsic, or perhaps even unacceptable to Muslims and adherents of other monotheistic faiths? It seems he did. After the reproduction of the 'ancient' text follows a discussion on the texts content between Ibn Waḥshiyya and al-Maghribī al-Qamarī. Ibn Waḥshiyya asks his interlocutor:

> Ibn Waḥshiyya: '[…] What this book stipulates concerning the characteristics of the beginning, the Eternal, He is God, mighty and majestic is He, our Lord, contradicts the belief of the Muslims (*al-muwaḥiddūn*). […] How can one accept what is written in an old book from the city of Memphis of which one does not know who its author was and what kind of person he was?'[50]

Al-Maghribī al-Qamarī refutes Ibn Waḥshiyya's theological concerns and counters that what he finds abominable does not necessarily have an impact on the fact whether the presented ideas in this ancient book are true or false. Already the German Arabist and scholar of alchemy, Ingolf Vereno, has pointed out that Hermetic treatises such as *The Epistle of the Secret* (*Risālat al-Sirr*) and *The Greater Epistle of the Celestial Bodies* (*al-Risāla al-falakiyya al-kubrā*) present theories contrary to Islamic dogma. He wondered in which circles such works were read.[51] Pseudotranslations might have been a suitable means for alchemists to alleviate their Muslim readers' suspicions and outright rejection of these heterodox doctrines. They might have been much more than 'literarisches Rankenwerk'. They were rather evidence of a literary strategy that allowed alchemists to present their rather controversial ideas and unconventional wisdom in disguise to their prospective readers.

48 Toury, 'Enhancing Cultural Changes', p. 4.

49 On the refutation of alchemy by Ibn Khaldūn, see Al-Azmeh, *Ibn Khaldun*, p. 115.

50 Pseudo-Ibn Waḥshiyya, *Das Kitāb Sidrat al-muntahā*, p. 85 (Arabic text); p. 129 (German trans.).

51 Vereno, *Studien*, p. 36.

Bibliography

Manuscripts

Beirut, Bibliothèque Orientale de l'Université Saint-Joseph, MS 252
Erfurt, Forschungsbibliothek Gotha, MS 85
Erfurt, Forschungsbibliothek Gotha, MS 1162
Vatican City, Vatican Apostolic Library, MS 926

Primary Sources

Abū Jaʿfar al-Idrīsī, *Anwār ʿulwī al-ajrām fi-l-kashf ʿan asrār al-ahrām*, ed. by Ulrich Haarmann (Stuttgart and Beirut: Steiner, 1991)

ʿAbd al-Laṭīf al-Baghdādī, *The Eastern Key: Kitāb al-Ifādah wa-l–iʿtibār of ʿAbd al-Laṭīf al-Baghdādi*, trans. by Kamal H. Zand, John A. Videan, and Ivy E. Videan (London: Allen and Unwin, 1965)

al-Balāḏurī, Aḥmad b. Yaḥyā, *Ansāb al-ašrāf*, vol. 4.2, ed. by ʿAbd al-ʿAzīz al-Dūrī and ʿIṣām ʿUqla, Bibliotheca islamica, 28e (Berlin: Klaus Schwarz, 2001)

al-Dimashqī, *Nukhbat al-dahr fī ʿajāʾib al-barr wa-l-baḥr*, ed. by Ghassān Dāwūd al-Nāṣīr, Ṭalāl Sālim al-Ḥadithī, and Aḥmad Muḥammad Walīd Ayyūb (Damascus: Dār al-ʿArrāb and Nūr, 2013)

Ibn Baṭṭūṭa, *The Travels of Ibn Battuta*, trans. by Hamilton A. R. Gibb, 3 vols (Cambridge: Cambridge University Press, 1958–1971)

Ibn Waḥshiyya, *Kitāb Shawq al-mustahām fī maʿrifat rumūz al-aqlām / Ancient Alphabets and Hieroglyphic Characters Explained: With an Account of the Egyptian Priests, their Classes, Initiation, and Sacrifices*, ed. and trans. by Joseph von Hammer-Purgstall (London: Bulmer, 1806)

——, *al-Filāḥa al-nabaṭiyya*, ed. by Toufic Fahd, 3 vols (Damascus: al-Maʿhad al-ʿIlmī al-Faransī li–l-Dirāsāt al-ʿArabiyya, 1993–1998); English translation: Hämeen-Anttilla, Jaakko, *The Last Pagans of Iraq: Ibn Waḥshiyya and his Nabatean Agriculture* (Leiden: Brill, 2006)

Pseudo-Ibn Waḥshiyya, *Das Kitāb Sidrat al-muntahā des Pseudo-Ibn Waḥšīya. Einleitung, Edition und Übersetzung eines hermetisch-allegorischen Traktats zur Alchemie*, ed. and German trans. by Christopher Braun, Islamkundliche Untersuchungen, 327 (Berlin: Klaus Schwarz Verlag, 2016)

Pseudo-Mağrīṭī, *Das Ziel des Weisen 1. Arabischer Text*, ed. by Hellmut Ritter (Leipzig: B. G. Teubner, 1933); German translation: *Picatrix: das Ziel des Weisen, von Pseudo-Mağrīṭī*, trans. by Helmut Ritter and Martin Plessner (London: Warburg Institute, 1962)

Secondary Studies

Al-Azmeh, Aziz, *Ibn Khaldun: An Essay in Reinterpretation* (New York: Frank Cass, 1982)

Braun, Christopher, '"Who Began with this Art? Where did it Emerge?": A Hermetic Frame Story on the Origins of Alchemy in Pseudo-Ibn-Waḥshīya's *The Book of the Ziziphus Tree of the Furthest Boundary*', *Al-Qanṭara. Revista de Estudios Árabes*, 37.2 (2016), 373–98

Brentjes, Sonja, 'Narratives of Knowledge in Islamic Societies: What Do They Tell Us about Scholars and their Contexts?', *Almagest*, 4.1 (2013), 74–95

Chwolsohn, Daniel, *Über die Überreste der altbabylonischen Literatur in arabischen Übersetzungen*, Académie impériale des sciences de St Pétersbourg, Mémoires des savants étrangers, VIII. 2, repr. (Amsterdam: Oriental Press, 1968)

D'Ancona, Cristina, 'Greek into Arabic', in *Encyclopaedia of Islam, THREE*, ed. by Kate Fleet, Gudrun Krämer, Denis Matringe, John Nawas, and Everett Rowson, 1 (2016), pp. 116–34

Endreß, Gerhard, 'Die wissenschaftliche Literatur', in *Grundriß der Arabischen Philologie. Band 2. Literaturwissenschaft*, ed. by Helmut Gätje (Wiesbaden: Reichert, 1987), pp. 400–506

Fahd, Toufic, 'Nabaṭ', in *Encyclopaedia of Islam: New Edition*, ed. by C. E. Bosworth, E. van Donzel, W. P. Heinrichs, and Ch. Pellat, assisted by F. Th. Dijkema, P. J. Bearman, and Mme S. Nurit (Leiden: Brill, 1993), vol. 7, pp. 834–38

Fodor, Alexander, 'The Origins of the Arabic Legends of the Pyramids', *Acta Orientalia Academiae Scientiarum Hungaricae*, 23 (1970), 335–63

Fowden, Garth, *The Egyptian Hermes: A Historical Approach to the Late Pagan Mind* (Cambridge: Cambridge University Press, 1986)

Gürçağlar, Şehnaz Tahir, 'Pseudotranslation on the Margin of Fact and Fiction', in *A Companion to Translation Studies*, ed. by Sandra Bermann and Catherine Porter (Chichester: Wiley Blackwell, 2014), pp. 516–27

Gutas, Dimitri, *Greek Thought, Arabic Culture: The Graeco-Arabic Translation Movement in Baghdad and Early 'Abbāsid society (2nd–4th / 8th–10th centuries)* (London: Routledge, 2006)

Gutschmid, Alfred von, 'Die Nabatäische Landwirthschaft und ihre Geschwister', *Zeitschrift der Deutschen Morgenländischen Gesellschaft*, 15 (1861), 1–110

Haarmann, Ulrich, 'Der Schatz im Haupte des Götzen', in *Die islamische Welt zwischen Mittelalter und Neuzeit. Festschrift für Hans Robert Roemer zum 65. Geburtstag*, ed. by Ulrich Haarmann and Peter Bachmann (Wiesbaden: Steiner, 1979), pp. 198–229

Hämeen-Anttila, Jaakko, *The Last Pagans of Iraq: Ibn Waḥshiyya and his Nabatean Agriculture* (Leiden: Brill, 2006)

Heinrichs, Wolfhart P., 'Ramz', in *Encyclopaedia of Islam: New Edition*, ed. by C. E. Bosworth, E. van Donzel, W. P. Heinrichs, and G. Lecomte, assisted by P. J. Bearman, and Mme S. Nurit (Leiden: Brill, 1995), vol. 8, pp. 426b–8b

Martelli, Matteo, 'L'alchimie en syriaque et l'œuvre de Zosime in *Les sciences en Syriaque*, ed. by Émilie Villey (Paris: Geuthner, 2014), pp. 191–214

Nöldeke, Theodor, 'Noch Einiges über die "nabatäische Landwirtschaft"', *Zeitschrift der Deutschen Morgenländischen Gesellschaft*, 29 (1876), 445–55

Pertsch, Wilhelm, *Die orientalischen Handschriften der Herzoglichen Bibliothek zu Gotha*, 3 vols (Wien: Hof- und Staatsdruckerei Perthes, 1859–1893)

Rath, Brigitte, 'Pseudotranslation', *The 2014–2015 Report on the State of the Discipline of Comparative Literature, Ideas of the Decade*, 01 April 2014 <https://stateofthediscipline.acla.org/entry/pseudotranslation> (accessed 01 March 2017)

Rizzi, Andrea, 'When a Text is Both a Pseudotranslation and a Translation: The Enlightening Case of Matteo Maria Boiardo (1441–1494)', in *Beyond Descriptive Translation Studies: Investigations in Homage to Gideon Toury*, ed. by Anthony Pym, Miriam Shlesinger, and Daniel Simeoni (Amsterdam: Benjamins, 2008), pp. 153–62

Ruska, Julius, *Tabula Smaragdina: ein Beitrag zur Geschichte der hermetischen Literatur*, Arbeiten aus dem Institut für Geschichte der Naturwissenschaft, 4 (Heidelberg: Winter, 1926)

——, 'Quelques problèmes de littérature alchimiste', *Annales Guebhard-Séverine*, 7 (1931), 156–73

Savage-Smith, Emilie, 'Introduction', in *Magic and Divination in Early Islam*, ed. by Emilie Savage-Smith (Aldershot: Ashgate Variorum, 2004), pp. xiii–li

Schütt, Hans-Werner, *Auf der Suche nach dem Stein der Weisen: die Geschichte der Alchemie* (München: C. H. Beck, 2000)

Sezgin, Fuat, *Geschichte des arabischen Schrifttums*, 17 vols (Leiden: Brill, 1967–2015)

Stapleton, Henry E., 'Further Notes on the Arabic Alchemical Manuscripts in the Libraries of India', *Isis*, 26.1 (1936), 127–31

Strohmaier, Gotthard, 'Elixir, Alchemy and the Metamorphoses of Two Synonyms', *Al-Qanṭara. Revista de Estudios Árabes*, 37.2 (2016), 423–34

Toury, Gideon, 'Enhancing Cultural Changes by Means of Fictitious Translations', in *Translation and Cultural Change*, ed. by Eva Hung (Amsterdam: Benjamins, 2005), pp. 3–18

——, *Descriptive Translation Studies – and Beyond*, 2. expanded and revised edn (Amsterdam: Benjamins, 2012)

Ullmann, Manfred, *Die Natur- und Geheimwissenschaften im Islam*, Handbuch der Orientalistik, Abt. 1, Erg.-Bd. 6, Abschn. 2 (Leiden: Brill, 1972)

——, 'Ḫālid ibn Yazīd und die Alchemie: Eine Legende', *Der Islam*, 55 (1978), 181–218

——, 'Khālid b. Yazīd', in *Encyclopaedia of Islam: New Edition*, ed. by Hamilton A. R. Gibb and others (Leiden: Brill, 1978), pp. 929a–30a

——, 'al-Kīmiyā'', in *Encyclopaedia of Islam: New Edition*, ed. by Hamilton A. R. Gibb and others (Leiden: Brill, 1986), vol. 5, pp. 110–15

——, *Wörterbuch der klassischen arabischen Sprache*, 2 vols (Wiesbaden: Harrassowitz, 1970–2009)

Van Bladel, Kevin, *The Arabic Hermes: From Pagan Sage to Prophet of Science* (Oxford: Oxford University Press, 2009)

Vereno, Ingolf, *Studien zum ältesten alchemistischen Schrifttum. Auf der Grundlage zweier erstmals edierter arabischer Hermetica* (Berlin: Klaus Schwarz Verlag, 1992)

Viaud, Gérard, *Magie et coutumes populaires chez les Coptes d'Égypte* (Sisteron: Éditions Présence, 1978)

Wallenstein, Uta, '"Ich habe mehr gefunden, als ich erwartete …" – Seetzen und die Ägyptensammlung Gotha', in *Ulrich Jasper Seetzen (1767–1811). Leben und Werk. Die arabischen Länder und die Nahostforschung im napoleonischen Zeitalter*, ed. by Hans Stein (Gotha: Forschungs- und Landesbibliothek, 1995), pp. 65–76

Weisser, Ursula, 'Hellenistische Offenbarungsmotive und das Buch Geheimnis der Schöpfung', *Journal for the History of Arabic Science*, 2.1 (1978), 101–25

Wüstenfeld, Ferdinand, 'Die älteste Aegyptische Geschichte nach den Zauber- und Wundererzählungen der Araber', in *Orient und Occident insbesondere in ihren gegenseitigen Beziehungen. Forschungen und Mitteilungen*, ed. by Theodor Benfey, 3 vols (Göttingen: Dieterich, 1862–1866)

ALEXANDER FIDORA

Philology and Polemics in the Prologues to the Latin Talmud Dossier

The thirteenth century deserves a special place in the long history of Christian-Jewish relations, since it heralded the discovery of the Talmud by the Christian world. Earlier authors such as Peter Alfonsi and Peter the Venerable had already referred to the Talmud and subjected it to a critique; however, a greater awareness of this fundamental post-biblical Jewish corpus among Christian authors did not arise until the late 1230s when the Jewish convert Nicholas Donin submitted a Latin anthology of Talmudic fragments to Pope Gregory IX.

Nicholas Donin's translation, also known as the thirty-five articles against the Talmud, was to have an enormous impact on Christian attitudes towards Judaism. Thus, in 1239 the pope wrote to kings and bishops across Europe urging them to seize and examine the manuscripts of the Talmud within their dominions, as a result of which proceedings against the Talmud were launched in Paris in 1240. Though the Talmud was put to the torch at the Place de Grève in 1241/1242,[1] the controversy in its regard continued during the years to come, since Gregory's successor, Pope Innocent IV, called for a review of its condemnation. At the centre of this review lay the *Extractiones de Talmud* — a translation of almost 2000 passages from the Babylonian Talmud prepared in 1245 for Odo of Châteauroux, Legate of the Apostolic See, which served as the basis for his final condemnation of the Talmud in May 1248.

The texts surrounding this infamous controversy have survived in several manuscripts, the most complete — though not the original — of which is

* The research giving rise to the current results has received funding from the Spanish Ministry of Science and Innovation ('The Latin Talmud: Edition and Study of the Dossier', PID2020–112592GB-I00).

1 The exact date of its burning is disputed. See Rose, 'When Was the Talmud Burnt in Paris?'.

Alexander Fidora (alexander.fidora@icrea.cat) is an ICREA research professor in the Department of Ancient and Medieval Studies of the Universitat Autònoma de Barcelona. His research focuses on medieval philosophy as well as the intercultural and interreligious dimensions of medieval thought. He has directed the ERC Starting Grant 'Latin into Hebrew' (2008–2012) and the ERC Consolidator project 'The Latin Talmud' (2014–2019).

Narratives on Translation across Eurasia and Africa: From Babylonia to Colonial India, ed. by Sonja Brentjes in cooperation with Jens Høyrup and Bruce O'Brien, CAT 3, pp. 219–228 (Turnhout: Brepols, 2022) BREPOLS PUBLISHERS 10.1484/M.CAT-EB.5.127942

MS Paris, Bibliothèque nationale de France, lat. 16558.[2] This manuscript offers a comprehensive 'dossier' on the Talmud affair, whose first part contains the aforementioned *Extractiones de Talmud*, while its second part includes Nicholas Donin's thirty-five articles against the Talmud, along with other materials. Though scholars have been dealing with this dossier for over 130 years, we still lack a thorough interpretation of the two parts of this dossier, of which until recently there was no complete critical edition.[3]

In this paper I shall focus on the prologues pertaining to the two parts of the dossier, i.e. the prologue to the *Extractiones de Talmud*, on the one hand, and the prologue to Nicholas Donin's thirty-five articles, on the other, while addressing the prominent role that philology plays within both.

The Prologue to the *Extractiones de Talmud*

The first prologue, written by the anonymous compiler of the Latin Talmud dossier, consists of three major sections. The first of these gives a brief introduction to the Talmud *qua* Oral Torah as well as to the parts thereof, listing the Six Orders of the Talmud along with their Hebrew names and the respective Latin translations. The Hebrew subdivisions of the Talmud are simultaneously introduced, using once more the Hebrew technical terms, which are subsequently explicated in Latin. Here the reader learns, among other things, that each Order of the Talmud is called a 'Seder', and that the plural of Seder is 'Sedarim', and that these Sedarim are divided into 'Masekhtot' (the singular of which is 'Masekhta'), i.e. tractates, which are in turn subdivided into 'Perakhim' (the singular of which is 'Perekh'), i.e. chapters, which themselves contain the 'halakhik' material.[4]

The second section of the prologue offers a glossary of recurrent Hebrew terms in the Talmud, since 'necesse est quarundam dictionum, quae frequenter occurrunt, significationem et interpretationem agnoscere' (it is necessary to know the meaning and the rendering of some terms, which appear

2 For the manuscript tradition of the Latin Talmud, see, among others, Fidora, 'Die Handschrift 19b des Arxiu Capitular de Girona'.

3 A critical edition of the *Extractiones de Talmud* was published by Ulisse Cecini and Óscar de la Cruz in 2018 in the Corpus Christianorum Continuatio Mediaevalis series. One year later, Piero Capelli published a critical edition of Nicholas Donin's thirty-five articles (Capelli, '*De articulis litterarum papae*: A Critical Edition', pp. 36–57) that replaces Isidore Loeb's nineteenth-century text which was based on a single manuscript (Loeb, 'La controverse de 1240 sur le Talmud').

4 Cf. *Praefatio* in *Extractiones de Talmud*, ed. by Cecini and de la Cruz, p. 4: 'Continet autem sex libros [...] Istorum quilibet cezer, id est "ordinatio" et gallice *attirement*, nuncupatur, et *cezarym* dicitur in plurali. Horum etiam quilibet in plures *macectot*, id est in plures "libros", dividitur partiales, et *macecta*, id est "fundamentum", dicitur in singulari. Sed etiam quaelibet *macecta* plures *parakym* continet, id est "iuncturas" aut "copulas", *perec* in singulari, quod nos "capitulum" appellamus. Item unusquisque *perec* suas continet *halakoth*, id est "sententias" [...]; *halaka* est singulare'.

frequently).[5] This list contains more than twenty notions, such as 'goy', i.e. a non-Jewish person, explicated in Latin as 'gens'; 'Hanukkah', explicated as 'festum Judith'; 'Shemhamphorash', explicated as God's name expressed by means of forty-two letters; and so on.[6]

The third section draws attention to the difficulties in transcribing Hebrew and Aramaic terms into Latin, because of differences regarding their respective phonetic systems:

> Postremo sciendum quod Latinarum defectus litterarum miram nobis difficultatem generat et quasi inpossibilitatem scribendi gallicum et hebraeum, ut primas sillabas gallici istarum dictionum: 'venite', 'tenete', 'sedete' et similium, et ultimam harum: 'dominae', 'domina', 'dominam' et omnium huiusmodi, ita frequenter est in hebraeo.[7]
>
> (Moreover, one has to know that the limitedness of the Latin alphabet poses great problems to us, since it is almost impossible to write French or Hebrew words in Latin, as is the case with the first syllables of the following words in French: 'come', 'hold', 'sit', etc., and the last syllable of words like 'lady', etc. And the same occurs with regard to Hebrew.)

This passage is of particular interest, since it makes use of Old French in order to explicate the problems of transcribing from Hebrew, which problems the text goes on to discuss in further detail.[8]

Altogether, the three major sections of the prologue to the *Extractiones de Talmud* show the compiler's aim of providing a rigorous philological introduction to the Latin translation of the Talmud that explains: a) the structure of the text; b) difficult terms; as well as c) problems of transcription.

The philological sensitivity of the compiler also becomes manifest in his description of the translation process of the Talmud. In an intriguing passage from the prologue to the *Extractiones de Talmud*, we are told that

> Deus autem duos sibi providit interpretes catholicos in hebraea lingua quam plurimum eruditos. Hoc autem fidelitatis eorum infallibile mihi praestitit argumentum: quod, cum multa magna et notabilia de praedictis libris diversis temporibus, posteriore ignorante quae vel qualiter, ab ore

5 *Praefatio* in *Extractiones de Talmud*, ed. by Cecini and de la Cruz, p. 5.

6 *Praefatio* in *Extractiones de Talmud*, ed. by Cecini and de la Cruz, pp. 5–7. During the Middle Ages, the story of Judith gained increasing importance among the Hanukkah tales; this explains why the compiler associates the Festival of Lights, which in fact commemorates the rededication of the Second Temple in Jerusalem, with the feast of Judith. See Gera, 'The Jewish Textual Traditions', pp. 30–31.

7 *Praefatio* in *Extractiones de Talmud*, ed. by Cecini and de la Cruz, p. 8. The examples refer to the various pronunciations of the vowel 'e' in French, in words such as 'venez', 'tenez' or 'dame', for which there is no phonetic equivalent in Latin script, as the compiler claims.

8 On the transcription of Hebrew and Aramaic terms in the *Extractiones de Talmud*, see Vernet i Pons, 'On the Latin Transcription of Hebrew and Aramaic', pp. 197–219.

prioris interpretis transtuleram, etsi propter difficultatem et obscuritatem hebraici, quandoque variaverint verba, eandem tamen sententiam et sensum tenuerunt.[9]

> (God sent two Catholic translators who were very learned in the Hebrew language. For me, unquestionable proof of their reliability lay in the fact that some time after I had translated many important and remarkable passages from the aforesaid books from the mouth of the first translator (*ab ore prioris interpretis transtuleram*), this translation, as well as that of the second translator — who did not know what I had previously translated or how it had been rendered — both expressed the same opinions and yielded the same sense, though they sometimes used different words because of the difficulty and obscurity of the Hebrew language.)

The factual information which can be gained from this passage is as follows: at a certain point in time the compiler of the Talmud dossier and a translator, T_1, collaboratively rendered portions from the Talmud into Latin via an intermediary oral vernacular translation. Later the compiler had the opportunity to compare their joint translation with that of a different, independent translator, T_2. This comparison revealed that both translations were extremely close to each other: in fact, they yielded the same sense, though their wording was different.

As well as providing valuable insights into the practical work of the translators, this passage also evokes important literary motifs and traditions. *Prima facie*, the account shows striking parallels to the translation of the Septuagint, which is said to have been translated by seventy learned men, who, working independently from one another, produced identical translations. The account of this miraculous translation of the Old Testament into Greek was made known to the Latin world through Irenaeus of Lyon. In his *Adversus haereses*, III. 21. 2, the Bishop of Lyon describes the translation process in the following manner:

> Convenientibus autem ipsis in unum apud Ptolomaeum et comparantibus suas interpretationes, Deus glorificatus est et Scripturae vere divinae creditae sunt, omnibus eadem et isdem verbis et isdem nominibus recitantibus ab initio usque ad finem, uti et praesentes gentes cognoscerent quoniam per aspirationem Dei interpretatae sunt Scripturae.[10]

---

9 *Praefatio* in *Extractiones de Talmud*, ed. by Cecini and de la Cruz, p. 4. In a second version of the prologue, which the anonymous compiler of the *Extractiones de Talmud* prepared for his thematic rearrangement of the texts translated, one reads that the two translators were converts: 'Deus autem ad hoc duos sibi providit interpretes ab errore iudaico ad fidem conversos' (transcribed in *Extractiones de Talmud*, ed. by Cecini and de la Cruz, p. 11, from MS Schaffhausen, Stadtbibliothek, ms. Min. 71, fol. 60r).

10 Irenaeus of Lyon, *Contre les hérésies*, p. 404.

> (When [the translators of the Old Testament] came together in the same place before Ptolemy, and each of them compared his own translation with that of every other, God was glorified, and the Scriptures were acknowledged as truly divine. For all of them pronounced the same text with the same expressions and words, from beginning to end, so that even the gentiles present realized that the Scriptures had been translated by the inspiration of God.)

While the idea of textual coincidence in processes of multiple translation clearly connects the Latin Talmud translation to the account of the Septuagint, the compiler of the Talmud dossier also states a categorical difference: in the case of the Septuagint, one is dealing with literal coincidence, whereas in the translations of the Talmud only the sense is stable throughout its various translations, while the wording differs (*variaverint verba*).

This latter affirmation echoes Jerome's classical *dictum* concerning literal versus sense-for-sense translation; the first of these is reserved by him for the Bible, while the second is used for the translation of secular texts. Thus, in his famous Letter to Pammachius (Epistula 57), Jerome claims:

> Ego enim non solum fateor, sed libera voce profiteor me in interpretatione Graecorum absque Scripturis sanctis, ubi et verborum ordo mysterium est, non verbum e verbo, sed sensum exprimere de sensu. Habeoque huius rei magistrum Tullium.[11]
>
> > (Not only do I acknowledge, but also overtly profess that for the translation of Greek texts I do not translate word for word — which I do only in the case of Holy Scripture, where even the order of the words is a mystery —, but rather I translate sense for sense. My teacher in this is Cicero.)

The blend of these two *loci classici* of medieval translation theory, namely the Septuagint and Jerome, is meant to confirm, once more, the philological accuracy of the Latin translation of the Talmud. As in the case of the Septuagint, such accuracy is confirmed by independent yet coincident translations, the proviso being, however, that in our own case the coincidence accommodates Jerome's rule for the translation of non-revealed texts.

The Prologue to Donin's Thirty-five Articles

The detailed description of the translation process in the first prologue and the emphasis therein upon coincident translations should not, however, be taken as an unbiased scholarly plea for the quality of the translation. In my view, the following passage from the second prologue, i.e. the one preceding

11 *Sancti Hieronymi Epistulae LIII–LXX*, p. 59.

Nicholas Donin's thirty-five articles, is key to understanding the far-reaching implications of the issue at stake:

> Quoniam in ore duorum vel trium testium stat omne verbum [Deuteronomy 19. 15] ad maiorem praecedentium firmitatem et certitudinem quaedam repetere quaedam superaddere utile iudicavi quae ex ore alterius interpretis sunt translata v vel vi annis prius, licet hic ponantur posterius […].[12]
>
> > (Since every charge rests upon the statements of two or three witnesses [Deuteronomy 19. 15], in order to increase the firmness and certainty of what has been said, I thought it useful to repeat and to add some passages which were translated from the mouth of the other translator (*ex ore alterius interpretis*) [e.g. Donin's thirty-five articles] some five or six years earlier, even though here they are placed afterwards […].)

Elsewhere, Ulisse Cecini and I have discussed the consequences of this passage for our understanding of the details of the actual translation process described in the first prologue. Thus, when, in the first prologue, the anonymous compiler refers to his translation *à quatre mains* with T_1, he is actually referring to his participation in the translation of Nicholas Donin's thirty-five articles. These articles were translated first of all, as the compiler states in both the first and second prologues, but, as included in the dossier, follow the *Extractiones de Talmud*, i.e. sequentially speaking, they come second.[13]

I shall not dwell on this point, however, in this particular instance. Here I should like to highlight instead how, in the second prologue, the idea of multiple but coincident translations shifts from being an apparently noble philological argument, as had emerged from the first prologue, to assume the character of certain accusatory procedures associated with legal disputes. This almost tacit shift is achieved by the above quotation from Deuteronomy 19. 15, which introduces the so-called 'two-witness rule'.[14] The rule, which also found its way into the New Testament as 'fraternal correction' (Matthew 18. 16), postulates the existence of at least two qualified witnesses for every accusation.[15]

It is certainly more than pure coincidence that this legal principle features very prominently in Pope Gregory IX's *Liber Extra*, the authoritative

---

12 The *Prologus in secundam partem* is now edited in Capelli, '*De articulis litterarum papae*: A Critical Edition', p. 36 (only fragments thereof — which do not include the present passage — were edited in Loeb, 'La controverse de 1240 sur le Talmud').

13 For example, Fidora and Cecini, 'Nicholas Donin's Thirty-Five Articles Against the Talmud'.

14 Deuteronomy 19. 15: 'One witness alone shall not take the stand against a man in regard to any crime or any offense of which he may be guilty; a judicial fact shall be established only on the testimony of two or three witnesses'.

15 The rule was already present in the *Decretum Gratiani*: C. II, q. 4, c. 3: 'Quorum vero vita adeo laudabilis est, ut omnibus imitanda appareat, de quorum assertione nulla dubitatio nasci poterit, eorum testimonio duorum vel trium testium quilibet iure convinci et dampnari poterit' (*Corpus Iuris Canonici*, ed. by Friedberg, i, col. 466).

compilation of Canon Law by Ramon de Penyafort, which the pope had only recently sent to the Masters of the University of Paris, i.e. in 1234. In Titulus XX 'De testibus et attestationibus', the 'two-witness rule' is referred to no fewer than three times. In the first instance, in Chapter 4, it is connected with the discussion of fraternal correction in general; later on, in Chapter 28, it is said that the firmness of any judgement (*firmitas*) — a term which is also used in the passage quoted above — fundamentally depends upon the number of witnesses. And lastly, Chapter 20 (*Licet universis*), underscores the importance of relying upon more than one witness when in litigation with Jews, the title of this chapter being: 'Ad decisionem causae, maxime pro parte Iudaei, non sufficit regulariter unius testimonium'.[16] In the present context, this explicit connection between the 'two-witness rule' and legal disputes with Jews is very telling, for it strongly suggests that the compiler's insistence on independent yet coincident translations of the Talmud is not only invoking *topoi* from the history of translation, but also introducing legal categories and procedures (with the aim of dealing with Jewish people in particular) as laid out in the pope's *Liber Extra*.

* * *

In view of the account I have offered, the idea of multiple yet coincident translations serves not merely as an indicator of the quality of a translation and the faithfulness thereof. Rather, it acquires an additional dimension which ties together the philological aspects of the Talmud translation with its polemical purpose, insofar as the repeated references to multiple yet coincident translations are intended ultimately to confer formal legal validity upon the accusations against the Talmud raised within the dossier.

Forming an integral part of the legal procedures which led to the final condemnation of the Talmud in May 1248, the different versions of the Latin Talmud within the dossier, i.e. the *Extractiones de Talmud* and Nicholas Donin's thirty-five articles, were, in fact, 'summoned' as qualified textual witnesses in the trial of the Talmud, a trial which, as such, had to conform to the 'two-witness rule'. From this perspective, the detailed reflections upon

16 *Liber Extra*, X 2.20.23: 'Mandamus, quatenus, si inter vos et quoscunque *Christianos sive* Iudaeos emerserit quaestio, *pro nullius vocatione ad saecularem curiam, ut ibi de negotio tractetis aut iudicemini, accedere praesumatis, sed, sicut exigit iustitia et aequitatis ratio postulat,* in qualibet causa Christiani, et maxime clerici, non minus quam duorum vel trium virorum, qui sint probatae vitae et fidelis conversationis, testimonium admittatis, iuxta illud dominicum: In ore duorum vel trium testium stat omne verbum, quia, licet quaedam sint causae, quae plures quam duos exigant testes, nulla est tamen causa, quae unius *tantum* testimonio, quamvis legitimo, *rationabiliter* terminetur' (*Corpus Iuris Canonici*, ed. by Friedberg, II, col. 323). The italicised expressions, namely the so-called *partes decisae,* were not included in Ramon de Penyafort's compilation of the *Liber Extra,* though they are printed in modern editions. His version gives the impression, much more than do the original texts which he collected, of formulating a general rule as regards how to handle cases of litigation with Jewish people.

language and translation contained in the prologues should be understood in connection to the legal strategies employed in the Talmud proceedings, which, in turn, provide the missing link between the dossier's philological concerns and its polemical aims.

This interplay of differing motifs and professional approaches in the Talmud affair is corroborated by the list of signatories to the final condemnation of the Talmud in the year 1248: four ecclesiastical authorities; eleven 'magistri theologiae'; and no fewer than twelve 'boni viri' and fourteen 'magistri decretorum'.[17] Interestingly enough, it is not the masters of theology who represent the largest group within this commission, but, rather, the 'boni viri', among whom might have featured the anonymous compiler and translator(s) of the *Extractiones de Talmud*, as well as the masters of law: in other words, the two groups by which and for which the dossier was prepared.

17 For the document and the list of signatories, see Denifle and Chatelain, *Chartularium universitatis parisiensis*, pp. 209–11. The theologians and masters of law in this list have been identified in Gorochov, *Naissance de l'Université*, pp. 535 and 544–45.

Bibliography

Manuscripts

Paris, Bibliothèque nationale de France, lat. 16558
Schaffhausen, Stadtbibliothek, MS Min. 71

Primary Sources

Capelli, Piero, '*De articulis litterarum papae*: A Critical Edition', in *The Talmud in Dispute During the High Middle Ages*, ed. by Alexander Fidora and Görge K. Hasselhoff (Bellaterra: Servei de Publicacions de la Universitat Autònoma de Barcelona, 2019), pp. 29–57

Corpus Iuris Canonici, ed. by Emil Friedberg, 2 vols (Leipzig: Bernhard Tauchnitz, 1879–1881)

Extractiones de Talmud per ordinem sequentialem, ed. by Ulisse Cecini and Óscar de la Cruz, Corpus Christianorum Continuatio Mediaevalis, 291 (Turnhout: Brepols, 2018)

Irenaeus of Lyon, *Contre les hérésies (Livre III, tome 2)*, ed. by Adeline Rousseau and Louis Doutreleau (Paris: Cerf, 2002)

Sancti Hieronymi Epistulae LIII–LXX, ed. by Jérôme Labourt (Paris: Cerf, 1953)

Secondary Studies

Denifle, Heinrich, and Émile Chatelain, *Chartularium universitatis parisiensis*, vol. 1 (Paris: Delalain, 1886)

Fidora, Alexander, 'The Latin Talmud and its Influence on Christian-Jewish Polemic', *Journal of Transcultural Medieval Studies*, 1.2 (2014), 337–42

——, 'Die Handschrift 19b des Arxiu Capitular de Girona: Ein Beitrag zur Überlieferungsgeschichte des lateinischen Talmud', in *Zwischen Rom und Santiago. Festschrift für Klaus Herbers zum 65. Geburtstag*, ed. by Claudia Alraum, Andreas Holndonner, Hans-Christian Lehner, Cornelia Scherer, Thorsten Schlauwitz, and Veronika Unger (Bochum: Winkler, 2016), pp. 49–56

Fidora, Alexander, and Ulisse Cecini, 'Nicholas Donin's Thirty-Five Articles Against the Talmud: A Case of Collaborative Translation in Christian-Jewish Polemic', in *'Ex Oriente Lux'. Translating Words, Scripts and Styles in Medieval Mediterranean Society. Selected Papers*, ed. by Charles Burnett and Pedro Mantas-España (Córdoba/London: CNERU/The Warburg Institute, 2016), pp. 187–99

Friedman, John, Jean Connell Hoff, and Robert Chazan, eds, *The Trial of the Talmud: Paris, 1240* (Toronto: PIMS, 2012)

Gera, Deborah L., 'The Jewish Textual Traditions', in *The Sword of Judith: Judith Studies Across the Disciplines*, ed. by Kevin R. Brine, Elena Ciletti, and Henrike Lähnemann (Cambridge: Open Book Publishers, 2010), pp. 23–40

Gorochov, Nathalie, *Naissance de l'Université. Les écoles de Paris d'Innocent III à Thomas d'Aquin (v. 1200-v. 1245)* (Paris: Honoré Champion, 2012)

Loeb, Isidore, 'La controverse de 1240 sur le Talmud', *Revue des études juives*, 1 (1880), 247–61; 2 (1881), 248–70; 3 (1881), 39–57

Rose, Paul Lawrence, 'When Was the Talmud Burnt in Paris? A Critical Examination of the Christian and Jewish Sources and a New Dating. June 1241', *Journal of Jewish Studies*, 62 (2011), 324–39

Vernet i Pons, Eulàlia, 'On the Latin Transcription of Hebrew and Aramaic Proper Names in the Latin Talmud (Tract. Sanhedrin): Phonetic Features of the Translation', *Journal of Transcultural Medieval Studies*, 2.2 (2015), 197–219

LUCIA FINOTTO

Faraj ben Salīm of Agrigento

Translation, Politics, and Jewish Identity in Medieval Sicily

> I decided to make a great effort in the present subject, even if I realize that it is not for a man like me to climb and ascend this high mountain, the mountain of translation. The way is too long for me and the stumbling blocks too numerous.
>
> Jacob Anatoli, *Preface to Expositio Isagogis by Averroes*[1]

Among the pages of a Latin manuscript preserved at the Bibliothèque nationale de France in Paris, the portrait of a Jewish doctor receiving a book from the hands of a king captures the attention of the observer.[2] Experts believe that it is probably the first authentic figurative representation of a Jewish person in premodern Europe.[3] The doctor, distinguished by the typical hat worn by physicians in medieval southern Italy, is also portrayed in three subsequent vignettes: translating, the original book on a pedestal with the translation manuscript on his lap; delivering his completed manuscript; and finally receiving payment. The colophon of the manuscript reveals that the royal figure is Count Charles I of Anjou, King of Sicily, Naples and Jerusalem (r. 1266–1282), while the translator of the book is Faraj ben Salīm of Agrigento, also known in the registers (or *Registri*) of the royal chancellery as Faracius Judeus, Farasche Moyse, and other homophones. The authenticity of the picture is considered indisputable.[4]

The illumination on this manuscript is in itself a narration of one of many translation stories which characterized the intellectual life of medieval southern Italy. Together with chancellery documents and personal writings,

---

1 Parma, Biblioteca Palatina, MS 2762, fol. 2ʳ. The translation is mine.
החלטתי להתאמצ בענין הנוכחי ואם ידעתי כי לא יעות ליש כמוני לחרוש ולהעלות על.
ההר הגדול, הר העתקה. הדרך ארוכה והאבני הנגף רבות ד׳ והותר.

2 Paris, BnF, MS Latin 6912, fol. 1ᵛ.

3 Durrieu, 'Un portrait de Charles Ier d'Anjou', p. 199; Kaufmann, 'Un portrait de Faradj, le Traducteur', pp. 152–54.

4 Durrieu, *Les archives angevines de Naples*, pp. 46–51; Minieri-Riccio, *Della dominazione angioina nel reame di Sicilia*; Durrieu,'Un portrait de Charles Ier d'Anjou', pp. 195–97.

Lucia Finotto (PhD, Brandeis University, luciafi@brandeis.edu) is a cultural historian of the Jews in the medieval Mediterranean. She is currently a research fellow at the Frankel Institute for Advanced Judaic Studies, University of Michigan, Ann Arbor.

Narratives on Translation across Eurasia and Africa: From Babylonia to Colonial India, ed. by Sonja Brentjes in cooperation with Jens Høyrup and Bruce O'Brien, CAT 3, pp. 229–248 (Turnhout: Brepols, 2022) BREPOLS PUBLISHERS 10.1484/M.CAT-EB.5.127943

it relates how and why the translation of one of the most influential works of medicine produced in the Islamic world, *Kitāb al-Ḥāwī fī l-ṭibb*, by the Persian clinician and philosopher Abū Bakr Muḥammad ibn Zakariyyà' al-Rāzī (Rhazes in Latin), (d. *c.* 925 CE) was performed by the physician Faraj ben Salīm in thirteenth-century Naples. Recent scholarship in Jewish Studies though has ignored his story, not only for the mentioned scarcity of sources, but because Faraj's translation work into Latin is traditionally seen as having little relationship with the development of the Jewish communities. After all, medieval Jews wanted little to do with Latin texts. They saw them as closely connected to the Church or to other Christian powers, and therefore as texts aimed at a predominantly Christian public.[5] I will argue instead that Faraj is a representative figure and that, exactly like many of his modern counterparts, he excelled in translation as well as in other disciplines. He was both a reliable and extremely competent court expert in various disciplines, and a Jew, an individual with a definite identity and a well-defined role within his community. This paper also intends to show that, even though most narratives on the modes and motives of the translation of *al-Ḥāwī* derive from official royal and administrative sources, they are closely connected to the intellectual milieu outside the court and to the life of individual Jews. Therefore studying the views and preoccupations of single actors, Jewish, Muslim, or Christian, translators, rulers, or end users of the texts in question, can both reinforce or challenge and subvert those official narratives.

From the royal registers, hints about Faraj's family history can be gleaned, as well as the reason for his emigration to Naples:

> Magistro Faragio Judeo de Agrigento familiari et fratribus, provisio quod non molestentur in bonis suis, qua tempora rebellionis Agrigenti ipsi in nostra curia nostri servitiis commorabantur.[6]
>
> > (I provide that Master Faraj, Jew of Agrigento, his family and brothers should not be molested in their possessions, because at the time of the rebellion of the city of Agrigento, we have retained him at our court and in our service.)

This brief statement, reported in 1269, sheds some light not only on Faraj's personal circumstances but also on the political situation of the Angevin kingdom. Sicily had been the theatre of a violent rebellion against the newly established king, Charles I. He had conquered the island just two years before, after defeating the last Swabian king, Manfred, Frederick II's illegitimate son, in response to a papal plea, that of Innocent IV, to rid the world of the

---

5 Freudenthal, *Science in the Medieval Hebrew and Arabic Traditions*, pp. 89–99.

6 Register of Charles of Anjou (1268–69) Filangieri XV 1269 n. 1053 — 'Quaternus Extravagantium' in Minieri-Riccio, *Brevi notizie intorno all'archivio angioino di Napoli*; Scandaliato, 'Gli ebrei di Sicilia nel Medioevo', pp. 115–33; Lagumina, *Codice diplomatico dei Giudei di Sicilia*. III, pp. 74–75 — two physicians Faraj ben Faraj were reported in 1425 and 1453.

Hohenstaufen family who had ruled over Sicily and southern Italy since 1195. The local barons did not tolerate the heavy taxation, the assignment of old feudal lands to French and Provencal newcomers, or the excessive privileges granted to ecclesiastic entities. In Sicily, Charles was officially a vassal of the Church. The recognition of certain rights and exemptions to the papal supporters was crucial to guarantee the very existence of his reign.[7] The king was therefore obliged to create a convincing image of his monarchy as a way of gaining popularity and maintaining control.

From Agrigento to Naples: Translation, Diplomacy, and Jewish Affairs

Agrigento was a dangerous city for Jews in those years. Not only were they subject to continuous extortions of money by unauthorized royal officers, but they suffered several incursions into their quarters. Newcomers, both officers and private persons, sent their servants to pillage Jewish residences 'violently taking from them beds, clothes, furniture, vases and many other items'.[8]

The Jewish community petitioned the king to obtain justice. Charles intervened immediately to ensure that the royal officers stop requiring undue contributions and cease mistreating and robbing the Jews.[9] The king, as part of a project of restoring consensus on the island, took action to ensure that these assets be returned to Faraj and his brothers in the year 1270.[10] Faraj, however, remained at the court for at least twelve more years.

Faraj's name is mentioned for the first time in the surviving royal registers in 1267. His oath, taken according to the Jewish law, had been inscribed in the royal register. He was now ready to become a translator from Arabic to Latin and to start translating 'certain books' for the king.[11] Later that year, the royal chancellery compiled a list of all the books of 'medical science' that Faraj had translated because the physician of the king had urged him to do so.[12] Although the official documents are not sufficiently clear and do not expand on Faraj's exact role at the court, we can infer that he had been active as a translator since the early days of Charles's reign, and that he was allowed to take an oath according to his religion. He was also confirmed in the role of medical expert and translator from Arabic to Latin.

7 Catalioto, *Terre, baroni e città in Sicilia*, pp. 51–52; Malaspina, *Rerum Sicularum Historia*, ed. by Muratori and Argelati, p. 296; Bartolomeo de Neocastro, *Historia Sicula*, XIII, Part 1–3, p. 86; Altamura, *Cronaca di Partenope*, pp. 128-–31.

8 Houben, 'Neue Quellen', pp. 347–48.

9 Houben, 'Neue Quellen', pp. 347–48; Minieri-Riccio, *Diario Angioino dal 4 gennaio 1284 al 7 gennaio 1285*.

10 Catalioto, *Terre, baroni e città in Sicilia*, pp. 143, 262, 283.

11 Filangieri, *I registri della cancelleria angioina*, Reg. 91, XXI, no. 221.

12 Filangieri, *I registri della cancelleria angioina*, Reg. 91, XXI, no. 225.

Moreover, Faraj must have served as a sort of liaison between the court and the Jewish community. In 1270 King Charles, writing from Palermo, confirmed his approval of the newly elected presbyter of the synagogue of Palermo, Maborach Faddalckassem, who was also to be a butcher and a notary for the Jews of that city. His election and the legality of the process had been ascertained by the excellent evaluation of Faraj, 'our faithful man and interpreter at our court', who diligently examined the case and the people involved in approving the individual's capabilities and fitness for the role. The king also granted Maborach a licence for all his activities and enjoined both him and the community to be faithful to the king while respecting their own customs.[13]

Meat had a political valence in medieval Palermo. Several sources attest to the existence of two slaughter-houses, the *bocciaria magna* for the general public and the *bocciaria Judeorum* located near the synagogue in the Jewish quarter of Cassaro. A number of petitions to the royal chancellery reveal that part of the ritually slaughtered animals ended up being sold not only in Jewish stores but also in the main market, mostly by authorized non-Jewish dealers. Jews had obtained from previous rulers the 'privilege' of selling ritually imperfect animals or those parts of animals whose consumption was forbidden by the Jewish law. Christians, for their part, were outraged that what they perceived as the 'scraps of the Jews' were being offered for purchase in the *bocciaria magna*. Since the meat market of medieval Palermo seemed to be a theatre of more than just buying and selling, it is legitimate to conclude that Faraj was sent on a delicate mission requiring not only transcultural abilities but also mediation power. For this he must have been highly trusted by the court. Adjectives like 'faithful', 'reliable', 'trusted', and our 'familiare', that is to say part of the court inner circle, are used in almost every document referring to Faraj and testify that he was very close to the king.[14]

In 1272, though, Faraj was sent on a diplomatic mission of a more conventional type. Charles's envoys visited the sultan of Tunis to exact the newly increased yearly tribute to be paid by the North African ruler. Faraj was probably selected because he could serve as an interpreter of Arabic and also as an expert in coins and silver. He was paid forty *uncias* as an advance for his services.[15] We do not know if it is on this occasion that the Tunisian ruler handed the manuscript of *al-Ḥāwī* to the royal ambassadors. The court documents only

---

13 Simonsohn, *The Jews in Sicily*, I, pp. 464–65.

14 Luzzati, 'Carne "cristiana" e carne "ebraica"', pp. 135–37. The designation of 'familiare' was traditionally reserved to members of the king's inner circle. On this subject, see the article by Takayama, 'Familiares Regis and the Royal Inner Council in Twelfth-Century Sicily'.

15 *Cartulaire général de l'ordre des Hospitaliers*, III, n. 3473, in data Monteforte 2 settembre 1272; Borghese, *Carlo I d'Angiò e il Mediterraneo*, pp. 152–53; Filangieri, *I Registri Cancelleria Angioina*, p. 158. This document reports a 'Farachio [Sicilian version of the name Faraj], espertis ad cognescendam monetam et argentum …' being compensated for his expertise on top of his interpreting abilities. One *uncia* (or ounce) was the equivalent of thirty *taris* (Arabic gold coins) as in use in Sicily at the time (see also footnote n. 38 below).

report that at least two emissaries were part of this delegation.[16] The sultan was a ruler of the Ḥafṣid dynasty, either Abū ʿAbdallāh Muḥammad al-Mustanṣir (1249–1277) or his son Abū Zakariyyàʾ Yaḥyà II, nicknamed al-Wāthiq (the Trustful) (1277–1279), with whom Charles seems to have had an especially positive relationship.[17] The manuscript of the *Ḥāwī*, though, portrays three almost identical figures sitting in front of the Tunisian ruler — the latter is clearly recognizable by the typical North African garb and headpiece.

The introduction of the *Liber Continens*, the name with which *al-Ḥāwī* became known in Latin Europe, also sheds some light on the process of acquisition of the text and the appointment of the translator:

> Predicto itaque libro a rege Tunisii per sollempnes nuntios conquisito virum fidelem adhibuit lingue tam arabice quam latine peritum, et in libro ipso, in quo sub arabice lingue tenebris tanta nobis occultabatur utilitas, mandavit et fecit lucernam latine translationis accendi.[18]
>
> > (And after he had acquired the aforementioned book from the ruler of Tunis by means of official envoys, he found a faithful man, an expert in both Arabic and Latin, and delivered to him the book whose great utility to us was hidden in the darkness of the Arabic language, and he made it luminous with the light of the Latin translation.)

Despite the necessity of balancing his position between allegiance to the pope and local control, which took up most of his personal and military energies, Charles I did not neglect culture. His involvement with Jewish intellectuals and translators is perhaps not as evident as in the case of his flamboyant predecessor, Frederick II, whose influence on the transmission of Islamic sciences to the west had been enormous.[19] Yet, the king fully embraced and sustained the cultural policy of his predecessors, including the use of the university as a branch of government. He hosted at his court a number of Jewish intellectuals.[20]

Translating the *Kitāb al-Ḥāwī*

The history of the translation of *al-Ḥāwī* allows a glimpse into the relationship between arts, and especially between translation and power. The royal registers show that the king was personally involved in the process of translation and followed closely all the phases of the work, even when he was residing

---

16 Minieri-Riccio, *Della dominazione angioina nel reame di Sicilia*, p. 32.

17 Durrieu, 'Un portrait de Charles Ier d'Anjou', p. 193 no. 1; Fischer and Weisser, 'Das Vorwort zur lateinischen Übersetzung von Rhazes', p. 240; Bryson, 'The Kitāb al-*Ḥāwī* of Rāzī (ca. 900 AD)', p. 95.

18 Paris, BnF, MS Latin 6912, fol. 2r.

19 Houben, 'Federico II e gli ebrei', pp. 325–46.

20 Sirat, 'Les traducteurs juifs à la cour des Rois de Sicile et de Naples', pp. 169–91.

outside Naples.[21] Moreover, Charles commissioned genealogies, legitimization histories, and copies of the works of classical authors preciously decorated, for the realization of which he even consulted with the higher ranks of the local clergy.[22] Translation was not, in most cases, a purely intellectual exercise or simply a response to practical needs but rather a political instrument. Medicine, especially the highly-respected Islamic one, was a tool for monarchic propaganda. In addition, Charles was trying to both project power and attract French intellectual elites to join his court and the University of Naples.

Two centuries earlier, the Islamic rulers of Sicily had brought with them sophisticated scientific interests together with a taste for beautifully decorated manuscripts. Both the Norman and Hohenstaufen rulers who succeeded them continued this tradition by commissioning copies and translations.[23] Charles was aware that his image was at stake and he understood the necessity of maintaining a library containing both state of the art and aesthetically pleasing texts. He also knew that in order to translate an important text such as Rhazes' *al-Ḥāwī*, he needed a translator who not only knew Arabic well, but who was also an expert in medicine.[24] Faraj, who belonged to the medical school of Salerno, was also well versed in Latin.

The court documents of Naples and the manuscripts of the *Liber Continens* establish that Faraj started translating the *Ḥāwī* on 6 February 1278, and completed his work on 13 February 1279. Once the translator handed his work to the royal officers, two richly illuminated manuscripts were prepared. The Paris manuscript was copied by several scribes and illustrated by the monk Giovanni da Montecassino. Giovanni was invited to come to Naples where he spent two and a half months 'making images of certain precious books of medicine belonging to the king'.[25] Faraj contributed to and supervised not only the translation but also the illumination process. He made the decision to add by his own hand a number of corrections, some of which are quite lengthy, in order to improve the quality of this luxury copy for the king's library. The king had to grant his permission for Faraj to collect the texts to be translated and useful glossaries, and to bring all the necessary volumes to his home.[26] He also had the opportunity to correct the illuminated copy of the *Ḥāwī*, now *Liber Continens*, even after the scribes had finished their work.[27] Paris manuscript 6912 still contains the additions in Faraj's own hand. At the

21 Minieri-Riccio, *Diario Angioino dal 4 gennaio 1284 al 7 gennaio 1285*, see 21 to 25 February.

22 Boüard, *Actes et lettres*, Doc. 6 June 1278; also Paris, BnF, MS Latin 5005a, *Chronicle Lemovicensis* (circa 1280) compiled by Johannis de Nigellis (or Jean de Néelle).

23 On this subject consult: Wood, and Fyfe, ed, *The Art of Falconry: Being the De Arte Venandi Cum Avibus of Frederick II of Hohenstaufen*; Kantorowicz, *Frederick the Second*.

24 Coulter, 'The Library of the Angevin Kings of Naples', pp. 141–55.

25 Del Giudice, *Codice diplomatico del regno di Carlo I. e II*, RA 1282 A, fol. 163.

26 Boüard, *Actes et lettres de Charles Ier d'Anjou*, pp. 53–59.

27 Minieri-Riccio, *Diario Angioino dal 4 gennaio 1284 al 7 gennaio 1285*.

same time, another copy was made based on the corrected version. The latter is now preserved in the Vatican library.[28]

A Single Translator or a Translation Team?

Some scholars are sceptical about the fact that Faraj could have translated Rāzī's monumental work in only a year, and this doubt has led some to hypothesize that he may have supervised a team of translators.[29] However, he is the only one to whom authorship is attributed in the *Continens* manuscript. All the professionals involved in the project and members of the royal *scriptorium* are carefully listed by name in the royal registers, whereas Faraj figures in all the available documents as the sole translator. Even though occasionally other translators are mentioned in the *Registri*, they are never prominent, nor are their names connected to this prestigious work of medicine. Even though the manuscript's illuminations only provide a limited view of the acquisition of the text and its translation, it seems noteworthy that only a single translator is portrayed, especially considering that the pictures were prepared only a few months after the translation was completed. In addition, it is not physically impossible for a skilled and hard-working translator to translate a source of a little less than six hundred pages in the course of one year, even while attending to other activities and obligations.

It has also been speculated that Faraj must have been paired with a Christian scholar, possibly Master Mattheus of Salerno, who is mentioned together with Faraj in a document of 16 June 1278.[30] However, the latter only proves that they were both to receive compensation for work they had completed; it does not specify that they worked together on any particular project. Given that Charles's mandates to the treasurers often contain orders of payment for disparate activities, I would not conclude that Faraj and Mattheus necessarily cooperated.[31]

The Process and Technique of Translation

Despite the remarkable wealth of details available about the practical aspects of the translation activities carried out at the court of Charles I, we do not know much about Faraj's motivations or the techniques he used for translating. Neither do we have any information about the manuscript he worked on, nor do we know which dictionaries, glossaries, or earlier translations he used.

28 Lattanzi Daneu, 'Una bella copia di al-*Ḥāwī*', pp. 149–69.

29 Fischer and Weisser, 'Das Vorwort zur lateinischen Übersetzung', p. 240.

30 Boüard and Durrieu, *Documents en français des archives Angevines de Naples*, pp. 53–59, II Doc 41; On the necessity of being a physician as well: Lattanzi Daneu, 'Una bella copia di al-*Ḥāwī*', pp. 149–69, plates 1–14.

31 Boüard and Durrieu, *Documents en français des archives angevines de Naples*, p. 110 no. 81.

However, scholars of medieval translation have been able to identify, at least tentatively, the most common forms of medieval translation.

Generally, two different techniques were adopted by Jewish translators for their texts from Arabic into Hebrew or from Arabic into Latin. One is the literal translation, which reproduces the original almost word for word. According to Mauro Zonta, this 'literal' method was the domain only of professional translators who were rendering texts for other experts into Hebrew or Latin.[32] Their purpose was to give their rendering an authentically scientific character, which could be used as a reliable source by philosophers, astronomers, mathematicians, and physicians.

Another frequently used method of translation is the interpretive rendering, in which the original word is translated by using two or more words or an entirely different expression. The syntax may or may not be respected, and almost no neologisms of Arabic or Latin words are used. Quotations from the Qurʾān are replaced by Biblical or Talmudic ones. The medieval translators were well aware of their choices and sometimes they discussed this subject in their prefaces or *explicit*. Judah Ibn Tibbon, who leaned toward the literalist camp, explains his choice in the preface to one of his translations:

> I have been careful, according to my capacity, not to deviate from the paths of the wording of the author, and whenever it was possible for me, I have translated the text word for word, although the language was not always as appropriate as I would have liked. In the cases where I was not able to translate this way, I have tried to understand the text in order to make it understandable, and then I have translated it according to my capacity. I have studied what was doubtful to me in other books devoted to this science [...]. Those who read this translation should not accuse me of having, in some points, conjugated certain verbs and declined certain nouns according to patterns which do not exist in our language, because the fact is due to the paucity of the Hebrew language.[33]

In other cases, translators extol the virtues of interpretive translation but do not in fact adopt it. Although Jewish translators may seem to abide by the traditional literalism which characterized the translation of scriptural texts, this attitude would be rather problematic if applied to philosophical and scientific texts. In this case, not only would they attribute to Arabic the same sacred status reserved to biblical Hebrew, but they would raise philosophy or science to a similar rank.[34] On the contrary, Charles Burnett has shown that

32 Zonta, 'Medieval Hebrew Translations: Methods and Textual Problems', pp. 129–42.

33 Ibn Paquda, *Sefer Hovot ha-levavot*, p. 6. Translation in: Zonta, 'Medieval Hebrew Translations', p. 131. Parts of this passage by Judah ibn Tibbon are mentioned in several works. Among them: Robinson, 'The Ibn Tibbon family', pp. 201–02; Rothschild, 'Motivations et méthodes des traductions', pp. 283–84.

34 On this subject, Zonta holds a different opinion. See Hamesse, *Les traducteurs au travail*, p. 132.

while word-for-word translation became predominant, there was originally a wide range of approaches to the translation of philosophical and scientific texts, from strict literalism to more creative adaptations.[35] Even though Faraj does not express directly which method he intends to adopt, the very end of the introduction to the *Liber Continens* explains:

> Hanc nichilominus artis medicine professorum familiarium medicorum suorum ac aliorum Neapoli et Salerni regentium examinationi provisioni et correctioni supposuit, et eis ad id non summariu, set ordinarium tempus indulsit. Qui omnes et singuli de translatione huismodi statuto ad hoc die relationem in publico facientes una voce et una omniunn concordi sententia dignissimos laudum preconjis extulerunt interpretem cum auctore. Nam si arabica verborum proprietas a latino interprete forsan alicubi videatur corrupta, vera tamen et integra conpilationis huius sententia virginitatis gratiam non amisit.
>
> > (Nevertheless, professors of the medical arts, the king's physicians and others at the universities of Naples and Salerno put the translation under examination, review and correction and they dedicated to this task not a short but a reasonable amount of time. They reported about the translation both as a group and individually, publicly, at an appointed day, and they unanimously extolled with the highest praise both the author and the translator. Even though the translator may have here and there altered the Arabic words, this collective work is true and intact and has not lost the grace of its original sentences.)[36]

Faraj may have not been a convinced literalist, but he nevertheless wanted to preserve the Arabic feel of his document. Modern translation theorists would rather say that he was 'source-language oriented.'[37] We have no way to establish if that was his personal choice or rather done in response to a *diktat* from the court medical milieu.

A few more technical details can be gleaned about the translation process from the court documents. Faraj received the text for translations gradually as originally the manuscript was divided into a number of booklets. It is not clear how many there were.

> Faresche le juif deus bons coffes grans et larges lesqueux nous voulons que vous pregniez en nostre chastiau de Salvateur en mer, liquel est etc. [...] et nous envoiez (par le dit Faresche les cinc livres encians d'arabis

35 Burnett, 'Humanism and Orientalism', pp. 22–31.

36 Paris, BnF, MS Latin 6912, fol. 2r. The translation is mine. A German translation can be found in Fischer and Weisser, 'Das Vorwort zur lateinischen Übersetzung', p. 227.

37 Eco, *Experiences in Translation*, pp. 20–22; Munday, *Translation as Intervention*, pp. 18–23; Venuti, *The Translator's Invisibility*, pp. 11–14. See also by the same author *Translation and Minority*; *Rethinking Translation*.

qui vindrent de Tunes, et les cinc premiers livres en arabic des vint […] chastiau de l'Euf a vos, quant nous en partimes derreannement […][38]

> ((To) Faraj the Jew two good trunks big and large which we want you to take from our Castle of Salvatore a Mare, which is, etc. […] and send us through the above mentioned Faraj the five ancient books in Arabic that arrived from Tunis, and the first five in Arabic of the twenty […] Castel dell'Uovo […] to you, when we left last time.)

However, on 2 June 1278 Charles wrote a letter to Faraj asking him to continue translating the book he was working on, while Faraj waited for a certain treatise on the diseases of the ear, which was due to arrive from Palermo. As soon as he received the text, the translator was to insert it in the book with the utmost urgency. For the exact positioning of it, he was to make sure that a sufficient number of blank pages were at his disposal. Armand, the king's physician, was also to provide advice on pagination.[39]

A few weeks later the king wrote to 'Faraj, the Jew, his servant' again:

> Miratur non immerito nostra serenitas, quod licet dodum et oretenus et per litteras nostras mandaverimus tibi expresse, ut tractatum super passione aurium nobis transmitteres sine mora, tu tamen nichil inde facere curavisti. Ideoque tibi sub pena gracie nostre iterato districte precipiendo mandamus, quatinus statim receptis presentibus tractatum ipsum omni mora et difficultate sublatis nobis mittere non obmittas, ita quod ulterius tibi super hoc scribere non cogamur.[40]

> ([…] Although we have already written to you asking that you send us the treatise on the disease of ears without hesitation, you have not bothered to do so. […] Send me the book immediately, lest you fall out of my graces, and put aside all other difficult tasks, so that we will not be obliged to write to you again on this matter.)

Given the tone of the letter, one could reasonably conclude that there was a certain familiarity between the king and his translator, which further confirms the high status that Faraj enjoyed at the court. One can also infer that the translation process was not always a smooth one, that it could involve several people and require permissions and materials. However, despite the threat of a withdrawal of the king's 'good graces' this episode had a positive conclusion for Faraj, who was timely and handsomely paid:

---

38 Filangieri *I registri della cancelleria angioina*, XXI, p. 208.

39 R.A. 32 (1278), published by Houben, 'Neue Quellen', p. 349. The translation into English is mine.

40 Houben, 'Neue Quellen', pp. 349–50.

> a Faresche le juif, notre translateur, ses depens des le tens que nous partimes de la Tour de Capes et de tant comme il sera en notre service, a la raison d'un tarin et demi d'or par jour [...] le quint livre de l'oeuvre qu'il a encommenciee a tranlater, lequel nous voulons qu'il tranlate, et de toute comme il metra a tranlater le dit quint livre, nous voulons que vous le paiez a la raison dessus dite.[41]
>
> ([*Mandate to the royal treasurers* to pay:] to Faresche, the Jew, our translator his expenses starting from the time of our departure for Torre del Capo and until when he will be at our service, in the amount of one and a half gold *tarì* per day and to: give the aforementioned Faraj the fifth book of the work he has already started translating, which we want him to translate; at the moment when he starts translating the above mentioned fifth book, we want you to pay it to him because of the abovementioned reason.)

One year after Faraj had completed the translation of *al-Ḥāwī*, in 1280, the king ordered his translator, whom he calls 'Faracio the Jew, our translator and *familiare*' to go to the treasury of Castel dell'Uovo to get the Arabic book called *De expositionibus vocabulorum simplicis medicine*, allowing him to take the book home to be used for a certain work that he was compiling for the king.[42] This suggests that Faraj used glossaries, as did many of his Christian counterparts.

Intellectual Life Outside the Court: The Medical Milieu

Sicily was an ideal territory for Jewish translators, be they natives or visitors from other areas. The southern Italian cultural setting was such that Jews could remain profoundly connected to their identity and at the same time live in symbiosis, although not always an idyllic one, with the Christian society.[43]

Faraj's principal connection with the Christian world outside the court was almost certainly the medical school of Salerno. He is referred to in most documents as *Magister*, a title reserved since the time of Frederick II to

---

41 Boüard and Durrieu, *Documents en français des archives angevines de Naples*, p. 110 no. 81, in old French. The translation is mine. The *tarì* was one of the Sicilian currencies. It roughly corresponds to a quarter dinar of the time. Faraj was very well paid compared to other professionals and intellectual workers. For example, a professor of logic at the University of Naples would earn 16 and a half gold *grains* per day. Thomas of Aquinas in 1272 was paid 20 grains a day for teaching theology in the *Studium* of Naples. One gold grain was one twentieth of a *tarì*. A chicken cost from eight to ten gold grains. Books were very expensive: from one *tarì* for a psalter to six for a French 'roman'. See Fuiano, *Carlo I d'Angiò in Italia*, pp. 289–90.

42 Del Giudice, *Codice diplomatico del regno di Carlo I. e II.*, 1, p. 268.

43 Ben Solomon of Salerno, *Un glossario filosofico ebraico-italiano*, pp. 33–40 (on the relationship between Moses of Salerno and Christian and Jewish scholars).

individuals trained according to a strict curriculum and examined by officers of the king. Secondly, the preface of Faraj's translation of *al-Ḥāwī* states clearly that his translation was reviewed by the doctors of Salerno who found both translator and translation excellent. Third, Salvatore De Renzi, author of a carefully documented history of medicine in Italy published 1884, cites Faraj as one of the prominent Jewish physicians of the School.

Renzi consulted at least two manuscripts of Faraj's translations from Arabic into Latin, the *Tacuynum de febribus* (*Taqwīm al-abdān fī l-tadbīr al insān* [*The Almanac of the bodily parts for the treatment of people*]) by Yaḥyá ʿĪsá (Abū l-Ḥasan) Ibn Jazlah and another work, *Tacuynum aegritudinum* (*Almanac of illnesses*) generally attributed to Ibn Jazlah as well. The latter's introduction states that it was undertaken in 1280 for use by the 'chambers of the most excellent King Charles' by 'Faragium Judeum, fidelem ejus'.[44] As for the former, a document of the Giudice collection confirms that Faraj did translate it.[45] It contains orders for a scribe to copy the compendium called *Tacuinum de febribus (Almanac on Fevers)* 'quod trasferri fecimus per Faracium Judeum' (that we had translated by Faraj, the Jew). Although, to my knowledge, no original manuscript of the translation remains, some of the later printed editions do attribute the translation to Faraj.[46]

Faraj (Moses) and/or Master Musa?

A recent article, dedicated to Charles' scribal workshop and its personnel during the translation of *al-Ḥāwī*, hypothesizes that Faraj may also be the same person as a certain Master Musa, who cooperated with with Mattheus Scillato, a translator who worked at the court at the time of Faraj ben Salīm. It also posits that since the name of Faraj was Faraj Moses ben Salīm, Musa may as well be identified with him 'if we adopt the Arabic version of his name Moses Ferragut'.[47]

However, in all the documents from the royal registers that I was able to consult, the name of Faraj in its various versions appears to the exclusion of others in the Latin documents. The name Moses (Moyse) appears instead in the documents in Old French but is always accompanied by the French version of Faraj's name (Farache or Faresche). It is also doubtful that in an arabophone environment, such as Sicily remained until the sixteenth century, the form Moses Ferragut was ever adopted. Moreover, given the familiarity between Faraj and his patron that emerges from both registers and personal

44 De Renzi, *Storia della medicina in Italia*, II, pp. 130–31.

45 Del Giudice, *Codice diplomatico del regno di Carlo I. e II.*, I, p. 314; also quoted by Steinschneider, *Die hebräischen Übersetzungen des Mittelalters*, p. 582, although he took the information from another collection.

46 Byngezla, *Tacuini aegritudinum et morborum*; trans. by ben Salim.

47 Gurrado, 'Traduction et copie à la cour des Angevins de Naples', p. 263.

correspondence, it is very unlikely that the king would name his translator so inconsistently. Lastly, the documents talk about a 'Musa of Palermo' but never mention Faraj's onomastic 'of Girgenti' with which he is identified in most of the documentation.

Finally, a French document may be conclusive on this issue:

> Challes [...] A Jehan Trousevache etc. Nos te mandos que tu balles et livres a Perot des Estables, vallet du Rois de France et a Moises li Iuif translateur quatres unces de bon or en florins a choscun d'eus unces deus, que Nous donnous audit Perrot des Estables et deus autres que Nous prestons audit Moises de Juif. De rechef balles et livres a Faresche le Juif trois unces d'or iu florins aussit, les quales Nous li prestons et en recef bone apodixe a tu cautele de l'un de eus, de ce que tu leur balleras, seelée de son seel.[48]
>
> > (*For the representative of the King of France*
> > Challes [...] To Jean Trousevache etc. We are asking you that you pay and deliver to Perot des Estables, valet of the king of France and to Moses, the Jew, translator, four ounces of good gold in florins, two ounces each which we give to Perrot des Estable and lend to the said Moses, the Jew. Moreover, pay and deliver to Faraj the Jew three ounces of gold in florins as well, which we lend him and you should take care of collecting a receipt from one of them for what you will lend them, sealed with his seal.)

Although the identity of Moses is not specified and the document is in French, which does not utilize the Sicilian 'Musa' but uses Moyse instead, one can conclude that Faraj and Moses were two different persons and that they knew each other.

As far as Master Musa is concerned, not much can be inferred from the Angevin registers. An ordinance from the king only clarifies that he is a translator and that he is from Palermo, not Agrigento. 'We order that Master Musa of Palermo come to us to translate books of Arabic literature into Latin'. Another mandate, given in Brindisi on 8 April 1277, orders that two ounces of gold be paid to Moses to cover his travel expenses from Palermo to Naples. At the time Faraj was already a 'sworn' and busy translator as pointed out earlier in this chapter. It seems unlikely that he was still learning Latin ten years later. Moreover, another mandate asks Mattheus Scillato to assist Moses 'who needs to translate books from Arabic to Latin in Salerno'. On 10 June 1277, a royal letter is sent from the city of Venosa, in Apulia to Mattheus:

> cum magister Musam de Panormo fidelem pro translatandis quibusdam libris Camere nostre de arabico in latinum apud Salernum providerimus commorari, [...] mandamus quatenus cum eodem magistro Musa esse

48 Boüard and Durrieu, *Documents en français des archives angevines de Naples*, p. 354.

debeas ad docendum et informandum eum de licteratura latina, donec libri ipsi fuerint translati[49]

> (Since we have arranged that Master Moses of Palermo … should sojourn at Salerno in order to translate sundry books of our chamber from Arabic into Latin [...] we order that you should be with the aforesaid Master Moses to teach and instruct him in Latin learning, until those books are translated.)

Mattheus, who was asked to be Moses' Latin teacher, can probably be identified with Faraj's colleague Mattheus who is mentioned in a royal letter of 16 June 1278.[50] Since Moses needs instruction in Latin, he cannot have received a university education in a European context as Faraj did.

Why and for Whom Should One Translate?

Although Faraj must have been exposed to philosophy and especially to logic, an essential part of medical training, nothing can be gleaned about his philosophical opinions, neither from his translation, nor from any other paratext. However, in the preface of the translation of *al-Ḥāwī*, or *Liber Continens*, it is stated that it was the author's intention to correct the errors of the philosophers for whom sickness and death are mere accidents, whereas they are in fact a consequence of human errors, sin, and fall from divine grace. Klaus Fisher and Ursula Weisser have retrieved in the introduction the philosophical and theological influences of theologians such as Augustine, Thomas of Aquinas, and Peter of Spain. Based on that, they concluded that Faraj probably did not write the introduction himself, but that one of his Christian colleagues at the court may have been the author. The name cannot for the moment be identified. The writer may had been close to the king and had a patron-client relationship with him. The surviving records mention several clerics but do not provide enough data or reliable evidence. The author, Fischer and Weisser claim, must have been a religious doctor or a theologian interested in medicine, or even both in one person, which at the time was not uncommon.[51] The language of the preface borrows from typical expressions of Christian theology. Already the first paragraph uses words taken from the profession of faith: it speaks of a universe created from nothing and in time by one supreme principle from which everything, visible and invisible, physical and spiritual, derives. However, as opposed to the profession of faith, the text emphasizes only one God 'primo, solo et summo principio' and does not mention Jesus,

---

49 Minieri-Riccio, *Diario Angioino dal 4 gennaio 1284 al 7 gennaio 1285* (Registri Angioini), XVI, 41 and 76–77.

50 Boüard and Durrieu, *Documents en français des archives angevines de Naples*, pp. 53–59, II, Doc 41.

51 Fischer and Weisser, 'Das Vorwort zur lateinischen Übersetzung von Rhazes', p. 211.

the Trinity, or the Church. This is quite unique if one recollects that most texts of the time would start with 'In the name of the Father, the Son and the Holy Ghost, who created everything'. The preface to *al-Ḥāwī* sounds instead like a kind of *Basmalah*:

> Incipit prohemium libri elhauy ad honorem dei, cuius nomen sit benedictus in secula seculorum amen.[52]
>
> The introduction to the book of *al-Ḥāwī* begins in the honour of God, whose name is blessed forever, amen.

Although the correspondences between the Latin text of the introduction and expressions used by several Christian authors are numerous in the introduction to the *Continens*, the possibility of Faraj's authorship cannot be ruled out completely. Even if his education in Salerno cannot be proven, the introduction and the royal registers which mention him always refer to him as *magister*, suggesting that he was either teaching or lecturing at the school. Given that, he certainly was familiar with a number of expressions and *topoi* used to introduce medical books or books created at or for the court in general. One should also take into account that the medical school activities were heavily influenced by the clergy during Charles's reign, after a more secular parenthesis under the Swabian rulers. The compulsory expressions connected to working under a patron who did not possess secular inclinations included the necessity of praising God and the religious virtues of the sovereign. The highly rhetorical nature of the entire preface proves that patronage had conventions and limitations for translators and intellectuals. Moreover, the royal chancellery was a controlling environment when it came to communicating, whether in writing or otherwise. At the time, the southern Italian ruling dynasties had started formalizing their language directed towards the outside, marking the beginning of state control over documentation and circulation of people and ideas.[53]

Although the preface to the *Liber Continens* is no exception to the conventional style, a closer analysis reveals that it is an original document. The first five paragraphs are dedicated to philosophical and theological reflections about God, creation, the body and the soul and the process through which the body can become ill: as the soul which used to be innocent can nevertheless fall into guiltiness, so the body which is intact can become sick and in pain.[54] The text continues by saying that because of the original sin, the body is forced to withstand many afflictions, such as pain, defects, labour, maladies, and the ultimate punishment of death. It is this latter paragraph which excludes Faraj

52 Paris, BnF, MS Latin 6912, fol. 2r. The translation is mine. A German translation can be found in Fischer and Weisser, 'Das Vorwort zur lateinischen Übersetzung', p. 221.

53 Grévin, *Rhétorique du pouvoir médiéval*, pp. 1–13.

54 Fischer and Weisser, 'Das Vorwort', p. 220. The English translation from Latin is mine.

from the authorship of the introduction unless, as it has been speculated, he had converted to Christianity. If this indeed ever happened, it must have been years after he completed the translation of *al-Ḥāwī* as the documents refer to him as 'the Jew' until at least 1282. Even though original sin is mentioned, in general, the theological concepts to which the author refers in the introduction do not necessarily clash with Jewish theology. Moreover, it still remains quite noteworthy that neither Jesus nor the Trinity are ever mentioned.

In the Sicilian context, cooperation between Jewish and Christian intellectuals took the form of dialogue and learned exchange. Christian interlocutors are often referred to in the writings of Jewish authors as 'ha-ḥakam she itḥabarti 'immo' (the scholar with whom I cooperated).[55] Lengthy discussions of philosophical subtleties are reported. Jewish intellectuals thought, following the ideas put forward by Moses Maimonides, that the value of science and exegesis was independent from the religious affiliation of the interpreter. Most significantly, the absence of public disputations also made religious arguments assume an entirely different tone. As for Faraj ben Salīm, we have no elements allowing us to establish that he took part in any intellectual exchange besides those in the court and in the medical milieu.

The translations carried out by Jews in Sicily did not necessarily have Jews as the intended audience. The introduction of the *Liber Continens* makes it clear that the book was translated for the benefit of a Christian public.

> Sed post longua (*sic*) annorum curricula christianissimus Dominus
>
> Karolus, Iherusalem et Sicilie Rex, eiusdem libri fama conmotus et ardore tam captabilis utilitatis illectus, non sibi solum sed christicolis omnibus prodesse desiderans, bellicis curis liberalium studiorum sollicitudinem ad ipsius libri translationem miscere delegit.[56]
>
> After long years, the most Christian lord, Charles, King of Jerusalem and Sicily, was moved by the fame of this book, and was captivated by the desire of an object so easy to acquire. And he decided not only for his benefit, but for the benefit of all Christians to unite his knowledge with his military might in an effort to attend to the translation of this book.

Sicilian Jews used Arabic in their daily life until their expulsion from the island in 1492 and could therefore read most Arabic works in their original language. Although patronage had its inconveniences, the fact that the king paid such close attention to the learned men who surrounded him made the role of intellectuals pivotal and allowed translation to be an act of power in which Jews actively participated.

---

55 Anatoli, *Il pungolo dei discepoli*, p. 161; the colophon is in Oxford, Bodleian Library, MS Hunt 410, fol. 146^{v}.

56 Fischer and Weisser, 'Das Vorwort', p. 226. The English translation from Latin is mine.

Bibliography

Manuscripts

Oxford, Bodleian Library, MS Hunt 410
Paris, Bibliothèque nationale de France, MS Latin 5005a
——, MS Latin 6912
Parma, Biblioteca Palatina, MS 2762
Parma, Collezione De Rossi, MS cod. 3162–3
Madrid, Real Biblioteca del Escurial, MS árabe 846
——, MS árabe 858

Primary Sources

Altamura, Antonio, *Cronaca di Partenope* (Naples: Società Editrice Napoletana, 1974)

Anatoli, Jacob ben Abba Mari ben Samson, *Il Pungolo Dei Discepoli = Malmad Ha-Talmidim: Il Sapere Di Un Ebreo E Federico II* [text in Hebrew with Italian translation], ed. by Luciana Pepi (Palermo: Officina di Studi Medievali: Fondazione Federico II, 2004)

Bartolomeo de Neocastro, *Historia Sicula*, in *Rerum Italicarum Scriptores*, ed. by Lodovico Antonio Muratori and Filippo Argelati (Sala Bolognese: A. Forni, 1977)

Byngezla, Buhahylyha, *Tacuini Aegritudinum Et Morborum Ferme Omnium Corporis Humani, Cum Curis Eorundem / Ex Arabico Transtulit Farragus*, trans. by Faraj ben Salim (Strasbourg: Adolf Occo, 1532)

Boüard, A. de, and Paul Durrieu, *Documents en français des archives angevines de Naples: (Règne de Charles Ier)*, ed. by Archivio di Stato di Napoli (Paris: E. de Boccard, 1933)

Boüard, Alain de, *Actes et lettres de Charles Ier d'Anjou, roi de Sicile, concernant la France (1257–1284), extraits des Registres angevins de Naples* (Paris: de Boccard, 1926)

Compagna, Adele Maresca, Filangieri, Riccardo, and Pontaniana Accademia, *I registri della cancelleria angioina* (Naples: Accademia Pontaniana, 1982)

Del Giudice, Giuseppe, *Codice diplomatico del regno di Carlo I e II d'Angiò, ossia Collezione di leggi, statuti e privilegi, mandati, lettere regie e pontificie … concernenti la storia ed il diritto politico … delle province meridionali d'Italia dal 1265 al 1309* (Naples: Stamperia della R. Univesità, 1863)

Filangieri, Riccardo, *I registri della Cancelleria angioina (Testi e documenti di storia napoletana, v. 1–50)* (Naples: L'Accademia Pontaniana, 1950–2010)

Ibn Paquda, Bahya ben Joseph, Yehuda Ibn Tibbon, tr., and Refa'el Mendl, com., *Sefer Ḥovot ha-levavot* (Vilna: Y. R. Rom, 621 [1860])

Lagumina, Bartolomeo, and Giuseppe Lagumina, *Codice Diplomatico dei Giudei di Sicilia* (Palermo: Tip. di M. Amenta, 1884)

Malaspina, Saba, *Rerum Sicularum Historia (1250–1285)*, in *Rerum Italicarum Scriptores*, ed. by Lodovico Antonio Muratori and Filippo Argelati (Sala Bolognese: A. Forni, 1977)
Simonsohn, Shlomo, *The Jews in Sicily* (Leiden: Brill, 1997)

Secondary Studies

Amari, Michele, *La guerra del vespro siciliano* (Turin: Cugini Pomba e Compagnia, 1852)
Ben Solomon of Salerno, Moses, *Un glossario filosofico ebraico-italiano del XIII secolo*, ed. by Giuseppe Sermoneta (Rome: Edizioni dell'Ateneo, 1969)
Borghese, Gian Luca, *Carlo I d'Angiò e il Mediterraneo: Politica, Diplomazia e Commercio Internazionale prima dei Vespri* (Rome: École française de Rome, 2008)
Bryson, Jennifer S, 'The *Kitāb Al-Ḥāwī* of Rāzī (ca. 900 AD): Book One of the *Ḥāwī* on Brain, Nerve, and Mental Disorders: Studies in the Transmission of Medical Texts from Greek into Arabic into Latin' (Ph.D. Dissertation, New Haven, Yale University, 2000)
Burnett, Charles, 'Humanism and Orientalism in the Translations from Arabic into Latin in the Middle Ages', in *Wissen über Grenzen: arabisches Wissen und lateinisches Mittelalter*, ed. by Andreas Speer and Lydia Wegener (Berlin: de Gruyter, 2006), pp. 22–31
Catalioto, Luciano, *Terre, baroni e città in Sicilia nell'età di Carlo I d'Angiò* (Messina: Intilla, 1995)
Coulter, Cornelia, 'The Library of the Angevin Kings of Naples', *Transactions and Proceedings of the American Philological Association*, 75 (1944), 141–55
Delaville Le Roulx, Joseph, *Cartulaire général de l'ordre des Hospitaliers de S. Jean de Jérusalem (1100-1310)*, tome III (Paris: Ernest Leroux, 1894–1906)
De Renzi, Salvatore, *Storia documentata della Scuola Medica di Salerno* (Salerno: Ed. Ripostes, 2000)
Durrieu, Paul, 'Un portrait de Charles Ier d' Anjou, roi de Sicile, frère de Saint Louis dans un manuscrit aujourd'hui à la Bibliothèque Nationale de Paris', *Gazette archéologique*, 11 (1886), 192–201
——, *Les archives angevines de Naples: études sur les registres du roi Charles 1er (1265–1285)* (Paris: E. Thorin, 1886)
Eco, Umberto, *Experiences in translation*, Toronto; Buffalo: University of Toronto Press, 2001
Fischer, Klaus-Dietrich, and Ursula Weisser, 'Das Vorwort zur lateinischen Übersetzung von Rhazes' *Liber Continens* (1282): Text, Übersetzung und Erläuterungen', *Medizinhistorisches Journal*, 21.3–4 (1986), 211–41
Freudenthal, Gad, *Science in the Medieval Hebrew and Arabic Traditions*, Variorum Collected Studies Series (Aldershot: Ashgate, 2005)
——, *Science in Medieval Jewish Cultures* (New York: Cambridge University Press, 2011)
Fuiano, Michele, *Carlo I d'Angiò in Italia: studi e ricerche* (Naples: Liguori, 1974)

Grévin, Benoît, *Rhétorique du Pouvoir Médiéval: Les Lettres de Pierre de La Vigne et la Formation du Langage Politique Européen, XIIIe–XVe Siècle* (Rome: École française de Rome, 2008)

Grévin, Benoît, and Giuseppe Mandalà, 'Le rôle des communautés juives siciliennes dans la transmission des savoirs arabes en Italie, XIIIe–XVe siècles', in *La Frontière Méditérranéenne du XVème au XVIIIème siècle: échanges, circulations et affrontements*, ed. by Bernard Heyberger and Albrecht Fuess (Turnhout: Brepols, 2013), pp. 283–99

Gurrado, Maria, 'Traduction et copie à la cour des Angevins de Naples, L'Encyclopédie médicale *al-Ḥāwī* et le personnel du scriptorium de Charles Ier (1277–1282)', *Scriptorium*, 67.2 (2013), 259–91

Hamesse, Jacqueline, *Les traducteurs au travail: leurs manuscrits et leurs méthodes: Actes du Colloque International organisé par le 'Ettore Majorana Centre for Scientific Culture' (Erice, 30 Septembre-6 Octobre 1999)*, Textes et Etudes de Moyen Âge, 18 (Turnhout: Brepols, 2001)

Houben, Hubert, 'Neue Quellen zur Geschichte der Juden und Sarazenen im Königreich Sizilien (1275–1280)', *Quellen und Forschungen aus italienischen Bibliotheken und Archiven*, 74 (1994), 335–59

——, 'Federico II e gli Ebrei', *Nuova Rivista Storica*, 85.2 (2001), 325–46

Kantorowicz, Ernst Hartwig, *Frederick the Second, 1194–1250* (New York: Ungar, 1957)

Kaufmann, David, 'Un portrait de Faradj, le traducteur', *Revue des Etudes Juives*, 19 (1889), 152–54

Lattanzi Daneu, Angela, 'Una bella copia di al-*Ḥāwī*, tradotto dall'arabo di Farag Moyse per Carlo I d'Angió: ms. Vat. Lat. 2398–2399', *Miscellanea di studi in memoria di Anna Saitta Revignas, Biblioteca di bibliografia italiana*, 86 (1978), 149–69

Luzzati, Michele, 'Carne "cristiana" e carne "ebraica", La *bocciaria* della Judaica di Palermo', in *Ebrei e Sicilia*, ed. by Nicolo Bucaria (Palermo: Flaccovio, 2002), pp. 135–36

Minieri-Riccio, Camillo, *Brevi notizie intorno all'archivio angioino di Napoli, dopo le quali si pubblica per la prima volta parte di quei registri ora non piu' esistenti* (Naples: Alberto Detken, 1862)

——, *Diario Angioino dal 4 Gennaio 1284 al 7 Gennaio 1285 formato su' registri angioini del grande Archivio di Napoli da Camillo Minieri Riccio* (Naples: Stamperia della R. Università, 1873)

——, *Della dominazione angioina nel reame di Sicilia: studii storici estratti da' registri della Cancelleria Angioina di Napoli* (Naples: R. Rinaldi e G. Sellitto, 1876)

Munday, Jeremy, *Translation as Intervention* (London: Continuum, 2007)

Robinson, James T, 'The Ibn Tibbon Family: A Dynasty of Translators in Nedieval "Provence"', in *Be'erot Yitzhak: Studies in Memory of Isadore Twersky*, ed. by Jay M. Harris (Cambridge, MA: Harvard University Press, 2005), pp. 193–224

Rothschild, Jean-Pierre, 'Motivations et méthodes des traductions en hébreu du milieu du XII à la fin du XVeme siècle', in *Traduction et Traducteurs au Moyen Age: Actes du Colloque International du CNRS organisé à Paris, 26–28 Mai 1986*, ed. by Geneviève Contamine (Paris: CNRS, 1989), pp. 279–302

Scandaliato, Angela, 'Gli ebrei di Sicilia nel Medioevo cultura e lingua', *Archivio Storico Siciliano*, series 4, 21–22 (1995–1996), 113–32

Sirat, Colette, 'Les traducteurs juifs à la cour des rois de Sicile et de Naples', in *Traduction et traducteurs du Moyen Âge. Les actes du Colloque International du CNRS organisé à Paris, Institut de Recherche et d'histoire des Textes, 26–28 Mai 1986*, ed. by Geneviève Contamine (Paris: CNRS, 1989), pp. 169–91

Steinschneider, Moritz, *Die Hebräischen Übersetzungen des Mittelalters und die Juden als Dolmetscher* (Graz: Akademische Druck u. Verlagsanstalt, 1956)

Takayama, Hiroshi, 'Familiares Regis and the Royal Inner Council in Twelfth-Century Sicily', *The English Historical Review*, 104.411 (1989), 354–72

Venuti, Lawrence, *Rethinking Translation: Discourse, Subjectivity, Ideology* (London: Routledge, 1992)

——, *Translation and Minority* (Manchester: St Jerome, 1998)

——, *The Translator's Invisibility: A History of Translation* (Hoboken: Taylor and Francis, 2012)

Wood, Casey Albert, and Florence Marjorie Fyfe, ed, *The Art of Falconry: Being the De Arte Venandi Cum Avibus of Frederick II of Hohenstaufen* (Stanford: Stanford University Press, 1961)

Zonta, Mauro, 'Medieval Hebrew Translations: Methods and Textual Problems', in *Les traducteurs au travail: leurs manuscrits et leurs méthodes: actes du colloque international organisé par le 'Ettore Majorana Centre for Scientific Culture' (Erice, 30 Septembre-6 Octobre 1999)*, Textes et Etudes de Moyen Âge, 18 (Turnhout: Brepols, 2001), pp. 129–42

ERIC GUREVITCH

Practices of Translation in Medieval Kannada Sciences

'Removing the Conflict Between Textual Authority and the Worldly'

kēcid bhāṣāntarakṛtatayā kāmaśāstraprabandhā
durvijñēyā gurutaratayā kēcid alpārthakāś ca

Some texts on the science of erotics are difficult to understand on account of their being composed in other languages, while some are too dense, and some have only a little meaning.

Padmaśrī, *Everything a Townsman Needs (Nāgarasarvasva)*, written in Sanskrit[1]

Old Science in New Kannada

There was much talk of newness in the Deccan in the first half of the eleventh century, where the warring dynasties of the Paramāras, the Cōḷas, and the Western Caḷukyas jostled for prestige and revenue in the aftermath of the collapse of the Rāṣṭrakūṭa empire in 937. To the north, in what is now Madhya Pradesh, the Paramāra king Bhōja (r. 1010–1055) undertook an architectural and literary programme of monumental proportions, rewriting the Sanskrit canon and renovating the landscape.[2] In the deep south, in what is now Tamil

1 Padmaśrī, *Nāgarasarvasva* 1.2[ab]. All translations are my own. Many of my thoughts about the texts discussed in this paper were produced in conversation with N. S. Tharanatha in 2017. I thank Sonja Brentjes, Whitney Cox, Marko Geslani, Zoë High, Andrew Ollett and Jason Schwartz for helping me to sharpen the argument. The paper benefited from comments received at the *Premodern Experience of the Natural World in Translation* conference held at Max Planck Institute for the History of Science in June 2019 organized by Katja Krause, Maria Avksentyevskaya, and Dror Weil.

2 For an explication of Bhōja's political and literary imagination, see Cox, Bhoja's Alternate Universe', pp. 61–71.

Eric Moses Gurevitch is a PhD candidate at the University of Chicago in the Department of South Asian Languages and Civilizations and the Committee on the Conceptual and Historical Studies of Science. His article 'The Uses of Useful Knowledge and the Languages of Vernacular Science: Perspectives from Southwest India' recently appeared in *History of Science*.

Narratives on Translation across Eurasia and Africa: From Babylonia to Colonial India, ed. by Sonja Brentjes in cooperation with Jens Høyrup and Bruce O'Brien, CAT 3, pp. 249–270 (Turnhout: Brepols, 2022) BREPOLS PUBLISHERS 10.1484/M.CAT-EB.5.127944

Nadu, King Rājarāja (r. 985–1014) consolidated Cōḷa power and re-segmented the territory under his control into new political divisions based on a survey conducted around 1001.[3] And in the upstart Western Caḷukya court of Jayasiṃha II (r. 1015–1043) in the heart of the Deccan, there was talk of a new regional language, 'New Kannada', that had burst onto the literary and political scene 150 years earlier, and which was now being put to new uses.[4]

More particularly, a group of authors writing within the orbit of Jayasiṃha II used the language they called 'New Kannada' to write new scholarly texts — *śāstras* — that were related to, but different from, earlier Sanskrit textual models. These texts included dictionaries, grammars, astrological, veterinary, and agricultural manuals, as well as texts that described other so-called worldly sciences.[5] These authors used a diverse set of translingual practices such as translation, citation, quotation, summation, and commentarial expansion to position themselves against a prior tradition, while defining a new epistemic space for themselves. Translation for these authors was a part of an activity of archive building, a way of pointing towards the past as relevant, but insufficient for the present.

These New Kannada texts provide an opportunity to think about translation outside of dominant models developed in the mid-twentieth century — largely by anthropologists — to account for colonial interactions, where linguistic translation is equated with cultural translation.[6] From this historiographic perspective, which is one that is often emphasized in the history of science, translation is presented as a mode of bridging cultural gaps. It appears as a sort of economic encounter, one in which epistemic goods are exchanged; sometimes fairly, often unfairly. Related to movement, translation is presented as a way of transporting or transmitting knowledge from one place to another, and culture ultimately is something that can itself be translated.[7] There is nothing wrong with this narrative when it is used to describe specific cases, but when it is

3 Subbarayalu, 'Quantifying Land Revenue', pp. 100–15. For an overview, see Cox, *Politics, Kingship, and Poetry*, pp. 42–52.

4 On the early history of Kannada in the Rāṣṭrakūṭa court, see Pollock, *Language of the Gods*, pp. 330–79 and Taylor, *Aesthetics of Sovereignty*, pp. 51–116.

5 For an introduction to this corpus, see Gurevitch, 'The Uses of Useful Knowledge'.

6 For the classic statement critiquing the metaphor of cultural translation, see Asad, 'The Concept of Cultural Translation', pp. 141–64 and later Liu *Translingual Practice*, pp. 1–44 and Hart, 'Translating the Untranslatable', pp. 45–50. For programmatic discussions of the creation of dominant semiotic ideologies in global colonial encounters, see Bauman and Briggs, *Voices of Modernity*, pp. 1–18 and Keane, *Christian Moderns*, pp. 6–25.

7 For an example of this general model, see Montgomery *Science in Translation*, pp. 1–16. For insightful thinking about these problems in the history of science, and about a colonial moment when translation was linked with movement, see Elshakry, 'Knowledge in Motion', pp. 701–05 and Elshakry and Nappi, 'Translations', pp. 372–83. For a critique of the dominant metaphor of cross-cultural interaction as translation among medievalists, see Brentjes, Fidora, and Tischler 'Towards a New Approach to Medieval Cross-Cultural Exchanges', p. 23. And for the relationship between the colonial and medieval historiographies, see Ragab 'In a Clear Arabic Tongue', pp. 612–20.

extended to all acts of translation, and when it comes to encompass all uses of translation, it can have a distorting effect. There are many moments when translation is used to affect the movement of information to new contexts, but when that is the case, it is a specific historical achievement, and it should not be presumed to be the norm, or even the goal, of most translations.

Things look different from the medieval Deccan, where Kannada literacy existed alongside and was mediated in every instance by Sanskrit literacy. As Sheldon Pollock has put it, 'translation as we normally conceive of it — rendering a text from a language the intended reader does not understand into a language he does — makes no cultural sense in this world'.[8] To put it simply, the Kannada texts of this period were suffused with lexical items taken from Sanskrit, long Sanskrit compounds, and complete Sanskrit verses. Translation appears in texts from this period, but it was not used to introduce unfamiliar knowledge to new audiences. It was not used to make knowledge more mobile. Translation is used for different reasons at different times, and we would do well to attend to the pragmatic uses translation has been put to. By turning to texts that appear under the double effacement of the non-modern and non-west, we have an opportunity to think through problems of translation and science without much of the normal baggage.

It is important to walk a thin line here. It is often assumed that translation did not occur at all in precolonial India. There is much scholarship that holds that 'there was in India no "translation" in the Western sense throughout the first three thousand years of its literary history, until the colonial impact'.[9] Adaptations, transcreations, yes. Translations, no. Statements such as this are wrong — and for many reasons. They are premised on an exclusive focus on expressive literature; the excision of Tibetan and Sinhalese translations of Buddhist texts as well as Arabic and Persian translations from South Asian history; and a refusal to acknowledge the complex relationships between Sanskrit and Prakrit.[10] Further, as is the central contention of this paper, translation did, in fact, play an important role in the development of regional literary languages across South Asia. And it is in vernacular scholarly texts in

8 Pollock, *Language of the Gods*, pp. 244–45.

9 Trivedi, 'In Our Own Time, on Our Own Terms', p. 102. The *locus classicus* for the more nuanced version of the argument that something called 'literal translation' did not exist in precolonial South Asia is Ramanujan, 'Three Hundred Rāmāyaṇas', pp. 44–46. More useful is recent scholarship that treates translation in the light of commentary, see for instance Patel, 'Source, Exegesis, and Translation', pp. 262–65; Cort, 'Making It Vernacular in Agra', pp. 61–69; and Williams, 'Commentary as Translation', pp. 99–125. The ongoing work of Elaine Fisher promises to rewrite the history of religious translations in early modern southern India; see Fisher, 'Coconut in the Honey'.

10 For recent studies, see Ricci, *Islam Translated*, pp. 31–65. Truschke, *Culture of Encounters*, pp. 64–100. For astronomical texts in translation, see Pingree, 'Islamic Astronomy in Sanskrit', pp. 315–30 and for medical texts, see Speziale, *Culture Persane*.

particular that we can see the uses to which translation was put in premodern South Asia.[11]

The New Kannada texts produced in the court of Jayasiṃha II present an opportunity to bracket semantic questions about the possibility of literal translation as well as more abstract discussions of cultural translation and the movement of knowledge, and instead focus on the pragmatic uses of translation in a particular context. This paper focuses on one of the texts produced in this court, Candrarāja's *Ornament of Desire* (*Madanatilakam*), and how Candrarāja used translation as a part of his larger project of writing a new type of science of erotics. This text, along with the other scholarly works produced in the court of Jayasiṃha II, is not a translation of a single Sanskrit text, nor is it an attempt to bring a particular text to a new audience. Rather, Candrarāja uses translations from multiple texts as well as a host of other indexical practices to strategically frame his composition, and to present his project as something new: an opportunity to combine the science of erotics, the astral sciences, and literature. Authors writing in regional languages used shifts in language as opportunities to make epistemic interventions. There is a difference between how we approach 'translation' as the product that is a translated text and 'translation' as a process of translating. By drawing attention to this latter sense of translation, by attending to translating as a practice, we can start to see how language was used in different ways to create new types of sciences in south-west India.

Between Textual Authority and the Worldly

Candrarāja begins the *Ornament of Desire* with a long introduction that positions his work in relation to the past as well as the courtly context in which it was produced. This was a peripatetic court in the wake of the collapse of the Rāṣṭrakūṭa state that strove to control a kingdom on the make. It was a place to which ambitious courtiers travelled in order to exhibit their skills — both literary as well as administrative. Writing a New Kannada text was one of many ways to ascend the Western Cāḷukya chancellery, and authors used their literary productions as vehicles to advertise their resumé accomplishments. Candrarāja explicates the virtues of his patron, a general named Reca, as well as his suzerain, Jayasiṃha II, and then goes on to describe his own qualifications. In the course of establishing his intellectual capabilities and accomplishments, Candrarāja brazenly insults the most prominent author on erotics in South Asia, Vātsyāyana (third century), the author of the massively influential *Manual on Pleasure* (*Kāmasūtram*), together with the set of authorities upon whom Vātsyāyana relies, writing:

---

11 But see the discussion of the general dismissal of non-Sanskrit *śāstra* in Pollock, 'The Languages of Science', p. 25.

sakalavyākaraṇārthaśāstragaṇitālaṃkārasatkāvyanā-
ṭakavātsyāyananṛttagītahayaśāstrādvaitagāṃdharvatā- |
rkakavīṃdrāgamavaidyavādyaśakunōdyad[d]hṛdyavidyākadaṃ-
bakamaṃ caṃdrakavīṃdran orvane valaṃ ballaṃ peṟar ballarē ||
anakaṃ kuṃdali bābhravīyan atilaulyaṃ kūbaraṃ kātaraṃ
kinipaṃ bhadran arūpi kētu kuviṭaṃ vātsyāyanaṃ gōṇikā- |
tanayaṃ ni[r]dayan alpavīryan enipam cārāyaṇaṃ jatta[kaṃ]
tanuhīnaṃ dorey allar iṃt' inibaruṃ pratyakṣakaṃdarpanoḷ ||

> (Surely, it is only the lord of poets Candra who knows the collection of sciences that are pleasing and upright: the entire meaning of the science of grammar, mathematics, poetic ornamentation, good poetry, drama, erotics, song and dance, the science of horses, non-dualist philosophy, music, logic, magic, medicine, musical instruments, and augury. How could others know all that?
>
> Kuṃdali is lowly and Bābhravīya very fickle, Kūbara is timid, Bhadra is angry, Ketu is bodiless, Vātsyāyana is a knave, the son of Gōṇikā is cruel, Cārāyaṇa is said to be impotent, Jattaka has a flawed body. All these people do not equal Candrarāja, who is Kāmadeva incarnate.)[12]

In this versified argument, Candrarāja presents himself as someone qualified to write a new text owing to his training in a diverse set of disciplines, as well as his personal experience in sex. Citing both Vātsyāyana and the collection of scholars of erotics whom Vātsyāyana cites in his *Manual on Pleasure*, Candrarāja presents himself as knowledgeable in the history of the erotic sciences, while, in a sense, superseding it. His attack is *ad hominem*, drawing out the personal flaws of his predecessors, which in turn may have had negative epistemic entailments. How could an ugly or timid person write well about erotics? But immediately after making this attack on his predecessors, Candrarāja scales his claims back, and asserts that he has faithfully studied and summarized earlier scholarship, but in a new medium: New Kannada (*posagannaḍa*).[13]

ene negaḻda caṃdran abjā-
nanacaṃdraṃ śvētakētujattakavātsya- |
yanapāṃcāḷādimahā-
munimata[mane] pēḻdan eseye posagannaḍadiṃ ||

12 Candrarāja, *Madanatilakam*, 1.51–52.

13 For a discussion of the rhetorical uses of *paḻagannaḍa* (Old Kannada) in the massively influential Kannada text on poetics, the *Way of the King of Poets* (*Kavirājamārgam*), see Pollock, *Language of the Gods*, pp. 339–42.

> (The famous Candra, who is a moon for those whose faces are lotuses, narrated the thoughts of the great scholars such as Śvētakētu, Jattaka, Vātsyāyana, and Pāṃcāḷa, shining, in the New Kannada.)[14]

Candrarāja negotiates a thin line between his Sanskrit predecessors and his 'New Kannada' contemporaries, repositioning Kannada as fully capable — perhaps even more capable — of doing the work that Sanskrit had done earlier. His project asserts that Sanskrit and Kannada are both appropriate for expression of the same propositional content, a claim that was most systematically expressed by Candrarāja's contemporary in the Western Caḷukya court, the grammarian and lexicographer Nāgavarma, who repurposed linguistic tools that were developed to analyse Sanskrit in order to systematically describe Kannada in a series of bilingual dictionaries, grammars, and poetic manuals.[15]

After this discussion of his resumé, Candrarāja translates into New Kannada the brief history of the science of erotics that Vātsyāyana gives at the start of his *Manual on Pleasure*. Here, Candrarāja returns to the scholars whom Candrarāja named in his derisive verses. By translating Vātsyāyana's description of earlier authors, Candrarāja brings himself within the same reportive frame as Vātsyāyana, re-presenting this earlier event of discourse, while reflexively marking the representation as not quite the same.[16] This translation is an opportunity for Candrarāja to interpolate himself at the end of a long historical lineage of scholars of erotics, one that was initially described by Vātsyāyana and which included gods and ancient sages as well as more widely-acknowledged authorities in the erotic sciences. At the same time, he creates a new epistemic space for himself — one occasioned, but not defined by a new language — placing himself at the end of this lineage. Below are the two passages from the *Ornament of Pleasure* and *The Manual on Erotics*. The first is in *Kāmasūtram* (Sanskrit) and the second is in *Madanatilakam* (Kannada).

> *prajāpatir hi prajāḥ sṛṣṭvā tāsāṃ sthitinibandhanaṃ trivargasya sādhanam adhyāyānāṃ śatasahastrēṇāgrē prōvāca | tasyaikadēśikaṃ manuḥ svāyambhō dharmādhikārikaṃ pṛthak cakāra | bṛhaspatir arthādhikārikam | mahādēvānucaraś ca nandī sahasrēṇādhyāyānāṃ pṛthak kāmasūtraṃ prōvāca | tad ēva tu pañcabhir adhyāyaśatair auddālakiḥ śvētakētuḥ sañcikṣēpa | tad ēva tu punar adhyardhēnādhāyaśatēna sādhāraṇasāmprayōgikakanyāsa mprayuktaka-bhāryādhikārikapāradārikavaiśikaupaniṣadikaiḥ saptabhir adhikaraṇair bābhravyaḥ pāñcālaḥ sañcikṣēpa | tasya ṣaṣṭhaṃ vaiśikam adhikaraṇaṃ pāṭaliputrikāṇāṃ gaṇikānāṃ niyōgād dattakaḥ pṛthak cakāra | tatprasaṅgāt cārāyaṇaḥ sādhāraṇam adhikaraṇaṃ pṛthak prōvāca | suvarṇanābhaḥ sāmprayōgikam | ghōṭakamukhaḥ kanyāsamprayuktakam*

14 Candrarāja, *Madanatilakam*, 1.53.

15 For an overview of the relationship between the Kannada language sciences and Sanskrit, see Pollock, 'A New Philology', pp. 389–406.

16 Here I follow Nakassis, 'Citation and Citationality', p. 54.

gōnardīyō bhāryādhikārikam | gōṇikāputraḥ pāradārikam | kucumāra aupaniṣadikam iti | ēvaṃ bahubhir ācāryais tac chāstraṃ khaṇḍaśaḥ praṇītam utsannakalpam abhūt | tatra dattakādibhiḥ praṇītānāṃ śāstrāvayavānām ēkadēśatvāt mahad iti ca bābhravīyasya duradhyēyatvāt saṃkṣipya sarvam artham alpēna granthēna kāmasūtram idaṃ praṇītaṃ |

> Indeed, in the beginning, the creator, upon creating creatures, explicated the means of accomplishing the three goals of life, which are the basis of stability, in 100,000 chapters. The Manu known as 'Svāyambhu' separated out a single portion of that and made an authoritative text on *dharma*. And Bṛhaspati [likewise] created an authoritative text on *politics*. And Nandin, the attendant of Śiva, explicated an authoritative text on erotics in 1000 chapters. And Auddālaki Śvetaketu abridged that in 500 chapters. And Bābhravya Pāñcāla abridged that in 150 chapters on the topics of: general principles, sex, having sex with virgins, wives, other men's wives, courtesans, and erotic esoterica. The sixth topic, namely courtesans, was produced independently by Dattaka for the use of the courtesans of Pāṭaliputra. Cārāyaṇa explicated a separate book on general principles, because of his attachment to that. Suvarṇanābha on sex, Ghoṭakamukha about having sex with virgins, Gonardīya an authoritative text on wives, Goṇikāputra on other men's wives, and Kucumāra on erotic esoterica. Thus, that science, because it has been taught piecemeal by many different scholars, is now on the verge of disappearing. Because the different portions of the science that were taught by Dattaka and the rest are portions of a larger whole, and because the text of Bābhravīya is difficult to study, this *Kāmasūtram* was taught, having condensed all the meaning into a small book here.[17]

modaloḻ abjasaṃbhavaṃ dharmārthakāmaśāstraṃgaḷan oṃdu lakṣādhyāya[vaṃ] māḍidan. alli[ṃ] tegedkoṃḍu caturmukhaputraṃ svāyaṃbhuv eṃba manudharmamaṃ pēḻdaṃ | bṛhaspatiy' arthaśāstraṃ pēḻdaṃ | mahādēvara gaṇaṃ naṃdikēśvaraṃ sahasrādhyāyadiṃ kāmaśāstramaṃ pēḻdaṃ | kiṟidaroḻ uddālakamuniya magaṃ [aid]nūṟadhyāyadiṃ pēḻdan. adaṃ pirid' eṃdu babhruvina magaṃ pāṃcāḷaṃ nūṟayvattadhyādiṃ sādhāraṇa[sāṃ]prayōgi[kaka]nyāsaṃprayukta-bhāryādhikārikapāradārika] vai[śyayikaupaniṣadādika]m eṃb' ēḻ adhikaraṇamaṃ pēḻdan | alli āṟaney adhikaraṇamaṃ vaiśyayika[maṃ] dattakaṃ pāṭaliputraṃ gaṇikeyarge pēḻdan | allade sādhāraṇam eṃb' adhikaraṇamaṃ cārāyaṇaṃ, sāṃprayōgikamaṃ svarṇanābhaṃ, kanyāsaṃprayuktamaṃ ghōṭa[ka]mukhaṃ, bhāryādhikaraṇamaṃ gōna[rdīyaṃ], pataṃjaḷiy ā pāradārikamaṃ, [gō]ṇikāputraṃ [kucu]māran aupaniṣadādikamaṃ pēḻda[r | iṃ]tu pāṃcāḷaniṃd itta palavarum ācāryariṃd avyavacchinnam āda madanāgamaman

17 Vātsyāyana, *Kāmasūtram*, 1.1.5–14.

oṃdumāḍi vātsyāyanaṃ mūvattāṟ adhyāyam ēḻ adhikaraṇado[ḷaṃ] nālvatteṃṭ akkarada samapādasahasragraṃthadiṃ pēḻdan | alli caṃdrarājan āgamalaukikavirōdhamaṃ kaḷedu sārāṃśamaṃ koṃḍu palavu mataṃgaḷan oṃdumāḍi padin eṃṭ' adhikaraṇaṃgaḷiṃd aḷaṃkā[rālaṃ]kṛtam āge nānāchaṃdadin ainūṟu gadyapadyaṃgaḷiṃ viśrutaṃ māḍi pēḻdan |

> In the beginning, the creator made a single work of the sciences of *dharma*, politics, and erotics in 100,000 chapters. Selecting from among them, the son of Brahma, the Manu known as 'Svāyambhu', taught *dharma*. Bṛhaspati taught the science of politics, and Naṃdikēśvara, who is one of the attendants of Śiva, taught the science of erotics in 1000 chapters. In an abridgement consisting of 500 chapters, the son of the sage Uddālaka taught it. Pāṃcāḷa, the son of Babhru, thinking it to be excessive, taught seven topics with 150 chapters, which were known as: general principles, sex, sex with virgins, wives, the wives of other men, courtesans, and erotic esoterica. Among them, the sixth topic, relating to courtesans, was taught by Dattaka for the courtesans from Pāṭaliputra. Moreover, Cārāyaṇa taught a text on general principles, Svarṇanābha on sex, Ghōṭakamukha on sex with virgins, Gōnardīya Patañjali on wives, Gōṇikāputra on the wives of others, and Kucumāra on the erotic esoterica. Then, from the work of Pāṃcāḷa, and from the many scholars, Vātsyāyana made a single authoritative text on erotics, which was uninterrupted. He taught thirty-six chapters in seven books and 1000 even verses with forty-eight syllables. Of that, Candrarāja, removing the conflict between authoritative texts (*āgama*) and the worldly (*laukika*), taking the [most] essential part of it, united the many schools and taught it in eighteen chapters, decorated with ornaments, with various metres, and with 500 celebrated verses, together with prose.[18]

Candrarāja translates Vātsyāyana's history of scholarship on erotics in order to place himself at its conclusion — to mark himself as competent in and yet separate from the work of his predecessors. Writing in a new language allows for Candrarāja to assert that his relationship with textuality is different from that of his predecessors, and he asserts that his own text is better for it. He is able, as he claims, to 'remove the conflict between authoritative texts and the worldly'. Candrarāja asserts that he is authoring a new text that places, as we will see, real-world experience at the centre of a *śāstric* endeavour. Candrarāja dwells on this theme of negotiating the space between authoritative texts and worldly experience, introducing his poetic competence as a mark of his difference from his predecessors, writing:

18 Candrarāja, *Madanatilakam*, pp. 16–17.

chaṃdad' aḷaṃkāraṃ kara-
m oṃdi manōjāgamōktamaṃ laukikamaṃ |
saṃdisi nītig oḍaṃbaḍu
vaṃdadin ār peḻvar iṃtu caṃdrana teṟadiṃ ||

(Joining the beauty of poetic ornaments with metrics, uniting what has already been said in authoritative texts (*āgama*) on erotics and the worldly (*laukika*), being agreeable to propriety — who can write the way that Candra can?)[19]

Throughout the *Ornament of Desire*, Candrarāja walks this line that he traces between earlier textual authorities and his own experiences.[20] Knowledge of erotics, for him, has to be produced somewhere between the worldly and the textual, and his ways of dealing with textuality open a view onto how translation was used in the medieval Deccan.

From Astrology to Erotics

One of Candrarāja's most significant sources is Varāhamihira, a sixth-century author of a series of texts on mathematical astronomy, divination, and astrology that would become standard reference works in the medieval period. Candrarāja makes the work of Varāhamihira present in various ways — through citation, quotation, and translation — and he deftly jumps across languages in his presentation of Varāhamihira's astrological and divinatory manual, the *Large Collection* (*Bṛhatsaṃhitā*), which provides him with justification for writing a science of erotics.

Candrarāja echoes both Vātsyāyana and Varāhamihira in arguing that without a systematic science passion will ruin people, and so it is necessary to have a science of erotics just as it is necessary to have systematic sciences of politics and law. He combines his own Kannada verses with Sanskrit verses extracted from Varāhamihira's *Large Collection*, writing:

kūrale vēḻpudu satiyar
kūradoḍ' avariṃd av' asuharaṃ vasuharam i- |
nn' ārayvoḍ' uḻida sāhasa-
m ār aḷavū mihiravākyamaṃ kēḻdaṟiyā ||

śastrēṇa vēṇīvinigūhitēna
vidūrathaṃ tanmahiṣī jaghāna |

19 Candrarāja, *Madanatilakam*, 1.56.

20 This theme of the science of erotics being dependent on experience would be taken up by the early thirteenth-century author Janna in his *Mirror of Experience* (*Anubhavamukuram*), who consistently argues (Janna, 'Anubhavamukuram', ed. by Krishnakumar, vv. 41, 59, 60, 109) that the principles of erotics need to be established through experience (*anubhavasiddham*).

viṣapradigdhēna ca nūpurēṇa
dēvī viraktā kila kāśirājaṃ ||

> (Wives should be loving. If they do not love, they will take one's life and one's wealth.
>
> If one were to consider this, who would behave so rashly? Who has not heard the speech of Varāhamihira?
>
> 'Vidūratha was killed by his own chief queen with a weapon that was hidden in her hair. It is said that the wife of the king of Kāśī, having fallen out of love with him, killed him with her anklet, which was smeared with poison.'[21])

The audience of this New Kannada *śāstra* is presumed to already know Sanskrit and to have no difficulty switching between the two languages. Translation here is used alongside multilingual quotation as a part of the same exercise of composing a new text.

In addition to presenting verses from Varāhamihira's *Large Collection* in their Sanskrit original, Candrarāja also translates select verses — and sometimes portions of verses — from sections of the *Large Collection* about pregnancy and gestation. Take, for instance, the following selection from the end of the introduction of the *Ornament of Desire* and the verses it draws on from the *Large Collection*:

***Madanatilakam* (Kannada)**	**English**
ratiya padadalli garbha- *sthitiyoḷ śuklaṃ viśēṣam ādoḍe puruṣaṃ* | *sati raktādhikadiṃdaṃ* *satataṃ saman' āge ṣaṃḍar appar makkaḷ* || *MT* 1.82	At the time of sex, should semen predominate inside the womb, there will be a male child. There will always be a female when blood predominates. And when they are equal, non-gendered children are born.
ṛtuvina ratiyoḷ peraraṃ *sati bayasidoḍ' ava[ḷa] bayasidavanaṃ pōlvar* | *sutar adariṃ strīg' anura-* *ktateyaṃ māḍalke kāmatattvave mukhyaṃ* || *MT* 1.83	When a woman is ovulating and has sex, if the woman desires another man, her children will resemble he whom she desires. Therefore, the principles of erotics are extremely important in order to make women desirous of the right person.
balagelad' eḍeyoḷ garbhaṃ *nile puruṣaṃ vāmabhāgadiṃ strīy' eraḍuṃ* | *keladoḷ amaḷgaḷ naḍuvaṇa* *neleyiṃdaṃ ṣaṃḍar āgi puṭṭuvar eṃduṃ* || *MT* 1.84	When the foetus stays on the right side of a woman's womb, it is male, and it is female on the left portion. When it is in both spots, it becomes twins, and when it stays in the middle, it is said that third-gendered children born.[22]

21 Candrarāja, *Madanatilakam*, 1.72–73. The second verse is in Sanskrit and is excerpted from Varāhamihira, *Bṛhatsaṃhitā*, 77.1.

22 Candrarāja, *Madanatilakam*, 1.82–84.

Bṛhatsaṃhitā (Sanskrit)	English
raktē 'dhikē strī puruṣas tu śukrē napuṃsakaṃ śōṇitaśukrasāmyē | yasmād ataḥ śukravivṛddhidāni niṣēvitavyāni rasāyanāni ||	When blood predominates, a female will be born, but when semen predominates a male will be born. When there is equal blood and semen, a third-gendered child will be born. Therefore, one should use medicines that increase one's semen.[23]
jātyaṃ manōbhavasukhaṃ subhagasya sarva- m ābhāsamātram itarasya manōviyōgāt | cittena bhāvayati dūragatāpi yaṃ strī garbhaṃ bibhartti sadṛśaṃ puruṣasya tasya ||	Every pleasure of love that is noble comes to a handsome man, while a mere semblance comes to a man who is otherwise, since he is separated from the heart. A woman conceives a foetus similar to whichever man she imagines in her mind, even if she is far away from him.[24]
dakṣiṇapārśvē puruṣō vāmē nārī yamāv ubhayasaṃsthau | yad udaramadhyōpagataṃ napuṃsakaṃ tan nibōddhavyam ||	When a foetus is on the right side, it is male. When it is on the left, it is female. When they are on both sides, they are twins. It should be understood that that foetus which is situated in the middle of the womb is third-gendered.[25]

Here we see Candrarāja translating full verses from Varāhamihira's *Large Collection* as well as half-verses. In each instance, Candrarāja repurposes statements from Varāhamihira in order to show the practical nature of understanding erotics. It is a science with real results in the world, important for selecting the sex of one's future child, with results that were enumerated earlier by Varāhamihira.[26] Candrarāja draws content from individual verses spread across different chapters in Varāhamihira's *Large Collection*, bringing them together within a single sequence of Kannada verses in his new work, using his text to present these disparate verses from Varāhamihira as providing a coherent argument for the importance of studying the science of erotics based on its practical efficacy.

Varāhamihira's writing would also serve as the basis for Cāvuṃḍarāya's *Assistance for the World* (*Lōkōpakāram*), which was composed in Jayasiṃha II's court in 1025, as well as for Śrīdhara's *Ornament of Astrology* (*Jātakatilakam*), which was written in the subsequent court of Āhavamalla in 1049. Across these texts, Varāhamihira's scholarship — which consisted of manuals for the

23 Varāhamihira, *Bṛhatsaṃhitā*, 76.1.

24 Varāhamihira, *Bṛhatsaṃhitā*, 75.1.

25 Varāhamihira, *Bṛhatsaṃhitā*, 78.24.

26 On the various procedures for selecting the sex of one's progeny in Sanskrit medical literature, see Das, *Origin of the Life of a Human Being*, pp. 445–52 and Selby, 'Narratives of Conception', pp. 258–65.

astral sciences as well as astral-inflected divination — was disarticulated by later authors and appropriated to describe other realms of investigation.[27] As Daud Ali has put it while describing medieval Sanskrit texts of erotics, 'the *types* of characteristics enumerated for the basic divisions of lovers in later *kāmaśāstra* seem to build upon the kinds of characteristics detailed in the *Bṛhatsaṃhitā* [Varāhamihira's *Large Collection*]', which served as the basis for 'other nascent fields of worldly knowledge like *śilpaśāstra, gandhaśāstra* and *vṛkṣāyurveda* [architecture, perfumery, and agriculture]'.[28] When we follow Ali's observations into the realm of vernacular sciences, we can see the ways in which the typological analysis developed in Varāhamihira's texts could be challenged, while being simultaneously invoked to describe new phenomena. Candrarāja uses typological analysis enumerated by earlier authors in a manner that is subtly subversive, and is another place in which we can see his complex engagement with worldly experience, with earlier authoritative texts, and with the types of indexical practices that often come along with translation.

Beyond a System of Human Marks

After his introduction, Candrarāja proceeds to give a series of brief chapters explaining various typologies of women based on age, country of origin, and various physical and psychological qualities in a manner that is reminiscent of these descriptions given in the roughly contemporaneous Sanskrit texts *The Secrets of Sex* (*Ratirahasyam*) by Kokkoka and *Everything a Townsman Needs* (*Nāgarasarvasva*) by Padmaśrī.[29]

One hallmark of this medieval scholarship on erotics is a schema that divided women into four different classes: lotus-type (*padminī*), artistic-type (*citriṇī*), conch shell-type (*śaṅkhinī*), and elephant-type (*hastinī*) based on physical and psychological characteristics.[30] This schema seems to have been taken up by later authors from Kokkoka's *Secrets of Sex*, and became the basic form of analysis in most later texts on erotics, as well as by poets and scholars

---

27 Geslani, 'Astrological Vedism', pp. 305–13 provides an important reassessment of Varāhamihira's influences and sources outside of the astral sciences.

28 Ali, 'Padmaśrī's "Nāgarasarvasva" and the World of Medieval Kāmaśāstra', p. 46. Emphasis in original.

29 Priority and influence are difficult to determine, since neither of these two Sanskrit texts has been convincingly dated more precisely than a 400-year timeframe. But it is clear that by the early eleventh century there was a robust discourse about pleasure that drew on the changing fields of medicine, astrology, divination, physiognomy, and dramaturgy, and which was influenced by, but which had different concerns from Vātsyāyana. On the difficulty of dating these two texts precisely, see Ali, 'Padmaśrī's "Nāgarasarvasva"', pp. 42–44. For further discussions of this general late medieval courtly 'kāma world', see McHugh, 'The Incense Trees of the Land of Emeralds', pp. 63–100 and Desmond, 'The Pleasure Is Mine', pp. 16–23.

30 See the discussions in Ali 'Padmaśrī's "Nāgarasarvasva"', pp. 45–47 as well as Zysk, 'Animal Usage in the Sanskrit Traditions of Lovemaking', 287–304. Perhaps the most comprehensive examination of this history remains Raghavan, 'Introduction', pp. 14–116.

writing in other genres.[31] The science of erotics was reoriented around this fourfold classification, which gradually displaced the typologies that appear in Vātsyāyana's *Manual on Pleasure*.[32]

Because *The Secrets of Sex* is difficult to date, Candrarāja's *Ornament of Desire* provides the earliest securely dateable instance of the fourfold typology of women into the classes when it is discussed in its second chapter.[33] Curiously, the *Ornament of Desire* provides the names of these four classes of women in a non-standard form derived from Sanskrit — they are *padmini, cittini, śaṃkini,* and *hastini* — suggesting a possible Prakrit source for changes in the medieval science of erotics. Kokkoka's *Secrets of Sex* also cites a Prakrit predecessor, *The Belt of Hara* (*Haramēkhalā*), and the early astral text, *The Astral Sciences of Garga* (*Gārgīyajyotiṣa*) contains a chapter on human marks of a style that would become standard in later texts on erotics, and which seems to have relied on a similarly non-Sanskrit predecessor.[34] In explicating these changes, we need to open up our analysis beyond the simple equation of *śāstra* with Sanskrit, and turn towards more diverse sources.

In presenting this fourfold classification of women, Candrarāja does not seem quite comfortable with its explanatory power. After explaining the typology, he writes:

> *iṃt' ī nālkuṃ jātiya*
> *kāṃteyar avayavaguṇaṃgaḷ oṃdoṃdaṟoḷ a-* |
> *tyaṃtaṃ koḍidoḍ' aṟi nīṃ*
> *bhrāṃt' ēṃ saṃkīrṇajātiy eṃd' ā vadhuvaṃ* ||
>
> (Those are the qualities of the parts of the body of women of the four types. If they are given in a high degree of combination in any individual, and you come to know that, what is your confusion? That woman is said to be of the 'complex' type.)[35]

---

31 For general remarks about the life of this schema outside of erotics, see Patel, 'Shared Typologies of Kāmaśāstra', pp. 101–21.

32 The new fourfold schema appears in *The Secrets of Sex* alongside Vātsyāyana's typologies of women. The two systems would be superimposed in *The Delight of the Mind* (*Mānasōllāsa*) — produced in the Western Cāḷukya court of the twelfth century — combines the fourfold typology with the classificatory system of women in Vātsyāyana's *Manual on Pleasure,* yielding a six-fold typology (Someśvara, *Mānasollāsa,* 20.1718c–19b *et* passim). This text has been excluded from all scholarly narratives of the development of *kāmaśāstra.*

33 This fact that has not been noted in recent scholarly discussions of erotics. Kokkoka seems to suggest that this fourfold classification came from the schools of thought propounded by Nandikeśvara and Goṇikāputra (see *The Secrets of Sex,* prose before 1.9; left untranslated in the English translation by Upadhyaya). The texts of these authors are no longer extant.

34 For *The Astral Sciences of Garga,* see Geslani and others, 'Garga and Early Astral Science', p. 161. There has been a general neglect of *śāstras* written in Apabhraṃśa and Prakrit. For the best overview, see Jain, *History and Development of Prakrit,* pp. 424–77. Ollett, *Language of the Snakes,* pp. 1–25 provides an important reassessment of the role Prakrit played in the Sanskrit cosmopolis focused on literature and the language sciences.

35 Candrarāja, *Madanatilakam,* 2.6.

Candrarāja presents a series of typologies that seem to be taken from earlier authoritative texts only to conclude — time and again — by rejecting them as insufficient to describe the complexity of things in the world. Some women, Candrarāja explains, might be classified as 'godly', 'sage-like', or 'demonic', but many are more complex than any typology would allow.[36] Some women may be dominated by the phlegmatic, bilious, or airy humours, and it might be best to approach them for sex during certain times of the year, but Candrarāja again tells his audience — after narrating the effects of the humours on women — that things are more complicated than any typology might let on. He writes:

iṃt' ī prakṛtiguṇaṃgaḷ
kāṃteyaroḷ berasi tōṟe saṃkīrṇeyar ā- |
d' iṃt' ivara bhēdamaṃ naya-
diṃ tiḷid' oḍagūḍi geldoḍ' ātaṃ caduraṃ ||

> (When these natural qualities appear to unite in a woman, she is a 'complex' woman. That man is clever if clear knowledge of these differences leads him to sexual conquests.)[37]

Once he has laid out the typological thinking of his predecessors in New Kannada verse, Candrarāja rejects the possibility of such systematic description of the world. Time and again, he invokes the notion of complexity to show that the expected classifications of *śāstra* are more motley in everyday experience. Every typology will ultimately fail, Candrarāja argues, to describe the complexity of sexual experiences in the world. In reality, most things are more mixed up than simple typologies would allow. Candrarāja here shows what it means to 'remove the conflict between authoritative texts and the worldly'. By invoking and summarizing earlier schematizations of the world of erotics, Candrarāja positions himself as having the opportunity to supersede it by bringing in his observations about the complexity of the world that is not captured in *śāstra*.

Between Science and Literature

By the eighth chapter of the *Ornament of Desire*, the typological analysis breaks down even further. While Candrarāja still discusses different social roles as well as the different possible emotional states and their external symptoms, the chapters in the latter half of the text tend to be longer and less systematic, and often contain poetic dialogues of erotic situations written in the first- and second-person rather than straightforward exposition in a third-person voice as would be expected in *śāstra*. By switching towards dialogues explaining erotic situations, Candrarāja was able to cement his reputation as a poet, while once again pushing the boundaries of what it meant to write an

36 Candrarāja, *Madanatilakam*, 3.6.

37 Candrarāja, *Madanatilakam*, 5.13.

authoritative text.[38] Take, for instance, the following verses, which record various poetic — and somewhat misogynistic — conversations lovers might find themselves having:

> *kālan ott' engum t[a]mb[u]lam ikk' engum taleyan uguris' engum āgulikum*
> *mēle nemmugum urigum bīs' engum appikoḷ cumbanammāḍu nīm bēgam engum* |
> *[sō]le niḍusuygum naḍugugum mēlvāygum poḍa[maḍu]gum kathēvēḻ' engum*
> *bāle soḍaram maguḻc' engum kemmane manam aṟiyalk' emdu[m ā] viṭam* ||
>
> *paḍiyan eyede teṟe gharmam id' engum*
> *naḍugi kuttam aḍasitt' enas' engum* |
> *miḍukad' umte maralumdida pāmgim*
> *maḍadi ṟōḍisugum egganan emdum* ||
>
> *ēkārāmtam akkum-*
> *eley ēk' ēlegē, kēḷ ene, kēḷ em; neney ene, neney em; ēk' emb' ene,*
> *nened' ēvem. kēḷ eḍegeydem; neleyem, nereyem, neṟevēḻvem* ||
>
> *emdu bēṟ' ūrge pōdanam pōgi bamdanam puruḍisuvar* |
>
> (A libertine will say, 'massage my leg!' and he will say, 'give me some betel!' and he will say 'scratch my head!' and he will yawn, and lean on top of a woman, and he will say, 'I'm burning, fan me!' and he will say 'quickly! You! Hug and kiss me!' and growing tired and sighing deeply, he will tremble and jump up and give praise and say, 'tell me a story!' and then he will say, 'Listen, woman! Turn the lamp away!' for no reason, just to know her heart.
>
> A woman will say: 'It's hot, go to the door and open it!' and then she will say: 'Now I'm shivering and getting sick!' Thus, even when she is unanimated, and seems to be asleep, a woman will annoy an idiotic man.
>
> This verse contains only the vowel 'e' —
>
> 'Why, oh why, woman?!' 'I'm speaking, listen!' 'I won't listen!' 'I'm speaking, remember!' 'I won't remember!' 'What was said? I'm speaking!' 'What will I get from remembering?' 'Listen! I'll give you space!' 'I won't stay!' 'I won't have sex with you!' 'I'll tell it all!'
>
> That is what envious people say when one of them has gone to another village and then returned.)[39]

38 It is from these chapters — and not the ones at the start of the *Ornament of Desire* — that Mallikārjuna's later anthology of Kannada poetry, *The Ambrosial Ocean of Beautiful Verses* (*Sūktisudhārṇavam*), would excerpt verses. Recontextualized in Mallikārjuna's anthology, these verses stand as self-contained poems, independent of their scholarly context. Mallakavi's *Essence of Poetry* (*Kāvyasāra*) would in turn reproduce some of the verses from the *Ornament of Desire* that were presented in Mallikārjuna's earlier anthology.

39 Candrarāja, *Madanatilakam*, 10.85–87.

There is still a logic to the second half of the *Ornament of Desire*, but it is a different logic than that which animates the first half. It is a logic informed by poetic topoi as well as by the psychological investigations staged by earlier authors of scholarly texts. It is a logic that is dialogical, that can best be expressed by writing poetry in the first- and second-person narrative frame. Candrarāja combines single-verse poems that resemble those of the poets Hāla, Amaru, or Gōvardhana within a larger śāstric apparatus. Poetry and the sciences — often contrasted in Sanskrit intellectual discourse — are elegantly woven together in the hands of Candrarāja.[40]

In the middle of the eleventh chapter of the *Ornament of Desire*, a single verse written in an unusual metre stands out. The verse, as it has survived, is damaged, but it seems to be written in *ṣaṭpadi* metre, a non-Sanskrit-derived metre that would later become standard in Kannada poetry, but which was incredibly rare in the early stages of Kannada literature.[41] Even though it is somewhat corrupt, much of the meaning is still clear. The eminent Kannada philologist T. V. Venkatachala Sastry has attempted to reconstruct this verse with the following emendations:[42]

Madanatilakam **(Kannada)**	**English**
māsaprasūte ṣa- *ṇmāsagarbhiṇi tāṃ [kru-* *ddhā]sati me[ytiḷid' e̱lcarta]vaḷ* | *māsaranṛtyavi-* *ḷāsinigaṃ kāma-* *[m ā] sukhaṃ kūṭamuṃ tatkālamē* ||	A woman who is one-month post-partum, a woman who is six months pregnant, [conj. an angry woman, a woman whose body has been cleansed after her period, a woman who has woken up from sleep]: Those are the proper times for erotics, for pleasure, and for sexual union for a woman who plays at the theatre as her supreme refuge.[43]

Using this verse, Venkatachala Sastry argues that 'It is likely that Candrarāja … knew about *The Secrets of Sex* either directly or indirectly', and that 'while there is a difference between Candrarāja's verse and that of *The Secrets of Sex*, it may be its source'.[44] And indeed, the verse — especially after Venkatachala Sastry's emendations — seems to reflect the following verse in Kokkoka's text:

40 On the distinction between *kāvya* and *śāstra* generally, see Pollock, 'Sanskrit Literary Culture from the Inside Out', pp. 41–61.

41 For the history of this metre in Kannada, see Venkatachala Sastry, *Kannaḍa Chandaḥsvarūpa*, pp. 432–75. On metres in the *Ornament of Desire* more generally, see Venkatachala Sastry, 'Madanatilakam: Chandassu'.

42 For explanations of these emendations, see Venkatachala Sastry, 'Madanatilakada Ṣaṭpadiya Padyapāṭha'.

43 Candrarāja, *Madanatilakam*, 11.10.

44 *bahuśaḥ caṃdrarājanu horatu uḷida kannaḍa kavigaḷu pratyakṣavāgiyō parōkṣavāgiyō 'ratirahasya'vannu ballavarāgiddāre … caṃdrarājana padyakke 'ratirahasya'kkiṃta bēreyāda mattāvudādarū oṃdu ākaravirabahudu*: Venkatachala Sastry, 'Madanatilakada Ṣaṭpadiya Padyapāṭha', p. 82.

***Ratirahasyam* (Sanskrit)**	**English**
adhvaklāntatanur navajvaravatī nṛtyaślathāṅgī tathā māsaikaprasavā dadāti suratē ṣaṇmāsagarbhā sukham | vikhyātā virahayya saṅgamavidhau kruddhaprasannē ṛtu-snānē nūtanasaṅgamē madhumadē rāgāspadaṃ yōṣitaḥ ||	A woman whose body is worn out from travel, a woman who has recently contracted fever, a woman whose limbs are loosened from dancing, a woman who is one-month post-partum, and a woman who is six months pregnant give pleasure during sex. Women are well-known to be the seat of passion upon the moment of coming together again, when they have been separated from their loves, when their anger has been soothed, after bathing for menstruation, and when they are drunk on wine.[45]

But it seems more likely, given the wording of the verse and its markedly non-Sanskrit metre and setting in second half of the *Ornament of Desire*, that it is in fact a Kannada translation of a similar Prakrit verse from Hāla's earlier Prakrit anthology, *Seven Hundred Verses* (*Sattasaī*).

***Sattasaī* (Prakrit)**	**English**
māsapasūaṃ chammāsagabbhiṇiṃ ēkkadiahajariaṃ ca | raṃguttiṇṇaṃ ca piaṃ puttaa kāmaṃtaō hohi || SS 259	You should have sex with a woman who is one-month post-partum, who is six months pregnant, who has had a fever for a single day, or who is skilled in stagecraft, dear boy![46]

The order of the presentation of information, as well as the precise wording (*māsapasūaṃ chammāsagabbhiṇiṃ*) corresponds closely between the Kannada and Prakrit verses, and Candrarāja has already shown his willingness to use non-Sanskrit sources and to use translation more generally. In translating this verse, Candrarāja situates it in a new context, one that is part literary and part scholarly, and in which newness is the epistemic virtue par excellence. Candrarāja constructs a dense network of allusion in which he points towards many earlier textual models in order to appropriate them to new ends. In his *Ornament of Erotics*, systematic expositions can sit alongside poetic dialogues. He has used translation to turn science into poetry and poetry into science. If, as Hāla argues at the start of *The Seven Hundred Verses*, people who investigate the principles of erotics should feel shame if they do not appreciate the nectar that is Prakrit poetry, Candrarāja shows a way in which these two different realms can be coordinated.[47] Poetry can safely sit alongside sciences as long as the poetry is mediated by the set of translingual practices that Canrarāja brings to interact with earlier texts.

45 Kokkoka, *Ratirahasyam*, 4.28.

46 Hāla, *Sattasaī*, v. 259.

47 The verse in question is: *amiaṃ pāuakavvaṃ* | *paḍhiuṃ sōuṃ ca jē ṇa āṇaṃti* | *kāmassa tattattiṃ* | *kuṇaṃti tē kaha ṇa lajjaṃti* || Hāla, *Sattasaī*. For an important interpretation of Hāla's argument, see Ollett *Language of the Snakes*, pp. 59–60.

Conclusions: A Pragmatic View of Science in Translation

By turning to translation as a practice, and as a particular practice centred around scholarly texts in the medieval Deccan, we can see something that is often overlooked in philosophic and literary accounts of translation: More often than not, people do not translate entire texts. It is far more common to translate portions of texts, to use translation as part of a process of selective excerpting and of archive building. In the *Ornament of Desire,* Candrarāja creates a new text out of a patchwork of older texts brought into a new language, New Kannada. Translation here is part of a larger toolkit of indexical practices — including citation, quotation, summation, and elaboration — that allow authors to position themselves critically with the past, to appropriate earlier scholarship while moving beyond it.[48] Translation is one possible way for authors to assert that they are 'doing the same thing' as earlier authors and that it is possible to 'say the same thing' in two separate languages. But translation also reveals a gap, a difference, and this gap is the site for further possible epistemic interventions. It is an opportunity for new scholarly inquiry.

Daud Ali has argued that 'the entanglement between the realms of literature and *kāma* (erotics) [...] is deep and mutually constitutive'.[49] It is perhaps in regional language scholarly texts that we can see this relationship most clearly. Candrarāja, together with his colleagues in the Western Cāḷukya court, saw himself as breaking new ground in *śāstra,* and one of the ways in which he differentiated his project was through his use of language. In the *Ornament of Desire,* Candrarāja brings together an intellectual world that includes Sanskrit theorists, Prakrit poets, and New Kannada scholars. Candrarāja was not concerned with using translation to bring texts written in a different language to a new audience. He presumed that his audience would already know Sanskrit; in any case it would be nearly impossible for them to understand the *Ornament of Desire* without it. Translation here was not a tool to make already extant knowledge mobile, and it was not a means of exchanging knowledge across geographic or cultural boundaries but quite the opposite: Candrarāja used translation to take knowledge that had been asserted to be universal and to root it in a specific place. He used translation to mark himself as making new knowledge, but new knowledge that was not mobile. By writing in Kannada, he committed himself to writing in a language that was seen not to travel beyond a delimited region.[50] For Candrarāja, translation was an opportunity to show how he is different from the past, and thus to introduce new sources and to open up a new epistemic space for his

---

48 For a useful discussion of this larger toolkit, see Cox, *Modes of Philology,* pp. 40–43.

49 Ali, 'Rethinking the History of the "Kāma" World', p. 9.

50 For the scope of the geographic region asserted to be concurrent with Kannada speakers and the assertion of Kannada as a language rooted to a specific place, see Pollock, *Language of the Gods,* pp. 330–79.

own experience. Translation, in this context, was one of many indexical tools an author could deploy and was a practice that Candrarāja drew attention to in different ways at different moments in his text. It was a way of making the past present, while also marking it as not quite contemporary and as not quite complete.

Bibliography

Primary Sources

Candrarāja, *Madanatilakam*, ed. by R. S. Panchamukhi (Dharwar: Kannada Research Institute, 1953)

——, *Madanatilakam*, ed. by T. V. Venkatachala Sastry (Bangalore: Sapna Book House, 2012)

Hāla, *Das Saptaçatakam des Hâla*, ed. by Albrecht Weber (Leipzig: F. A. Brockhaus, 1881)

Janna, 'Anubhavamukuram', in *Janna Saṃpuṭa*, ed. by C. P. Krishnakumar, Samagra Kannaḍa Jaina Sāhitya Saṃpuṭa, 13 (Hampi: Prasaranga, Kannada University, 2007), pp. 247–90

Kokkoka, *Ratirahasyam*, ed. by Rāmānanda Śarmā (Vārāṇasī: Kr̥ṣṇadāsa Akādamī, 1994)

Padmaśrī, *Nāgarasarvasva*, ed. by Amal Shib Pathak (New Delhi: Chaukhambha Publications, 2014)

Someśvara, *Mānasollāsa*, ed. by G. K. Shrigondekar, Gaekwad's Oriental Series, 28, 74, 138, 3 vols (Baroda: Oriental Insitute of Baroda, 1925)

Varāhamihira, *Br̥hatsaṃhitā*, ed. and trans. by M. Ramakrishna Bhat (Delhi: Motilal Banarsidass, 1981)

Vātsyāyana, *Kāmasūtram*, ed. by Rāmānanda. Śarmā, Biṭṭhaladāsa Saṃskr̥ta sīrija, 4 (Vārāṇasī: Kr̥ṣṇadāsa Akādamī, 2001)

Secondary Studies

Ali, Daud, 'Rethinking the History of the "Kāma" World in Early India', *Journal of Indian Philosophy*, 39 (2011), 1–13

——, 'Padmaśrī's "Nāgarasarvasva" and the World of Medieval Kāmaśāstra', *Journal of Indian Philosophy*, 39 (2011), 41–62

Asad, Talal, 'The Concept of Cultural Translation in British Social Anthropology', in *Writing Culture: The Poetics and Politics of Ethnography*, ed. by James Clifford and George E. Marcus (Berkeley: University of California Press, 1986), pp. 141–64

Bauman, Richard, and Charles Briggs, *Voices of Modernity: Language Ideologies and the Politics of Inequality* (Cambridge: Cambridge University Press, 2003)

Brentjes, Sonja, Alexander Fidora, and Matthias M. Tischler, 'Towards a New Approach to Medieval Cross-Cultural Exchanges', *Journal of Transcultural Medieval Studies*, 1.1 (2014), 9–50

Cort, John E., 'Making It Vernacular in Agra: The Practice of Translation by Seventeenth-Century Jains', in *Tellings and Texts*, ed. by Francesca Orsini and Katherine Butler Schofield, Music, Literature and Performance in North India, 1st edn (Open Book Publishers, 2015), pp. 61–106

Cox, Whitney, 'Bhoja's Alternate Universe', *Journal of the Royal Asiatic Society*, 22 (2012), 57–72

——, *Politics, Kingship, and Poetry in Medieval South India: Moonset on Sunrise Mountain* (Cambridge: Cambridge University Press, 2016)

——, *Modes of Philology in Medieval South India* (Boston: Brill, 2016)

Das, Rahul Peter, *Origin of the Life of a Human Being: Conception and the Female According to Ancient Indian Medical and Sexological Literature* (Delhi: Motilal Banarsidass Publishers, 2003)

Desmond, Laura, 'The Pleasure Is Mine: The Changing Subject of Erotic Science', *Journal of Indian Philosophy*, 39 (2011), 15–39

Elshakry, Marwa S., 'Knowledge in Motion: The Cultural Politics of Modern Science Translations in Arabic', *Isis*, 99.4 (2008), 701–30

Elshakry, Marwa, and Carla Nappi, 'Translations', in *A Companion to the History of Science*, ed. by Bernard Lightman (Chichester: Wiley Blackwell, 2016), pp. 372–86

Fisher, Elaine M., 'Coconut in the Honey: Multilingual Cosmopolitanism in Early Modern South India' (conference paper presented at the South Asia Seminar, University of Chicago, 2019)

Geslani, Marko, 'Astrological Vedism: Varahamihira in Light of the Later Rituals of the Atharvaveda', *The Journal of the American Oriental Society*, 136 (2016), 305–23

Geslani, Marko, Bill Mak, Michio Yano, and Kenneth G. Zysk, 'Garga and Early Astral Science in India', *History of Science in South Asia*, 5 (2017), 151–91

Gurevitch, Eric Moses, 'The Uses of Useful Knowledge and the Languages of Vernacular Science: Perspectives from Southwest India', *History of Science*, forthcoming

Hart, Roger, 'Translating the Untranslatable: From Copula to Incommensurable Worlds', in *Tokens of Exchange: The Problem of Translation in Global Circulations*, ed. by Lydia H. Liu (Durham, NC: Duke University Press, 1999), pp. 45–73

Jain, Jagdish Chandra, *History and Development of Prakrit Literature* (New Delhi: Manohar, 2004)

Keane, Webb, *Christian Moderns: Freedom and Fetish in the Mission Encounter* (Berkeley: University of California Press, 2007)

Liu, Lydia, *Translingual Practice: Literature, National Culture, and Translated Modernity – China, 1900–1937* (Stanford, CA: Stanford University Press, 1995)

McHugh, James, 'The Incense Trees of the Land of Emeralds: The Exotic Material Culture of Kāmaśāstra', *Journal of Indian Philosophy*, 39 (2011), 63–100

Montgomery, Scott L., *Science in Translation: Movements of Knowledge through Cultures and Time* (Chicago: The University of Chicago Press, 2000)

Nakassis, Constantine V., 'Citation and Citationality', *Signs and Society*, 1 (2013), 51–77

Ollett, Andrew, *Language of the Snakes: Prakrit, Sanskrit, and the Language Order of Premodern India*, South Asia across the Disciplines (Oakland: University of California Press, 2017)

Patel, Deven M., 'Shared Typologies of Kāmaśāstra, Alaṅkāraśāstra and Literary Criticism', *Journal of Indian Philosophy*, 39 (2011), 101–22

——, 'Source, Exegesis, and Translation: Sanskrit Commentary and Regional Language Translation in South Asia', *Journal of the American Oriental Society*, 131 (2011), 245–66

Pollock, Sheldon, 'Sanskrit Literary Culture from the Inside Out', in *Literary Cultures in History*, ed. by Sheldon Pollock (Berkeley: University of California Press, 2003), pp. 39–130

——, 'A New Philology: From Norm-Bound Practice to Practice-Bound Norm in Kannada Intellectual History', in *South-Indian Horizons: Felicitation Volume for François Gros*, ed. by Jean-Luc Chevillard (Pondichery: Institut Français de Pondichéry, 2004), pp. 389–406

——, *The Language of the Gods in the World of Men: Sanskrit, Culture, and Power in Premodern India* (Berkeley: University of California Press, 2006)

——, 'The Languages of Science in Early Modern India', in *Forms of Knowledge in Early Modern Asia: Explorations in the Intellectual History of India and Tibet, 1500–1800*, ed. by Sheldon Pollock (Durham, NC: Duke University Press, 2011), pp. 19–48

Pingree, David, 'Islamic Astronomy in Sanskrit', *Journal for the History of Arabic Science*, 2 (1978), 315–30

Ragab, Ahmed, '"In a Clear Arabic Tongue": Arabic and the Making of a Science-Language Regime', *Isis*, 108.3 (2017), 612–20

Raghavan, V., 'Introduction', in Akbar Shāh, *Śṛṅgāra Mañjarī of Saint Akbar Shāh, Based on Old Sanskrit Manuscripts in Devanagari and Telugu Scripts*, ed. by V. Raghavan (Hyderabad: Hyderabad Archaeological Dept., 1951), pp. 1–116

Ramanujan, A. K., 'Three Hundred Rāmāyaṇas: Five Examples and Three Thoughts on Translation', in *Many Rāmāyaṇas: The Diversity of a Narrative Tradition in South Asia*, ed. by Paula Richman (Berkeley: University of California Press, 1991), pp. 22–49

Ricci, Ronit, *Islam Translated: Literature, Conversion, and the Arabic Cosmopolis of South and Southeast Asia* (Chicago: University of Chicago Press, 2011)

Selby, Martha Ann, 'Narratives of Conception, Gestation, and Labour in Sanskrit Āyurvedic Texts', *Asian Medicine*, 1.2 (2018), 254–75

Speziale, Fabrizio, *Culture Persane et Médecine Ayurvédique En Asie Du Sud* (Leiden: Brill, 2018)

Subbarayalu, Y., 'Quantifying Land Revenue of the Chola State', in *South India Under the Cholas* (New Delhi: Oxford University Press, 2012), pp. 100–15

Taylor, Sarah Pierce, *Aesthetics of Sovereignty: The Poetic and Material Worlds of Medieval Jainism* (unpublished dissertation, University of Pennsylvania, 2016)

Trivedi, Harish, 'In Our Own Time, on Our Own Terms: "Translation" in India', in *Translating Others*, ed. by Theo Hermans (Manchester: St Jerome, 2006), I, 102–19

Truschke, Audrey, *Culture of Encounters: Sanskrit at the Mughal Court*, South Asia across the Disciplines (New York: Columbia University Press, 2016)

Venkatachala Sastry, T. V., *Kannaḍa Chandaḥsvarūpa* (Maisūru: Ḍi. Vi. Ke. Mūrti, 1978)

——, 'Madanatilakada Ṣaṭpadiya Padyapāṭha, Sadṛśapadyagaḷu', in *Śāstrīya* (Bangalore: Sapna Book House, 1999), I, pp. 78–82

——, 'Madanatilakam: Chandassu', in *Śāstrīya* (Bangalore: Sapna Book House, 1999), II, pp. 242–73

Williams, Tyler, 'Commentary as Translation: The Vairāgya Vṛnd of Bhagvandas Niranjani', in *Text and Tradition in Early Modern North India*, ed. by Tyler Walker Williams, Anshu Malhotra, and John Stratton Hawley (Oxford: Oxford University Press, 2018), pp. 99–125

Zysk, Kenneth G., 'Animal Usage in the Sanskrit Traditions of Lovemaking, Lawful Conjugal Love, and Medicine', in *Penser, dire et représenter l'animal dans le monde indien*, ed. by Nalini Balbir and Georges-Jean Pinault (Paris: Champion, 2009), pp. 287–304

EVA WILDEN

The Trope of Sanskrit Origin in Premodern Tamil Literature

Introduction

A claim frequently expressed in Tamil literature, both poetic and theoretical, and even epigraphic, is that of a Sanskrit origin for a Tamil work. In many cases evidence can be brought forth that Tamil versions of Sanskrit texts existed or exist. In other cases, this is dubious, in other words, we are also dealing with a trope that pervades Tamil prefatory material and may be related to tropes about a lost or corrupted source text throughout the Sanskrit literary transmission. Of course, the phenomenon of multiple versions in the various Indian learned and vernacular languages is far more wide-ranging and does not only imply the relations between Sanskrit and Tamil. But even the influx of Sanskrit into Tamil is very much understudied and the methodological framework for describing it has as yet to be developed. Roughly we may distinguish three types of situation; firstly, the case that a Sanskrit school or tradition exists and that a freshly composed text in Tamil seeks affiliation (and thus participation in an already established authority). Secondly, narrative material wanders between the regions and the languages, in which case we have to think rather in terms of retelling and adaptation to various local genres. Thirdly, especially in the theoretical domains but also in the narrative realm there is evidence for particular, named source texts being brought into Tamil. Tamil authors do occasionally refer to what they do, when adopting Sanskrit sources, as an act of translation (*moḻippeyarppu*),[1] and in one of the verses quoted below from the grammatical tradition we even get a glimpse at a terminology of translation developed in the Sanskrit tradition that was adopted to Tamil (cf. below). But before actually finding out in which way the notion of translation applies in the creation of such parallel versions it seems useful to collect some of the widely scattered pertinent material.

1 Wilden, 'Translation and Transcultural Adaptation', pp. 93–110.

Eva Wilden is professor of Tamilistics and manuscriptology at the University of Hamburg. She was the PI of the ERC Advanced grant NETamil (Going from Hand to Hand: Networks of Intellectual Exchange in the Tamil Learned Traditions) jointly held by the Hamburg Centre for the Study of Manuscript Cultures and the Pondicherry centre of the École Française d'Extrême-Orient.

Narratives on Translation across Eurasia and Africa: From Babylonia to Colonial India, ed. by Sonja Brentjes in cooperation with Jens Høyrup and Bruce O'Brien, CAT 3, pp. 271–296 (Turnhout: Brepols, 2022) BREPOLS PUBLISHERS 10.1484/M.CAT-EB.5.127945

Indications of what I would like to call multilingual synergies are, on the one hand, found in titles, proper names, loanwords, and calques. On the other hand, the issue of predecessors and sources, even of translation, is often discussed in the prefatory material, in satellite stanzas such as those naming the authors or in the prefaces themselves. In brief, the situation is complicated because we have to keep apart three issues, namely the prolific theory about prefaces, the usages that can be observed in the surviving manuscripts and the conventions established in the early print tradition.

The first distinction is whether a preface is written by the author himself or by somebody else (a disciple, a friend, or a patron). This might or might not be discernible by the use of the first person (singular or plural). An author writing about himself or his text might give information useful to the understanding of the composition and its tradition, but he might also simply be fulfilling the claims of a poetic convention, for example by writing a 'submission to the assembly' (*avaiyaṭakkam*) where he denigrates himself for his meagre poetic capacities and his daring in producing the work nevertheless. The assembly (*avai*, from Skt. *sabhā-*) refers here to the social gathering of connoisseurs at a court or temple, or even a mere village common, the traditional place where poetic works were presented and discussed, possibly after having been commissioned — hence the sub-topos of having produced a work of poetry on demand. Another person writing about the author fulfils the convention of lauding him and his work, a task where verisimilitude and poetic hyperbole are not always well balanced. Both these types of verse are closely connected with the origin of the text and its first presentation. A satellite stanza, however, may serve as a mnemonic verse as part of the further transmission and in general have the purpose of preserving a minimum of information for the chain of transmitters.

Secondly, the preface material is fluid and not always identical in all the sources. Thirdly, in print part of the free-floating anonymous mnemonic stanzas, that in the manuscript tradition are found in colophons or in unnumbered folios at the beginning or end, are relocated as a preface.[2] Since for most texts the manuscript transmission has not been studied, the sources will be marked where in doubt. The three primary domains under scrutiny here will be grammar (*ilakkaṇam*), the longer poetic forms often referred to as epic (Skt. *mahākāvya-*, Tamil *peruṅkāppiyam*), and finally *purāṇam*, one of the genres taken over from Sanskrit which have developed a new regional meaning, in this case a sort of semi-mythological, semi-historiographical temple chronicle — what would in Sanskrit rather be called a *sthalapuraṇa*.

While already the earliest layer of transmitted Tamil literature, the *Caṅkam* ('Academy') corpus, going back roughly to the beginning of the Common Era, contains some 220 Indo-Aryan loanwords,[3] the growing influence of northern

2 For a more detailed discussion, see Wilden, 'Tamil Satellite Stanzas'.

3 According to my current counting of base forms (irrespective of the derivation variants),

narrative mythology from the late *Caṅkam* period onwards is mirrored in a growing number of loanwords and calques from Indo-Aryan. Epic episodes from the *Mahābhārata* and the *Rāmāyaṇa* are alluded to, and from the *Tēvāram*, the Śaiva devotional texts of the seventh century onwards, we find references to generic Sanskrit texts like *vētam* and *ākamam* (Skt. *vēda-* and *āgama-*). More specific titles are missing, however, and even the *Tirumantiram* ('Holy Mantra') remains vague with a section on the excellence of the Veda and the Āgama (*vētacciṟappu* and *ākamacciṟappu*). Also in the devotional Vaiṣṇava canon, the *Tivviyappirapantam* ('Heavenly Compositions'; sixth to tenth centuries), expertise in the Veda becomes a trope and this is continued into the court-poetic traditions (*kāppiyam*/*kāvya*) in the form of the ideal of blending Sanskrit and Tamil knowledge, ever recurrent in the praise of god, but also in the description of sages, scholars, and poets. One example from the *Kallāṭam*, a Śaivite court poem of perhaps the eleventh century, should suffice to illustrate the point:

> *kuṟu-muṉi tēṟa neṭu maṟai virittōy*
> *āṟu tiru eḻuttum kūṟu nilai kaṇṭu*
> *niṉ tāḷ pukaḻunar kaṇṇuḷ polintōy,*
> *maṇi-kāl aṟiñar perum kuṭi tōṉṟi*
> *iṟaiyōṉ poruṭku paraṇar mutal kēṭpa*
> *perum tamiḻ viritta arum tamiḻ pulavaṉum*
> *pāy pār aṟiya nīyē ātaliṉ*
>
> (*Kallāṭam*, *Vēlaṉ Vaṇakkam* 49–55; ed. by Mīṉāṭcicuntarampiḷḷai, p. 2)

> (You who expounded the long Vedas so that they were clear to the short sage, You who saw the allotted position of the six holy syllables [and] prospered in the eyes of those who praise your feet, because You are to be known on the extended earth as a scholar of rare Tamil who, appearing in a great family of people knowledgeable about gems, expounded the great Tamil, for Paraṇar and so forth to hear, of the lord's poetics)

Here the Tamil god Murukaṉ (identified with the Northern Skanda) is hailed as an expert in Vedic lore, in Śaiva mysticism (the mantra being *om namaḥ śivāya*), in gem lore (unclear what is the significance here) and in Tamil literature and poetics: the event alluded to is his intervention, in human form, in the learned academy in Madurai where he explained the *Iṟaiyaṉār Akapporuḷ*, an important treatise on poetics, to the scholars. The latter feat does not seem to conform to the most frequently told versions of this widely known

---

partly based on critical editions and manuscript evidence, partly on the existing indexes; for a list of Indo-Aryan words in the Caṅkam corpus and the *Cilappatikāram*, see Vaidyanathan, *Indo-Aryan Loanwords in Old Tamil*; for distribution, frequency and morphology in particular texts, see *Naṟṟiṇai*, ed. by Wilden; *Kuṟuntokai*, ed. by Wilden; and *Akanāṉūṟu Kaḷiṟṟiyāṉainirai*, ed. by Wilden.

story, just as here he seems to be made intermediary between his father Śiva and the 'short sage', Akattiyaṉ (Skt. Agastya), the Tamil ur-grammarian and all-round scholar.[4] My point is that the divine Tamil expert in the first place is also expected to be a Sanskrit expert.

Grammar

The first domain where Sanskrit influence is perceivable on a conceptual level is grammar (*ilakkaṇam*), a wider domain of actual grammar plus poetics and metrics, which includes the Sanskrit sub-disciplines of *vyākaraṇa* (grammar), *alaṅkāra* (poetics), and *candas* (metrics). From the earliest layers onwards, we find both loanwords and calques, and sometimes it is possible to observe conflicting strategies of simply using loans or of avoiding Sanskrit terminology with the help of more of less apt translation. A case in point is the *sūtra* that defines the term *kaḷavu* (the phase of secrecy which is a recurrent topic in love poetry). This is usually explained as a Tamil version of the Gandharva marriage (the type of marriage based on simple consent between the couple). In one treatise, the *Iṟaiyaṉār Akapporuḷ* already mentioned above, the word employed in the first *sūtra* is *kantaruvam*, a Tamil adaptation of Skt. *gandharva-*. The parallel *sūtra* 89 in the *Tolkāppiyam Poruḷatikāram* uses the circumscription *tuṟai amai nal yāḻt tuṇaimaiyōr*, 'the companions of the good lute who reside by the ghat', that is, heavenly musicians living close to the water, i.e. Gandharvas.

The famous laudatory preface (*ciṟappuppāyiram*) to the *Tolkāppiyam* contains one of the early direct references to Sanskrit influence in the domain of Tamil grammar, by asserting that the author studied *Aintiram*, the grammar related to Indra, one of the lesser schools of Sanskrit grammar whose source text is contested.[5]

The first substantial and verifiable claim of a Sanskrit source is attested in the eleventh century with the *Vīracōḻiyam*, a Buddhist grammatical work that tries to map Tamil on the system of Sanskrit grammar. While traditional Tamil poetics (*poruḷ*) is more concerned with poetic content and with metrics than with what we in the West would call rhetoric and figures of speech, it comes as no surprise that here the Tamil range of topics is extended to what in Sanskrit is called *Alaṅkāraśāstra*, the 'teachings in ornamentation'. In the beginning of the chapter on poetics, called the *alaṅkārap paṭalam*, Daṇḍin is explicitly mentioned as a source for this chapter. In fact, Daṇḍin's *Kāvyādarśa* (Mirror of Poetry) has become a source text for regional adaptations in quite a number of Indian vernacular languages, including Tamil, Tibetan, and

---

4 For an extensive discussion of these academy stories, see Wilden, *Manuscript, Print and Memory*, pp. 216–95; for the stories on Akattiyaṉ, see Chevillard, 'The Pantheon of Tamil Grammarians', pp. 243–68.

5 Burnell, *On the Aindra school of Sanskrit Grammarians*, p. 8 et passim.

Simhala; the analysis of the extended tradition in all its regional ramifications is a comparatively recent subject of study.[6]

The verse in question is *Vīracōḻiyam* 143 and part of the treatise itself, not a satellite stanza as is the more frequent case with this type of information, as shall be shown in what follows:

urai uṭal āka uyir poruḷ āka uraitta vaṇṇam
nirai niṟam ā naṭaiyē celav' ā niṉṟa ceyyuṭkaḷ ām
tarai mali māṉiṭar tam ***alaṅkāraṅkaḷ taṇṭi coṉṉa***
karai mali nūliṉ paṭiyē *uraippaṉ kaṉafkuḻaiyē!*

(*Vīracōḻiyam* 143, ed. by Tāmōtarampiḷḷai, p. 138)

(I shall expound, oh lady with heavy earrings, in the very manner of the treatise that spreads to the [other] shore [of knowledge] which Daṇḍin uttered on the ornaments of the human beings, abundant on earth, that are poems in which words stand as [their] body, meaning as [their] soul, the series of alliterative patterns as [their] complexion, style/[rhythmic] motion as [their] walk.)

The verse is based on a well-known metaphor of a poem perceived as a beautiful woman wearing ornaments. The part of interest here is just the brief phrase *alaṅkāraṅkaḷ taṇṭi coṉṉa karai mali nūliṉ paṭiyē*, that is, the author here will continue to describe the poetic ornaments (*alaṅkāras* = figures of speech) in a way that corresponds to the comprehensive treatise of the Sanskrit poet Daṇḍin in his *Kāvyādarśa*. The wording does not suggest an act of translation but rather an adaptation.[7] A closer parallelism is found with the *Taṇṭilalaṅkāram* ('[treatise on] ornamentation of Taṇṭi (~ Skt. Daṇḍin)'; twelfth century?), named after the author of the original Sanskrit work. Moreover, there we find one of those free-floating stanzas mentioned above, missing in many editions but printed as a 'laudatory preface' (*ciṟappuppāyiram*) or quoted in the editor's introduction:[8]

(vaṭa ticai iruntu teṉ malaikk' ēki
mati tavaḻ kuṭumip potiya māl varai
irum tavaṉ taṉ-pāl arum tamiḻ uṇarnta

6 For example, Monius, 'The Many Lives of Daṇḍin'; a long-term project started by David Shulman presented its output in a conference in December 2015, entitled 'A Lasting Vision: Dandin's Mirror in the World of Asian Letters'.

7 For a more detailed discussion, see Chevillard, 'The Pantheon of Tamil Grammarians'.

8 In the Tamil print tradition, a satellite stanza can either be made part of the text transmission itself, in which case it is put in the beginning as a *ciṟappuppāyiram*, or its independent character is preserved in not adding it to the text but just quoting it as anonymous source in the introduction. The former is usually done with author verses, the latter with the verses higher up in the level of abstraction such as verses enumerating the works belonging to a corpus (such as the *Caṅkam* corpus) or the structure of a particular text (Wilden, 'Tamil Satellite Stanzas', pp. 172–73).

paṉṉiru pulavariṉ muṉṉavaṉ pakarnta
tolkāppiyam neṟi palkāppiyattum
***aṇi peṟum ilakkaṇam** aritiṉiṉ terintu*
vaṭa nūl vaḻi muṟai marapiṉiṉ vaḻāat'
īr-iraṇṭ' ellaiyiṉ ikavā mummaip
pārata ~ilakkaṇam paṇṭitar taḻīit
*tiruntiya maṇi muṭic **cempiyaṉ avaiyatt'***
arum poruḷ yāppiṉ amaiv' uṟa vakuttaṉaṉ
nāṭaka maṉṟattu nāṭakam naviṟṟum
vaṭa nūl uṇarnta tamiḻ nūl pulavaṉ
*pū viri taṇ poḻil **kāviri nāṭṭu***
*vamp' aviḻ teriyal **ampikāpati***
mēvarum tavattiṉ il payanta
*tā arum cīrttit **taṇṭi** eṉpavaṉē.*[9]

(*Taṇṭiyalaṅkāram, ciṟappuppāyiram*, ed. by T. Vē. Kōpālaiyar, p. 14)

After having understood with difficulty **the grammar that pertains to poetic figures** of all the *Palkāppiyam*, on the path of the *Tolkāppiyam* that was composed by the first of twelve scholars that had understood difficult Tamil from the great ascetic on the vast Poti mountain of him in whose top the moon crawls after going from the northern direction to the southern mountain, **without swerving from the custom, sequence [and] way of the northern (~ Sanskrit) treatise**, without transgressing the twice two boundaries, in a metrically suitable way he assigned difficult meaning in **the assembly of Cempiyaṉ**, with a jewel crown, that was perfect in encompassing scholars of Indian grammar threefold, – the one who is called **Taṇṭi**, of a fame difficult to generate, brought forth by the house of a penance that is befitting for **Ampikāpati** with a wreath on which new [flowers] open, in **the land of the Kāviri** with flower-spread cool groves, **of a scholar of the Tamil treatises who had understood the northern (~ Sanskrit) treatises**, having also proclaimed a drama in the drama hall.)

This verse, while avoiding precise information as to what was done with the source text, is nevertheless clear about the origin in that the Tamil author 'did not swerve from the custom, sequence [and] way of the northern (~ Sanskrit) treatise' (*vaṭa nūl vaḻi muṟai marapiṉiṉ vaḻāatu*). He also 'had understood with difficulty the grammar that pertains to poetic figures | of all the *Palkāppiyam*' (*palkāppiyattum | aṇi peṟum ilakkaṇam aritiṉiṉ terintu*), in other words, he had

9 The text quoted and translated here follows the print version — as is the case with all the material discussed in this article — but the verse is also found in at least one manuscript (Tañcāvūr MSSML 631), with textual deviations so significant that they deserve a discussion in a special paper that will make, first of all, the point that it is not possible to work on this kind of paratextual material only on the basis of printed texts.

integrated both the Sanskrit and the Tamil tradition into a single work. The word employed to refer to 'poetic figures' in the translation, is *aṇi*, the Tamil calque of Skt. *alaṅkāra-*, both literally meaning 'decoration'. It also informs us that the *Palkāppiyam* (a lost text!) follows the highest credentials of the Tamil grammatical tradition, namely the *Tolkāppiyam* (whose laudatory preface was discussed above) and, yet again, the Tamil ur-grammarian Akattiyaṉ (here referred to as the ascetic of the Poti mountain, whose twelve disciples are the alleged authors of the *Palkāppiyam*). The Tamil author is credited with having presented his text in the learned assembly of the Cōḻa king Cempiyaṉ (one of the Cōḻa titles)[10] that comprised scholars of 'Indian grammar' (*pārata ilakkaṇam*), presumably a reference to the grammatical works of more than one Indian language (both Sanskrit and Tamil are mentioned). Accordingly, he is called a scholar of Tamil grammatical theory who has also mastered Sanskrit theory (*vaṭa nūl uṇarnta tamiḻ nūl pulavaṉ*). He is supposed to have also presented a drama (lost). The verse culminates, as is customary, with his birth place, here remaining vague as the land of the Kāviri, that is, the Cōḻa land, the name of his father, Ampikāpati,[11] and his own name, Taṇṭi. This name, Taṇṭi, is easily recognizable as the Tamil form of Daṇḍin, the Sanskrit author. In the present context, it need not be discussed whether this name is an argument to discount the whole verse as spurious or whether it should be seen just as a case of a Tamil author's actual name being replaced by an allusion to one of his major achievements, in this case, the fact that he translated Daṇḍin's work into Tamil.

In about the sixteenth century, there is one more text bearing the title *alaṅkāram* in Tamil with the *Māṟaṉalaṅkāram* ([treatise on] ornamentation of Māṟaṉ), a continuation of the Vaiṣṇava poetic tradition that started with the *Māṟaṉakapporuḷ* (Love Poetics of Māṟaṉ) of Perumāḷ Kavirāyaṉ from Tirukkurukai, a treatise of poetic themes in love poetry in the line of the *Iṟaiyaṉār Akapporuḷ* and *Nampiyakapporuḷ* (Nampi's Love Poetics; twelfth century), to which the *Alaṅkāram* adds the part on poetic figures. In its laudatory preface (l. 11) it still claims to be in the tradition of Daṇḍin, though whether this refers to the Sanskrit *Kāvyādarśa* or just the Tamil *Taṇṭiyalaṅkāram* is debatable:

mutumoḻit teṇṭi mutaṉūl aṇiyōṭum
putu moḻip pulavar puṇarttiya aṇiyaiyum
taṉātu nuṇ uṇarvāl taru pala aṇiyaiyum
maṉāt' uṟat tokuttum vakuttum virittum

10 This Cōḻa king is generally identified with Aṉapayaṉ Kulōttuṅkaṉ II (ruling from 1133–1150 CE).

11 The name of his father as mentioned in this verse links up with the set of literary legends around the poet Kampaṉ, author of the *Kamparāmāyaṇam*. As the son of Kampaṉ and court poet of the Cōḻa, so a romantic story goes, Ampikāpati would have fallen in love with a Cōḻa princess, been caught in her quarters and excuted, declenching a series of retaliations between the king and Kampaṉ.

potuviyal poruḷ col aṇi eccaviyal eṉac
catur peṟa iraṇṭ' iṭam taḻīiya cārp' eṉal āyk
kāri tant' aruḷ kalaik kaṭal iyal peyar puṉaint'
āriyar tuvaṉṟa avaik kaḷatt' uraittaṉaṉ

(*Māṟaṉ Alaṅkāram, ciṟappuppāyiram*, ed. by T.Vē. Kōpālaiyar, pp. 2 f.)

> (bringing together, dividing and expanding so as to be taken in by the mind, **with the poetic figures (*aṇi*) from the primary treatise of Teṇṭi** with ancient wisdom **the poetic figures (*aṇi*) brought together by scholars in new words and the many poetic figures (*aṇi*) given by his own subtle perception as a tertiary treatise (*cārpu*)** that encompasses two sections so as to obtain four [chapters], namely Potuviyal, Poruḷ- and Col- Aṇi[viyal and] Eccaviyal, he decorated [it] with natural words from the ocean of arts graciously given by Kāri [and] taught [it] in the assembly full of Āriyars ...)

Here the poetic figures are referred to with the Tamil calque of Skt. *alaṅkāra-*, which is *aṇi*. Without wishing to enter a full discussion of this passage redolent with grammatical erudition, here the choice of words might suggest that Teṇṭi, a colloquial version of Taṇṭi, which goes back to Skt. Daṇḍin, does not just refer to the author of the *Taṇṭiyalaṅkāram* but to the Sanskrit author: among the types of treatises (*nūl*) defined in the Tamil grammatical tradition[12] a *mutal nūl* is the primary treatise that starts a tradition, a *vaḻi nūl* is a secondary treatise that follows in its wake, one way of doing so being translation (*moḻippeyarppu*). Since the word *vaḻi nūl* is not used here, but the word *mutal nūl* is, we would have to assume either that Daṇḍin is meant, or that the origin by translation of the *Taṇṭiyalaṅkāram* has been forgotten meanwhile (which cannot be excluded in those troubled times). However, there is an intermediate step between the *mutal nūl*, namely the 'poetic figures brought together by scholars in new words', and the contribution of Perumāḷ Kavirāyaṉ, the author of the *Māṟaṉalaṅkāram* ('the many poetic figures given by his own subtle perception'). This makes the latter a tertiary treatise, a *cārpu nūl*, as is affirmed in line 16. The implication might be that the primary treatise alluded to is the *Kāvyādarśa*, the unnamed secondary treatise the *Taṇṭiyalaṅkāram*, and the tertiary treatise the *Māṟaṉalaṅkāram*, one possible way of avoiding the issue of translation.

Much more explicit is, in the seventeenth century, the *Pirayōkavivēkam*. Some five to six centuries after the *Vīracōḻiyam* quoted above, it is the second Tamil grammatical treatise to strongly affiliate Tamil with the Sanskrit tradition. The very title is an adaptation from Sanskrit, meaning perhaps an

12 For example, Nakkīraṉ on *Iṟaiyaṉār Akapporuḷ*, 1, pp. 14–16, *Tolkāppiyam Poruḷatikāram Iḷampūraṇam, Marapiyal*, 639–42, pp. 574–75 and *Naṉṉūl*, 4–6, pp. 8.11; the chronological order among these texts is far from established.

'Investigation of [Linguistic] Usage'. The preface, according to the editor by the author Cuppiramaṇiya Tīṭcitar himself, pays obeisance not only to lord Śiva and to Pārvati (alias Sarasvatī) but also to the illustrious triad of Sanskrit grammarians, Pāṇini, Katyāyana, and Patañjali:

1. *ta<u>r</u>ci<u>r</u>appuppāyiram*
nīr koṇṭa ce<u>n</u>ni makēccura<u>n</u> ***pāṇi<u>n</u>i*** *nīḷ kaṭal cū<u>l</u>*
pār koṇṭa kīrtti ***vararuci*** *ñā<u>n</u>a* ***patañcali*** *pūm*
tār koṇṭa vā<u>n</u>avar kō<u>n</u> pārati ivar tāḷ vaṇaṅki
ēr koṇṭa col pirayōkavivēkam iyampuva<u>n</u>ē.

(*Pirayōkavivēkam*, ed. by T. Vē. Kōpālaiyar, p. 1)

> (Mahesvara whose head receives the water [of the Gaṅgā], **Pāṇi<u>n</u>i**, **Vararuci** whose fame took the earth surrounded by the large ocean, knowledgeable **Patañcali**, Pārati, king of the celestials with a flower garland, having bowed at the feet of these I shall proclaim the *Pirayōkavivēkam* in beautiful words.)

Even more interesting in the current context is the stanza that follows, headed by the editor with 'authority of the teachers', since it contains some evidence on how the Sanskrit sources were used for their transfer into Tamil:

2. *āciriyari<u>n</u> mē<u>r</u>kōḷ*
po<u>r</u>p' amar teyva-mo<u>l</u>ip pākupāṭum pot' e<u>l</u>utt' āyp
pal-pala ākit tirivatum cā<u>rr</u>i<u>n</u>ar paṇṭ' uṇarntōr
mu<u>n</u> pakar nūluḷ ci<u>r</u>upā<u>n</u>mai pērkku mo<u>l</u>ipeyarttām
ta<u>r</u>pavam ta<u>r</u>camamē perumpā<u>n</u>maiyum cā<u>rr</u>i<u>n</u>amē.

(*Pirayōkavivēkam*, ed. by T. Vē. Kōpālaiyar, p. 8)

> (The earlier scholars have proclaimed the subdivisions of the elegant Sanskrit language, there being common letters, and the deviations, there being many, many [of them]. We have translated from the treatise taught before for nouns [that are] in a minority. We have proclaimed *tatsama*-s and *tadbhava*-s for a majority.)

Here the author employs the word for translating (*mo<u>l</u>ipeyarttal*) when referring, presumably, to the technique of bringing over nouns for Sanskrit technical terms, stating that in a minority of cases he translated, preferring, however to use Tamil equivalents that either did not need changes of letters (for the voiced consonants and aspirates that are missing in the Tamil alphabet) or equivalents that needed such changes. Examples for the latter we see in the verse itself with *ta<u>r</u>pavam* for Skt. *tadbhāva-* and *ta<u>r</u>camam* for Skt. *tatsama-*. This appears to be a simple phonetician's point of view, without apparent ideological implications. How such processes took place in detail obviously is a question not to be answered without a full analysis of the treatise.

Epic (peruṅkāppiyam/mahākāvya)

The second domain where Sanskrit influence is tangible, though in a manner very different from that of grammar, are the long narrative poems that are called *mahākāvya-* (large poetry) in Sanskrit, half translated and half adapted into Tamil with *perum* ('large') plus *kāppiyam* for *kāvya-*, but mostly referred to as 'epic' in the West. The tradition starts in Tamil perhaps in the early sixth century with the *Cilappatikāram* (Story of the Anklet), followed by what often is known as its twin, the *Maṇimēkalai* (Jewel Belt) which tells the story of the daughter of one of the *Cilappatikāram*'s protagonists. Both of the two early poems have connections to the North via their religious affiliation, the former Jain, like the majority of Tamil narrative poems, the latter Buddhist. Both have their share of loanwords, especially the *Maṇimēkalai* whose last canto is notorious for discussing Buddhist doctrine, but the story lines are apparently Tamil, as are the names of the protagonists. The satellite stanzas, still moderate in number, do not make any allusion to sources or predecessors.

A second set, made up of the majority of Tamil epics before or around the turn of the millennium have titles that are translated or calqued from Sanskrit, and the heroes, heroines, and places bear names of a similar kind. For the following two, the *Cīvaka Cintāmaṇi* (Thought Jewel; ninth century) and the *Nīlakēci* (tenth century), both Jain in outlook, no actual northern parallels or possible sources are known although the protagonists, to give just these two examples, are named, respectively, Cīvakaṉ (~ Skt. *jīvaka-*, 'soul') and Nīlakēci (~ Skt. *nīla-* + *kēśinī-*, 'she with blue hair'). No allusions to any source text are found in the *Cintāmaṇi*, but the *Nīlakēci* comes with a 'submission to the assembly' (*avaiyaṭakkam*) — one of the standard sets of satellite stanzas to be expected with the longer poetic forms from the *Cintāmaṇi* onwards — that suggests if not a Sanskrit original, then northern predecessors for the discussion of doctrine (ranking high on the agenda of this poem) which are called 'Āgama':

3. *avaiyaṭakkam*
paṇṭ' ākamattuḷ payilā urai eṉṟu mikkār
viṇṭ' īṅk' itaṉai vekuḷār viṭal vēṇṭuvaṉ yāṉ
taṇ tāmarai mēḷ naṭantāṉ taṭam tāḷ vaṇaṅkik
kaṇṭēṉ kiṭantēṉ kaṉaviṉ itu kaṇṭa-v-āṟē.

(*Nīlakēci, avaiyaṭakkam*, ed. by Pō. Vē. Cōmacuntaraṉār, p. 15)

(Being at variance with those who are excellent, saying '[these] words have not been uttered in the old Āgamas', I must let go of those who do not dislike this [book] here. Bowing to the large feet of him who walked on a cool lotus I have seen this [book] when I was lying, by the way of seeing it in a dream.)

Here the point seems to be an excuse, as befits the stanza's expected tenor of humility, for the fact that the work presented is not in line with earlier teaching on the same subject matter. The reason added in the second half may sound fanciful at first, but a dream, in the given cultural context, has to be seen as an equivalent to divine inspiration. Whether or not the earlier Āgamas might have been composed in Sanskrit or Tamil appears to be of no concern to the author.

With two further texts we have further indications that they base their narration on material taken over from Sanskrit or Prakrit, either because parallel versions in other languages still exist or because there is an explicit reference. In the case of the *Peruṅkatai* (seventh century?) we know that it retells portions of the stories belonging to the 'great story', the *Bṛhatkathā*, although no paratextual material elucidates the background, either because the custom of such reference was not yet well established or because the beginning and the end of the Tamil text have been lost.[13]

The *Cūḷāmaṇi* (Crest Jewel) in about the tenth century, then, is the first text to come with a stanza that refers back to a source, if in a slightly allusive way. Verse 3 and 4 of the prefatory verses, the 'submission to the assembly' and its sequel specifying the assembly where the text was first presented, stress the fact that this version was composed in Tamil:

3. *avaiyaṭakkam*
koṟṟam kōṉ nēmi neṭumāl kuṇam kūṟa ippāl
uṟṟ' iṅk' or kātal kiḷarat tamiḻ nūṟkal uṟṟēṉ.
maṟṟ' iṅk' or kuṟṟam varum āyiṉum naṅkaḷ pōlvār
aṟṟaṅkaḷ kāppār aṟiviṉ periyārkaḷ aṉṟē.

(*Cūḷāmaṇi*, ed. by Cāminātaiyar, p. 4)

> (So as to speak hereafter of the qualities of Neṭumāl with a discus, victorious king, I have undertaken to string Tamil, so that [my] unique love here may emerge. Again, even if here comes a mistake, people great in knowledge will take guard against the failings of the like of us, isn't it?)

Verse 6, the 'way the text has come [down to us]', however, mentions the Sanskrit source, generally identified as the Jaina *Mahāpurāṇa* (dated to the late ninth century):

6. *nūl vanta vaḻi*
viñcaikk' iṟaivaṉ virai cūḻ muṭi vēntaṉ maṅkai
pañcikk' aṉuṅkum cilamp' ār aṭip pāvai pū ār
vañcik koṭi pōlpavaḷ kāraṇam āka vanta
cem col purāṇatt' uraiyiṉ vaḻic cēṟum aṉṟē.

(*Cūḷāmaṇi*, ed. by Cāminātaiyar, p. 6)

---

13 For an analysis of the story and its relations to the surviving parallel versions, see Vijayalakshmy, *A Study of the Peruṅkatai*, pp. 56–155.

(We will join, won't we?, the path of the words of the *Purāṇam* with refined words that came, the reason being her like a mahua creeper full of flowers, the girl whose feet wear anklets muffled with cotton, the woman of the king whose crown is surrounded with fragrance, the lord of knowledge.)

Here the bigger part of the stanza is devoted to an allusive description of the poem's heroine, but in the last line (in Tamil) the author in a royal 'we' states his intention to follow the 'path of words', that is, the tradition and story line of an untitled Purāṇa that is, however, endowed with an attribute otherwise reserved for Tamil, as in *cen-tamiḻ*, 'refined Tamil'. Translation is not an issue.

The matter becomes clearer with the famous Indian epics, the *Mahābhārata* and the *Rāmāyaṇa*. The earliest epigraphic reference is found in a Pāṇṭiya copperplate of the early tenth century:

mahābhāratan tamiḻp paṭuttum madhurāpuric caṅkam vaittum

(*Inscriptions of the Early Pāṇḍyas (c. 300 B.C. to 984 A.D.)*, ed. by Krishnan, p. 96)

(having the *Mahābhārata* brought into Tamil and establishing the academy (*caṅkam*) in Maturai)

Here the inscription clearly mentions among the deeds of the current Pāṇṭiya's unnamed ancestors the foundation of the famous Maturai academy and the translation of the *Mahābhārata* into Tamil and from Sanskrit, as the title with its grantha letters for the voiced aspirate *bh* suggests. Evidence to support the claim made in this much-discussed passage is scant but available. Apart from the name of a poet who composed the invocation stanzas for five of the 'Eight Anthologies' (*Eṭṭuttokai*), Pāratam pāṭiya Peruntēvaṉār ('Peruntāvaṉār who sang the [Makā]pāratam') there is a number of quotations from a lost text entitled *Pāratam* that is quoted in Nacciṉārkkiṉiyar's commentary on the *Tolkāppiyam Poruḷatikāram* (the famous fourteenth-century commentary on the poetics portion of the oldest grammatical treatise), already brought together by S. Kiruṣṇasāmi Aiyaṅkār in his 1925 edition of the *Pāratavenpā*. The latter is another early version of the epic in Tamil, fragmentary with a mere 800 stanzas, but associated with the Pallavas (third to ninth century), not with the Pāṇṭiyas (sixth to tenth century).

There is another big version in Tamil, but in chronological order another epic comes first, and that is, in about the twelfth century, the *Irāmāyaṇam* by Kampaṉ, the monumental Tamil adaptation of Valkmīki's *Rāmāyaṇa*. This is not the place to discuss further possible sources; what is of interest here is that the preface (*ciṟappuppāyiram*) contains exactly the type of stanza we are looking for. With all the lengthy texts of the second millennium (and even with a number of less voluminous ones) the preface with a plethora of subcategories for verses has become an important institution.[14]

14 How many of these verses actually occur in all the manuscripts of a particular tradition is an

Verse 10 deals with the history of transmission for the work:

10. *nūlvaralāṟu*
tēva-pāṭaiyiṉ ik katai ceytavar
mūvar āṉavar tammuḷum muntiya
nāviṉāṉ uraiyiṉ paṭi nāṉ tamiḻp
pāviṉāl it' uṇarttiya paṇp' arō.

(*Kamparāmāyaṇam*, ed. by Cuppiramaṇyaṉ, p. 17)

(In the manner of the words by the poet (Valmīki) who is foremost among those that have become the Three[15] who have made this story in the language of the gods (Sanskrit) this is the one brought to notice by me in Tamil verses.)

So here Kampaṉ, if we want to believe him to be the author of the stanza, evokes as his predecessor the Sanskrit author Valmīki along with the mythological tellers of the story, Lava and Kuśa. The issue at stake here is probably not so much translation as affiliation: the goal of retelling a story is still different from the demands of a theoretical domain like grammar where technical terms have a bearing on what one is trying to say. It is stressed, however, that this version is not in the 'language of the gods', i.e., Sanskrit but in Tamil. This is the earliest occasion for the use of the Tamil loan *tēva-pāṭai* I could locate for Skt. *deva-bhāṣā*, not a compound as yet of wide currency in the North either.

The topos of changing language when retelling the story develops into a standard constituent of prefatory verses throughout the second millennium and we find it again with the great Tamil version of the *Mahābhārata*, in the early fifteenth century. The *Villipputtūr Pāratam* devotes two verses, one a 'submission to the assembly', the other a 'reason for composing the song', to the language issue:

1.7 *avaiyaṭakkam*
muṉ col ākiya col elām muḻut' uṇar muṉivaṉ
taṉ col ākiya māp peruṅkāppiyam taṉṉait
teṉ colāl uraiceytaliṉ, ceḻum cuvai illāt
puṉ col āyiṉum, poṟutt' aruḷ purivarē, pulavōr.

(*Makāpāratam, Viḷḷiputtūrāḻvār iyaṟṟiya*, 1, ed. by Kōpālakiruṣṇam, p. 5)

(Because of [my] speaking with Southern words the great *Mahākāvya* that existed in the words of the sage who perceived the whole of the words that were the words before, even if they be low words without rich taste, will they indulge [and] be gracious, the scholars?)

open question. Judging from the few texts where an investigation along those lines is at least on the way, such as the *Tirumurukāṟṟuppaṭai*, a certain number is more or less ubiquitous while others tend to be more fluid or even restricted to a single manuscript (cf. Francis, 'Supplementing Poetry and Devotion', forthcoming).

15 Kuśa, Lava, and Valmīki.

Here the author of the *Mahābhārata*, Vyāsa, is alluded to as 'sage', and the epic is not perceived as an *itihāsa* — what would correspond roughly to 'epic' but as a 'major poem' (*peruṅkāppiyam* in Tamil, for the Skt. poetological term *mahākāvya-*), bringing it into a context of court literature on a par with the environment where he worked, namely the minor court of Vakkapākai. This stanza sadly becomes a bit insipid in English because it is impossible to emulate the rhyme word *col* (word) repeated five times. The author plays on the standard designation of Sanskrit as *vaṭa moḻi*, 'the northern language', by referring to his native Tamil as *teṉ col*, 'Southern word'.

The following verse hints at the labour share between Sanskrit and Tamil and at the reasons for producing a Tamil version:

1.8 pāṭaluṟṟa kāraṇam
muṉṉum mā maṟai muṉivarum, tēvarum, piṟarum
paṉṉum mā moḻip pāratap perumaiyum pārēṉ
maṉṉum mātavaṉ caritamum iṭai iṭai vaḻaṅkum
eṉṉum ācaiyāl, yāṉum ītu iyamputaṟku icaintēṉ.

(*Makāpāratam, Viḷḷiputtūrāḻvār iyaṟṟiya*, ed. by Kōpālakiruṣṇam, p. 6)

> (I who did not see the greatness of the *Pāratam* in the great words spoken by great Vedic sages, gods and others in the past, I too made this harmonious so as to sound [musically], out of longing that the life story of lasting Mādava may wander from place to place.)

Here it is not perfectly clear why the author would not have been able to see the 'greatness' of the Sanskrit *Mahābhārata*, but I believe the point is made in the second half of the stanza: while the Sanskrit version is made by sages and gods, to be enjoyed by those who speak the language of the gods, the Tamil version and its beauties are of immediate access to the author himself as to his audience: thus, the great story can survive and spread even further.

Śaiva Cycles and purāṇam-s

By far the most fertile domain, both for satellite stanzas in general and for the mention of Sanskrit predecessors, are the Śaiva narrative cycles that go under the heading of a *purāṇam*, for the most part of the type that would in Sanskrit be called a *sthalapurāṇa*, that is, a town- or temple chronicle that freely mixes mythological, legendary and historical events and persons, and we can do no more here than just outline the tip of the iceberg. The first text to go under such a title is not yet of that kind; Cēkkiḻār's *Tiruttoṇṭar-* or *Periyapūraṇam*, of the twelfth century, tells the life stories of the sixty-three *nāyaṉmār*, the Śaiva saints, and it does so without reference to any Sanskrit source, which would indeed have been surprising with these proverbially Southern stories.

None of the texts to follow have been translated as yet, although the Maturai stories centred on the sixty-four games lord Śiva has with the mortals of the Pāṇṭiya country have received some attention lately.[16] This cycle comes in an as yet uncounted number of versions in at least three languages (Tamil, Sanskrit, Telugu) that create a web of intertextual relationship including, besides retelling, reformulating, and bringing into a different genre, several acts of translation. Undisputedly the oldest complete version (containing all the sixty-four episodes) is the fourteenth-century *Tiruviḷaiyāṭaṟpurāṇam* by Perumpaṟṟappuliyūr Nampi. In the complicated setup of prefatory material, the structure (and growth) of which awaits analysis, the topic of Sanskrit sources and Tamil rendering appears several times. The first occurrence is in one of the invocation stanzas, this one to Vināyakar, i.e. Gaṇeśa, and it simply mentions the fact that a Sanskrit story was retold in Tamil verse:[17]

> *kaṭavuḷ vāḻttu 17 Vināyakar*
> *kuṟaiv' aṟa vaṭa col collum katait tamiḻk kottiṉālē*
> *niṟaiv' uṟa naṭattutaṟku nīḷ paṉait taṭak kai veṟṟic*
> *ciṟu patap peru vayiṟṟuc cekkar mukkaṇ kaḷiṟṟai*
> *uṟav' uṟa itaya-kūṭatt' uriya pācattāl cērppām.*
>
> (*Cellinakarp Perumpaṟṟappuliyūr Nampi iyaṟṟiyatu Tiruviḷaiyāṭaṟpurāṇam*, ed. by Cāminātaiyar, p. 6)

> (In order to set in motion, so as to be complete, in a collection of Tamil [verses] the story that was spoken in faultless northern words, we join, out of attachment befitting to the heart temple, so as to experience it, the Bull elephant with three red eyes, a big belly, small feet, victorious, with a broad trunk [like] a long Palmyra tree.)

So here the author, true to convention, invokes the help of the elephant-headed god in order to turn his task to good, namely to retell the story that was told in Northern words (*vaṭa col*) now in Tamil. The word for story is *katai*, the Tamil adaptation of Sanskrit *kathā*, often used in the context of our verses (see above for the *Ramāyaṇam*) to denote not a literary genre but indeed a narrative content, as in English 'story'. The Tamil version is specified with a less frequent word, *kottu*, that might simply designate a collection [of verses].[18]

---

16 For example, Wilden, *Manuscript, Print and Memory*, pp. 247–74; Fisher, *Hindu Pluralism*, pp. 137–82.

17 The following numbering follows the 1972 reprint of U. Vē. Cāminātaiyar's edition (Cāminātaiyar, *Śrī Mīṉāṭcicuntaram Piḷḷai avarkaḷ carittiraccurukkam*).

18 It has to be derived from the verb *kottutal*, 'to chop, to carve', and U. Vē. Cāminātaiyar gives two alternative glosses in his commentary on difficult/rare words (*arumpatavurai*), namely either *tamiḻc ceyyuṭkaḷiṉ tokuti* or *tamiḻ nūlkaḷiṉ tokuti*, that is, presumably, a 'collection of Tamil verse' or a 'collection of Tamil theoretical aphorisms'.

The next instance is found in the second 'submission to the assembly':

> *avaiyaṭakkam 2*
> *avai-naṭu ōṅkum teyva akattiyaṉ muṉṉam coṉṉa*
> *kavi poti kataiyai yāṉum tamiḻ ceyvēṉ eṉ kai kāṇiṉ*
> *puvi-micai vicumpiṉ nīṭum porupp' iṭai muṭavaṉ ēṟic*
> *cuvai-taru tēṉai uṇṇa eṇṇuvāṉ tuṇital pōlum.*

(*Cellinakarp Perumpaṟṟappuliyūr Nampi iyaṟṟiyatu Tiruviḷaiyāṭaṟpurāṇam*, ed. by Cāminātaiyar, p. 8)

> (In the assembly, when they see in the hand of me, who has made it in Tamil, the story that is a treasure of a poem spoken first by the high divine Akattiyaṉ, it will on earth be like a lame man venturing to climb a mountain that reaches up to the sky who counts on eating tasty honey.)

Here it is difficult to tell whether the tone of humility is simply due to the genre conventions or whether it conveys some real feeling of being daunted by the task, and then it still would not be clear whether the point is bringing the story from Sanskrit into Tamil or following in the path of a figure like Akattiyaṉ, the Vedic seer and Tamil ur-grammarian (already referred to in the *Kallāṭam* verse cited at the end of the introduction).

The often-cited verse is the following one, which for some unexplained reason is not part of the preface but is imbedded into the first chapter:

> 1.35 *ōt' ariya uttara-māpurāṇam taṉṉuḷ uṇmai taru cāracamuccayattu muṉṉa*
> *mētaku nal katai viriviṉ kaṇṭ' eṉakku viyāta vāṉmīki eccaṉ coṉṉa eṇ eṇ*
> *tīt' il viḷaiyāṭalkaḷiṉ piṟaṅkum intat tiruviḷaiyāṭaliṉ parappai curukki iṉṟu*
> *pōtam uṟa numakk' uraittēṉ yāṉum cokkaṉ pukaḻiṉai yār karai kaṇṭu pukaḻuvārē.*

(*Cellinakarp Perumpaṟṟappuliyūr Nampi iyaṟṟiyatu Tiruviḷaiyāṭaṟpurāṇam*, ed. by Cāminātaiyar, p. 29)

> (Today I am telling you, for [your] enjoyment, after having compressed [its] extent, this sport that is redolent with the flawless eight [times] eight sports related to me by the deity of Vyāsa [and] Valmīki, after seeing in detail the good story, eminent with the intention of the **Sārasamuccaya**, that gives the essence in the **highest Mahāpurāṇa** difficult to recite. Who are those that praise the fame of Cokkaṉ to the full?[19])

Here, with the reference to the Sanskrit authors of the *Mahābhārata* and the *Rāmāyaṇa*, the *Tiruviḷaiyāṭaṟpurāṇam* is grafted on the great epic tradition, but what started the debate was the mention of a direct Sanskrit predecessor, which in re-sanskritized form would have been the *Sārasammuccaya*, it in turn

19 *karai-kaṇṭu*: literally 'after having seen [the other] shore [of this ocean of fame]'.

a condensation of the *Uttaramahāpurāṇa*. Neither is available, and since both names do not look like actual titles but more like generic terms for genres of literature, I would argue that here we are dealing with a trope: just like the other two epics mentioned were first told in Sanskrit and then also brought into Tamil, the *Tiruviḷaiyāṭaṟpurāṇam* follows in their wake.[20]

Arguably the next version is, perhaps in about the fifteenth century, but definitely before the seventeenth one, the *Hālāsyamāhātmya*, a Sanskrit adaptation without satellite stanzas in the one available edition,[21] which in turn became the source for the second great Tamil version of the seventeenth century, Parañcōti's *Tiruviḷaiyāṭāṟpurāṇam*.[22] In the preface (*pāyiram*) of Āṟumukanāvalar's 1912 edition of this well-ordered text, there is a sequence of three stanzas (*pāyiram* 23–25) which are in turn entitled by the editor as 'the origin of the primary text', 'the reason for producing [this version of] the text', and 'the result of translating':

23. *mutaṟnūlvaḻi*
aṇṇal-pāl teḷinta nanti aṭikaḷ-pāl caṉaṟkumāraṉ
uḷ niṟai aṉpiṉ āyntu viyātaṉukk' uṇartta vantap
puṇṇiya muṉivaṉ cūtaṟk' ōtiya purāṇam mū āṟu
eṇṇiya ivaṟṟuḷ kāntatt' īca caṅkitaiyiṉ mātō.

(*Cuttacaivarākiya Parañcōtimuṉivar moḻipeyrttaruḷiya Tiruviḷaiyāṭaṟpurāṇam*, ed. by Āṟumukanāvalar, p. 6)

> (Among these that are counted as the three [times] six *Purāṇams* recited to the bard by the meritful sage (Akattiyaṉ) who came after having been taught by Vyāsa, after Sanatkumāra had examined [it]

20 Thus also the conclusion drawn by Fisher, *Hindu Pluralism*, p. 150; with respect to her argument about the designation of *purāṇam*, however, that would not be confirmed by the manuscript transmission, one cannot help but notice that her extensive list of manuscript sources (cf. pp. 251–52) does not contain a single specimen of Nampi's text. A spot check among the fourteen manuscripts in the IFP collection counts eight copies of Parañcōti and six of Nampi, many in very bad condition, but at least one, RE47715, containing a head colophon dated to Kollam 1043 (~ 1868) and giving the title as *Tiruviḷaiyāṭaṟpurāṇam*. This is admittedly late but still precedes the era of widespread print and the Tamil renaissance.

21 The one edition I have managed to get hold of is an old *grantha* print from the EFEO collection, which has sadly lost its title page; however, the manuscript transmission is extraordinarily strong with thirty copies in the IFP collection alone (i.e., twice as many as both Tamil versions together), testimony to the fact that this was an important and widespread text. The task of collecting a more complete picture of the surviving evidence and of actually sifting through all this material has not even begun.

22 Fisher, *Hindu Pluralism*, p. 159, argues with strong rhetoric against this sequence, claiming that the *Hālāsyamāhātmya* and the Parañcōti's *Tiruviḷaiyāṭaṟpurāṇam* would be 'twin texts' of the seventeenth century, where the Sanskrit text would have been produced from the Tamil in order to provide it with a Sanskrit original, without, however, adducing a convincing argument why this should be so; in fact analysis of textual details shows unequivocally that the *Hālāsyamāhātmya* contains narrative elements that are found in Nampi's text, but no longer in that of Parañcōti (cf. Wilden, *Manuscript, Print and Memory*, pp. 223–24).

with love filling [his] inside at the feet of Nandi who had understood it from the Majesty, [is this not] in the *Skāndīśa Saṃhitā*?)

Here the framing is similar to that of Nampi but brings in once more the ubiquitous Akattiyaṉ and simply states that among the eighteen Purāṇas told by him, this one is part of the *Skandīśa Samhitā*. This, now, reminds the educated reader of the frame story of the *Hālāsyamāhātmya*, explicitly told by Agastya and claiming, at the end of each chapter, to be part of the '*Hālāsyamāhātmya* in the *Agastyasaṃhitā* in the holy *Skandamahāpuraṇa*' (*śrī skāmde mahā-purāṇe agastya-saṃhitāyāṃ hālāsya-māhātmya*). This might be mere mythic reference, but it just might also be an acknowledgement of an actual and extant source. The following verse mentions the creation of a Tamil version on the basis of a Sanskrit source as an explicit task, recurrent with puranic texts:

24. *nūlceytaṟkukkāraṇam*
aṟaint' iṭap paṭṭatu ākum ālavāy pukaḻmai antac
ciṟant' iṭum vaṭanūl taṉṉait teṉ colāl ceyti eṉṟ' iṅku
uṟaint' iṭum periyōr kūṟak kaṭaippiṭitt' uṟuti intap
piṟant' iṭum piṟappil eytap peṟutum eṉṟu uḷḷam tēṟō.

(*Cuttacaivarākiya Parañcōtimuṉivar moḻipeyrttaruḷiya Tiruviḷaiyāṭaṟpurāṇam*, ed. by Āṟumukanāvalar, pp. 6 f.)

(Cheer up, mind, in the thought that we'll obtain reaching, in this birth we are born into, liberation,[23] as the great people who live here speak: 'make with Southern words that excellent Northern work in praise of Ālavāy that is the thing spoken about'.)

This makes sense if we keep in mind that much of the poetry of this period was in fact poetry on demand, patronized by the notables of a city and/or temple.[24] The title of the third verse leads us to expect it to speak about translating, but actually it just seems to point out a discrepancy between the number of sports on the part of Śiva, the famous sixty-fours, and the number of chapters which would be sixty-eight:

25. *moḻipeyarttavitam*
tirunakar tīrttam mūrttic ciṟappu mūṉṟ' anta murtti
aruḷ viḷaiyāṭal eṭṭ' eṭṭ' aruccaṉai viṉai oṉṟ' āka
varal muṟai aṟupatt' eṭṭām maṟṟavai paṭalam āka
viri muṟai viruttac ceyyuḷ vakaimaiyāl viḷampal uṟṟēṉ.

(*Cuttacaivarākiya Parañcōtimuṉivar moḻipeyrttaruḷiya Tiruviḷaiyāṭaṟpurāṇam*, ed. by Āṟumukanāvalar, p. 7)

---

23 *kaṭaippiṭittu uṟuti eyta* might be understood literally as 'grasping the [other] end [and] reaching certainty/stability'.

24 Ebeling, *Colonizing the Realm of Words*, pp. 103–64.

(I have undertaken to proclaim, by the way of Viruttam verses in expanded manner, the worship of eight [times] eight sports graciously done by that form of threefold excellence, the form from the ghat of the holy city, the work being one, the chapters being, in the sequence of coming, those others that are sixty-eight.)

Here we get into deep waters since the wording is ambiguous and the number of chapters does not conform to what we find in the editions. Parañcōti's version actually comes in sixty-five chapters. If we take it that the number of sixty-eight does not refer to the chapters of his text, but to that of the Sanskrit predecessor he evoked in verse 23, we might once more be inclined to think of the *Hālāsyamāhātmya* which has, in the book, sixty-four sports but seventy-one chapters — a real answer to such a question, however, would presuppose a study of the manuscript transmission and the very likely various ways of counting chapters not only of both these texts, but also of the numerous other parallel versions. Moreover, we can never discount the possibility that some texts in the chain of transmission have in fact been lost.

Parallels could be multiplied, but suffice it to bring in two less controversial examples. With the Āṉantak Kūttar's *Tirukkāḷattippurāṇam* we move backwards in time to about the sixteenth century and find, just as with Nampi, a bewildering amount and variety of prefatory material, with all the topoi and the corresponding phraseology already in place: adaptation of a Sanskrit text, commission from the local people and spiritual effect of the composition, even if it may be flawed. Again in location and designation of the verses I can do no more than follow U. Vē. Cāminātaiyar's edition from 1912. The first protective verse at the beginning is once more dedicated to Gaṇeśa who guards the process of bringing the text from Sanskrit to Tamil:

1. *kāppu*
ceḻuviya vaṭamoḻi teṉmoḻip paṭa
moḻi uṟu māk katai muḻutum kākkumāl
kuḻaviyam tiṅkaḷ veḷ kōṭṭu mum matat
taḻai cevip pukar mukat taṭak kai vēḻamē.

(*Tirukkāḷattipurāṇam of Āṉantakkūttar*, ed. by Cāminātaiyar)

(When the excellent northern language is brought into southern language, he guards the whole great story rich in words, the bull elephant with tusks the white of the child moon, three[fold] must, leaf ears, [and] a broad trunk in [his] spotted face.)

Since also some of the verses to follow reveal more about the problem of translation than most it might not be out of place to perceive a certain concern here, namely that of keeping the story intact in the process of bringing it from one language to the other. This still does not tell us, however, whether the anxiety is focused simply on the narrative sequence or on the exact wording of the text. Verse 22 in this section gives a partial answer that might tally with a situation familiar from some nineteenth-century sources (on which below), namely the intervening element of oral explanation:

22. *vaṭanūlai moḻipeyarttaḷitta paurāṇikar*
eṇṇiya ik katai emakk' uṇarttiya
naṇṇiya caṅkaranāraṇaṉ eṉṉum
puṇṇiyaṉ vīrai vāḻ purāṇikaṉ taṉai
vaṇmai vētiyar kulam maṇiyai vāḻttuvām.

(*Tirukkāḷattipurāṇam of Āṉantakkūttar*, ed. by U. Vē. Cāminātaiyar)

> (We praise the gem of the generous Veda-scholar family, the Purāṇa scholar, living in Puṇṇiyaṉvīrai(?!) who is called Caṅkaranāraṇaṉ who is nearby, who has explained to us this respected story.)

Here the heading refers to the 'Purāṇa scholar who provided [help in] translating the northern work'. Tradition has it that the *Tirukāḷattipurāṇam* goes back to the Sanskrit *Kālahastimāhātmya* of Caṅkaranārāyaṇa Aiyar, that is, presumably, the scholar named in this verse (without his caste name). But here yet another function is ascribed to him, namely that of explaining the Sanskrit text to the prospective Tamil author. Read from the information available on the nineteenth century, we would expect this to mean that Āṉantak Kūttar did not or did not sufficiently master the Sanskrit language to be capable of producing a Tamil version on his own. Whether such was a common situation already in the sixteenth century or whether the stanza rather evokes a learned discussion between authors could perhaps be ascertained by a detailed comparison of the two texts.

A few more verses from the extensive preface section (*patikam*) touch upon the same topic, although the details remain illusive without further study. The first stanza revealing 'the reason for composing the work' just refers to the inhabitants of Kāḷatti asking the poet to act.[25] The second one, however, while referring to the salvific aspect, also expresses worry about the author's being up to his task, possibly as a translator:

nūliyaṟṟutaṟkukkāraṇam 2
tericaṉap pēṟ' immaiyilē tiru aruḷ pālittat' eṉap
peru kavuḷam kaḷi ciṟantēṉ kavitai nalam peṟṟ' aṟiyēṉ

---

25 *nūliyaṟṟutaṟkukkāraṇam 1.*
poṉ koḻikkum veḷ ṭaraṅkap poṉ mukari cūḻ pōnta.
teṉ kayilai māl varaiyāyt tikaḻ tirukkāḷatti-nakar.
nal kataiyai nūl muṟaiyē teṉ moḻiyiṉ naṭāttuk(a) eṉa.
aṉpoṭu coṟṟaṉar eṉṉaic cannitik-kaṇ amar periyōr.

> (Set in motion in the southern language in the sequence of the work the good story. | of the city of shining Tirukkāḷatti, being on the great mountain of southern Kailash. | where come, surrounded by golden Mukari, white waves that wash ashore gold', | those who told me so with love are great people abiding in the vicinity).

urai ceyum-āṟ' eṉ-kol eṉa olkiṉēṉ āṉālum
periyavar tam tiru vākku maṟāmai pēṟ' eṉat tuṇintēṉ.

(*Tirukkāḷattipurāṇam of Āṉantakkūttar*, ed. by Cāminātaiyar)

> (Thinking 'it will impart the grace of obtaining seeing God (*darśaṇa*) in this birth', I, exuberant in great cheeky pride, I who don't know how to achieve the goodness of a poem, I was disheartened, thinking 'what is the way to make the words?' However, I have resolved: 'the achievement is not to change the sacred words of great people'.)

The point made here seems to be that poetic quality has to be sought in faithfulness to the source text and its wording. More detail appears to be added in three consecutive verses on 'the origin of the text' (*nūlvaralāṟu*), sadly cryptic without knowledge of the textual and perhaps also the theological background, but it is still interesting to see that the topic is discussed:

1. *vāynta pal purāṇam-toṟum kāḷatti mahimai*
   āynt' iṭum-poḻut' aḷapp' ila eṉakk' avai aṭaṅkā
   kānta nūliṉuḷ tīrttavai pavam eṉum kaṇṭat
   tēynta poṉ mukar ik kataiyiṉ cila eṭuttu.

(*Tirukkāḷattipurāṇam of Āṉantakkūttar*, ed. by Cāminātaiyar)

> (Beyond measure at the time of appreciating the greatness of the *Kāḷatti* among all the many excellent *Purāṇams*, [even] a section in the *Skānda* work that was submitted to the assembly by me, taking up [only] a few of these stories sealed with worn gold is said to finish off sin.)

Here the topic is the salvific effect of the composition; the adjective *kānta* may once more be a derivation of Sanskrit *skānda-* and locate the Kāḷatti- just as the Maturai Tiruviḷaiyāṭal texts within the bigger fold of puranic traditions.

2. *cūta caṅkitai taṉṉilum iyaṉṟavai tokuttu*
   mā toṭaip paṭak kūṭṭupu vāciṭṭalaiṅkatt'
   ētam iṉṟiya cila terint' ivaṟṟoṭum iyaintē
   ātaritta kāḷatti māṉmiyam eṉa araintēṉ.

(*Tirukkāḷattipurāṇam of Āṉantakkūttar*, ed. by Cāminātaiyar)

> (Collecting those agreeable to a bardic anthology, joining [them] so as to be firmly linked, testing as few that are free from the faults of the *Vāciṭṭalainkam/Vāsiṣṭhalaiṅga*, I proclaimed the *Kāḷatti Māṉmiyam/Kālahasti Māhātmyam*, honoured as being in harmony with these.)

The gist of this verse might be that the source text, although authoritative, was lacking in some respect, whether because the manuscript was damaged, or for poetic reasons or even doctrinal ones cannot be discerned without a careful study of both the Sanskrit original, the *Vāciṭṭalainkam/Vāsiṣṭhalaiṅga* (one of the Sanskrit Śaiva *Upapurāṇas* or its Tamil version?) and the *Tirukāḷattipurāṇam* itself, incidentally referred to as *māṉmiyam* (~ Skt. *māhātmya*) rather than as a *purāṇam*. The last verse adds another *caveat*:

3. *talattu māṉmiyam vēṟ' iṉik kāṇiṉum tamiḻiṉ*
pulappaṭutt' iṭal vēṇṭumēl pulamaiyiṉ vallōr
nalat takum-paṭi pāṭuka. nāṉ aṟint' uḷat' āyc
colat takum katai kaṇṭataik koṇṭ(u) yāṉ coṟṟēṉ.

(*Tirukkāḷattipurāṇam of Āṉantakkūttar*, ed. by Cāminātaiyar)

(Even though now one sees the *Māhātmya* of the site as different, if one must make it comprehensible in Tamil, let those capable by erudition sing [its] in a way befitting [its] goodness. It being known to me I have spoken, taking up what I have seen, the story that is fit to be told.)

Whether the poet here forestalls once more criticism because of his poetic capacities, for his insufficient mastery of Sanskrit or because of deviations in content is not clear.

The last example comes from the nineteenth century, the *Tiruvamparppurāṇam* of one of the last famous traditional poets, Mīṉāṭcicuntaram Piḷḷai.[26] The phraseology still remains the same, but here more is known about the social milieu and the background. The biography written by U. Vē. Cāminātaiyar about his teacher recounts how the great man was looking for a copy of the original Sanskrit *Sthalapurāṇa* which he finally located in the Caracuvatimakāl library in Tañcāvūr. In order to enable him to understand it he had to commission a Tamil prose translation (*vacaṉam*) on the basis of which he then produced his Tamil verse version.[27] In verse 29 of the preface (*pāyiram*), the 'origin of the work' (*nūlvaralāṟu*) reads like this:

perumaiyiṉ poliyum amparp perum tirukkōyil mēya
karumaiyiṉ poliyum kaṇṭak-kaṭavuḷār tiruppūrāṇam
arumaiyiṉ pāṭuk(a) eṉṉa vaṭamoḻi aṉaittum ārāynt'
orumaiyiṉ pāṭal uṟṟēṉ tamiḻiṉāl urai maṟātē.

(*Tiruvamparppurāṇam of Mīṉāṭcicuntaram Piḷḷai*, ed. by Taṇṭapāṇitēcikar)

(As the devotees of the god with a throat in which blackness thrives, who dwells[28] in the big holy temple of Ampar that thrives with greatness, said: 'sing with difficulty the holy Purāṇam', having examined the whole [of it] in the northern language I have undertaken to sing in uniqueness without leaving off a word by Tamil.)

---

26 Ebeling, *Colonising the Realm of Words*, pp. 33 ff.

27 This information is found in Cāminātaiyar, *Śrī Mīṉāṭcicuntaram Piḷḷai avarkaḷ carittiraccurukkam*, I, p. 161, *Amparppurāṇam iyaṟṟa toṭaṅkiyatu*, kindly brought to my notice by Sascha Ebeling; a similar anecdote about the *Kumbhakonapurāṇam* is recounted by Fisher, *Hindu Pluralism*, pp. 175–76.

28 *mēya*: either the god dwells in or the devotees are attached to the temple.

So here we hear once more that the composition of the text was instigated by the local people. It was based on a source in Sanskrit. The topos of faithfulness to the original is taken up as well, only in this case we may be sure that it does not refer to translation: the two remaining possibilities are that the Tamil version is true to the content of the Sanskrit *Purāṇa* or, and this is at least as likely, that Mīṉāṭcicuntaram Piḷḷai pays homage to yet another poetic convention.

Conclusion

The revision of material on the translation from Sanskrit into Tamil in various literary domains brought to light similar conventions but different motivations and strategies. Convention appears to demand that among the growing number of customary prefatory verses at least one and often several deal with the topic of sources and of language. In the grammatical tradition such a point is made already in the preface (*pāyiram*) to the earliest extant treatise, the *Tolkāppiyam*, probably setting the trend for the later tradition (mark, however, that the temporal delay for the addition of the preface is unclear; it is definitely not believed to have been added by the author himself): the author of the *Tolkāppiyam* is said to have studied the Northern grammatical school of *Aintiram*, presumably a statement of theoretical and terminological affiliation. In the further tradition, both claims of affiliation (*Māṟaṉalaṅkāram* and *Pirayōkavivēkam*) and of direct translation (*Vīracōḻiyam* and *Taṇṭiyalaṅkāram*) are found.

Even earlier than in grammar, references to Sanskrit sources are found in the epic-poetic tradition, and for good reason since often the narrative material travels over the subcontinent, most obviously of course in the case of the two great Indian epics, the *Mahābhārata* and the *Rāmāyaṇa*. For both of them there are (although partly lost) multiple versions in Tamil, and here the issue never appears to be direct translation but rather the adaptation of a story. In several stanzas, the evocation of Sanskrit predecessors appears to imbue both historical depth (by the number and/or fame of earlier authors) and spiritual authority (Sanskrit as the language of the gods), and this may be one reason why Sanskrit origin becomes a veritable trope in the puranic tradition.

Here Sanskrit origin is inevitably mentioned although it is not possible to argue for its plausibility in every case, as in the earliest versions of the narrative cycle focused on Śiva and the royal lineage of the Pāṇṭiyas in Maturai, that clearly tells local, southern stories. The poetic topoi to be covered are threefold, although not all three of them are covered in every instance. First, there is the task of converting a story (*katai*, from Skt. *kathā*) from the northern language into Tamil verse. Secondly, it is not the poet's idea, but rather he is asked to write this verse by the people of the place about which he is singing. Thirdly, complying with their wishes brings spiritual benefit and even salvation to the poet, reminding us that a Tamil *purāṇam* deals not just with poetry but with religious poetry. So on the one hand, apparently a Sanskrit background added to the credibility and weight of a work. On the other hand, translation became a real issue, although without detailed textual work it is not possible to be sure what exactly is at stake: the mere story lines, the precise wording, or concerns about doctrine. In some cases, documented for the nineteenth century, translation becomes a double issue, because the Tamil poets do not master enough Sanskrit to properly understand their source texts, in which case the remedy may be oral explanations or even an intermittent Tamil prose translation (*vacaṉam*) on which to base the verse version.

We should keep in mind, however, that the present article outlines the rhetoric of translation and not its practice.

Bibliography

Manuscripts

Pondicherry, French Institute, RE 47715

Mahārājā Serfoji Sarasvati Mahāl Library (MSSML), Tañcāvūr 631

Primary Sources

Akanāṉūṟu Kaḷiṟṟiyāṉainirai, Critical Edition and Annotated Translation; Glossary and Statistics, ed. by Eva Wilden, 3 vols, Critical Texts of Caṅkam Literature 4.1, 4.2, 4.3, collection indologie 134.1–3, NETamil series 1.1–3 (Pondicherry: EFEO / IFP, 2018)

Cilappatikāram mūlamum arumpatavuraiyum aṭiyārkkunallāruraiyum, ed. by U. Vē. Cāminātaiyar (Ceṉṉai: Kapīr Accukkūṭam, 1960; reprint of 6th edn)

Cīvaka Cintāmaṇi mūlamum nacciṉārkkiṉiyaruraiyum, ed. by U. Vē. Cāminātaiyar (Ceṉṉai: Kapīr Accukkūṭam, 1969; reprint of 7th edn)

Cūḷāmaṇi, ed. by U. Vē. Cāminātaiyar (Ceṉṉai: U. Vē. Cāminātaiyar Nūlnilaiyam, 1962; 2nd edn)

Cuntarapāṇṭiyam of Aṉatāri, ed. by T. Chandradekharan (Madras: Government Oriental Manuscript Library, 1955)

Cuttacaivarākiya Parañcōtimuṉivar moḻipeyarttaruḷiya Tiruviḷaiyāṭaṟpurāṇam, ed. by Āṟumukanāvalar (Yāḻppāṇam: Vittiyāratnākara Accukkūṭam, 1912)

Iṟaiyaṉār Akapporuḷ mūlamum Nakkīrar uraiyum, ed. by Kā.Ra. Kōvintarāja Mutaliyar (Ceṉṉai: Pavāṉantar Kaḻakam, 1939)

Inscriptions of the Early Pāṇḍyas (c. 300 B.C. to 984 A.D.), ed. by K. G. Krishnan (New Delhi: Indian Council of Historical Research, Northern Book Centre New Delhi, 2002)

Kallāṭam, ed. by Mīṉāṭcicuntarampiḷḷai (Ceṉṉai: Attinīyam Aṉṭ Ṭēliniyūs Pirāṉs Accukkūṭam, 1868)

Kamparāmāyaṇam mutalāvatu Pālakāṇṭam, ed. and comm. by Vai. Mu. Kōpālakiruṣṇamācāryar (Ceṉṉai: Vai. Mu. Kōpālakiruṣṇamācāryar Kampēṇi, 1964; 7th edn)

Kamparāmāyaṇam, ed. by Ca. Vē. Cuppiramaṇyaṉ (Ceṉṉai:Maṇivācakar Patippakam, 2008)
Kuṟuntokai, Critical Edition and Annotated Translation + Glossary and Statistics, ed. by Eva Wilden, 3 vols, Critical Texts of Caṅkam Literature 2.1–2.3 (Ceṉṉai: Tamilmann Patippakam / EFEO, 2010)
Makāpāratam, Villiputtūrāḻvār iyaṟṟiya, ed. by Vai. Mu. Kōpālakiruṣṇam, 6 vols (Ceṉṉai: Vai. Mu. Kōpālakiruṣṇamācāriyār Kampaṉi, 1970)
Maṇimēkalai, ed. by U. Vē. Cāminātaiyar (Ceṉṉai: Kapīr Accukkūṭam, 1965; reprint of 6th edn)
Māṟaṉ Alaṅkāran, mūlaiyum paḻaya uraiyum viḷakkaṅkaḷuṭaṉ, ed. by T.Vē. Kōpālaiyar (Ceṉṉai: Śrīmat Āṇṭavaṉ Ācciramam, 2005)
Naṉṉūl mulamum Caṅkaranamaccivāyaruraiyum, ed. by U.Vē. Cāminātaiyar (Ceṉṉai: Kapīr Accukkūṭam, 4th edn)
Naṟṟiṇai, Critical Edition and Annotated Translation + Glossary, ed. by Eva Wilden, 3 vols, Critical Texts of Caṅkam Literature 1.1–1.3 (Ceṉṉai: Tamilmann Patippakam / EFEO, 2008)
Nīlakēci, the Original Text and the Commentary of Samayadivarakara-vamana-muni, ed. by Pō. Vē. Cōmacuntaraṉār (Kumbakonam Government College: [n.pub.], 1936)
Pārataveṇpā, uttiyōka, vīṭum, turōṇa paruvaṅkaḷ, ed. by S. Kiruṣṇasāmi Aiyaṅkār (Mayilappūr: Centamiḻ Mantira Pustakacālai, 1925)
Peruṅkatai mūlamum kuṟippuraiyum, ed. by U. Vē. Cāminātaiyar (Ceṉṉai: U. Vē. Cāminātaiyar Nūlnilaiyam, 1968, 4th edn)
Pirayōkavivēkam mūlamum uraiyum, ed. by T. Vē. Kōpālaiyar (Kumpakōṇam: Jemiṉi Accakkam, 1973)
Taṇṭiyalaṅkāram mūlamum paḻaiyavuraiyum, ed. by T. Vē. Kōpālaiyar (Kumpakōṇam: Jemiṉi Accakkam, 1st edn1967, reprint Ceṉṉai: Umā Patippakam, 2016)
Tirukkāḷattipurāṇam of Āṉantakkūttar, ed. by U. Vē. Cāminātaiyar (Ceṉṉai: Vaijayanti Accukkūṭam, 1912)
Tiruvamparppurāṇam of Mīṉāṭcicuntaram Piḷḷai, ed. by Ca. Taṇṭapāṇitēcikar (Ceṉṉai: U.Vē. Cāminātaiyar Nūlnilaiyam, 1965)
Tiruviḷaiyāṭaṟpurāṇam, Cellinakarp Perumpaṟṟappuliyūr Nampi iyaṟṟiyatu, ed. by U. Vē. Cāminātaiyar (Ceṉṉai: Kapīr Accukkūṭam, 1972, 3rd edn)
Tiruviḷaiyāṭaṟpurāṇam, Cuttacaivarākiya Parañcōtimuṉivar moḻipeyrttaruḷiya, ed. by Āṟumukanāvalar (Ceṉṉai: Vittiyāratnākara Accukkūṭam, 1912)
Tolkāppiyam Poruḷatikāram Iḷampūraṇam, no editor (Tirunelvēli-Ceṉṉai: Tirunēlvelit Teṉṉintiya Caivacittānta Nūṟpatippuk Kaḻakam, 1967; 3rd reprint of 1st edn1953)
Vīracōḻiyam peruntēvaṉāruraiyōṭu, ed. by Ci. Vai. Tāmōtarampiḷḷai (Ceṉṉapaṭṭaṉam: Vittiyāvarttaṉai Accukkūṭam, 1881)

Secondary Studies

Burnell, Arthur Coke, *On the Aindra School of Sanskrit Grammarians: Their Place in the Sanscrit and Subordinate Literatures* (Mangalore: Basel Mission Book & Tract Depository, 1875)

Cāminātaiyar, U. Vē., *Śrī Mīṉāṭcicuntaram Piḷḷai avarkaḷ carittiraccurukkam*, 2 vols (Ceṉṉai: U. Vē. Cāminātaiyar Nūlnilaiyam, 1965)

Chevillard, Jean-Luc, 'The Pantheon of Tamil Grammarians: A Short History of the Myth of Agastya's Twelve Disciples', in *Écrire et transmettre en Inde classique*, ed. by Gerard Colas and Gerdi Gerschheimer, Études thématiques, 23 (Paris: École Française d'Extrême-Orient, 2009), pp. 243–68

——, 'The Retrospective Horizon of *Vīracōḻiyam* 143 — at the Advent of Daṇḍin Doctrine in Tamil Nadu', presentation for the workshop 'A Lasting Vision: Dandin's Mirror in the World of Asian Letters', organised by Yigal Bronner, Charles Hallisey, and David Shulman at the Hebrew University of Jerusalem, 13–17 December 2015 (URL: https://halshs.archives-ouvertes.fr/halshs-02179709)

Ebeling, Sascha, *Colonizing the Realm of Words: The Transformation of Tamil Literature in Nineteenth-Century South India* (New York: Suny Press, State University of New York, 2010)

Fisher, Elaine N., *Hindu Pluralism : Religion and the Public Sphere in Early Modern South India* (Oakland: University of California Press, 2017)

Francis, Emmanuel, 'Supplementing Poetry and Devotion: The Additional Stanzas to the *Tirumurukāṟṟuppaṭai*', in *Colophons, Prefaces, Satellite Stanza – Towards a Transmission History of Classical Tamil Literature*, ed. by Jonas Buchholz and Eva Wilden, Collection indologie, NETamil Series (Pondichéry: École Française d'Extrême/Institut Français de Pondichéry, 2019, forthcoming)

Monius, Anne, 'The Many Lives of Daṇḍin: The "Kāvyādarśa" in Sanskrit and Tamil', *International Journal of Hindu Studies*, 4.1 (2000) 1–37

Pandian, P., trans., *Cūḷāmaṇi, Tōlāmoḻi Tēvar*, 2 vols (Ceṉṉai: Department of Jainology, University of Madras, 2002)

Vaidyanathan, S., *Indo-Aryan Loanwords in Old Tamil* (Madras: Rajan Publishers, 1971)

Vijayalakshmy, R., *A Study of the Peruṅkatai, an Authentic Version of the Story of Udayana* (Madras: International Institute of Tamil Studies, 1981)

Wilden, Eva, 'Definitions of *kaḷavu* in the Old Poetological Tradition (*Tolkāppiyam Poruḷatikāram* + *Iṟaiyaṉār Akapporuḷ*): The Convergence of Interests' *Rivista di Studi Sudasiatici*, 1 (2006) 89–106

——, *Manuscript, Print and Memory: Relics of the Caṅkam in Tamilnadu*, Studies in Manuscript Cultures, 3 (Berlin: de Gruyter, 2014)

——, 'Translation and Transcultural Adaptation in a Multi-Lingual Environment: Tamil and Sanskrit Versions of the *Tiruviḷaiyāṭaṟpurāṇam*' in *La traduction dans l'histoire des idées linguistiques*, ed. by Emilie Aussant (Paris: Librairie orientaliste Paul Geuthner, 2015), pp. 93–110

——, 'Tamil Satellite Stanzas: Genres and Distribution', in *The South Asian Manuscript Book: Material, Textual and Historical Investigations*, ed. by Daniele Cuneo, Camillo Formigatti, and Vincenzo Vergiani, Studies in Manuscript Cultures (Berlin: de Gruyter, 2017), pp. 163–92

NICOLA CARPENTIERI

Ibn al-Quff the Translator, Ibn al-Quff the Physician

Language and Authority in a Medieval Commentary on the Hippocratic Aphorisms

Introduction

The Hippocratic *Aphorisms*, thought to have been composed between the late fifth and early fourth centuries BC, exerted a long and lasting influence over medical writing, inspiring the production of a vast body of exegetical literature. The *Aphorisms* were particularly prized for their didactic potential as concise, easily learned utterances that summarized a large amount of medical knowledge. As for the Arabic tradition, the subject of this article, no other Greek secular text received comparable attention: over a dozen commentaries penned from the eleventh to the sixteenth century, preserved in over a hundred manuscripts. As recent studies have demonstrated, these commentaries were as much venues for exegetical work as they were venues for debate and critical engagement with other sources.[1] Recent scholarship has

1 In particular, Gianna Pomata has argued for a distinction between 'epistemic' and 'literary' genres with medical case narrative belonging to the first group, that is, those kinds of texts that develop in tandem with scientific practices. Pomata advocated that medical case narrative should be studied in a long-term perspective, adopting Franco Moretti's 'distant reading', in order to 'trace the history of the medical case narrative as a genre that evolved over a very long period of time, from antiquity to modern medicine'.

Medical commentaries lend themselves excellently to such an approach, and recent attempts in this sense have proven fruitful for exploring the evolution of medical theory. A successful attempt in this sense is represented by the pioneering study by Pormann and Joosse on the commentaries on the Hippocratic *Aphorisms* in the Arabic tradition, which allowed for a preliminary exploration of such a rich tradition, highlighting the varying approaches of Arabic commentators following a six-century-long tradition.

Nicola Carpentieri (University of Padova) (nicola.carpentieri@unipd.it) researches Maghribī Arabic literature and the history of medicine. Dr Carpentieri received his PhD in Arabic and Islamic studies from Harvard University and has held research positions at the University of Manchester and at the Autonomous University of Barcelona. His most recent publication is the volume *Sicily, al-Andalus and the Maghreb: Writing in Times of Turmoil* for Amsterdam University Press.

Narratives on Translation across Eurasia and Africa: From Babylonia to Colonial India, ed. by Sonja Brentjes in cooperation with Jens Høyrup and Bruce O'Brien, CAT 3, pp. 297–308 (Turnhout: Brepols, 2022) BREPOLS PUBLISHERS 10.1484/M.CAT-EB.5.127946

only in part addressed the issue of how translation impacted medical theory and how the knowledge of languages and the job of the translator intertwined with epistemic practices. Notably, Overwien and Strohmaier have focused respectively on Ḥunayn ibn Isḥāq's (d. 877) translation technique and his domestication of pagan texts for Muslim and Christian audiences.[2] And yet, the degree to which medical theory and translation issues became intertwined in the formation of the Islamicate medical corpus has not received adequate attention. It is remarkable, for instance, that Ḥunayn resorted not only to Arabic terms and transliterations of the original Greek words in order to create an Arabic medical lexicon, but that he also adopted terminology borrowed from neighbouring linguistic traditions, such as the Persian. This practice caused, in some cases, an overlap in terminology that had repercussions on the classification of certain diseases. In what follows, I will be discussing one instance of this occurrence, investigating the implications of the imperfect overlapping between Greek, Persian, and Arabic terminology and its usage. It is my aim to show how knowledge of languages impacted on the exegetical text, as well as to reveal how such knowledge contributed to the shaping of medical vocabulary and even of medical theory and practice. I shall focus my analysis on a specific commentary on the Hippocratic *Aphorisms*: the one penned by the Syrian physician Ibn al-Quff (1232–1286) in the thirteenth century.[3]

A further nuancing of the medical commentary as discourse has been carried out by Nahyan Fancy in his study of Ibn al-Nafīs' medical commentaries. In the study, Fancy has compared the introductory and physiological sections of two of Ibn al-Nafīs's medical commentaries (*shurūḥ*) to his *Mūjaz* and compounded this comparison by discussing also two commentaries on the *Mūjaz*, thereby highlighting the salient aspects of each genre. He thus further documented the epistemological character of the commentary by investigating how the commentators situated their own theories on specific physiological issues vis-à-vis the source text, its commentaries, and/or the discussions found in the works of other medical authorities on these same issues. A distant reading of the Arabic commentary tradition on the Hippocratic *Aphorisms* has been carried out by T. Mimura and this author in their study of *Aphorisms*, 6. 11 in the Arabic commentary tradition, which documents the evolution of exegetical approaches to a variant reading of the lemma of *Aphorisms*, 6. 11. Yet another example of distant reading in approaching the medical commentary is this author's study of the meaning of *Birsām* and *Sirsām* in the Arabic commentaries on the Hippocratic *Aphorisms*, which examines the semantic shift of the two terms as attested by some of the most relevant Arabic commentaries on the *Aphorisms*. For this study, this author relied in part on Dols's groundbreaking monograph 'Majnūn', which itself allowed for an overarching narrative of mental disorder as attested by Arabic medical literature, as well as on Danielle Jacquart's own discussion of phrenitis and its aetiology in Ibn Sīnā and al-Rāzī, bringing into the discussion the importance of translation towards the shaping of medical theories on mental health. See Pomata, 'The Medical Case Narrative', Pormann and Joosse, 'Commentaries on the Hippocratic Aphorisms', Carpentieri, Mimura, 'Arabic Commentaries on the Hippocratic Aphorisms', Carpentieri, 'On the Meaning of *Birsām* and *Sirsām*', Dols, *Majnūn*, Jacquart, 'Les avatars de la phrénitis chez Avicenne et Rhazès', Fancy, 'Medical Commentaries'.

2 Overwien, 'The Art of the Translator'; Strohmaier, 'Galen the Pagan and Ḥunayn the Christian'.

3 For a biography of Ibn al-Quff, see Hamarneh, *The Physician, Therapist and Surgeon Ibn al-Quff*.

In his comment on *Aphorisms*, 4. 51, Ibn al-Quff addressed issues of translation and usage, delving into the Persian etymologies of two terms that, according to him, were used erratically by some Arabic physicians and medical writers. I will show that Ibn al-Quff's passage is substantially a rephrasing of a statement by Ibn Sīnā (d. 1037) that appears in his *Qānūn fī al-ṭibb*. I will propose a hypothesis around Ibn al-Quff's borrowing of this passage: namely, that he used Ibn Sīnā's argument to document his own competence as a translator, thereby enhancing his authority as an exegete.

Ibn al-Quff is best known for his surgical compendium *ʿUmdat al-iṣlāḥ* or *al-ʿUmda fī ṣināʿat al-jirāḥa*. But he also was the author of the longest Arabic commentary on the Hippocratic *Aphorisms*, a painstaking exegetical endeavour in which he engaged with both Galenic works as well as other Arabic commentaries on Hippocrates' treatise. The present paper focuses on this remarkable and thus far almost ignored work. Basing my analysis on the comment on 4. 51, it will be my aim to show how issues of translation played a role in medical theories on mental illness and in the social history of medicine.

Ibn al-Quff on Translation

Ibn al-Quff was born in Karak, modern-day Jordan. Encouraged to enter the medical profession by his father, he enjoyed a privileged upbringing, studying with some of the most distinguished physicians of his time: Ibn Abī Uṣaybiʿa (d. 1270), Shams al-Dīn al-Khusrāwshāhī (d. 1254), and Najm al-Dīn Ibn Minfākh (d. 1254), himself the author of a commentary on the Hippocratic *Aphorisms*. A precocious and talented learner, after his medical training Ibn al-Quff served as a physician in the fortress of ʿAjlūn (Jordan) and subsequently at the citadel of Damascus. His keen interest in surgery was likely the result of his service at these two military outposts, where, particularly during the turbulent times in which he lived, the necessity to treat ruinous battle wounds would have been frequent. Ibn al-Quff's education was carefully supervised by his father, Muwaffaq al-Dīn Yaʿqūb (d. after 1233), a bureaucrat in the Ayyubid administration who served as a scribe in the *Diwān al-Birr*, a palace bureau in charge of charitable endowments. Ibn al-Quff followed his father in his various employments in Damascus and Sarkhad before he began practicing as a physician. We have a vivid portrait of Ibn al-Quff's father in the words of Ibn Abī Uṣaybiʿa, who dedicated an entry to Ibn al-Quff in his *ʿUyūn al-Anbāʾ*. Ibn Abī Uṣaybiʿa was, apparently, a good friend of Ibn al-Quff's father, whom he lavishes with praise for his knowledge of poetry and of the Arabic language, his elegant calligraphy, and his impeccable writing style. The young Ibn al-Quff clearly benefited from the cultural milieu of the court administrators (*kātib*, pl. *kuttāb*) to which his father belonged. In addition to practicing as a physician, he authored a number of remarkable works both on medical practice and theory, some of which reflect his keen interest in language and philology. Among these works, Ibn al-Quff's commentary on the Hippocratic *Aphorisms*, entitled *Kitāb al-Uṣūl fī Sharḥ al-Fuṣūl* (The Book of the Principles on the Explanation of the *Aphorisms*), was a unique feat. It is by far the longest among the Arabic commentaries on the *Aphorisms* still extant, both a work of exegesis and a compendium of medical theories. The work follows a consistent arrangement: each entry begins with the Hippocratic lemma (based on Ḥunayn ibn Isḥāq's translation), followed by the commentary (*al-sharḥ*) which is subdivided into enquiries (*mabāḥith*), the first enquiry dealing, invariably, with the connection between the aphorism being commented upon and the one that precedes it.

In the introduction to his work, Ibn al-Quff states his wish to engage with every important commentary on the *Aphorisms* available in his time. Throughout the work, he frequently quotes from his colleagues, validating their theories or dismissing them with counterarguments. The length of Ibn al-Quff's commentary, unparalleled in the corpus of the Arabic commentaries on the Hippocratic *Aphorisms*, suggests that he did aim to compose the most exhaustive exegetical work on the Hippocratic text. In his introduction, the author corroborates this impression:

> وبعد ... فقد سألني بعد من يشتغل علي أن أشرح له كتاب الفصول للإمام أبقراط قدس الله روحه وأن أذكر له مع ذلك الإيرادات التي للرازي وغيره وأجيبَ عنها وأرتب له على كل كلمة من كلمات فصوله بحثا خاصا. فأجبته إلى ذلك مستعينا بالله تعالى وسميته بكتاب الاصول في شرح الفصول.

> (One of my students asked me to explain for him the book of *Aphorisms* by the Imām Hippocrates, may God sanctify his soul, and that I quote the opinions of Rāzī and the others, and that I engage with these opinions and that I compose a specific enquiry on each word contained in the book of the *Aphorisms*. So I undertook the task, relying upon God almighty and I called my work: 'The Book of the Principles on the Explanation of the *Aphorisms*'.)[4]

Ibn al-Quff's declared intention to engage with his predecessors often leads him to back up their theories with further evidence, or to elaborate counter-arguments to dispel their views. One such argument is based precisely on an issue of translation and will be the topic of this article.

The passage under scrutiny is contained in Ibn al-Quff's comment on 4. 51. There, the commentator distinguishes between two illnesses which cause mental derangement with fever: diaphragmatic fever and brain fever. In Arabic, each of the two illnesses goes under a Persian name: *birsām* for the former, *sirsām* for the latter. While the two pathologies affect different body parts, their similar symptoms, that is fever, dyspnoea — shortness of breath — and delirium, led physicians and commentators to confuse one

4 Ibn al-Quff, *Commentary on the Hippocratic Aphorisms*, ed. by Pormann and others, p. 1 (my translation).

for the other, and to use the two terms *birsām* and *sirsām* inappropriately to translate the Greek φρενίτις. In order to settle the confusion, Ibn al-Quff provides accurate Arabic translations for the two Persian words, explaining how, according to the etymologies, the two terms describe two discrete illnesses: namely, brain fever (*sirsām*) and diaphragmatic fever (*birsām*). As their names suggest, the first is a fever arising from an inflammation in or around the brain, while the latter is a fever arising from an inflammation of the diaphragm. This division mirrors the old feud between encephalocentrists and cardiocentrists, but Ibn al-Quff's remarks are also highly reminiscent of a passage from Ibn Sīnā's *Canon*, which I will introduce in what follows.

Ibn Sīnā on *sirsām* and *birsām*

Ibn Sīnā's great medical encyclopaedia, *al-Qānūn fī al-ṭibb*, is arguably the single most influential Arabic work in the history of medicine. Ibn Sīnā laid it out as a systematic compendium of Galenic medicine, and its outstanding pedagogical quality ensured it a lasting success both in the East and in the West.[5] The *Canon* enjoyed a status of the highest regard in the Arabic medical tradition, a status attested to by the great number of manuscripts preserved, as well as by the many commentaries on it, glosses, and imitations. Ibn Sīnā laid out his project clearly in the work's preface, where he declares that he chose to treat 'the general aspects of medicine, with its two parts, the theoretical and the practical, plus some general principles concerning the power of simple medicaments, and finally the illnesses which may affect each body-part'. The *Canon* is organized into books (*kitāb*, pl. *kutub*), parts (or arts, *fann*, pl. *funūn*), chapters (or teachings/speeches, *taʿlīm/maqāla*, pl. *taʿlīmāt/maqālāt*), sub-chapters (or propositions, *jumla*, pl. *jumal*) and sections (*faṣl*, pl. *fuṣūl*). Book One covers general aspects such as anatomy, physiology, nosology, prophylaxis, hygiene, and therapeutics. Book Two comprises about 760 simple medicaments, arranged alphabetically. Book Three covers the illnesses that affect each body-part, arranged from head to toes. Book Four deals with illnesses affecting the whole body, while Book Five explains how to prepare composite medicaments.

---

5 Ibn Sīnā (known in the West by his latinised name 'Avicenna') *al-Qānūn fī al-Ṭibb* is arguably the single most influential Arabic work in the history of Western medicine. Europe gained access to this work through Gerard of Cremona's Latin translation, which he completed in Toledo sometime before his death in 1187. The Latin *Canon* was subsequently read in European universities up to the end of the seventeenth century; its influence on medical theory, practice, and didactics was immense, as generations of physicians were trained based on this text. The influence of the *Canon* on both Arabic and Latin medical discourse and the translation technique of Gerard of Cremona have been the object of multiple studies by Danielle Jacquart. See Jacquart, 'Les traductions médicales de Gérard de Crémone, dans P. Pizzamiglio', Jacquart 'Remarques préliminaires à une étude comparée des traductions médicales de Gérard de Crémone'.

The *Canon* was as much a compendium as it was an endeavour to systematize a body of knowledge plagued with inconsistencies, discrepancies, and imprecisions largely caused by the progressive layering of terminology, multiple interpretations, and faulty transmissions. In her 1992 article 'Les avatars de la phrénitis chez Avicenne et Rhazes', Danielle Jacquart called attention to Ibn Sīnā's effort to systematize the nomenclature used in Arabic for the disease known in the Hippocratic Corpus as phrenitis. Jacquart proffered a translation and analysis of book three, *fann* one, *maqāla* three, a rather convoluted passage in which Ibn Sīnā distinguishes between a 'common' name (*ism ʿāmmī*) — *birsām* — and a 'technical' name (*ism ṣināʿī*) — *sirsām* — for the Greek φρενίτις (which appears also in a corrupted transliteration as قرانيطس – *qarānīṭis*).[6] According to Ibn Sīnā, the term *sirsām* underwent an evolution from its vulgar use, which referred to symptoms of phrenitis — delirium accompanied by high fever — to a technical use, which was employed properly by physicians to indicate an inflammation in the meninges:

فإن قرانيطس والسرسام مخصوص بورم حجاب الدماغ إذا كان حاراً وإن كان في بعض المواضع قد أُطلق أيضاً على ورم جوهر الدماغ وهو الاستعمال الخاص لهذا الاسم إلا أنه منقول من اسم العرض الذي يلزمه وهو الهذيان واختلاط العقل مع حرارة محرقة، فالاسم العامي واقع على هذا العرض، والصناعي على هذا الورم.

(*Qarānīṭis* and *sirsām* are the specific names for an inflammation which happens in the membrane enveloping the brain, when the inflammation is hot — even if in some passages the name has been used for an inflammation of the matter of the brain — and this is the specific use for this name, but the name is derived from the term used for the symptoms that accompany it, which are delirium and mental derangement with a burning fever. And the common name refers to these symptoms, while the technical name refers to the inflammation.)[7]

Jacquart underscored the influence of Galen on Ibn Sīnā's preoccupation with distinguishing between illness and symptom. This is a particularly important distinction, in that, since the common use of *sirsām* referred only to a symptom, that is delirium with fever, such common use comprised not only the disease described by the technical use, but also a host of other illnesses which displayed the symptoms of delirium and fever.[8]

Further in the passage, Ibn Sīnā addresses yet another crucial issue regarding the Arabic taxonomy of phrenitis. The issue concerns the erratic usage of the two terms *birsām* and *sirsām*:

6 Jacquart, 'Les avatars de la phrénitis chez Avicenne et Rhazès'.

7 Ibn Sīnā, *al-Qānūn fī al-Tibb*, ed. by al-Ḍinnāwī, Book 3, Fann, 1 Maqāla, p. 76.

8 Jacquart, 'Les avatars de la phrénitis chez Avicenne et Rhazès', p. 184.

... ومن الناس من لا يعرف اللغات بحسب أن البرسام اسم لهذا الورم، وأن السرسام أخف منه، وليس ذلك بشيء، فإن البرسام هو لفظة فارسية، والبر هو الصدر، والسام هو الورم، والسرسام هو أيضا لفظة فارسية: فالسر هو الرأس والسام هو الورم والمرض.

> (And there are people who do not know languages that think that *birsām* is the name for this inflammation, and that *sirsām* is lighter than that, but this is nonsense. In fact, *birsām* is a Persian term, *bar* being the chest and *sām* being the inflammation, and *sirsām* is also a Persian term, *sar* being the head and *sām* being the inflammation and the disease.)[9]

Ibn Sīnā is intervening in a situation of confusion about the terms *birsām* and *sirsām*. Jacquart underscores how the two terms had been used interchangeably since the early Arabic translations from the Greek. The two Persian words made their way into Arabic through their usage in pre-Islamic poetry, and were used, according to Pormann, 'nearly synonymously' in Arabic medical works to designate the Greek phrenitis.

Jacquart rightly pointed out the clash between such an ambiguous usage and Ibn Sīnā's concern for clarity. It seems that Ibn Sīnā is attempting to retrospectively force his classification of the two illnesses, based on their Persian etymology, upon the actual usage of the terms. But, Jacquart explains, Ibn Sīnā is mistaken about such history: the ambiguous usage of the two terms, one referring to the head and the other to the chest, reflected the ancients' hesitation about the seat of the illness: the brain or the diaphragm.[10]

In contrast with the concurrent use of the two terms, Ibn Sīnā proposes a clear-cut separation. He bases his distinction on a philological enquiry: those that are not trained in languages consider *sirsām* a lighter form of *birsām*. However, the origin of the two terms reveals how the latter is an inflammation located in the chest, while the former an inflammation of the brain. Tangentially, Ibn Sīnā's accusation towards 'those who do not know languages' may also be interpreted as an indirect attack against al-Rāzī, who in fact used *farāniṭis*, *birsām*, and *sirsām* interchangeably.

Ibn al-Quff's Reflections

Ibn Sīnā's etymologies resurface — without acknowledgement — in Ibn al-Quff's commentary on *Aphorisms*, 4. 51.[11] The lemma of the Hippocratic *Aphorism* which appears in Ibn al-Quff's commentary reads as follows:

---

9 Ibn Sīnā, *al-Qānūn fī al-Tibb*, ed. by al-Ḍinnāwī, Book 3, Fann, 1 Maqāla, p. 76.

10 Jacquart, 'Les avatars de la phrénitis chez Avicenne et Rhazès', pp. 182–83.

11 In Ibn al-Quff's commentary 4. 51 appears as 4. 50 due to a variant arrangement.

4.50
قال أبقراط: إذا حدث في حمّى غير مفارقة رداءة فى التنفّس واختلاط فى العقل فذلك من علامات الموت.

(Hippocrates said: When in a fever not of the intermittent type dyspnoea and delirium come on, they are signs of death.)

In Ibn al-Quff's second enquiry, we read:

البحث الثاني: مراده بالمرض المذكور ههنا البرسام وذلك لأنه ذكر أعراضه وذكر الحمى اللازمة ورداءة التنفس واختلاط العقل. فلما ذكر هذه علم من ذكره لها أن مراده بالمرض المذكور هاهنا بالبرسام لأن الأعراض دالة على الأمراض والبرسام ورم حار يحدث في الغشاء المسمى أفرغما وهذه اللفظة فارسية والسرسام أيضا ورم حار يحدث في أحد غشائي الدماغ أو في جرمه، خلافا لالرازي. وهذه اللفظة أيضا فارسية والسر هو الدماغ، والسام هو الورم، والبر هو الصدر والسام هو الورم. وهذا المرض يلزمه من الأعراض ما ذكره. أما الحمى فلأن الورم حادث عن مواد حادة عفنة. وذلك لأن الغشاء الصفاقية لا ينفذ فيه شيء من المواد إلا ما لطف منها. وكذلك الحال في ذات الجنب على ما ستعرفه. وأيضا لكون الآفة حالّة في محلّ شريف فتجتهد الطبيعة في دفعها والاجتهاد حركة وهي مسخنة. وأيضا فإن القلب يتضرر بالمشاركة والمحاذاة ومن جهة اختلال التنفس على ما ستعرفه.[Th4 55a] وأما رداءة التنفس فلتضرر الأعصاب المحركة للصدر لتضرر مبادئها بالمشاركة ... والبرسام أعراضه شبيهة بأعراض السرسام. والفرق بينهما من وجهين أحدهما أن السرسام يتقدم فيه اختلاط الذهن على ضرر التنفس والبرسام بعكس هذا. وثانيهما أن السرسام لا تكون الحمى معه قوية كما في البرسام[Th4 55b] . وذلك لقرب الآفة من القلب في البرسام وبعدها عنه في السرسام.[12]

(Second enquiry: What he means by 'aforementioned illness' here is *birsām*, since he mentions its symptoms and he mentions the inevitable fever, dyspnoea and delirium. And since he mentions these, it is clear from what he says that here he means, by 'the aforementioned illness', *birsām*, because the symptoms reveal the illness, and *birsām* is a hot inflammation that happens in the membrane called *afraghmā*, and this is a Persian word, and *sirsām* is also a hot inflammation, which happens in one of the two membranes of the brain or in the brain itself, contrary to what Rāzī says. And this word is also Persian, *sar* being the brain and *sām* being the inflammation, while *bar* is the chest and *sām* the inflammation. And this illness is accompanied by the symptoms which have been described. As for the fever [it happens] because this inflammation is caused by sharp, rotten humours. And this is because the peritoneal lining [*al-ghishā' al-ṣifāqiya*] does not expel matters except for those that soften it. And this is the same case with pleurisy, as you will learn. And also because the illness is settled in a noble part, and nature needs to repel it and the effort is a

12 Ibn al-Quff, *Commentary on the Hippocratic Aphorisms, Book 6*, ed. by Pormann and others, pp. 80–81 (my translation).

> movement, and it is warming. And also because the heart is damaged sympathetically and in parallel, and because of the impairment in breathing, as you will learn. As for dyspnoea, it happens because of the damage occurring to the nerves that move the chest, due to the damage to their beginnings because of sympathy… and the symptoms of *birsām* are similar to those of *sirsām*, but the two illnesses have two main differences. The first is that in *sirsām* mental derangement comes before complications in breathing, while in *birsām* there happens the contrary. Second, that *sirsām* does not cause a fever as strong as the fever in *birsām*. And this is because of the closeness of *birsām* to the heart, while *sirsām* is more removed.)

In the passage above, the translations from Persian already proffered by Ibn Sīnā are put forward as the preliminary argument for identifying the Hippocratic illness in the lemma as *birsām*, that is, diaphragmatic fever, as opposed to *sirsām*, brain fever. Ibn al-Quff follows closely Ibn Sīnā's classification as it appears in the *Canon*, complementing his argument with a discussion of the symptomatology of *birsām*: the fever arising from the inflammation of the diaphragm, caused by the lodging of sharp humours in it and the sympathetic involvement of the heart, and the damage to nerves located in the chest and departing from the diaphragmatic area, which determines dyspnoea. While such symptoms point to *birsām*, Ibn al-Quff underscores that the symptoms of *birsām* and of *sirsām* are similar, and that the physician can best discern between diaphragmatic and brain fever based on the intensity of the fever and on the time of insurgence of dyspnoea. This passage thus reveals how a translation issue is, in this case, instrumental in intervening in issues of medical theory: the classification of diaphragmatic vs brain fever, nicely encapsulated in the Persian etymologies provided by Ibn Sīnā, affects the interpretation of the symptoms associated with each of the two illnesses. For example, the fever in *birsām* is stronger than in *sirsām* because of the closeness of the former illness to the heart, which is involved sympathetically, and because of it affecting the nerves of the chest at their origin.

Let us now focus our attention on Ibn al-Quff's translations from the Persian. Ibn al-Quff's phrasing overlaps with the passage from the *Canon* seen above. This points to the likelihood that he is here borrowing directly from Ibn Sīnā. Ibn al-Quff was steeped in the *Canon*, having composed a commentary on it. Yet, in this instance, he fails to quote his source, and he adds a new, rather obscure, Persian word: *afraghmā*, which we infer to be the diaphragm. This term is remarkably absent not only from Ibn Sīnā's passage seen above but also from the entire *Canon*. When referring to the diaphragm, Ibn Sīnā consistently opts for *al-ḥijāb al-hājiz* (the separating veil or membrane). Ibn al-Quff also uses the term *al-ḥijāb al-hājiz* in several instances in his commentary, while in this passage he opts for *al-ghishā' al-ṣifāqiya* (peritoneal lining). *Afraghmā*, instead, occurs only in this instance in the entire commentary and it is virtually unattested before Ibn al-Quff, that is to say, in all earlier commentaries. Phonetically, the term *afraghmā* resembles the Greek διαφράγμα (diaphragma) and we can only assume that 'afraghmā' was employed in Arabic medical circles as a synonym for *al-ḥijāb al-hājiz*. If that was indeed the case, Ibn al-Quff would have had a direct channel to become acquainted with the term: namely, by way of his teacher Shams al-Dīn al-Khusrawshāwī, who hailed from Tabriz, and was a pupil of Fakhr al-Dīn al-Rāzī. But Ibn al-Quff's mention of *afraghmā* in this context is an addendum devoid of the argumentative value of Avicenna's etymologies: while the etymology of *birsām* and *sirsām* are in fact instrumental to the classification of diaphragmatic fever and brain fever according to the affected part, *afraghmā* adds nothing to this argument. Why then is Ibn al-Quff introducing this new allegedly Persian term in the discussion?

One possible interpretation is that, by weaving this word into Ibn Sīnā's enquiry, Ibn al-Quff is suggesting his competence in Persian. It will be useful to recall what Ibn al-Quff states in the passage quoted above: namely, that *birsām* is a hot inflammation that happens in the membrane called *afraghmā*, which is a Persian word; that *sirsām* is also a hot inflammation, and this noun is also Persian, *sar* being the brain and *sām* being the inflammation, while *bar* is the chest and *sām* the inflammation.

I suggest that we read this passage as an implicit participant narrative. It is implicit, in that Ibn al-Quff does not describe his activity as a translator but rather suggests such an activity by, on the one hand, appropriating Ibn Sīnā's etymology without acknowledgement, and on the other, adding a new Persian term, *afraghmā*. The implicit narrative thus presents the commentator Ibn al-Quff as competent in Persian. It endows him with the authority to intervene in the classification of brain fever vs diaphragmatic fever, by advocating a fitting usage of the Persian terms *birsām* and *sirsām*.

This short narrative thus reveals how the issue of translation, raised by Ibn Sīnā in a text which enjoyed such an immense popularity as the *Canon*, affected epistemic practices in the medical domain. Only 'people who do not know languages', as Ibn Sīnā has it, would commit the gross mistake of grouping together *birsām* and *sirsām* and use them synonymously.[13] The result of such confusion in terms would also have a deleterious impact on therapeutics, as confusing diaphragmatic and brain fever results necessarily in an imprecise, if not altogether wrong diagnosis. In light of this, we can explain Ibn al-Quff's preoccupation with demonstrating his competence as a translator. Knowing how to look into a Persian etymology becomes an argumentative tool against colleagues less steeped in languages, whose theories can be partly discredited based on their faulty usage in foreign terms. Knowledge of languages thus becomes a requisite of the competent physician and an indispensable tool towards a correct classification, diagnosis, and treatment of disease.

---

13 See n. 2.

Conclusion

While participant narratives in Arabic medical translations are extremely rare, Arabic authors did engage in methodological enquiries about translation and the usage of foreign words in order to back up their arguments. Above, I have given an account of one such enquiry, showing how Ibn Sīnā criticized his colleagues who lacked a proper training in languages and used foreign lexicon haphazardly. I also argued that Ibn al-Quff may have manipulated Ibn Sīnā's remarks in order to acquire authority as an exegete of the Hippocratic text. Not only did he appropriate Ibn Sīnā's argument about the etymology of *birsām* and *sirsām*, he also tampered with it by adding a third allegedly Persian word to the original text. By doing so, I argue, Ibn al-Quff crafted an implicit participant narrative aimed at asserting his own knowledge of Persian. With my argument, I have attempted to document one instance in which issues of translation came to play a crucial role in medical epistemic practices, and to how the knowledge of languages could be used by writers as an argument to refute rival theories.

Bibliography

Manuscript

Istanbul, Süleymaniy Library, Yeni Camii, MS 919

Primary Sources

Ibn al-Quff, لطيالمقالة الرابعة من شرح فصول أبقراط لأبي الفرج ابن القف (Commentary on the Hippocratic Aphorisms, Book 6), ed. by Peter Pormann, Kamran Karimullah, Nicola Carpentieri, Taro Mimura, Emily Selove, Aileen Das, Hammood Obaid, Elaine Van Dalen, and Sherif Masry (Manchester: University of Manchester, 2017), DOI: https://doi.org/10.3927/52132236

Ibn Abī Uṣaybiʿa, *ʿUyūn al-anbāʾ fī ṭabaqāt al-aṭibbāʾ*, vol. 2, ed. by August Müller (Cairo: al-Maṭbaʿa al-wahbiyyah, 1884)

Ibn Sīnā, *al-Qānūn fī al-Ṭibb*, ed. by Muḥammad Amīn al-Ḍinnāwī (Beirut: Dār al-Kutub al-ʿIlmiyya, 1999)

Secondary Studies

Carpentieri, Nicola, and Taro Mimura, 'Arabic Commentaries on the Hippocratic Aphorisms, vi.11: A Medieval Medical Debate on Phrenitis', *Oriens*, 45 (2017), 176–202

Carpentieri, Nicola, 'On the Meaning of *Birsām* and *Sirsām*, a Survey of the Arabic Commentaries on the Hippocratic *Aphorisms*', *Mélanges de l'Institut dominicain d'études orientales*, 32 (2017), 81–92

Dols, Michael, *Majnūn, the Madman in Medieval Islamic Society* (Cambridge: Cambridge University Press, 1992)

Fancy, Nahyan, 'Medical Commentaries: A Preliminary Examination of Ibn al-Nafīs's Shurūḥ, the Mūjaz and Subsequent Commentaries on the Mūjaz', *Oriens*, 41 (2013), 525–45

Hamarneh, Sami Khalaf, *The Physician, Therapist and Surgeon Ibn al-Quff (1233–1286)* (Cairo: The Atlas Press, 1974)

Jacquart, Danielle, 'Les avatars de la phrénitis chez Avicenne et Rhazès', in *Maladie et maladies: histoire et conceptualisation. Mélange en l'honneur de Mirko Grmek*, ed. by Danielle Gourevitch (Geneva: Droz, 1992), pp. 181–92

——, 'Les traductions médicales de Gérard de Crémone, dans P. Pizzamiglio', in *Gerardo da Cremona*, ed. by Pierluigi Pizzamiglio (Cremona: Annali della Biblioteca statale e libreria civica di Cremona XLI, 1992), pp. 57–70

——, 'Remarques préliminaires à une étude comparée des traductions médicales de Gérard de Crémone', in *Traduction et traducteurs au Moyen Age*, ed. by Geneviève Contamine (Paris: Editions du CNRS, 1989), pp. 109–18

Overwien, Oliver, 'The Art of the Translator, or: How did Ḥunayn ibn Isḥāq and his School Translate?' in *Epidemics in Context*, ed. by Peter E. Pormann (Berlin: de Gruyter, 2012), pp. 151–69

Pomata, Gianna, 'The Medical Case Narrative: Distant Reading of an Epistemic Genre', *Literature and Medicine*, 31.1 (2014), 1–23

Pormann, Peter, 'Theory and Practice in the Early Hospitals in Baghdad – al-Kaškarī on Rabies and Melancholy', *Zeitschrift für Geschichte der Arabisch-Islamischen Wissenschaften*, 15 (2002–2003), 197–248

Pormann, Peter E., and Peter N. Joosse, 'Commentaries on the Hippocratic Aphorisms in the Arabic Tradition', in *Epidemics in Context*, ed. by Peter E. Pormann (Berlin: de Gruyter, 2012), pp. 211–50

Strohmaier, G., 'Galen the Pagan and Ḥunayn the Christian: Specific Transformations in the Commentaries on *Airs, Waters, Places* and the *Epidemics*', in *Epidemics in Context*, ed. by Peter E. Pormann (Berlin: de Gruyter, 2012), pp. 171–84

Ullmann, Manfred, *Islamic Medicine* (Edinburgh: Edinburgh University Press, 1978)

FEDERICO DAL BO

'If you will judge me to have merit'

Isaac Aboab da Fonseca's Preface to his Hebrew Translation of Abraham Cohen de Herrera's Puerta del Cielo

Kabbalistic literature began its dissemination in Europe, outside the Jewish world, especially thanks to translations from Hebrew (or Aramaic) into western languages — mostly Latin.[1] This was almost an obvious decision, due to the prestige of Latin and its diffusion among intellectuals in Europe until very recent times. One can mention, for instance, the private library of Kabbalistic texts that the Italian erudite and philosopher Giovanni Pico della Mirandola had had translated to Latin in 1486 by the Jewish convert Guglielmo Raimondo Moncada, alias Flavius Mithridates.[2] Another important example is the famous anthology of Kabbalistic texts *Kabbala Denudata* translated

1 In the present paper, I cannot treat the historical importance of the dissemination of the Kabbalah in Arabic and also in the Ottoman Empire. On the reception of Kabbalah in the Arabic-speaking world, see especially Anidjar, *'Our Place in al-Andalus'*, pp. 166–245. For another insight into the modern, Asian context, see also Huss, 'The Sufi Society of America'. On the emergence of Kabbalistic literature in the Ottoman context, see also Lehmann, *Ladino Rabbinic Literature and Ottoman Sephardic Culture*, pp. 56–57.

2 Academic interest for Flavius Mithridates' translations of the Kabbalah for Giovanni Pico della Mirandola began with the pioneering work of Wirszubski, *Pico della Mirandola's Encounter with Jewish Mysticism*, pp. 69–120. See also the several papers collected in Perani, ed., *Guglielmo Raimondo Moncada alias Flavio Mitridate*, and Perani and Corazzol, eds, *Flavio Mitridate mediatore fra culture nel contesto dell'ebraismo siciliano del XV secolo*. Few volumes of Mithridates' translations have also been published. See: Busi, Campanini, and Bondoni, *The Great Parchment*; Campanini, ed., *The Book of Bahir*; Corazzol, ed., *Commentary on the Daily Prayers*; Martini, ed., *The Book of Punctuation*; Jurgan and Campanini, eds, *The Gate of Heaven*.

Federico Dal Bo holds a PhD in Translation Studies (Bologna, 2005) and a PhD in Jewish Studies (Berlin, 2009). He currently is a post-doctoral research assistant at the University of Heidelberg / Hochschule für Jüdische Studien in the project 'Material Text Cultures'. His most recent publications are: *Emanation and Philosophy of Language: An Introduction to Josef ben Abraham Giqatilla* (Cherub Press, 2019), *Deconstruting the Talmud: The Absolute Book* (Routledge, 2019), and *Qabbalah e traduzione. Un saggio su Paul Celan* (Orthotes, 2019), *Il linguaggio della violenza. Estremismo e ideologia nella filosofia contemporanea* (Biblioteca Clueb, 2020). (<https://www.federicodalbo.eu/>)

Narratives on Translation across Eurasia and Africa: From Babylonia to Colonial India, ed. by Sonja Brentjes in cooperation with Jens Høyrup and Bruce O'Brien, CAT 3, pp. 309–323 (Turnhout: Brepols, 2022) BREPOLS PUBLISHERS 10.1484/M.CAT-EB.5.127947

into Latin in 1678 by the German Christian Hebraist Christian Knorr von Rosenroth.[3] In most cases, the dissemination of Kabbalistic literature appears to be unidirectional and monolingual — from the Jewish to the Christian world and from Hebrew (or Aramaic) to Latin — according to this common route in Jewish-Christian intellectual history. Yet there is a significant exception: the famous Kabbalistic work *Puerta del Cielo* ('Gate of Sky')[4] — written by Abraham Cohen de Herrera and disseminated among European intellectuals, thanks to its translations into Hebrew and into Latin.

The Work *Puerta del Cielo*: Content and Dissemination

Puerta del Cielo — probably elaborated from an expression in Genesis 28. 17 — is a long, syncretistic collection of Kabbalistic traditions. It was originally written in Spanish, between 1620 and 1635 in Amsterdam, by the Jewish-born Abraham Cohen de Herrera, who intended to rescue the Kabbalah from the neglect of philosophers and the obscurantism of other Kabbalists, whom Herrera believed not to be interested in reaching many readers.[5] The text was inspired by a large number of Jewish sources: the *Sefer Yetzirah*,[6] the prominent Spanish Rabbi Joseph ben Abraham Gikatilla,[7] the teachings from the monumental book of the *Zohar*,[8] and the works of important Kabbalists like Rabbi Moshe Cordovero,[9] and Rabbi Israel Sarug.[10] Along with this genuine Jewish Kabbalistic background, Herrera's *Puerta del Cielo* also integrated several

3 Scholarship on Christian Knorr von Rosenroth (1636–1689) is very extensive. For brevity's sake, I refer here only to Kilcher, ed., *Die Kabbala Denudata. Text und Kontext.*

4 Please note that I render *puerta* as 'gate' rather than the literal translation as 'door' which is non-idiomatic and confusing.

5 For the dating of Herrera's works and other biographical details, see the Introduction in Krabbenhoft, ed., *Abraham Cohen De Herrera. Gates of Heaven*, pp. xi–xxxiv.

6 The short treatise *Sefer Yetzirah* was probably composed in Palestine in the sixth–seventh century and is transmitted in three versions: the short version, the long version, and the so-called Sa'adia version. See Hayman, ed., *Sefer Yetzira, Edition, Translation and Text-Critical Commentary*, pp. 59–195 and Hayman, 'The "Original Text" of the Sefer Yesira or the "Earliest Recoverable Text"'.

7 Rabbi Joseph ben Abraham Gikatilla (1248–*c.* 1325) was one of the most prominent Kabbalists in Spain. See the three monographs Blickstein, *Between Philosophy and Mysticism*, Morlok, *Rabbi Joseph Gikatilla's Hermeneutics*, and Dal Bo, *Emanation and Philosophy of Language*.

8 On the genesis of the *Zohar* with respect to the medieval attitude to literary production and the circle of Kabbalists working with Moshe de León, see in particular Abrams, 'The Invention of the *Zohar* as a Book'.

9 Rabbi Moshe Cordovero (1522–1570) was one of the most influential Kabbalists active in Safed, Israel. He published *Pardes Rimmonim* (An Orchard of Pomegranates) and especially *Or Yakar* (Precious Light), a comprehensive commentary on the *Zohar*.

10 On Israel Sarug (?–1610), the classic work is Scholem, 'Israel Sarug, the Ari's Disciple?' [Hebrew]. See also Idel, 'Between the Kabbalah of Jerusalem and the Kabbalah of Israel Sarug' [Hebrew].

non-Jewish sources from Platonic, Aristotelian, Neoplatonic metaphysics, medieval Islamic and Jewish theology, and Scholasticism. Herrera's style imitated that of the thirteenth-century introductions to the Kabbalah of the aforementioned Gikatilla: a clean, expository writing that might reach the largest audience possible. The fundamentally didactic purposes of Herrera's text also oriented his selection of Kabbalistic material and especially justified his attitude not to choose one strand of the Jewish mystical tradition to the exclusion of another. Therefore, Herrera emphasizes whether specific teachings on a topic have been received in the Jewish tradition.

This text underwent a very complex chain of transmission: it was originally written in Castilian, then translated into Hebrew in 1647 with the title *Shaʿar ha-Shamaim* ('The Gate of the Skies'), then translated into Latin in 1678 with the Latin title *Porta Coelorum* ('The Gate of the Skies'), and eventually included in the aforementioned anthology *Kabbala Denudata*. The reception of this text is very peculiar in its origin, language, and dissemination. First, Cohen de Herrera is believed to descend from a *converso* family that had a solid Jewish background and probably introduced him to the secrets of Kabbalistic literature. Second, the text was obviously written in a non-Jewish language — Castilian — and therefore represents an exception in the dissemination of Kabbalistic knowledge; it is neither written by a genuine Jewish scholar nor exclusively depends on Jewish tradition. Third, the text underwent a complex linguistic mediation — from Castilian to Hebrew and from Hebrew to Latin — with a particular impact on its content and phraseology, especially because both the Hebrew and the Latin translation have considerably abridged the source text.

The Translator's *Preface* to the Hebrew Translation

The Hebrew translation was done by an important Jewish scholar, Rabbi Itzhak Aboab da Fonseca, who was active as poet, writer, and a rabbi.[11] As a member of the Amsterdam congregation, he witnessed the excommunication of Baruch Spinoza — whom he probably made aware of Herrera's work.[12] Aboab himself came from a *converso* family from Portugal that eventually reconverted back to the Jewish faith in 1612, when moving to Amsterdam, where he was eventually ordained as a rabbi. Consequently, Aboab was appointed to office in 1642 at the *Kahal Tzur Israel*, a synagogue in the city of Recife (Brazil) — the oldest Jewish community in the New World — where Sephardic Jews had lived under Dutch rule since 1624. Shortly after Aboab's arrival, the city of Recife underwent a nine year-long siege by Portuguese forces that reoccupied the region after a harsh struggle. Only in 1654 did the siege end and Aboab eventually left for Amsterdam shortly thereafter, being

11 On Rabbi Isaac Aboab de Fonseca, see the entire monograph Orfali, *Isaac Aboab da Fonseca*.

12 See Beltran, *The Influence of Abraham Cohen de Herrera's Kabbalah on Spinoza's Ethics*, p. 3.

appointed as Chief Rabbi in 1656, when he was one of the signatories of the excommunication of Baruch Spinoza. Presumably after his return from Brazil, Aboab translated, elaborated, and abridged Herrera's *Puerta del Cielo* into Hebrew which was eventually published under the title *Shaʿar ha-Shamayim* ('The Gate of the Skies').

Most interestingly, Aboab wrote a long *Preface* that provides insight in the so-called narratives of translation.[13] The text essentially consists of an uninterrupted series of quotations from Scripture, Rabbinic texts, the *Zohar*, and other Jewish texts in an effort to produce a coherent, readable, and evocative text. In the translation that follows, I have segmented the text in four minor units and I have ignored minor changes in orthography and writing when they clearly reflected the indention of joining different verses. I have, however, emphasized changes with respect the original source if particularly relevant:

הקדמת המעתיק

אמר המעתיק, אחרי ההודאה והתהלה לפני מלך מלכי המלכים מלכו של עולם, *כל ברואי מעלה ומטה יעידון יגידון* (סידור ספרד, תפילת ישרים, זמירות ללֵיית שבת) כי הוא האלהם המוציא *לאור כל תעלומה* (תיקוני זוהר א קכב ע››א), *ותולה ארץ על בלימה* (איוב כו ז), בהוציאו יש מאין, כאשר *ראתה כל עין* (ישעיה סד ג), *סבת הסבות ועלת כל העלות* (תיקוני זוהר יז ע››א), לפני *פני הודה והדרה* (בעל הטורים, בראשית כח, י) *הכל היה הוה ויהיה* (סידור ספרד, שמע), *והיא לא שזפתה עין היא* (איוב כח ז), כי החיות והאופנים משאי הכבוד להעלימו, המכריזים ואומרים *ברוך כבוד ה׳ ממקומו* (יחזקאל ג יב). ממקומו *הפליא לעשות* עמנו (בן סירא לי ט), *כי הוציאנו מכור* הבראזי››ל *ממצרים* (דברים ד כ), אשר הציקונו אויבינו, *בלעג וקלס לסביבותינו* (תהלים עט ד), *מחוץ תשכל חרב ומחדרים אימה* (דברים לב כה), באלף החמישי וד› מאות וששה, עברו על האומה החשוקה כמה וכמה תלאות, לא יכילום ספרים ומגילות, *כי הדת נתנה* (אסתר ג טו) *בפמליא של מעלה* (ב› סנהדרין לח ע››ב), *פשט הגדוד* (הושע ז א) *וישטחו להם שטוח* (במדבר טב לב), ביער ובשדה, זה יעט אל *השלל* (א שמעאל טו יט) וזה הנפש צודה, כי בא האויב לעקור את הכל *בכלה ונחרצה* (ישעיה י כג), *צבאו ופקודיו* (במדבר ב ו) *מקרבם* (שופטים י יו) בא מארץ *גזרה* (ויקרא יו כב), אלו נהרגו אלו מחוסר *כל נאספו אל אבות׳* (שופטים ב י), *ינוחו שלום על משכבות׳* (ישעיהו נז ב), ואנחנו נשארו במתי *מעט* (דברים כו ה) נטויים להרג ולבזיון, *האוכלים למעדנים* (איכה ד ה) *אפתורא דדהבא* (ב› תענית כה ע››א), ערבה להם *לחם יבש* (יהשועה ט ה) *ופת חרבה* (משלי טח א), ואין שלום בה, וגם הוא אזל מבתינו, *חסר הצפחת והכד כלה* (א מלכים טח טז), *העם שב עד המכהו* (ישעהו ט יג) *ויצעקו* אל ה› (תהלים קז ו) אלהיהם, *אומנות אבותיהם* (מכילתא דר› ישמעאל יד יא) בידיהם, *ויעתר*(בראשית כה כא) להם *וימטר* (שמות ט כג) עליהם

13 I have transcribed it from the early print *Sefer Sha'ar ha-Shamayim* (Amsterdam: Immanuel Benveniste, 1655) p. 2a, and the later print *Sefer Sha'ar ha-Shamayim* (Warshaw: Chaim Kelter' i Spółki, 1864), pp. 23–24. I have found Biblical, Talmudic, and Rabbinic sources with help of The Global Jewish Database (The Responsa Project) Version 24, Bar Ilan University and the on-line Database: http://www.sefaria.org/. I would like to thank Dr Ruben Kiperwasser (Free University of Berlin), Dr Cedric Cohen Skalli (University of Haifa), and Dr Dror Weil (King's College London) for reading a first draft of this translation.

מן לאכול *צידה שלח להם לשובע* (תהלים עח כה), ויהי לנס. ואחרי כמה *צרות רבות ורעות* (תהלים עא כ) זו לזו תכופות קלות וחמורות, *קל מן שמיא נפל* (דניאל ד כח) *כלה גרש יגרש* (שמות יא א) *זעיר שם זעיר שם* (ישעיהו כח יג), מהם ערומים *מהם יחפים* (ישעהו כ ב), *דרך אניות בלב ים* (משלי ל יט), האלהים אנה לידם, כי קרא ה› *דרור בארץ* (ויקרא כה י) *והיה המחנה הנשאר שארית ישראל לפליטה* (בראשית לב ט) *וה' הולך לפניהם להנחותם הדרך* (שמות יג כא) *לעבור גאולים* (ישעהו נא י), *ולהחיות רוח שפלים* (ישעהו נז יה), *כי לא נפקד איש* (במדבר לא מט) מכל הקהלה, *ואני מתוך הגולה* (יחזקאל א א), *וישיבני אל* (יחזקאל מז א) המקום הזה *להתעדן בגן עדנה* (תפילת בקשה לשבת) של תורה, מנעורי *גרסה נפשי לתאבה* (תהילם קיט כ), *ואבא היום אל העין*(בראשית כד מב) עין הקורא, *להוכיח במישור* (ישעהו יא ד) *שמץ דבר* (איוב כו יד) ממעלת החכם המחבר, *מבינתו יאבר* (איוב לט כו), *נס להתנוסס* (תהלים ס ו), *המקרה בים* האלהיות *מעלותיו* (תהלים קד ג), *וכל הבארות אשר חפר* (בראשית כו טו), בספר *ספור וספר* (ספר יצירה א א), *כלם נכוחים למבין* (משלי ח ט) בסודות המבלה אשר קבל מהרב כמהור››ר **ישראל סרוג** עה››ש *אשר יצק מים ע'*'י (מלכים ב ג יא) הקדוש כמהור››ר **יצחק לוריא** אשכנזי וז››ל, כאשר יעידון בכרכי› הכרוכי› אשר היום בידי, *כתובים באצבע אלהים* (שמות לי טז), "ספר אדם קדמון", וביאור "אדרת האזינו", "סדר האצילות", או "כנפי יונה", וספר "מטי ולא מטי", *ואלה המלכים אשר מלכו בארץ אדום* (בראשית לו לא), וביאורם נחמדים, *יכלום עיני הרואים* (ישעיהו לב ג), *ויסכם אברהם* (בראשית כב ג) לעשות אזנים *לתושיה* (איוב כא ו), והחכמה הנעלמה *על אדני פז* (שיר השירים ה יה) יסדה, כי חכמה ושכלנותא השתכח› ביה *בחכמות הטבעיות ואלהיות* (ספר הקוזרי ג, לט) הקודמות והנצריכות לעבודת משמרת, דעת המקובלת אשר *בעטו יורה* (דברים יא יט), הרב המורה, *וה' ברוך את הברהם בכל* (בראשית כד א), וחיבור אלו השני הספים, מספירים יקרים, "השער השמים" עם "בית אלהים". וזה "שער השמים", האחד אשר על "מעשה בראשית" דיבר נכונה, והאחד "במעשה מרכבה", *שפתותיו* (שיר השירים ה יג) *מרבבה* (שיר השירים ה י), בראשון *שפתיו ברור מללו* (איוב לג ג), ועל סדר מהצליות ועשר ספירות, ועל החמש פרצופי› במתקלא של עולם, אדם קדמון, עלום הא››ס,[14] סוד שבירת הכלים, וחסרונות המלכים ותיקונם, *פום ממלל רברבן* (זוהר ב סז ע››א) ואלהים נסה את אברהם (בראשית כב א), ומן הגלגל עלה בית אל (בראשית לה א) בשני, ועל עשר כחות המלאכים דבר נפלאות, אופני מערכותם, וסוד התקשרותם, ועבודת משמרת החיות *האופנים לעומתם* (יחזקאל ג יג), *ויעל מהם באר שבע* (בראשית כו כג) היכלות, כסא הכבוד, ואופן בריאות› ומהותו, ואחריו גלה סוד הספירות, וכל העלומים הנעלמים, והתאצלותם, קשורם ואחדות›, עם מקור מעיינם וסיבתם, *וה' אמר המכסה אני מאברהם* (בראשית יח יז), והדברים עתיקים אך בלשון לועז ונכרי, כי לא נסה לדבר בארש העברי, ואותי צוה להעתיקם ולהוציא לאור משפטם, וביום העלותו אל האלהים, לא היתה עינו צרם בממונו, להוציא לאור פרי *מעלליו* (ירמיהו יז י), זהב הזיל ממכמניו, *מרגלית טובה תלויה בצוארו של אברהם* (בבא בתרא טז ע››ב), מרגלית *דלית ביה טימא* (תוספות מסכת ברכות דף יב ע››א), ולו *תהיה צדקה* (דברים ו כה), בזכותו את הרבים, *ואברהם עודנו עומד לפני ה'* (בראשית יח כב). ועתה *אנוש כערכי* (תהלים נה יד) *לא נעלם ממני* (אבן תיבון, הקדמה) כמה וכמה תנאים מחוייב מציאותם, למעתיק מלשון אל לשון, ומתכונת הדברים ועבודתם, מ››שכ הרב שמואל אבן תיבון ראש המעתיקי› בהקדמתו לספר "מורה הנבוכים" ומה ששלח אליו הרב באגרתו, כי ירא

14 I correct here עלוה הא"ם (?) with עלום הא"ס ('the world of the *En Sof*). I owe this suggestion to Dr Dror Weil.

אנכי אותו (בראשית לב יב), בהיות *גלוי וידוע לפני* (תפלית ברכת יצר) *מיעוט שלימותי* [...] וקוצר השגתי (אבן תיבון, הקדמה), בלשון *מדברת גדולות* (תהלים יב ד), ממני *נפלאות* (איוב מב ג), *כי לא כן אנכי עמדי* (איוב ט לה), במדת המתפאר מחכמתו ורזים *משחק לו* (חבקוק א י), מסתכל בדבריו כמסתכל הטווס בנוצתו, כי יביט לרגליו והנה חשך הודו ותפארתו, ונהפך לאבל גאותו, אמנם לצאת ידי חובתי, אזרתי כגבור חלצי, וארכיב ידי על קשתי, כי מצוה לקיים דברי המת, ואם הוא חי. *ועתה שא נא חטאתי*(שמות י יז) אם תמצאנו, אולי ימצאו לי עון אשר חטא זולתי גרם, ולך *תהיה צדקה* (דברים כד יג) *כי תדינני לכף זכות, ולא לכף חובה* (ב‹ ברכות לא ע››ב), *ותפטר באהבה רבה* (ב‹ ברכות יא ע››ב), ממני דורש שלומך וחושק אהבתך, הצעיר יצחק אבוהב

(The translator's introduction

(1) The translator said after confessing and beginning before the king of the kings of the kings, the king of the world: *all the creatures of above and below confirm* (Siddur Sefard, Tefillat Yesharim, Shabbat Evening Meal, Zemirot) that it is God who makes *all the hidden things come to light* (Tikkuney Zohar 1. 122a) and *hangeth the earth upon nothing* (Job 26. 7), while making something out of nothing, as every *eye has seen* (Isaiah 64. 3) *the supernal of all supernals, the cause of all causes* (Tikkuney Zohar 17a), in front of [God's] *glory and splendour* (Ba'al ha-Turim on Genesis 28. 10) [to] *everything that was, is, and will be* (Siddur Sefarad, Shema), and *the vulture's eye hath not seen* (Job 28. 7) that the beasts and the wheels supporting the Glory [of God] forever.

(2) They recall and say: *blessed the Glory of the Lord from His place* (Ezra 3. 12), from His place *hath done wonderful things* (Sirach 31. 9), since [he has] *brought you forth out of the furnace* of Brazil *even out of Egypt* (Deuteronomy 4. 20), where we were harassed by our enemies. While [being] *a scorn and a derision to those who are round about us* (Psalms 79. 13), *outside the sword shall bereave, and in the rooms, terror* (Deuteronomy 32. 25) [in the year] 5406 (= 1646), the nation in need has suffered a great deal of hardship [that] books and scrolls will not include, because *the decree was given* (Esther 3. 15) *in the entourage from above* (Babylonian Talmud, Tractate Sanhedrin 38b), *bands raiding* (Hosea 7. 1), *spread them out* (Numbers 11. 32) in the city and the field *and swoop down on the spoil* (1 Samuel 15. 19) and the soul became the pray of a hunter, because the enemy came to uproot everything with *a determined end* (Isaiah 10. 23) and *his host, and those that were numbered of them* (Numbers 2. 6) *from among them* (Judges 10. 16) came from *an inaccessible region* (Leviticus 16. 22), some were killed, some dispersed, *all gathered to [their] fathers* (Judges 2. 10), [they] *shall rest in peace on* [their] *couch* (Isaiah 57. 3) and we were left with *a meagre number* (Deuteronomy 26. 6) prone to killing and disgrace. *Those who fasted in dainties* (Lamentations 4. 5) [on] *a golden table* (Babylonian Talmud, Tractate Ta'anit 25a) satisfied their hunger with *dry bread* (Joshua 9. 5) and *dry crust* (Proverbs 17. 1) and there was no

peace from it and even this run out of our homes and *flour lacked in the jugs* (1 Kings 17. 16) *for the people turned back to him who struck them* (Isaiah 9. 12) *and they cried to the Lord* (Psalms 107. 6), their God, *the trade of their fathers* (Mekhilta de-Rabbi Ishmael 14. 11) in their hands. *And* [God] *pleaded with* (Genesis 25. 21) them *and rained down* (Exodus 9. 23) upon them *meal, He sent them provision in plenty* (Psalms 78. 25). And a miracle took place. And after *many troubles and misfortunes* (Psalms 71. 20), often to each other, light and severe, *a voice fell from the skies* (Daniel 4. 28): *He will drive you out of here one and all* (Exodus 11. 1) *a little here, a little there* (Isaiah 28. 13), some of them *naked,* some of them *barefoot* (Isaiah 20. 2), *how* ships *make* their *way through the high seas* (Proverbs 30. 19), because the Lord *proclaimed release throughout the land* (Leviticus 25. 10) and *the other camp* of the rest of Israel *may yet escape* (Genesis 32. 9) *and the Lord went before them in a pillar to guide them along the way* (Exodus 13. 21) *to the redeemer might walk* (Isaiah 51. 10) *and to the lowly in spirit* (Isaiah 57. 15), *because none was missing* (Numbers 21. 49) from the Community of Israel. *I was in the midst of the exile* (Ezra 1. 1) *and he led me back to* (Ezra 47. 1) this place *to be softened in the Garden of Delight* (Tefilat Bakashah le-Shabbat) of Scripture.

(3) From my youth *my soul was longing* (Psalms 119. 20) *and I came today to the spring* (*'ayn*) (Genesis 24. 42), the eye (*'ayn*) of the reader *to judge with equity* (Isaiah 11. 4) *a small portion* (Job 26. 14) from the supernal knowledge of the author *from his wisdom that grows* (Job 39. 26), *a banner for rallying* (Psalms 60. 6), *the rafters of his lofts in the* divine *waters* (Psalms 104. 3) *and all the wells which* he *had dug* (Genesis 26. 15) with *number, writing and speech* (Sefer Yetzirah 1. 1), *all are straightforward to the intelligent man* (Proverbs 8. 9) with the secrets of the Kabbalah that he received from the Rav, our honored master and teacher the great Rabbi Israel Sarug, the peace may be on him, who *poured water on the hands of* (2 Kings 3. 11) the Holy Rabbi, our honored master and teacher the great Rabbi Isaac Luria Ashkenazi, of blessed memory, as it will be discussed in the bound volumes that are in my hand today, *inscribed with the finger of God* (Exodus 31. 18): the 'Sefer Adam Kadmon', the explanation to the 'Idrat ha-Azinu', 'Seder ha-Atzilut' or 'Kanfey Yonah', and the Book 'Mete we-lo-Mate'.[15] *These are the kings who reigned in the land of Edom* (Genesis

15 These four texts — *Sefer Adam Kadmon*, the explanation to the *Idrat ha-Azinu*, *Seder ha-Atzilut* (also known as *Kanfey Yonah*) and the Book *Mete we-lo-Mate* — are Luranic homilies and Hayyim Vital's commentaries thereon. These are texts that Herrera might have received from Sarug and possibly handed over to Aboab himself. This list agrees with usual collections of Kabbalistic works of the time. See, for instance, the seventeenth-century copy of Hayyim Vital's *Tree of Life* (EH 47 B 25), published online here: http://etshaimmanuscripts.nl/manuscripts/eh-47-b-25/. As remarked by Altmann, no authorized collections of Luria's writing had yet been published, at the time of Herrera's studying with Sarug, see Altmann, 'Lurianic Kabbala in a Platonic Key'.

36. 31), and [other] pleasant explanations, included *the eyes of those who have sight* (Isaiah 32. 3). *And Abraham* agreed (Genesis 22. 3) to make ears *to sagacity* (Job 21. 6) and the hidden knowledge is set *in socket of fine gold* (Song of Solomon 5. 15), because knowledge and intellect are found in *natural and divine wisdoms* (Sefer ha-Kuzari 3.39) that once were and are highly required for worship have been forgotten, and the established opinion that our great master teaches,[16] *and the Lord blessed Abraham with everything* (Genesis 24. 2) and the author of these two books from the precious books: 'The Gate of the Skies' together with 'The House of God'. This is 'The Gate of the Skyes'. The one is on the 'Work of Creation', a correct speech, and one is on 'The Work of Chariot', *his lips* (Song of Solomon 5.13) *among thousand* (Song of Solomon 5. 10). In the first [book], *his lips utter honest words* (Job 33. 3) on the order of emanation, on the ten *sefirot*, on the five Faces, on the balance of the world, the First Man, the world of the *En Sof*, the secret of the Breaking of the Vessels, the shortcomings of the kings and their corrections, *his mouth speaks in a bombastic manner* (Zohar 2. 67 a) *and God put Abraham to the test* (Genesis 22. 1) and from the wheels [of the skies] *he went up to Bethel* a second time and on the ten angelic powers he spoke wondrously, [on] the wheels of their system and the secret of their connection and the worship of the service of the beasts and the *wheels beside them* (Ezra 3. 13) *and* from them *he went up to Beersheba* (Genesis 26. 23) to the Palace, the Throne of Glory, the art of their creation and their essence, and after that he revealed the secret of the *Sefirot* and all the hidden worlds and their emanation, their connection and their unity, with the source of their purpose and their reason *and the Lord said: Shall I hide from Abraham* (Genesis 18. 17) and these things are ancient but [written] in Romance and foreign language because he did not try to speak in sound Hebrew and he appointed me to translate and bring to light their sentences. And in the day when he went up to God, he had no interest at all in money in order to bring to light *the fruit of his deeds* (Jeremiah 17. 10) and he took gold from his treasures *and a precious gem hung on the neck of Abraham* (Babylonian Talmud, Tractate Baba Batra 27b), *a precious gem that is priceless* (Tosafot on Babylonian Talmud, Tractate Berakhot 12a) *and* he *had the merit* (Deuteronomy 6. 25), and in light of his benefiting the public *and Abraham remained standing before the Lord* (Genesis 18. 22).

16 The sentence is a homophonic wordplay with a verse from Deuteronomy that literally reads 'in its time, early rain' (בעתו יורה) (Deuteronomy 11. 19). The term *yoreh* (early rain) is interpreted as the homograph present participle *yoreh* from the verb *yarah* ('to teach'), whereas the prepositional syntagma *be-'ito* (בעתו) ('in its time') is transformed spelled as almost homophonic *be-'eṭo* (בעטו) ('with his pen').

(4) And now, *my equal* (Psalms 55. 14), *it is not hidden to me* (Ibn Tibbon, Translator's Preface) how many conditions require their existence to translate language by language and the structure of words and their function, as Rabbi Samuel Ibn Tibbon, the head of the translators wrote in his introduction to the Book 'The Guide for the Perplexed' and that the Rav send to him by letter, *for I fear him* (Genesis 32. 12), as it is *revealed and known before me* (Siddur Sefard, Birkat Asher Yatzar) *the fewness of my perfection* [...] *and the shortness of my accomplishment* (Ibn Tibbon, Translator's Preface) in *every tongue that speaks arrogance* (Psalms 12. 4) *things beyond me* (Job 42. 3) *for I know myself not to be so* (Job 9. 35) in a measure that boasts his knowledge and secrets *are a joke to him* (Habakkuk 1. 10), he looks into his words just as a peacock looks into his feathers, because he will look at his feet and, behold, the darkness of his honor and his splendour, and he became a grief of pride. It is true that I performed my duty, I gathered myself as a hero, I hold my hand on my request because of the commandment of fulfilling the words of a dead, as if he were alive. *Forgive my offence* (Genesis 1. 17), if you will find any. Maybe you will find a fault that I have committed inadvertently *and it will be your merit* (Deuteronomy 24. 13) if you will *judge me to have merit and not to have obligation* (Babylonian Talmud, Tractate Berakhot 31b) and you will *exempt me by abundant love* (Babylonian Talmud, Tractate Berakhot 11b) from me, who I seek your wellness and desire your love, the young Itzhak Aboab.)

Analysis: Texts and Subtexts in Aboab's *Preface*

This erudite *Preface* of the 'translator' (literally: 'the copyist') clearly has a main purpose — magnifying the figure of Abraham Cohen de Herrera, whom Aboab only mentions by his given-name Abraham, in clear resonance with the Patriarch Abraham. The text flows uninterruptedly but clearly exhibits an internal structure in four main units: (1) a general invocation to God, (2) a description of the duress during the siege of Recife, (3) a description of Herrera's sources, and (4) the difficult task of translating Herrera's works. Each of these units is particularly interesting and deserves a specific treatment.

(1) Aboab's short invocation to God is conventional at its very beginning ('the king of the kings of the kings, the king of the world') but then recurs to a few important quotations from a specific section of the *Zohar* — the *Tikkuney ha Zohar* — exalting the arcane, mysterious atmosphere of Herrera's text. This invocation is also counterpointed with frequent quotations from the Book of Job that spread a general sense of pessimism over the text and emphasize the man's limited existence with respect of the depth of the divine mysteries.

(2) The second unit is larger and historically very interesting. Aboab evokes the siege of Recife in 1646, which he biblically describes as *an iron furnace out of Egypt* (Deuteronomy 4. 20), by playing on the similarity between the

words *barzel* ('iron') and *Brazil* ('Brazil'). There is apparently no justification for recalling this historical event. Yet Aboab is clearly elaborating on Job's assumption, mentioned earlier, that *the earth hangeth upon nothing* (Job 26. 7) and therefore is exposed to risks and duress. Particularly interesting is the assumption that this 'great deal of hardship' was not reported in 'books and scrolls' for a theological reason: '*because the decree was given* (Esther 3. 15) *in the entourage from above*' (Babylonian Talmud, Tractate Sanhedrin 38b).

At first, Aboab appears to accuse God of delivering these hard times upon him and his community in Brazil. In truth, a closer examination of the sources — from the Book of Esther and from the Talmud — provides a subtler reading of this already surprising sentence. Rather than accusing God of being ignorant of the suffering of His people in Brazil, Aboab significantly quotes from the Book of Esther: a text describing a failed persecution against the Jews and the secret life of Queen Esther, who had covertly lived as Jewess. He does so in order to emphasize a deep contrast between historiography ('books and scrolls') and truest history — the one that takes place 'in the entourage from above'. Interestingly enough, the enemy's actions are described with verses from the historical books of Scripture that describe Israel's military actions, the duress and famine during the siege are described with eloquent verses from the Proverbs, and the beginning of deliverance is announced with a verse from the Prophet Daniel and from Exodus: '*a voice fell from the skies* (Daniel 4. 28), *He will drive you out of here one and all*' (Exodus 11. 1). The mystery of deliverance is then amplified with the allusion to the other camp of the rest of Israel and culminates with a sagacious elaboration from a prayer that well describes Aboab's joy for being back in Amsterdam, devoting his life to study: '*and he led me back to* (Ezra 47. 1) this place *to be softened in the Garden of Delight* (Tefilat Bakashah le-Shabbat) of Scripture'.

(3) The third unit is particularly important because it provides a specific chain of tradition that elaborates on Herrera's autobiographical remarks. In his concise, almost terse introduction to *Puerta del Cielo*, Herrera wrote that he came from a Jewish family and had been educated directly by Israel Sarug — one of the most prominent Kabbalists of his time, direct pupil of Isaac Luria and former lecturer in Amsterdam:[17]

> Breve introducción y compendio de alguna parte de la divina sabiduría, que por tradición vocal y sucesiva vino de Moisés, nuestro preceptor y maestro, a los ancianos, a los profetas y sapientes el pueblo israelítico, y finalmente, por merced del autor de ella, y de todos los bienes, a mí, Abraham Cohen de Herrera, hijo del honorado y prudente viejo rabí David Cohen de Herrera, colegida de la ordinaria doctrina de R. Simeón ben Yohai, R. Moisés Barnahman [= Nachmanides], R. Azroel, R. Yosef Chiquitilla, *Ma'arekhet ha-Elohut* y su expositor R. Judá Hayyat, R. Moisés

17 Original text from Beltran, *The Influence of Abraham Cohen De Herrera*, pp. 43–44. English translation from Krabbenhoft, *Gates of Heaven*, pp. 1–2.

> de León, R. Meir Gabbai, R. Menahem Recanati, R. Menahem Azaria de Fano, y de otros cabalistas de loable memoria, y principalmente del eminente Hakam Rabí Moisés Cordovero, que está en paz recibida y platicada de la viva voz del Hakam Rabí Israel Saruq de feliz memoria, mi preceptor y maestro. (*Puerta del Cielo*, fol. I^{r})
>
> (Brief introduction and summary of some of the divine wisdom that has come by continuous oral tradition from our teacher and guide Moses to the ancient ones, prophets, and wise men of the people of Israel, by the grace of its author and every blessing to me, Abraham Cohen de Herrera, son of the prudent and honorable elder, Rabbi David Cohen de Herrera, drawn from the established teachings of R. Simeon ben Yohai, R. Moses bar Nahman, R. Aziel, R. Joseph Gikatilla, the Maarekhet ha-Elohut and R. Judah Hayyat its espositor, R. Moses de León, R. Meir Gabbai, R. Menahem Recanti, Rabbi Menahem Azaria da Fano, and other Kabbalists of praiseworthy memory, and especially from the eminent Hakam Rabbi Moses Cordovero, who rests in peace, and orally expounded by Hakam Rabbi Israel Sarug of blessed memory, my teacher and guide.)

Herrera describes Jewish mysticism as since its very beginning modelling the chain of tradition — 'Moses', 'the ancient ones', 'prophets', and 'wise men of the people of Israel' — on the one, famously presented in Tractate *Avot*: 'Moses received Scripture from Sinai and transmitted it to Jehoshua and Jehoshua to the Elders, and the Elders to the Prophets, and the Prophets to the Men of the Great Assembly' (Mishnah, Tractate Avot 1. 1). In addition to this, Herrera also establishes another, supplementary chain of tradition, consisting of Kabbalists: Simeon ben Yohai, R. Moses bar Nahman, R. Aziel, R. Joseph Gikatilla, R. Judah Hayyat, R. Moses de León, R. Meir Gabbai, R. Menahem Recanti, Rabbi Menahem 'Azaria da Fano, Rabbi Moses Cordovero, and Rabbi Israel Sarug. While supplementing Talmudic with Kabbalistic genealogy, Herrera is radically positing himself at the end of a tradition that departs from Moses. In other terms, Herrera clearly intends to place himself within an established chain of tradition, specifically emphasizing that he is the last disciple, who had been educated *orally* by Isaac Sarug — a master, whose expertise and knowledge descend from ancient times and depend on a large number of previous prominent scholars.

This genealogy dramatically changes in Aboab's *Preface*. Aboab exalts Herrera's work in a more sophisticated way. Firstly, Aboab follows a number of options simultaneously: he emphasizes the figure of Isaac Sarug over the other Kabbalists who are no longer mentioned but juxtaposes it to the more prominent, authoritative figure of Isaac Luria.[18] More especially, he removes

18 This seems to be reflected also in the later colophon, usually published before the

Herrera's autobiographical remark — 'Abraham Cohen de Herrera, son of the prudent and honorable elder, Rabbi David Cohen de Herrera' — and speaks only of an individual named Abraham. Accordingly, Aboab explains virtues and qualities of Abraham (Cohen de Herrera) by quoting from Scripture speaking of Abraham (the Patriarch). The conflation of the Kabbalist with the Patriarch has the obvious purpose of rhetorically postdating the text that Aboab is presenting to a Hebrew reader for the first time: *Shaʿar ha-Shamayim*. Particularly relevant is the mention of the fact that the text was not originally written in Hebrew but rather 'in Romance and foreign language'. Nevertheless, Aboab appears to suggest that Abraham (Cohen de Herrera) simply 'did not try to speak in sound Hebrew', although he might do so. Differently from Herrera's original *Puerta del Cielo*, Aboab's *Preface* is very poor in biographical details but very rich in reporting a comprehensive list of topics that are examined in this Kabbalistic text. More specifically, Aboab provides some details on Herrera's works — *Puerta del Cielo* and *Casa de la Divinidad* — that are aptly described in terms of cosmology ('The Work of Creation') and metaphysics ('The Work of Chariot'), respectively. Aboab's last autobiographical remark — 'he appointed me to translate and bring to light their sentences' — suggests that Herrera himself, before dying, had asked Aboab to translate the text into Hebrew. Although it cannot be excluded that Aboab is only being emphatic, especially when alluding to the fact that Herrera wanted to be translated for neither vanity nor money, it seems plausible that some kind of agreement took place before Herrera's death.

(4) The fourth and final unit has an exquisite Translation Studies nature. As Translation Studies have well established in time, the act of translating is never the mere, trivial fact of transposing texts from a language into another. Translating essentially consists in *negotiating* between cultures.[19] Accordingly, this act involves a number of assumptions both about the source and target cultures: first, the idea that a work *can* be translated, as there is no actual linguistic hindrance to this; second, the idea that a work *may* be translated, as there is no cultural resistance to this; third, the idea that a work *should* be translated, as there is a need for cultural transmission. These three assumptions altogether show that translation can be well received only when there is consensus on practicability, liability, and morality. In other terms, a translation can fully be accepted only when it is actually possible, when it is allowed, and where it is culturally suggested. Failing to meet with all these three requirements usually causes a translation to be biased, rejected, or stigmatized. This event is particularly frequent when there are particular cultural issues at stake and the context is ethnically marked. For instance, when focusing on the context of Jewish literature, it is evident that the notion of translating Scripture

aforementioned passage from *Puerta del Cielo*. See Beltran, ed., *Abraham Cohen De Herrera. Puerta del Cielo*, p. 41 and Knabbenhoft, *Gates of Heaven*, p. 1.

19 Eco, *Mouse or Rat?*, p. 5; cf. Eco, *Dire quasi la stessa cosa*, p. 4.

underwent long, fierce discussions among scholars. Some famous passages from the Talmud, for instance, show that opposition to translating Scripture could be motivated by objecting that Scripture *cannot* be translated, *may not* be translated, or *should* be limited in form and content. For instance, early Aramaic translations of Scripture (*targum*) were subject to a specific discipline and cultural homogeneity was far more important than, say, linguistic accuracy. Accordingly, Aramaic translations of Scripture could culturally be accepted, although they clearly diverted from the 'literal' sense.[20]

The present case involves the translation of Kabbalistic literature but reflects the same cultural issues. Aboab is clearly aware that the act of translating implies that a translator takes the responsibility for trespassing both the very linguistic and cultural limits that the author has originally posed. As he understands the challenge implied in moving beyond the perimeter traced by the original work, Aboab elaborates on the fact that he is translating a difficult and challenging work. For this reason, he excuses himself for his limited qualities as a translator and recalls the famous *Preface* that the prominent twelfth-century Jewish scholar and translator Samuel ben Yehuda Ibn Tibbon wrote after translating Maimonides' *Guide for the Perplexed* from Arabic into Hebrew. The explicit reference to this translation and the clear mention of the *Guide for the Perplexed* probably reflects a rhetorical strategy. While he is imitating Ibn Tibbon's humility in asking for forgiveness for the mistakes in his translation, Aboab is equating Herrera's *Puerta del Cielo* with Maimonides' *Guide for the Perplexed*. Aboab is not simply exalting Herrera and juxtaposing him to Maimonides. He is implicitly admitting that Herrera's *Puerta del Cielo* is not purely 'Kabbalistic' but refers to a number of supplementary sources; just as Maimonides' *Guide for the Perplexed* was not entirely 'Jewish' but largely referred to Aristotle. This implication is particularly surprising, because Aboab took specific care to remove all the non-Jewish sources from Herrera's original *Puerta del Cielo* before translating it into Hebrew. In this respect, when comparing himself to Ibn Tibbon, Aboab seems inadvertently to admit how invasive his Hebrew translation has actually been with respect to the richness of Herrera's original *Puerta del Cielo* — and one might wonder if this really is the achievement that the reader shall 'judge [him] to have merit'.

---

20 For a Translation Studies insight into the Aramaic translation of Scripture, see, for instance, Shepherd *Targum and Translation*, pp. 220–21. See also Smelik, *Rabbis, Language, and Translation in Late Antiquity*, pp. 323–497.

Bibliography

Early Prints

Abraham Cohen de Herrera, *Sefer Shaar ha-Shamayim* (Amsterdam: Immanuel Benveniste, 1655)

Abraham Cohen de Herrera, *Sefer Shaar ha-Shamayim* (Warshaw: Chaim Kelter' i Spółki, 1864)

Primary Sources

Beltran, Miquel, ed., *Abraham Cohen De Herrera. Puerta del Cielo* (Madrid: Trotta, 2015)

Hayman, A. Peter, ed., *Sefer yetzira, Edition, Translation and Text-Critical Commentary* (Tübingen: Mohr Siebeck, 2004)

Secondary Studies

Abrams, Daniel, 'The Invention of the *Zohar* as a Book', in *Kabbalistic Manuscripts and Textual Theory: Methodologies of Textual Scholarship and Editorial Practice in the Study of Jewish Mysticism* (Jerusalem: Cherub Press, 2010) pp. 224–438

Altmann, Alexander, 'Lurianic Kabbala in a Platonic Key: Abraham Cohen Herrera's "Puerta Del Cielo"', in *Hebrew Union College Annual*, 53 (1982), 317–55

Anidjar, Gil, *'Our Place in al-Andalus': Kabbalah, Philosophy, Literature in Arab Jewish Letters* (Stanford: Stanford University Press, 2002)

Beltran, Miquel, *The Influence of Abraham Cohen de Herrera's Kabbalah on Spinoza's Ethics* (Leiden: Brill, 2016)

Blickstein, Shlomo., *Between Philosophy and Mysticism: A Study of the Philosophical-Qabbalistic Writings of Yosef Gikatila* (PhD thesis, Jewish Theological Seminary, New York, 1983)

Busi, Giulio, Saverio Campanini, and Simonetta Bondoni, eds, *The Great Parchment* (Turin: Aragno, 2004)

Campanini, Saverio, ed., *The Book of Bahir* (Turin: Aragno, 2005)

Corazzol, Giacomo, ed., *Commentary on the Daily Prayers* (Turin: Aragno, 2008)

Dal Bo, Federico, *Emanation and Philosophy of Language. An Introduction to Joseph ben Abraham Gikatilla* (Jerusalem: Cherub Press, 2019)

Eco, Umberto, *Dire quasi la stessa cosa. Esperienze di traduzione* (Milano: Bompiani, 2012)

——, *Mouse or Rat? Translation as Negotiation* (Hachette: Phoenix, 2013)

Hayman, Peter A., 'The "Original Text" of the Sefer Yesira or the "Earliest Recoverable Text"', in *Reflections and Refraction: Studies in Biblical Historiography in Honour of A. Graeme Auld*, ed. by R. Rezetko, T. Lin and B. Aucker (Leiden: Brill, 2007), pp. 175–86

Huss, Boaz, 'The Sufi Society of America: Theosophy and Kabbalah in Poona in the Late Nineteenth Century', in *Kabbalah and Modernity: Interpretations, Transformations, Adaptations*, ed. by B. Huss, M. Pasi and K. Stuckrad (Leiden: Brill, 2010), pp. 167–96

Idel, Moshe, 'Between the Kabbalah of Jerusalem and the Kabbalah of Israel Sarug' [Hebrew] *Shalem*, 6 (1992), 165–73

Jurgan, Susanne, and Saverio Campanini, eds, *The Gate of Heaven* (Turin: Aragno, 2012)

Kilcher, Andreas B., ed., *Die Kabbala Denudata. Text und Kontext* (Berlin: Lang, 2006)

Krabbenhoft, Kenneth, ed., *Abraham Cohen De Herrera. Gates of Heaven* (Leiden: Brill, 2002)

Lehmann, Matthias B., *Ladino Rabbinic Literature and Ottoman Sephardic Culture* (Bloomington: Indiana University Press, 2005)

Martini Annett, ed., *The Book of Punctuation* (Turin: Aragno, 2012)

Morlok, Elke, *Rabbi Joseph Gikatilla's Hermeneutics* (Tübingen: Mohr Siebeck, 2011)

Orfali, Moisés, 'Observaciones sobre el Parafrásis comentado del Pentateuco de R. Isaac da Fonseca', *eHumanista*, 20.2 (2012), 215–38

——, *Isaac Aboab da Fonseca: Jewish Leadership in the New World* (Eastbourne: Sussex University Press, 2014)

Perani, Mauro, ed., *Guglielmo Raimondo Moncada alias Flavio Mitridate: un ebreo converso siciliano* (Palermo: Officina di Studi Medievali, 2008)

Perani, Mauro, and Giacomo Corazzol, eds, *Flavio Mitridate mediatore fra culture nel contesto dell'ebraismo siciliano del XV secolo* (Palermo: Officina di Studi Medievali, 2012)

Scholem, Gershom, 'Israel Sarug, the Ari's Disciple?' [Hebrew], *Zion*, 5 (1940), 214–41

Shepherd, David, *Targum and Translation. A Reconsideration of the Qumranic Aramaic Version of Job* (Assen: Van Grocum, 2004)

Smelik, Willem F., *Rabbis, Language, and Translation in Late Antiquity* (Cambridge: Cambridge University Press, 2013)

Wirszubski, Chayym, *Pico della Mirandola's Encounter with Jewish Mysticism* (Cambridge, MA: Harvard University Press, 1989)

TERESA SOTO

Mahometism in Translation

Joseph Morgan's Version of Mohamad Rabadán's Discurso de la Luz *(1723–1725)*

In 1723 the first volume of *Mahometism Fully Explained; or Discourse of the Light and Lineage of the Prophet Muhammad* was printed in London by freemason William Mears, followed by a second volume two years later. The book was presented as the English translation of the original *Discurso de la Luz* (1603), a compilation on Islamic-related topics, written in Spanish verse by a Morisco poet from Aragón, Mohamad Rabadán, 'translated from the original manuscript, and illustrated with large Explanatory notes by Mr Morgan'. Diplomatic assistant, polymath, translator, and historian, Joseph Morgan is an elusive figure who seems to have preferred the sidelines over the centre stage.[1] Himself a freemason, his contacts and references included freethinkers, deists, orientalists, and North African diplomats.[2]

* The research for this paper was conducted within the framework of the national research, development and innovation project 'Género y santidad: experiencia religiosa y papel social a través de las vidas de mujeres santas en el Norte de Marruecos (Tánger, Tetuán)' (PID2019-104300GB-I00), funded by MCIN/AEI/10.13039/501100011033 and FEDER 'A way to make Europe'.

1 Almost all known biographical information about Jospeh Morgan comes from his own works. He mentions his appointment as *Cancellera* to Robert Cole in Algiers in the Preface to his *Complete History of Algiers*, p. xii, and his twenty-year stay in North Africa in several parts of *Mahometism Fully Explained*. He identifies himself as a freemason in the Dedication to the Duke of Richmond in *Phoenix Britannicus*.

2 Few studies have addressed the figure of Joseph Morgan or his works independently. Ann Thomson has discussed Morgan and Islam in her article 'Joseph Morgan et L'Islam', and Harry Sirr has written about his freemasonery and the *Phoenix Britannicus* in 'J. Morgan and his "Phoenix Britannicus" with Notes about His Other Works'. Finally, Nabil Matar has touched on his vision of Islam and comparatives cultures in 'Islam in Britain, 1689–1750', pp. 293–98.

Teresa Soto holds a PhD in Arabic and Islamic Studies from the University of Salamanca and was member of the CORPI project (Conversion, Overlapping Religiosities, Polemics and Interaction: Early Modern Iberia and Beyond) at the CCHS-CSIC (Madrid). Her research focuses on Morisco literature and poetics, cultural transfer, and intellectual networks in Europe and the Islamic world. She is a member of the Seminario de Estudios Árabo Románicos (SEAR), at the University of Oviedo.

Narratives on Translation across Eurasia and Africa: From Babylonia to Colonial India, ed. by Sonja Brentjes in cooperation with Jens Høyrup and Bruce O'Brien, CAT 3, pp. 325–340 (Turnhout: Brepols, 2022) BREPOLS PUBLISHERS 10.1484/M.CAT-EB.5.127948

After his twenty-year stay in North Africa as a chancellery assistant to the English consul Robert Cole, he moved back to England where he started his literary career with *Mahometism Fully Explained*, based on a manuscript he had acquired in Tunisia in 1719.[3] His extensive lived experience in Algiers and Tunisia seems to be one of the main axes that define his intellectual interest and writing career, which ranged from a history of Algiers to the translation of Alberto Radicati's treatise on suicide. When introducing his version of *Discurso de la Luz*, Joseph Morgan borrows a gardening metaphor that compares translating to transplanting: 'It was an ingenious Thought, of a late celebrated Writer, to compare *Translations*, more especially those of ancient *Poetry*, to *Vegetables*, removed from their own natural, and *warmer* Climate, and transplanted in a *colder*. They may be, indeed, *forced* to grow; but few, or rather none, ever arrive to a compleat Perfection'.[4] He could be referring here to Joseph Addison (1672–1719) who had died recently and whose literary writings in *The Spectator* — the journal he founded with Richard Steele (1672–1729) — often addressed translated poetry and employed several similar metaphors. Addison amply praised, among others, Pope's and Dryden's versions of Homer and Virgil but still considered that English could not rival languages such as Greek or Latin.

> The Works of Ancient Authors, which are written in dead Languages, have a great Advantage over those which are written in Languages that are now spoken. Were there any mean Phrases or Idioms in Virgil and Homer, they would not shock the Ear of the most delicate Modern Reader, so much as they would have done that of an old Greek or Roman, because we never hear them pronounced in our Streets, or in ordinary Conversation.[5]

If Milton's *Paradise Lost* (1667) falls short of the *Aeneid* it is just 'from the Fault of the Language in which it is written':

> There is an unquestionable Magnificence in every Part of *Paradise Lost*, and indeed a much greater than could have been formed upon any Pagan System.[6]

---

3 Morgan dedicated his first volume to Lord Harley and bequeathed the manuscript to his Harleian Library. Today the manuscript is held at the BL, MS Harley 7501. There is another copy, also from the seventeenth century, in France, BnF, MS Esp. 251 and a later copy from the eighteenth century in Madrid, Palacio Real, MS II/1767. Morgan acquired the manuscript from Hamooda Bussisa: 'I was told for a Truth, that there now are but Two Men remaining alive, who can read the Spanish Tongue, of which one is *Hamooda Bussisa*, the Person from whom I had this Manuscript. He is by Profession a Barber Surgeon. There is one miserable little Town, whose Inhabitants are Catalonian Moors, and who use that Dialect. The best of those Towns are *Suliman*, *Zaguan* and *Tessatore*'. Rabadán, *Mahometism Fully Explained*, trans. by Morgan, I, The Author's Preface n.a.

4 Rabadán, *Mahometism Fully Explained*, trans. by Morgan, II, p. ii.

5 Addison, *The Spectator*, II. No. 285, Saturday, January 26, 1712.

6 Addison, *The Spectator*, II. No. 267, Saturday, January 5, 1712.

Both Pope and Addison were advocates of the natural world over the man-made and showed their enthusiasm for natural landscapes over formal gardens.[7] That preference is revealed in Addison's literary critique as well: whereas the *Aeneid* is a 'well ordered Garden', the *Metamorphoses* are a 'Strange, enchanted Ground', richer for the imagination.[8]

Morgan's preoccupation with language and its natural correlation seemed to be of a different nature however. He surely is, like Addison, aware of the gap between the languages, but he is more interested in practical matters. Morgan opts for a version in prose rather than in verse, and even omits Rabadán's reflections on poetry from the prologue. This is contrary to Rabadán's own ideas on poetry, a medium he considered indispensable in order to commit the ideas to memory, and a way of honouring and celebrating the prophets by singing.

> Hiçe la composiçión en berso apaçible y | llano para que con más suabidad y gusto se cauleben en la memoria | cosas tan dignas de ser tractadas y memoradas.
>
> > (I made the composition in verse placid and | even, so that they would more gently and pleasantly enter the memory, | things so worthy of being discussed and remembered.)[9]

With his characteristic brand of blunt sarcasm, Morgan labels versification as a form of 'confinement' under which Rabadán 'laid himself, of cramping all his Lines into *Number, Feet,* or *Measure*',[10] a constraint that also leads to a lack of accuracy. For example, when commenting on Rabadán's use of '*Triumphant Leader*!',[11] he labels it as an instance of poetic licence, a quirk his poet 'boldly and copiously assumes throughout his Work not to lame his Metre'.[12] Morgan places emphasis instead on delivering the 'Author's Sense, and do[ing] my best to make intelligible to every Capacity some of the most intricate Passages I meet with'.[13] When 'liberties' are taken it is because 'his affected Conciseness has left the Sense scarce intelligible; at least, too obscure

7 Hoppit, *A Land of Liberty? England 1689–1727*, pp. 373–74.

8 Addison, *The Spectator*, III, No. 417, Saturday, June 28, 1712.

9 BnF, MS Esp. 251, fol. 4ᵛ.

10 Rabadán, *Mahometism Fully Explained*, trans. by Morgan, II, p. ii.

11 'MAHOMET the *Triumphant Leader*!', 'The Four Sects which are among the *Mahometans* esteemed as Orthodox, viz. The *Hanifeen*, the *Makileen*, the *Shaffisen*, and the *Hanbileen*, all unanimously agree, That the Name of the Impostor was, long before the Creation, Engraven all over the Heavens, and Recorded in the Sacred Registers thereof, in those well-known Words; *La illah illallah, Mohammed resoul Allah*: but our Author has here, it seems, given us a different Expression; I suppose, Licentia Poetica (which he boldly and copiously assumes throughout his Work) not to lame his Metre'. Rabadán, *Mahometism Fully Explained*, trans. by Morgan, I, pp. 27, 27a.

12 Rabadán, *Mahometism Fully Explained*, trans. by Morgan, i, p. 27a.

13 Rabadán, *Mahometism Fully Explained*, trans. by Morgan, II, p. lxi.

for the Comprehension of every Reader'.[14] Such unpacking is justified by his own 'Advantage of being more capable of guessing what a *Mussulman* would say on such, or any other Subjects, than one who has had less Intercourse with those People than myself'.[15] His claim that 'Scarce one *European* in a Million is capable of extracting the real Sense of ten Pages from the whole Manuscript'[16] because the language in which it is written is 'an unaccountable *Jargon*, peculiar to the *Spanish Moors*',[17] might be just a selling point for subscribers. However, hyperbole aside, the texts Morgan is translating are not easy, to be sure. An important part of this difficulty resides in the presence of both '*Arragonian* and *Valencian* Idioms [...] with innumerable *Arabick* Words'[18] written in Latin characters and often adapted to Spanish phonetics and morphology, a common characteristic of Morisco writings. He describes the task of guessing the Arabic words behind the Romanized variants as one bordering on sorcery: 'So many Arabick Words, and most of them in such uncooth Disguises, that I have been very frequently puzzled to know what to make of them; and, not without some Grounds it may be presumed, I was somewhat apprehensive of being charged with practicing the Black Art, especially by my Female Readers'.[19] Ultimately, his objective, he says, is to keep 'the Standard of the Oriental Style, and to render, at the

---

14 Rabadán, *Mahometism Fully Explained*, trans. by Morgan, II, p. iii.

15 Rabadán, *Mahometism Fully Explained*, trans. by Morgan, II, p. iii.

16 Rabadán, *Mahometism Fully Explained*, trans. by Morgan, II, p. vi.

17 Rabadán, *Mahometism Fully Explained*, trans. by Morgan, II, pp. v–vi.

18 Rabadán, *Mahometism Fully Explained*, trans. by Morgan, I, p. viii.

19 Rabadán, *Mahometism Fully Explained*, trans. by Morgan, II, p. lxi. An avid reader of Spanish sources, (he draws on Bernardo de Aldrete, Diego de Haedo, and Luis del Mármol Carvajal in his *Complete History of Algiers*), he appears to have spoken the language fluently. As for his knowledge of Arabic, based on the different uses he makes of local testimonies, grammar explanations, and his ability to read the Arabic words written in Latin characters, we might deduce that he has sound knowledge of the language and was a fluent speaker, but it is also true that he never uses any Arabic written source directly. When refering to Arabic sources, he is vague: 'Whatsoever Books our Author has consulted for this, he seems to be very much out in his Chronology, by the Relations I have heard my self, and by what I find written by their own Doctors', Rabadán, *Mahometism Fully Explained*, trans. by Morgan, I, p. 84a, or when refering to the Tafsir in a footnote: 'A book so called. It should be rather Tafsir [Rabadán writes *Tazfir*], which signifies an Expositor, and is the Title of many Books', Rabadán, *Mahometism Fully Explained*, trans. by Morgan, I, p. 24a. He almost always cites through other European scholars, for the most part Adrian Reland (1676–1718) and Barthélemy d'Herbelot (1625–1695) as in: 'I find it in Reland, taken, as that Author says, word for word from the Arabick Taarich or Chronicle: 1. Adam, 2. Seth, 3. Enos, 4. Kainan [...] 42. Jesus or Isa', Rabadán, *Mahometism Fully Explained*, trans. by Morgan, I, pp. 63–64c. or in 'The Arabians generally express themselves in a manner peculiar to them alone; for here Abou el Khabar, is the Title of a Book which literally signifies, The Father of the News, and is also the Sirname of several Men. Those who are remarkable for any Perfection or Imperfection of Body or Mind, or are addicted to any one Thing in particular, they call him the Father of it. See *d'Herbelot* in *Abou*, and Dr Prideaux L. *Mahom.* p. 82', Rabadán, *Mahometism Fully Explained*, trans. by Morgan, I, p. 24b.

same Time, the Reading not altogether unfamiliar to an English ear',[20] which he admits may, in some parts of the book, necessitate 'rather a *Paraphrase* than a *Translation*' but also to 'give my countrymen, more just ideas of the notions of the Mahometans, than they have hitherto received'.[21]

Morgan's own results, however, are irregular. When compared against the original, it quickly becomes apparent that his translation is indeed a very free one. One encounters many striking departures and embellishments. His decision to dispense with Rabadán's versification stands in contrast with the florid poetics of his own prose. For example, in the 'Historia del espantoso día del Juyçio' (The Terrors of the Last Day), Morgan renders the simple phrase 'quando la luna escurezca | aquel claror plateado | y el color de las estrellas | se ponga amarillo y baço', as, 'When the Moon shall wax dim and wan, deprived of all its wonted *Silver* Brightness, and the beautiful Twinkling of the Stars shall be changed to a dismal, faint, immutable and sickly Yellowness'.[22] This example is by no means an isolated one, but is rather the norm. In the nineteenth century, Morgan's translation was harshly judged by Henry E. J. Stanley (1827–1903), who would in turn publish his own edition of the *Complete Poetry of Muhamad Rabadán* in the *Journal of the Royal Asiatic Society*.[23] According to Stanley, Morgan's version was too English, not only linguistically but also in terms of how the ideas themselves were articulated:

> [H]is translation is not good; for besides shirking all the difficult passages, he is a very unfaithful translator, constantly adding words not in his text, and giving too English a form to the ideas of his author: he has, however, added some very good notes and interesting anecdotes in various parts of the work.[24]

Stanley's book could not be more different from Morgan's, highlighting the extent to which Morgan's project, while also taking Rabadán's material as a starting point, ultimately follows a path of its own. To begin with, Stanley published the text in the original Spanish, and prepared an introduction focused on both literary elements and doctrinal aspects. More in the vein of

---

20 Rabadán, *Mahometism Fully Explained*, trans. by Morgan, II, p. iii.

21 Rabadán, *Mahometism Fully Explained*, trans. by Morgan, I, p. iv.

22 A more literal rendering would be: 'when the moon darkens | that silver shine | and the color of the stars | becomes yellow and dim'.

23 Henry E. J. Stanley, a member of an aristocratic family from a freethinking context, was the first Member of Parliament to convert to Islam. He entered Trinity College in 1846 to study Arabic and pursued the diplomatic service before running for a seat in Parliament. In 1847 he entered the Foreign Office as assistant précis writer to Foreign Secretary Palmerston. After Palmerston was replaced in 1851, he took mission abroad at the British Embassy of Constantinople where Stratford Canning was ambassador. See Gilham, *Loyal Enemies: British Converts to Islam*, pp. 19–51.

24 Stanley, 'The Poetry of Mohamed Rabadan, of Arragon', pp. 1–2.

Addison's literary preoccupations, he compared Rabadán with Milton's *Paradise Lost*, postulating the two authors' common use of the same Hebrew sources.[25]

While Morgan's book is put forth as a translation of Rabadán, upon closer inspection, and when contrasted with the original, it seems to amount to something else. Despite offering a rather comprehensive and relatively unbiased account of Islamic beliefs to English readers that appears to closely follow its original text, Morgan also frequently adapts, expands, and contrasts the original text with other sources. For example, of the four books that make up Rabadán's manuscript, Morgan will translate just three of them, leaving out the treatise on *The 99 names of God*, considering it a 'tedious Bead-Roll of explanatory Notes', which would 'have been found very Little to the Taste of an English Reader'.[26] On the other hand, he adds a remarkable number of external materials. In the first volume, he includes the text of a separate *aljamiado* manuscript, *The Mahometan Confession of Faith* (I, pp. xi–xxvi),[27] as well as a supplement to the Ninth Chapter of Rabadán's text (I, pp. 218–56), on Jews, patriarchs Saleh and Heber, Lot, Job, prophet Samuel and King Saul, and fairies, genii, etc. The second volume will expand even further by providing extensive preliminary remarks (II, pp. i–lxxxiv), including some notes on 'Numidians and other Mahometans', and a whole appendix on the 'The Case of the *Moriscoes*, or Spanish Moors' (II, pp. 225–366) which contains original documents, among them an English translation of the anti-Christian (or rather anti-Catholic, anti-Inquisitorial) treatise by Abdelkarim Ben Aly Pérez.[28] The rather substantial addition of materials — almost entirely from the Morisco milieu — but also the use of European sources — such as Humphry Prideaux, Michael Geddes, Adrian Reland, and Barthélemy d'Herbelot, among others[29] — make us wonder in the first place what sort of intellectual

---

25 'The cantos describing the Creation have an additional interest from the passages in it which are parallel to Milton; some of these are necessarily similar, from the subject matter, such as the explanation of Man's Free Will; in other cases there may be a common Rabbinical origin of the ideas of both poets. Rabadan frequently refers to the Hebrew commentary. In his description of the Universal Deluge, Rabadan sometimes uses the same words and phrases in his description of the laying waste of the world before the Great Judgment, and he appears to draw a parallel between the two'. Stanley, 'The Poetry of Mohamed Rabadan, of Arragon', p. 3.

26 'A tedious Bead-Roll of explanatory Notes, no less than Ninety Nine in number, by way of Paraphrase upon the Attributes they give to God, which are so many it would, in my Opinnion, have been found very Little to the Taste of an English Reader, upon which Consideration I have omitted it, though the whole may seem properly enough adapted to the Palates of those *to whom, and no others,* the Author professes to have directed it'. Rabadán, *Mahometism Fully Explained*, trans. by Morgan, II, p. 220.

27 The 'Thirteen articles of the Muslim Faith', composed by Yça de Gebir (fl. about 1450) is a fundamental text that circulated widely among the Moriscos in Spain. See Wiegers, *Islamic Literature in Spanish and Aljamiado*, pp. 151–81, 243–65.

28 This fragementary English translation is the only surviving version of the original manuscript. On polemical literature written by Moriscos in this period in North Africa, see Wiegers, 'Las obras de polémica religiosa escritas por los moriscos fuera de España', pp. 391–413.

29 On their influence, see later comments in this paper and particularly footnotes 20 and 45.

project lies behind *Mahometism Fully Explained*, and how it negotiates the boundaries between authorship and translating.

Morgan expresses admiration of Rabadán as an author of 'more than common Genius', who had 'copiously and not unelegantly' treated his subject, and whose style is defined by 'beautiful Extravagance' and 'uncultivated Elegancy', not just to his mind, 'but in the Opinion of several Gentlemen of Learning and Sense'.[30] He also is sure to mention that 'The Name and Memory of this Author are still held in no small Veneration among the Off-spring of the Moriscoes', especially in Tunis, where the Morisco population was greater and Spanish had remained in use. Emphasizing the extent of Rabadán's continued renown, Morgan tells how the person who sold him the manuscript 'was very apt to swear by the Head of Sheikh Mohamet Rabadan'.[31] At the same time, however, Morgan explicitly distances himself from both subject and author by saying that he is 'not setting up my self in an obstinate Vindication, either of the Mussulmans in general, or of the Author, whose Work I publish, in particular'.[32] This is an idea that will recur in his subsequent books, as in his quite emphatic 'No!' in the *History of Algiers*: 'Let not the Public [...] imagine me their Advocate. No!'[33] In *Mahometism Fully Explained*, he claims not to mingle his own judgements with the text, declaring that 'if I pretend to give the World a Translation, I must give the real Meaning of my Author, and not my own, except I did it separately from the Work itself'.[34] Thus, there is a clear effort to, on a formal level, remain on a plane *external* to the text: his comments are contained in footnotes or, if in the main text, in brackets.

The emphasis on his unbiased opinion and impartiality seems to be deeply connected with his own personal beliefs. Morgan was a freemason with connections to the heterogeneous context of the Radical Enlightenment. The second volume of *Mahometism Fully Explained* is dedicated to his patron Richard Mead (1673–1754), a known freemason. From police records we know that he translated a book by radical materialist Alberto Radicati, for which he was arrested alongside Radicati and Mears, the publisher of both Radicati and Morgan's books.[35] In his last book, *Phoenix Britannicus*, Morgan openly declares

30 Rabadán, *Mahometism Fully Explained*, trans. by Morgan, II, p. ii.

31 Rabadán, *Mahometism Fully Explained*, trans. by Morgan, II, p. viii.

32 Rabadán, *Mahometism Fully Explained*, trans. by Morgan, II, p. lix.

33 Morgan, *A Complete History of Algiers*, p. i.

34 Rabadán, *Mahometism Fully Explained*, trans. by Morgan, I, p. 215.

35 Concerning his translation of Alberto Radicati's treatise *A Philosophical Dissertation upon Death*, published by Mears, the translation was anonymous but court records have revealed his involvement. Radicati, Morgan, and Mears were arrested and the publication caused a great scandal. See Cavallo, '"Atheist or Deist, more Charitable than Superstitious Zealots": Alberto Radicati's Intellectual Parabola', pp. 179–83; Jacob, *Radical Enlightenment*, pp. 173–74; and Venturini, *Saggi sull'Europa illuminista*, p. 209. In the Table of Contents to his *History of Algiers*, Joseph Morgan calls himself a 'Lover of Truth': '[The author] Is a Lover of Truth, and condemns those who are not. He hopes some will like him the better for that very good, tho' not very common Quality'. It is interesting to note that the full English title of another one

himself to be a mason, and dedicates the book to the Duke of Richmond, his Grand-Master.[36] Further evidence offering a glimpse of the intellectual context Morgan belonged to are his books' lists of subscribers. Subscribers to *Mahometism* included well-known freethinkers such as Anthony Collins and Barnham Goode, associated with the circle of the prominent deist John Toland. Collins subscribed to the *Complete History of Algiers* as well, alongside sceptical thinkers such as Thomas Morgan and Samuel Clark, in addition to renowned orientalist George Sale, translator of the Koran. In keeping with this milieu, the main targets of Morgan's criticism are superstition, bigotry, irrationality, and fanaticism, from which Christianity is not exempted. He repeatedly qualifies his criticism of Muslims with statements such as, 'I cannot say I like to see those who have but half an Eye laugh at others who have lost one of theirs',[37] or 'Yet I detest undeserved Calumny; the which wherever I light on I still endeavour to detect and refute'.[38] This back-and-forth approach may be motivated by a real fear of accusations by a public 'already by far too prone to Prejudice and Prepossession',[39] or even a desire to disappear altogether, as implied in his reference to himself as 'nameless': 'Why should the obscure, the unknown, the nameless I, make such a Bustle?'[40]

As a result, in portraying himself as a translator he oscillates between his uniqueness, the 'one *European* in a Million', and his self-proclaimed secondary role. What makes him such a unique translator appears to be not only his language skills and experience abroad, but also his ability to *guess* what a Muslim would say, almost — we might understand — a nearness that allows him to actually *think* like one? Or even *be* like one? Such a position is clearly connected to the urge to challenge preconceptions about religiosity. An anecdote in the *History of Algiers* recounts the offence a certain '*Englishman*' took at being told he bore a mere physical resemblance to 'a certain *Moor*':

> It is not long since I here met with one (who has no very great Reason, that I know of, so to value himself, except that valuable Reason of being a *True-born Englishman*, and that truly valuable one of living under so good, so mild, and so happily constituted a Government,) who was highly affronted at my saying, 'That had I met him with a Beard, and in a *Moorish* Garb,

---

of Alberto Radicati's treatises was *Discourses concerning Religion and Government, Inscribed to all Lovers of Truth and Liberty*. Also, his *Philosophical Dissertation upon Death* is signed by the pen-name 'a Friend to Truth'.

36 'The worthy Fraternity, whereof I have the Happiness of being a Member'. He proudly defends the movement against criticism: 'Are not the MASONS, obviously in the eye of the Sun, a very numerous, a respectable BODY of MEN?' Importantly, he praises the community's 'Proneness to countenance and assist their Brethren' likely an allusion to financial support for the book. Morgan, *Phoenix Britannicus*, Dedication.

37 Rabadán, *Mahometism Fully Explained*, trans. by Morgan, II, p. lix.

38 Morgan, *A Complete History of Algiers*, p. iii.

39 Morgan, *A Complete History of Algiers*, p. ii.

40 Morgan, *A Complete History of Algiers*, p. xi.

> I should have taken him for a certain *Moor* of Quality, I knew in Barbary; and whom he really much resembles'. 'Pithee!' returned my scornful, choleric Chap; 'Don't compare Me to any of your scoundrel Barbarians'.[41]

Returning to the image of the transplanted word and the foreign tree, the analogy seems to be further from Addison's garden and closer to naturalist Richard Bradley's (1688–1732) description of the pomegranate in *Philosophical Treatise on Husbandry and Gardening* (1721–1724), which states that while the pomegranate, originally from Tunis, will grow in England, 'I find it very difficult to ripen its Fruit with us'.[42] I believe that the *cold* and *not natural* Climate described in Morgan's metaphor reaches further than language or landscape ideology to offer a judgement of the intellectual context of reception, and in doing so underlines its own hostility. We should bear in mind that even after the 1689 Act of Toleration, Catholics, non-Anglican Protestants, anti-Trinitarians, and atheists were still subject to legal discrimination in Britain.[43] Indeed, in the remarks to his *Mahometism Fully Explained,* he recounts how some readers alleged it was 'dangerous for such who were not well grounded in their Faith, to read it', to which he retorts that 'a Portuguese Inquisitor could not have said more!' Literature on Islam and North Africa was not uncommon by the time Morgan was writing but tended toward religious polemics and travel literature. In any case, very few of the books that addressed Islam seemed, in his opinion, to have a proper approach to the subject,[44] with two notable exceptions. The first is the 'learned Dean *Prideaux*' of Norwich, author of *The True Nature of Imposture Fully Displayed in the Life of Mahomet* (1697), whose endorsement Morgan requested for *Mahometism Fully Explained,* despite Prideaux's markedly polemical stance on both Islam and Deism. The other is 'the impartial Monsier *Reland*', i.e. Dutch orientalist Adrian Reland (1676–1718), author of *De Religione Mohammedica* (1705), which exhibits a markedly more neutral approach.[45] Morgan relies heavily on David Durand's

---

41 Morgan, *A Complete History of Algiers,* p. viii.

42 Bradley, *A General Treatise of Husbandry and Gardening,* II, p. iv.

43 In the words of John Locke, 'Toleration has now at last been established by law in our country. Not perhaps so wide in scope as might be wished for… Still, it is something to have progressed so far'. Cited in Hoppit, *A Land of Liberty? England 1689–1727,* pp. 33–34.

44 In the *Complete History of Algiers,* he acknowledges the abundance of Histories of North Africa, but adds that none are sufficiently well informed and honest. When asking if there are enough of these stories already, he replies: 'We have [many]: But the Question is, have we one, that is not rather Romance than History? Doubtless, those of other Parts are not free from Falsities: But of those I am not so good of a Judge'. Morgan, *A Complete History of Algiers,* p. iii.

45 'Till the impartial Monsier *Reland,* and our late learned Dean *Prideaux* appeared, we knew very little, worthy Credit, either of the daring *Impostor* himself, or of his ill connected Doctrine; both the *one* and the *other,* by Pens too much biased, having been painted out to us with the same ungenerous Virulency as we ourselves by *Rome's* zealous Votaries, our never-failing Well-Wishers, who (as is daily too obvious) with an indefatigable Perseverance, lay hold of every Opportunity, that offers, of representing all who dissent from them in

(1680?–1763) 1721 expanded French edition of Reland's book for the notes and comments. This is also the source for the *Confession of Faith* that appears in *Mahometism Fully Explained*, in addition to three engravings that Morgan will likewise employ: Turks at prayer, Muḥammad's genealogy, and the Kaʿaba. It is worth noting that variations on these last two plates also show up in Bernard Picart's (1673–1733) contemporary *Cérémonies et coutumes religieuses de tous les peuples du monde* (1723–1743), whose illustrations have long been noted for their objective and ethnographic depiction of a wide range of religions and sects. Thus Reland's work appears to function as a model for Morgan's own book, which aspires to a similar impartiality. In their study on Bernard and Picart's *The Religious Ceremonies and Customs of all the Peoples of the World*, Margaret C. Jacob, Lynn Hunt, and Wijnand Mijnhardt showed how, in the Early Enlightenment, Bernard and Picart's book challenged the religious assumptions of its readers by giving them first-hand accounts, comparative essays, and ethnographic perspectives on the various religions found around the world. This implicitly invited the readers to 'distance themselves from their own beliefs and customs and to think about religious practices more generally', a process deemed to be significant in order to achieve complete tolerance. I believe that a similar process is at work here as well.[46]

The heavy apparatus of notes and the additional material are thus aimed at offering a well-informed and knowledgeable, almost encyclopedic, treatise, with an important focus on the case of the Moriscos, a community that suffered the consequences of religious persecution and intolerance. At the same time, it renders the book more accessible in the context of Britain where, as he sarcastically says, 'My Subject is unpopular! What care we, say Folks, whether there is any such rascally Place, as Algiers, existing on God's Earth? It is nothing to us! Lord! Half a Dozen of our small Ships would blow all those Scrubs to the Devil, and farther!'[47] By his account, apart from this disdain and fear, Morgan was also up against outright ignorance of geography, as in the following anecdote told in the *History of Algiers*:

> It was at a Coffee-House, where I was fitting with several Persons, to all whom I was a Stranger, and with them ingaged in promiscuous Discourses, that this *Butterfly* came fluttering in among us shaking his taudry Plumes. Listening some Minutes to our Talk, which then happened to be about *Tunis*, and the Ruins of *Carthage*: 'Sir, said he judiciously; as you lived so long in the Country, I admire you never had the Curiosity to take a *Ride*, to see the *Pyramids* which you hinted just now never to have visited'. 'Really,

any of their, even more than *Mahometan*, Inconsistencies, in Colours directly opposite to Truth, and also of making them other more effectual Tenders of their pious Benevolence, whenever it is thought practicable'. Rabadán, *Mahometism Fully Explained*, trans. by Morgan, I, pp. vi–vii.

46 Jacob, 'The Nature of Early Eighteenth-Century Religious Radicalism', pp. 6–7.

47 Morgan, *A Complete History of Algiers*, p. xi.

> Sir, replied I modestly, as became my present Vocation; that must have been a good smart *Ride*. But I never was in any Part of *Egypt*, I assure you, Sir'. '*Egypt*, Sir, Why, pray, is not *Carthage* in *Egypt*, Sir?'[48]

Despite the use of polemical language directed towards Islam ('Impostor', 'pernicious sect' etc.) and Catholicism ('Zeal of the Romish Clergy', 'detestable Tribunal'), it seems hard to place Morgan's project in a purely polemical context. Polemical language is not employed consistently in the book. Also, doctrinal elements are not contested with recourse to their Christian counterparts, and many of his criticisms are aimed at manifestations of *vulgar beliefs*, bigotry and superstition. Even when faced with openly polemical segments of the source text, such as Rabadán's refutation of the Trinity, Morgan refuses to get involved and urges the reader to withhold judgement: 'This Doctrine is, indeed, very Anti-Christian, but they are the Words of a Moor, and not of a Christian. He writes the real Sentiments of his honest well-meaning Heart',[49] thus urging the reader to consider the Muslim point of view. Importantly, his discussion of superstition, bigotry and also morals is equally applied to Christians:

> I never heard of any viler Action committed among the Infidels of Barbary than, some of our own Villanies; naming both Events and Persons, thought it very idle, I say, for them to make Answer: 'Well; however they were Christians, and not Heathens' as if Christianity privileged them to be Villains: Strange Doctrine![50]

I find particularly interesting to note his position towards aspects he ascribes to mere popular belief, a concept he applies across faiths. Here, as we have seen with how and what he chooses to translate, his own judgement shines through more clearly. A key aspect of the book that Joseph Morgan assigns to this category is the 'prophetick light which glares throughout his whole Work'.[51] This 'mysterious Light, which makes so very refulgent a Figure in almost every Page' is in fact one of the central teachings of the *Discurso de la Luz*, as the title suggests. This light is known in Arabic as *Nūr Muḥammadī*, the self-manifestation of divine consciousness held to precede not only Muḥammad's birth but the creation of Adam as well, and plays an important role in the Sufi conception of sainthood. In short, all prophets before Muḥammad derived their prophetic ability from this Muḥammadan light.[52] The most famous

48 Morgan, *A Complete History of Algiers*, p. xvii.

49 Rabadán, *Mahometism Fully Explained*, trans. by Morgan, I, pp. 214–15, 215a.

50 Morgan, *A Complete History of Algiers*, p. ix.

51 Rabadán, *Mahometism Fully Explained*, trans. by Morgan, II, pp. lix–lx.

52 Schimmel, *And Muhammad Is His Messenger*, p. 26 and p. 125; Rubin, 'Pre-Existence and Light: Aspects of the concept of Nūr Muḥammad', pp. 62–117; Katz, *The Birth of the Prophet Muhammad*, pp. 9–10. There are many *aljamiado* versions of this text among the Moriscos. A manuscript of Morisco origin containing al-Bakrī's original in Arabic is held at the Vatican Library, BAV, MS Borg. Ar. 125. The use of the book to celebrate the birth of the prophet

version of this tradition among the Moriscos was that of the *Kitāb al-anwār* or *Libro de las luces*, by al-Bakrī from the thirteenth century.[53] Despite the tradition's abundant presence among the Moriscos, it was not always well received in other Sunni contexts.[54] Although Morgan harshly criticizes this concept, he makes sure to add that this prophetic light is 'not one Jot less ridiculous and even inconsistent with common Reason, than Lord Peter's Mutton, his Father's Sign-Post, or the itinerant House'. He assures the reader that the 'prophetic light' is taken in the literal sense by only the less learned and more 'credulous Mahometans, with Views not unlike those which induce the Romish Clergy to forbid reading the Bible, and to force their passive Sheep to swallow Transubstantiation, and other Mysteries [...], into which they are not by any Means to pry'. Thus, in criticizing Islam he is also able to pass judgement on attitudes held within Christianity, and, by questioning the prophetic light specifically, he is perhaps implying his rejection of divine light and other mystical aspects of traditional Catholicism or Methodism, forms that stood in conflict with the 'masonic vision of true wisdom where knowledge must be achieved socially'.[55] He adds that this light is properly understood allegorically, particularly by 'the Majority of their Learned', 'and nay, several Moors, but more Turks, have frankly owned as much, upon my Inquiry'.[56] He adopts a similar stance toward the 'Prophet's amazing Pilgrimage, through the Seven Heavens', admitting its absurdity, but arguing it was no more absurd than the belief 'that St Dennis, after his Decollation, carried his Head under his Arm, for I don't know how many Miles, as he is recorded to have done'.[57]

To return one last time to the gardening metaphor that opened this paper, Morgan's approach to translation emphasizes a process of 'transplanting' that takes into consideration the environmental context, attempting to provide the most optimal conditions in order for the sense of the text to flourish, even in adverse circumstances. Such optimal conditions involve both stylistic considerations as well as a wide array of supplementary materials, in an attempt to provide a more comprehensive image of Islamic beliefs. It is interesting to note that in a letter sent to John Locke, which he includes in his *Four Letters concerning Toleration* (1685), 'true religion' is described as a 'foreign

---

Muḥammad is also documented, and Morgan mentions its use in the Morisco comunity in Tunisia for the *mawālid*. See Katz, *The Birth of the Prophet Muhammad*, pp. 9–10 and García-Arenal, 'Shurafa in the Last Years of al-Andalus and in the Morisco Period: Laylat al-Mawlid and Genealogies of the Prophet Muhammad', pp. 161–84.

53 Boaz Shoshan suggested the possibility of an earlier composition date to the ninth century, *Popular Culture in Medieval Cairo*, pp. 35–36. There are several *aljamiado* versions of this book in prose, collected in at least five manuscripts in the Gayangos Collection at the Royal Academy of History, in Madrid. María Luisa Lugo Acevedo has prepared an edition based on the different manuscripts, entitled *El libro de las luces*.

54 See Fierro, 'El Kitāb al-anwār y la circulación de libros en al-Andalus', pp. 100–04.

55 Jacob, *The Radical Enlightenment*, p. 55.

56 Rabadán, *Mahometism Fully Explained*, trans. by Morgan, II, pp. v–vi.

57 Rabadán, *Mahometism Fully Explained*, trans. by Morgan, II, pp. lix, lx.

plant' whereas 'false religions and atheism' seemed to be more 'agreeable to the soil', implying that one must constantly tend the faith lest the weeds creep in. This is another reading of the garden, as a space prone to invasion and contamination, mirroring contemporary political visions of the world. In this interpretative context, it is not difficult to see that seeking out new elements to be inserted in the landscape is also a way of trying to change the landscape altogether. While Morgan's wit and sarcasm borders at times on classic interreligious polemics, this may also be understood in terms of the satirist style so present in other contemporary creators of opinion such as Swift in *Tale of a Tub*, or Addison and Steele in *The Spectator*, seeking to affect and change ways of seeing. Joseph Morgan uses his own personal accounts, local testimonies, original texts, and documents to provide a multilayered object of study that challenges the readers' ideas and urges them to reconsider their position towards it.

Bibliography

Manuscripts

London, British Library, MS Harley 7501
Paris, Bibliotèque nationale de France, MS Esp. 251 (*olim* 8162)
Madrid, Palacio Real, MS II/1767
Città del Vaticano, Biblioteca Apostolica Vaticana, MS Borg. Ar 125

Primary Sources

Addison, Joseph, and Richard Steele, *The Spectator: A New Edition Reproducing the Original Text Both as First Issued and as Corrected by its Authors, with Introduction, Notes, and Index*, ed. by Henry Morley, 3 vols (London: George Routledge and Sons, 1891)

Bradley, Richard, *A General Treatise of Husbandry and Gardening; Containing a New System of Vegetation*, 3 vols (London: T. Woodward and J. Peele, 1723)

Geddes, Michael, *Several Tracts against Popery: Together with the Life of Don Alvaro de Luna* (London: E. J., 1715)

Haedo, Diego de, *Topographia e Historia General de Argel, repartida en cinco tratados, do se veran casos estraños, muertes espantosas, y tormentos exquisitos, que conviene se entiendan en la Christiandad: con mucha doctrina y elegancia curiosa* (Valladolid: Diego Fernández de Córdova y Oviedo, 1612)

d'Herbelot, Barthélemy, *Bibliothèque orientale ou Dictionnaire universel contenant généralement tout ce qui regarde la connoissance des Peuples de l'Orient* (Paris: Compagnie des Libraires, 1697)

Morgan, Joseph, *A Complete History of Algiers, to which is Prefixed an Epitome of the General History of Barbary from the Earliest Times, Interspersed with Many Curious Passages and Remarks not Touched on by any Writer Whatever* (London: J. Bettenham, 1731)

——, *Phoenix Britannicus, Being a MISCELLANEOUS COLLECTION Of Scarce and Curious TRACTS, Historical Political Biographical Satirical Critical Characteristical &c, Prose and Verse, Only to be found in the Cabinets of the Curious, Interspersed with Choice PIECES from Original MSS* (London: Printed for T. Edlin and J. Wilford, 1732)

Prideaux, Humphry, *The True Nature of Imposture Fully Displayed in the Life of Mahomet: With a Discourse Annexed for the Vindicating of Christianity from This Charge* (London: Printed for William Rogers, 1697)

Rabadán, Mohamad, *Mahometism Fully Explained; or Discourse of the Light and Lineage of the Prophet Muhammad*, trans. by Joseph Morgan, 2 vols (London: W. Mears, 1723–1725)

Radicati, Alberto, *A Philosophical Dissertation upon Death Composed for the Consolation of the Unhappy*, trans. by Joseph Morgan (London: W. Mears, 1732)

Reland, Hadrian, *La Religion des Mahométans exposée par leurs propres docteurs avec des éclaircissemens sur les opinions qu'on leur a faussement attribuées, tiré du latin de M. Reland et augmenté d'une Confession de foi mahométanne qui n'avait point encore paru*, trans. by David Durand (La Haye: J. Faillant, 1721)

Secondary Studies

Cavallo, Tomaso, '"Atheist or Deist, More Charitable than Superstitious Zealots": Alberto Radicati's Intellectual Parabola', in *Atheism and Deism Revalued: Heterodox Religious Identities in Britain, 1650–1800*, ed. by Wayne Hudson, Diego Lucci, and Jeffrey R. Wigelsworth (Burlington: Ashgate, 2014), pp. 173–91

Fierro, Maribel, 'Opposition to Sufism in al-Andalus', in *Islamic Mysticism Contested: Thirteen Centuries of Controversies & Polemics*, ed. by Frederick de Jong and Bernd Radtke, Bernd (Leiden: Brill, 1999), pp. 174–206

——, 'El Kitāb al-anwār y la circulación de libros en al-Andalus', *Sharq al-Andalus*, 20 (2011–2013), 97–108

García-Arenal, Mercedes, *Messianism and Puritanical Reform: Mahdīs of the Muslim West* (Leiden: Brill, 2006)

——, 'Musulmanes arabófonos y musulmanes aljamiados', *Al-Qantara*, 31.1 (2010), 295–310

——, 'Shurafa in the Last Years of al-Andalus and in the Morisco Period: Laylat al-Mawlid and Genealogies of the Prophet Muhammad', in *Sayyids and Sharifs in Muslim Societies. The Living Links to the Prophet*, ed. by Kazuo Morimoto, New Horizons in Islamic Studies (New York: Routledge, 2012), pp. 161–84

Gilham, Jamie, *Loyal Enemies: British Converts to Islam, 1850–1950* (London: Hurst & Company, 2014)

Hoppit, Julian, *A Land of Liberty? England 1689–1727*, The New Oxford History of England (Oxford: Clarendon Press, 2000)

Hunt, Lynn, Margaret C. Jacob, and Wijnan Mijnhardt, ed., *Bernard Picart and the First Global Vision of Religion* (Santa Monica: Getty Trust Publications, 2010)

Jacob, Margaret C., *The Radical Enlightenment: Pantheist, Freemasons and Republicans*, Early Modern Europe Today (London: Allen & Unwin, 1981)

——, 'The Nature of Early Eighteenth-Century Religious Radicalism', *Republics of Letters: A Journal for the Study of Knowledge, Politics, and the Arts*, 1.1 (2009); <https://arcade.stanford.edu/rofl/nature-early-eighteenth-century-religious-radicalism> (accessed 15 June 2017)

Katz, Marion Holmes, *The Birth of the Prophet Muhammad: Devotional Piety in Sunni Islam* (London: Routledge, 2007)

Lasarte López, José Antonio, *Poemas de Mohamad Rabadán* (Zaragoza: Diputación General de Aragón, 1991)

Lugo Acevedo, María Luisa, *El libro de las luces. Leyenda aljamiada sobre la genealogía de Mahoma. Estudio y edición crítica* (Madrid: Sial, 2008)

Matar, Nabil, *Britain and Barbary, 1589–1689* (Gainesville: University Press of Florida, 2005)

——, 'Islam in Britain, 1689–1750', *Journal of British Studies*, 47 (2008), 284–300

Mulsow, Martin, 'Socinianism, Islam and the Radical Uses of Arabic Scholarship', *Al-Qantara*, 31.2 (2010), 549–86

Rodríguez Rodríguez, A. Vespertino, 'El Discurso de la luz de Mohámed Rabadán y la literatura aljamiada de los últimos moriscos en España', in *Actes du IV Symposium international d'études morisques sur: Métiers, vie religieuse et problématiques d'histoire morisque, Zaghouan (Tunisia)* (Zaghouan: Ceromdi, 1990), pp. 279–91

Rubin, Uri, 'Pre-Existence and Light: Aspects of the Concept of Nūr Muhammad', *Israel Oriental Studies*, 5 (1975), 62–117

——, *The Eye of the Beholder: The Life of Muḥammad as Viewed by the Early Muslims* (Princeton: The Darwin Press, 1995)

Schimmel, Annemarie, *Mystical Dimensions of Islam* (Chapel Hill: University of North Carolina, 1975)

——, *And Muhammad Is His Messenger: The Veneration of the Prophet in Islamic Piety* (Chapel Hill: University of North Carolina Press, 1985)

Shoshan, Boaz, *Popular Culture in Medieval Cairo* (Cambridge: Cambridge University Press, 1993)

Sirr, Harry, 'J. Morgan and his "Phoenix Britannicus" with Notes about his Other Works', *Quator Coronati Lodge*, 19 (1906), 127–36

Stanley, Henry E. J., 'The Poetry of Mohamad Rabadan of Aragon', *The Journal of the Asiatic Society*, 3 (1869), 81–104; 4 (1870), 138–77; 5 (1871), 303–37; 6 (1873), 165–212

Thomson, Ann, *Barbary and Enlightenment: European Attitudes towards the Maghreb in the 18th Century* (Leiden: Brill, 1987)

——, 'Joseph Morgan et L'Islam', *Dix-Huitième siècle*, 27 (1995), 349–63

Venturi, Franco, *Saggi sull'Europa illuminista*, vol. 1: *Alberto Radicati di Passerano* (Torino: Giulio Einaudi, 1954)

Wiegers, Gerard, *Islamic Literature in Spanish and Aljamiado: Iça of Segovia (fl. 1450): His Antecedents and Successors* (Leiden: Brill, 1994)

——, 'Las obras de polémica religiosa escritas por los moriscos fuera de España', in *Los moriscos: expulsión y diáspora. Una perspectiva internacional*, ed. by Mercedes García-Arenal and Gerard A. Wiegers (València, Granada, Zaragoza: Universitat de València, Universidad de Granada, Universidad de Zaragoza, 2013), pp. 391–413

REBEKAH CLEMENTS

The Possibility of Translation

A Comparison of the Translation Theories of Ogyū Sorai and Ōtsuki Gentaku

此ノ方ノ学者以二方言一ヲ読レ書ヲ号シテ曰二和訓一ト。
取レリ二諸コレヲ訓詁ノ之義一ニ。其ノ実訳ヤ也

(Scholars from this country read [Chinese] books using our regional language. We call this *wakun* (glossing in Japanese). This is taken to mean an interpretive gloss, but in reality it is a translation.)[1]

Ogyū Sorai, *Yakubun Sentei*.

In the early decades of the eighteenth century, the Japanese scholar of Chinese learning, Ogyū Sorai (1666–1728), made what was at the time an extraordinary claim: classical Chinese was in fact *Chinese* and not Japanese. This seemingly obvious statement was made possible, necessary, even, by the way Japanese readers had interacted with Chinese texts in history. The Chinese writing system is logographic, and over the centuries Japanese scholars had developed ways of reading Chinese logographs as though they represented Japanese rather than Chinese words. Such methods included glossing Chinese logographs with Japanese words and rearranging the syntax of Chinese texts to correspond with Japanese word order. By so doing Japanese readers were able to bypass the spoken Chinese language and 'read' Chinese source texts as if they were Japanese. Such methods were known, among other things,

1 Ogyū Sorai, *Yakubun sentei*, 1, fol. 2^{r}. Unless otherwise stated, English translations are my own. For a complete English translation of Sorai's preface to *Yakubn sentei*, see Pastreich, 'Grappling with Chinese Writing as a Material Language', pp. 143–66.

Rebekah Clements is research professor at the Catalan Institution for Research and Advanced Studies (ICREA), and is based at the Autonomous University of Barcelona. She is the author of *A Cultural History of Translation in Early Modern Japan* (Cambridge University Press, 2015) and the co-editor of *Genji monogatari no kinsei: Zokugoyaku, hon'an, eiribon de yomu koten* (*The Tale of Genji in the Early Modern Period: Reading a Classic through Vernacular Translation, Adaptation, and Illustrated Editions* (Benseisha, 2019). She is currently the Principal Investigator of a new project on the aftermath of Toyotomi Hideyoshi's invasions of Korea 1592–1598, funded by a European Research Council Starting Grant.

Narratives on Translation across Eurasia and Africa: From Babylonia to Colonial India, ed. by Sonja Brentjes in cooperation with Jens Høyrup and Bruce O'Brien, CAT 3, pp. 341–351 (Turnhout: Brepols, 2022) BREPOLS PUBLISHERS 10.1484/M.CAT-EB.5.127949

as *wakun* (Japanese/simplified glosses). Sorai claimed that using *wakun* produced not a reading but a translation, and a bad translation at that; the traditional Japanese readings associated with Chinese characters were, he argued, so archaic and confusing that attempting to understand classical Chinese texts mediated in this way was like 'scratching at an itch through a leather shoe' — impossible to get to the essence.[2] To circumvent this problem, Sorai advocated that classical Chinese texts should either be read as Chinese using contemporary Chinese pronunciation and the original word order, or, when teaching less capable readers, texts should at least be translated freely into more natural Japanese. As Emmanuel Pastreich has pointed out, Sorai was grappling with Chinese as a 'material language', the product of a foreign country, the reality of which was becoming increasingly apparent to Japanese readers thanks to the large numbers of vernacular Chinese novels that were imported to Japan in the seventeenth and eighteenth centuries and which depicted the everyday realities of contemporary China to an extent never before witnessed in Japan.[3]

By pointing to the essential otherness of classical Chinese, Sorai launched a series of discussions on language, translation, and reading that would reverberate within the walls of Japanese Sinology throughout the eighteenth and nineteenth centuries, although few had the time or skill to follow his exhortation to abandon Japanese glosses in favour of learning spoken Chinese from scratch. The effects were also felt beyond Sinology. This chapter examines the echoes of Sorai's writings in the work of Ōtsuki Gentaku (1757–1827), a leading scholar of Rangaku (Dutch Learning), who was active almost a century after Sorai first made his claims about Chinese. By examining the work of Sorai and Gentaku in dialogue, I shall flesh out the ways in which Gentaku applied Sorai's arguments to the study of Dutch, and compare their attitudes towards the foreignness of the source languages from which they were translating.

Sorai and the Nagasaki Method

The narrative that Ogyū Sorai chose to tell about his childhood goes some way to illuminating his views on translation. In *Yakubun sentei*, the text in which Sorai's claims about the Chineseness of classical Chinese were first published in print, Sorai describes his time spent away from the shogunal capital of Edo from the age of fourteen to twenty-five. Sorai was exiled to Kazusa (in modern-day Chiba prefecture) with his father when his father fell out of favour with the shogun Tokugawa Tsunayoshi. Surrounded by 'field labourers and old rustics', Sorai had only his father and a copy of Hayashi Razan's *Daigaku genkai* (Vernacular Explanation of the Greater Learning) to turn to for help

2 Ogyū Sorai, *Yakubun sentei*, I, fol. 2ᵛ.

3 Pastreich, 'Grappling with Chinese Writing as a Material Language'; Pastreich, *The Observable Mundane*.

in understanding the Chinese classics: 'After I had studied this [i.e. *Daigaku genkai*] diligently for a long time, I found that I was able to understand all the classics without the need of any lectures'.[4] Hayashi Razan (1583–1657), author of *Daigaku genkai*, was one of the most important Japanese Confucian scholars of the early seventeenth century; he had produced something in the region of forty vernacular explanations of the Chinese classics, of which *Daigaku genkai* was one.[5] Razan's vernacular explanations were written in Japanese using the *katakana* phonographic script and logographic Chinese characters, and took the form of translations or combinations of translations with commentary and paraphrase. Sorai was fortunate to have been exiled with a copy of one of Razan's works of this nature because, despite Razan's stature as a scholar and his later influence, Japanese translation was not a method widely adopted by other Confucianists.[6] Sorai's encounter with Razan's vernacular explanation of the canonical *Daxue* (Greater Learning) provided him with the opportunity to learn to read Chinese texts via the medium of translation and explanation in natural, vernacular Japanese, rather than the archaic pronunciations and highly bound Chinese-Japanese hybrid language that characterized traditional reading methods as taught in mainstream academies in the capital.

Such methods required students to first repeatedly practice intonating the Japanese reading of a canonical text aloud in class until memorization of the sounds of the reading had been achieved. This was not accompanied by instruction in the meaning of the text or its vocabulary. In-class intonation was followed by private reading practice, in which students were expected to decipher the correct reading of texts using dictionaries and asking questions of their teacher. *Wakun* annotations, and the stilted 'readings' they produced (as Sorai pointed out, these were in fact translations), were thus essential guides for scholars when approaching Chinese texts. It was only when such methods had been mastered that students moved onto receiving instruction in the contents of the texts themselves.[7]

For all his claims to have learned to approach Chinese texts in their correct syntactical order while in exile, there is no evidence that Sorai learned to *speak* contemporary Chinese or to read classical Chinese with Chinese pronunciation during that period. However, when he returned to Edo, he encountered native Chinese speaking monks from the Ōbaku Buddhist tradition[8] and interpreters born or adopted into the Nagasaki hereditary interpreter families who had learned to speak Chinese in the port city but had come to Edo to seek their

---

4 Ogyū Sorai, *Yakubun sentei*, 1, fol. 2[v].

5 Kornicki, 'Hayashi Razan's Vernacular Translations and Commentaries'.

6 Clements, *A Cultural History of Translation in Early Modern Japan*, pp. 120–24.

7 Takeda, *Kinsei nihon gakushū hōhō no kenkyū*.

8 Ōbaku (Ch. Huangbo) Buddhism began as a branch of Rinzai (Ch. Linji) Zen (Ch. Chan) Buddhism and was not formally recognized as a separate sect in Japan until 1876. See, Baroni, *Ōbaku Zen*.

fortune.[9] Sorai became a retainer of Yanagisawa Yoshiyasu (1658–1714), the most powerful feudal lord (daimyo) of his day, who had close connections with Chinese Ōbaku monks and who sponsored the study of contemporary spoken Chinese among the Confucian scholars in his employment, including Sorai.[10] After leaving Yoshiyasu's service, Sorai founded a 'Translation Society' (*yakusha*) in 1711 for the study of vernacular, spoken Chinese.

It is important to remember that although Sorai wrote extensively about translation, his ideal was not Japanese translation but rather to become so familiar with Chinese texts that one could understand them via their original syntax and vocabulary. The 'Nagasaki method', based on the approach of interpreters in the port city who knew Chinese as a living language, was the means to achieve this by reading Chinese texts aloud using contemporary Chinese pronunciation and the original word order; vernacular Japanese was used in the classroom for instruction and translation. In *Yakubun sentei* Sorai writes:

> 先為シ二崎陽ノ之学ヲ一教ニ以二俗語ヲ一。誦スルニ以二華音ヲ一訳スルニ以二此ノ方ノ俚語ヲ一。絶シテ不レ作二和訓廻環ノ之読ヲ一。
>
> (One must above all practice the Nagasaki method. When teaching, use vernacular language; when reciting texts, use Chinese pronunciation. And when translating use the common words of our region. You must not make a reading based on *wakun* and reversed word order.)[11]

Despite his dislike of *wakun* annotations when reading aloud, Sorai was resigned to the use of such glosses in the printed word: his works contain the seeming contradiction that his classical Chinese prose, while advocating direct reading through the Nagasaki Method, is printed with the traditional reading marks used to indicate the Japanese glosses and syntactical rearrangement necessary so that it can be read in the Japanese manner, and *Yakubun sentei* is no exception.

Ōtsuki Gentaku and the Nagasaki Method

As his retention of *wakun* annotations as a necessary evil suggests, Sorai's call to read Chinese as Chinese was not followed by many beyond his immediate disciples. However, we may observe echoes of his scholarship nearly seventy years later in the work of one of the leaders of Dutch Learning, Ōtsuki Gentaku. But was Gentaku directly referencing Sorai's work or does his source of inspiration lie elsewhere?

---

9 Pastreich, 'Grappling with Chinese Writing as a Material Language', pp. 126–28.

10 Clements, 'Speaking in Tongues?'.

11 Ogyū Sorai, *Yakubun sentei*, I, fol. 7r.

Gentaku came to Rangaku or 'Dutch Learning' via the study of medicine, having received an education in the Chinese classics that traditionally served as the basic education for men of letters, and to which the scholarship of Sorai belongs. Branching out from the Chinese style medicine that informed mainstream medical knowledge at the time, Gentaku became a pupil of the influential Rangaku scholar-medics Sugita Genpaku (1733–1817) and Maeno Ryōtaku (1723–1803). After a period of study in Nagasaki, Gentaku became an Edo-based medic for the Sendai domain and in 1786 opened the first private academy for the study of Dutch, the Shirandō.[12] Grammatical inaccuracies in Gentaku's instructional works suggest his Dutch language skills were not comparable with those of Nagasaki interpreters who had been engaging with the language since childhood as part of their training. Conversely, Gentaku was trained in Japanese and Chinese academic writing, something in which the interpreters were not traditionally proficient. As De Groot has argued, Gentaku's success in fact lay in his collaboration with a series of interpreter assistants, such as Baba Teiyū (1787–1822), who was his deputy at the shogunate Office for the Translation of Barbarian Books (*Bansho wage goyō*), rendering their translations in an acceptable form of Japanese academic prose.[13]

Through collaboration with interpreters, Gentaku overcame his linguistic shortcomings to become a Rangaku field leader. He was asked by his mentor Sugita Genpaku to revise *Kaitai Shinsho* (A New Treatise on Anatomy), the influential work of Western anatomy translated by Edo-based scholars in 1774. He was also one of the initiators of the *Haruma wage* (*Halma Translated*, 1796) project which used François Halma's Dutch-French *Woordenboek* to produce the first Dutch-Japanese language dictionary,[14] and in 1811 Gentaku was appointed to be the first head of the newly-created shogunate Office for the Translation of Barbarian Books (*Bansho wage goyō*). Important for our purposes here, Gentaku also authored the first widely available manual for students of Dutch in Japan, *Rangaku kaitei* (A Guide to Dutch Studies).[15] *Rangaku kaitei* was finished in 1783 and circulated in manuscript before being published in print five years later. Perhaps because of Gentaku's own struggles with the language, *Rangaku kaitei* is a very detailed and basic introduction to mastering Dutch, which clearly articulates what he saw as the necessary methodology.

Rangaku kaitei begins with an introduction to the history of Dutch studies in Japan, after which Gentaku explains various characteristics of the Dutch language such as letters, numbers, spelling, and pronunciation. He then recommends study methods and translation strategies. His instructions are divided into two stages, which mirror the traditional learning methods

12 Hesselink, 'A Dutch New Year at the Shirandō Academy', pp. 192–93.

13 De Groot, 'The Study of the Dutch Language in Japan', pp. 125–28.

14 Inamura, and others, *Haruma wage*, 204–106–1, 2965.

15 De Groot, 'The Study of the Dutch Language in Japan', p. 127.

employed in approaching Chinese texts, outlined above. It is only after mastering the art of pronouncing the sounds of Dutch texts aloud — reading without comprehending — that the student may begin to understand their contents first by translating individual words, and from there moving on to translating entire sentences. Gentaku advises affixing word and sentence-level translations as glosses, using the term *kun'yaku* (glossed translation), from Japanese methods for approaching classical Chinese. Once glosses have been affixed to each word, Gentaku continues, the beginner may progress to understanding entire sentences. It is significant that he explains the approach by reference to the Japanese encounter with classical Chinese:

> サテ訳字ノコラス付ケ終ラハ一章ヲ貫キテノ意味ヲ其師ニ就テ質問（タヽシトフ）スヘシ其師精ク説キ教ユルトイヘトモ文章ノ語路是マテ読ミ馴レタル支那ノ書籍ノ趣キニアラサレハ初学ハ容易ニ暁リ難シ其教ヲ受タル訓訳ノ全文ヲヒラキ塾中ニコモリテ幾遍トモ無ク熟読暗誦スレハ自然ニ水釈シテ其義通スルモノナリ其文毎語訳字ヲ加フルトイヘトモ支那ノ書ヲ和読スル意ロ持ニテ顚倒ヲ用ヒテ読ミ解セサレハ通セヌナリ
>
> (Now, once you have finished affixing translations at a word level, you should discuss the meaning of entire sentences with your teacher. Your teacher will explain this in great detail; however, the syntax is not the same as that you have encountered hitherto in the Chinese books you are used to reading and so in the initial stages of learning it will be difficult to understand with ease. Comprehension will come to you as a matter of course after you have opened up the complete text equipped with the glosses in which you have been instructed, shut yourself up in school, read the texts aloud innumerable times, and can recite them by heart. Although you will have affixed a translation to each word, unless you reverse the word order to read and understand the way one makes a Japanese reading of a Chinese text then you will not grasp the meaning.)[16]

So far, Gentaku is advocating the traditional method of textual approach, identical to that which was used for reading classical Chinese books: reversal of word order and the use of glosses. However, he then goes on to suggest an approach that mirrors Sorai's methods. For the advanced reader, Gentaku advocates reading Dutch in its original word order:

> 近ロ吾黨ノ士研精ノ余リ少シク得ル所アリテ其読書ノ際タ文意ノ至テ難カラサル所ナレハ一遍ヲ読下シテ直ニ訳文ノ出来ルヨウニハナレリ是唐音ニテ書ヲ読ムニ上ヨリ下ヘ順直ニ読ミ下シテ其義通スルト同シキ理ニテ

16 Ōtsuki Gentaku, *Rangaku kaitei*, II, fols 15^{v}–16^{r}.

> (Recently, particularly learned colleagues of mine have reached the point where they are able to read entire works and translate them immediately, provided the works in question do not contain any extremely complex sections. This is like reading texts from top to bottom using vernacular Chinese pronunciation and understanding the meaning.)[17]

The expression 'top to bottom' reading (*ue yori shita e junchoku ni yomikudashite*) refers to reading classical Chinese without syntactical rearrangement — that is to say, following the Chinese syntax, reading in order from the top of the line to the bottom. Like Sorai, Gentaku ultimately advocated this form of direct reading of the original language followed by a vernacular translation as a better way to grasp the full meaning of a text:

> 元来彼方ノ言辞遥ニ別ナルコトナレハ蘭語ヲ悉ク倭語漢語トナシテ読ントスレハ却テ其義ヲ失フコト多シ只大方ニ翻訳シテ意義ノ尽シ難キ所ニ至リテハ其旨ヲ心ニ合得シテ訳ヲナスヘシ是其大法ナリ
>
> (By its very nature, this language is highly distinct from our own, and so if you read Dutch by turning every word of it into Japanese or Chinese words you in fact lose much of the meaning. Rather you should translate it in a broad sense, and keep the gist of this translation in mind when you come to a particularly difficult part. This is the greatest rule.)[18]

Dutch language interpreters in Nagasaki were trained on the job, apprenticed at a young age to learn Dutch as a living language from the traders themselves, rather than relying on glossed texts.[19] Gentaku is known for his close collaborations with Nagasaki interpreters and so the question remains as to whether he was drawing directly on Sorai's teachings about Chinese or whether he was actually influenced by the interpreters with whom he worked. After all, Sorai himself was merely advocating the 'Nagasaki Method' of reading Chinese that was based on the work of interpreters in the port city. However, it is significant that before branching out into Dutch Learning, Gentaku received a traditional education in the Chinese classics, and that it is in relation to the sinological tradition that he locates his recommended practices for Dutch in *Rangaku kaitei*. The oblique mention of 'learned colleagues' above may be a reference to Gentaku's interpreter collaborators, but if it is he does not spell this out in more detail, nor does he justify the direct reading methodology by explicit reference to interpreter practices.

At the time, the reputation of interpreters suffered in part because many were not well trained and even those who were skilled had to make do without the aid of adequate dictionaries for much of the eighteenth century. They

---

17 Ōtsuki Gentaku, *Rangaku kaitei*, II, fol. 16^{r}.

18 Ōtsuki Gentaku, *Rangaku kaitei*, II, fol. 16^{v}.

19 Sugimoto, *Nagasaki tsūji monogatari*.

were also victims of intellectual snobbery because they lacked the sinological training that formed the educational basis for most serious scholars. Gentaku's mentor, Sugita Genpaku, had led a team of Edo-based scholars to translate an influential Dutch anatomy book into classical Chinese, and had told the story of this so-called 'beginning' of Dutch Learning in his *Rangaku kotohajime* (The Beginning of Dutch Studies, 1815);[20] in doing so, he wrote earlier vernacular translation work by interpreters out of the picture. Based in Edo, rather than Nagasaki, and part of the scholarly establishment, Gentaku naturally located his work on Dutch within the sinological tradition, to which Sorai and his work on reading methods belonged. Whatever the actual origin of his inspiration, this explains why Gentaku's work echoes Sorai's writing about classical Chinese, rather than referencing the Nagasaki interpreters directly.

Sorai and Gentaku on Cultural Distance

This comparison of Gentaku and Sorai's writings on Chinese and Dutch is also revealing for what it tells us about changing attitudes towards these two source languages. There is no suggestion in Gentaku's work that Chinese and Dutch are languages of different value or closeness to Japan, and he clearly believes that understanding Dutch and translating it is possible for someone from Japan. This is in marked contrast to the earlier work of Sorai.

Although *Yakubun sentei* and the lectures upon which it was based were written several decades before the peak of Rangaku in the late eighteenth century, Sorai was aware of the Dutch language texts circulating in Japan in his day. For Sorai, the cultural distance between Holland and the lands of the Sinosphere rendered Dutch more difficult to understand than classical Chinese. In fact, using Dutch as a contrast to Chinese he suggests that such cultural difference meant that the language of 'countries like Holland' (Jp., *Oranda*, i.e. the Dutch Republic), was closer in comprehensibility to that of animals than it was to the languages of Japan and China:

> 如キハ二其荷蘭等ノ諸国。性禀異ナルカ一常ニレ当有下難キレ解シ語。
> 如ク二鳥鳴獣叱不ルレ近二人情ニ一者上。而中華ト之与二此ノ方一情態全同。

> (In the same way that the common sensibility of countries like Holland is far removed from what is normal [for us], their languages are difficult to understand, and are as distant from human sentiment as the squawking of birds or the baying of beasts. In contrast, the sensibility here and in China is completely the same.)[21]

20 Sugita, *Rangaku kotohajime*.
21 Ogyū Sorai, *Yakubun sentei*, fol. 4r.

Sorai goes on to argue that it is a shared sensibility (he uses the compound 人情, Jp. *ninjō*, Ch. *ren qing*, human feelings) that makes understanding across languages possible, whether the texts in question are separated by time or by region. This concept was key to his argument that Chinese texts could be translated into Japanese:

> 人多言フ三古今人不ト二相及一。予読ニ三代以前ノ書ヲ一人情世態。
> 如レ合タルカ二符契ヲ一。
>
> > (People often say that ancient and modern peoples are not equal. But when I read [Chinese] texts from before the Three Ages [i.e. from idealized time of the Sages] the human sentiments and customs match perfectly with my own.)[22]

He uses that argument as a foundation to make the point that the Chinese classics could just as easily have been written in Japanese, if the sages had lived in Japan:

> 仮使聖人生ルトモ二於此方ニ一。豈能外ニシテ二此ノ方ノ言ニ一。
> 別ニ為ンヤ二深奥難解キレ語ヲ一哉。
>
> > (Imagine if the Sages had been born in our land — would they have come up with some obscure, difficult language different to our own?)[23]

This, in turn, justifies his call for the translation of the Chinese classics into Japanese. If sensibility, rather than language, is what is important, then the source language is not inviolate. Sorai was concerned with placing the Japanese language on an equal footing with Chinese in the hierarchy of languages. His work may be understood in the context of attitudes held by some in Japan, that in the wake of the Ming Dynasty's collapse to Qing 'barbarians', Japan was the inheritor of the intellectual traditions of East Asia.[24] In contrast, Dutch was placed beyond the realm of human sentiment by Sorai, in the same category as the languages of birds and beasts.

There is no such agenda apparent in Gentaku's work. Although in the quote above he writes that the Dutch language is 'highly distinct from our own', he does not use the language of civilized versus uncivilized and, unlike Sorai, clearly believes that translation from Dutch into Japanese is possible. By categorizing Chinese and Dutch together with very little justification, Gentaku was also clearly aware of the foreignness of Chinese, an argument Sorai had to make from scratch. This shows that much had changed in the seven decades since *Yakubun sentei* appeared. It is worth noting that Gentaku was

---

22 Ogyū Sorai, *Yakubun sentei*, fol. 4r.

23 Ogyū Sorai, *Yakubun sentei*, fol. 4r.

24 Nakai, 'The Naturalization of Confucianism in Tokugawa Japan'.

also writing at a time when written Japanese as opposed to classical Chinese was coming into its own as an acceptable language of scholarship in Japan.[25]

These changing attitudes go some way towards explaining why freer forms of translation were such a fundamental part of Dutch Learning from its earliest beginnings, rather than Japanese glosses becoming the main method as they had with Chinese. Since by the time the field of Dutch Learning grew in popularity in the late eighteenth century, the sense of Japanese versus foreign languages such as Chinese and Dutch was well established, translation was an obvious and appropriate method of approach. Of course, Dutch texts were never canonical in the way that Chinese texts had been, and so there was little perceived need to preserve them through highly bound glossed translation methods, nor was Dutch characterized by the use of logographs that lent themselves to Japanese annotation. Nonetheless, the writings of Gentaku suggest that an understanding of the foreignness of Dutch, together with an acceptance of vernacular written Japanese as a language of scholarship was also a factor in the choice of vernacular translation as a key strategy in Rangaku.

---

25 Clements, *A Cultural History of Translation*, pp. 228–29.

Bibliography

Archival Sources

Inamura Sanpaku, and others, *Haruma wage* (Manuscript, microfilm), Shizuoka Prefectural Library, 204–106-01, 2965コマ, A

Ogyū Sorai, *Yakubun sentei*, 5 vols (Chion'in monzen, Rakutō: Reitakudō, 1715), Tokyo, Waseda University Library, 文庫17 W0039

Ōtsuki Gentaku, *Rangaku kaitei*, 2 vols ([n. p.]: [n. pub.], 1783), Tokyo, Waseda University Library, 文庫08 E0077

Sugita, Genpaku, *Rangaku kotohajime* (Tenshinrō, Tokyo, 1869), Tokyo, Chiba University Library, 50813–14

Secondary Studies

Baroni, Helen Josephine, *Ōbaku Zen: The Emergence of the Third Sect of Zen in Tokugawa Japan* (Honolulu: University of Hawai'i Press 2000)

Clements, Rebekah, *A Cultural History of Translation in Early Modern Japan* (Cambridge: Cambridge University Press, 2015)

——, 'Speaking in Tongues? Daimyo, Zen Monks, and Spoken Chinese in Japan, 1661–1711', *Journal of Asian Studies*, 76.3 (2017), 603–26

De Groot, Henk W. K., 'The Study of the Dutch Language in Japan During its Period of National Isolation (ca.1641–1868)' (Unpublished doctoral thesis, University of Canterbury, 2005)

Hesselink, Reinier H., 'A Dutch New Year at the Shiranō Academy, 1 January 1795', *Monumenta Nipponica*, 50.2 (1995), 189–234

Kornicki, Peter, 'Hayashi Razan's Vernacular Translations and Commentaries', in *Towards a History of Translating: In Celebration of the Fortieth Anniversary of the Research Centre for Translation*, ed. by Lawrence Wong (Hong Kong: Chinese University of Hong Kong, 2013), vol. 3, pp. 189–212

Nakai, Kate Wildman, 'The Naturalization of Confucianism in Tokugawa Japan: The Problem of Sinocentrism', *Harvard Journal of Asiatic Studies*, 40.1 (1980), 157–99

Pastreich, Emanuel, 'Grappling with Chinese Writing as a Material Language: Ogyū Sorai's *Yakubunsentei*', *Harvard Journal of Asiatic Studies*, 61.1 (2001), 119–70

——, *The Observable Mundane: Vernacular Chinese and the Emergence of a Literary Discourse on Popular Narrative in Edo Japan* (Seoul: Seoul University Press, 2011)

Sugimoto Tsutomu, *Nagasaki tsūji monogatari: Kotoba to bunka no hon'yakusha* (Tokyo: Sōtakusha, 1990)

Takeda Kanji, *Kinsei nihon gakushū hōhō no kenkyū* (Tokyo: Kōdansha, 1969)

DHRUV RAINA

The Hermeneutics of Mathematical Reconciliation

Two Pandits and the Benares Sanskrit College

The encounter of South Asian and European scholarship has a long history dating back to the early modern period. This history is a rather chequered one, characterized by several interpretive movements. The present chapter discusses one such site of encounter, the Benares Sanskrit College in the nineteenth century. The special focus of the chapter is the activity that entailed the translation of texts from two European languages (Latin and English) to Sanskrit and from Sanskrit into English and Hindi. The College was a colonial institution, where Orientalist and local Sanskrit scholars worked and interacted, exchanged, produced and co-produced texts and translations of texts. Orientalism was indubitably the dominant discourse framing this encounter, nevertheless local scholars did manage to get their perspectives across. The chapter pointedly addresses the translation activity of two Sanskrit scholars, mathematicians who were faculty members of the College, and contextualizes their translation projects and the hermeneutics of mathematical reconciliation that they practised. Thus while contesting the deficit theories of the Orientalists, they went on to establish one of the genealogies of the modern history of mathematics writing in India. Nevertheless, a phase of translation activity came to an end with their work.

* The corpus of work of Bāpu Deva Śāstrī and Sudhākar Dvivedī has preoccupied me for some time now. My doctoral student Ritesh Gupta was generous enough to share three of the primary sources that appear in this reconstruction.

Dhruv Raina is professor at the Jawaharlal Nehru University, New Delhi. He studied physics at the Indian Institute of Technology, Mumbai and received his PhD in philosophy of science from Göteborg University. His research has focused on the politics and cultures of scientific knowledge in South Asia, as well as on the history and historiography of mathematics. He has published books and papers on the history and philosophy of science and his most recent (co-edited with Hans Harder) is entitled *Hans Harder, Disciplines and Movements: Scientific Exchanges between India and the German Speaking World*, (Orient Blackswan 2022). Among many positions, he has been a Fellow of the Institute of Advanced Study, Berlin; the first incumbent of the Heinrich Zimmer Professorship at Heidelberg University and in 2018 was elected Fellow of the Indian National Science Academy.

Narratives on Translation across Eurasia and Africa: From Babylonia to Colonial India, ed. by Sonja Brentjes in cooperation with Jens Høyrup and Bruce O'Brien, CAT 3, pp. 353–382 (Turnhout: Brepols, 2022) BREPOLS PUBLISHERS 10.1484/M.CAT-EB.5.127950

The Early Years of Benares Sanskrit College as the Embodiment of the Orientalist Episteme

Orientalist scholarship on India and elsewhere in the nineteenth century was instrumentalized in and by the colonial states to legitimate their rule. Nevertheless, in India the colonial state turned to those it considered to be experts in the domain of knowledge, these being the Sanskrit pandits and Persian-speaking scholars, for legitimacy. These scholars in turn adapted and appropriated the conceptual and institutional panoply of Orientalist discourse and thereby reshaped the identity of Hinduism.[1] But post-Saidian scholarship departed from the linear historical determination of Orientalism in the absence of a cartography of the different shades of Orientalism as well as the constantly shifting ground of Orientalist discourse.[2] Furthermore, for Said the victims of Orientalism were docile participants in its construction.[3] Orientalism's well-developed conceptual apparatus and equally sophisticated institutional structure facilitated its reproduction as it enrolled local participants and interlocutors. Running against the grain of the linear account of diffusion of imperial perspectives in Orientalist discourse, contemporary research signals how local elites and interlocutors managed to articulate their perspectives.[4]

Benares Sanskrit College (also referred to as Government Sanskrit College and today renamed Sampuranand Sanskrit Vishwavidyalaya) was founded in 1791 following a proposal submitted by Jonathan Duncan, the then resident at Benares to Earl Cornwallis, the Governor General, to set apart support for a Hindu College 'for the preservation and cultivation of the Sanskrit Literature and religion of that nation, at this centre of their faith and common resort of their tribes'.[5] The college was officially inaugurated on 18 October 1791 and was mandated to pursue formal studies on the Sanskrit literary tradition, ensure its conservation, and promote and disseminate Sanskrit learning. Vasudha Dalmia approaches the history of the College as a location to follow the evolution of this encounter with the worlds of knowledge, its acquisition and the methods of learning. Her study suggests that in the encounter between Orientalist and Oriental scholars at the College based on '... a thorough mutual exposure to the method of the other, the unsilenced oriental showed a breadth of vision and a generosity' rarely found in the contemporary academic world.[6]

While postcolonial histories of science have explored the dialectic between imperial structures of power and knowledge,[7] the complexity of the knowledge-making process, its different logics and the reckoning with other

1 Dodson, *Orientalism, Empire and National Culture*, p. 1.

2 Dalmia, 'Sanskrit Scholars and Pandits of the "Old School"', p. 321.

3 Said, *Orientalism*.

4 Bayly, *Empire and Information*; Vajpayei, *Righteous Republic*.

5 Nicholls, *Sketch of the Progress*, p. 1.

6 Dalmia, 'Sanskrit Scholars and Pandits of the "Old School"', p. 321.

7 Pinch, 'Same Difference in India and Europe'.

ways of knowing, without discounting the oppressiveness of colonial rule are still issues that require elaboration. Thus moving beyond the simplistic binaries of 'collaboration and resistance', Dodson suggests the need to reckon with these differentiated colonial spaces where '… hierarchies are worked out, universalist notions tested, and ultimately, understandings of difference to oppose European superiority constructed'.[8] The Government Sanskrit College and the vocation of the two mentioned mathematical interlocutors could for our purposes serve as one such differentiated space.

The subsequent discussion focuses upon the translation of mathematical and astronomical texts either from Sanskrit to English or the other vernaculars undertaken by Indian scholars, sometimes with their European colleagues at the College, in the nineteenth century. The attempt is to follow the emergence of a shared hermeneutic that was an outcome of the efforts of the European Orientalists and the Sanskrit scholars from Benares in the second half of the nineteenth century. The work of the two Sanskritists and mathematicians at the Benares Sanskrit College, discussed are Bāpū Deva Śāstrī (1821–1900) and Sudhākara Dvivedī (1855–1910). The works of these scholars will be placed against the larger institutional backdrop of learning in the second half of the nineteenth century.

Situating Translation Activities from Sanskrit in the Nineteenth Century

The histories of most translation projects of the nineteenth century have been framed in relation to the history of colonial rule, the history of Orientalist discourse, the birth of 'Indianisme' or Indology, the history of the circulation and production of knowledge.[9] The underlying theories of translation and the agenda of translation activity, as disclosed by each of them, distinguishes the genres from each other, although that is not the only ground on which that distinction is drawn.[10] As Bernard Cohn, Ronald Inden and others have suggested the process of translation from the modern European into the classical as well as modern South Asian languages was shaped by the idea of the civilizing mission and characterized by a hermeneutics of deficit.[11] This deficit theory may have its roots in part in a stadial theory of the development of language. Thus, the language of colonialism was itself premised upon a colonial perspective of the languages of South Asia, wherein Sanskrit had an ethereal beauty but was inadequate to express the truths of modern European science.

Nevertheless, there existed several imaginaries of India among the Europeans, some of them even tinged with Utopianism. From the work of French Jesuits

8 Dodson, *Orientalism, Empire and National Culture*, p. 11.

9 Kejariwal, *The Asiatic Society of Bengal*; Murr, 'Les conditions d'emergence', pp. 233–84; Schwab, *The Oriental Renaissance*; Županov, *Missionary Tropics*.

10 Kumar, *Political Agenda of Education*.

11 Cohn, *Colonialism and its Forms of Knowledge*; Inden, *Imagining India*.

in the late seventeenth century to those of the early generation of British Indologists such as Reuben Burrow, Samuel Davis, and H. T. Colebrooke, there was a deep recognition of the presence of the rational sciences alongside systems of logic and formal debate in the region.[12] Evidently, these modes of knowing embodied in the textual tradition referred to as the *Siddhāntas* confronted the legends of the *Purāṇas*. In the first decades of the nineteenth century, Lancelot Wilkinson, the political agent of the state of Bhopal and a scholar of Indology, had translated one of the *Siddhāntas* and published an article entitled 'On the Use of the *Siddhāntas* in the Work of Native Education'. In the article he identified three Hindu cosmologies of the day: the Buddhist and Jaina cosmologies; the Brahmānical or Purāṇic system; and the *Siddhāntas* or astronomical systems. Wilkinson saw similarities between the Buddhist, Jaina, and Purāṇic systems while the *Siddhāntas* engaged with the '… the true theory of eclipses', the shape and size of the earth. In support of this view, he cited Bhāskarāchārya's *Siddhānta Śiromaṇi*.[13] The *Siddhāntas* had become for this generation of English scholars and administrators the repositories of rational and naturalist thought of India.

Consequently, the translation of scientific texts from the European languages into the South Asian ones was oriented by the desire to modernize South Asian languages, to infuse them with the 'new knowledge', so that it would be possible to express the insights of the European sciences. Initially these translations were initiated by British colonial administrators, officials, teachers, or doctors employed by the East India Company and all of them worked in close collaboration with vernacular scholars, intellectuals, and school teachers.[14] There is a tendency to see the renewal in Sanskrit studies in the nineteenth century as entirely shaped by the Orientalist imaginaries. This picture, however problematic, needs to be amended by the dialectic created by the colonial compulsion to spread Western learning and the need to co-opt the local intellectual elites so as to impart Western learning in a world that had a semblance to the European one but was inferior to the aforementioned traditions of learning.[15] And so it was that the Sanskrit Colleges of the late

---

12 Murr, *L'indologie du Père Coeurdoux*; Raina, 'Science East and West', pp. 1934–44.

13 Wilkinson quoted in Sarma, 'Sanskrit as Vehicle for Modern Science', p. 190; cf. also Bayly, *Empire and Information*, p. 186.

14 Dalmia, 'Sanskrit Scholars and Pandits of the "Old School"'; Raj, 'Refashioning Civilities, Engineering Trust'.

15 In the third decade of the nineteenth century, a disagreement broke out between two camps as to the educational policy to be adopted by the East India Company in India. On the one hand, there was the camp of the so-called 'Anglicists' who were predisposed to the utilitarian argument, such as that of T. H. Macaulay, that 'traditional' systems of learning and teaching should be supplanted by Western ones. On the other hand, the British Orientalists suggested a reconciliatory policy of 'engraftment' of modern science onto a Sanskritic and Persianate base be adopted. And although the Anglicists managed to have their policy promulgated in the famous (or infamous) Minute of 1835, the project of engraftment, despite the Minute, continued till the end of the nineteenth century.

eighteenth and nineteenth centuries, the Benares Sanskrit College being one of them, and other Anglo-Oriental Colleges employed local scholars, Muslim maulvis and Hindu pandits. Amongst them were those who set the terms for the renewal of 'traditional scholarly debate' in order to promote and ensure the reach of modern learning.[16] The Sanskrit College Library in Benares was dedicated to the collection of original Sanskrit texts. Texts on the specific *darśanas* (literally: view, perspective; here: philosophy, doctrine, teaching), such as the *Nyāya-Vāiśeṣika*, were instrumentalized in the process of naturalizing modern sciences.[17] Faculty were appointed early in the history of the College to teach *Nyāya*, possibly in the early decades of the nineteenth century, Candra Narayāṇa Panḍit (Bhaṭṭāchārya) being the first of the lecturers.[18] He was later recognized as one of 'the most celebrated logicians in India'.[19] On his death, his son Śiromaṇi Bhaṭṭāchārya was appointed to the professorship of logic.[20] It is not clear whether the succession was a matter of chance or primogeniture, or maybe a combination of both, as encountered in several institutions of learning.

In the mid- and late nineteenth century, the works undertaken for translation into Sanskrit from the European canon included the writings of Berkeley, Locke, and Bacon. A little later works from the Sanskrit canon were translated into English and the modern South Asian languages. Local intellectuals participated in the task of translating works from the European languages and Sanskrit into modern Indian languages. Literary figures from across India and Europe formed communities participating in translation activities. One of the most visible domains in this context was that of *Siddhāntajyotiṣa* (the astral sciences) and *gaṇita* (mathematics). The books in question were either the classics from the canon or even textbooks for school children and college students. In short, this space of translation was not bilingual but densely multilingual.

These multilingual vernacular cultures leave their tracks in dictionaries and textbooks with glossaries of technical terms produced from the second quarter of the nineteenth century. It was not uncommon to find glossaries ranging in combinations: English–Sanskrit–Hindi, English–Persian–Urdu, English–Sanskrit–Marathi. The trilingual approach sought to bridge the semantic distance maintained between the vernacular, the Classical South Asian, and modern Western scientific spheres. With the passage of time the trilingual dictionaries made way for bilingual vernacular dictionaries, as classical learning was eclipsed by modern regimes of education both at the school and collegiate levels.

16 Bayly, *Empire and Information*, pp. 224–25.

17 Bayly, *Empire and Information*, p. 228; Raina, 'Translating the "Exact" and "Positive" Sciences'.

18 Nicholls, *Sketch of the Progress*, p. 29.

19 Nicholls, *Sketch of the Progress*, p. 78.

20 Nicholls, *Sketch of the Progress*, p. 85.

Utilitarianism and the Colonial Agenda of Education

In the first quarter of the nineteenth century, there was a very close relationship between Indological research undertaken by East India Company officials and educational policy. Towards the last decades of the nineteenth century, and most certainly by the early decades of the twentieth century the connections between Indological research and education were disrupted, as Indology dug its roots deep into Indian classical learning and was preoccupied with researching Indian antiquity. The focus here is on translation in the scientific disciplines.

While following the internal trajectory of scholarship within one of the cities of Sanskrit learning,[21] it is difficult to separate out this literary activity as totally divorced from the encounter with Europe; the symmetry condition requires that we study this encounter as a two-way exchange of knowledge between Europe and India.[22] Prior to the encounter with Europe, the Sanskrit tradition had a prehistory of encounters with Persian- and Arabic-speaking scholars. This was reflected in the literary cultures and knowledge production of the times.[23] Specialist scholarship has recently highlighted the circulation of knowledge and knowledge-related practices from worlds hitherto considered disconnected. The first European missionary encounters impacted upon the translation practices of South Asian intellectuals writing in Sanskrit and the vernaculars.[24]

In his discussion on the Indian oikumene in the nineteenth century, Bayly points out that in the 1830s, colonial ideologues and leaders of Indian opinion initiated a discussion on 'public instruction' and 'useful knowledge' and drew both on European and precolonial South Asian traditions of communication and argument. Four decades before an incipient nationalism began to colour these debates, matters of concern included the interpretations of history.[25] As suggested above, the debates drew upon local norms and conventions as well as incorporating European ones.[26] However, with the spread of the print medium Hindu and Muslim literati responded to colonial and missionary provocation in written form. This they undertook in their capacity as literary arbiters, practitioners of the astral sciences, and men of medicine.[27] Bayly points out that 'the ecumene had always worked unevenly beneath the network of

---

21 Pollock, 'New Intellectuals in Seventeenth Century India'.

22 Clarke, *Oriental Enlightenment*; Blackburn, 'Early Books and New Literary Practices'.

23 Pollock, 'The Death of Sanskrit'; Truschke, *Culture of Encounter*.

24 Xavier and Županov, *Catholic Orientalism*; Rubiés, 'Reassessing "the Discovery of Hinduism"'.

25 The framework of nationalist discourse in the Indian languages had been influenced by orientalist historiography, but local historians had critically examined and 'reshuffled it according to their own preoccupations' concerning the nature of history, its identity and the validity of its sources. Orsini, *The Hindi Public Sphere*, p. 176.

26 Bayly, *Empire and Information*, pp. 180–81.

27 Bayly, *Empire and Information*, p. 191.

the most enlightened intelligentsia. *In this, India was not qualitatively different from other societies with emergent public spheres'* [emphasis mine].[28] Utilitarian thinkers who influenced colonial policy in India believed that the English educational system would destabilize the foundations of Hinduism and rouse Hindus out of their state of slumber. This constellation of utilitarian ideas was developed with India in mind but circulated as much in India as in Britain thereby reshaping the imaginary of the respective citizenry.[29]

The process of translation within this contact or trading zone was premised on the encounter of distinct and shared intellectual values that were comprised of notions of the rational and scientific. These values, though embedded in different cultural contexts, encounter each other at particular historical junctures and spaces of negotiation, finally authorizing a body of knowledge as knowledge. There were multiple genealogies of encounter that were conjoined because civilizational knowledge that travelled across trade and silk routes for millennia became resources that were mobilized to reposition distinct-knowledge systems. In this process, as Dodson argues, the Sanskrit pandit plays an important role in presenting 'Western knowledge', as articulating a 'specific version of Indian knowledge'.[30] This process is observed in multiple historical contexts across time and civilizational encounters, with differences.[31] But in the process of this repositioning, the persona of the Sanskrit pandit is metamorphosed into that of the professor, and this is part of the present story wherein the Sanskrit pandit becomes professor of astronomy and mathematics.[32]

Translation as Engraftment: The Benares Sanskrit College as the Site of an Experiment

The history of the circulation of scientific knowledge in nineteenth-century India draws attention to the relationship between a variety of learned associations and societies established under imperial rule, the changing character of traditional or local institutions of higher learning, as well as the agenda of colonial education. The primary vehicle for the transmission of formal scientific knowledge was the school and college textbook, produced for a culturally alien readership.[33] The translator had to confront not just the problem of knowability but the problem of translatability.[34]

---

28 Bayly, *Empire and Information*, p. 211.
29 Van Der Veer, *Imperial Encounters*, pp. 6–7.
30 Dodson, *Orientalism, Empire and National Culture*, pp. 13–16.
31 Raina, 'Revisiting Social Theory and History of Science India'.
32 Deshpande, 'Pandit and Professor'.
33 Kumar, *Political Agenda of Education*.
34 Raina, 'Iterative Learning in the Modernisation of the Indian Mathematical Tradition'.

The standard historiography of transmission through translation has proved inadequate.[35] Since the ontogeny of transmission through translation reckons with a process that is all inclusive (the sciences and the accompanying philosophy travel together), the recipient culture is seen as passive or docile, and translation activity is scholarly activity. This historiography evidently requires more nuance arising from the recognition of the complexity of translation in distinct cultural and chronological contexts.[36] The ontogeny of scientific translations recognizes the deep connection between translation activity and research on what preceded the translation or was contemporaneous with it. The aim of translation was not merely to contribute to the evolution of the sciences, but it was also intended as an enabling activity, to train students, to present researchers with textual sources, to inspire and to facilitate education.[37] There were three premises of the translation-research dialectic. Firstly, translation was in part stimulated by current trends in research and teaching and integrated that which was external to the tradition. Secondly, translation and research could be linked in particular historical circumstances, and the critical translation of works were undertaken to surpass them. Finally, and as a consequence of the previous premise these translations occasionally stimulated the extension of translated knowledge and the elaboration of a new theory.[38]

The faculty members of the Benares College comprised a cohort of Sanskrit scholars credentialised in the world of the Sanskrit humanities, astral, and medical sciences. These scholars encountered the contemporaneous world of learning within the precincts of the College, through collegial ties with their European colleagues, or through processes of self-study and collaborative research. From this cohort of Sanskrit scholars would emerge some of the leading thinkers of the late nineteenth-century Sanskrit ecumene. In order to acquire an appreciation of this tradition (परम्परा), it is important to pin down in institutional and scholarly memory the spectrum of scholarship that emerged between the middle of the nineteenth and the early decades of the twentieth century. Fortunately, Paṇḍit Baldev Upādhyāya's काशी की पाण्डित्य परम्परा (*Kāshī Kī Pāṇḍitya Paramparā*) provides us with the biographies of the faculty of the College and its history in over 1200 pages. This work is based not just on documents but on interviews with present and former faculty members who knew other scholars, as well as families and friends of the scholars concerned. The book provides detailed biographies of ninety-five Sanskrit scholars employed between 1840 and 1890 including those of the principals of the College who were largely Europeans in the nineteenth century and European faculty.

---

35 Montgomery, *Science in Translation.*
36 Rashed, 'Problems of the Transmission', p. 199.
37 Rashed, 'Problems of the Transmission', p. 202.
38 Rashed, 'Problems of the Transmission', p. 208.

Upādhyāya's account of the emergence of *jyotiṣaśāstra* and *gaṇita* at the College for the early period also relies on an unpublished work of George Nichols cited above namely *Sketch of the Rise and Progress of the Benares Patshala*. A handwritten version of the book was available in the Queen's College Library, Benares and the work was published in 1907 by Government Press in Uttar Pradesh. Nicholls was the headmaster of the College in 1847 and the book was written at the request of John Ballantyne, in order to put in one place, the evolution of the 'oldest Government Education Institution'.

These works offer us a glimpse of the early generation of the *Jyotiṣa Śāstrīs*, such as Paṇḍit Lakshmipathy (1748–1820), specializing in *both phalajyotiṣa* and *gaṇitajyotiṣa*.[39] His students included Paṇḍit Kṛṣṇadev and Paṇḍit Lajjaśaṅkar Śarmā. The latter was known to be a reputed astrologer. The college when founded was mandated to improve upon and cultivate eighteen branches of learning of the Sanskrit tradition in the humanities, astral and medical sciences. This entailed an analysis of the literature from the *Agni Purāṇas*, the four *Vedas*, in particular the *Atharvaveda*, and *Āyurveda*, *Gandharvavidya*, *Dhanurveda*, *Śikṣā*, *Nirukta*, *Kalpa*, *Mīmāṃsā*, *Nyāya*, *Dharmaśāstras*, the eighteen *Purāṇas*, *Vyākaraṇa*, *Jyotiṣa* and *Vedānta*.[40]

The faculty members were not just employed as teachers but pursued extra-mural research in those areas concerned with the world of Sanskrit learning. These included *vyākaraṇa* (grammar); *mīmāṃsā* (hermeneutics); *nyāya* (logic); *dharmaśāstra* (traditional law); *alaṅkāraśāstra* (poetics or aesthetics), *āyurveda* (medicine) and finally *jyotiṣa* and *gaṇita*.[41] From this cohort, we shall focus on two who contributed to *jyotiṣa* and *gaṇita*, namely Bāpū Deva Śāstrī and Sudhākara Dvivedī.

The College was a site of knowledge where scholars not only taught or acquired knowledge but where they also acquired scholarly reputations.[42] The importance of the College in the world of Sanskrit learning was reflected in the claim that any scholar who mattered in that century had passed under its portals as student, teacher, or visitor.[43] Amongst the principals was John Muir, who was born in Glasgow in 1810 and like most East India Company officials graduated from Haileybury. On 13 April 1844, he was appointed by the Lieutenant Governor as principal of Benares College.[44] He was subsequently associated with the establishment of Muir College, Allahabad

39 *Phalajyotiṣa* was a branch of *jyotiṣa* engaging with the interpretation of astronomical events and the place of the stellar constellations in the firmament in relation to the conditions on earth. The concern was with the *grahas* (astral houses), *nakśatras* and their positive impact on humans and different aspects of creation. *Gaṇitajyotiṣa*, on the other hand, dealt with the positive aspects of astrology.

40 Nicholls, *Sketch of the Progress*, pp. 3–4.

41 Pollock, 'New Intellectuals in Seventeenth Century India'.

42 Jacob, 'Lieux de Savoir'.

43 Upādhyāya, *Kāshi Ki Pāṇḍītya Paramparā*, p. 60.

44 Nicholls, *Sketch of the Progress*, p. 128.

that later developed into the science faculty of Allahabad University.[45] On taking over as principal of the Benares College, he issued a memorandum in 1845, wherein students could opt for grammar and arithmetic or poetry and grammar. Those opting for the arithmetic courses were expected to read the *Jyotiṣ Candrikā (jyotiṣa)* and the *Padārtha Vidyāsar* to be taught by Bāpū Deva Śāstrī or Lajjaśaṅkar. The advanced students were expected to read these works in Sanskrit.[46]

Among the early pandits associated with the College was Keśav Śāstrī Marathe, who is supposed to have published a work entitled *Jñānasiddhāntachandrikā*, a translation of George Berkeley's *A Treatise concerning the Principles of Human Knowledge*. The translation into Sanskrit was published in a periodical called *The Pandit* in English and the *Kāśividyāsudhāniddhi* in Sanskrit between 1873 and 1875 — more about the journal later (see Figure 2, opposite). A critical edition of this book was prepared by Radheyśām Das Dvivedī. Thus from the second half of the nineteenth century, Sanskrit philosophers, either at the suggestion of their European colleagues or out of the need to respond to the swell tide of European learning began to produce translations of important works from the European epistemological and wider philosophical canon. Evidently, epistemology was of the essence, the beacon guiding the conversation between traditions.[47] Similarly, a contemporary work was produced by Ḍhuṇḍirāja Śāstrī when he undertook a translation of John Locke's *An Essay Concerning Human Understanding*, the Sanskrit translation was entitled *Mānavīyajñānaviṣayakaśāstrāvatāra*. This translation was also serialized in *The Pandit*. He then went on to translate into Hindi two important works from the Sanskrit epistemological canon, namely from the *Nyāya* called the *Nyāyadarśanam* and on the *Vāiśeṣika* called the *Vāiśeṣikadarśana*. Clearly, the translations into Hindi also reflected a move of this enclosed community of Sanskrit scholars to reach out to a wider audience who could read Hindi. This was then part of the vernacularization of the *darśanas*.

Muir was trying to push the Sanskrit pandits to learn English and come out of their singular mastery of the Sanskrit language, for he felt that even their command over their respective vernaculars was limited to highly local patois. He went on to argue for a standardization of the grammar and orthography of Hindi.[48]

Beyond the colonial lens, J. R. Ballantyne, another of the principals of the College, also appears as a utilitarian votary of languages. As principal of the college, among his many initiatives was to publish a work entitled *Synopsis of Science* in 1850 in order to facilitate a comparison of Western and Eastern ways

---

45 Gour, *Three Rivers and a Tree*.

46 Nicholls, *Sketch of the Progress*, pp. 135–36.

47 Upādhyāya, *Kāshi Ki Pāṇḍītya Paramparā*, p. 93.

48 Nicholls, *Sketch of the Progress*, p. 139.

काशीविद्यासुधानिधिः

THE PANDIT.

A MONTHLY PUBLICATION

OF THE

BENARES COLLEGE,

DEVOTED TO

SANSKRIT LITERATURE.

NEW SERIES.

VOL. II.

BENARES:

PRINTED AND PUBLISHED BY THE PROPRIETORS,

E. J. LAZARUS AND CO., AT THE MEDICAL HALL PRESS.

1878.

Figure 2. Frontispiece of one of the issues of *The Pandit* (Sanskrit title *Kāshīvidyāsudhānidhi*).

of obtaining and validating knowledge.[49] The work was written in English accessible to the Sanskrit pandits such as Bāpū Deva Śāstrī and Vitthala Rao and discussed Western logic, the history of science, and natural theology.[50] The foundational text for staging this encounter was Francis Bacon's *Novum Organum*, although a work at the time considered as passé in Europe, but it was presented to an Indian readership as the seminal text in Western philosophy that engaged with rational scientific methodology. As Dodson writes, the *Novum Organum* 'was thereby characterised as the text which best represented Europe's transition into modernity through the presentation of an enabling

49 *A Synopsis of Science from the Standpoint of the Nyāya Philosophy. Part I, Hindi and English.*

50 Dodson, *Orientalism, Empire and National Culture*, pp. 102–05.

scientific methodology' — its treatment of the '… scientific methodology of induction correlated closely with the discussion of the method for apprehending invariable concomitance (*vyāpti-grahopāya*) found in the *Nyāya* and as such represented a measure of the intellectual common ground between Indians and Britons'.[51] By placing a dated Aristotelian syllogistic reasoning, and not Baconian inductivism on the same plane as the *Nyāya*, Ballantyne was chronologically placing contemporaneous Indian civilization on par with ancient and medieval Europe and not modern Europe. In this manner, the importance of Bacon's *Novum Organum* was located within Orientalism's constructive educational programme and its theory of deficit.[52] Ballantyne's programme becomes clear in his *Minute* of 1846 that is reproduced in Nicholl's *Sketch*.

> All improvement must be in the way of addition, not substitution. The most perfect European education bestowed upon a young Brahman, however great a blessing it might be to himself, would exert no beneficial influence beyond his own breast, if unaccompanied by the amount of Sanskrit education which is indispensable for securing any degree of respectful attention to his words. How little moral influence do the very best pupils of the college exert on the mind of the learned natives, if indeed neglecting so much as they do their vernacular tongue, they be supposed capable of communicating much of what they have learned to any native at all. But if we succeed in establishing in the Sanskrit College the standard of training which I propose, we shall have in the case of each pupil so trained a Brahman whose acquirement in Sanskrit learning must command respect, and consequent attention, whose thoughts (by the hypothesis) are to a certain extent influenced acquaintance with correct modes of thinking and who will find acute men of his own class sufficiently disposed to argue with him and no wise disposed to yield a single point that can be by any means contested.
>
> From Ballantyne's Report 1846.[53]

Ballantyne's collaborator in this project was Vitthala Rao, a leading scholar of this generation,[54] best known for his translation of the first book of Francis Bacon's *Novum Organum*. Vitthala Rao had been a student of Ballantyne and was later appointed assistant professor at the College in 1853. He alongside Bāpu Deva Śāstrī were Ballantyne's interlocutors.[55] With Ballantyne, Vitthala Rao co-authored a work in English entitled *An Explanatory Version of Bacon's*

51 Dodson, *Orientalism, Empire and National Culture*, p. 106.

52 Dodson, *Orientalism, Empire and National Culture*, p. 107.

53 Reproduced in Nicholls, *Sketch of the Progress*, p. 142.

54 Vitthala Rao belonged to the Konkan region of Maharashtra, and was mentored in the *Nyāya* school by the reputed logician Bhau Śāstrī from what is now Andhra Pradesh. Upādhyāya, *Kāshī Kī Pāṇḍitya Paramparā*, p. 94.

55 Dodson, *Orientalism, Empire and National Culture*, pp. 285–91.

Novum Organum in Sanskrit and English. The book is interestingly structured. Ballantyne wrote the preface to the book, followed by a translation from the Latin of the *Novum Organum* into English. This translation is accompanied by explanatory notes for the pandits. The remarkable feature is that many of the footnotes are in Sanskrit and deal with conceptually obtuse sections of the text or attempt to introduce a concept that does not exist in the Indian *darśanas*. The third part reproduces the original Latin text.

Vitthala Rao and his colleagues collaborated with European Indologists in the translation of original texts into English, such as Kannāda's *Vāiśeṣikāsūtra*. In addition, as was the case with Ḍhuṇḍirāja Śāstrī, they participated in creating a linguistic identity for Hindi, by not just writing in Hindi but translating the canon into Hindi and reaching out to a widening readership that extended beyond the Sanskrit *sampradāya*.[56] The pandits of Benares and Allahabad played no small role in conferring a Sanskritized lexicon and prestige on the constructed language. As a result, these translations were instrumentalized for their historical preoccupations and thereby played a significant role in shoring up Hindu identity. But as Nicholson points out, till the eighteenth century the intellectuals of the Sanskrit cosmopolis had no such awareness of an exclusively Hindu identity.[57]

As colonial officials became more confident of the scholarship of British Indologists, their enthusiasm for the translation activity of the College may have waned, for this activity was temporarily suspended at the College, only to be revived in 1882. Ballantyne proposed that an important Sanskrit text on logic, the *Nyāya-Kaumudī*, be translated and that the *Nyāya sūtras* of Gāutama and Bacon's *Novum Organum* be studied in detail. Fritz Edward Hall was then His Majesty's Inspector for Public Instruction in the Central Provinces. Nehemiah Nīḷakaṇṭha Śāstrī Goreh and Edward Hall translated a work from Hindi called the *Shad-darśana-darpana* into English. The English translation was called *A Rational Refutation of the Hindu Philosophical Systems* that was published in 1860. The original work in Hindi was in two parts: the first was the *Shad-darśana-darpana* and the second the 'Hindu Philosophy examined by a Sanskrit Pandit'. In 1897 this work was translated into English to remedy the dismal outreach of the work among Hindi readers at the time.

---

56 The movement to create Hindi as a distinct modern language of the Hindus descended from Sanskrit roots began to pick up in second half of the nineteenth century. Orsini, *The Hindi Public Sphere*.

57 Nicholson, *Unifying Hinduism*, pp. 1–2. Nicholson refers to the historiographic divide in interpretations of Hinduism. According to one historiographic frame, Hinduism is a term referring to Sanātana Dharma, and according to the other, it is an invention of Orientalism internalized by English-educated Indians. Both, Nicholson contends, are oversimplifications of premodern Indian history and that between 1200 and 1600 CE, 'some' intellectuals approached Saddārśana as the 'mainstream of Hindu philosophy'. European thinkers in the nineteenth century influenced by the explanatory category of 'world religions' as well as the works of medieval philosophers and doxographers developed the term 'Hinduism'.

The authors then decided to reach out to 'Hindu students of English', as well as evangelizers who sought 'to acquaint themselves with the abstruse matters of their ancestral religion'.[58]

The other European scholars who were either faculty of the College or passed through at different points in time included A. E. Gough, J. Nesfield, G. Thibaut, and R. O. H. Griffith who was at the College between 1861 and 1879. Thibaut and Griffith shifted the focus of their activity from translating European texts into Sanskrit to that of translating from Sanskrit into English.[59] This activity depended on the deepening of their collegial ties with their Indian counterparts, the Sanskrit pandits. This did not mean that the pandits followed the interpretative trail of their European colleagues, but rather what resulted from the collaboration was a *métissage*. Secondly, the output of this activity was published in a journal named *Vidyasudhāniddhi* in Sanskrit and *The Pandit* in English. The title page was bilingual, and so were the publications in the journal. Publication commenced in 1866 and the mandate was to publish consolidated versions of rare Sanskrit manuscripts and translations of these as well as complex and important works that were difficult to trace or comprehend. *The Pandit* was published regularly till 1917 and in some years it appeared tri-annually. The translated texts included works on Indian philosophy, the astral and medical sciences.[60] The role of journals like *The Pandit* was also to popularize historical research pursued by associations and institutes on ancient India and bring history into the arena of public debate.[61]

The German Indologist Georg Wilhelm Friedrich Thibaut (b. 1848) joined the college in 1875, became its principal in 1888 and occupied the position till 1894. During this period, he worked on Indian philosophy, the astral sciences, and mathematics. With Sudhākara Dvivedī, he produced an edition of Varāhamihira's *Pañcasiddhāntikā*. In addition to Dvivedī, he was indebted to three other scholars who aided him with the translations, these being, Rām Mishra Śāstrī, Gangādhara Śāstrī, and Pandit Keśav Śāstrī.[62] As pointed out earlier, the Anglo-Sanskrit Department that served as an institutional umbrella for the translation activity was shut down. Shortly after Thibaut arrived, a memorandum was issued to consider reviving the department. Thibaut reckoned that the earlier mandate of the department was framed at a time when there was dearth of facilities for imparting a knowledge of the European languages and the sciences. By the third quarter of the nineteenth century, that situation had changed. Against this backdrop, Thibaut was reworking the mandate. He writes: 'The task [...] of improving the method on which the study of Sanskrit is at present carried on in the Benares Sanskrit

58 Goreh, *A Rational Refutation of the Hindu Philosophical Systems*.

59 Upādhyāya, *Kāshī Kī Pāṇḍitya Paramparā*, p. 97.

60 Upādhyāya, *Kāshī Kī Pāṇḍitya Paramparā*, p. 95.

61 Orsini, *The Hindi Public Sphere*, p. 176.

62 Upādhyāya, *Kāshī Kī Pāṇḍitya Paramparā*, p. 99.

College, and of converting Pandits of the old school into accomplished Sanskrit scholars, in the European sense of the word'.[63] Thus while recognizing the accomplishments of the pandits of the Old school, Thibaut sought to reorient the research activity of the College in the direction of European Indology; this entailed imparting its methods and responding to its concerns.

Engraftment: From Educational Policy to the Hermeneutics of Reconciliation

Postcolonial scholarship has underlined the epistemological violence that accompanies the encounter of knowledge systems involving distinct cultures under colonial rule. Other framings of encounter, particularly those departing from diffusionism and subscribing to interactionist or constructivist models, scrutinize the process of cultural redefinition. Drawing upon the literature on psychotherapy, this process of cultural redefinition may also be conceived as one of cultural psychotherapy.[64] The recipient culture's narrative acquires form when there is a sense of hopefulness as opposed to devastation. The possibility of reconciliation within the recipient culture arises when features of this culture provide meaning and resources to engage not just with the self but with the other. This possibility was on offer through the colonial policy of engraftment reworked by the local culture as a hermeneutics of reconciliation as a narrative for transformation. The clash of cultures can be deeply problematic, and it has been viewed through different frames. So while the same cultural encounter can be viewed by some as the 'clash of civilizations', there could be aspects at the other end that make sense as dialogical. Perhaps both frames oversimplify, occupying opposite ends of the spectrum. Intercultural contact that alters ways of being and quotidian practices could provoke hostility and antagonism, accompanied by destabilization and confusion arising from the very dynamics of encounter. At Benares College the oeuvre of our interlocutors begins to make sense, in all its complexity and the burden of a past inherited and mediated by the colonial experience, in terms of a hermeneutics of reconciliation, which itself is a form of cultural therapy. The next section maps this process in the lives of two Sanskrit pandits.

Śāstrī, Dvivedī, and the Hermeneutics of Reconciliation

The first of these interlocutors was Bāpu Deva Śāstrī who was born into a Brahmin family in what is now Maharashtra on 24 October 1819 and was schooled in the Southern Indian Sanskrit tradition. This meant that he was instructed in the Sanskrit classics such as the *Aṣṭādhyāyī*, *Piṅgalasūtram*,

63 Nicholls, *Sketch of the Progress*, pp. 154–55.

64 Foster and James, 'Narratives of Hope and Reconciliation'.

Rūpāvali, *Amarakoṣa*, and *Āyurveda*. He later acquired knowledge of the *Vedas*, *Raghuvaṃśa*, and the *Laghu-Kaumudī* and then studied mathematics in Pune at the school of mathematics run by Pāndurang Tatya Divekar.[65] From Pune he proceeded to Nagpur where he undertook the study of the mathematical classics namely the *Līlāvatī* and the *Bīja-Gaṇita* with Pandit Dhundiram Mishra. Lancelot Wilkinson, mentioned earlier, was impressed with Bāpu's knowledge of algebra and invited him to Sehor where the former was stationed, and where Bāpu learned English and undertook research in mathematics with Pandit Sewaram.[66] Between 1830 and 1840, Wilkinson was also the administrative head in Sehor; and it is here that their collaboration on the classics of *gaṇita* commenced. Their foremost contributions included the *Siddhāntaśiromaṇi*, *Bīja-Gaṇita*, and *Rekhāgaṇita*.[67]

Wilkinson was moulded or programmatically committed to the idea of engrafting modern science on a Sanskritic base. And within this schema the works of Bhāskarachārya had a special place. This is evident from the following passage:

> How readily may a knowledge of the science, as taught in the Siddhāntas, be recommunicated, especially to the Jotshis (*sic*). With what exultation will every man of ingenious mind amongst them receive explanations making plainand clear what is now all unintelligible and dark. They will not stop in simply admitting what is taught in the Siddhāntas. Grateful to their European Instructors for bringing them back to a knowledge of the works of their own neglected, but still revered, masters, they will … also readily receive the *additions made during the last few hundred years in science* (emphasis added).
>
> > […] there can be little or nothing which we have to teach in Geometry, Surveying, and Trigonometry generally, in Geography or Astronomy, of which Bhaskar Acharya has not already given us the first principles, and for enabling us to explain which, he will not afford us many new and also the most appropriate arguments, in as much as they will be best suited to Hindu taste'[68]

Wilkinson felt that in addition to Bhāskara's *Bīja-Gaṇita*, *Līlāvatī*, and *Siddhānta Śiromaṇi*, other books required translation in order to provide a comprehensive understanding of jyotiṣa, this being Gaṇeśa Daivajña's *Gṛhalāghava*. By the

65 Upādhyāya, *Kāshī Kī Pāṇḍitya Paramparā*, p. 190.

66 Bāpu Deva was easily the brightest among Wilkinson's pupils, who went on to master Euler's *Algebra* in addition to that of Bhāskara, that qualified him to teach European mathematics at the College. For Wilkinson's account of Bāpu Deva's reaction to Euler's work see Sarma, 'Sanskrit as Vehicle for Modern Science'.

67 *Translation of the Sūrya Siddhānta by Pandit Bapu Deva Sastri and of the Siddhānta Śiromani, by the late Lancelot Wilkinson, revised by Bapu Deva Sastri.*

68 Wilkinson quoted in Sarma, 'Sanskrit as Vehicle for Modern Science', p. 191.

time Wilkinson succeeded in emphasizing the importance of these works, the translations of H. T. Colebrooke, Edward Strachey, and John Taylor of the *Bīja-gaṇita* and the *Līlāvatī* were available. Hence a decision was taken to publish the *Rekhāgaṇita*, a work on geometry.[69] The *Rekhāgaṇita* was none other than Jagannātha Samrāṭ's Sanskrit translation from the previous century of a recension of Euclid's *Elements* by the polymath Naṣīr al-Dīn al-Ṭūsī. Samrāṭ, in his own words, had written that his *Siddhāntasārakaustubha* was a translation of Ṭūsī's astronomical work whose title he abbreviated as *mijāstī* (*al-Majisṭī*):

अरबीभाषया ग्रन्थो मजिास्तीनामकस्थतिः।
गणकानां सुबोधाय गीर्वाण्या प्रकटीकृतः।।

He also claimed that the *Rekhāgaṇita* was a translation of a geometrical work.[70] According to Hawadia Chakala who wrote the 'introduction' to the 1901 edition of the book, the *Rekhāgaṇita* was a 'version of Euclid's *Elements*'. Books I to IV and Book VI were on plane geometry, Book V was on the law of proportions that was then used in Book VI, Books VII, VII, and IX were on arithmetic and discussed the principles of numbers or number theory, and Book XI onwards were on solid geometry.[71] Pages 188–219 of the manuscript that was Book X of the translation covering propositions 16 to 101 were missing from the manuscript.[72]

A committee had earlier been appointed that was headed by J. T. Marshall of Fort Williams College, Calcutta and Jaynarayan Tarkapanchannan to review the courses of the Benares Sanskrit College. From the mid 1830s, there was a growing sense that the academic standards in the College were declining despite earlier curricular reforms. The students seemed to prefer *jyotiṣa* in their pursuit of astrological researches rather than the so-called 'scientific attainments' of mathematics, astronomy, and algebra.[73] A local committee inquired into the causes of the decline. Among others, the *Nyāya* pandit Krishna Chander and the astronomy pandit Lajjaśaṅkar identified the causes to reside outside the system.[74] A perusal of the syllabus indicated that the students of astronomy were expected to have read several *Siddhāntas, Rekhāgaṇita, Bīja-Gaṇita,* and *Līlāvatī*.

The committee suggested the inclusion of instruction on natural philosophy and Sanskrit mathematics [संस्कृत गणति]. Bāpu Deva was appointed as a faculty member of the College in 1842. Since there was a dearth of textbooks

---

69 Sarma, 'Sanskrit as Vehicle for Modern Science', p. 195. The work was actually published sixty years later in the Bombay Sanskrit series.

70 Trivedi, 'Introduction' to *The Rekhāganita or Geometry in Sanskrit*, pp. 35–39, 41. This book is a 1901 republication of Samrāṭ's work first translated in the first half of the eighteenth century.

71 *The Rekhāganita or Geometry in Sanskrit*, p. 11.

72 *The Rekhāganita or Geometry in Sanskrit*, p. 8.

73 Nicholls, *Sketch of the Progress*, p. 116.

74 Nicholls, *Sketch of the Progress*, p. 120.

at the time, Bāpu Deva edited and published critical editions of important works. At the request of Ballantyne and Macleod, he went on to produce and publish a translation of the *Bīja-Gaṇita* in 1850 from Mumbai. The book was so well received that an award of ₹ (rupees) 2000 was bestowed on him. In 1859, he collaborated with Fritz Edward Hall to produce a comprehensive edition of the Sanskrit text of the *Sūrya-Siddhānta* based on a collation of nine manuscripts, several of which were procured from pandits working in Benares or were faculty members of the College such as Lajjaśaṅkar.[75] He then published a textbook called the *Saraltrikonomiti*. This work puts Western trigonometry in a Sanskrit idiom, and in the process introduces Western mathematics to the *jyotiṣastri*. In 1865, he published a work entitled the *Manamandira Observatory in Benares*. The observatory had been established by Mān Singh, an ancestor of Jai Singh of Amber. Jai Singh had installed additional astronomical instruments (*yantra*) at the observatory. Śāstrī's pamphlet in English describes and discusses the workings of these instruments bringing them from the realm of the quaint into the realm of contemporary astronomical familiarity.[76] He was then professor of astronomy and mathematics at the Benares College. As professor he requested Pandit Pravir Neelambar to write a book on Eastern and Western mathematics called *Gol Prakash* that appeared in 1871. This was the period when he authored a number of books in Sanskrit and Hindi.[77] In addition, he went to author a book in English in two parts entitled *Elements of Algebra* and *Elements of Arithmetic*.[78] Purely in the realm of speculation, it could be suggested that the inspiration for these works came from Augustus De Morgan's two books of the same name that had been translated into Marathi towards the end of the 1830s, and as a student of *gaṇita* in Pune, Bāpu Deva was possibly aware of them.[79] He was inducted as a member of the Asiatic Society, London in 1864, in recognition of his scholarship. Clearly, this recognition came not just for his work on mathematics but as the first Indian pursuing the modern history of mathematics.

After his 1850 book, Bāpu Deva Śāstrī had emerged within the Benares College as a scholar of renown in the astral sciences and mathematics with few competitors. The moment was both opportune and remarkable. This was the period when Western mathematical systems began to be introduced in schools and colleges in India. I have elsewhere discussed the process of the cultural translation of modern mathematics within the mathematics curriculum of the subcontinent.[80] As suggested earlier, the issue as it posed itself for Bāpu Deva Śāstrī was one of reconciliation (समन्वय) of the Western

75 Hall and Śāstrī, *The Sūrya Siddhānta*.

76 Śāstrī, *The Manamandira Observatory*.

77 For a listing of the titles of his books, see Upādhyāya, *Kāshī Kī Pāṇḍitya Paramparā*, pp. 192–93.

78 Śāstrī, *Elements of Algebra and Elements of Arithmetic*.

79 Raina, 'A Transcultural History'.

80 Raina, 'Mathematics Education in Modern India', pp. 382–84.

and Eastern traditions.[81] From the colonial perspective, this was a project in engraftment, to remedy the deficit in Sanskrit *gaṇita*, even while acknowledging its accomplishments. From the point of view of the local interlocutors, it was one of harmonizing Western mathematics with ancient Indian mathematics.

In 1861 a book was published in two parts comprising a translation of the *Sūrya Siddhānta* by Bāpu Deva and of the *Siddhānta Śiromaṇi* by Wilkinson. Since Wilkinson had by then passed on, the completion of the translation of the latter too was undertaken by Bāpu Deva. But going back to their working years, the translation earned him Wilkinson's recommendation for a position in the department of *Jyotiṣśāstra* at the Benares Sanskrit College.[82]

Ballantyne had embarked on a project of engrafting modern mathematics onto a Sanskrit and Persian mathematical medium to initiate the modernization of Indian mathematics. Bāpu Deva Śāstrī set about reconciling Western mathematics anchored in the Sanskritic tradition. While it was already recognized that the two systems were not radically incommensurable, they reckoned that they were mutually comprehensible, though with different starting points. Thus both sides moved in opposite directions and rather than pass each other they did meet up. The fact that both sides shared an institutional locus facilitated this process. In any case, there were mathematicians around in the nineteenth century who did not see the emergence of modern mathematics as a radical break with the past.

There are several genealogies of modern mathematics, all of which develop along separate trajectories of solving polynomial equations of order three or greater than three. Bāpu Deva Śāstrī's work explicitly locates the ostensibly ancient Indian tradition of mathematics within the narrative frame of the evolution of mathematics rather than just Western mathematics. In 1858, Bāpu Deva published a paper on the history of mathematics, probably one of the first papers on the subject published by an Indian in a Western research periodical. He proposes in the paper to correct the impression that the 'principle of differential calculus' was unknown to the ancient Hindu mathematicians and he proceeds to remedy this situation by turning to the work of Bhāskara. A question that acquires salience here is as to why the differential calculus was so important. In earlier writing I have tried to address the question internally and from constructivist perspectives of how calculus was introduced into India. It seemed then the modernity of mathematics and science was entwined with the invention of calculus that then set the boundary between the less developed ancient mathematics and modern mathematics. Bāpu Deva reveals Bhāskara's approach to calculating the *tātkālika* which is the differential of

81 Upādhyāya, *Kāshī Kī Pāṇḍitya Paramparā*, p. 189.

82 Upādhyāya, *Kāshī Kī Pāṇḍitya Paramparā*, p. 191. Wilkinson had collegial ties with a number of Sanskrit scholars that included Durgasankara Pathak who authored *Sarva-Siddhānta Tattva Cintamani* (The Crest Jewel of the Essence of all Astronomical Systems) comprising star maps 'meticulously drawn from Islamic and European sources', his relative and a teacher at the College Lajjashankar Pathak. Sarma, 'Sanskrit as Vehicle for Modern Science', p. 194.

the longitude of the planet. The demonstration of this computation of the *tātkālika* is directed towards establishing that it corresponds with the principle of differential calculus. He concludes by pointing out that since Bhāskara treated the subject briefly and his followers never fully appreciated its salience its import was never recognized.[83]

H. H. Wilson communicated Bāpu Deva's note to the mathematician W. Spottiswoode. The latter's comment too was published in the Journal. Spottiswoode felt that Bāpu Deva's claim that Bhāskara was 'fully aware with the principal of the differential calculus was overstated', which still left the window for admitting that there was something to it nevertheless. On the positive side, Spottiswoode recognized that: [1] there was a method of comparing the successive positions of a planet in motion, [2] that the motion of the planet was assumed constant during the interval, [3] there was a 'rudimentary idea' of representing the arc of a curve by an auxiliary straight line.[84] But the most substantial criticism was the absence of the idea of the infinitesimal magnitude of the 'intervals of time and space thereof employed' — an essential feature of the differential calculus. And finally, in Bhāskara there is no recognition of the approximate nature of the method.[85] In that sense the principle is not the same. But, as often happens in mathematics; the result Bhāskaracharya obtains for the instantaneous velocity: $U' - U = x' - x \pm \{a \cos y/R\}\{(y' - y)/R\}$, bears according to Spottiswoode '... more than a resemblance — a strong analogy to the corresponding process in modern mathematical astronomy'. So a correction is proposed in Bāpu Deva's derivation of Bhāskara's formula; while the formula in modern analysis is:

$$\begin{aligned} du &= d(x \pm a \sin y) \\ &= dx \pm a \cos y \, dy. \end{aligned}$$

In this process, Bāpu Deva raised an important historiographic point by disrupting the narrative of mathematical progress within the history of European mathematics by widening the context of discussion, and bringing the separated domains of civilizational history into the domain of encounter through this hermeneutics of reconciliation. On the other hand, closer to home he had reconfigured the agenda of *gaṇita* and *jyotiṣa* by bringing the former into an active relation with modern mathematics and proposed to draw on the new mathematics and astronomy for improving the predictions of the latter. This task was subsequently taken up by none other than Sudhākara Dvivedī.

Unlike Bāpu Deva Śāstrī, Sudhākara Dvivedī was no outsider to the College. His father Pandit Kripaludutt Dvivedī was a student of Pandit Nandlal Sharma, a teacher at the College. Sharma was considered an expert on *phalajyotiṣa*.

83 Śāstrī, 'Bhāskara's Knowledge of the Differential Calculus', pp. 215–16.

84 Spottiswoode, 'Note on the Supposed Discovery', p. 222.

85 Spottiswoode, 'Note on the Supposed Discovery', p. 222.

Devkrishan Sharma was another expert on *jyotiṣa* at the College and Sudhākar Dvivedī was his leading student.[86]

Dvivedī was considered one of the leading proponents of the *Siddhānta Jyotiṣa*, for within the field of *jyotiṣśāstra*, he, in the tradition of Bāpu Deva, threw new light on ancient texts (*gaṇita*), offering new explanations, interpretations, and commentaries. In substantial measure he participated in the birthing process of Hindi as a language in the late nineteenth and early twentieth century. He was born in 1830 into a family that had links with the town of Gorakhpur and he was named after what probably was a well-known periodical of the time *Sudhākara*.[87] His father desired that the young Sudhākara mastered Sanskrit grammar and the astral sciences, to earn his living by drawing horoscopes and divining auspicious moments for important events. Sudhākara, however, apprenticed himself to an associate of Bāpu Deva Śāstrī, namely Pandit Devkrishna Mishra (Sharma).[88]

In addition to his being a faculty member at the Sanskrit College, he was also appointed the chief librarian of the Saraswati Bhawan Library by which time he had commenced his own writing. His dedication to the cause of Hindi is further reflected in the poetry he wrote in Hindi and among his admirers he was considered as the greatest commentator on the *Siddhāntaśāstra*s after Gaṇeśa Daivajña.[89] Much of his work was published in the important series of publications referred to as the *Benares Sanskrit Series*. While his basic training was in Sanskrit *gaṇita*, he was essentially self-taught in Western mathematics. During his time, the BSc mathematics class and those of the Sanskrit College were held in the same premises. Dvivedī doubled sometimes as a mathematics lecturer in the BSc programme.[90]

In addition to his historical writing, he produced a work entitled *Gaṇaka Tāraṅgiṇī*, which contained biographies of Indian astronomers from antiquity onwards, marking a new trend in the Sanskrit cosmopolis in the nineteenth century, where historical accounts and biographies began to be produced about scholars themselves. The work is in Sanskrit and contains an author's (Sudhākara Dvivedī) and an editor's (his son Padmakar) preface. The contents pages are comprised of a listing, in alphabetical order, of the long line of astronomers, and their work.[91] While the contents page lists the astronomers in alphabetical order, the actual order of appearance of the biographies is chronological. The first historical astronomer to appear then is Āryabhaṭa, who chronologically inaugurates the Indian astronomical

86 Upādhyāya, *Kāshī Kī Pāṇḍitya Paramparā*, p. 188.

87 Upādhyāya, *Kāshī Kī Pāṇḍitya Paramparā*, p. 301.

88 A listing of his works in Hindi and Sanskrit are available in Upādhyāya, *Kāshī Kī Pāṇḍitya Paramparā*, p. 306. The relationship between Bāpu Deva and Dvivedī is also discussed in Upādhyāya's work including the stuff of legend.

89 Upādhyāya, *Kāshī Kī Pāṇḍitya Paramparā*, pp. 306–07.

90 Upādhyāya, *Kāshī Kī Pāṇḍitya Paramparā*, p. 311.

91 Dvivedī, *Gaṇaka Taraṅgiṇī*, pp. 1–7.

(Siddhāntic) tradition. The book is about 150 pages in length and begins with an invocation, customary in the Sanskrit literary tradition, praising the contributions of the sages of yore. After two pages the book gets down to business with a summary account of the work of the first of the *Siddhāntins* — Āryabhaṭa, who receives ten pages. *Gaṇaka Taraṅgiṇī* ends with biographies of Neelambara Sharma (b. 1745) and Govind Dev Śāstrī (b. 1756). For example, in discussing Āryabhaṭa he mentions the astronomer-mathematician's provenance, drawing upon the evidence provided by the scholar Bhau Daji; then he proceeds to elaborate upon the notation Āryabhaṭa employs when dealing with large numbers.[92] Dvivedī's sources are very comprehensive, drawing upon local and international scholarship, both past and present. For example, in the entry on Varāhamihira, the discussion on the *Pañcasiddhāntikā* alludes to the edition of the work prepared by Thibaut and himself.[93] In addition to the original texts, he takes recourse to the work of European Indologists as well as work of the Khwārazmian scholar al-Bīrūnī. The important point to note here is that while the early Indologists worked with local scholars as interlocutors or informants, the latter were often invisible. Gradually local scholars began to acquire a voice of their own, while some of them collaborated as scholars with their European counterparts. Eventually, through this joint translation activity the canon of the sciences of ancient India were compiled. In this context, Bāpu Deva Śāstrī and Sudhākara Dvivedī represent the beginnings of the modern history of astronomy and mathematics in Sanskrit and Hindi.

In 1910, Dvivedī published a work on the history of mathematics in Hindi entitled *Gaṇita kā Itihās*, thus reaching out to a wider readership and recognizing the place of big history.[94] The work was a product of a set of lectures he delivered on the history of mathematics in his mathematics course. At some point, he decided to remedy the dearth of material on the subject in Hindi and rather than translate an already existing book, he decided to put together his lectures and publish them. Dvivedī informs us in the preface that the lectures were based on what he had internalized within the *gurūparamparā* (गुरूपरम्परा) — the tradition of learning from the guru, the ancient Sanskrit works, and the available work of 'European pandits'. While the work mentioned here is the volume of arithmetic, he also planned a volume on algebra.[95] Within a larger context of the Hindi language movement, it has been pointed out that the preoccupation of Hindi intellectuals with history was to inform the Hindi readership that they were an integral part of 'a common, if vaguely defined national community'. Orsini points out that there was a semblance of an idea

92 Dvivedī, *Gaṇaka Taraṅgiṇī*, pp. 2–5.

93 Dvivedī, *Gaṇaka Taraṅgiṇī*, p. 15.

94 Dvivedī, *Gaṇita kā Itihās*.The Wikipedia page on Sudhākara Dvivedī lists among his publications in Hindi a *History of Hindu Mathematics*, while the Hindi Wikipedia correctly mentions the book as *Ganita ka Itihas* (History of Mathematics).

95 Dvivedī, *Gaṇita kā Itihās*.

at the beginning of the twentieth century that the nation was 'already there'. The historical discourse within the Hindi public sphere, as in other parts of India, was shaped by the colonial encounter, oriental scholarship, and the new institutional context.[96]

A recent study of two translations of the *Brāhmasphuṭa Siddhānta* with the commentary by Pṛthūdhaka, one by Colebrooke and the other by Dvivedī, illustrates contrasting translation and editorial practices of the latter two scholars, and the changing landscape of the historiography of mathematics in the nineteenth century.[97] The commentary was important for illustrating the workings of and unpacking the meaning of mathematical algorithms.

Both Colebrooke and Dvivedī approached the work they translated quite distinctly due to their different understandings of structure, commentary, and the concept of number. Besides, Colebrooke's selection of chapters from the texts he had gathered appear in Dvivedī's translation and constitute the canon. A retrospective rational reconstruction that runs against the grain of the actual chronological development enables Colebrook to prepare *Algebra* as a text on the history of Indian mathematics accessible to historians of mathematics.[98] Colebrooke's translation was paraphrastic in that it made sense of the Sanskritic text in the idiom of the language of translation, rather than exhibit, as philologists would do, the nuance in the original text.

On the other hand, both Thibaut and Dvivedī too flaunted style in favour of the content and the mathematical cogency of the rules, even though Thibaut was receptive to the philology of the concepts employed. While Dvivedī draws upon German philological practices that he picked up from Thibaut, the latter too was influenced by the local Benares Pāṇḍitya. But for Dvivedī, the editing of a text required that it be conferred with a coherence of form and content rather than ensured as philologically authentic or being the original'. Dvivedī subsequently proceeded to produce a spectrum of translations of Sanskrit mathematical texts.[99] Evidently Dvivedī's historiography is shaped not just by the Benares *paramparā*, but equally by the Indological tradition with which he was in conversation.[100]

The process of engraftment or reconciliation, depending on which side of the story one is narrating, continued for a long time in Hindi and Sanskrit as well. This is evident in the work of Lakshmi Shankar Mishra entitled *Saraltrikonomiti kī Upkramaṇikā* with several worked examples and the *Samīkarṇa Mīmāṃsā* by Sudhākar Dvivedī. That the process of engraftment in some form continued, not as colonial policy, but as a theory of translation, is

96 Orsini, *The Hindi Public Sphere*, p. 175.

97 Keller, 'Shaping a Mathematical Text in Sanskrit'.

98 Keller, 'Shaping a Mathematical Text in Sanskrit'; Colebrooke, *Algebra with Arithmetic and Mensuration*.

99 Keller, 'Overlooking Mathematical Justifications in the Sanskrit Tradition'.

100 Keller raises the important issue of how Thibaut's reading of the Indian tradition too was reshaped by the scholars with whom he collaborated.

also reflected in the publication of another work by Dvivedī written in Sanskrit and Hindi entitled *Calarāśikalanam*, a work on the differential and integral calculus, and republished from Benares in 1917.[101] In the republished edition of the work, the preface to the first edition is reproduced and interestingly enough several decades after the publication of Ramchandra's work, the figures of De Morgan and Ramchandra again reappear. Ramchandra's work was probably seen as a first attempt to introduce calculus in Urdu and Dvivedī saw his effort as doing the same with differential and integral calculus. It is pointed out by Dvivedī that 'Ramchandra, a native of Delhi, besides translating numerous works on mathematics, ... from English into Urdu, produced a generation ago, at least one work ... distinguished by accredited originality. Reference is here intended to his "Problems of Maxima and Minima ..."', and De Morgan's role in supporting the publication of the second edition from London is mentioned. Further: 'And now we have to announce the appearance [...] of a kindred treatise, but one of much ampler scope, "Chalana-kalana", bearing an alternative title "A Hindi Treatise on the Differential Calculus"'.[102] In other words, the project of mathematical reconciliation of two mathematical traditions was prevalent beyond the portals of the College and extended well beyond the domain of Sanskrit and Hindi into Urdu and the other regional languages. Further as Dvivedī himself concludes by pointing out that:

> I earnestly request all learned gentlemen to understand that this book is not written to show off talent, but to encourage and incite our own countrymen towards the cultivation of Western science. Why should we not improve our own language and advance with the aid of Western science to the attainment of which we are applying our heart and soul.[103]

And then slightly ahead, as in Ramchandra's case, he wishes that the readership of the book is European as well: 'Now-a-days there being mutual communication between Europeans and Indians [...] Therefore this treatise will be useful to those Europeans who are interested in the history and development of Indian mathematics'.[104] In more ways than one, this hermeneutics of mathematics reconciliation that commenced in the 1830s acquired momentum and visibility in the projects and research of Bāpu Deva Śāstrī and more or less ambled towards closure in the sense of a disjuncture between teaching modern mathematics and research on Sanskrit *gaṇita* in the work of Dvivedī.[105]

---

101 Dvivedī, *Calarāśikalanam*. This work was translated into Hindi with the title *Chalan Kalan*.

102 Dvivedī, *Calarāśikalanam*, p. 4.

103 Dvivedī, *Calarāśikalanam*, p. 4.

104 Dvivedī, *Calarāśikalanam*, p. 5.

105 Raina, 'A Transcultural History of the Shaping of Mathematics Education in India by the History of Mathematics'.

Conclusion

The nineteenth century was marked by many efforts and projects in different parts of the subcontinent, that were either under direct or indirect colonial rule. Benares fell under directly administered India but with the passage of time the number of Sanskrit Colleges in indirectly administered India mushroomed. Benares Sanskrit College was among the first of the Anglo-Oriental Colleges. Similar colleges and projects flowered in Maharashtra, Baroda, Travancore, Mysore, and other locations. The focus of this essay is solely on Benares. But a more comprehensive history of translation activity in South Asia from Sanskrit into the vernaculars and English needs to be written — the canvas of this paper is miniscule compared with the scale of this activity. In the case of Benares, one of the agendas of this kind of literary activity was directed at consolidating a sense of Hindu identity. But since the period discussed covers close to a century the mandate, agendas, and objectives kept shifting — the crystallization of Hindu identity emerges in the last phase of this activity.[106] Naturally, as scholarly activity it went beyond this social reduction, for it was also a project in conservation and reaching out to sections of society, hitherto with little access to the Sanskrit canon. Whether this was one of the outcomes of the modernization of education, or a response of the educated upper castes to the incursion of missionary education or to European cultural imperialism, or a combination of all these and other factors is difficult to tell. The situation was indeed complicated and any singular causal explanation will fall by the roadside.

But this paper is preoccupied with the world of mathematics and in this world translation activity was linked with teaching both ancient and medieval Indian mathematics and modern mathematics. The algebraization of the mathematics curriculum in Western and central India is reflected in the circulation of De Morgan's work both in English and in translation.[107] The work of British Indologists alongside the influence of the British 'analytics', as long as it lasted, provided the conceptual justification for educationists who were working towards the development of a mathematical curriculum for an empire in the making. On the other hand, the *Bīja-Gaṇita* and other mathematical texts from India, as Joan Richards' work points out, played an important role in debates on the foundations of mathematical knowledge.[108]

The colonial policy of engraftment created a space for an exchange on logic and mathematics, and the local interlocutors transformed what the

---

106 For the Hindi intellectual, history played the role of collapsing the diversity of Indian identity to essentially Hindu identity. This was quite contrary to what happened in other regions, e.g. Marathi historiography provided critical and conflicting voices that shaped an alternate historiography. Orsini, *The Hindi Public Sphere*, p. 176.

107 For a detailed discussion, see Raina, 'A Transcultural History of the Shaping of Mathematics Education in India by the History of Mathematics'.

108 Richards, 'Augustus De Morgan, the History of Mathematics, and the Foundations of Algebra'.

colonizers considered engraftment into a hermeneutics of reconciliation. Śāstrī and Dvivedī may have sartorially donned vestments of Benares pandits, but they wore two hats, that of the modern mathematician and that of the teacher of Sanskrit *gaṇita*, amphibians comfortable in both traditions. The long gestation of mathematics and *Nyāya* in Benares, of *jyotiṣa* and *Nyāya*, would stimulate an interest in mathematics and history. A modern disciplinary field had been created at the intersection of the history of science and Indology. The field of the history of science and mathematics had moved away from the penumbra of Indology.[109]

109 Raina, 'The European Construction of Hindu Astronomy (1700–1900)'.

Bibliography

Primary Sources

A Synopsis of Science from the Standpoint of the Nyaya Philosophy. Part I, Hindi and English, prepared in Sanskrit by Pandit Vitthala Śástrí, and in English by James R. Ballantyne, Part I (Mirjapore: Orphan School Press, 1852)

An Explanatory Version of Lord Bacon's Novum Organum, prepared in Sanskrit by Pandit Vitthala Śástrí, and in English by James R. Ballantyne. Part I. [Containing a Sanskrit version of book 1, with commentary in Sanskrit, together with an English translation of the text of aphorisms 1–37, and of the commentary thereon.] (Benares: Benares Recorder Press, 1852)

Colebrooke, H. T., *Algebra with Arithmetic and Mensuration from the Sanscrit of Brahmagupta and Bhāscara*, trans. by H. T. Colebrooke (London: John Murray, 1817)

Dvivedī, Sudhākara, *Gaṇita kā Itihās* (गणति का इतहिास: पहला भाग – पतगिणति) (Benares: Prabhakar Printing Works, 1910)

——, *Calarāśikalanam* (Vārānāsī: Sampuranānd Saṃskrit Vishwavidyālaya, 1917)

——, *Gaṇaka Tāraṅgiṇī* (गणक तारंगणिी) (Lives of Hindu astronomers), ed. by Padmakar Dvivedī (Benares: Prakash Press, 1933)

Goreh, Rev. Nehemiah Niḷakaṇṭa Śāstrī, *A Rational Refutation of the Hindu Philosophical Systems*, trans. from the original Hindi (London, India: Christian Literary Society for India, SPCK Press, 1897)

Hall, Fritz Edward, and Bāpu Deva Śāstrī, *The Sūrya Siddhānta: An Ancient System of Hindu Astronomy with Ranganatha's Exposition* (Calcutta: Baptist Mission Press, 1859)

Nicholls, George, *Sketch of the Progress of the Benares Pathshala [With a supplement bringing the story to 1906]* (Benares: Government Press, Uttar Pradesh, 1907; republished by Varanasi: Sampuranand Sanskrit University, 2005)

Śāstrī, Ḍhuṇḍirāja, 'Mānavīyajnānavishayakaśastrāvatara', *The Pandit*, 2 (1878), 54, 102, 166, 230, 359

——, 'Nyayadarśanam', *The Pandit*, 2 (1878), 60, 109, 311, 363

——, *Vaiśeṣikasūtropaskāraḥ with the Prakāśikā in Hindi Commentary* (Benares: Kashi Sanskrit Series, reprinted by Chowkhamba, 1969)

Śāstrī, Bāpu Deva, 'Bhaskara's Knowledge of the Differential Calculus', *Journal of the Asiatic Society of Bengal*, 27.1–5 (1858), 213–16

——, *The Manamandira Observatory* (Benares: Medical Hall Press, 1865)

——, *Elements of Algebra and Elements of Arithmetic*' (Benares: Medical Hall Press, 1875)

Spottiswoode, W. 'Note on the Supposed Discovery of the Principle of Differential Calculus by an Indian Astronomer', *Journal of the Royal Asiatic Society*, 17 (1860), 221–22

The Rekhāganita or Geometry in Sanskrit composed by Samrād Jagannātha, vol. 1, Books I–VI, 1719/1901, *The Rekhaganita or Geometry in Sanskrit*, vol. 1 (Bombay: Central Book Depot, 1901)

Translation of the Sūrya Siddhānta and of the Siddhānta Śiromaṇi, by the late Lancelot Wilkinson, revised by Bāpu Deva Śāstrī from the Sanskrit, Bibliotheca Indica, 32 (Calcutta: Baptist Mission Press, 1861)

Secondary Studies

Bayly, C. A. 1997. *Empire and Information: Intelligence Gathering and Social Communication in India, 1770–1880* (Cambridge: Cambridge University Press, 1997)

Blackburn, Stuart, 'Early Books and New Literary Practices', in *The History of the Book in South Asia*, ed. by Francesca Orsini (Farnham: Ashgate, 2013), pp. 105–58

Clarke, J. J. *Oriental Enlightenment: The Encounter Between Asian and Western Thought* (London: Routledge, 1997)

Cohn, Bernard S., *Colonialism and its Forms of Knowledge: The British in India* (Oxford: Oxford University Press, 1997)

Dalmia, Vasudha, 'Sanskrit Scholars and Pandits of the "Old School": The Benares Samskrit College and the Constitution of Authority in the Nineteenth Century', *Journal of Indian Philosophy*, 24 (1996), 321–37

Deshpande, Madhav M., 'Pandit and Professor: Transformations in Nineteenth Century Maharashtra', in *The Pandit: Traditional Scholarship in India*, ed. by Axel Michaels (New Delhi: Manohar, 2001), pp. 119–53

Dodson, Michael S., *Orientalism, Empire and National Culture: India 1770–1780* (Delhi: Cambridge University Press, 2010)

Foster, Gary, and Evans James, 'Narratives of Hope and Reconciliation', *Constructivism in the Human Sciences*, 9.2 (2004), 67–76

Gour, Neelam Saran, *Three Rivers and a Tree: The Story of Allahabad University* (New Delhi: Rupa Publications, 2015)

Inden, Ronald, *Imagining India* (Oxford: Basil Blackwell, 1990)

Jacob, Christian, 'Lieux de savoir: Places and Spaces in the History of Knowledge', *Know: A Journal on the Formation of Knowledge*, 1.1 (2017), 85–102

Kejariwal, Om P., *The Asiatic Society of Bengal and the Discovery of India's Past 1784–1838* (Delhi: Oxford University Press, 1988)

Keller, Agathe, 'Overlooking Mathematical Justifications in the Sanskrit Tradition: the Nuanced Cas of G. F. Thibaut', in *History of Mathematical Proof in the Ancient Tradition*, ed. by Karine Chemla (Cambridge: Cambridge University Press, 2012) pp. 260–73

——, 'Shaping a Mathematical Text in Sanskrit: H. T. Colebrooke, Sudhākara Dvivedin and Pṛthūdaka's Commentary on the Twelfth Chapter of the *Brāhmasphuṭasiddhānta*', in *Shaping the Sciences of the Ancient World*, ed. by Karine Chemla and Agathe Keller (Springer, WSAWM, forthcoming)

Kumar, Krishna, *Political Agenda of Education: A Study of Colonialist and Nationalist Ideas* (New Delhi: Sage Publications, 1991)

Murr, Sylvia, 'Les conditions d'emergence du discours sur l'Inde au siècle des lumières', *Collection Purusartha*, 7 (1983), 233–84

Murr, Sylvia, *L'indologie du Père Coeurdoux: stratégies, apologétique et scientificité* (Paris: École Française d'Extrême-Orient, 1987)

Montgomery, Scott L., *Science in Translation: Movements of Knowledge through Cultures and Time* (Chicago and London: University of Chicago Press, 2000)

Nicholson, Andrew J., *Unifying Hinduism: Philosophy and Identity in Intellectual History* (New York: Columbia University Press, 2010)

Orsini, Francesca, *The Hindu Public Sphere: Language and Literature in the Age of Nationalism* (Oxford: Oxford University Press, 2009)

Pinch, William R., 'Same Difference in India and Europe', *History and Theory*, 38.3 (1999), 389–407

Pollock, Sheldon, 2001. 'The Death of Sanskrit', *Comparative Studies in Society and History*, 43.2 (2001), 392–426

——, 'New Intellectuals in Seventeenth Century India', *The Indian Economic and Social History Review*, 38.1 (2001), 3–32

Raina, Dhruv, 'Science East and West', in *Encyclopedia of Science, Technology and Medicine in Non-Western Cultures*, ed. by Helaine Selin (Heidelberg: Springer, 2008), pp. 1934–44

——, 'Revisiting Social Theory and History of Science in Early Modern South Asia and Colonial India', *Special Issue on Human Mobility and the Circulation of Technical Knowledge (17th–19th Centuries), Extrême-Orient Extrême-Occident*, 36 (2013), 191–210

——, 'Mathematics Education in Modern India', in *Handbook on the History of Mathematics Education*, ed. by Alexander Karp and Gert Schubring (Heidelberg: Springer, 2014), pp. 376–84

——, 'Iterative Learning in the Modernisation of the Indian Mathematical Tradition', in *Wissen in Bewegung: Institution–Iteration–Transfer*, ed. by Eva Cancik-Kirschbaum and Anit Traninger (Wiesbaden: Harrassowitz, 2015), pp. 29–47

——, 'Translating the "Exact" and "Positive" Sciences: Early Twentieth Century Reflections on the Past of Science in India', *Transcultural Studies*, 1 (2015), 8–33

——, 'A Transcultural History of the Shaping of Mathematics Education in India by the History of Mathematics', in *Writing Historiographies of Mathematics (18th to the 21st Century)*, ed. by Karine Chemla and Agathe Keller (Heidelberg: Springer, forthcoming)

——, 'The European Construction of Hindu Astronomy (1700–1900)', in *Handbook of Hinduism* ed. by Knut Jacobsen (forthcoming)

Raj, Kapil, 'Refashioning Civilities, Engineering Trust: William Jones, Indian Intermediaries and the Production of Legal Knowledge in Eighteenth Century Bengal', *Studies in History*, 17.2 (2001), 175–209

Rashed, Roshdi, 'Problems of the Transmission of Greek Scientific Thought into Arabic: Examples from Mathematics and Optics', *History of Science*, 37 (1989), 199–209

Richards, Joan L. 'Augustus De Morgan, the History of Mathematics, and the Foundations of Algebra', *Isis*, 78 (1987), 7–30

Rubiés, Joan-Pau, 'Reassessing "the Discovery of Hinduism": Jesuit Discourse on Gentile Idolatry and the European Republic of Letters', in *Intercultural Encounter and the Jesuit Mission in South Asia*, ed. by Anand Amaladass and Ines G. Županov (Bangalore: Asia Trading Corporation, 2014), pp. 113–54

Said, Edward W., *Orientalism* (London: Penguin, 1978)

Sarma, Sreeramula Rajeswara, 'Sanskrit as Vehicle for Modern Science: Lancelot Wilkinson's Efforts in the 1830s', *Studies in History of Medicine and Science*, 14.1–2 (1995–1996), 189–99

Schwab, Raymond, *The Oriental Renaissance: Europe's Discovery of India and the East 1680–1850*, trans. by Gene-Patterson Black and Victor Reinking (New York: Columbia University Press, 1984) [first French edn appeared 1950]

Truschke, Audrey, *Culture of Encounter: Sanskrit at the Mughal Court* (New York: Columbia University Press, 2018)

Upādhyāya, Āchārya Pandit Baldev, *Kāshī Kī Pāṇḍitya Paramparā* (काशी की पाण्डित्य परम्परा) (Vārānāsī: Vishwavidyālaya Prakashan, 1983)

Xavier, Ângela Barreto, and Ines G. Županov, *Catholic Orientalism: Portuguese Empire, Indian Knowledge 16th–18th Centuries* (New Delhi: Oxford University Press, 2015)

Vajpayei, Ananya, *Righteous Republic: The Political Foundations of Modern India* (Cambridge, MA: Harvard University Press, 2012)

Van Der Veer, Peter, *Imperial Encounters: Religion and Modernity in India and Britain*. (Princeton, Princeton University Press, 2001)

Županov, Ines G., *Missionary Tropics: The Catholic Frontier in India (16th–17th Centuries)* (Ann Arbor: University of Michigan Press, 2005)

General Index

Index of Names

Contact and Transmission

Intercultural Encounters from Late Antiquity to the Early Modern Period

Titles in Series

Isaac Lampurlanés Farré, *Excerptum de Talmud: Study and Edition of a Thirteenth-Century Latin Translation* (2020)

Premodern Translation: Comparative Approaches to Cross-Cultural Transformations, ed. by Sonja Brentjes and Alexander Fidora (2021)